LUDWIG W

Ray Monk gained a first-class degree in Philosophy at York University and went on to Oxford, where he wrote his M.Litt. thesis on Wittgenstein's philosophy of mathematics.

Logic and ethics are fundamentally the same,
they are no more than duty to oneself.

Otto Weininger, *Sex and Character*

'This biography transforms Wittgenstein into a human being. It shows his capacity for love, bumps away the hagiolatry, and cuts through a strange layer of po-faced schlock which is perhaps unique to his memory. It ties the philosophy to the life and brings clearly into view the immoderate, brilliant, moving and regularly insupportable genius... For nearly 600 pages Monk moves between quotations, drawing on interviews and letters, diaries, and memoirs of Wittgenstein and his family and friends. He works them intelligently into continuity. His own speculative interventions about Wittgenstein's feelings and motivations are never pushy or insistent, but well-supported, plausible and at the same time self-effacing... His handling of the early philosophy is admirable. He has a gift for simple exposition, and knows what it is worth trying to get across to a largely non-philosophical audience.'

Independent On Sunday

'With a subject who demands passionate partisanship, whose words are so powerful, but whose actions speak louder, it must have been hard to write this definitive, perceptive and lucid biography. Out goes Norman Malcolm's saintly Wittgenstein, Bartley's tortured, impossibly promiscuous Wittgenstein, and Brian McGuinness's bloodless, almost bodiless Wittgenstein. This Wittgenstein is the real human being: wholly balanced and happily eccentric, with nothing much in common with his suicidal brother Rudolf, except his homosexuality. Allowed to speak for himself by a self-effacing author, this Wittgenstein knows his own military mind and nature, of which the suicidal gestures were deeply felt, but still gestures.'

The Times

'Ray Monk studied philosophy as an undergraduate and went on to write a dissertation on the philosophy of mathematics. In writing this book he has shown himself a more than competent biographer and historian of ideas... It is both readable and easy to use, with a full index and bibliography. It is much to be recommended not least for its tolerant, non-judgmental, but sometimes sardonic tone.'

Observer

'Monk presents a portrait of real complexity: a sceptic (who in his early years was sceptical enough to disagree with Russell that it could be proved that "there was not a rhinoceros in the room") and yet a mystic for whom certainty of a kind existed – the certainty of unknowing. Monk's biography is deeply intelligent, generous to the ordinary reader, and restrained about Wittgenstein's homosexual relationships. It is a beautiful portrait of a beautiful life. After such rigour, such strictness and moral torment, there is a beauty and a release in Wittgenstein's famous last words, "Tell them I've had a wonderful life".'

Guardian

'Monk's energetic enterprise is remarkable for the interleaving of the philosophical and the emotional aspects of Wittenstein's life. The biographical method here is comparative: Monk *shows* certain connections, but he does not *argue* them. He honours the master by his very method and renovates biography in the process.'

Sunday Times

Ray Monk

LUDWIG WITTGENSTEIN

The Duty of Genius

𝒱

VINTAGE

TO JENNY

First published in Vintage 1991

3 5 7 9 10 8 6 4

© Ray Monk 1990

'The Strayed Poet' from *Internal Colloquies* by I. A. Richards
is reproduced by permission of Routledge & Kegan Paul

The right of Ray Monk to be identified as the author of this work has
been asserted by him in accordance with the Copyright, Designs and
Patents Act, 1988

First published by Jonathan Cape Ltd, 1990

Vintage Books
Random House UK Ltd, 20 Vauxhall Bridge Road, London SW1V 2SA

Random House Australia (Pty) Limited
20 Alfred Street, Milsons Point, Sydney,
New South Wales 2061, Australia

Random House New Zealand Limited
18 Poland Road, Glenfield
Auckland 10, New Zealand

Random House South Africa (Pty) Limited
PO Box 337, Bergvlei, South Africa

Random House UK Limited Reg. No. 954009

A CIP catalogue for this book
is available from the British Library

ISBN 0 09 988370 8

Printed and bound in Great Britain by
Cox & Wyman Ltd, Reading, Berkshire

CONTENTS

ILLUSTRATIONS

The author and publishers would like to thank the following for permission to use photographs: Dr Milo Keynes (13); Anne Keynes (15); Dr Norman Malcolm (46); Michael Nedo (1–7, 9–12, 19–34, 36, 39–43, 47, 50–54); Neue Pinakothek, Munich (photo: Artothek: 7); Gilbert Pattisson (37–8, 41–2, 44–5); Ferry Radax (16–18, 48), Technische Hochschule, Berlin (now the Technical University of Berlin: 8); Trinity College, Cambridge (14, 35).

ACKNOWLEDGEMENTS

My first thanks must go to Monica Furlong, without whose support this book would never have been started. It was she who persuaded David Godwin (then Editorial Director of Heinemann) to consider the possibility of financing the project. No less essential has been the undying enthusiasm and kind encouragement of David Godwin himself and the equally unstinting support given me by my American publisher, Erwin Glikes of the Free Press.

It was initially feared that the project would founder for lack of co-operation from Wittgenstein's literary heirs. I am happy to report that the exact opposite has been the case. Wittgenstein's three literary executors, Professor Georg Henrik von Wright, Professor G. E. M. Anscombe and the late Mr Rush Rhees have all been exceptionally kind, co-operative and helpful. In addition to granting me permission to quote from Wittgenstein's unpublished manuscripts, they have been assiduous in replying to my many questions and very generous in providing me with information that I would not otherwise have found out.

To Professor von Wright I am particularly grateful for his very patient and detailed replies to my (initially rather primitive) speculations concerning the composition of *Philosophical Investigations*. His articles on the origins of Wittgenstein's two great works and his meticulous cataloguing of Wittgenstein's papers have been indispensable. Professor Anscombe agreed to meet me on a number of occasions to speak to me about her own memories of Wittgenstein and to answer my enquiries. To her I am especially grateful, for allowing me access to Francis Skinner's letters to Wittgenstein.

The kindness shown to me by Mr Rhees was far above and beyond the call of duty. Despite his advancing years and frail health he devoted many hours to discussions with me; during which he revealed his incomparable knowledge of Wittgenstein's work and his many insights into both Wittgenstein's personality and his philosophy. He further showed me many documents, the existence of which I would not otherwise have known. So concerned was he to impart to me as much of what he knew as possible that on one occasion he insisted on paying for me to stay in a hotel in Swansea, so that our discussions would not have to be curtailed by my having to return to London. News of his death came just as I finished work on the book. He will be sorely missed.

Sadly, a number of other friends of Wittgenstein's died while I was researching this book. Roy Fouracre had been ill for a long time, but his wife was kind enough to see me and to supply me with copies of the letters from Wittgenstein to her husband. Similarly kind was Katherine Thomson, whose late husband, Professor George Thomson, expressed a wish to meet me shortly before he died, in order to discuss Wittgenstein's visit to the Soviet Union. Mrs Thomson also showed me some letters and discussed with me her own memories of Wittgenstein. Dr Edward Bevan I met a year or so before his death. His recollections, and those of his widow, Joan Bevan, form the basis of Chapter 27. Tommy Mulkerrins, who provided Wittgenstein with indispensable help during his stay on the west coast of Ireland, was an invalided but exceptionally alert octogenarian when I met him in his cottage in the spring of 1986. His reminiscences have been incorporated into Chapter 25. He too, alas, is no longer with us.

Other friends, happily, are alive and well. Mr Gilbert Pattisson, a close friend of Wittgenstein's from 1929 to 1940, met with me a number of times and provided me with the letters quoted in Chapter 11. Mr Rowland Hutt, a friend of both Wittgenstein and Francis Skinner, took a lively and helpful interest in my work and provided me with the letters quoted in Chapter 23. I am grateful also to Mr William Barrington Pink, Sir Desmond Lee, Professor Basil Reeve, Dr Ben Richards, Dr Casimir Lewy, Mr Keith Kirk, Mrs A. Clement, Mrs Polly Smythies, Professor Wolfe Mays, Mrs Frances Partridge and Madame Marguerite de Chambrier, all of whom took the trouble to speak to me – in some cases over the course of several meetings – about their recollections of Wittgenstein. To Professor Georg Kreisel,

Professor F. A. von Hayek, Mr John King, Professor Wasif A. Hijab, Professor John Wisdom, the late Professor Sir Alfred Ayer and Father Conrad Pepler, I am grateful for replies by letter to my enquiries.

The account of Wittgenstein's work at Guy's Hospital and the Royal Infirmary at Newcastle could not have been written without the help of Wittgenstein's colleagues: Mr T. Lewis, Dr Humphrey Osmond, Dr R. T. Grant, Miss Helen Andrews, Dr W. Tillman, Miss Naomi Wilkinson, Dr R. L. Waterfeld, Dr Erasmus Barlow and Professor Basil Reeve. To Dr John Henderson I am grateful for help in contacting many of these colleagues. Dr Anthony Ryle kindly showed me the letter from his father quoted in Chapter 21, and allowed me to quote from the diary he kept as a child. To him and to Professor Reeve I am also grateful for reading and commenting on an earlier draft of this chapter.

To Mr Oscar Wood, Sir Isaiah Berlin and Dame Mary Warnock I am grateful for their recollections of the meeting of the Jowett Society described in Chapter 24, the only occasion on which Wittgenstein took part in a philosophical meeting at Oxford.

Many people who did not meet Wittgenstein also provided me with valuable help, and in this context I am pleased to acknowledge my gratitude to Professor W. W. Bartley III, Professor Quentin Bell, Mrs Margaret Sloan, Mr Michael Straight, Mr Colin Wilson and Professor Konrad Wünsche, who all replied helpfully to my letters, and to Mrs Anne Keynes, Dr Andrew Hodges and Professor George Steiner, who were kind enough to arrange to meet me to discuss matters arising from my research. Mrs Keynes also kindly provided me with a dissertation on philosophy written by her uncle, David Pinsent.

My research took me far and wide, but two trips in particular should be mentioned; those to Ireland and to Austria. In Ireland I was chauffeured around Dublin, County Wicklow and County Galway by my friend Jonathan Culley, who showed inexhaustible patience and supplied a much-needed (but otherwise missing) sense of urgency and punctuality. In Dublin I was helped by Mr Paul Drury, in Wicklow by the Kingston family and in Connemara by Tommy Mulkerrins. Mr and Mrs Hugh Price, Mrs R. Willoughby, Mr J. Mahon and Mr Sean Kent gave much appreciated assistance along the way. My trip to Austria was made pleasant and comfortable by the kindness shown to me by my friend Wolfgang Grüber and by the hospitality of his brother, Heimo. In Vienna I had the pleasure of meeting Mrs Katrina

Eisenburger, a granddaughter of Helene Wittgenstein, and another member of the family, Dr Elizabeth Wieser. I also received the kind help of Professor Hermann Hänsel. On my visit to the Wechsel mountains, where Wittgenstein taught at the schools of Trattenbach and Otterthal, I was helped enormously by Dr Adolf Hübner, who not only escorted me around the area and supplied me with copies of the fascinating material he has collected for the Documentation Centre in Kirchberg, but also – with quite extraordinary kindness – took the trouble to re-shoot a series of photographs that I had taken after it had been discovered that my own pictures had been ruined.

To Dr T. Hobbs of the Wren Library, Trinity College, Cambridge; Dr A. Baster of the Wills Library, Guy's Hospital; Miss M. Nicholson of the Medical Research Council Archives; and the staff of the British Library, the Bodleian Library, Oxford, and the Cambridge University Library, I extend my gratitude for their undying courtesy and helpful assistance. To my friend Mr Wolf Salinger I am grateful for the trouble he took on my behalf to uncover whatever records exist at the Technical University of Berlin of the time that Wittgenstein spent as a student of engineering there (when it was the Technische Hochschule). I am grateful also to the staff of the university library for the help they gave Mr Salinger.

One of the most important collections of letters used in the book is that held by the Brenner Archive at the University of Innsbruck. This is a collection of several hundred letters to Wittgenstein (including those from Bertrand Russell and Gottlob Frege used in chapters 6, 7, 8 and 9) that has only recently been made available. I am grateful to Dr P. M. S. Hacker of St John's College, Oxford, for drawing my attention to the existence of this collection, and to Dr Walter Methlagl and Professor Allan Janik of the Brenner Archive for their kindness in allowing me access to it, and for giving up their time to discuss the contents of the letters with me. For permission to quote these and other letters from Bertrand Russell my thanks go to Kenneth Blackwell of the Russell Archive, McMaster University, Hamilton, Ontario.

I owe a special debt of gratitude to Dr Michael Nedo of Trinity College, Cambridge, whose knowledge of Wittgenstein's manuscripts is unrivalled, and who has, over the years, collected photographs, documents and copies of documents connected with Wittgenstein that constitute an immensely useful archive. He not only gave me completely free access to this material, but also devoted much of his time to the discussion of many and various aspects of my research. I am also greatly indebted to him for providing me with copies of his careful transcriptions of the coded remarks in Wittgenstein's manuscripts.

Dr Paul Wijdeveld has been enormously helpful in a similarly varied fashion. He has given me the benefit of the meticulous research he has conducted in connection with his book on the house that Wittgenstein designed, alerted me to the existence of published sources that I would not otherwise have known about, and provided me with copies of drafts of his own work and of the many documents he has discovered relating to Wittgenstein's relationship with Paul Engelmann.

For reading and passing comments on earlier drafts of parts of this book, I am grateful to Dr G. P. Baker of St John's College, Oxford, and Professor Sir Peter Strawson of Magdalen College, Oxford. Dr Baker and his colleague Dr P. M. S. Hacker were also kind enough to make available to me work that they are currently engaged upon. Professor Stephen Toulmin kindly read through the whole manuscript, and made a number of helpful suggestions and constructive criticisms. My editors, David Godwin and Erwin Glikes, have read many earlier drafts, and have also made a great number of useful suggestions. In preparing the manuscript for publication, Alison Mansbridge pointed out many errors that I would not otherwise have noticed, and I am greatly indebted to her for the enthusiasm and meticulousness with which she undertook her difficult task. Dr David McLintock kindly checked the accuracy of my translations of Frege's letters and Wittgenstein's diary entries. He made many important corrections and drew my attention to a number of interesting nuances and allusions I would otherwise have missed. Any errors that remain are, of course, entirely my responsibility.

Without the help of my agent, Mrs Gill Coleridge, I could not have survived the last four years. To Jenny, I owe my most heartfelt thanks for having survived them with me.

London
December 1989   RAY MONK

INTRODUCTION

The figure of Ludwig Wittgenstein exerts a very special fascination that is not wholly explained by the enormous influence he has had on the development of philosophy this century. Even those quite unconcerned with analytical philosophy find him compelling. Poems have been written about him, paintings inspired by him, his work has been set to music, and he has been made the central character in a successful novel that is little more than a fictionalized biography (*The World as I Found It*, by Bruce Duffy). In addition, there have been at least five television programmes made about him and countless memoirs of him written, often by people who knew him only very slightly. (F. R. Leavis, for example, who met him on perhaps four or five occasions, has made his 'Memories of Wittgenstein' the subject of a sixteen-page article.) Recollections of Wittgenstein have been published by the lady who taught him Russian, the man who delivered peat to his cottage in Ireland and the man who, though he did not know him very well, happened to take the last photographs of him.

All this is, in a way, quite separate from the ongoing industry of producing commentaries on Wittgenstein's philosophy. This industry too, however, continues apace. A recent bibliography of secondary sources lists no fewer than 5,868 articles and books about his work. Very few of these would be of interest (or even intelligible) to anyone outside academia, and equally few of them would concern themselves with the aspects of Wittgenstein's life and personality that have inspired the work mentioned in the previous paragraph.

It seems, then, that interest in Wittgenstein, great though it is, suffers from an unfortunate polarity between those who study his work in isolation from his life and those who find his life fascinating but his work unintelligible. It is a common experience, I think, for someone to read, say, Norman Malcolm's *Memoir*, to find themselves captivated by the figure described therein, and then be inspired to read Wittgenstein's work for themselves, only to find that they cannot understand a word of it. There are, it has to be said, many excellent introductory books on Wittgenstein's work that would explain what his main philosophical themes are, and how he deals with them. What they do not explain is what his work has to do with *him* – what the connections are between the spiritual and ethical preoccupations that dominate his life, and the seemingly rather remote philosophical questions that dominate his work.

The aim of this book is to bridge that gap. By describing the life and the work in the one narrative, I hope to make it clear how this work came from this man, to show – what many who read Wittgenstein's work instinctively feel – the unity of his philosophical concerns with his emotional and spiritual life.

I
1889–1919

I

THE LABORATORY FOR
SELF-DESTRUCTION

W hy should one tell the truth if it's to one's advantage to tell a
lie?'

Such was the subject of Ludwig Wittgenstein's earliest recorded
philosophical reflections. Aged about eight or nine, he paused in a
doorway to consider the question. Finding no satisfactory answer, he
concluded that there was, after all, nothing wrong with lying under
such circumstances. In later life, he described the event as, 'an experience which if not decisive for my future way of life was at any rate
characteristic of my nature at that time'.

In one respect the episode is characteristic of his entire life. Unlike,
say, Bertrand Russell, who turned to philosophy with hope of finding
certainty where previously he had felt only doubt, Wittgenstein was
drawn to it by a compulsive tendency to be struck by such questions.
Philosophy, one might say, came to him, not he to philosophy.
Its dilemmas were experienced by him as unwelcome intrusions,
enigmas, which forced themselves upon him and held him captive,
unable to get on with everyday life until he could dispel them with a
satisfactory solution.

Yet Wittgenstein's youthful answer to this particular problem is,
in another sense, deeply uncharacteristic. Its easy acceptance of dishonesty is fundamentally incompatible with the relentless truthfulness
for which Wittgenstein was both admired and feared as an adult. It is
incompatible also, perhaps, with his very sense of being a philosopher.
'Call me a truth-seeker', he once wrote to his sister (who had, in a
letter to him, called him a great philosopher), 'and I will be satisfied.'

This points not to a change of opinion, but to a change of character —

the first of many in a life that is marked by a series of such transforma-
tions, undertaken at moments of crisis and pursued with a conviction
that the source of the crisis was himself. It is as though his life was an
ongoing battle with his own nature. In so far as he achieved anything,
it was usually with the sense of its being in spite of his nature. The
ultimate achievement, in this sense, would be the complete overcoming of himself – a transformation that would make philosophy
itself unnecessary.

In later life, when someone once remarked to him that the childlike
innocence of G. E. Moore was to his credit, Wittgenstein demurred. 'I
can't understand that', he said, 'unless it's also to a *child*'s credit. For
you aren't talking of the innocence a man has fought for, but of an
innocence which comes from a natural absence of a temptation.'

The remark hints at a self-assessment. Wittgenstein's own character – the compelling, uncompromising, dominating personality recalled in the many memoirs of him written by his friends and
students – *was* something he had had to fight for. As a child he had a
sweet and compliant disposition – eager to please, willing to conform, and, as we have seen, prepared to compromise the truth. The
story of the first eighteen years of his life is, above all, the story of this
struggle, of the forces within him and outside him that impelled such
transformation.

He was born – Ludwig Josef Johann Wittgenstein – on 26 April 1889,
the eighth and youngest child of one of the wealthiest families in
Habsburg Vienna. The family's name and their wealth have led some
to suppose that he was related to a German aristocratic family, the
Seyn-Wittgensteins. This is not so. The family had been Wittgensteins
for only three generations. The name was adopted by Ludwig's
paternal great-grandfather, Moses Maier, who worked as a land-agent
for the princely family, and who, after the Napoleonic decree of 1808
which demanded that Jews adopt a surname, took on the name of his
employers.

Within the family a legend grew up that Moses Maier's son,
Hermann Christian Wittgenstein, was the illegitimate offspring of a
prince (whether of the house of Wittgenstein, Waldeck or Esterházy
depends on the version of the story), but there are no solid grounds for
believing this. The truth of the story seems all the more doubtful, since
it appears to date from a time when the family was attempting

(successfully, as we shall see later) to have itself reclassified under the Nuremberg Laws.

The story would no doubt have suited Hermann Wittgenstein himself, who adopted the middle name 'Christian' in a deliberate attempt to dissociate himself from his Jewish background. He cut himself off entirely from the Jewish community into which he was born and left his birthplace of Korbach to live in Leipzig, where he pursued a successful career as a wool-merchant, buying from Hungary and Poland and selling to England and Holland. He chose as his wife the daughter of an eminent Viennese Jewish family, Fanny Figdor, but before their wedding in 1838 she too had converted to Protestantism.

By the time they moved to Vienna in the 1850s the Wittgensteins probably no longer regarded themselves as Jewish. Hermann Christian, indeed, acquired something of a reputation as an anti-Semite, and firmly forbade his offspring to marry Jews. The family was large – eight daughters and three sons – and on the whole they heeded their father's advice and married into the ranks of the Viennese Protestant professional classes. Thus was established a network of judges, lawyers, professors and clergymen which the Wittgensteins could rely on if they needed the services of any of the traditional professions. So complete was the family's assimilation that one of Hermann's daughters had to ask her brother Louis if the rumours she had heard about their Jewish origins were true. '*Pur sang*, Milly', he replied, '*pur sang*.'

The situation was not unlike that of many other notable Viennese families: no matter how integrated they were into the Viennese middle class, and no matter how divorced from their origins, they yet remained – in some mysterious way – Jewish 'through and through'.

The Wittgensteins (unlike, say, the Freuds) were in no way part of a Jewish community – except in the elusive but important sense in which the whole of Vienna could be so described; nor did Judaism play any part in their upbringing. Their culture was entirely Germanic. Fanny Wittgenstein came from a merchant family which had close connections with the cultural life of Austria. They were friends of the poet Franz Grillparzer and known to the artists of Austria as enthusiastic and discriminating collectors. One of her cousins was the famous violin virtuoso, Joseph Joachim, in whose development she and Hermann played a decisive role. He was adopted by them at the age of twelve and sent to study with Felix Mendelssohn. When the composer asked what he should teach the boy, Hermann Wittgenstein replied: 'Just let him breathe the air you breathe!'

Through Joachim, the family was introduced to Johannes Brahms, whose friendship they prized above any other. Brahms gave piano lessons to the daughters of Hermann and Fanny, and was later a regular attender at the musical evenings given by the Wittgensteins. At least one of his major works – the Clarinet Quintet – received its first performance at the Wittgenstein home.

Such was the air the Wittgensteins breathed – an atmosphere of cultural attainment and comfortable respectability, tainted only by the bad odour of anti-Semitism, the merest sniff of which was sufficient to keep them forever reminded of their 'non-Aryan' origins.

His grandfather's remark to Mendelssohn was to be echoed many years later by Ludwig Wittgenstein when he urged one of his students at Cambridge, Maurice Drury, to leave the university. 'There is', he told him, 'no oxygen in Cambridge for you.' Drury, he thought, would be better off getting a job among the working class, where the air was healthier. With regard to himself – to his own decision to stay at Cambridge – the metaphor received an interesting twist: 'It doesn't matter for me', he told Drury. 'I manufacture my own oxygen.'

His father, Karl Wittgenstein, had shown a similar independence from the atmosphere in which he was brought up, and the same determination to manufacture his own. Karl was the exception among the children of Hermann and Fanny – the only one whose life was not determined by their aspirations. He was a difficult child, who from an early age rebelled against the formality and authoritarianism of his parents and resisted their attempts to provide him with the kind of classical education appropriate to a member of the Viennese bourgeoisie.

At the age of eleven he tried to run away from home. At seventeen he got himself expelled from school by writing an essay denying the immortality of the soul. Hermann persevered. He tried to continue Karl's education at home by employing private tutors to see him through his exams. But Karl ran off again, and this time succeeded in getting away. After hiding out in the centre of Vienna for a couple of months, he fled to New York, arriving there penniless and carrying little more than his violin. He managed nevertheless to maintain himself for over two years by working as a waiter, a saloon musician, a bartender and a teacher (of the violin, the horn, mathematics, German and anything else he could think of). The adventure served to establish that he was his own master, and when he returned to Vienna in 1867 he was allowed – indeed, encouraged – to pursue his practical and technical bent, and to study engineering rather than follow his father and his brothers into estate management.

After a year at the technical high school in Vienna and an apprenticeship consisting of a series of jobs with various engineering firms, Karl was offered the post of draughtsman on the construction of a rolling mill in Bohemia by Paul Kupelwieser, the brother of his brother-in-law. This was Karl's great opportunity. His subsequent rise within the company was so astonishingly swift that within five years he had succeeded Kupelwieser as managing director. In the ten years that followed he showed himself to be perhaps the most astute industrialist in the Austro-Hungarian Empire. The fortunes of his company – and, of course, his own personal fortune – increased manifold, so that by the last decade of the nineteenth century he had become one of the wealthiest men in the empire, and the leading figure in its iron and steel industry. As such, he became, for critics of the excesses of capitalism, one of the archetypes of the aggressively acquisitive industrialist. Through him the Wittgensteins became the Austrian equivalent of the Krupps, the Carnegies, or the Rothschilds.

In 1898, having amassed a huge personal fortune which to this day provides comfortably for his descendants, Karl Wittgenstein suddenly retired from business, resigning from the boards of all the steel companies he had presided over and transferring his investments to foreign – principally US – equities. (This last act proved to be remarkably prescient, securing the family fortune against the inflation that crippled Austria after the First World War.) He was by this time the father of eight extraordinarily talented children.

The mother of Karl Wittgenstein's children was Leopoldine Kalmus, whom Karl had married in 1873, at the beginning of his dramatic rise through the Kupelwieser company. In choosing her, Karl was once again proving to be the exception in his family, for Leopoldine was the only partly Jewish spouse of any of the children of Hermann Christian. However, although her father, Jakob Kalmus, was descended from a prominent Jewish family, he himself had been brought up a Catholic; her mother, Marie Stallner, was entirely 'Aryan' – the daughter of an established (Catholic) Austrian land-owning family. In fact, then (until the Nuremberg Laws were applied in Austria, at least), Karl had not married a Jewess, but a Catholic, and had thus taken a further step in the assimilation of the Wittgenstein family into the Viennese establishment.

The eight children of Karl and Leopoldine Wittgenstein were baptized into the Catholic faith and raised as accepted and proud members of the Austrian high-bourgeoisie. Karl Wittgenstein was even given the chance of joining the ranks of the nobility, but declined the invitation to add the aristocratic 'von' to his name, feeling that such a gesture would be seen as the mark of the parvenu.

His immense wealth nevertheless enabled the family to live in the style of the aristocracy. Their home in Vienna, in the 'Alleegasse' (now Argentinergasse), was known outside the family as the Palais Wittgenstein, and was indeed palatial, having been built for a count earlier in the century. In addition to this, the family owned another house, in the Neuwaldeggergasse, on the outskirts of Vienna, and a large estate in the country, the Hochreit, to which they retired during the summer.

Leopoldine (or 'Poldy' as she was known to the family) was, even when judged by the very highest standards, exceptionally musical. For her, music came second only to the well-being of her husband, as the most important thing in her life. It was owing to her that the Alleegasse house became a centre of musical excellence. Musical evenings there were attended by, among others, Brahms, Mahler and Bruno Walter, who has described 'the all-pervading atmosphere of humanity and culture' which prevailed. The blind organist and composer Josef Labor owed his career largely to the patronage of the Wittgenstein family, who held him in enormously high regard. In later life Ludwig Wittgenstein was fond of saying that there had been just six *great* composers: Haydn, Mozart, Beethoven, Schubert, Brahms – and Labor.

After his retirement from industry Karl Wittgenstein became known also as a great patron of the visual arts. Aided by his eldest daughter, Hermine – herself a gifted painter – he assembled a noteworthy collection of valuable paintings and sculptures, including works by Klimt, Moser and Rodin. Klimt called him his 'Minister of Fine Art', in gratitude for his financing of both the Secession Building (at which the works of Klimt, Schiele and Kokoschka were exhibited), and Klimt's own mural, *Philosophie*, which had been rejected by the University of Vienna. When Ludwig's sister, Margarete Wittgenstein, married in 1905, Klimt was commissioned to paint her wedding portrait.

The Wittgensteins were thus at the centre of Viennese cultural life during what was, if not its most glorious era, at least its most dynamic. The period of cultural history in Vienna from the late nineteenth century to the outbreak of the First World War has, quite justifiably, been the centre of much interest in recent years. It has been described as a time of 'nervous splendour', a phrase which might also be used to characterize the environment in which the children of Karl and Poldy were raised. For just as in the city at large, so within the family, beneath the 'all-pervading atmosphere of culture and humanity', lay doubt, tension and conflict.

The fascination of *fin de siècle* Vienna for the present-day lies in the fact that its tensions prefigure those that have dominated the history of Europe during the twentieth century. From those tensions sprang many of the intellectual and cultural movements that have shaped that history. It was, in an oft-quoted phrase of Karl Kraus, the 'research laboratory for world destruction' – the birthplace of both Zionism and Nazism, the place where Freud developed psychoanalysis, where Klimt, Schiele and Kokoschka inaugurated the *Jugendstil* movement in art, where Schoenberg developed atonal music and Adolf Loos introduced the starkly functional, unadorned style of architecture that characterizes the buildings of the modern age. In almost every field of human thought and activity, the new was emerging from the old, the twentieth century from the nineteenth.

That this should happen in Vienna is especially remarkable, since it was the centre of an empire that had, in many ways, not yet emerged from the eighteenth century. The anachronistic nature of this empire was symbolized by its aged ruler. Franz Josef, Emperor of Austria since 1848 and King of Hungary since 1867, was to remain both *kaiserlich* and *königlich* until 1916, after which the ramshackle conglomeration of kingdoms and principalities that had formed the Habsburg Empire soon collapsed, its territory to be divided between the nation states of Austria, Hungary, Poland, Czechoslovakia, Yugoslavia and Italy. The nineteenth-century movements of nationalism and democracy had made its collapse inevitable a long time before that, and for the last fifty or so years of its existence the empire survived by teetering from one crisis to the next, its continuing

survival believed in only by those who turned a blind eye to the
oncoming tides. For those who wished it to survive, the political
situation was always 'desperate, but not serious'.

The emergence of radical innovation in such a state is not, perhaps,
such a paradox: where the old is in such transparent decay, the new *has*
to emerge. The empire *was* a home for genius, after all, as Robert Musil
once famously observed: 'and that, probably, was the ruin of it'.

What divided the intellectuals of *Jung Wien* from their forebears was
their recognition of the decay around them, a refusal to pretend that
things could go on as they always had. Schoenberg's atonal system
was founded on the conviction that the old system of composition had
run its course; Adolf Loos's rejection of ornament on the recognition
that the baroque adornments to buildings had become an empty shell,
signifying nothing; Freud's postulation of unconscious forces on
the perception that beneath the conventions and mores of society
something very real and important was being repressed and denied.

In the Wittgenstein family this generational difference was played
out in a way that only partly mirrors the wider dissonance. Karl
Wittgenstein, after all, was not a representative of the Habsburg old
order. Indeed, he represented a force that had curiously little impact on
the life of Austria–Hungary – that of the metaphysically materialistic,
politically liberal and aggressively capitalistic entrepreneur. In England, Germany or – especially, perhaps – in America, he would have
been seen as a man of his times. In Austria he remained outside the
mainstream. After his retirement from business he published a series
of articles in the *Neue Freie Presse* extolling the virtues of American free
enterprise, but in doing so he was addressing an issue that had only a
marginal place in Austrian politics.

The absence of an effective liberal tradition in Austria was one of the
chief factors that set its political history apart from that of other
European nations. Its politics were dominated – and continued to be
so until the rise of Hitler – by the struggle between the Catholicism of
the Christian Socialists and the socialism of the Social Democrats. A
side-show to this main conflict was provided by the opposition to both
parties – who each in their different ways wished to maintain the
supra-national character of the empire – of the pan-German movement led by Georg von Schoenerer, which espoused the kind of
anti-Semitic, *Volkisch*, nationalism that the Nazis would later make
their own.

Being neither members of the old guard, nor socialists – and certainly not pan-German nationalists – the Wittgensteins had little to contribute to the politics of their country. And yet the values that had made Karl Wittgenstein a successful industrialist were, in another way, the focus of a generational conflict that resonates with the wider tensions of the age. As a successful industrialist, Karl was content to *acquire* culture; his children, and especially his sons, were intent on contributing to it.

Fifteen years separated Karl's eldest child, Hermine, from his youngest, Ludwig, and his eight children might be divided into two distinct generations: Hermine, Hans, Kurt and Rudolf as the older; Margarete, Helene, Paul and Ludwig the younger. By the time the two youngest boys reached adolescence, the conflict between Karl and his first generation of children had dictated that Paul and Ludwig grew up under quite a different régime.

The régime within which Karl's eldest sons were raised was shaped by Karl's determination to see them continue his business. They were not to be sent to schools (where they would acquire the bad habits of mind of the Austrian establishment), but were to be educated privately in a way designed to train their minds for the intellectual rigours of commerce. They were then to be sent to some part of the Wittgenstein business empire, where they would acquire the technical and commercial expertise necessary for success in industry.

With only one of his sons did this have anything like the desired effect. Kurt, by common consent the least gifted of the children, acquiesced in his father's wishes and became in time a company director. His suicide, unlike that of his brothers, was not obviously related to the parental pressure exerted by his father. It came much later, at the end of the First World War, when he shot himself after the troops under his command had refused to obey orders.

On Hans and Rudolf, the effect of Karl's pressure was disastrous. Neither had the slightest inclination to become captains of industry. With encouragement and support, Hans might have become a great composer, or at the very least a successful concert musician. Even by the Wittgenstein family – most of whom had considerable musical ability – he was regarded as exceptionally gifted. He was a musical prodigy of Mozartian talents – a genius. While still in infancy he mastered the violin and piano, and at the age of four he began composing his own work. Music for him was not an interest but an all-consuming passion; it had to be at the centre, not the periphery, of his life. Faced with his father's insistence that he pursue a career in industry, he did what his father had done before him and ran away to America. His intention was to seek a life as a musician. What exactly happened to him nobody knows. In 1903 the family were informed that a year earlier he had disappeared from a boat in Chesapeake Bay, and had not been seen since. The obvious conclusion to draw was that he had committed suicide.

Would Hans have lived a happy life had he been free to devote himself to a musical career? Would he have been better prepared to face life outside the rarefied atmosphere of the Wittgenstein home if he had attended school? Obviously, nobody knows. But Karl was sufficiently shaken by the news to change his methods for his two youngest boys, Paul and Ludwig, who were sent to school and allowed to pursue their own bent.

For Rudolf, the change came too late. He was already in his twenties when Hans went missing, and had himself embarked upon a similar course. He, too, had rebelled against his father's wishes, and by 1903 was living in Berlin, where he had gone to seek a career in the theatre. His suicide in 1904 was reported in a local newspaper. One evening in May, according to the report, Rudolf had walked into a pub in Berlin and ordered two drinks. After sitting by himself for a while, he ordered a drink for the piano player and asked him to play his favourite song, 'I am lost'. As the music played, Rudi took cyanide and collapsed. In a farewell letter to his family he said that he had killed himself because a friend of his had died. In another farewell letter he said it was because he had 'doubts about his perverted disposition'. Some time before his death he had approached 'The Scientific-Humanitarian Committee' (which campaigned for the emancipation of homosexuals) for help, but, says the yearbook of the organization, 'our influence did not reach far enough to turn him away from the fate of self-destruction'.

Until the suicides of his two brothers, Ludwig showed none of the self-destructiveness epidemic among the Wittgensteins of his generation. For much of his childhood, he was considered one of the dullest of this extraordinary brood. He exhibited no precocious musical, artistic or literary talent, and, indeed, did not even start speaking until he was four years old. Lacking the rebelliousness and wilfulness that marked the other male members of his family, he dedicated himself from an early age to the kind of practical skills and technical interests his father had tried unsuccessfully to inculcate into his elder brothers. One of the earliest photographs of him to survive shows a rather earnest young boy, working with apparent relish at his own lathe. If he revealed no particular genius, he at least showed application and some considerable manual dexterity. At the age of ten, for example, he constructed a working model of a sewing machine out of bits of wood and wire.

Until he was fourteen, he was content to feel himself surrounded by genius, rather than possessed of it. A story he told in later life concerned an occasion when he was woken at three in the morning by the sound of a piano. He went downstairs to find Hans performing one of his own compositions. Hans's concentration was manic. He was sweating, totally absorbed, and completely oblivious of Ludwig's presence. The image remained for Ludwig a paradigm of what it was like to be possessed of genius.

The extent to which the Wittgensteins venerated music is perhaps hard for us to appreciate today. Certainly there is no modern equivalent of the form this veneration took, so intimately connected was it with the Viennese classical tradition. Ludwig's own musical tastes – which were, as far as we can judge, typical of his family – struck many of his later Cambridge contemporaries as deeply reactionary. He would tolerate nothing later than Brahms, and even in Brahms, he once said, 'I can begin to hear the sound of machinery.' The true 'sons of God' were Mozart and Beethoven.

The standards of musicality that prevailed in the family were truly extraordinary. Paul, the brother closest in age to Ludwig, was to become a very successful and well-known concert pianist. In the First World War he lost his right arm, but, with remarkable determination, taught himself to play using only his left hand, and attained such proficiency that he was able to continue his concert career. It was for him that Ravel, in 1931, wrote his famous Concerto for the Left Hand. And yet, though admired throughout the world, Paul's playing was not admired within his own family. It lacked taste, they thought; it was too full of extravagant gestures. More to their taste was the refined, classically understated playing of Ludwig's sister Helene. Their mother, Poldy, was an especially stern critic. Gretl, probably the least musical of the family, once gamely attempted a duet with her, but before they had got very far Poldy suddenly broke off. *'Du hast aber keinen Rhythmus!'* ('You have no sense of rhythm at all!') she shrieked.

This intolerance of second-rate playing possibly deterred the nervous Ludwig from even attempting to master a musical instrument until he was in his thirties, when he learnt to play the clarinet as part of his training to be a teacher. As a child he made himself admired and loved in other ways – through his unerring politeness, his sensitivity to others, and his willingness to oblige. He was, in any case, secure in the knowledge that, so long as he showed an interest in engineering, he could always rely on the encouragement and approval of his father.

Though he later emphasized the unhappiness of his childhood, he gave the impression to the rest of his family of being a contented, cheerful boy. This discrepancy surely forms the crux of his boyhood reflections on honesty quoted earlier. The dishonesty he had in mind was not the petty kind that, say, allows one to steal something and then deny it, but the more subtle kind that consists in, for example, saying something because it is expected rather than because it is true. It was in part his willingness to succumb to this form of dishonesty that distinguished him from his siblings. So, at least, he thought in later life. An example that remained in his memory was of his brother Paul, ill in bed. On being asked whether he would like to get up or to stay longer in bed, Paul replied calmly that he would rather stay in bed. 'Whereas I in the same circumstances', Ludwig recalled, 'said what was untrue (that I wanted to get up) because I was afraid of the bad opinion of those around me.'

Sensitivity to the bad opinion of others lies at the heart of another example that stayed in his memory. He and Paul had wanted to belong to a Viennese gymnastic club, but discovered that (like most such clubs at that time) it was restricted to those of 'Aryan' origin. He was prepared to lie about their Jewish background in order to gain acceptance; Paul was not.

Fundamentally, the question was not whether one should, on all occasions, tell the truth, but rather whether one had an overriding obligation to *be* true – whether, despite the pressures to do otherwise, one should insist on being oneself. In Paul's case, this problem was made easier following Karl's change of heart after the death of Hans. He was sent to grammar school, and spent the rest of his life pursuing the musical career that was his natural bent. In Ludwig's case, the situation was more complicated. The pressures on him to conform to the wishes of others had become as much internal as external. Under the weight of these pressures, he allowed people to think that his natural bent was in the technical subjects that would train him for his father's preferred occupation. Privately he regarded himself as having 'neither taste nor talent' for engineering; quite reasonably, under the circumstances, his family considered him to have both.

Accordingly, Ludwig was sent, not to the grammar school in Vienna that Paul attended, but to the more technical and less academic Realschule in Linz. It was, it is true, feared that he would not pass the rigorous entrance examinations set by a grammar school, but the primary consideration was the feeling that a more technical education would suit his interests better.

The Realschule at Linz, however, has not gone down in history as a promising training ground for future engineers and industrialists. If it is famous for anything, it is for being the seedbed of Adolf Hitler's *Weltanschauung*. Hitler was, in fact, a contemporary of Wittgenstein's there, and (if *Mein Kampf* can be believed) it was the history teacher at the school, Leopold Pötsch, who first taught him to see the Habsburg Empire as a 'degenerate dynasty' and to distinguish the hopeless dynastic patriotism of those loyal to the Habsburgs from the (to Hitler) more appealing *Völkisch* nationalism of the pan-German movement. Hitler, though almost exactly the same age as Wittgenstein, was two years behind at school. They overlapped at the school for only the year 1904–5, before Hitler was forced to leave because of his poor record. There is no evidence that they had anything to do with one another.

Wittgenstein spent three years at the school, from 1903 to 1906. His school reports survive, and show him to have been, on the whole, a fairly poor student. If one translates the five subject-grades used in the school into a scale from A to E, then he achieved an A only twice in his school career – both times in religious studies. In most subjects he was graded C or D, rising to a B every now and again in English and natural history, and sinking to an E on one occasion in chemistry. If there is a pattern to his results, it is that he was, if anything, weaker in the scientific and technical subjects than in the humanities.

His poor results may in part be due to his unhappiness at school. It was the first time in his life he had lived away from the privileged environment of his family home, and he did not find it easy to find friends among his predominantly working-class fellow pupils. On first setting eyes on them he was shocked by their uncouth behaviour. '*Mist!*' ('Muck!') was his initial impression. To them he seemed (as one of them later told his sister Hermine) like a being from another world. He insisted on using the polite form 'Sie' to address them, which served only to alienate him further. They ridiculed him by chanting an alliterative jingle that made play of his unhappiness and of the distance between him and the rest of the school: '*Wittgenstein wandelt wehmütig widriger Winde wegen Wienwärts*' ('Wittgenstein wends his woeful windy way towards Vienna'). In his efforts to make friends, he felt, he later said, 'betrayed and sold' by his schoolmates.

His one close friend at Linz was a boy called Pepi, the son of the Strigl family, with whom he lodged. Throughout his three years at the school, he experienced with Pepi the love and hurt, the breaks and reconciliations, typical of adolescent attachment.

The effect of this relationship, and of his difficulties with his classmates, seems to have been to intensify the questioning and doubting nature implicit in his earlier reflections. His high marks in religious knowledge are a reflection, not only of the comparative leniency of priests compared with school teachers, but also of his own growing preoccupation with fundamental questions. His intellectual development during his time at Linz owed far more to the impetus of these doubts than to anything he may have been taught at school.

The biggest intellectual influence on him at this time was not that of any of his teachers, but that of his elder sister Margarete ('Gretl'). Gretl was acknowledged as the intellectual of the family, the one who kept abreast of contemporary developments in the arts and sciences, and the one most prepared to embrace new ideas and to challenge the views of her elders. She was an early defender of Freud, and was herself psychoanalysed by him. She later became a close friend of his and had a hand in his (perilously late) escape from the Nazis after the *Anschluss*.

It was no doubt through Gretl that Wittgenstein first became aware of the work of Karl Kraus. Kraus's satirical journal *Die Fackel* ('The Torch') first appeared in 1899, and from the very beginning was a huge success among the intellectually disaffected in Vienna. It was read by everyone with any pretence to understanding the political and cultural trends of the time, and exerted an enormous influence on practically all the major figures mentioned previously, from Adolf

Loos to Oskar Kokoschka. From the first, Gretl was an enthusiastic reader of Kraus's journal and a strong sympathizer of almost everything he represented. (Given the protean nature of Kraus's views, it was more or less impossible to sympathize with quite everything he said.)

Before founding *Die Fackel*, Kraus was known chiefly as the author of an anti-Zionist tract entitled *Eine Krone für Zion* ('A Crown for Zion'), which mocked the views of Theodor Herzl for being reactionary and divisive. Freedom for the Jews, Kraus maintained, could come only from their complete assimilation.

Kraus was a member of the Social Democrat Party, and for the first few years of its publication (until about 1904) his journal was regarded as a mouthpiece for socialist ideas. The targets of his satire were, to a large extent, those a socialist might like to see hit. He attacked the hypocrisy of the Austrian government in its treatment of the Balkan peoples, the nationalism of the pan-German movement, the *laissez-faire* economic policies advocated by the *Neue Freie Presse* (in, for example, Karl Wittgenstein's articles for the paper), and the corruption of the Viennese Press in its willingness to serve the interests of the government and of big business. He led an especially passionate campaign against the sexual hypocrisy of the Austrian establishment, as manifested in the legal persecution of prostitutes and the social condemnation of homosexuals. 'A trial involving sexual morality', he said, 'is a deliberate step from individual to general immorality.'

From 1904 onward, the nature of his attacks became less political than moral. Behind his satire was a concern with spiritual values that was alien to the ideology of the Austro-Marxists. He was concerned to uncover hypocrisy and injustice, not primarily from a desire to protect the interests of the proletariat, but rather from the point of view of one who sought to protect the integrity of an essentially aristocratic ideal of the nobility of truth. He was criticized for this by his friends on the Left, one of whom, Robert Scheu, told him bluntly that the choice before him was that of supporting the decaying old order or supporting the Left. 'If I must choose the lesser of two evils', came Kraus's lofty reply, 'I will choose neither.' Politics, he said, 'is what a man does in order to conceal what he is and what he himself does not know'.

The phrase encapsulates one of the many ways in which the outlook of the adult Wittgenstein corresponds to that of Kraus. 'Just improve yourself', Wittgenstein would later say to many of his friends, 'that is all you can do to improve the world.' Political questions, for him, would always be secondary to questions of personal integrity. The question he had asked himself at the age of eight was answered by a kind of Kantian categorical imperative: one *should* be truthful, and that is that; the question 'Why?' is inappropriate and cannot be answered. Rather, all other questions must be asked and answered within this fixed point – the inviolable duty to be true to oneself.

The determination not to conceal 'what one is' became central to Wittgenstein's whole outlook. It was the driving force that impelled the series of confessions he was to make later in life of the times when he had failed to be honest. During his time at school in Linz, he made the first of these attempts to come clean about himself, when he made some confessions to his eldest sister, Hermine ('Mining'). What formed the subject of these confessions, we do not know; we know only that he was later disparaging about them. He described them as confessions 'in which I manage to appear to be an excellent human being'.

Wittgenstein's loss of religious faith, which, he later said, occurred while he was a schoolboy at Linz, was, one supposes, a consequence of this spirit of stark truthfulness. In other words, it was not so much that he lost his faith as that he now felt obliged to acknowledge that he had none, to confess that he could not believe the things a Christian was supposed to believe. This may have been one of the things he confessed to Mining. Certainly he discussed it with Gretl, who, to help him in the philosophical reflection consequent on a loss of faith, directed him to the work of Schopenhauer.

Schopenhauer's transcendental idealism, as expressed in his classic, *The World as Will and Representation*, formed the basis of Wittgenstein's earliest philosophy. The book is, in many ways, one that is bound to appeal to an adolescent who has lost his religious faith and is looking for something to replace it. For while Schopenhauer recognizes 'man's need for metaphysics', he insists that it is neither necessary nor possible for an intelligent honest person to believe in the literal truth of religious doctrines. To expect that he should, Schopenhauer says, would be like asking a giant to put on the shoes of a dwarf.

Schopenhauer's own metaphysics is a peculiar adaptation of Kant's. Like Kant, he regards the everyday world, the world of the senses, as mere appearance, but unlike Kant (who insists that noumenal reality is unknowable), he identifies as the only true reality the world of the ethical will. It is a theory that provides a metaphysical counterpart to the attitude of Karl Kraus mentioned earlier – a philosophical justification of the view that what happens in the 'outside' world is less important than the existential, 'internal' question of 'what one is'. Schopenhauer's idealism was abandoned by Wittgenstein only when he began to study logic and was persuaded to adopt Frege's conceptual realism. Even after that, however, he returned to Schopenhauer at a critical stage in the composition of the *Tractatus*, when he believed that he had reached a point where idealism and realism coincide.*

Taken to its extreme, the view that the 'internal' has priority over the 'external' becomes solipsism, the denial that there is any reality *outside* oneself. Much of Wittgenstein's later philosophical thinking about the self is an attempt once and for all to put to rest the ghost of this view. Among the books that he read as a schoolboy which influenced his later development, this doctrine finds its most startling expression in *Sex and Character*, by Otto Weininger.

It was during Wittgenstein's first term at Linz that Weininger became a cult figure in Vienna. On 4 October 1903, his dying body was found on the floor in the house in Schwarzspanierstrasse where Beethoven had died. At the age of twenty-three, in an act of self-consciously symbolic significance, he had shot himself in the home of the man whom he considered to be the very greatest of geniuses. *Sex and Character* had been published the previous spring, and had received, on the whole, fairly bad reviews. Had it not been for the sensational circumstances of its author's death, it would probably have had no great impact. As it was, on 17 October, a letter from August Strindberg appeared in *Die Fackel*, describing the work as: 'an awe-inspiring book, which has probably solved the most difficult of all problems'. Thus was the Weininger cult born.

Weininger's suicide seemed to many to be the logical outcome of the argument of his book, and it is primarily this that made him such a *cause célèbre* in pre-war Vienna. His taking of his own life was seen, not as a cowardly escape from suffering, but as an ethical deed, a brave acceptance of a tragic conclusion. It was, according to Oswald Spengler, 'a spiritual struggle', which offered 'one of the noblest

---

* See p. 144.

spectacles ever presented by a late religiousness'. As such, it inspired a number of imitative suicides. Indeed, Wittgenstein himself began to feel ashamed that he had not dared kill himself, that he had ignored a hint that he was *de trop* in this world. This feeling lasted for nine years, and was overcome only after he had convinced Bertrand Russell that he possessed philosophic genius. His brother Rudolf's suicide came just six months after Weininger's, and was, as we have seen, executed in an equally theatrical manner.

Wittgenstein's acknowledgement of Weininger's influence, more than that of any other, ties his life and work to the environment in which he was raised. Weininger is a quintessentially Viennese figure. The themes of his book, together with the manner of his death, form a potent symbol of the social, intellectual and moral tensions of the *fin de siècle* Vienna in which Wittgenstein grew up.

Running throughout the book is a very Viennese preoccupation with the decay of modern times. Like Kraus, Weininger attributes this decay to the rise of science and business and the decline of art and music, and characterizes it, in an essentially aristocratic manner, as the triumph of pettiness over greatness. In a passage reminiscent of the prefaces Wittgenstein would write in the 1930s, for his own philosophical work, Weininger denounces the modern age as:

. . . a time when art is content with daubs and seeks its inspiration in the sports of animals; the time of a superficial anarchy, with no feeling for Justice and the State; a time of communistic ethics, of the most foolish of historical views, the materialistic interpretation of history; a time of capitalism and of Marxism; a time when history, life and science are no more than political economy and technical instruction; a time when genius is supposed to be a form of madness; a time with no great artists and no great philosophers; a time without originality and yet with the most foolish craving for originality.

Like Kraus, too, Weininger was inclined to identify those aspects of modern civilization that he most disliked as Jewish, and to describe the social and cultural trends of the age in terms of the sexual polarity between the masculine and the feminine. Unlike Kraus, however, Weininger emphasizes these two themes to an obsessive, almost lunatic, extent.

Sex and Character is dominated by an elaborately worked out theory intended to justify Weininger's misogyny and anti-Semitism. The central point of the book, he says in the preface, is to 'refer to a single principle the whole contrast between men and women'.

The book is divided into two parts: the 'biological-psychological', and the 'logical-philosophical'. In the first he seeks to establish that all human beings are biologically bisexual, a mixture of male and female. Only the proportions differ, which is how he explains the existence of homosexuals: they are either womanly men or masculine women. The 'scientific' part of the book ends with a chapter on 'Emancipated Women', in which he uses this theory of bisexuality to oppose the women's movement. 'A woman's demand for emancipation and her qualification for it', he claims, 'are in direct proportion to the amount of maleness in her.' Such women are, therefore, generally lesbians, and as such are on a higher level than most women. These masculine women should be given their freedom, but it would be a grave mistake to let the majority of women imitate them.

The second, and much larger, part of the book discusses Man and Woman, not as biological categories, but as 'psychological types', conceived of as something like Platonic ideas. As actual men and women are all mixtures of masculinity and femininity, Man and Woman do not exist *except* as Platonic forms. Nevertheless, we are all psychologically either a man or a woman. Curiously, Weininger thinks that, whereas it is possible for a person to be biologically male but psychologically female, the reverse is impossible. Thus, even emancipated, lesbian, women are psychologically female. It follows that everything he says about 'Woman' applies to all women and also to some men.

The essence of Woman, he says, is her absorption in sex. She is nothing but sexuality; she is sexuality itself. Whereas men possess sexual organs, 'her sexual organs possess women'. The female is completely preoccupied with sexual matters, whereas the male is interested in much else, such as war, sport, social affairs, philosophy and science, business and politics, religion and art. Weininger has a peculiar epistemological theory to explain this, based on his notion of a 'henid'. A henid is a piece of psychical data before it becomes an idea. Woman thinks in henids, which is why, for her, thinking and feeling are the same thing. She looks to man, who thinks in clear and articulated ideas, to clarify her data, to interpret her henids. That is why women fall in love only with men cleverer than themselves. Thus, the essential difference between man and woman is that, whereas 'the male lives consciously, the female lives unconsciously'.

Weininger draws from this analysis alarmingly far-reaching ethical implications. Without the ability to clarify her own henids, woman is incapable of forming clear judgements, so the distinction between true and false means nothing to her. Thus women are naturally, inescapably, untruthful. Not that they are, on this account, immoral; they do not enter the moral realm at all. Woman simply has no standard of right or wrong. And, as she knows no moral or logical imperative, she cannot be said to have a soul, and this means she lacks free will. From this it follows that women have no ego, no individuality, and no character. Ethically, women are a lost cause.

Turning from epistemology and ethics to psychology, Weininger analyses women in terms of two further Platonic types: the mother and the prostitute. Each individual woman is a combination of the two, but is predominantly one or the other. There is no moral difference between the two: the mother's love for her child is as unthinking and indiscriminate as the prostitute's desire to make love to every man she sees. (Weininger will have nothing to do with any explanation of prostitution based on social and economic conditions. Women are prostitutes, he says, because of the 'disposition for and inclination to prostitution' which is 'deep in the nature of women'.) The chief difference between the two types is the form that their obsession with sex takes: whereas the mother is obsessed with the object of sex, the prostitute is obsessed with the act itself.

All women, whether mothers or prostitutes, share a single characteristic – 'a characteristic which is really and exclusively feminine' – and that is the instinct of match-making. It is the ever present desire of all women to see man and woman united. To be sure, woman is interested first and foremost in her own sexual life, but that is really a special case of her 'only vital interest' – 'the interest that sexual unions shall take place; the wish that as much of it as possible shall occur, in all cases, places and times'.

As an adjunct to his psychological investigation of woman, Weininger has a chapter on Judaism. Again, the Jew is a Platonic idea, a psychological type, which is a possibility (or a danger) for all mankind, 'but which has become actual in the most conspicuous fashion only amongst the Jews'. The Jew is 'saturated with femininity' – 'the most manly Jew is more feminine than the least manly Aryan'. Like the woman, the Jew has a strong instinct for pairing. He has a poor sense of individuality and a correspondingly strong instinct to preserve the race. The Jew has no sense of good and evil, and no soul. He is non-philosophical and profoundly irreligious (the Jewish religion being 'a mere historical tradition'). Judaism and Christianity are opposites: the latter is 'the highest expression of the highest faith'; the former is 'the extreme of cowardliness'. Christ was the greatest of all men because he: 'conquered in himself Judaism, the greatest negation, and created Christianity, the strongest affirmation and the most direct opposite of Judaism'.

Weininger himself was both Jewish and homosexual (and therefore possibly of the psychologically female type), and the idea that his suicide was, in some way, a 'solution' could therefore be easily assimilated within the most vulgar anti-Semitic or misogynist outlook. Hitler, for example, is reported as having once remarked: 'Dietrich Eckhart told me that in all his life he had known just one good Jew: Otto Weininger who killed himself on the day when he realised that the Jew lives upon the decay of peoples.' And the fact that fear of the emancipation of women, and, particularly, of Jews, was a widespread preoccupation in Vienna at the turn of the century no doubt accounts to some extent for the book's enormous popularity. It would later provide convenient material for Nazi propaganda broadcasts.

But why did Wittgenstein admire the book so much? What did he learn from it? Indeed, given that its claims to scientific biology are transparently spurious, its epistemology obvious nonsense, its psychology primitive, and its ethical prescriptions odious, what could he *possibly* have learnt from it?

To see this, we have, I think, to turn aside from Weininger's – entirely negative – psychology of Woman, and look instead at his psychology of Man. Only there do we find something in the book other than bigotry and self-contempt, something that resonates with themes we know to have been central to Wittgenstein's thoughts as a teenager (and, indeed, for the rest of his life), and that provides at least some hint as to what Wittgenstein may have found to admire in it.

Unlike Woman, Man, according to Weininger, has a choice: he can, and must, choose between the masculine and the feminine, between consciousness and unconsciousness, will and impulse, love and sexuality. It is every man's ethical duty to choose the first of each of these pairs, and the extent to which he is able to do this is the extent to which he approximates to the very highest type of man: the genius.

The consciousness of the genius is the furthest removed from the henid stage; 'it has the greatest, most limpid clearness and distinctness'. The genius has the best developed memory, the greatest ability to form clear judgements, and, therefore, the most refined sense of the distinctions between true and false, right and wrong. Logic and ethics are fundamentally the same; 'they are no more than duty to oneself'. Genius 'is the highest morality, and, therefore, it is everyone's duty'.

Man is not born with a soul, but with the potential for one. To realize this potential he has to find his real higher self, to escape the limitations of his (unreal) empirical self. One route to this self-discovery is love, through which 'many men first come to know of their own real nature, and to be convinced that they possess a soul':

> In love, man is only loving himself. Not his empirical self, not the weaknesses and vulgarities, not the failings and smallnesses which he outwardly exhibits; but all that he wants to be, all that he ought to be, his truest, deepest, intelligible nature, free from all fetters of necessity, from all taint of earth.

Naturally, Weininger is here talking of Platonic love. Indeed, for him, there *is* only Platonic love, because: 'any other so-called love belongs to the kingdom of the senses'. Love and sexual desire are not only not the same thing; they are in opposition to one another. That is why the idea of love after marriage is make-believe. As sexual attraction increases with physical proximity, love is strongest in absence of the loved one. Indeed, love *needs* separation, a certain distance, to preserve it: 'what all the travels in the world could not achieve, what time could not accomplish, may be brought about by accidental, unintentional, physical contact with the beloved object, in which the sexual impulse is awakened, and which suffices to kill love on the spot'.

The love of a woman, though it can arouse in a man some hint of his higher nature, is, in the end, doomed either to unhappiness (if the truth about the woman's unworthiness is discovered) or to immorality (if the lie about her perfection is kept up). The only love that is of enduring worth is that 'attached to the absolute, to the idea of God'.

Man should love, not woman, but his own soul, the divine in himself, the 'God who in my bosom dwells'. Thus he must resist the pairing instinct of the woman and, despite pressure from women, free himself from sex. To the objection that this suggestion, if adopted universally, would be the death of the human race, Weininger replies that it would be merely the death of the *physical* life, and would put in its place the 'full development of the spiritual life'. Besides, he says: 'no one who is honest with himself feels bound to provide for the continuity of the human race':

> That the human race should persist is of no interest whatever to reason; he who would perpetuate humanity would perpetuate the problem and the guilt, the only problem and the only guilt.

The choice that Weininger's theory offers is a bleak and terrible one indeed: genius or death. If one can only live as a 'Woman' or as a 'Jew' – if, that is, one cannot free oneself from sensuality and earthly desires – then one has no right to live at all. The *only* life worth living is the spiritual life.

In its strict separation of love from sexual desire, its uncompromising view of the worthlessness of everything save the products of genius, and its conviction that sexuality is incompatible with the honesty that genius demands, there is much in Weininger's work that chimes with attitudes we find Wittgenstein expressing time and again throughout his life. So much so, that there is reason to believe that of all the books he read in adolescence, Weininger's is the one that had the greatest and most lasting impact on his outlook.

Of particular importance, perhaps, is the peculiar twist that Weininger gives to Kant's Moral Law, which, on this account, not only imposes an inviolable duty to be honest, but, in so doing, provides the route for all men to discover in themselves whatever genius they possess. To acquire genius, on this view, is not merely a noble ambition; it is a Categorical Imperative. Wittgenstein's recurring thoughts of suicide between 1903 and 1912, and the fact that these thoughts abated only after Russell's recognition of his genius, suggest that he accepted this imperative in all its terrifying severity.

So much for Wittgenstein's intellectual development as a schoolboy, which, we have seen, was inspired primarily by philosophical reflection and (under Gretl's guidance) fuelled by the reading of philosophers and cultural critics. But what of his development in the technical subjects – his advancement in the skills and knowledge required to succeed in his chosen profession?

Of this we hear surprisingly little. The works by scientists which he read as a teenager – Heinrich Hertz's *Principles of Mechanics*, and Ludwig Boltzmann's *Populäre Schriften* – suggest an interest, not in mechanical engineering, nor even, especially, in theoretical physics, but rather in the philosophy of science.

Both (like the works previously discussed) espouse a fundamentally Kantian view of the nature and method of philosophy. In *Principles of Mechanics* Hertz addresses the problem of how to understand the mysterious concept of 'force' as it is used in Newtonian physics. Hertz proposes that, instead of giving a direct answer to the question: 'What is force?', the problem should be dealt with by restating Newtonian physics without using 'force' as a basic concept. 'When these painful contradictions are removed', he writes, 'the question as to the nature of force will not have been answered; but our minds, no longer vexed, will cease to ask illegitimate questions.'

This passage of Hertz was known by Wittgenstein virtually word for word, and was frequently invoked by him to describe his own conception of philosophical problems and the correct way to solve them. As we have seen, philosophical thinking *began* for him with 'painful contradictions' (and not with the Russellian desire for *certain* knowledge); its aim was always to resolve those contradictions and to replace confusion with clarity.

He may well have been led to Hertz by reading Boltzmann's *Populäre Schriften*, a collection of Boltzmann's more popular lectures, published in 1905. The lectures present a similarly Kantian view of science, in which our models of reality are taken *to* our experience of the world, and not (as the empiricist tradition would have it) derived from it. So ingrained in Wittgenstein's philosophical thinking was this view that he found the empiricist view difficult even to conceive.

Boltzmann was Professor of Physics at the University of Vienna, and there was some talk of Wittgenstein's studying with him after he had left school. In 1906, however, the year that Wittgenstein left Linz, Boltzmann committed suicide, despairing of ever being taken seriously by the scientific world.

Independently of Boltzmann's suicide, it seems, it had been decided that Wittgenstein's further education should advance his technical knowledge rather than develop his interest in philosophy and theoretical science. Accordingly, after leaving Linz he was sent – no doubt urged by his father – to study mechanical engineering at the Technische Hochschule (now the Technical University) in Charlottenburg, Berlin.

Of Wittgenstein's two years in Berlin very little is known. The college records show that he matriculated on 23 October 1906, that he attended lectures for three semesters and that, having completed his diploma course satisfactorily, he was awarded his certificate on 5 May 1908. Photographs of the time show him to be a handsome, immaculately dressed young man, who might well have been – as he is reported to have been a year later in Manchester – a 'favourite with the ladies'.

He lodged with the family of one of his professors, Dr Jolles, who adopted him as their own 'little Wittgenstein'. Much later, after the First World War had produced in him a transformation comparable to, and perhaps even deeper than, the change he had undergone in 1903–4, Wittgenstein was embarrassed by the intimacy he had shared with the Jolles family, and replied to the friendly and affectionate letters he received from Mrs Jolles with stiff politeness. But while he was in Berlin, and for a number of years after he left, he was grateful enough for the warm concern they showed him.

It was a time of competing interests and obligations. Wittgenstein's sense of duty towards his father impelled him to stick at his engineering studies, and he developed an interest in the then very young science of aeronautics. But, increasingly, he found himself gripped, almost against his will, by philosophical questions. Inspired by the diaries of Gottfried Keller, he began to write down his philosophical reflections in the form of dated notebook entries.

In the short term, his father's wishes prevailed, and on leaving Berlin he went to Manchester to further his studies in aeronautics. But in the long term, it was probably already clear to him that the only life he could consider worthwhile was one spent in fulfilment of the greater duty he owed to himself – to his own genius.

2
MANCHESTER

Suppressing his growing preoccupation with philosophical questions, Wittgenstein, in the spring of 1908, at the age of nineteen, went to Manchester to pursue research in aeronautics. It was his apparent intention to construct, and eventually to fly, an aeroplane of his own design.

These were the very pioneering days of aeronautics, when the subject was in the hands of rival groups of amateurs, enthusiasts and eccentrics from America and the various European nations. Orville and Wilbur Wright had not yet amazed the world by staying in the air for a full two and a half hours. Though no substantial successes had been made, and the subject was treated with some amusement and derision by the Press and public, scientists and governments alike were aware of the potential importance of the research. It was a field in which successful innovation could expect handsome rewards, and Wittgenstein's project no doubt had the complete support of his father.

He began his research by experimenting on the design and construction of kites. For this purpose he went to work at the Kite Flying Upper Atmosphere Station, a meteorological observation centre near Glossop, where observations were made using box-kites carrying various instruments. The centre had been set up by the recently retired Professor of Physics Arthur Schuster, who continued to maintain an active interest in its work. The head of the centre was J. E. Petavel, lecturer in meteorology at Manchester, who developed a keen interest in aeronautics and later became one of the leading authorities on the subject.

While working at the observatory Wittgenstein lived at the Grouse Inn, an isolated roadside pub on the Derbyshire Moors. From here, on 17 May, he wrote to Hermine, describing the conditions under which he worked, exulting in the glorious isolation of the Grouse Inn, but complaining of the incessant rain and the rustic standards of the food and the toilet facilities: 'I'm having a few problems growing accustomed to it all; but I am already beginning to enjoy it.'

His job, he said, 'is the most delightful I could wish for':

> I have to provide the observatory with kites – which formerly were always ordered from outside – and to ascertain through trial and error their best design; the materials for this are ordered for me by request from the observatory. To begin with, of course, I had to help with the observations, in order to get to know the demands which would be made of such a kite. The day before yesterday, however, I was told that I can now begin making independent experiments . . . Yesterday I began to build my first kite and hope to finish it by the middle of next week.

He goes on to describe his physical and emotional isolation, and his deep need for a close companion. At the inn he was the only guest apart from 'a certain Mr Rimmer who makes meteorological observations', and at the observatory the only time he had company was on Saturdays, when Petavel arrived with some of his students:

> Because I am so cut off I naturally have an *extraordinarily strong* desire for a friend and when the students arrive on Saturday I always think it will be one of them.

He was too reticent to approach the students, but shortly after this letter a friend came to him. William Eccles, an engineer four years older than himself, came to the observatory to conduct meteorological research. On his arrival at the Grouse Inn, Eccles walked into the common living room to find Wittgenstein surrounded with books and papers which lay scattered over the table and floor. As it was impossible to move without disturbing them, he immediately set to and tidied them up – much to Wittgenstein's amusement and appreciation. The two quickly became close friends, and remained so, with interruptions, until the Second World War.

In the autumn of 1908 Wittgenstein registered as a research student in the Engineering Department of Manchester University. In those days Manchester had very few research students, and the arrangements made for them were somewhat casual. No formal course of study was organized, nor was a supervisor provided to oversee the research. It was not expected that Wittgenstein should work for a degree. Instead, it was understood that he would pursue his own line of research, having at his disposal the laboratory facilities of the university and the interested attention, should he require it, of its professors.

Among these professors was the mathematician Horace Lamb, who held a seminar for research students to which they could bring their problems for his consideration. Wittgenstein seems to have availed himself of this provision. In a letter to Hermine of October he describes a conversation he had had with Lamb, who, he says:

. . . will try to solve the equations that I came up with and which I showed him. He said he didn't know for certain whether they are altogether solvable with today's methods and so I am eagerly awaiting the outcome of his attempts.

His interest in the solution of this problem was evidently not confined to its aeronautical applications. He began to develop an interest in pure mathematics, and to attend J. E. Littlewood's lectures on the theory of mathematical analysis, and one evening a week he met with two other research students to discuss questions in mathematics. These discussions led to a consideration of the problems of providing mathematics with logical foundations, and Wittgenstein was introduced by one of his fellow students to Bertrand Russell's book on the subject, *The Principles of Mathematics*, which had been published five years previously.

Reading Russell's book was to prove a decisive event in Wittgenstein's life. Though he continued for another two years with research in aeronautics, he became increasingly obsessed with the problems discussed by Russell, and his engineering work was pursued with an ever-growing disenchantment. He had found a subject in which he could become as absorbed as his brother Hans had been in playing the piano, a subject in which he could hope to make, not just a worthwhile contribution, but a *great* one.

The central theme of *The Principles of Mathematics* is that, contrary to the opinion of Kant and most other philosophers, the whole of pure mathematics could be derived from a small number of fundamental, *logical*, principles. Mathematics and logic, in other words, were one and the same. It was Russell's intention to provide a strictly mathematical demonstration of this by actually making all the derivations required to prove each theorem of mathematical analysis from a few trivial, self-evident axioms. This was to be his second volume. In fact, it grew into the monumental three-volume work *Principia Mathematica*. In this, his 'first volume', he lays the philosophical foundations of this bold enterprise, taking issue principally with Kant's at that time widely influential view that mathematics was quite distinct from logic and was founded on the 'structure of appearance', our basic 'intuitions' of space and time. For Russell, the importance of the issue lay in the difference between regarding mathematics as a body of certain, *objective*, knowledge, and regarding it as a fundamentally *subjective* construction of the human mind.

Russell did not become aware until *The Principles of Mathematics* was being printed that he had been anticipated in the main lines of his enterprise by the German mathematician Gottlob Frege, who in his *Grundgesetze der Arithmetik* (the first volume of which was published in 1893) had attempted precisely the task that Russell had set himself. He made a hurried study of Frege's work and appended to his book an essay on 'The Logical and Arithmetical Doctrines of Frege', praising the *Grundgesetze*.

Until then, the *Grundgesetze* had been a much neglected work. Few had bothered to read it, and even fewer had understood it. Russell was perhaps the first to appreciate its importance. In his quick study of Frege's work, however, he had noticed a difficulty that Frege had overlooked. The problem it raised seemed at first a minor one, but its solution was soon to become the cardinal problem in the foundations of mathematics.

To provide a logical definition of number, Frege had made use of the notion of a class, which he defined as the extension of a concept. Thus, to the concept 'man' corresponds the class of men, to the concept 'table', the class of tables, and so on. It was an axiom of his system that to every meaningful concept there corresponds an object, a class, that is its extension. Russell discovered that, by a certain chain of reasoning, this led to a contradiction. For on this assumption there will be some classes that belong to themselves, and some that do not: the class of all classes is itself a class, and therefore belongs to itself; the class of men is not itself a man, and therefore does not. On this basis we form 'the class of all classes which do not belong to themselves'. Now we ask: is *this* class a member of itself or not? The answer either that it is or that it is not leads to a contradiction. And, clearly, if a contradiction can be derived from Frege's axioms, his system of logic is an inadequate foundation upon which to build the whole of mathematics.

Before publishing his discovery, Russell wrote to Frege at the University of Jena to inform him of it. Frege was then preparing the second volume of his *Grundgesetze*, and though he included in it a hasty and unsatisfactory reaction to the paradox, he realized it showed his entire system to be fundamentally flawed. Russell himself proposed to avoid the contradiction by a strategy he called the 'Theory of Types', an outline of which formed the second appendix to the *Principles*. This postulates a hierarchy of *types* of objects, collections of which can legitimately be grouped together to form sets: thus, the first type is individuals, the second, classes of individuals, the third, classes of classes of individuals, and so on. Sets must be collections of objects of the same type; thus, there is no such thing as a set which is a member of itself.

The Theory of Types does indeed avoid the contradiction, but at the expense of introducing into the system a somewhat *ad hoc* measure. It may be true that there are different types of things; it may also be true that there is no such thing as a set which is a member of itself – but these are hardly the sort of trivial, self-evident truths of logic from which Russell had originally intended to proceed. Russell himself was dissatisfied with it, and his book ends with a challenge:

> What the complete solution of the difficulty may be, I have not succeeded in discovering; but as it affects the very foundations of reasoning, I earnestly commend the study of it to the attention of all students of logic.

It was precisely the bait needed to hook Wittgenstein, and, as Russell recommends, he dedicated himself earnestly to the solution of the paradox. He devoted much of his first two terms at Manchester to a close study of both Russell's *Principles* and Frege's *Grundgesetze*, and, some time before April 1909, formulated his first attempt at a solution, which he sent to Russell's friend, the mathematician and historian of mathematics Philip E. B. Jourdain.

That Wittgenstein sent his solution to Jourdain rather than to Russell or Frege perhaps indicates some degree of tentativeness. He presumably came across Jourdain's name in a 1905 issue of the *Philosophical Magazine*, which contains an article by Jourdain on the foundations of mathematics and an article by his professor at Manchester, Horace Lamb. An entry in Jourdain's correspondence book, dated 20 April, shows that he replied to Wittgenstein's attempted solution after first discussing it with Russell. Neither, it seems, were inclined to accept it:

> Russell said that the views I gave in reply to Wittgenstein (who had 'solved' Russell's contradiction) agree with his own.

According to his sister Hermine, Wittgenstein's obsession with the philosophy of mathematics at this time caused him to suffer terribly from the feeling of being torn between conflicting vocations. It may have been Jourdain's dismissal of his 'solution' that persuaded him, for the time being, to stick to aeronautics. Not for another two years did he return to the fray, when he finally contacted both Frege and Russell directly to present to them a more considered philosophical position. Though he had taste enough for philosophical problems, he was yet to be persuaded he had talent for them.

Though still convinced he had neither talent nor taste for aeronautical engineering, Wittgenstein persevered with his attempts to design and construct an aircraft engine. Plans of his proposed engine survive, and show that his idea was to rotate the propeller by means of high-speed gases rushing from a combustion chamber (rather in the way that the pressure of water from a hose is used to turn a rotating lawn sprinkler). The idea was fundamentally flawed, and quite impractical for propelling an aeroplane. It was, however, successfully adopted during the Second World War in the design of certain helicopters.

Wittgenstein had a combustion chamber built specially for him by a local firm, and much of his research consisted of experimenting on this with various discharge nozzles. He was helped by a laboratory assistant called Jim Bamber, whom he later described as: 'one of the very few people with whom I got on well during my Manchester period'. His general irritability at having to dedicate himself to engineering work was compounded by the fiddly nature of the task, and, recalls Bamber, 'his nervous temperament made him the last person to tackle such research':

> . . . for when things went wrong, which often occurred, he would throw his arms about, stamp around and swear volubly in German.

According to Bamber, Wittgenstein would ignore the midday meal break and carry on until the evening, when he would relax either by sitting in a very hot bath ('He used to brag about the temperature of the water') or by going to a concert given by the Hallé Orchestra, occasionally accompanied by Bamber, who has described how 'he used to sit through the concert without speaking a word, completely absorbed'.

Other diversions included outings with Eccles, who by this time had left the university to take up an engineering job in Manchester. One Sunday afternoon remained in Eccles's memory. Wittgenstein had decided he would like to go to the seaside, to Blackpool. On finding that there was no suitable train, he did not seek an alternative but suggested they hire a special train, just for the two of them. He was eventually dissuaded from this by Eccles, and induced to adopt the less expensive (though still, to Eccles's mind, extravagant) option of taking a taxi to Liverpool, where they had a trip on the Mersey ferry.

During his second year at Manchester, Wittgenstein abandoned his attempt to design and construct a jet engine and concentrated instead on the design of the propeller. His work on this was taken sufficiently seriously by the university for him to be elected to a research studentship for what was to be his last year there, 1910–11. He himself was confident enough about the importance and originality of his work to patent his design. His application, together with a provisional specification of his design for 'Improvements in Propellers applicable for Aerial Machines', is dated 22 November 1910. On 21 June 1911 he left a complete specification, and the patent was accepted on 17 August of that year.

By this time, however, Wittgenstein's obsession with philosophical problems had got the better of his resolve to pursue a vocation in engineering. Though his studentship was renewed for the following year, and he is still listed as a student of Manchester University in October 1911, his days as an aeronaut were finished during the summer vacation of that year, when, 'in a constant, indescribable, almost pathological state of agitation', he drew up a plan for a proposed book on philosophy.

3
RUSSELL'S PROTÉGÉ

At the end of the summer vacation of 1911 Wittgenstein, having drawn up a plan of his projected book on philosophy, travelled to Jena to discuss it with Frege – presumably with a view to finding out whether it was worth going on with, or whether he should instead continue with his work in aeronautical research. Hermine Wittgenstein knew Frege to be an old man and was anxious about the visit, fearing that he would not have the patience to deal with the situation, or the understanding to realize the momentous importance the meeting had for her brother. In the event, so Wittgenstein later told friends, Frege 'wiped the floor' with him – one reason, perhaps, why nothing of this proposed work has survived. Frege was, however, sufficiently encouraging to recommend to Wittgenstein that he go to Cambridge to study under Bertrand Russell.

The advice was more propitious than Frege could have known, and was not only to lead to a decisive turning point in Wittgenstein's life, but also to have a tremendous influence on Russell's. For at the very time when Wittgenstein needed a mentor, Russell needed a protégé.

The year 1911 was something of a watershed in Russell's life. He had, in the previous year, finished *Principia Mathematica*, the product of ten years of exhausting labour. 'My intellect never quite recovered from the strain', he writes in his *Autobiography*. 'I have been ever since definitely less capable of dealing with difficult abstractions than I was before.' With the completion of *Principia* Russell's life, both personally and philosophically, entered a new phase. In the spring of 1911 he fell in love with Ottoline Morrell, the aristocratic wife of the Liberal MP Phillip Morrell, and began an affair that was to last until 1916. During the height of his passion he wrote Ottoline as many as three letters a day. These letters contain an almost daily record of Russell's reactions to Wittgenstein – a record which provides a useful corrective to some of the anecdotes he told about Wittgenstein in his later years, when his love of a good story frequently got the better of his concern for accuracy.

Partly under the influence of Ottoline, and partly from the debilitating effect of finishing *Principia*, Russell's work in philosophy began to change. His first work after *Principia* was *The Problems of Philosophy*, his 'shilling shocker', the first of many popular works and the book that first revealed his remarkable gift for the lucid expression of difficult ideas. At the same time he took up the post of lecturer in mathematical logic at Trinity College. His teaching and his work on a book popularizing his thought – together with the fact that *Principia* had left him exhausted – combined to persuade him that from now on his chief task in the development of the ideas of *Principia* lay in encouraging others to continue from where he had left off. At the end of 1911 he wrote to Ottoline: 'I did think the technical philosophy that remains for me to do very important indeed.' But now:

> I have an uneasiness about philosophy altogether; what remains for *me* to do in philosophy (I mean in *technical* philosophy) does not seem of first-rate importance. The shilling shocker really seems to me better worth doing . . . I think really the important thing is to make the ideas I have intelligible.

The influence of Ottoline during this time is most clearly seen in Russell's plans for a book on religion, to be called *Prisons*, which he began while he was still finishing *The Problems of Philosophy*, and which he abandoned some time in 1912. The title of the work comes from a line in *Hamlet* – 'The world's a prison and Denmark one of the worst wards' – and its central idea was that 'the religion of contemplation' could provide the means of escape out of the prisons into which we enclose human life. By 'the religion of contemplation' Russell did not mean a belief in God or immortality – even his infatuation with the deeply religious Ottoline could not persuade him to believe in those. He meant, rather, a mystical union with the universe in which our finite selves are overcome and we become at one with infinity.

For, as he told Ottoline (with dubious accuracy), 'What you call God is very much what I call infinity.'

The project might plausibly be seen as an attempt by Russell to reconcile his own sceptical agnosticism with Ottoline's devout faith. The central conceit of the book reappears in a letter to Ottoline describing the liberating effect of her love for him:

> . . . now there is no prison for me. I reach out to the stars, & through the ages, & everywhere the radiance of your love lights the world for me.

The Russell Wittgenstein met in 1911, then, was far from being the strident rationalist, the offender of the faith, he later became. He was a man in the grip of romance, more appreciative than he had been before, or was to become, of the irrational and emotional side of human character – even to the extent of adopting a kind of transcendental mysticism. Perhaps more important, he was a man who, having decided that his contribution to technical philosophy was finished, was looking for someone with the youth, vitality and ability to build upon the work which he had begun.

There are some indications that Wittgenstein was initially inclined to ignore Frege's advice and to continue with his work at Manchester. Thus we find him still listed as a research student in engineering for the start of the autumn term, his studentship having been renewed for the coming year. It may be that, having been floored by Frege in argument, he had resolved to overcome his obsession with the philosophy of mathematics and to persist with his vocation as an engineer.

He had not, apparently, made any prior arrangement with Russell, when, on 18 October – about two weeks into the Michaelmas term – he suddenly appeared at Russell's rooms in Trinity College to introduce himself.

Russell was having tea with C. K. Ogden (later to become the first translator of *Tractatus Logico-Philosophicus*) when:

> . . . an unknown German appeared, speaking very little English but refusing to speak German. He turned out to be a man who had learned engineering at Charlottenburg, but during his course had

acquired, by himself, a passion for the philosophy of mathematics & has now come to Cambridge on purpose to hear me.

Two omissions in Wittgenstein's self-introduction are immediately striking. The first is that he does not mention that he had been advised to come to Russell by Frege. The second is that he omits to tell Russell he had studied (indeed, officially, *was studying*) engineering at Manchester. These omissions, though strange, are perhaps indicative of nothing more than Wittgenstein's extreme nervousness; if Russell had the impression that he spoke very little English, he must indeed have been in quite a state.

From what we know of the weeks that followed, it seems to have been Wittgenstein's intention not simply to hear Russell lecture, but to impress himself upon him, with a view to finding out, once and for all – from the horse's mouth, as it were – whether he had any genuine talent for philosophy, and therefore whether he would be justified in abandoning his aeronautical research.

Russell's lectures on mathematical logic attracted very few students, and he often lectured to just three people: C. D. Broad, E. H. Neville and H. T. J. Norton. He therefore had reason to feel pleased when, on the day he first met Wittgenstein, he found him 'duly established' at his lecture. 'I am much interested in my German', he wrote to Ottoline, '& shall hope to see a lot of him.' As it turned out, he saw a lot more of him than he had bargained for. For four weeks Wittgenstein plagued Russell – dominating the discussions during the lectures, and following him back to his rooms after them, still arguing his position. Russell reacted to this with a mixture of appreciative interest and impatient exasperation:

> My German friend threatens to be an infliction, he came back with me after my lecture & argued till dinner-time – obstinate & perverse, but I think not stupid. [19.10.11]

> My German engineer very argumentative & tiresome. He wouldn't admit that it was certain that there was not a rhinoceros in the room . . . [He] came back and argued all the time I was dressing. [1.11.11]

> My German engineer, I think, is a fool. He thinks nothing empirical is knowable – I asked him to admit that there was not a rhinoceros in the room, but he wouldn't. [2.11.11]

[Wittgenstein] was refusing to admit the existence of anything except asserted propositions. [7.11.11]

My lecture went off all right. My German ex-engineer, as usual, maintained his thesis that there is nothing in the world except asserted propositions, but at last I told him it was too large a theme. [13.11.11]

My ferocious German came and argued at me after my lecture. He is armour-plated against all assaults of reasoning. It is really rather a waste of time talking with him. [16.11.11]

In later life Russell made great play of these discussions and claimed he had looked under all the tables and chairs in the lecture room in an effort to convince Wittgenstein that there was no rhinoceros present. But it is clear that for Wittgenstein the issue was metaphysical rather than empirical, to do with what kind of things make up the world rather than the presence or otherwise of a rhinoceros. In fact, the view that he is here so tenaciously advancing prefigures that expressed in the famous first proposition of the *Tractatus*: 'The world is the totality of facts, not of things.'

It will be seen from the above extracts that Russell had, as yet, no great conviction of Wittgenstein's philosophical ability. And yet the responsibility for Wittgenstein's future was soon to rest with him. On 27 November, at the end of the Michaelmas term, Wittgenstein came to Russell to seek his opinion on the question that mattered to him above all else, the answer to which would determine his choice of career and finally settle the conflict of interests with which he had struggled for over two years:

My German is hesitating between philosophy and aviation; he asked me today whether I thought he was utterly hopeless at philosophy, and I told him I didn't know but I thought not. I asked him to bring me something written to help me judge. He has money, and is quite passionately interested in philosophy, but he feels he ought not to give his life to it unless he is some good. I feel the responsibility rather as I really don't know what to think of his ability. [27.11.11]

Before he left Cambridge, Wittgenstein met Russell socially and, for once, was relaxed enough in Russell's company to reveal something of himself apart from his all-consuming involvement with philosophical problems. Russell finally discovered that he was Austrian rather than German, and also that he was 'literary, very musical, pleasant-mannered . . . and, I *think* really intelligent'. The consequence of which was: 'I am getting to like him.'

The real turning point, however, came when Wittgenstein returned to Cambridge in January 1912 with a manuscript he had written during the vacation. On reading it, Russell's attitude towards him changed immediately. It was, he told Ottoline, 'very good, much better than my English pupils do', adding: 'I shall certainly encourage him. Perhaps he will do great things.' Wittgenstein later told David Pinsent that Russell's encouragement had proved his salvation, and had ended nine years of loneliness and suffering, during which he had continually thought of suicide. It enabled him finally to give up engineering, and to brush aside 'a hint that he was *de trop* in this world' – a hint that had previously made him feel ashamed he had *not* killed himself. The implication is that, in encouraging him to pursue philosophy and in justifying his inclination to abandon engineering, Russell had, quite literally, saved Wittgenstein's life.

Over the next term Wittgenstein pursued his studies in mathematical logic with such vigour that, by the end of it, Russell was to say that he had learnt all he had to teach, and, indeed, had gone further. 'Yes', he declared to Ottoline, 'Wittgenstein has been a great event in my life – whatever may come of it':

> I love him & feel he will solve the problems I am too old to solve – all kinds of problems that are raised by my work, but want a fresh mind and the vigour of youth. He is *the* young man one hopes for.

After supervising him for just one term, Russell had identified in Wittgenstein the protégé he was looking for.

What philosophical work Wittgenstein actually did during the three months of this term, we do not know. Russell's letters to Ottoline contain only the most tantalizing hints. On 26 January Wittgenstein proposed: 'a definition of logical *form* as opposed to logical *matter*'. A

month later he: 'brought a very good original suggestion, which I
think is right, on an important point of logic'. These hints, though, are
enough to suggest that Wittgenstein's work was, from the beginning,
not directed to the problem: 'What is mathematics?' but to the still
more fundamental question: 'What is logic?' This, Russell himself felt,
was the most important question left unanswered by *Principia*.

On 1 February 1912 Wittgenstein was admitted as a member of
Trinity College, with Russell as his supervisor. Knowing that he had
never received any formal tuition in logic, and feeling that he might
benefit from it, Russell arranged for him to be 'coached' by the
eminent logician and Fellow of King's College, W. E. Johnson. The
arrangement lasted only a few weeks. Wittgenstein later told F. R.
Leavis: 'I found in the first hour that he had nothing to teach me.'
Leavis was also told by Johnson: 'At our first meeting he was teaching me.' The difference is that Johnson's remark was sardonic,
Wittgenstein's completely in earnest. It was actually Johnson who put
an end to the arrangement, thus providing Russell with the first of
many occasions on which he had to use all his tact and sensitivity to
point out Wittgenstein's faults to him without upsetting him:

> While I was preparing my speech Wittgenstein appeared in a great
> state of excitement because Johnson (with whom I had advised him
> to coach) wrote and said he wouldn't take him any more, practically
> saying he argued too much instead of learning his lesson like a good
> boy. He came to me to know what truth there was in Johnson's
> feeling. Now he is terribly persistent, hardly lets one get a word in,
> and is generally considered a bore. As I really like him very much, I
> was able to hint these things to him without offending him.

Wittgenstein made quite a different impression on G. E. Moore,
whose lectures he began to attend during this term. 'Moore thinks
enormously highly of Wittgenstein's brains', Russell told Ottoline;
'– says he always feels W. *must* be right when they disagree. He says
during his lectures W. always looks frightfully puzzled, but nobody
else does. I am glad to be confirmed in my high opinion of W. – the
young men don't think much of him, or if they do it is only because
Moore and I praise him.' For Wittgenstein's part, he 'said how much
he loves Moore, how he likes and dislikes people for the way they

think – Moore has one of the most beautiful smiles I know, and it had
struck him'.

Wittgenstein's friendship with Moore was to develop later. But,
with Russell, an affectionate bond quickly developed. Russell's
admiration knew no bounds. He saw in Wittgenstein the 'ideal pupil',
one who 'gives passionate admiration with vehement and very intelligent dissent'. As opposed to Broad, who was the most *reliable* pupil he
had had – 'practically certain to do a good deal of useful but not
brilliant work' – Wittgenstein was 'full of boiling passion which may
drive him anywhere'.

Russell came increasingly to identify with Wittgenstein, to see in
him a fellow-spirit, one who brought all his force and passion to bear
on *theoretical* questions. 'It is a rare passion and one is glad to find it.'
Indeed: 'he has more passion about philosophy than I have; his
avalanches make mine seem mere snowballs'. Again and again, one
comes across the word 'passion' in Russell's descriptions: 'a pure
intellectual passion' that Wittgenstein (like Russell himself) had 'in the
highest degree'; 'it makes me love him'. It was almost as though he
saw in Wittgenstein a mirror image of himself – or, perhaps more
apposite, as though he saw him as his own offspring:

> His disposition is that of an artist, intuitive and moody. He says
> every morning he begins his work with hope, and every evening he
> ends in despair – he has just the sort of rage when he can't under-
> stand things that I have. [16.3.12]

> I have the most perfect intellectual sympathy with him – the same
> passion and vehemence, the same feeling that one must understand
> or die, the sudden jokes breaking down the frightful tension of
> thought. [17.3.12]

> . . . he even has the same similes as I have – a wall parting him from
> the truth which he must pull down somehow. After our last
> discussion, he said 'Well, there's a bit of wall pulled down.'
> His attitude justifies all I have hoped about my work. [22.3.12]

Russell noted with approval that Wittgenstein had excellent
manners, but, even more approvingly, that: 'in argument he forgets
about manners & simply says what he thinks':

No one could be more sincere than Wittgenstein, or more destitute of the false politeness that interferes with truth; but he lets his feelings and affections appear, and it warms one's heart. [10.3.12]

When, for example, Wittgenstein met a student who happened to be a monk, Russell could report gleefully to Ottoline that he was 'far more terrible with Christians than I am':

He had liked F., the undergraduate monk, and was horrified to learn that he is a monk. F. came to tea with him and W. at once attacked him – as I imagine, with absolute fury. Yesterday he returned to the charge, not arguing but only preaching honesty. He abominates ethics and morals generally; he is deliberately a creature of impulse and thinks one should be. [17.3.12]

'I wouldn't answer for his technical morals', Russell concluded.

The remark jars. It shows that he had misunderstood the thrust of Wittgenstein's argument. For, if Wittgenstein was preaching honesty, he was obviously not abominating ethics in the sense of arguing for a licence for immorality. He was arguing for a morality based on integrity, on being true to oneself, one's impulses – a morality that came from inside one's self rather than one imposed from outside by rules, principles and duties.

It was a question upon which, for Wittgenstein, a great deal would have hung. In abandoning engineering for philosophy, had he not forsaken what might have been seen as his duty in favour of pursuing something that burned *within* him? And yet, as we have seen – and as Russell was originally told – such a decision needed the justification that, in doing so, he was not simply pursuing a whim, but following a course in which he might conceivably make an important contribution.

Russell's misunderstanding of the point is a hint of things to come, a suggestion that his 'theoretical passion' and Wittgenstein's were not, after all, as similar as he had supposed. By the end of term their relationship was such that Wittgenstein felt able to tell Russell what he liked *and disliked* about his work. He spoke with great feeling about the beauty of *Principia*, and said – what was probably the highest praise he could give it – that it was like music. The popular work, however, he disliked strongly – particularly 'The Free Man's Worship' and the last chapter of *The Problems of Philosophy*, on 'The Value of Philosophy'. He disliked the very idea of saying philosophy had *value*:

> . . . he says people who like philosophy will pursue it, and others won't, and there is an end of it. *His* strongest impulse is philosophy. [17.3.12]

It is hard to believe that Wittgenstein's attitude was quite as straightforward as Russell suggests. After all, for years before becoming Russell's pupil, he had suffered deeply from the conflict of duty and impulse engendered by the fact that philosophy was his strongest impulse. He indeed believed that one *should* be – as his father had been, and as his brother Hans had been, and as all geniuses are – a creature of impulse. But he also had an almost overbearing sense of duty, and was prone to periodically crippling self-doubts. Russell's encouragement had been necessary precisely because it enabled him to overcome these doubts, and to follow his strongest impulse *happily*. His family had been struck by the immediate change that came over him after he had been encouraged to work on philosophy by Russell. And he himself, at the end of this term, told Russell that the happiest hours of his life had been spent in his rooms. But this happiness was caused not simply by his being allowed to follow his impulses, but also by the conviction that – as he had an unusual talent for philosophy – he had the *right* to do so.

It was important to Wittgenstein that Russell should understand him on this point, and on the day he returned to Cambridge for the following term, the theme was renewed. Russell found that he 'wears well . . . quite as good as I thought. I find him strangely exciting', and was still inclined to see no fundamental difference in their temperamental outlook: 'He lives in the same intense excitement as I do, hardly able to sit still or read a book.' Wittgenstein talked about Beethoven:

> . . . how a friend described going to Beethoven's door and hearing him 'cursing, howling and singing' over his new fugue; after a whole hour Beethoven at last came to the door, looking as if he had been fighting the devil, and having eaten nothing for 36 hours because his cook and parlour-maid had been away from his rage. That's the sort of man to be.

But, again, this is not just *anybody* 'cursing, howling and singing'. Would Wittgenstein have felt this to be 'the sort of man to be' if all this fierce absorption had produced only mediocre works? What is implied is that, if one's strongest impulse is to write music, and if, by surrendering completely to that impulse one is able to write sublime music, then one not only has the right to behave impulsively; one has a duty to do so.

Similarly, Russell gave Wittgenstein the licence to behave in the same way, because he recognized in him the quality of genius. He later described Wittgenstein as:

> . . . perhaps the most perfect example I have ever known of genius as traditionally conceived, passionate, profound, intense, and dominating.

He had already come to see in Wittgenstein these qualities at the beginning of this summer term. In his letter to Ottoline of 23 April, he told her: 'I don't feel the subject neglected by my abandoning it, as long as he takes it up', adding, as if in illustration of the qualities needed for the task: 'I thought he would have smashed all the furniture in my room today, he got so excited.'

Wittgenstein asked him how he and Whitehead were going to end *Principia*. Russell replied that they would have no conclusion; the book would just end 'with whatever formula happened to come last':

> He seemed surprised at first, and then saw that was right. It seems to me the beauty of the book would be spoilt if it contained a single word that could possibly be spared.

This appeal to the beauty of the work would no doubt have been sympathetically received by Wittgenstein, who was to take to new heights, with the sparse prose of the *Tractatus*, the austere aesthetic here advanced by Russell.

Already, by the beginning of the summer term, the relationship between the two was beginning to change. Although he was still formally Wittgenstein's supervisor, Russell became increasingly anxious for his approval. Over the Easter vacation he had begun work on a paper on 'Matter', to be delivered to the Philosophical Society at Cardiff University. It was, he hoped, to be a work which demonstrated a renewed vigour – 'a model of cold passionate analysis, setting forth the most painful conclusions with utter disregard of human feelings'. Cold *and* passionate? Russell explained:

> I haven't had enough courage hitherto about matter. I haven't been sceptical enough. I want to write a paper which my enemies will call 'the bankruptcy of realism'. There is nothing to compare to passion for giving one cold insight. Most of my best work has been done in the inspiration of remorse, but any passion will do if it is strong. Philosophy is a reluctant mistress – one can only reach her heart with the cold steel in the hand of passion.

'Cold steel in the hand of passion' – the phrase conjures up perfectly Wittgenstein's own combination of a rigorously logical mind and an impulsive and obsessional nature. He was the very personification of Russell's philosophical ideal.

Russell was, however, to be disappointed with Wittgenstein's reaction to the project. He dismissed the whole subject as 'a trivial problem':

> He admits that if there is no Matter then no one exists but himself, but he says it doesn't hurt, since physics and astronomy and all the other sciences could still be interpreted so as to be true.

A few days later, when Wittgenstein actually read parts of the paper, Russell was relieved to note a change of mind: Wittgenstein was delighted by its radicalism. Russell began his paper by stating baldly that all the arguments advanced hitherto by philosophers intending to prove the existence of matter were, quite simply, fallacious. This, declared Wittgenstein, was the best thing Russell had done. When he saw the rest of the paper he changed his mind again and told Russell that he did not like it after all, 'but only', Russell told Ottoline, clutching at straws, 'because of disagreement, not because of its being badly done'. The paper, for which Russell originally had such high hopes, remained unpublished.

The extraordinarily high opinion which Russell had of Wittgenstein was bound to arouse the curiosity of his friends at Cambridge, particularly among the Apostles, the self-consciously élite conversation society (of which Russell himself was a member) which was at the time dominated by John Maynard Keynes and Lytton Strachey. Wittgenstein became what, in Apostolic jargon, was known as an 'embryo' – a person under consideration for membership. Strachey (who lived in London) came to tea with Wittgenstein at Russell's rooms to inspect this potential Apostle for himself. Wittgenstein had recently read Strachey's *Landmarks in French Literature*, but had not liked it. He told Russell that it made an impression of effort, like the gasps of an asthmatic person. He nevertheless took the trouble to shine at tea sufficiently to impress Strachey. 'Everybody has just begun to discover him', Russell told Ottoline afterwards; 'they all now realize he has genius.'

As to whether Wittgenstein would want to join the Apostles, Russell had doubts:

Somebody had been telling them about Wittgenstein and they wanted to hear what I thought of him. They were thinking of electing him to the Society. I told them I didn't think he would like the Society. I am quite sure he wouldn't really. It would seem to him stuffy, as indeed it has become, owing to their practice of being in love with each other, which didn't exist in my day – I think it is mainly due to Lytton.

Whether or not he was right in supposing that Wittgenstein would object to the 'stuffy' atmosphere of the homosexual affairs which dominated the Society at that time, he was, as it turned out, right to suggest that Wittgenstein would not like the Apostles.

Strachey's impressions of Wittgenstein, meanwhile, were somewhat mixed. On 5 May he invited him for lunch, but on this second meeting he was not impressed. 'Herr Sinckel-Winckel lunches with me', he wrote to Keynes; 'quiet little man'. Two weeks later the two met again in the rooms of Strachey's brother, James. This time the impression gained was one of exhausting brilliance:

Herr Sinckel-Winckel hard at it on universals and particulars. The latter oh! so bright – but *quelle souffrance!* Oh God! God! 'If A loves B' – 'There may be a common property' – 'Not analysable in that way at all, but the complexes have certain qualities.' How shall I manage to slink off to bed?

There, for the moment, Wittgenstein's connections with the Apostles rested, until the following October when, after meeting Keynes, 'Herr Sinckel-Winckel' became, briefly and disastrously, 'Brother Wittgenstein'.

From being 'generally considered a bore' by the young men at Cambridge, Wittgenstein was now considered 'interesting and pleasant, though his sense of humour is heavy'. That, at least, was the judgement of one of them, David Pinsent, who met him at one of Russell's 'squashes' (social evenings) early in the summer term. Pinsent was then in his second year as a mathematics undergraduate. The previous year he had himself been an Apostolic 'embryo', but had not been elected. This perhaps indicates how he was seen by the fashionable intellectual élite at Cambridge – interesting but not fascinating, bright but not possessed of genius.

To Wittgenstein, however, Pinsent's musical sensitivity and his equable temperament made him the ideal companion. He seems to have recognized this very swiftly, within a month of knowing Pinsent surprising him by inviting him on a holiday in Iceland, all expenses to be met by Wittgenstein's father. 'I really don't know what to think', Pinsent wrote in his diary:

> . . . it would certainly be fun, and I could not afford it myself, and Vittgenstein [sic] seems very anxious for me to come. I deferred my decision and wrote home for advice: Iceland seems rather attractive: I gather that all inland travelling has to be done on horse back, which would be supreme fun! The whole idea attracts and surprises me: I have known Vittgenstein only for three weeks or so – but we seem to get on well together: he is very musical with the same tastes as I. He is an Austrian – but speaks English fluently. I should say about my age.

Until then their acquaintance had been confined to Pinsent's acting as a subject in some experiments that Wittgenstein was conducting in the psychological laboratory. It seems to have been his intention to investigate scientifically the role of rhythm in musical appreciation. For this he presumably needed a subject with some understanding of music. In his diary Pinsent does not describe what the experiments involved, recording only that taking part in them was 'not bad fun'.

Wittgenstein was helped in this work by the psychologist C. S. Myers, who took the experiments seriously enough to introduce a demonstration of them to the British Society of Psychology. The chief result obtained from them was that, in some circumstances, subjects heard an accent on certain notes that was not in fact there.

Apart from taking part in these experiments two or three times a week, Pinsent's only contact with Wittgenstein before being invited to spend a holiday with him had been at Russell's Thursday evening 'squashes'. After one of these, on 30 May, he reports that he found Wittgenstein 'very amusing':

> . . . he is reading philosophy up here, but has only just started systematic reading: and he expresses the most naive surprise that all the philosophers he once worshipped in ignorance are after all stupid and dishonest and make disgusting mistakes!

But it was not until after Wittgenstein's unexpected invitation that a close friendship began to develop. The following day the two attended a concert together, after which they went to Wittgenstein's rooms, where they stayed talking until 11.30. Wittgenstein was 'very communicative and told me lots about himself'. It was then that he told Pinsent that Russell's encouragement to pursue philosophy had been his salvation, after nine years of suicidal loneliness and suffering. Pinsent added:

> Russell, I know, has a high opinion of him: and has been corrected by him and convinced that he (Russell) was wrong in one or two points of Philosophy: and Russell is not the only philosophical don up here that Vittgenstein has convinced of error. Vittgenstein has few hobbies, which rather accounts for his loneliness. One can't thrive entirely on big and important pursuits like Triposes. But he is quite interesting and pleasant: I fancy he has quite got over his morbidness now.

After this Wittgenstein and Pinsent saw much of each other, going to concerts at the Cambridge University Musical Club, dining together at the Union and meeting for tea in each other's rooms. Wittgenstein even attended a service at the college chapel especially to hear Pinsent read the lesson.

Despite his earlier having been described by Russell as 'terrible' with Christians, this may not have been quite so out of character as it appears. At about the same time, in fact, he surprised Russell by suddenly saying how much he admired the text: 'What shall it profit a man if he gain the whole world and lose his own soul':

> [He] then went on to say how few there are who don't lose their soul. I said it depended on having a large purpose that one is true to. He said he thought it depended more on suffering and the power to endure it. I was surprised – I hadn't expected that kind of thing from him.

The stoicism expressed here seems related to something Wittgenstein later told Norman Malcolm. During one of his holidays at home in Vienna, his previously contemptuous attitude to religion had been changed by seeing a play, *Die Kreuzelscheiber* by the Austrian dramatist and novelist Ludwig Anzengruber.* It was mediocre drama, but in it one of the characters expressed the thought that no matter what happened in the world, nothing bad could happen to *him*. *He* was independent of fate and circumstances. This stoic thought struck Wittgenstein powerfully, and, so he told Malcolm, he saw, for the first time, the possibility of religion.

For the rest of his life he continued to regard the feeling of being 'absolutely safe' as paradigmatic of religious experience. A few months after the conversation with Russell quoted above, we find him reading William James's *Varieties of Religious Experience*, and telling Russell:

> This book does me a *lot* of good. I don't mean to say that I will be a saint soon, but I am not sure that it does not improve me a little in a way in which I would like to improve *very much*: namely I think that it helps me to get rid of the *Sorge* [worry, anxiety] (in the sense in which Goethe used the word in the 2nd part of Faust).

---

*He told Malcolm he was about twenty-one years old when this event took place, which would date it to 1910 or early 1911. Because of the change in Wittgenstein's attitude to religion noted by Russell in the summer of 1912, however, it is tempting to date the episode to the Easter vacation of that year.

Two days after the discussion on losing and retaining one's soul, Russell and Wittgenstein had another conversation which revealed something of the deep differences between their respective ethical views. It arose out of a discussion of Dickens's *David Copperfield*. Wittgenstein maintained that it was wrong for Copperfield to have quarrelled with Steerforth for running away with Little Emily. Russell replied that, in the same circumstances, he would have done the same. Wittgenstein was 'much pained, and refused to believe it; thought one could and should always be loyal to friends and go on loving them'.

Russell then asked him how he would feel if he were married to a woman and she ran away with another man:

> [Wittgenstein] said (and I believe him) that he would feel no rage or hate, only utter misery. His nature is good through and through; that is why he doesn't see the need of morals. I was utterly wrong at first; he might do all kinds of things in passion, but he would not practise any cold-blooded immorality. His outlook is very free; principles and such things seem to him nonsense, because his impulses are strong and never shameful.

'I think he is passionately devoted to me', Russell added. 'Any difference of feeling causes him great pain. My feeling towards him is passionate, but of course my absorption in you makes it less important to me than his feeling is to him.'

Russell seemed slow to appreciate that their differences of feeling were important to Wittgenstein because they touched upon issues of fundamental importance to him. He was slow, too, to understand that Wittgenstein's emphasis on personal integrity (and, in the above case, loyalty) was not something *opposed* to morality, but something which constituted a different morality. It is typical of their fundamentally opposed attitudes, for example, that Russell, even in this, perhaps his most introspective period, should think that keeping one's soul depended upon a 'large purpose that one was true to' – that he was inclined to look outside himself for something to sustain him. It was typical, too, for Wittgenstein to insist that the possibility of remaining uncorrupted rested entirely on one's self – on the qualities one found within. If one's soul was pure (and disloyalty to a friend was one thing that would make it impure), then no matter what happened to one 'externally' – even if one's wife ran away with another man –

nothing could happen to one's *self*. Thus, it is not external matters that should be of the greatest concern, but one's self. The *Sorge* that prevents one facing the world with equanimity is thus a matter of more immediate concern than any misfortune that may befall one through the actions of others.

When attitudes of the most fundamental kind clash, there can be no question of agreement or disagreement, for everything one says or does is interpreted from *within* those attitudes. It is therefore not surprising that there should be frustration and incomprehension on both sides. What is surprising is Russell's rather naïve assumption that he was faced, not with a different set of ideals to his own, but simply with a rather peculiar person, a person whose 'impulses are strong and never shameful'. It is as though he could make sense of Wittgenstein's views only by appealing to some *fact* about Wittgenstein that would make his holding such views intelligible. Finding Wittgenstein's outlook alien and incomprehensible, he could seek only to *explain* it, not to *make sense* of it. He was incapable. as it were, of getting *inside* it.

Again and again, in Russell's letters to Ottoline, one has the feeling that the spirit of Wittgenstein's 'theoretical passion' eluded him. The centrality of the notion of personal integrity in Wittgenstein's outlook was interpreted by him at various times as the rejection of conventional morality, the sign of a pure, uncorrupted nature – and even, on at least one occasion, as a joke. At one of Russell's 'quashes', Wittgenstein defended the view that a study of mathematics would improve a person's taste: 'since good taste is genuine taste and therefore is fostered by whatever makes people think truthfully'. From Russell's account to Ottoline, one gathers he found this argument impossible to take seriously. He describes Wittgenstein's view as a 'paradox', and says 'we were all against him'. And yet there is every reason to suppose that Wittgenstein was speaking in complete earnest: honesty and good taste were, for him, closely intertwined notions.

Wittgenstein was not one to debate his most fundamental convictions. Dialogue with him was possible only if one shared those convictions. (Thus, dialogue with Russell on ethical questions was soon to become impossible.) To one who did not share his fundamental outlook, his utterances – whether on logic or on ethics – would, as likely as not, remain unintelligible. It was a tendency that began to worry Russell. 'I am seriously afraid', he told Ottoline, 'that no one will see the point of what he writes, because he won't recommend it by arguments addressed to a different point of view.' When Russell told him he ought not simply to state what he thought, but should also provide arguments for it, he replied that arguments would spoil its beauty. He would feel as if he were dirtying a flower with muddy hands:

> I told him I hadn't the heart to say anything against that, and that he had better acquire a slave to state the arguments.

Russell had good reason to worry about whether Wittgenstein would be understood, for he increasingly came to feel that the future of his own work in logic should be placed in Wittgenstein's hands. He even felt that when his five-year lectureship at Trinity expired he should give it up and let Wittgenstein take his place. 'It is really amazing how the world of learning has grown unreal to me', he wrote. 'Mathematics has quite faded out of my thoughts, except when proofs bring it back with a jerk. Philosophy doesn't often come into my mind, and I have no *impulse* to work at it.' Despite what he had written in the last chapter of *Problems of Philosophy*, he had lost faith in the value of philosophy:

> I did seriously mean to go back to it, but I found I really couldn't think it was very valuable. This is partly due to Wittgenstein, who has made me more of a sceptic; partly it is the result of a process which has been going on ever since I found you.

The 'process' he mentions was his growing interest, inspired by Ottoline, in non-philosophical work. First, there was *Prisons*, his book on religion; then an autobiography (which he abandoned and, apparently, destroyed); and finally an autobiographical novella called *The Perplexities of John Forstice*, in which, no doubt using some of the material he had written for his autobiography, and quoting extensively from his own letters to Ottoline, he attempted to describe imaginatively his own intellectual pilgrimage from isolation, through moral and political confusion, to clarity and grace. Russell was not at his best with this sort of writing, and none of the works mentioned saw the light of day during his lifetime. 'I do *wish* I were more creative', he lamented to Ottoline. 'A man like Mozart makes one feel such a worm.' In later life he agreed to the posthumous publication of *Forstice*, but with serious reservations:

> . . . the second part represented my opinions during only a very short period. My view in the second part were very sentimental, much too mild, and much too favourable to religion. In all this I was unduly influenced by Lady Ottoline Morrell. .

For better or for worse, it was during this 'very short period' that Wittgenstein was making his phenomenal progress in the analysis of logic. And perhaps his acceptance as a philosophical genius owes something to the influence exerted by Ottoline over Russell. If Russell had not been going through such a sentimental phase, he may not have taken to Wittgenstein in the way that he did: 'Wittgenstein brought me the most lovely roses today. He is a treasure' (23.4.12); 'I love him as if he were my son' (22.8.12). And, perhaps, if he had not lost faith and interest in his own contribution to mathematical logic, he might not have been quite so prepared to hand the subject over to Wittgenstein.

As it was, by the end of his first year at Cambridge, Wittgenstein was being primed as Russell's successor. At the end of the summer term, when Hermine visited Cambridge and was taken to meet Russell, she was amazed to hear him say: 'We expect the next big step in philosophy to be taken by your brother.'

At the beginning of the summer vacation Wittgenstein was offered G. E. Moore's old college rooms. He had, until then, been living in lodgings in Rose Crescent, and he accepted Moore's offer gratefully. The rooms were perfectly situated for him, at the top of K staircase in Whewell's Court, with a splendid view of Trinity College. He liked being at the top of the tower, and kept the same set of rooms for the rest of his time at Cambridge, even when he returned in later life, when as a Fellow and, later, as a Professor he would have been entitled to larger and grander rooms.

Wittgenstein chose the furniture for his rooms with great care. He was helped in this by Pinsent:

> I went out and helped him interview a lot of furniture at various shops: he is moving into college next term. It was rather amusing: he is terribly fastidious and we led the shopman a frightful dance, Vittgenstein ejaculating 'No – Beastly!' to 90% of what he shewed us!

Russell, too, was drawn into Wittgenstein's deliberations on the matter, and found it rather exasperating. 'He is *very* fussy', he told Ottoline, 'and bought nothing at all yesterday. He gave me a lecture on how furniture should be made – he dislikes all ornamentation that is not part of the construction, and can never find anything simple enough.' In the end Wittgenstein had his furniture specially made for him. When it arrived it was judged by Pinsent to be 'rather quaint but not bad'.

Neither Pinsent nor Russell was well placed to understand Wittgenstein's fastidiousness in the matter. To appreciate his concern for design and craftsmanship, one would have to have had some experience of construction. Thus, a few years later, we find Eccles, his engineer friend from Manchester, sending him some furniture designs of his own for Wittgenstein's comments, and receiving in reply a carefully considered, and gratefully accepted, verdict.

And to understand the strength of Wittgenstein's feeling against superfluous ornamentation – to appreciate the *ethical* importance it had for him – one would have to have been Viennese; one would have to have felt, like Karl Kraus and Adolf Loos, that the once noble culture of Vienna, which from Haydn to Schubert had surpassed anything else in the world, had, since the latter half of the nineteenth century, atrophied into, in Paul Engelmann's words, an 'arrogated base culture – a culture turned into its opposite, misused as ornament and mask'.

On 15 July Wittgenstein returned to Vienna, having arranged with Pinsent (whose parents had given the proposed holiday in Iceland their blessing) to meet in London during the first week of September. Home life in Vienna was not easy. His father had cancer and had been operated on several times; Gretl was having a baby and experiencing a difficult birth; and he himself was operated on for a hernia, discovered during an examination for military service. This latter he kept secret from his mother, who was in a distraught state looking after the invalid father.

From Vienna he wrote to Russell telling him: 'I am quite well again and philosophizing for all I am worth.' His thought progressed from thinking about the meaning of logical constants (the Russellian signs 'v', '~', '⊃' etc.) to deciding that: 'our problems can be traced down to the *atomic* prop[osition]s'. But in his letters to Russell he gave only hints as to what theory of logical symbolism this progression would result in.

'I am glad you read the lives of Mozart and Beethoven', he told Russell. 'These are the actual sons of God.' He told Russell of his delight on reading Tolstoy's *Hadji Murat*: 'Have you ever read it? If not, you ought to, for it is wonderful.'

When he arrived in London on 4 September he stayed as a guest of Russell's in his new flat in Bury Street. Russell found him a refreshing change from Bloomsbury – 'a great contrast to the Stephens and Stracheys and such would-be geniuses':

We very soon plunged into logic and have had great arguments. He has a very great power of seeing what are really important problems.

. . . He gives me such a delightful lazy feeling that I can leave a whole department of difficult thought to him, which used to depend on me alone. It makes it easier for me to give up technical work. Only his health seems to me very precarious – he gives one the feeling of a person whose life is very insecure. And I think he is growing deaf.

Perhaps the reference to Wittgenstein's hearing problem is ironic; in any case, it was not true that he couldn't hear, simply that he wouldn't listen – especially when Russell offered some 'sage advice' not to put off writing until he had solved *all* the problems of philosophy. That day, Russell told him, would never come:

This produced a wild outburst – he has the artist's feeling that he will produce the perfect thing or nothing – I explained how he wouldn't get a degree or be able to teach unless he learnt to write imperfect things – this all made him more and more furious – at last he begged me not to give him up even if he disappointed me.

Pinsent arrived in London the next day, to be met by Wittgenstein, who insisted on taking him by taxi to the Grand Hotel, Trafalgar Square. Pinsent tried in vain to suggest some less luxurious hotel, but Wittgenstein would not hear of it. There was evidently, as Pinsent noted in his diary, to be no sparing of expense on this trip. Once at the hotel Pinsent was told the financial arrangements:

Wittgenstein, or rather his father, insists on paying for both of us: I had expected him to be pretty liberal – but he surpassed all my expectations: Wittgenstein handed me over £145 in notes, and kept the same amount in notes himself. He also has a letter of Credit for about £200!

From London they went by train to Cambridge ('I need hardly say we travelled first class!'), where Wittgenstein had to attend to some business connected with his new college rooms, and then on to Edinburgh, where they stayed overnight before the boat journey. At Edinburgh, Wittgenstein took Pinsent on a shopping trip; he had not, he insisted, brought enough clothes:

> . . . he is being very fussy about taking enough clothing: he himself has three bags of luggage, and is much perturbed by my single box. He made me buy a second rug in Cambridge and several other odds and ends in Edinborough★ this morning: I have resisted a good deal – especially as it is not my money I am thus spending. I got my own back on him, however, by inducing him to buy oilskins, which he has not got.

On 7 September they set off from Leith on the *Sterling*, which to Wittgenstein's disgust looked much like an ordinary cross-Channel steamer – he had expected something grander. He calmed down when they discovered a piano on board and Pinsent, who had brought a collection of Schubert's songs, sat down to play, heartily encouraged by the other passengers. It was a five-day boat journey across fairly rough sea, and both Pinsent and Wittgenstein suffered from it, although Pinsent notes with curiosity that Wittgenstein, though he spent a great deal of time in his cabin lying down, was never actually sick.

They reached Reykjavik on 12 September, and as soon as they had booked into the hotel, they hired a guide to take them on a journey inland, starting the following day. At the hotel they had their first argument – about public schools. The argument got quite heated, until, so Pinsent records, they found that they had misunderstood each other: 'He has an enormous horror of what he calls a "Philistine"

★ This, as are other eccentric spellings in Pinsent's letters, is authentic.

attitude towards cruelty and suffering – any callous attitude – and accuses Kipling of such: and he got the idea that I sympathised with it'.

A week later, the subject of 'Philistine' attitudes was renewed:

> Wittgenstein has been talking a lot, at different times, about 'Philistines' – a name he gives to all people he dislikes! (*vide supra* – Thursday Sept: 12th) I think some of the views I have expressed have struck him as a bit philistine (views – that is – on practical things (not on philosophy) – for instance on the advantage of this age over past ages and so forth), and he is rather puzzled because he does not consider me really a Philistine – and I don't think he dislikes me! He satisfies himself by saying that I shall think differently as soon as I am a bit older!

It is tempting to see in these arguments a contrast between the pessimism of Viennese *Angst* and the optimism of British stolidity (at least, as it existed before the First World War had weakened even the British faith in 'the advantage of this age over past ages'). But if so, then it was exactly the qualities in Pinsent that made it impossible for him to share Wittgenstein's cultural pessimism that also made him the ideal companion.

Even Pinsent's cheerful equanimity, however, could sometimes be strained by Wittgenstein's nervousness – his 'fussiness', as Pinsent called it. On their second day in Reykjavik they went to the office of the steamship company to secure their berths home. There was some trouble in making themselves understood, but the matter was eventually resolved, at least to Pinsent's satisfaction:

> Wittgenstein however got terribly fussy and talked about our not getting home at all, and I got quite irritated with him: eventually he went off alone and got a man from the bank to act as interpreter and go through the whole business again at the steamship office.

Such temporary lapses in Pinsent's good humour, though infrequent, disturbed Wittgenstein greatly. On 21 September we read:

> Wittgenstein was a bit sulky all the evening: he is very sensitive if I get, momentarily, a bit irritated over some trifle – as I did tonight – I forget what about: the result being that he was depressed and silent

for the rest of the evening. He is always imploring me not to be irritable: and I do my best, and really, I think, I have not been so often on this trip!

Ten days of the holiday were taken up with a journey inland on ponies. Again, no expense was spared. The cortège consisted of Wittgenstein, Pinsent and their guide, each on a pony, while in front they drove two pack ponies and three spare ponies. During the day they rode and explored the countryside, and in the evenings Wittgenstein taught Pinsent mathematical logic, which Pinsent found 'excessively interesting' – 'Wittgenstein makes a very good teacher'.

Occasionally they explored the countryside on foot, and even once attempted some rock-climbing, at which neither was very proficient. It made Wittgenstein 'terribly nervous':

His fussyness comes out here again – he is always begging me not to risk my life! It is funny that he should be like that – for otherwise he is quite a good travelling companion.

On their walks the talk would mostly be of logic, Wittgenstein continuing to educate Pinsent on the subject: 'I am learning a lot from him. He is really remarkably clever.'

I have never yet been able to find the smallest fault in his reasoning: and yet he has made me reconstruct entirely my ideas on several subjects.

When, after their excursion through the Icelandic countryside, they were back at the Reykjavik hotel, Pinsent took the opportunity of having some lighter conversation with 'a very splendid bounder' who had just arrived. It prompted a long discussion about 'such people': 'he simply won't speak to them, but really, I think, they are rather amusing'. The following day: 'Wittgenstein made an awful fuss.' He took such a violent dislike to Pinsent's 'splendid bounder' that he refused to contemplate eating at the same table. To ensure that this didn't happen, he gave orders that their meal was to be served an hour earlier than table d'hôte in all cases. At lunch they forgot, and rather than take the chance, Wittgenstein took Pinsent out to see if they could find anything in Reykjavik. They couldn't. So Wittgenstein ate a few biscuits in his room, and Pinsent went to table d'hôte. In the evening Pinsent found Wittgenstein 'still fairly sulky about the lunch business', but they got their supper an hour early as arranged, and had champagne with it, 'which cheered him up a bit, finally leaving him quite normal'.

Pinsent stayed receptive and cheerful throughout. On the boat home Wittgenstein took him into the engine room and explained to him how the engines worked. He also described the research he was doing in logic. 'I really believe he has discovered something good', Pinsent comments – without, unfortunately, mentioning what it was.

On the return journey, Pinsent persuaded Wittgenstein to spend a night with his family in Birmingham – he was keen to show him off to his parents. The inducement was a concert at the town hall, the programme for which was Brahms's *Requiem*, Strauss's *Salome*, Beethoven's Seventh Symphony and a Bach motet, 'Be not afraid'. Wittgenstein enjoyed the Brahms, refused to go in for the Strauss and left the hall as soon as the Beethoven had finished. At supper, Pinsent's father was suitably impressed when Pinsent got Wittgenstein to explain to him some of the logic that he had taught him during the holiday. 'I think father was interested', he writes, and – less hesitantly – 'certainly he agreed with me afterwards that Wittgenstein is really very clever and acute.'

For Pinsent it had been: 'the most glorious holiday I have ever spent!'

> The novelty of the country – of being free of all considerations about economising – the excitement and everything – all combine to make it the most wonderful experience I have ever had. It leaves almost a mystic-romantic impression on me: for the greatest romance consists in novel sensations – novel surroundings – and so forth, whatever they be provided they are novel.

Not so for Wittgenstein. What remained in his memory were their differences and disagreements – perhaps the very occasions mentioned in Pinsent's diary – Pinsent's occasional irritability, hints of his 'Philistinism', and the incident with the 'bounder'. He later told Pinsent that he had enjoyed it, 'as much as it is possible for two people to do who are nothing to each other'.

4
RUSSELL'S MASTER

> If we now turn to the gifted men, we shall see that in their case love frequently begins with self-mortification, humiliation, and restraint. A moral change sets in, a process of purification seems to emanate from the object loved.
>
> Weininger, *Sex and Character*

Wittgenstein returned to Cambridge from his holiday with Pinsent in an agitated and irritable state. Within days, he had his first major disagreement with Russell. In Wittgenstein's absence, Russell had published a paper on 'The Essence of Religion' in the *Hibbert Journal*. It was taken from his abandoned book, *Prisons*, and was an Ottoline-inspired attempt to present a 'Religion of Contemplation' centred on the notion of 'the infinite part of our life', which 'does not see the world from one point of view: it shines impartially, like the diffused light on a cloudy sea':

> Unlike the finite life, it is impartial; its impartiality leads to truth in thought, justice in action, and universal love in feeling.

In many ways the article anticipates the mystical doctrines that Wittgenstein himself was to advance in the *Tractatus*, particularly in its advocation of a Spinozistic 'freedom from the finite self' (what in the *Tractatus* is called contemplating the world *sub specie aeterni*) and in its repudiation of what Russell calls: 'the insistent demand that our ideals shall be already realized in the world' (compare *TLP* 6.41). Nevertheless, unlike the *Tractatus*, Russell's paper shows no hesitation in articulating this mysticism, and in, for example, using words like 'finite' and 'infinite' in ways that are, strictly speaking, meaningless. In any case, Wittgenstein hated the article and, within days of being back at Cambridge, stormed into Russell's rooms to make his feelings known. He happened to interrupt a letter to Ottoline:

Here is Wittgenstein just arrived, frightfully pained by my Hibbert article which he evidently *detests*. I must stop because of him.

A few days later Russell spelt out the reasons for Wittgenstein's outburst: 'He felt I had been a traitor to the gospel of exactness; also that such things are too intimate for print.' 'I minded very much', he added, 'because I half agree with him.' He continued to brood on the attack for a few more days:

Wittgenstein's criticisms disturbed me profoundly. He was so unhappy, so gentle, so wounded in his wish to think well of me.

He minded all the more because of his increasing tendency to look upon Wittgenstein as his natural successor. His own endeavours in the analysis of logic were becoming ever more half-hearted. Having prepared the first draft of a paper entitled 'What is Logic?' he found he couldn't get on with it and felt 'very much inclined to leave it to Wittgenstein'.

Moore, too, felt the force of Wittgenstein's forthright criticism during these first few weeks of October. Wittgenstein began the term by attending Moore's lectures on psychology. 'He was very displeased with them', writes Moore, 'because I was spending a great deal of time in discussing Ward's view that psychology did not differ from the Natural Sciences in subject-matter but only in point of view':

He told me these lectures were very bad – that what I ought to do was to say what *I* thought, not to discuss what other people thought; and he came no more to my lectures.

Moore adds: 'In this year both he and I were still attending Russell's Lectures on the Foundations of Mathematics; but W. used also to go for hours to Russell's rooms in the evening to discuss Logic with him.'

In fact, Wittgenstein – apparently undergoing the process of self-mortification and moral change described by Weininger – would spend these hours discussing himself as much as logic. He would, according to Russell, 'pace up and down my room like a wild beast for three hours in agitated silence'. Once, Russell asked: 'Are you thinking about logic or your sins?' 'Both', Wittgenstein replied, and continued his pacing.

Russell considered him to be on the verge of a nervous breakdown – 'not far removed from suicide, feeling himself a miserable creature, full of sin' – and was inclined to attribute this nervous fatigue to the fact that: 'he strains his mind to the utmost constantly, at things which are discouraging by their difficulty'. He was supported in this view by a doctor who, so concerned was Wittgenstein about his fits of dizziness and his inability to work, was called and who pronounced: 'It is all nerves.' Despite Wittgenstein's earnest desire to be treated *morally*, therefore, Russell insisted on treating him physically, advising him to eat better and to go out riding. Ottoline did her bit by sending some cocoa. 'I will remember the directions', Russell promised her, '& try to get W. to use it – but I'm sure he won't.'

Wittgenstein did, however, take Russell's advice to go riding. Once or twice a week for the rest of term he and Pinsent would hire horses and take them for what Pinsent regarded as 'tame' rides (i.e. rides that involved no jumping) along the river tow-path to Clay-hithe, or along the Trumpington road to Grantchester. If this produced any effect on Wittgenstein's temperament at all, it did not make him any the less inclined to sudden outbursts of wrath against the moral failings of himself and others.

On 9 November, Russell had arranged to take a walk with Wittgenstein. On the same day, however, he felt obliged to watch Whitehead's son, North, compete in a rowing race on the river. He therefore took Wittgenstein to the river, where they both watched North get beaten in his race. This led to, as Russell put it, a 'passionate afternoon'. He himself found the 'excitement and conventional importance' of the race painful, the more so because North 'minded being beaten horribly'. But Wittgenstein found the whole affair *disgusting*:

. . . said we might as well have looked on at a bull fight (I had that feeling myself), and that *all* was of the devil, and so on. I was cross North had been beaten, so I explained the necessity of competition with patient lucidity. At last we got on to other topics, and I thought it was all right, but he suddenly stood still and explained that the way we had spent the afternoon was so vile that we ought not to live, or at least he ought not, that nothing is tolerable except producing great works or enjoying those of others, that he has accomplished nothing and never will, etc. – all this with a force that nearly knocks one down. He makes me feel like a bleating lambkin.

A few days later, Russell had had enough: 'I told Wittgenstein yesterday that he thinks too much about himself, and if he begins again I shall refuse to listen unless I think he is quite desperate. He has talked it out now as much as is good for him.'

And yet, at the end of November, we find him drawn once more into a discussion with Wittgenstein about Wittgenstein:

I got into talking about his faults – he is worried by his unpopularity and asked me why it was. It was a long and difficult and passionate (on his side) conversation lasting till 1.30, so I am rather short of sleep. He is a great task but quite worth it. He is a little too simple, yet I am afraid of spoiling some fine quality if I say too much to make him less so.

Something of what Russell means by Wittgenstein's being 'a little too simple' (and also, perhaps, of the source of his supposed unpopularity) we can gather from an entry in Pinsent's diary. On the evening following Wittgenstein's 'passionate afternoon' on the river, he and Pinsent attended a concert at the Cambridge University Music Club, and afterwards went to Wittgenstein's rooms. Farmer, the undergraduate monk mentioned earlier by Russell, appeared. He was, says Pinsent, 'a man Wittgenstein dislikes and believes to be dishonest minded':

. . . [Wittgenstein] got very excited trying to induce him to read some good book on some exact science, and see what honest thought is. Which would obviously be good for Farmer – as indeed for any one – : but Wittgenstein was very overbearing and let Farmer know exactly what he thought of him, and altogether talked as if he was his Director of Studies! Farmer took it very well – obviously convinced that Wittgenstein is a lunatic.

Wittgenstein's conviction that he was unpopular needs some qualification. During this term, at the very peak of his nervous irritability,
he did succeed in making some new and important friendships. In
particular, he gained the respect and affection of John Maynard
Keynes, who was to be a valuable and supportive friend for the greater
part of Wittgenstein's life. Russell first brought the two together on 31
October – 'but it was a failure', he reports, 'Wittgenstein was too ill to
argue properly'. But by 12 November we find Keynes writing to
Duncan Grant: 'Wittgenstein is a most wonderful character – what I
said about him when I saw you last is quite untrue – and extraordinarily nice. I like enormously to be with him.'

Keynes's advocacy was powerful enough to overcome any doubts
Lytton Strachey may still have had about Wittgenstein's suitability for
membership of the Apostles, and, after his pronouncement of Wittgenstein's genius, the issue was decided. The only remaining doubt
was whether Wittgenstein would wish to become a member –
whether he really considered it worth his while to meet regularly for
discussions with the other members. This, from an Apostolic point of
view, was quite extraordinary. 'Have you heard', wrote Keynes in
astonishment to Strachey, 'how our new brother's only objection to
the Society is that it doesn't happen to be apostolic?'

Russell, with some misgivings, did his best to further the cause.
'Obviously', he wrote to Keynes:

from [Wittgenstein's] point of view the Society is a mere waste of
time. But perhaps from a philanthropic point of view he might be
made to feel it worth going on with.

Thus, 'philanthropically', he did what he could to present the
Society in a favourable light. He explained to Wittgenstein that,
though there was nothing to be got out of the Society in its present
state, in former days it had been good and might be again if he were
prepared to stick to it. As we have seen, Russell's own objections to
the Society centred on their predilection for homosexual 'intrigues'.
Wittgenstein's doubts, however, were to do with the fact that, though
he liked the 'angels' (graduates) in the Society (Moore, Russell and
Keynes, in particular), he had taken a fierce dislike to his fellow
'brothers' – the undergraduate members – and was uncertain
whether he could stand the prospect of regular discussions with them.

He objected to their immaturity, telling Keynes that to watch them at Apostolic meetings was to see those who had not yet made their toilets – a process which, though necessary, was indecent to observe.

The 'brothers' in question were Frank Bliss, who had come from Rugby to read classics at King's, and Ferenc Békássy, an aristocratic Hungarian who had been at Bedales before coming to King's. Both were involved in the intrigues that Russell objected to, particularly Békássy, who, it is reported by James Strachey, filled Keynes and Gerald Shove with such lust at his first meeting with the Apostles that they wanted to 'take him' right then and there on the ritual hearthrug. It can hardly have been their involvement in such affairs that made Wittgenstein object to them: otherwise, it would be quite inexplicable that he took no exception to Keynes. His dislike for Békássy may perhaps have had something in it of Austro-Hungarian rivalry. But it was principally Bliss that he objected to – 'He can't stand him', Russell told Ottoline.

With great hesitation and doubt, therefore, Wittgenstein accepted membership and attended his first Saturday meeting on 16 November. At the meeting Moore read a paper on religious conversion and Wittgenstein contributed to the discussion his view that, so far as he knew, religious experience consisted in getting rid of worry (the *Sorge* that he had mentioned to Russell) and had the consequence of giving one the courage not to care what might happen (for, to someone with faith, nothing *could* happen). After the meeting Lytton Strachey was optimistic about the future of the Society, finding the prospect of conflict and bitchiness offered by the new members 'particularly exhilarating':

> Our brothers B[liss] and Wittgenstein are so nasty and our brother Békássy is so nice that the Society ought to rush forward now into the most progressive waters. I looked in on B[liss] on Sunday night and he seemed quite as nasty as Rupert [Brooke] ever was.

On the same day he wrote at length to Sydney Saxon Turner about Russell's objections to Wittgenstein's membership:

> The poor man is in a sad state. He looks about 96 – with long snow-white hair and an infinitely haggard countenance. The election of Wittgenstein has been a great blow to him. He dearly hoped

to keep him all to himself, and indeed succeeded wonderfully, until
Keynes insisted on meeting him, and saw at once that he was a
genius and that it was essential to elect him. The other people (after
a slight wobble from Békássy) also became violently in favour.
Their decision was suddenly announced to Bertie, who nearly
swooned. Of course he could produce no reason against the election – except the remarkable one that the Society was so degraded
that his Austrian would certainly refuse to belong to it. He worked
himself up into such a frenzy over this that no doubt he got himself
into a state of believing it – but it wasn't any good. Wittgenstein
shows no signs of objecting to the Society, though he detests Bliss,
who in return loathes him. I think on the whole the prospects are of
the brightest. Békássy is such a pleasant fellow that, while he is in
love with Bliss, he yet manages to love Wittgenstein. The three
of them ought to manage very well, I think. Bertie is really a
tragic figure, and I am very sorry for him; but he is most deluded
too.

Strachey was wrong on several counts. Russell had no desire to
'keep Wittgenstein all to himself'; he would have been only too glad to
be spared the evening-long examinations of Wittgenstein's 'sins', to
which he had been subjected all term. His doubts about the wisdom of
electing Wittgenstein to the Apostles – apart from his own disapproval of their homosexuality – had to do chiefly with his feeling
that it would 'lead to some kind of disaster'. And in this he was not, as
Strachey thought, deluded.

At the beginning of December, Strachey was told by his brother
James that: 'The Witter-Gitter man is trembling on the verge of
resignation.' Prompted by Moore, Strachey came up to Cambridge to
try and persuade Wittgenstein to stay on, but, even after several
meetings with both Wittgenstein and Moore, he was unable to do so.
At the end of term Russell reported to Ottoline:

> Wittgenstein has left the Society. I think he is right, tho' loyalty to
> the Society wd. not have led me to say so beforehand.

He added, in terms which suggest he was very far indeed from
wanting to keep Wittgenstein all to himself:

I have had to cope with him a good deal. It is really a relief to think of
not seeing him for some time, tho' I feel it is horrid of me to feel
that.

To 'Goldie' Lowes Dickenson, Russell repeated his opinion that
Wittgenstein had been right to leave, and added that he had tried to
dissuade him: 'He is much the most apostolic and the ablest person I
have come across since Moore.'

Evidence for the nature of Wittgenstein's work during this Michaelmas term is scanty. On 25 October Pinsent records a visit from
Wittgenstein during which he announces a new solution to a problem – 'In the most fundamental Symbolic Logic' – which had puzzled
him greatly in Iceland, and to which he had then made only a
makeshift solution:

> His latest is quite different and covers more ground, and if sound
> should revolutionise lots of Symbolic Logic: Russell, he says,
> thinks it sound, but says nobody will understand it: I think I
> comprehend it myself however (!). If Wittgenstein's solution
> works, he will be the first to solve a problem which has puzzled
> Russell and Frege for some years: it is the most masterly and
> convincing solution too.

From this we can reconstruct neither the problem nor the solution,
although it seems quite likely that it had to do with Wittgenstein's
remark to Russell during the summer that: 'our problems can be traced
down to the *atomic* prop[osition]s'. Towards the end of term Wittgenstein gave a paper to the Moral Science Club, the philosophy society at
Cambridge, which can perhaps be seen as an expansion of this remark.
Wittgenstein had played a great part in the discussions of the club
during this term, and with Moore's help had persuaded them to adopt
a new set of rules, requiring a Chairman to be appointed with the duty
of preventing the discussion from becoming futile, and stipulating
that no paper should last longer than seven minutes. Wittgenstein's
own paper was one of the first to be given under these new rules. On
29 November the minutes record:

Mr Wittgenstein read a paper entitled 'What is Philosophy?' The paper lasted only about 4 minutes, thus cutting the previous record established by Mr Tye by nearly two minutes. Philosophy was defined as all those primitive propositions which are assumed as true without proof by the various sciences. This defn. was much discussed, but there was no general disposition to adopt it. The discussion kept very well to the point, and the Chairman did not find it necessary to intervene much.

After term, on his way back to Vienna, Wittgenstein called on Frege at Jena, and had a long discussion with him, so he told Russell, 'about our Theory of Symbolism of which, I think, he understood the general outline'. His letters to Russell during January show him to be concerned with 'the Complex Problem' – the question of what corresponds to an atomic proposition if it is true. Suppose, for example, 'Socrates is mortal' is such a proposition: is the fact which corresponds to it a 'complex' made up of the two 'things', Socrates and mortality? This view would require the Platonic assumption of the objective existence of forms – the assumption that there exists, not only individuals, but also abstract entities such as mortality. Such an assumption is, of course, made by Russell in his Theory of Types, with which Wittgenstein became increasingly dissatisfied.

During the vacation this dissatisfaction led to his announcement of one of the central conceptions of his new logic. 'I think that there cannot be different Types of things!' he wrote to Russell:

> . . . every theory of types must be rendered superfluous by a proper theory of symbolism: For instance if I analyse the prop[osition] Socrates is mortal into Socrates, Mortality and $(Ex, y)\epsilon l(x, y)$ I want a theory of types to tell me that 'Mortality is Socrates' is non-sensical, because if I treat 'Mortality' as a proper name (as I did) there is nothing to prevent me to make the substitution the wrong way round. *But* if I analyse [it] (as I do now) into Socrates and (Ex) x is mortal or generally into x and (Ex) (x) it becomes impossible to substitute the wrong way round, because the two symbols are now of a different *kind* themselves.

He told Russell that he was not quite certain that his present way of analysing 'Socrates is mortal' was correct. But on one point he was most certain: 'all theory of types must be done away with by a theory of symbolism showing that what seem to be *different kinds of things* are symbolised by different kinds of symbols which *cannot* possibly be substituted in one another's places'.

In the face of such a sweeping dismissal of his theory, Russell might have been expected to present a spirited defence of his position – or at least some tough questions as to how his logicist foundations of mathematics might avoid contradiction *without* a theory of types. But he had by this time abandoned logic almost entirely. He spent the vacation working on quite a different subject – the existence of matter. He had, in November, delivered a paper to the Moral Science Club on the subject, in which he reiterated the view expressed in Cardiff earlier in the year that: 'No good argument for or against the existence of matter has yet been brought forward', and posed the question: 'Can we, therefore, know an object satisfying the hypotheses of physics from our private sense-data?' During the vacation he sketched an outline of the way in which he proposed to treat the problem:

> Physics exhibits sensations as functions of physical objects.
>
> But epistemology demands that physical objects should be exhibited as functions of sensations.
>
> Thus we have to solve the equations giving sensations in terms of physical objects, so as to make them give physical objects in terms of sensations.
>
> That is all.

'I am sure I have hit upon a real thing', he told Ottoline, 'which is very likely to occupy me for years to come.' It would require 'a combination of physics, psychology, & mathematical logic', and even the creation of 'a whole new science'. In the letter of January 1913, Wittgenstein was faintly dismissive of the whole project: 'I cannot imagine your way of working from sense-data forward.'

By the beginning of 1913, then, we see Russell and Wittgenstein working on very different projects – Russell on the creation of his 'new science', and Wittgenstein on the analysis of logic. Russell was now fully prepared to accept the latter as Wittgenstein's field rather than his own.

The new basis of their relationship was detected by Pinsent, who

near the beginning of term describes an occasion when he and
Wittgenstein were together in his rooms:

> Then Russell appeared – to inform me of some alterations he is
> making in the hours of his lectures – and he and Wittgenstein got
> talking – the latter explaining one of his latest discoveries in
> the Fundamentals of Logic – a discovery which, I gather, only
> occurred to him this morning, and which appears to be quite
> important and was very interesting. Russell acquiesced in what he
> said without a murmur.

A couple of weeks after this, upon being convicted by Wittgenstein
that some of the early proofs in *Principia* were very inexact, Russell
commented to Ottoline: 'fortunately it is his business to put them
right, not mine'.

The co-operation between the two had come to an end. In the field
of logic, Wittgenstein, far from being Russell's student, had become
his teacher.

Wittgenstein was late returning for the start of term owing to his
father's long-expected death from the cancer he had suffered with for
over two years. The end, when it came, was something of a relief. On
21 January he wrote to Russell:

> My dear father died yesterday in the afternoon. He had the most
> beautiful death that I can imagine; without the slightest pains and
> falling asleep like a child! I did not feel sad for a single moment
> during all the last hours, but most joyful and I think that this death
> was worth a whole life.

He finally arrived in Cambridge on 27 January, going straight to
Pinsent's rooms. About a week later Pinsent records an argument that
shows yet another facet of the differences between Russell and Wittgenstein. In 1907 Russell had stood as a parliamentary candidate for
the Women's Suffrage Party. Perhaps prompted by this fact (they had
just returned from one of Russell's lectures), Wittgenstein and Pinsent
got into an argument about women's suffrage. Wittgenstein was 'very
much against it':

. . . for no particular reason except that 'all the women he knows are such idiots'. He said that at Manchester University the girl students spend all their time flirting with the professors. Which disgusts him very much – as he dislikes half measures of all sorts, and disapproves of anything not deadly in earnest.

Wittgenstein's work on logic did nothing, apparently, to improve the rigour of his thought on political questions.

It is perhaps this inability – or, more likely, unwillingness – to bring his analytical powers to bear on questions of public concern that prompted Russell to criticize Wittgenstein for being 'in danger of becoming narrow and uncivilised'. Russell suggested as a corrective some French prose – a suggestion that involved him in a 'terrific contest':

He raged & stormed, & I irritated him more & more by merely smiling. We made it up in the end, but he remained quite unconvinced. The things I say to him are just the things you would say to me if you were not afraid of the avalanche they wd. produce – & his avalanche is just what mine wd. be! I feel his lack of civilisation & suffer from it – it is odd how little music does to civilise people – it is too apart, too passionate & too remote from words. He has not a sufficiently wide curiosity or a sufficient wish for a broad survey of the world. It won't spoil his work on logic, but it will make him always a very narrow specialist, & rather too much the champion of a party – that is, when judged by the highest standards.

As the comparisons to his own situation with Ottoline indicate, Russell was bemused to find himself in the position of one advocating synthesis rather than analysis. But it should be remembered that even his philosophical preoccupations at this time were moving in that direction – away from the 'narrowness' of logical analysis and towards a broader synthesis of physics, psychology and mathematics. In consequence, his discussions with Wittgenstein became, for him, frustratingly one-sided:

I find I no longer talk to him about *my* work, but only about his. When there are no clear arguments, but only inconclusive considerations to be balanced, or unsatisfactory points of view to be set against each other, he is no good; and he treats infant theories with a ferocity which they can only endure when they are grown up. The result is that I become completely reserved, even about work.

As the wearer of Russell's mantle in logic (it is hard to remember that Wittgenstein was still only twenty-four, and officially an undergraduate reading for a BA), Wittgenstein was asked to review a textbook on logic – *The Science of Logic* by P. Coffey – for the *Cambridge Review*. This is the only book review he ever published, and the first published record of his philosophical opinions. In it he presents a Russellian dismissal of the Aristotelian logic advanced by Coffey, but expresses himself with a stridency that exceeds even Russell's, and borders on the vitriolic:

In no branch of learning can an author disregard the results of honest research with so much impunity as he can in Philosophy and Logic. To this circumstance we owe the publication of such a book as Mr Coffey's 'Science of Logic': and only as a typical example of the work of many logicians of to-day does this book deserve consideration. The author's Logic is that of the scholastic philosophers and he makes all their mistakes – of course with the usual references to Aristotle. (Aristotle, whose name is so much taken in vain by our logicians, would turn in his grave if he knew that so many Logicians know no more about Logic to-day than he did 2,000 years ago.) The author has not taken the slightest notice of the great work of the modern mathematical logicians – work which has brought about an advance in Logic comparable only to that which made Astronomy out of Astrology, and Chemistry out of Alchemy.

Mr Coffey, like many logicians, draws a great advantage from an unclear way of expressing himself; for if you cannot tell whether he means to say 'Yes' or 'No', it is difficult to argue against him. However, even through his foggy expression, many grave mistakes can be recognised clearly enough; and I propose to give a list of some of the most striking ones, and would advise the student of Logic to trace these mistakes and their consequences in other books on Logic also.

There follows a list of such mistakes, which are, for the most part, the weaknesses of traditional (Aristotelian) logic customarily pointed out by adherents of Russellian mathematical logic – for instance, that it assumes all propositions to be of the subject-predicate form, that it confuses the copula 'is' (as in 'Socrates is mortal') with the 'is' of identity ('Twice two is four'), and so on. 'The worst of such books as this', the review concludes, 'is that they prejudice sensible people against the study of Logic.'

By 'sensible people' Wittgenstein presumably meant people with some sort of training in mathematics and the sciences, as opposed to the classical training we can probably assume Mr Coffey (along with most traditional logicians) to have had. In this he was echoing a view held by Russell and expressed to Ottoline the previous December:

I believe a certain sort of mathematicians have far more philo-sophical capacity than most people who take up philosophy. Hitherto the people attracted to philosophy have been mostly those who loved the big generalizations, which were all wrong, so that few people with exact minds have taken up the subject. It has long been one of my dreams to found a great school of mathematically-minded philosophers, but I don't know whether I shall ever get it accomplished. I had hopes of Norton, but he has not the physique, Broad is all right, but has no fundamental originality. Wittgenstein of course is exactly my dream.

As we have seen, during the Lent term Russell somewhat modified this view: Wittgenstein was exact, but narrow. He had too little 'wish for a broad survey of the world', insisted on too great a degree of exactness from infant theories, showed too little patience with 'incon-clusive considerations' and 'unsatisfactory points of view'. Perhaps, faced with Wittgenstein's single-mindedness, Russell came to think that a love of the big generalizations was not such a bad thing after all.

For Wittgenstein, his absorption in logical problems was complete. They were not a part of his life, but the whole of it. Thus, when during the Easter vacation he found himself temporarily bereft of inspiration, he was plunged into despair. On 25 March he wrote to Russell des-cribing himself as 'perfectly sterile' and doubting whether he would ever gain new ideas:

Whenever I try to think about Logic, my thoughts are so vague that nothing ever can crystallize out. What I feel is the curse of all those who have only half a talent; it is like a man who leads you along a dark corridor with a light and just when you are in the middle of it the light goes out and you are left alone.

'Poor wretch!' Russell commented to Ottoline. 'I know his feelings so well. It is an awful curse to have the creative impulse unless you have a talent that can always be relied on, like Shakespeare's or Mozart's.'

The responsibility Wittgenstein had been given by Russell – for the 'next great advance in philosophy' – was a source of both pride and suffering. He assumed it with complete and utter seriousness. He assumed also the role of a kind of custodian in the field of Russellian mathematical logic. Thus, when Frege wrote to Jourdain telling him about his plans to work at the theory of irrational numbers, we find Jourdain ticking him off in Wittgenstein's name:

> Do you mean that you are writing a third volume of the *Grundgesetze der Arithmetik*? Wittgenstein and I were rather disturbed to think that you might be doing so, because the theory of irrational numbers – unless you have got quite a new theory of them – would seem to require that the contradiction has been previously avoided; and the part dealing with irrational numbers on the new basis has been splendidly worked out by Russell and Whitehead in their *Principia Mathematica*.

Wittgenstein returned from the Easter vacation in, according to Russell, a 'shocking state – always gloomy, pacing up and down, waking out of a dream when one speaks to him'. He told Russell that logic was driving him mad. Russell was inclined to agree: 'I think there is a danger of it, so I urged him to let it alone for a bit and do other work.'

There is no record of Wittgenstein's doing any other work during this period – only of his taking up, albeit briefly, an unexpected pastime. On 29 April Pinsent notes: 'I played tennis with Wittgenstein: he has never played the game before, and I am trying to teach him: so it was a rather slow game!' However, a week later: 'I had tea chez: Wittgenstein, and at 5.0, we went up to the "New Field" and played tennis. He was off his game today and eventually got sick of it and stopped in the middle of a game.' And that is the last we hear of tennis.

Wittgenstein came to think that what he needed was not a diversion, but greater powers of concentration. To this end he was prepared to try anything, even hypnosis, and had himself mesmerized by a Dr Rogers. 'The idea is this', writes Pinsent in his diary: 'It is, I believe, true that people are capable of special muscular effort while under hypnotic trance: then why not also special mental effort?'

> So when he is under trance, Rogers is to ask him certain questions about points of Logic, about which Wittgenstein is not yet clear, (– certain uncertainties which no one has yet succeeded in clearing up): and Witt: hopes he will then be able to see clearly. It sounds a wild scheme! Witt: has been twice to be hypnotised – but not until the end of the second interview did Rogers succeed in sending him to sleep: when he did, however, he did it so thoroughly that it took ½ hour to wake him up again completely. Witt: says he was conscious all the time – could hear Rogers talk – but absolutely without will or strength: could not comprehend what was said to him – could exert no muscular effort – felt exactly as if he were under anaesthetic. He felt very drousy for an hour after he left Rogers. It is altogether a wonderful business.

Wonderful it may have been; useful it was not.

Russell, apparently, knew nothing about the scheme (it would surely have made too good a story to omit from his many recorded reminiscences of Wittgenstein if he *had* known of it); by this time, Pinsent was the more trusted confidant. At one of Russell's 'squashes' they are described as 'talking to each other and ignoring the rest of the world'. Pinsent was, perhaps, the *only* person with whom Wittgenstein could relax, and, temporarily at least, take his mind off logic. With Pinsent, Wittgenstein found himself able to enjoy some of the recreations customary for Cambridge undergraduates – riding, playing tennis, and even, on occasion, 'messing about on the river':

> . . . went on the river with Wittgenstein in a canoo. We went up to 'the Orchard' at Grantchester, where we had lunch. Wittgenstein was in one of his sulky moods at first, but he woke up suddenly (as

always happens with him) after lunch. Then we went on above Byron's pool and there bathed. We had no towels or bathing draws, but it was great fun.

Their strongest common bond, however, was music. Pinsent's diary records innumerable concerts at the Cambridge University Music Club, and also times when they would make music together, Wittgenstein whistling the vocal parts of Schubert's songs while Pinsent accompanied him on the piano. They had the same taste in music – Beethoven, Brahms, Mozart, and above all Schubert. Wittgenstein also seems to have tried to arouse interest in Labor, and Pinsent tells of an occasion when Wittgenstein tried to get a Labor quintet performed at Cambridge. They shared, too, a distaste for what Pinsent describes as 'modern music'. Thus:

> . . . we went to the C.U.M.C., and found Lindley there . . . he and Wittgenstein got arguing about modern music, which was rather amusing. Lindley used not to like modern stuff, but he has been corrupted! These performers always do in the end. [30.11.12]

> Wittgenstein and Lindley came to tea: there was a lot of animated discussion about modern music – Lindley defending it against us two. [28.2.13]

> I came with him to his rooms. Soon afterwards one Mac'Clure turned up – a musical undergraduate – and there was a wild discussion on modern music – Mac'Clure against Witt: and myself. [24.5.13]

And so on. Music did not have to be *very* modern to be deprecated by Wittgenstein, and these entries are just as likely to refer to conversations about, say, Mahler, as Schönberg. Labor aside, neither Wittgenstein nor Pinsent are on record as admiring anything after Brahms.

Wittgenstein asked Pinsent to accompany him on another holiday, this time in Spain, again to be paid for by Wittgenstein, an offer which Pinsent's mother told him was 'too good to refuse'. No doubt intrigued by the munificence of their son's friend, Pinsent's parents were taken to tea at Wittgenstein's rooms. It was an occasion when his exceptionally good manners could be used to good effect. The tea was served in chemical beakers ('because ordinary crockery is too ugly for him!'), and 'except that he was somewhat preoccupied by his duties as host, [Wittgenstein] was in very good form'.

When Pinsent's parents had left, Wittgenstein proceeded to lecture his friend about his character. Pinsent was, he said, 'ideal in all respects':

> . . . except that he [Wittgenstein] feared that with others except himself I was lacking in generous instincts. He specially said – not with himself – but he feared I did not treat my other friends so generously. By 'generously' he did not imply the ordinary crude meaning – but meant feelings of sympathy etc.

Pinsent took all this very well. 'He was very nice about it all and spoke in no way that one could resent.' He was nevertheless inclined to demur at Wittgenstein's judgement. After all, Wittgenstein knew very little of his other friends and his relations with them. He conceded, however, that it might be true that he treated Wittgenstein differently – after all, Wittgenstein was so different from other people ('he is if anything a bit mad') that one *had* to treat him differently.

As Wittgenstein's friendship with Pinsent grew warmer, his relationship with Russell became increasingly strained. Russell was, more and more, inclined to see in Wittgenstein his own faults writ large – to feel that, faced with Wittgenstein, he knew how other people felt when faced with himself. 'He affects me just as I affect you', he told Ottoline:

> I get to know every turn and twist of the ways in which I irritate and depress you from watching how he irritates and depresses me; and at the same time I love and admire him. Also I affect him just as you affect me when you are cold. The parallelism is curiously close altogether. He differs from me just as I differ from you. He is clearer, more creative, more passionate; I am broader, more sympathetic, more sane. I have overstated the parallel for the sake of symmetry, but there is something in it.

Emphasis on this parallel may have misled Russell. He was inclined to see Wittgenstein's faults as those 'characteristic of logicians': 'His faults are exactly mine – always analysing, pulling things up by the roots, trying to get the exact truth of what one feels towards him. I see it is very tiring and deadening to one's affections.' But the story he tells in illustration of this could point to a different moral – not that Wittgenstein was too analytical, but that he himself was too remote:

I had an awful time with Wittgenstein yesterday between tea and dinner. He came analysing all that goes wrong between him and me and I told him I thought it was only nerves on both sides and everything was all right at bottom. Then he said he never knew whether I was speaking the truth or being polite, so I got vexed and refused to say another word. He went on and on and on. I sat down at my table and took up my pen and began to look through a book, but he still went on. At last I said sharply 'All you want is a little self-control.' Then at last he went away with an air of high tragedy. He had asked me to a concert in the evening, but he didn't come, so I began to fear suicide. However, I found him in his room late (I left the concert, but didn't find him at first), and told him I was sorry I had been cross, and then talked quietly about how he could improve.

Perhaps he had to keep himself aloof to stop himself being submerged. But though Russell could turn a deaf ear to Wittgenstein's personal haranguing, he could not withstand the power of his philosophical onslaughts. During this summer Wittgenstein had a decisive influence on Russell's development as a philosopher – chiefly by undermining his faith in his own judgement. Looking back on it three years later, Russell described it as: 'an event of first-rate importance in my life', which had 'affected everything I have done since':

Do you remember that at the time when you were seeing Vittoz [Ottoline's doctor] I wrote a lot of stuff about Theory of Knowledge, which Wittgenstein criticised with the greatest severity? . . . I saw he was right, and I saw that I could not hope ever again to do fundamental work in philosophy. My impulse was shattered, like a wave dashed to pieces against a breakwater. I became filled with

utter despair . . . I *had* to produce lectures for America, but I took a
metaphysical subject although I was and am convinced that all
fundamental work in philosophy is logical. My reason was that
Wittgenstein persuaded me that what wanted doing in logic was too
difficult for me. So there was no really vital satisfaction of my
philosophical impulse in that work, and philosophy lost its hold on
me. That was due to Wittgenstein more than to the war.

The 'stuff about Theory of Knowledge' that Russell mentions was
the beginning of what he hoped would be a major work. It grew out of
his work on matter, and was stimulated in part by an invitation to
lecture in America. He had already written the first chapter of it before
he even mentioned it to Wittgenstein. 'It all flows out', he wrote
euphorically to Ottoline on 8 May. 'It is all in my head ready to be
written out as fast as my pen will go. I feel as happy as a king.' His
euphoria lasted only so long as he kept his writing secret from
Wittgenstein. The fact that he did so seems to indicate that he was
never as convinced of its worth as his letters to Ottoline would
suggest. He seemed to know instinctively what Wittgenstein's reaction would be to a work that was metaphysical rather than logical in
character. Sure enough: Wittgenstein disliked the very idea of it. 'He
thinks it will be like the shilling shocker, which he hates. *He* is a tyrant,
if you like.'

Russell pressed on regardless, and before the end of May had
written six chapters of what was clearly becoming a sizeable volume.
Then came the blow that was to shatter his impulse and convince him
that he was no longer capable of fundamental work in philosophy. In
discussing the work, Wittgenstein made what at first seemed a
relatively unimportant objection to Russell's Theory of Judgement.
Initially, Russell was confident that it could be overcome. 'He was
right, but I think the correction required is not very serious', he told
Ottoline. Just a week later, however, it seemed to him that the very
basis of his work had been undermined:

> We were both cross from the heat – I showed him a crucial part of
> what I had been writing. He said it was all wrong, not realizing the
> difficulties – that he had tried my view and knew it couldn't work. I
> couldn't understand his objection – in fact he was very inarticu-
> late – but I feel in my bones that he must be right, and that he has

seen something I have missed. If I could see it too I shouldn't mind, but, as it is, it is worrying, and has rather destroyed the pleasure in my writing – I can only go on with what I see, and yet I feel it is probably all wrong, and that Wittgenstein will think me a dishonest scoundrel for going on with it. Well, well – it is the younger generation knocking at the door – I must make room for him when I can, or I shall become an incubus. But at the moment I was rather cross.

It is a measure of Russell's lack of confidence that, even though he did not understand Wittgenstein's objections, he *felt* they must be justified. 'But even if they are', he wrote with unconvincing equanimity, 'they won't destroy the value of the book. His criticisms have to do with the problems I want to leave to him.' In other words, Wittgenstein's criticisms were logical rather than metaphysical. But if, as Russell believed, the problems of philosophy were *fundamentally* logical, how could it not affect the value of the book? How could the book be sound if its foundations were not? When Wittgenstein was finally able to put his objections in writing, Russell admitted defeat, unreservedly. 'I am very sorry to hear that my objection to your theory of judgment paralyses you', Wittgenstein wrote. 'I think it can only be removed by a correct theory of propositions.' Such a theory was one of the things that Russell had wanted to leave to Wittgenstein. Being convinced that it was at once necessary and beyond his own capabilities, he came to think that he was no longer able to contribute to philosophy of the most fundamental kind.

The conviction produced in him an almost suicidal depression. The huge work on the Theory of Knowledge, begun with such vigour and optimism, was now abandoned. But as he was contractually obliged to deliver the series of lectures in America, he had to continue with his preparations for them, even though he was now convinced that the material he had written for them was fundamentally in error. 'I must be much sunk', he told Ottoline, 'it is the first time in my life that I have failed in honesty over work. Yesterday I felt ready for suicide.' Four months previously he had written: 'Ten years ago I could have written a book with the store of ideas I have already, but now I have a higher standard of exactness.' That standard had been set by Wittgenstein, and it was one he now felt unable to live up to. He did not recover faith in his work until Wittgenstein was out of the way – and even then he felt it necessary to reassure himself in his absence that: 'Wittgenstein would like the work I have done lately.'

It says much for the generosity of Russell's spirit that, although devastated by Wittgenstein's criticisms of his own work, he could yet rejoice when he heard from Wittgenstein – during the late summer of 1913 – that *his* work was going well. He wrote to Ottoline: 'You can hardly believe what a load this lifts off my spirits – it makes me feel almost young and gay.'

Wittgenstein felt himself to have made a substantial breakthrough. When, at the end of August, he met Pinsent in London, he gave him an almost ecstatic account of his 'latest discoveries', which were, according to Pinsent, 'truly amazing and have solved all the problems on which he has been working unsatisfactorily for the last year'. They constituted a system which was: 'wonderfully simple and ingenious and seems to clear up everything':

> Of course he has upset a lot of Russell's work (Russell's work on the fundamental concepts of Logic that is: on his purely Mathematical work – for instance most of his 'Principia' – it has no bearing. Wittgenstein's chief interest is in the very fundamental part of the subject) – but Russell would be the last to resent that, and really the greatness of his work suffers little thereby – as it is obvious that Wittgenstein is one of Russell's disciples and owes enormously to him. But Wittgenstein's work is really amazing – and I really believe that the mucky morass of Philosophy is at last crystallising about a rigid theory of Logic – the only portion of Philosophy about which there is any possibility of man knowing anything – Metaphysics etc: are hampered by total lack of data. (Really Logic is all Philosophy. All else that is loosely so termed is either Metaphysics – which is hopeless, there being no data – or Natural Science e.g.: Psychology.

And yet, frustratingly – despite the fact that he had, apparently, already developed a system of logic that completely transformed philosophy – there is still no written record of Wittgenstein's work. Whether the overstatements that the system 'cleared up everything' and 'solved all the problems' are due to Wittgenstein or to Pinsent is impossible to say. But a few weeks later we learn from a letter of

Wittgenstein's to Russell that: 'There are still some *very* difficult problems (and very fundamental ones too) to be solved and I won't begin to write until I have got some sort of a solution for them.'

Pinsent had arranged to meet Wittgenstein under the impression that he would then be taken on a holiday to Spain. When they met, however, he was told there had been a change of plan. Spain had (for some unspecified reason) given way to three other alternatives: Andorra, the Azores or Bergen, in Norway. Pinsent was to choose – 'He was very anxious to shew no preference for any particular scheme and that I should choose unbiased' – but it was quite obvious that Wittgenstein's choice was Norway, so Pinsent opted for that. (Actually, he would have preferred the Azores, but Wittgenstein feared they would meet crowds of American tourists on the boat, 'which he can't stand!')

> So we are going to Norway and not Spain after all! Why Wittgenstein should have suddenly changed his mind at the last moment I can't think! But I expect it will be great fun in Norway all the same.

Before they left, Wittgenstein travelled to Cambridge to explain his new work to Russell and Whitehead. Both, according to Pinsent, were enthusiastic, and agreed that the first volume of *Principia* would now have to be rewritten in the light of it (if this is so, Whitehead must have had a change of heart later on) with Wittgenstein himself perhaps rewriting the first eleven chapters: 'That is a splendid triumph for him!'

As he assumed (or appeared to assume) more and more responsibility for the future of Russellian mathematical logic, Wittgenstein became ever more nervously susceptible. As they set sail from Hull to Christiania (now Oslo), he revealed himself to be in an extraordinarily fraught frame of mind:

> Soon after we had sailed Wittgenstein suddenly appeared in an awful panic – saying that his portmanteau, with all his manuscripts inside, had been left behind at Hull . . . Wittgenstein was in an awful state about it. Then, just as I was thinking of sending a wireless message about it, – it was found in the corridor outside someone else's cabin!

They reached Christiania, where they stayed overnight, before taking the train to Bergen, on 1 September. At the hotel Wittgenstein, apparently thinking of their occasional differences in Iceland the previous year, remarked to Pinsent: 'We have got on splendidly so far, haven't we?' Pinsent responded with typically English reserve. 'I always find it exceedingly hard to respond to his fervent outbursts, and I suppose this time I instinctively tried to turn it off flippantly – I am horribly shy of enthusiasm about that sort of thing.' His reticence deeply offended Wittgenstein, who said not a word to him for the rest of the evening.

The following morning he was still 'absolutely sulky and snappish'. On the train they had to change their seats at the last moment because Wittgenstein insisted on being away from other tourists:

> Then a very genial Englishman came along and talked to me and finally insisted on our coming into his carriage to smoke – as ours was a non-smoker. Witt: refused to move, and of course I had to go for a short time at least – it would have been violently rude to refuse. I came back as soon as I could and found him in an awful state. I made some remark about the Englishman being a weird person – whereat he turned and said 'I could travel the whole way with him if I pleased.' And then I had it all out with him and finally brought him round to a normal and genial frame of mind.

'I have to be frightfully careful and tolerant when he gets these sulky fits', Pinsent adds. 'He is – in his acute sensitiveness – very like Levin in "Anna Karenina", and thinks the most awful things of me when he is sulky – but is very contrite afterwards':

> I am afraid he is in an even more sensitive neurotic state just now than usual, and it will be very hard to avoid friction altogether. We can always avoid it at Cambridge, when we don't see so much of each other: but he never will understand that it becomes infinitely harder when we are together so much as now: and it puzzles him frightfully.

The quarrel on the train seemed to mark some kind of turning point in their relationship. Wittgenstein is now referred to as 'Ludwig' for the remainder of Pinsent's diary.

On reaching Bergen they went to a tourist office to make enquiries as to where they could find the sort of place that Wittgenstein wanted: a small hotel, somewhere on a fjord, set in pleasant country and entirely away from tourists. A perfect place, in other words, for Wittgenstein to work on logic undisturbed. (It must by now have been obvious that this was the reason for the last-minute change in plan.) He had already begun his work in the hotel in Bergen. 'When he is working', Pinsent noted, 'he mutters to himself (in a mixture of German and English) and strides up and down the room all the while.'

The tourist office found them a place satisfying all their conditions – a small hotel in a tiny village called Öistesjo, on the Hardanger fjord, at which they would be the only foreign tourists, the other ten guests being Norwegian. Once there they went for a short walk, Pinsent, ever the keen photographer, taking his camera, 'which was the cause of another scene with Ludwig':

> We were getting on perfectly amicably – when I left him for a moment to take a photo: And when I overtook him again he was silent and sulky. I walked on with him in silence for half an hour, and then asked him what was the matter. It seemed, my keenness to take that photo: had disgusted him – 'like a man who can think of nothing – when walking – but how the country would do for a golf course'. I had a long talk with him about it, and eventually we made it up again. He is really in an awful neurotic state: this evening he blamed himself violently and expressed the most piteous disgust with himself.

In an ironically apt comparison, Pinsent remarks: 'at present it is no exaggeration to say he is as bad – (in that nervous sensibility) – as people like Beethoven were'. Perhaps he had not been told that Wittgenstein regarded Beethoven as *exactly* 'the sort of man to be'.

Henceforth, Pinsent took great care not to offend or irritate Wittgenstein, and the rest of the holiday passed without another scene. They very quickly settled into a routine that suited Wittgenstein perfectly: they worked in the morning, went walking or sailing in the early afternoon, worked in the late afternoon, and played dominoes in the evening. For Pinsent it was all rather dull – 'just enough to do to keep one from being bored'. There was none of the novelty and romance of a pony cortège through the Icelandic countryside, and in his diary he is forced to linger on what little excitement there was to be found in an empty hotel (the other guests having left soon after Pinsent and Wittgenstein arrived) in an isolated part of Norway – returning again and again, for example, to their attempts to rid the hotel of a wasps' nest they had found in the roof.

For Wittgenstein, however, it was perfect. He was able to write to Russell in a mood of great contentment:

I am sitting here in a little place inside a beautiful fiord and thinking about the beastly theory of types . . . Pinsent is an enormous comfort to me here. We have hired a little sailing boat and go about with it on the fiord, or rather Pinsent is doing all the sailing and I sit in the boat and work.

One question nagged at him:

Shall I get anything out??! It would be awful if I did not and all my work would be lost. However I am not losing courage and go on thinking . . . I very often now have the indescribable feeling as though my work was all sure to be lost entirely in some way or other. But I still hope that this won't come true.

Wittgenstein's mood – as always – fluctuated with his ability to work. And it fell to Pinsent to cheer him up when he was depressed about his progress. On 17 September, for example, we read:

During all the morning and most of the afternoon Ludwig was very gloomy and unapproachable – and worked at Logic all the time . . . I somehow succeeded in cheering him up – back to his normal frame of mind – and after tea we went for a stroll together (it was a fine sunny day). We got talking and it appeared that it had been some very serious difficulty with the 'Theory of Types' that had depressed him all today. He is morbidly afraid he may die before he has put the Theory of Types to rights, and before he has written out all his other work in such a way as shall be intelligable to the world and of some use to the science of Logic. He has written a lot already – and Russell has promised to publish his work if he were to die – but he is sure that what he has already written is not sufficient-ly well put, so as absolutely to make plain his real methods of

thought etc: – which of course are of more value than his definite
results. He is always saying that he is certain he will die within four
years – but today it was two months.

Wittgenstein's feeling that he might die before being able to publish
his work intensified during his last week in Norway, and prompted
him to write to Russell asking if Russell would be prepared to meet
him '*as soon as possible* and give me time enough to give you a survey of
the whole field of what I have done up to now and if possible to let me
make notes for you *in your presence*'. It is to this that we owe
the existence of *Notes on Logic*, the earliest surviving exposition of
Wittgenstein's thought.

In his anxiety, this feeling that he *might* die soon became an
unchangeable conviction that he was *bound* to do so. Everything he
said or did became based on this assumption. He was not *afraid* to die,
he told Pinsent – 'but yet frightfully worried not to let the few
remaining moments of his life be wasted':

> It all hangs on his absolutely morbid and mad conviction that he is
> going to die soon – there is no obvious reason that I can see why he
> should not live yet for a long time. But it is no use trying to dispel
> that conviction, or his worries about it, by reason: the conviction
> and the worry he can't help – for he is mad.

Another, related, anxiety was that his work on logic might perhaps,
after all, be of no real use: 'and then his nervous temperament had
caused him a life of misery and others considerable inconvenience – all
for nothing'.

Pinsent seems to have done a marvellous job of keeping Wittgenstein's spirits up throughout these attacks of crippling anxiety –
encouraging him, reassuring him, playing dominoes with him, taking
him out sailing and, above all, perhaps, playing music with him.
During the holiday they put together a repertoire of some forty
Schubert songs, Wittgenstein whistling the air and Pinsent playing the
accompaniment.

It is perhaps not surprising to find that their perceptions of the
holiday differed sharply. Wittgenstein said he had never enjoyed a
holiday so much. Pinsent was less enthusiastic: 'I am enjoying myself
pretty fairly . . . But living with Ludwig alone in his present neurotic

state is trying at times.' On his return, on 2 October, he swore that he would never go away with Wittgenstein again.

At the end of the holiday Wittgenstein 'suddenly announced a scheme of the most alarming nature':

> To wit: that he should exile himself and live for some years right away from everybody he knows – say in Norway. That he should live entirely alone and by himself – a hermits life – and do nothing but work in Logic. His reasons for this are very queer to me – but no doubt they are very real for him: firstly he thinks he will do infinitely more and better work in such circumstances, than at Cambridge, where, he says, his constant liability to interruption and distractions (such as concerts) is an awful hindrance. Secondly he feels that he has no right to live in an antipathetic world (and of course to him very few people are sympathetic) – a world where he perpetually finds himself feeling contempt for others, and irritating others by his nervous temperament – without some justification for that contempt etc:, such as being a really great man and having done really great work.

Part of this argument is familiar: if he is to behave like Beethoven, he ought, like Beethoven, to produce really great work. What is new is the conviction that this is impossible at Cambridge.

Wittgenstein's mind was not definitely made up on the scheme, however, and he continued with preparations for a course of lectures on philosophy that he had agreed to give at the Working Men's College in London. The issue was finally decided when they reached Newcastle on the way home. There Wittgenstein received a letter from Gretl telling him that she and her American husband, Jerome Stonborough, were coming to live in London. That appeared to settle the matter. He could not, he told Pinsent, stand to live in England if he were perpetually liable to visits from the Stonboroughs.

He even convinced Pinsent – who at first was inclined to think the idea absurd – that he *should*, after all, go to Norway to work on logic. For: 'He has settled many difficulties, but there are still others unsolved.' And: 'The great difficulty about his particular kind of work is that – unless he absolutely settles all the foundations of Logic – his work will be of little value to the world.' So: 'There is nothing between doing really great work & doing practically nothing.'

Pinsent appears to have accepted the force of this reasoning, even though it has nothing whatever to do with the fact of the Stonboroughs being in England, does not explain why Wittgenstein has to be alone, and is in sharp contrast to the view he had accepted just a week before (that Wittgenstein's *method* was the important thing, not his *results*). The argument appears, in fact, to be a restatement of the terrible dichotomy raised by Weininger – greatness or nothingness. But in order to make it an intelligible reason for living away from Cambridge, one would perhaps have to add to it two other Weiningerian themes: that love is conducive to greatness, sexual desire inimical to it; and that 'sexual desire increases with physical proximity; love is strongest in the absence of the loved one; it needs a separation, a certain distance to preserve it'.

The possibility of greatness, therefore, demands a separation from the loved one.

5
NORWAY

As might be expected, Russell thought Wittgenstein's plan to live alone in Norway for two years a wild and lunatic one. He tried to talk him out of it by presenting various objections, all of which were brushed aside:

> I said it would be dark, & he said he hated daylight. I said it would be lonely, & he said he prostituted his mind talking to intelligent people. I said he was mad & he said God preserve him from sanity. (God certainly will.)

Before Wittgenstein embarked again for Bergen, it was important for both him and Russell that a written record of his work should be made: for Wittgenstein, because of his conviction that he had only a few more years (or even months) to live; and for Russell, because he hoped to use Wittgenstein's ideas for his forthcoming series of lectures in America – and because he, too, thought it was now or never (he strongly suspected that Wittgenstein would go completely mad and/ or commit suicide during his solitary sojourn in Norway).

The difficulty was that Wittgenstein's 'artistic conscience' (as Russell called it) made him extremely reluctant to write his ideas out in an imperfect form, and – as he had not yet reached a perfect formulation of them – therefore loathe to write anything at all. He wanted simply to explain his ideas to Russell, orally. Russell, who considered Wittgenstein's work 'as good as anything that has ever been done on logic', did his best to follow Wittgenstein's explanations, but in the end, finding the ideas so subtle that he kept forgetting them, begged him to write them out:

> After much groaning he said he couldn't. I abused him roundly and we had a fine row. Then he said he wd. talk & write down any of his remarks that I thought worth it, so we did that, & it answered fairly well. But we both got utterly exhausted, & it was slow.

He was prevented from giving up only by his resolute determination to 'drag W's thoughts out of him with pincers, however he may scream with the pain'.

Eventually he managed to get some written record of Wittgenstein's thoughts by asking the secretary of Philip Jourdain (who had come into Russell's room to borrow a book) to take shorthand notes while Wittgenstein talked and Russell asked questions. These notes were supplemented by a typescript which Wittgenstein dictated a few days later while he was in Birmingham saying his goodbyes to Pinsent. Together, the dictation and typescript constitute *Notes on Logic* – Wittgenstein's first philosophical work.

The work might be seen as an expansion of his remark to Russell earlier in the summer, that the Theory of Types 'must be rendered superfluous by a proper theory of symbolism', and as a preliminary attempt to provide such a theory. In its details, and in its criticisms of Russell, it is indeed very subtle. But its fundamental thought is quite staggeringly simple. It is that: '"A" is the same letter as "A"' (a remark which prompted the shorthand writer to comment, 'Well, that's true anyway'). This apparently trivial truism was to lead to the distinction between showing and saying which lies at the heart of the *Tractatus*. The thought – here in an embryonic form – is that what the Theory of Types *says* cannot be said, and must be *shown* by the symbolism (by our *seeing* that 'A' is the same letter as 'A', the same *type* of letter as 'B', and a different type from 'x', 'y' and 'z').

In addition to this embryonic Theory of Symbolism, *Notes on Logic* contains a series of remarks on philosophy which state unequivocally Wittgenstein's conception of the subject, a conception that remained – in most of these respects at least – unchanged for the rest of his life:

> In philosophy there are no deductions: *it* is purely descriptive.
> Philosophy gives no pictures of reality.

Philosophy can neither confirm nor confute scientific investigation.

Philosophy consists of logic and metaphysics: logic is its basis.

Epistemology is the philosophy of psychology.

Distrust of grammar is the first requisite for philosophizing.

After bidding farewell to Pinsent, Wittgenstein left Birmingham on
8 October. 'It was sad parting from him', wrote Pinsent:

> . . . but it is possible he may pay a short visit to England next
> summer (remaining in Norway till then & going back thither
> afterwards) when I may see him again. Our acquaintance has been
> chaotic but I have been very thankful for it: I am sure he has also.

The outbreak of war the following summer meant that this was the
last time the two saw each other.

What Wittgenstein needed (or felt he needed) in 1913 was solitude. He
found the ideal place: a village called Skjolden, by the side of the Sogne
fjord, north of Bergen. There he lodged with the local postmaster,
Hans Klingenberg. 'As I hardly meet a soul in this place', he wrote to
Russell, 'the progress of my Norwegian is exceedingly slow.' Neither
statement is entirely true. In fact, he made friends with a number of the
villagers. As well as the Klingenbergs, there was Halvard Draegni, the
owner of a local crate-factory, Anna Rebni, a farmer, and Arne
Bolstad, then a thirteen-year-old schoolboy. And his progress in
Norwegian was so swift that within a year he was able to exchange
letters with these friends in their native language. Admittedly, the
language in these letters was not excessively complicated or sophisti-
cated. But this was due less to the limitations of his Norwegian than to
the nature of the friendships. They were, in fact, the kind of simple,
direct and brief letters he liked best: 'Dear Ludwig, how are you? We
often think of you' might be a typical example.

He was not, then, entirely divorced from human contact. But he
was – and perhaps this is most important – away from *society*, free
from the kind of obligations and expectations imposed by bourgeois
life, whether that of Cambridge or that of Vienna. His horror of the
bourgeois life was based in part on the superficial nature of the
relationships it imposed on people, but partly also on the fact that his

own nature imposed upon *him* an almost insufferable conflict when faced with it – the conflict between needing to withstand it, and needing to conform to it.

In Skjolden he could be free from such conflicts; he could be himself without the strain of upsetting or offending people. It was a tremendous liberation. He could devote himself entirely to himself – or, rather, to what he felt to be practically the same thing, to his logic. That, and the beauty of the countryside – ideal for the long, solitary walks he needed as both a relaxation and a meditation – produced in him a kind of euphoria. Together they created the perfect conditions in which to think. It was perhaps the only time in his life when he had no doubts that he was in the right place, doing the right thing, and the year he spent in Skjolden was possibly the most productive of his life. Years later he used to look back on it as the one time that he had had some thoughts that were entirely his own, when he had even 'brought to life new movements in thinking'. '*Then* my mind was on fire!' he used to say.

Within just a few weeks he was able to write to Russell with an announcement of important new ideas, the apparently startling consequence of which would be 'that the whole of Logic follows from one P.P. [primitive proposition] only!!'

Russell, meanwhile, was doing his utmost to digest the *Notes on Logic* in readiness for his Harvard lectures. In the preface to the published version of those lectures, he states:

In pure logic, which, however, will be very briefly discussed in these lectures, I have had the benefit of vitally important discoveries, not yet published, by my friend Mr Ludwig Wittgenstein.

But there were points about which he was still unclear, and he sent Wittgenstein a series of questions hoping for elucidation. Wittgenstein's answers were brief and, for the most part, helpful. But he was too full of new ideas to find the process of going over old ground congenial: 'An account of general indefinables? Oh Lord! It is *too* boring!!! Some other time!'

Honestly – I *will* write to you about it some time, if by that time you have not found out all about it. (Because it is all quite clear in the manuscript, I think.) But just now I am SO troubled with Identity

that I really cannot write any long jaw. All sorts of new logical stuff
seems to be growing in me, but I can't yet write about it.

In the excitement of this peak of intellectual creativity he found it
particularly irksome to give explanations of points he felt were already
clear and well established. In a letter of November he tried to explain
why he thought the whole of logic had to follow from a single
primitive proposition. But when Russell still did not get it, his
patience was exhausted:

> I beg you to think about these matters for yourself, it is INTOLER-
> ABLE for me, to repeat a written explanation which even the first
> time I gave only with the *utmost repugnance*.

Nevertheless, he did make an effort to clarify the point. It hinged on
his conviction that, given the correct method of displaying the truth
possibilities of a proposition, a *logical* proposition can be shown to be
either true or false without knowing the truth or falsity of its constituent parts. Thus: 'It is either raining or not raining' will be true
whether 'It is raining' is true or false. Similarly, we need know nothing
about the weather to know that the statement: 'It is both raining and
not raining' is certainly false. Such statements are *logical* propositions:
the first is a tautology (which is always true), and the second a
contradiction (always false). Now, if we had a method for determining whether or not any given proposition is a tautology, a contradiction or neither, then we would have a single rule for determining *all*
the propositions of logic. Express this rule in a proposition, and the
whole of logic has been shown to follow from a single (primitive)
proposition.

This argument works only if we accept that all true logical propositions are tautologies. That is why Wittgenstein begins his letter to
Russell with the following oracular pronouncement:

> All the propositions of logic are generalizations of tautologies and
> all generalizations of tautologies are propositions of logic. There are
> no other logical propositions. (I regard this as definitive.)

'The big question now', he told Russell, is: 'how must a system of
signs be constituted in order to make every tautology recognizable as

such IN ONE AND THE SAME WAY? This is the fundamental problem of logic!'

He was later to tackle this problem using the so-called Truth-Table Method (familiar to all present-day undergraduate students of logic). But, for the moment, the peak of the *crescendo* had passed. As Christmas approached, exhilaration gave way to gloom and Wittgenstein returned to the morbid conviction that he had not long to live, and that he would therefore never publish anything in his lifetime. 'After my death', he insisted to Russell, 'you must see to the printing of the volume of my journal with the whole story in it.'

The letter ends: 'I often think I am going mad.' The insanity was two-edged, the mania of the previous few months turning into depression as Christmas approached. For, at Christmas: 'I must UNFORTUNATELY go to Vienna.' There was no way out of it:

> The fact is, my mother very much wants me to, so much so that she would be grievously offended if I did not come; and she has such bad memories of just this time last year that I have not the heart to stay away.

And yet: 'the thought of going home appals me'. The one consolation was that his visit would be brief and he would be back in Skjolden before long: 'Being alone here does me no end of good and I do not think I could now bear life among people.'

The week before he left, he wrote: 'My day passes between logic, whistling, going for walks, and being depressed':

> I wish to God that I were more intelligent and everything would finally become clear to me – or else that I needn't live much longer!

Complete clarity, or death – there was no middle way. If he could not solve: 'the question [that] is fundamental to the *whole* of logic', he had no right – or, at any rate, no desire – to live. There was to be no compromise.

In agreeing to join his family for Christmas, Wittgenstein was compromising – going against his own impulses – in order to satisfy the duty he felt to his mother. Once there, further compromise would be inevitable. The energy he had successfully channelled into his logic would have once more to be dissipated in the strain of personal relationships. His real preoccupations would have to be driven underground, while, for the sake of his mother and the rest of his family, he adopted the persona of the dutiful son. And, worst of all, he did not have the strength or clarity of purpose to do anything different: he *could* not bring himself to do anything that would risk grievously offending his mother. The experience threw him into a state of paralysing confusion. He was forced to realize that, however close he might be to complete, uncompromising clarity in the field of logic, he was as far away from it as ever in his personal life – in himself. He alternated between resistance and resignation, between ferment and apathy. 'But', he told Russell:

> . . . deep inside me there's a perpetual seething, like the bottom of a geyser, and I keep hoping that things will come to an eruption once and for all, so that I can turn into a different person.

In this state he was, of course, unable to do any work on logic. But, in his torment, was he not squaring up to an equally important, even related, set of problems? 'Logic and ethics', Weininger had written, 'are fundamentally the same, they are no more than duty to oneself.' It was a view Wittgenstein echoed in his letter to Russell, who, as Wittgenstein knew from their discussions in Cambridge, was hardly likely to see it in the same light:

> Perhaps you regard this thinking about myself as a waste of time – but how can I be a logician before I'm a human being! *Far* the most important thing is to settle accounts with myself!

Like his logic, this work on himself could best be done in solitude, and he returned to Norway as soon as possible. 'It's VERY sad', he wrote to Russell, 'but I've once again no logical news for you':

> The reason is that things have gone terribly badly for me in the last weeks. (A result of my 'holidays' in Vienna.) Every day I was tormented by a frightful *Angst* and by depression in turns and even in the intervals I was so exhausted that I wasn't able to think of doing a bit of work. It's terrifying beyond all description the kinds of mental torment that there can be! It wasn't until two days ago

that I could hear the voice of reason over the howls of the damned
and I began to work again. And *perhaps* I'll get better now and be
able to produce something decent. But I *never* knew what it meant
to feel only *one* step away from madness. – Let's hope for the best!

He had returned with a determination to rid himself once and for all
of the sordid compromises in his life. And – though it was a bit like
kicking the dog to get even with the boss – he began with his
relationship with Russell. The opening salvo was mild enough – a
gentle, and disguised, ticking off about Russell's own tendency to
compromise:

All best wishes for your lecture-course in America! Perhaps it will
give you at any rate a more favourable opportunity than usual to tell
them your *thoughts* and not *just* cut and dried results. THAT is what
would be of the greatest imaginable value for your audience – to
get to know the value of *thought* and not that of a cut and dried
result.

This can hardly have prepared Russell for what was to follow. He
replied, as he told Ottoline, in 'too sharp' a manner. What he actually
said, we do not know, though it is a reasonable conjecture that he
showed some impatience with Wittgenstein's pointed remarks about
his forthcoming lectures, that he criticized Wittgenstein's perfection-
ism (as he had done in the past), and that he justified his own
willingness to publish imperfect work.

Whatever it was, it was sufficient – in Wittgenstein's present
mood – to convince him that the time had come to break off all
relations with Russell. In what was clearly intended to be the last letter
he ever wrote to Russell, he explained that he had thought a lot about
their relationship, and had 'come to the conclusion that we really don't
suit one another':

This is NOT MEANT AS A REPROACH! either for you or for
me. But it is a fact. We've often had uncomfortable conversations
with one another when certain subjects came up. And the uncom-
fortableness was not a consequence of ill humour on one side or the
other but of enormous differences in our natures. I beg you most
earnestly not to think I want to reproach you in any way or to

preach you a sermon. I only want to put our relationship in clear terms *in order to draw a conclusion.* – Our latest quarrel, too, was certainly not simply a result of your sensitiveness or my inconsiderateness. It came from deeper – from the fact that my letter must have shown you how totally different our ideas are, E.G. of the value of a scientific work. It was, of course, stupid of me to have written to you at such length about this matter: I ought to have told myself that such fundamental differences cannot be resolved by a letter. And this is just ONE instance out of *many*.

Russell's value-judgements, he conceded, were just as good and as deep-seated as his own, but – for that very reason – there could not be any *real* relation of friendship between them:

> *I shall be grateful to you and devoted to you* WITH ALL MY HEART *for the whole of my life, but I shall not write to you again and you will not see me again either.* Now that I am once again reconciled with you I want to part from you *in peace* so that we shan't sometime get annoyed with one another again and then perhaps part as enemies. I wish you everything of the best and I beg you not to forget me and to think of me often *with friendly feelings*. Goodbye!
>
> Yours *ever*
LUDWIG WITTGENSTEIN

'I dare say his mood will change after a while', Russell told Ottoline after showing her the letter; 'I find I don't care on his account, but only for the sake of logic.' And yet: 'I do really care too much to look at it. It is my fault – I have been too sharp with him.'

He managed to reply in a way that melted Wittgenstein's resolve never to write to him again. On 3 March Wittgenstein wrote saying Russell's letter had been: '*so* full of kindness and friendship that I don't think I have the *right* to leave it unanswered'. Wittgenstein remained, however, resolute on the central point: 'our quarrels don't arise *just* from external reasons such as nervousness or over-tiredness but are – at any rate on *my* side – *very* deep-rooted':

> You may be right in saying that *we ourselves* are not *so very* different, but *our ideals* could not be more so. And that's why we haven't been able and we shan't *ever* be able to talk about anything involving our

value-judgements without either becoming hypocritical or falling out. *I think this is incontestable*; I had noticed it a long time ago; and it was frightful for me, because it tainted our relations with one another; we seemed to be side by side in a marsh.

If they were to continue with any sort of relationship at all, it would have to be on a different basis, one in which, 'each can be completely frank without hurting the other'. And, as their ideals were fundamentally irreconcilable, these would have to be excluded. They could avoid hypocrisy or strife *only* by 'restricting our relationship to the communication of facts capable of being established objectively, with perhaps also some mention of our friendly feelings for one another':

Now perhaps you'll say, 'Things have more or less worked, up to the present. Why not go on in the same way?' But I'm *too* tired of this constant sordid compromise. My life has been one nasty mess so far – but need that go on indefinitely?

He therefore presented a proposal that would, he thought, allow their relationship to continue on a 'more genuine basis':

Let's write to each other about our work, our health, and the like, but let's avoid in our communications any kind of value-judgement.

It was a plan to which he adhered for the remainder of his correspondence with Russell. He continued to sign himself 'your devoted friend'; he wrote of his work and he described his health. But the intimacy which had previously enabled them to talk of 'music, morals and a host of things besides logic' was lost. And what intellectual sympathy survived *this* break was to disappear entirely as a result of the changes brought about in both of them by the First World War – changes that emphasized and heightened the differences in their natures.

As Wittgenstein repeatedly emphasized in his letters, his friendship with Russell had been strained by their differences for over a year – despite Russell's delusion that it was their *similarity* that caused the trouble. Even their philosophical discussions had, long before Wittgenstein left for Norway, lost their co-operative character. In fact, during his last year at Cambridge he had not really discussed his ideas with Russell at all; he had simply reported them – given him, as it were, logical bulletins. As early as the previous November, when he had written to Moore urging him to come to Norway to discuss his work, he had expressed the view that there was no one at Cambridge with whom this was possible – no one 'who is not yet stale and is *really* interested in the subject':

> Even Russell – who is of course most extraordinarily fresh for his age – is no more pliable for *this* purpose.

As his relationship with Russell was first severed, and then placed on a less intimate footing, Wittgenstein's overtures to Moore became ever more insistent. Moore was dragging his feet somewhat about the proposed visit, and was probably regretting ever having promised to undertake it. But Wittgenstein's demands would brook no refusal: '*You must come as soon as Term ends*', he wrote on 18 February:

> I am looking forward to your coming more than I can say! I am bored to death with Logik and other things. But I hope I shan't die before you come for in that case we couldn't discuss *much*.

'Logik' is probably a reference to a work which Wittgenstein was then in the process of writing, and which he planned to show Moore with the intention of its being submitted for the BA degree. In March he wrote: 'I *think*, now, that Logic must be very nearly done if it is not already.' And although Moore, meanwhile, had come up with a new excuse – he needed to stay at Cambridge to work on a paper – Wittgenstein would have none of it:

> Why on earth won't you do your paper *here*? You shall have a *sittingroom* with a splendid view ALL BY YOURSELF and I shall leave you alone as much as you like (*in fact the whole day, if necessary*). On the other hand we *could* see one another whenever both of us should like to. And we *could* even talk over your business (which *might* be fun). Or do you want *so* many books? You see – I've PLENTY to do myself, so I shan't disturb you a bit. *Do* take the

Boat that leaves Newcastle on the 17th arriving in Bergen on the 19th and do your work here (I might even have a good influence upon it by preventing too many repetitions).

Finally, Moore overcame his reluctance to face the rigours of the journey – and the even more daunting prospect of being alone with Wittgenstein – and agreed to come. He left for Bergen on 24 March and was met there by Wittgenstein two days later. His visit lasted a fortnight, every evening of which was taken up with 'discussions', which consisted of Wittgenstein talking and Moore listening ('*he* discusses', Moore complained in his diary).

On 1 April Wittgenstein began to dictate to Moore a series of notes on logic. Whether these constitute the whole of the work referred to above as '*Logik*', or simply a selection, we can at least assume they contain the most important parts of it. Their central point is the emphatic insistence on the distinction between *saying* and *showing*, which was only implicit in the notes dictated to Russell the previous year. The notes begin:

Logical so-called propositions *show* the logical properties of language and therefore of the Universe, but *say* nothing.

The notes outline how this distinction allows us to achieve what he had earlier told Russell must be achieved: a Theory of Symbolism which shows the Theory of Types to be superfluous. That there are different types of things (objects, facts, relations etc.) cannot be said, but is *shown* by there being different types of symbols, the difference being one which can immediately be *seen*.

Wittgenstein regarded the work as a considerable advance on the notes he had earlier dictated to Russell, and it was, for the moment at least, his last word on the subject. He wrote to Russell urging him to read Moore's notes. 'I have now relapsed into a state of exhaustion and can neither do any work nor explain what I did earlier':

However, I explained it *in detail* to Moore when he was with me and he made various notes. So you can best find it all out from him. Many things in it are new. – The best way to understand it all would be if you read Moore's notes for yourself. It will probably be some time before I produce anything further.

On his return to Cambridge, Moore – as he had been instructed by Wittgenstein – made enquiries as to whether '*Logik*' might serve as a BA thesis. In this, he sought the advice of W. M. Fletcher (Wittgenstein's tutor at Trinity), and was told that, according to the regulations governing such theses, Wittgenstein's work would not be eligible as it stood. It was required that the dissertation should contain a preface and notes indicating the sources from which information had been derived and specifying which parts of the dissertation were claimed to be original and which parts were based on the work of others.

Moore, accordingly, wrote to Wittgenstein to explain the situation. Wittgenstein was outraged. His work – 'the next big advance in philosophy' – not entitled to receive a BA!? And just because it was not surrounded with the usual paraphernalia of undergraduate scholarship! This was the limit. It was bad enough to have to offer pearls to swine; to have them rejected was intolerable. On 7 May he gave vent to his feelings in a fiercely sarcastic letter to Moore, which, for the time being, put an end both to his friendship with Moore and to his hopes of obtaining a Cambridge degree:

> Dear Moore,
> Your letter annoyed me. *When I wrote Logik I didn't consult the Regulations*, and therefore I think it would only be fair if you gave me my degree without consulting them so much either! As to a Preface and Notes; I think my examiners will easily see how much I have cribbed from Bosanquet. – If I am not worth your making an exception for me *even in some* STUPID *details* then I may as well go to HELL directly; and if I *am* worth it and you don't do it then – by God – *you* might go there.
>
> The whole business is too stupid and too beastly to go on writing about it so –
>
> L.W.

The attack on Moore was unjustifiable: he had not made the regulations, nor was it his job to enforce them – he was simply letting Wittgenstein know where he stood with regard to them. He was, moreover, not used to being addressed in such a manner, and was profoundly disturbed by the tone of the letter. The unjustness shocked him deeply, and the fierceness of it made him feel physically sick. His diary for 11–15 May shows him to be still reeling from the blow days after receiving it. He did not reply.

Nor did he reply when, nearly two months later, on 3 July, he received a somewhat friendlier, almost contrite letter, written after Wittgenstein had left Norway to spend the summer in Vienna.

Dear Moore,
Upon clearing up some papers before leaving Skjolden I popped upon your letter which had made me so wild. And upon reading it over again I found that I had probably no sufficient reason to write to you as I did. (Not that I like your letter a bit *now*.) But at any rate my wrath has cooled down and I'd rather be friends with you again than otherwise. I consider I have strained myself enough now for I would *not* have written this to many people and if you don't answer this I shan't write to you again.

'Think I won't answer it', Moore wrote in his diary, 'because I really don't want to see him again.' His resolve almost weakened several times during the next few years. Wittgenstein's name would come up in conversation with Russell or with Desmond MacCarthy, and whenever it did he would wonder whether he was right not to have replied. Even though Wittgenstein (indirectly, through Pinsent) pleaded with him to get in touch, however, he did not do so, and the breach in their friendship was not healed until, when Wittgenstein returned to Cambridge in 1929, they happened to meet each other on the train. But throughout these years, thoughts of Wittgenstein haunted him so much that he contemplated writing a diary devoted to: 'what I feel about Wittgenstein'.

After Moore's visit Wittgenstein relapsed, as we have seen, into a state of exhaustion. Incapable, for the moment, of doing further work in logic, he devoted himself instead to building a small house on the side of the Sogne fjord, about a mile away from the village. It was intended to be a more or less permanent residence – or at least a place to live until he had finally solved all the fundamental problems in logic. But work on it was not finished when, in July, he returned to Vienna to escape the tourist season in Norway. He intended to spend only the summer away, partly in Austria with his family and partly on holiday with Pinsent. But he was not to return to Norway until the summer of 1921, by which time the fundamental problems of logic had – temporarily at least – been solved.

6

BEHIND THE LINES

Wittgenstein arrived back at the Hochreit towards the end of June 1914. His intention was to spend the early part of the summer there, before taking a two-week holiday with Pinsent starting at the end of August, and, finally, visiting old friends in England (e.g. Eccles) before returning to Norway in the autumn, there to live in his new house and to complete his book.

Throughout July, as the crisis following the assassination of Archduke Franz Ferdinand worsened and the European powers prepared for war, Wittgenstein and Pinsent exchanged letters discussing their proposed holiday. Should they go to Spain as planned, or to somewhere more remote? Eventually they agreed to meet at the Grand Hotel in Trafalgar Square on 24 August, and to decide then where they should go. In his reply to a letter from Eccles dated 28 June (the very day of the assassination), in which Eccles had told Wittgenstein of his new house and of the baby – 'the little stranger' – that his wife was expecting some time in August, we find Wittgenstein promising, with complete confidence, to visit Eccles in Manchester around 10 September, after he and Pinsent had returned from wherever they had decided to go. 'I hope the little stranger keeps well', Wittgenstein replied, 'and I hope he'll turn out to be a boy.'

Eccles had written asking Wittgenstein's advice on a proposed suite of bedroom furniture – wardrobe, medicine chest and dressing table – which Eccles had designed and was proposing to have manufactured. Such faith did he have in Wittgenstein's judgement on these matters that his new drawing room was a copy of Wittgenstein's room in Cambridge: blue carpet, black paint, yellow walls. 'The effect,' he told Wittgenstein, 'is greatly admired by everyone.'

Eccles's own criteria of good design are outlined in the letter: the greatest utility, the easiest method of construction, and absolute simplicity were, he said, the only things he had considered. They were criteria which Wittgenstein could readily approve. 'Splendid' was his verdict on Eccles's designs, suggesting only some alterations to the wardrobe, based on purely functional considerations. 'I can't see any drawing of a bed', he added:

> . . . or do you wish to take the one which the furniture manufac-turers submitted? If so *do* insist that they cut off all those measly fancy ends. And why should the bed stand on rollers? You're not going to travel about with it in your house!? By all means have the other things made after *your* design.

Though Wittgenstein and Eccles were at one in their preference for functional design, stripped of any sort of ornamentation, we can, I think, assume that for Wittgenstein the issue had a cultural, even an ethical, importance that it did not for Eccles. To the intellectuals of *Jung Wien*, the abhorrence of unnecessary ornamentation was at the centre of a more general revolt against what they saw as the empty posturing that characterized the decaying culture of the Habsburg Empire. Karl Kraus's campaign against the *feuilleton*, and Adolf Loos's notoriously unadorned building on the Mischlerplatz, were but two aspects of the same struggle. That Wittgenstein, to some extent at least, identified with this struggle is evident from his admiration for the work of its two chief protagonists.

While in Norway Wittgenstein had had Kraus's *Die Fackel* sent to him, and came across an article written by Kraus about Ludwig von Ficker, a writer who was an admirer of Kraus, and who was himself the editor of a Krausian journal published in Innsbruck, called *Der Brenner* ('The Burner'). On 14 July Wittgenstein wrote to Ficker offering to transfer to him the sum of 100,000 crowns, with the request that he distribute the money 'among Austrian artists who are without means'. 'I am turning to you in this matter', he explained, 'since I assume that you are acquainted with many of our best talents and know which of them are most in need of support.'

Ficker was, quite naturally, dumbfounded by the letter. He had neither met Wittgenstein nor heard of him, and this offer to place at his disposal such a large sum of money (100,000 crowns was the equivalent of £4000 in 1914, and therefore of perhaps £40,000–£50,000 of today's currency) needed, he thought, to be checked. He replied asking whether he could really take it that the offer was meant in all seriousness, that it was not a joke. 'In order to convince you that I am sincere in my offer', Wittgenstein answered, 'I can probably do nothing better than actually transfer the sum of money to you; and this will happen the next time I come to Vienna.' He explained that upon the death of his father he had come into a large fortune, and: 'It is a custom in such cases to donate a sum to charitable causes.' He had chosen Ficker 'because of what Kraus wrote about you and your journal in the *Fackel*, and because of what you wrote about Kraus'.*

Having received this letter, and having arranged to meet Wittgenstein at Neuwaldeggergasse on 26–7 July, Ficker endeavoured to find out something about him from his Viennese friends. From the painter Max von Esterle he learnt that Wittgenstein's father had been one of the richest *Kohlen-Juden* in the empire, and a generous patron of the visual arts. Reassured as to the sincerity of Wittgenstein's offer, Ficker travelled to Vienna to meet him in person and to discuss the allocation of the money. He stayed two days in the Wittgenstein house in Neuwaldeggergasse. Wittgenstein (he said in a memoir published in 1954) reminded him of such figures as Aloysha in *The Brothers Karamazov* and Myshkin in *The Idiot*: 'a picture of stirring loneliness at the first glance'.

Somewhat to Ficker's surprise, very little of their weekend together

---

*Kraus had written of Ficker's journal: 'That Austria's only honest review is published in Innsbruck should be known, if not in Austria, at least in Germany, whose only honest review is published in Innsbruck also.' *Der Brenner* had been started in 1910. Its name echoes that of Kraus's journal ('The Torch'), and announces its intention of extending the work of Kraus. Where Kraus satirized the shoddy thinking and writing prevalent in Austria, Ficker attempted to publish work that was free from shoddiness. His greatest success, and perhaps his greatest claim to fame, was that he was the first to recognize the genius of the poet Georg Trakl. From October 1912 to July 1914, no issue of *Der Brenner* appeared without Trakl's work. He also published the work of Hermann Broch, Else Lasker-Schüler, Carl Dallago and Theodor Haecker, and *Der Brenner* had, by the time Wittgenstein wrote to Ficker, established a reputation as one of the leading literary journals of the German avant-garde.

was taken up with a discussion of the matter in hand. Indeed, the subject of the allocation was broached only on the second day of his visit. Wittgenstein, initially, seemed more anxious to tell Ficker a little about himself. He described his work on logic, and its relation to the work of Frege and Russell. He told also of his hut in Norway, and of how he now lived among Norwegian peasants, and of his intention to return to Norway to continue his work. It is difficult to resist the conclusion that Wittgenstein's offer to Ficker was motivated not only by philanthropy, but also by a desire to establish some contact with the intellectual life of Austria. After all, he had severed communication with his Cambridge friends, Russell and Moore, despairing of their ever understanding his ideals and sensitivities. Perhaps among Austrians he might be better understood.

While in Vienna Ficker introduced Wittgenstein to Adolf Loos. Ficker's introduction was, for Wittgenstein, the highlight of his visit. 'It makes me *very* happy to have been able to meet him', he wrote to Ficker on 1 August. Indeed, so close were their concerns and their attitudes at this time, that Loos himself is reported to have exclaimed on meeting Wittgenstein: 'You are me!'

When they eventually got around to discussing the disbursement of the money, Wittgenstein's one condition was that 10,000 crowns should go to the *Brenner* itself; the rest was to be left to Ficker himself to distribute.

Ficker had already decided who his three main beneficiaries should be: Rainer Maria Rilke, Georg Trakl and Carl Dallago. Each would receive 20,000 crowns. Rilke is one of the few modern poets that Wittgenstein is known to have admired, and he welcomed Ficker's suggestion. Trakl's name, too, he accepted readily. About Dallago he made no comment. Dallago was a bohemian figure, well known at the time as a writer and philosopher. A regular contributor to the *Brenner*, he espoused an anti-materialistic, anti-scientific outlook that embraced Eastern mysticism and a celebration of the emotional, 'feminine', side of human nature.

Of the remaining 30,000 crowns, 5000 each went to the writer Karl Hauer (a friend of Trakl's and an erstwhile contributor to *Die Fackel*) and the painter Oskar Kokoschka; 4000 to Else Lasker-Schüler (a poet and a regular contributor to *Der Brenner*); 2000 each to Adolf Loos and the writers Theodor Haecker, Theodor Däubler, Ludwig Erik Tesar, Richard Weiss and Franz Kranewitter; and 1000 each to

Hermann Wagner, Josef Oberkofler, Karl Heinrich and Hugo Neugebauer.

Another contributor to *Der Brenner*, the expressionist writer Albert Ehrenstein, also seems to have benefited from Ficker's allocation of the money. So, at least, Wittgenstein thought. 'Once I helped him financially without really meaning to', he later told Paul Engelmann. In gratitude, Ehrenstein had sent him two of his books, *Tubutsch* and *Man Screams*, which Wittgenstein declared were: 'just muck if I'm not mistaken'.

It is very doubtful whether he knew the work of most of the artists whom he helped, and still more doubtful that he would have admired it if he had. From his responses to the letters of gratitude that were passed on to him by Ficker, there is no sign at all of any admiration for most of these artists, and, indeed, his reactions reveal a certain disdain for the whole business. The first such letter he received was from Dallago. Wittgenstein sent it straight back to Ficker: 'I do not know whether you have any use for it, but I am returning it anyway.' And when he was later sent a collection of such letters, he returned them all, saying that he did not need them as documents, and: 'as thanks they were – to be frank – for the most part highly distasteful to me. A certain degrading, *almost* swindling tone – etc.'

Something of this distance from the 'needy' artists he had patronized was felt by at least one of the beneficiaries, Theodor Haecker, whose German translations of Kierkegaard were published in *Der Brenner*, and did much to stimulate the interest of Austrian intellectuals in the Danish philosopher before the First World War. Haecker was at first inclined to refuse the money. The condition specified in Wittgenstein's instructions to Ficker was that the money should go to artists *in need*, and this was, he argued, a condition he could not meet. It would be different if a rich person had been so taken by his translations of Kierkegaard that he wished to pay for them: 'but a gift which the sponsor has expressly tied to the condition of the neediness of the recipient, I cannot and will not accept'. In his reply Ficker urged that it was appropriate, and in accordance with the wishes of the benefactor, that Haecker should be granted a portion of the donation. Haecker was reassured, and accepted the money, but there is no sign that Wittgenstein took any more pride in having helped Haecker than in having helped Ehrenstein.

Of only three of the beneficiaries can one say with any certainty that

Wittgenstein both knew of their work and admired it: Loos, Rilke and Trakl. And even here we must add the provisos that, though he admired the tone of Trakl's work, he professed himself incapable of understanding it; that he came to dislike Rilke's later poetry; and that, after the war, he denounced Loos as a charlatan.

Nevertheless, Rilke's letter of thanks he described as 'kind' and 'noble':

> [It] both moved and deeply gladdened me. The affection of any noble human being is a support in the unsteady balance of my life. I am totally unworthy of the splendid present which I carry over my heart as a sign and remembrance of this affection. If you could only convey my deepest thanks and my faithful *devotion* to Rilke.

Of Trakl's poems, he probably knew nothing until he was sent a collection of them by Ficker. He replied: 'I do not understand them, but their *tone* makes me happy. It is the tone of true genius.'

The weekend during which Wittgenstein and Ficker discussed the allocation of money to the artists of the Austro-Hungarian Empire was the weekend that sealed the fate of that empire. The Austro-Hungarian ultimatum to Serbia had been presented on 23 July, and the deadline for their acceptance of its terms was Saturday 25 July, at 6 p.m. No acceptance was received, and accordingly, on 28 July, Austria declared war on Serbia.

Even at this late stage – and within a week, the whole of Europe would be at war – it was not generally realized that this would have any effect on relations between Austria-Hungary and Britain. Public opinion in Britain – in so far as it concerned itself with such things – was sympathetic to the Habsburgs and antagonistic towards the Serbians. The British newspapers were almost as passionate in their denunciation of the murder of the Archduke as were their Austrian counterparts.

Perhaps, then, it is not surprising to read, in a letter to Wittgenstein dated 29 July, Pinsent's confident confirmation of their arrangement to meet at the Grand Hotel on 24 August. The only doubt expressed by him concerns their destination. Should it be Andorra or the Faeroe Islands? Or perhaps somewhere else? 'I suppose Madeira wouldn't suit you', he suggested optimistically. 'Of course', he wrote, without any discernible enthusiasm, 'there are out of the way places in the British Isles.' But: 'I don't think we had better go to Ireland, as there will almost certainly be riots & civil war of a sort there soon!' Scotland might do (this had evidently been Wittgenstein's suggestion) – say, Orkney or Shetland, or the Hebrides. And, indeed, this might, in one respect, be preferable to a holiday on the Continent. For:

> Perhaps in view of this European War business we had better not go to Andorra – it might be difficult to get back.

By the absurd logic of what A. J. P. Taylor had called 'war by time-table', 'this European war business' had led, within a few days of Wittgenstein's receiving this letter, to his country and Pinsent's being on different sides in the First World War.

Wittgenstein's first reaction seems to have been to try and get out of Austria, perhaps to England or to Norway. When that failed, and he was told he could not leave, he joined the Austrian army as a volunteer, the rupture he had suffered the previous year having exempted him from compulsory service. 'I think it is magnificent of him to have enlisted', wrote Pinsent in his diary, 'but extremely sad and tragic.'

Although a patriot, Wittgenstein's motives for enlisting in the army were more complicated than a desire to defend his country. His sister Hermine thought it had to do with: 'an intense desire to take something difficult upon himself and to do something other than purely intellectual work'. It was linked to the desire he had felt so intensely since January, to 'turn into a different person'.

The metaphor he had then used to describe his emotional state serves equally to describe the feeling that pervaded Europe during the summer of 1914 – the sense of perpetual seething, and the hope that 'things will come to an eruption once and for all'. Hence the scenes of joy and celebration that greeted the declaration of war in each of the belligerent nations. The whole world, it seems, shared Wittgenstein's madness of 1914. In his autobiography, Russell describes how, walking through the cheering crowds in Trafalgar Square, he was amazed to discover that 'average men and women were delighted at the prospect of war'. Even some of his best friends, such as George Trevelyan and Alfred North Whitehead, were caught up in the enthusiasm and became 'savagely warlike'.

We should not imagine Wittgenstein greeting the news of war against Russia with unfettered delight, or succumbing to the hysterical xenophobia that gripped the European nations at this time. None the less, that he in some sense *welcomed* the war seems indisputable, even though this was primarily for personal rather than nationalistic reasons. Like many of his generation (including, for example, some of his contemporaries at Cambridge, such as Rupert Brooke, Frank Bliss and Ferenc Békássy), Wittgenstein felt that the experience of facing death would, in some way or other, *improve* him. He went to war, one could say, not for the sake of his country, but for the sake of himself.

The spiritual value of facing death heroically is touched upon by William James in *Varieties of Religious Experience* – a book which, as he had told Russell in 1912, Wittgenstein thought might improve him in a way in which he very much wanted to improve. 'No matter what a man's frailties otherwise may be', writes James:

> if he be willing to risk death, and still more if he suffer it heroically, in the service he has chosen, the fact consecrates him forever.

In the diaries Wittgenstein kept during the war (the personal parts of which are written in a very simple code) there are signs that he wished for precisely this kind of consecration. 'Now I have the chance to be a decent human being', he wrote on the occasion of his first glimpse of the enemy, 'for I'm standing eye to eye with death.' It was two years into the war before he was actually brought into the firing line, and his immediate thought was of the spiritual value it would bring. 'Perhaps', he wrote, 'the nearness of death will bring light into life. God enlighten me.' What Wittgenstein wanted from the war, then, was a transformation of his whole personality, a 'variety of religious experience' that would change his life irrevocably. In this sense, the war came for him just at the right time, at the moment when his desire to 'turn into a different person' was stronger even than his desire to solve the fundamental problems of logic.

He enlisted on 7 August, the day after the Austrian declaration of war against Russia, and was assigned to an artillery regiment serving at Kraków on the Eastern Front. He was immediately encouraged by the kindness of the military authorities in Vienna. 'People to whom thousands come each day to ask advice replied kindly and in detail', he commented. It was a good sign; it reminded him of the English way of doing things. He arrived in Kraków on 9 August in a state of excited anticipation: 'Will I be able to work now??! I am anxious to know what lies ahead.'

Wittgenstein's regiment was assigned to the Austrian First Army, and was therefore involved in one of the most absurdly incompetent campaigns of the early months of the war. Both the Russian and the Austrian commands pursued a strategy based on illusion: the Russians thought the mass of Austrian troops would be centred on Lemberg (now Lwów); the Austrians expected to find the bulk of Russian forces further north, around Lublin. Thus, while the Austrian army made easy headway into Russian Poland, the Russians advanced on Lemberg, the largest city in Austrian Galicia, both forces surprised at how little resistance they faced. By the time the Austrian commander, Conrad, realized what had happened, Lemberg had fallen and his First Army was in grave danger of being cut off from its supply lines by Russian troops to the south. He was therefore forced to order a retreat. What had begun as a bold offensive into Russian territory ended in an ignominious withdrawal to a line 140 miles *inside* Austria-Hungary. Had the Austrian army not withdrawn, however, it would have been annihilated by the numerically stronger Russian forces. As it was, 350,000 men out of the 900,000 under Conrad's control died in the confused and fruitless Galician campaign.

Wittgenstein spent most of this campaign on board a ship on the Vistula river – the *Goplana*, captured from the Russians during the initial advance. If he saw any active fighting during these first few months, there is no record of it in his diary. We read instead of great battles heard but not seen, and of rumours that 'the Russians are at our heels'. It is perhaps typical of Wittgenstein's pessimism (justified in this case) that he was all too ready to believe the stories coming in that the Russians had taken Lemberg, but quick to disbelieve the rumour that the Germans had taken Paris. From both stories he drew the same conclusion: 'Now I know that we are lost!' The rumour about Paris, particularly, prompted him, on 25 October, to reflect gloomily on the situation of the Central Powers:

Such incredible news is always a bad sign. If something really had gone well for us then *that* would be reported and people would not succumb to such absurdities. Because of this, today, more than ever, I feel the terrible sadness of our – the German race's – situation. The English – the best race in the world – *cannot* lose. We, however, can lose, and will lose, if not this year then the next. The thought that our race will be defeated depresses me tremendously, because I am German through and through.

The fact that he was inclined to see the war in racial terms perhaps goes some way towards explaining why he found it so difficult to get on with the majority of his fellow crew members. The Austro-Hungarian army was the most multi-racial of all the European armies. Although most of its officers were Germans or Magyars, the bulk of its ordinary soldiers came from the various subject Slavic nationalities of the empire. Wittgenstein's officers he found 'kind, and at times very fine', but as soon as he met his crew mates he pronounced them 'a bunch of delinquents': 'No enthusiasm for anything, unbelievably crude, stupid and malicious.' He could barely see them as human beings:

> When we hear a Chinese talk we tend to take his speech for inarticulate gurgling. Someone who understands Chinese will recognize *language* in what he hears. Similarly I often cannot discern the *humanity* in a man.

Surrounded as he was by alien beings – and appearing to them equally as alien – Wittgenstein found the situation rather like that he had faced at school in Linz. On 10 August, the day after he collected his uniform, the analogy had struck him in terms which suggest a repressed anxiety brought suddenly to the surface: 'Today, when I woke up I felt as though I were in one of those dreams in which, unexpectedly and absurdly, one finds oneself back at school.' And on the *Goplana*, after having been jeered at by the crew, he wrote: 'It was terrible. If there is one thing I have found out it is this: in the whole crew there is not one decent person':

> There is an enormously difficult time ahead of me, for I am sold and betrayed now just as I was long ago at school in Linz.

His sense of isolation was made complete by the knowledge that the people in his life who had helped him to overcome the feeling of loneliness he had had since a pupil at Linz – Russell, Keynes, Pinsent –

were 'on the other side'. 'The last few days I have often thought of Russell', he wrote on 5 October. 'Does he still think of me?' He received a letter from Keynes, but it was of a purely businesslike nature, asking him what should happen after the war to the money that he had arranged to give to Johnson.* 'It hurts to receive a letter of business from one with whom one was once in confidence, and especially in these times.' But it was, above all, to Pinsent that his thoughts turned: 'No news from David. I am completely abandoned. I think of suicide.'

To his few German and Austrian friends Wittgenstein sent greetings in the form of military postcards, and received in reply letters of encouragement and support. The Jolles family in Berlin, in particular, were frequent and enthusiastic correspondents. Elderly and patriotic, they took a vicarious pleasure in reading the news from the Front of their 'little Wittgenstein', and, throughout the war, badgered him to provide more detailed accounts of his exploits. 'I have never thought of you so often and with such joy in my heart as now', wrote Stanislaus Jolles on 25 October. 'Let us hear from you often and soon.' They 'did their bit' by sending him regular parcels of chocolate, bread and cigarettes.

From Frege, too, he received patriotic best wishes. 'That you have enlisted as a volunteer', Frege wrote on 11 October:

> I read with particular satisfaction, and am amazed that you can still dedicate yourself to scientific work. May it be granted to me to see you return from the war in good health and to resume discussions with you. Undoubtedly, we will then, in the end, come closer to each other and understand one another better.

What saved him from suicide, however, was not the encouragement he received from Jolles and Frege, but exactly the kind of personal transformation, the religious conversion, he had gone to war to find. He was, as it were, saved by the word. During his first month in Galicia, he entered a bookshop, where he could find only one book: Tolstoy's *Gospel in Brief*. The book captivated him. It became for him

---

* Before the war Wittgenstein had arranged with Keynes to donate £200 a year to a research fund administered by King's College to help Johnson continue in his work on logic.

a kind of talisman: he carried it wherever he went, and read it so often that he came to know whole passages of it by heart. He became known to his comrades as 'the man with the gospels'. For a time he – who before the war had struck Russell as being 'more terrible with Christians' than Russell himself – became not only a believer, but an evangelist, recommending Tolstoy's *Gospel* to anyone in distress. 'If you are not acquainted with it', he later told Ficker, 'then you cannot imagine what an effect it can have upon a person.'

His logic and his thinking about himself being but two aspects of the single 'duty to oneself', this fervently held faith was bound to have an influence on his work. And eventually it did – transforming it from an analysis of logical symbolism in the spirit of Frege and Russell into the curiously hybrid work which we know today, combining as it does logical theory with religious mysticism.

But such an influence does not become apparent until a few years later. During the first few months of the war, the spiritual sustenance that Wittgenstein derived from reading Tolstoy's *Gospel* 'kept him alive', in the sense that it allowed him, as he put it, to lighten his external appearance, 'so as to leave undisturbed my inner being'.

It allowed him, that is to say, to put into practice the thought that had struck him while watching *Die Kreuzelscheiber* two (or three) years previously – the idea that, whatever happened 'externally', nothing could happen to *him*, to his innermost being. Thus we find in his diary repeated exhortations to God to help him not to 'lose himself'. This, for him, was far more important than staying alive. What happened to his body was – or, he felt, should have been – a matter of indifference. 'If I should reach my end now', he wrote on 13 September (one of the days on which it was reported that the Russians were advancing towards them), 'may I die a good death, attending myself. May I never lose myself.'

For Wittgenstein, the body belonged only to the 'external world' – the world to which also belonged the 'crude, stupid and malicious' delinquents among whom he now lived. His *soul*, however, must inhabit an entirely different realm. In November he told himself:

Don't be dependent on the external world and then you have no fear of what happens in it . . . It is x times easier to be independent of things than to be independent of people. But one must be capable of that as well.

His job on the ship was to man the searchlight at night. The loneliness of the task made it much easier to achieve the independence from people he considered necessary to endure the conditions on the boat. 'Through it', he wrote, 'I succeed in escaping the wickedness of the comrades.' Perhaps also his intense desire to distance himself from his external surroundings made it easier for him to resume work on logic. On 21 August he had wondered whether he would ever be able to work again:

> All the concepts of my work have become 'foreign' to me. I do not SEE anything at all!!!

But during the following two weeks – a period spent working at night on the searchlight, and the time during which he first began to read, and find solace in, Tolstoy's *Gospel* – he wrote a great deal. At the end of these two weeks he remarked: 'I am on the path to a great discovery. But will I reach it?'

And yet, the separation between body and spirit was not complete. How could it be? He could distance himself from his surroundings, even from his fellow men, but he could not separate himself from his own body. In fact, coincident with his renewed ability to work on logic, was a revitalized sensuality. The almost jubilant remark quoted above is followed by: 'I feel more sensual than before. Today I masturbated again.' Two days previously he had recorded that he had masturbated for the first time in three weeks, having until then felt almost no sexual desire at all. The occasions on which he masturbated – though clearly not an object of pride – are not recorded with any self-admonition; they are simply noted, in a quite matter-of-fact way, as one might record one's state of health. What appears to emerge from his diary is that his desire to masturbate and his ability to work were complementary signs that he was, in a full sense, *alive*. One might almost say that, for him, sensuality and philosophical thought were inextricably linked – the physical and mental manifestations of passionate arousal.

There are no coded remarks in Wittgenstein's notebooks for the second half of September, the time of the Austrian retreat. It was during this time, however, that he made the great discovery he had felt was imminent. This consisted of what is now known as the 'Picture

Theory of language' – the idea that propositions are a picture of the reality they describe. The story of how this idea occurred to him was told by Wittgenstein in later life to his friend G. H. von Wright, and has since been retold many times. While serving on the Eastern Front, the story goes, Wittgenstein read in a magazine a report of a lawsuit in Paris concerning a car accident, in which a model of the accident was presented before the court. It occurred to him that the model could represent the accident because of the correspondence between the parts of the model (the miniature houses, cars, people) and the real things (houses, cars, people). It further occurred to him that, on this analogy, one might say a *proposition* serves as a model, or *picture*, of a state of affairs, by virtue of a similar correspondence between *its* parts and the world. The way in which the parts of the proposition are combined – the *structure* of the proposition – depicts a possible combination of elements in reality, a possible state of affairs.

From Wittgenstein's notebooks we can date this genesis of the Picture Theory to somewhere around 29 September. On that day he wrote:

> In the proposition a world is as it were put together experimentally. (As when in the law-court in Paris a motor-car accident is represented by means of dolls, etc.)

Throughout October, Wittgenstein developed the consequences of this idea, which he called his 'Theory of Logical Portrayal'. Just as a drawing or a painting portrays pictorially, so, he came to think, a proposition portrays *logically*. That is to say, there is – and must be – a logical structure in common between a proposition ('The grass is green') and a state of affairs (the grass being green), and it is this commonality of structure which enables language to represent reality:

> We can say straight away: Instead of: this proposition has such and such a sense: this proposition represents such and such a situation. It portrays it logically.
>
> Only in this way can *the proposition* be true or false: It can only agree or disagree with reality by being a *picture* of a situation.

Wittgenstein regarded this idea as an important breakthrough. It was, so to speak, a valuable fortress that had to be taken if logic were to be conquered. 'Worked the whole day', he wrote on 31 October:

Stormed the problem in vain! But I would pour my blood before this fortress rather than march off empty-handed. The greatest difficulty lies in making secure fortresses already conquered. And as long as the whole *city* has not fallen one cannot feel completely secure in one of its fortifications.

But while he himself was on the offensive, the Austrian army was in chaotic and disorderly retreat. The *Goplana* was making its way back towards Kraków, deep inside Austrian territory, where the army was to be quartered for the winter. Before they reached Kraków, Wittgenstein received a note from the poet Georg Trakl, who was at the military hospital there as a psychiatric patient. He had earlier been told of Trakl's situation by Ficker, who had been to Kraków to visit Trakl, and from there had written to Wittgenstein asking him to pay the poet a visit. Trakl felt extremely lonely, Ficker had written, and knew nobody in Kraków who would visit him. 'I would be greatly obliged', Trakl himself wrote, 'if you would do me the honour of paying a visit . . . I will possibly be able to leave the hospital in the next few days to return to the field. Before a decision is reached, I would greatly like to speak with you.' Especially in his present company, Wittgenstein was delighted by the invitation: 'How happy I would be to get to know him! When I arrive at Kraków I hope to meet him! He could be a great stimulus to me.' On 5 November, the day that the *Goplana* finally arrived at Kraków, he was: 'thrilled with the anticipation and hope of meeting Trakl':

I miss greatly having people with whom I can communicate a little . . . it would invigorate me a great deal . . . In Krakau. It is already too late to visit Trakl today.

This final sentence is charged with the most terrible, unwitting, irony. For as Wittgenstein found out the next morning when he rushed to the hospital, it was indeed too late: Trakl had killed himself with an overdose of cocaine on 3 November 1914, just two days before Wittgenstein's arrival. Wittgenstein was devastated: '*Wie traurig, wie traurig*!!!' ('What unhappiness, what unhappiness!!!') was all he could find to say on the matter.

For the next few days Wittgenstein's diary is full of the misery of his life, the brutality of his surroundings and the failure of his attempts to find a decent person to help him survive. Robbed of such a person in Trakl, he turned his thoughts to Pinsent: 'How often I think of him! And whether he thinks of me half as much.' He discovered that he could get mail through to England via Switzerland, and immediately sent a letter to 'the *beloved* David'. During the weeks that followed, he waited impatiently for a reply. When a letter from Pinsent finally did arrive, on 1 December, it came as such a relief that he kissed it.

In the letter Pinsent told Wittgenstein that he had tried to join the British army but had failed the medical test for a private ('I am too thin') and could not get a commission as an officer. So he was still, reluctantly, reading for his examinations in law. 'When this war is over', he wrote, 'we will meet each other again. Let's hope it will be soon!' 'I think it was *splendid* of you to volunteer for the Army', he added, 'though it is terribly tragic that it should be necessary.'

Wittgenstein answered straight away, and then waited with growing impatience for the reply. And so it went on. '*Keine Nachricht von David*' ('No news from David') and '*Lieben Brief von David*' ('Lovely letter from David') are phrases that appear repeatedly, throughout the winter, in his diary.

Wittgenstein's greatest worry about spending winter in Kraków was not the cold (although he complains of that frequently), but the thought that he would have to share sleeping quarters with the other men – 'from which', he prayed, 'may God release me'. In the event, his prayers were answered: he was, to his enormous relief, promised a room of his own. Even better, in December he was given an entirely new post, a chance to rid himself once and for all of the 'mass of scoundrels' whose company he had endured for four long months. He had wanted to join a balloon section, but when it was discovered that he had a mathematical training he was offered instead a job with an artillery workshop.

Actually, the task Wittgenstein was given at the workshop was mundane clerical work, requiring no mathematical expertise and consisting of compiling a list of all the vehicles in the barracks. For a while all he had to report in his diary was '*Ganzer Tag Kanzlei*' ('At the office all day'), which, so often did it recur, he began to abbreviate as '*G.T.K.*'. The job had its compensations, however, not the least of which was a decent room to himself: 'For the first time in 4 months I am alone in a proper room!! A luxury I *savour*.' He was also, more important, among people he could like and respect, and with whom he could communicate. With his immediate superior, Oberleutnant Gürth, particularly, he formed the nearest thing to a friendship he had yet experienced in the army.

Perhaps because he now had people with whom he could converse, his diary entries at this point become shorter and more formulaic. Apart from 'G.T.K.', the other constant refrain is: 'Nicht gearbeitet' ('Have not worked'). Paradoxically (but, upon reflection, perhaps not surprisingly), focussing his mind on logic after a long day at the office among congenial colleagues was more difficult than it had been while he was facing death manning a searchlight amid heavy fighting, and living among people whom he detested. At the workshop he had neither the opportunity nor the desire for the complete solitude he needed for absorption in philosophical problems.

He managed, however, to do some reading. In November he had begun to read Emerson's Essays. 'Perhaps', he thought, 'they will have a good influence on me.' Whether they did, he does not say, and Emerson is not mentioned again in his diary. Certainly there is no trace of Emerson's influence in the work that he wrote at this (or indeed at any other) time.

More stimulating was a writer whose view could not have been more antithetical to the Tolstoyan Christianity that Wittgenstein had come to embrace: Friedrich Nietzsche. Wittgenstein had bought in Kraków the eighth volume of Nietzsche's collected works, the one that includes The Anti-Christ, Nietzsche's blistering attack upon Christianity. In it, Nietzsche rails against the Christian faith as a decadent, corrupt religion, 'a form of mortal hostility to reality as yet unsurpassed'. Christianity has its origins, according to him, in the weakest and basest aspects of human psychology, and is at root no more than a cowardly retreat from a hostile world:

We recognize a condition of morbid susceptibility of the *sense of touch* which makes it shrink back in horror from every contact, every grasping of a firm object. Translate such a psychological *habitus* into its ultimate logic – as instinctive hatred of *every* reality, as flight into the 'ungraspable', into the 'inconceivable', as antipathy towards every form, every spatial and temporal concept, towards everything firm . . . as being at home in a world undisturbed by reality of any kind, a merely 'inner world', a 'real' world, an 'eternal' world . . . 'The kingdom of God *is within you*' . . .

This hatred of reality, and the idea to which it gives rise, of the need for redemption through the love of God, are, in Nietzsche's view, the consequence of: 'an extreme capacity for suffering and irritation which no longer wants to be "touched" at all because it feels every contact too deeply . . . The fear of pain, even of the infinitely small in pain – *cannot* end otherwise than in a *religion of love*.'

Though 'strongly affected' by Nietzsche's hostility towards Christianity, and though he felt obliged to admit some truth in Nietzsche's analysis, Wittgenstein was unshaken in his belief that: 'Christianity is indeed the only *sure* way to happiness':

> . . . but what if someone spurned this happiness? Might it not be better to perish unhappily in the hopeless struggle against the external world? But such a life is senseless. But why not lead a senseless life? Is it unworthy?

Even from this it can be seen how close Wittgenstein was, despite his faith, to accepting Nietzsche's view. He is content to discuss the issue in Nietzsche's psychological terms; he does not see it as a question of whether Christianity is *true*, but of whether it offers some help in dealing with an otherwise unbearable and meaningless existence. In William James's terms, the question is whether it helps to heal the 'sick soul'. And the 'it' here is not a *belief* but a practice, a way of living. This is a point that Nietzsche puts well:

> It is false to the point of absurdity to see in a 'belief', perchance the belief in redemption through Christ, the distinguishing characteristic of the Christian: only Christian *practice*, a life such as he who died on the Cross *lived*, is Christian . . . Even today *such* a life is possible, for *certain* men even necessary: genuine, primitive Christianity will be possible at all times . . . *Not* a belief but a doing, above all a *not*-doing of many things, a different *being* . . . States of consciousness, beliefs of any kind, holding something to be true for example – every psychologist knows this – are a matter of complete indifference and of the fifth rank compared with the value of the instincts . . . To reduce being a Christian, Christianness, to a holding of something to be true, to a mere phenomenality of consciousness, means to negate Christianness.

This, we may feel sure, was one of the passages in *The Anti-Christ* that persuaded Wittgenstein that there was some truth in Nietzsche's work. The idea that the essence of religion lay in feelings (or, as Nietzsche would have it, *instincts*) and practices rather than in beliefs remained a constant theme in Wittgenstein's thought on the subject for the rest of his life. Christianity was for him (at this time) 'the only *sure* way to happiness' – not because it promised an after-life, but because, in the words and the figure of Christ, it provided an example, an attitude, to follow, that made suffering bearable.

In the winter months of 1914–15 we read little more in Wittgenstein's diary about his faith. There are no more calls to God to give him strength, no more entries that end: 'Thy will be done.' To bear life in the workshop, it seems, required no divine assistance. Apart from the fact that he had very little time to himself to work on philosophy, life was almost pleasant, at least by comparison with the previous four months.

In any case, it was preferable to life in Vienna. The fact that he had no leave at Christmas to visit his family troubled him not a bit. On Christmas Eve he was promoted to *Militärbeamter* ('Military Official'); on Christmas Day he was invited to a meal in the officers' mess; and on Boxing Day he went out in the evening to a café with a young man he had got to know and like, who had been at college in Lemberg. So passed his Yuletide – quietly, and apparently without any longing to be at home with his family. Through the military post he received Christmas greetings from Jolles (complete, of course, with a chocolate parcel), from the Klingenberg family in Norway, and from Frege. ('Let us hope', wrote Frege, 'for the victory of our warriors and for a lasting peace in the coming year.')

On New Year's Eve, however, Wittgenstein was suddenly told that he had to accompany his superior officer, Oberleutnant Gürth, on a visit to Vienna, where Gürth had some official business to attend to. Wittgenstein's mother was, naturally, delighted by the surprise visit. From his diary, one gathers that Wittgenstein himself retained a cold aloofness. On being reunited with his family, he remarks only that, as New Year's Day was taken up entirely with being with them, he had managed to do no work. He adds, with dispassion (and apparent irrelevance): 'I wish to note that my moral standing is much lower now than it was, say, at Easter.' Of the ten days that he was in Vienna, two of them were spent with Labor, the by now elderly composer, and much of the rest of the time with Gürth. When he arrived back in Kraków his only comment on the visit was that he had 'spent many pleasant hours with Gürth'.

This coolness towards his family suggests a determination not to let them intrude on his inner life, and a fear, perhaps, that to do so would risk undoing the advances he had made in self-discovery and self-possession during his experience of the war. But it seems also to be part of a more general lethargy. He remarks on his exhaustion frequently during this period, especially in relation to his work. On 13 January, for example, he comments that he is not working with any great energy:

> My thoughts are tired. I am not seeing things freshly, but rather in a pedestrian, lifeless way. It is as if a flame had gone out and I must wait until it starts to burn again by itself.

He was dependent, he thought, on an external source of inspiration: '*Only* through a miracle can my work succeed. Only if the veil before my eyes is lifted from the outside. I have to surrender myself completely to my fate. As it has been destined for me, so will it be. I am in the hands of fate.'

His thoughts turned once more to his English friends. He wrote to Pinsent again, and waited impatiently for a reply. 'When will I hear something from David?!' his diary pleads on 19 January. He received a letter from Keynes, but pronounced it 'not very good'. It was, in fact, a very friendly note, but perhaps its tone was too flippant to be of any real comfort. 'I hope you have been safely taken prisoner by now', Keynes wrote:

> Russell and I have given up philosophy for the present – I to give my services to the govt. for financial business, he to agitate for peace. But Moore and Johnson go on just as usual. Russell, by the way, brought out a nice book at about the beginning of the war.
>
> Pinsent had not joined the army by the middle of October but I have not heard since.
>
> Your dear friend Békássy is in your army and your very dear friend Bliss is a *private* in ours.
>
> It must be much pleasanter to be at war than to think about propositions in Norway. But I hope you will stop such self-indulgence soon.

Finally, on 6 February, Wittgenstein was able to announce: 'Lovely letter from David!' The letter had been written on 14 January; in it Pinsent says he has little to say, 'except that I hope to God we shall see each other again after the War'. In contrast to the affectionate, but none the less distancing, 'cleverness' of Keynes's letter, this straightforward expression of friendship was exactly what was craved and needed.

More to Wittgenstein's taste also were probably the short notes he received from the villagers in Skjolden: Halvard Draegni, Arne Bolstad and the Klingenberg family. 'Thanks for your card. We are all healthy. Speak of you often', runs a typical card from Draegni. Wittgenstein's replies were no doubt just as brief, and just as warmly received. The news from Norway was that work on his hut had been completed. 'We all hope', wrote Klingenberg, 'that you will soon be able to return to your new house, which is now finished.' Wittgenstein paid the workers via Draegni, who was surprised to be sent the money; he had not expected Wittgenstein to pay, he wrote, until his return. Draegni was apologetic about the cost: 'If one wants to build as solidly as you have had it made', he explained, 'it will always be more expensive than one initially reckons.'

At the beginning of February Wittgenstein was put in charge of the forge in the workshop, and this added responsibility made it even harder for him to concentrate on philosophy. Apart from having to spend more time in the forge, his supervisory role imposed on him more trouble with his workmates. He was presumably chosen for this task because of his superior engineering skills, but even so it was difficult for him to assume the role of foreman. He reports many difficulties with the men whose work he was supervising, some of which led to great unpleasantness. On one occasion he came close to a duel with a young officer who, one supposes, disliked being told what to do by someone of inferior rank. The effort of trying to impose his will on an intransigent workforce, which neither respected his rank nor were willing to accept the authority of his superior knowledge, drained him of all his energy and strained his nerves almost to breaking point. After only a month of the job – a month in which he had written almost no philosophy at all – Wittgenstein was suicidal, despairing of ever being able to work again.

'One cannot go on like this', he wrote on 17 February. It was clear that something had to change: he had either to be promoted, or transferred to another post. He began to petition Gürth for a change in his situation, but, whether through inefficiency or neglect, nothing was done for a very long time. To add to the constant refrain of '*Nicht gearbeitet*', a new phrase finds its way into the diary at this point: '*Lage unverändert*' ('Situation unchanged'). It must be this period that Hermine had in mind when, in speaking of Wittgenstein's war experiences, she wrote of his repeated efforts to be sent to the Front, and of the 'comical misunderstandings which resulted from the fact that the military authorities with which he had to deal always assumed that he was trying to obtain an easier posting for himself when in fact what he wanted was to be given a more dangerous one'.

It is possible, I think, that Wittgenstein's requests to join the infantry were not so much misunderstood as ignored, and that he was perceived to be of more use to the army as a skilled engineer in charge of a repair depot than as an ordinary foot-soldier. Throughout March, despite repeated entreaties to Gürth, his situation remained unchanged.

Philosophically, the first three months of 1915 were almost completely barren. In other respects, too, Wittgenstein felt dead, unresponsive. (It puzzled him, however, that at such a time, when nothing else moved in him, he could feel sensual and have the desire to masturbate.) When, in February, Ficker sent a posthumously published edition of Trakl's works, his only comment was strikingly dull: 'probably very good'. Thanking Ficker for the volume, he explained that he was now in a sterile period and had 'no desire to assimilate foreign thoughts'. There was, however, something to be hoped for, even from his very unresponsiveness:

> I have this only during a decline of productivity, not when it has *completely* ceased. However – UNFORTUNATELY I now feel completely burnt out. One just has to be patient.

He had, he thought, just to wait for God, for the spirit, to help and inspire him.

Having, in the meantime, nothing to say, he fell silent. From Adele Jolles he received a letter gently berating him for the brevity of his communications from the field. One thing is certain, she told him – he would not make a satisfactory war correspondent or telegraphist.

1 The infant Ludwig Wittgenstein

2 The eleven sons and daughters of Hermann and Fanny Wittgenstein. From left to right: Fine, Karl (Ludwig's father), Anna, Milly, Lydia, Louis, Clothilde, Clara, Marie, Bertha and Paul

3 Ludwig, *c.* 1891

4 *Right:* The grand staircase in the Alleegasse

5 A family photograph taken on Karl and Leopoldine's silver wedding anniversary, 1898, at the family home in Neuwaldeggasse in Vienna. Ludwig is in the front row on the left

6 Ludwig, aged nine

Couldn't he, for once, send a decent letter, so that one could know where he was and how he was and what he was doing? What did he think of the Italians? Weren't they a pack of scoundrels, deserting the Triple Alliance as they had? 'If I were to write what I think of them', she said, 'my letter would most likely not get through the censors.' She kept up the supply of bread, chocolate and fruit cake, evidently taking pride in the part her 'little Wittgenstein' was playing in the struggle. 'That you willingly volunteered', she told him, 'pleases me ever anew.'

Her husband took pride in the fact that Wittgenstein was at last in a position to put his technical knowledge to some use. 'In any case', he wrote, 'with your skills you are at the right place and, what with the awful Galician roads there must surely be autos aplenty to repair!' Wittgenstein evidently replied that he would rather be with the infantry at the Front than repairing cars behind the lines. Jolles was surprised: 'Don't you think that you could use your technical talents more in the workshop?' His wife, too, despite her patriotic fervour, was concerned: 'Hopefully, your wish to go to the Front will not be fulfilled', she wrote, with motherly anxiety; 'there you are one of very many, and not one of the strongest, here you can play your part more safely.'

Such concern, though no doubt welcome, and perhaps even necessary, was not sufficient. And it was not until after he had received a letter from Pinsent that Wittgenstein was able to shake off his lethargy. On 16 March he was again able to write in his diary: 'Lovely letter from David.' And: 'Answered David. *Very* sensual.' A draft of a reply has been preserved. It reads:

My *dear* Davy,
Got today your letter dated January 27th. This is about the limit. I'm now beginning to be more fertile again.

Wittgenstein had asked Pinsent to pass on a message to Moore, and to explain to him how to get a letter through. This Pinsent had done, and 'I hope he will write to you.' It was a forlorn hope. 'I am so sorry if Moore won't behave like a Christian', Pinsent wrote in April; 'as a matter of fact he never acknowledged my letter.'

Not that Moore could keep Wittgenstein out of his thoughts entirely. On 12 October 1915 he recorded in his diary: 'Dream of Wittgenstein':

. . . he looks at me as if to ask if it is all right, and I can't help smiling as if it was, though I know it isn't; then he is swimming in the sea; finally he is trying to escape arrest as an enemy alien.

On 22 April Wittgenstein was put in charge of the whole workshop, but this, he reports, merely presented him with more unpleasantness to deal with. To help ease the situation he was allowed by Gürth to wear the uniform of an engineer and was provisionally given that title.*

On 30 April Wittgenstein records another 'lovely letter from David', which contained a piece of perhaps surprising news. 'I have been writing a paper on Philosophy', Pinsent told him, 'probably absolute rot!' It was, he said, an attempt to explain 'what Logic as a whole is *about* and what "Truth" is & "Knowledge"'. Though its subject-matter is identical to Wittgenstein's, the resultant work (which still survives) bears little resemblance either to the *Tractatus* or to the earlier *Notes on Logic*. Logic is defined by Pinsent using the notion of 'consistency' rather than that of 'tautology', and the general tenor of its thought owes more to the British empirical tradition (particularly to Moore and Russell) than to Wittgenstein. Nevertheless, Pinsent himself clearly thought of it as a contribution to the issues with which Wittgenstein was concerned. 'I wish you were here & could talk it over with me', he wrote. His letter ends:

I wish to God this horrible tragedy would end, & I am longing to see you again.

Whether inspired by Pinsent's letter or not, it is remarkable that during his last few months at Kraków – at a time when he was desperately unhappy and intensely frustrated at not being able to obtain another position – Wittgenstein found himself able to work again with renewed vigour. Throughout the months of May and June he was prolific. A large part (approximately a third) of the remarks published as *Notebooks: 1914–1916* were written during this period.

The problem with which he was principally concerned during this time was that of *how* language pictures the world – what features of

---

* Wittgenstein's status had still not been made official when, following the breakthrough of the Central Powers forces on the Eastern Front in the late summer of 1915, the whole depot was moved further north to Sokal, north of Lemberg.

both language and the world make it possible for this picturing to take place:

> The great problem round which everything I write turns is: Is there an order in the world *a priori*, and if so what does it consist in?

Almost against his will, he was forced to the conclusion that there was such an order: the world, as he had insisted to Russell, consists of *facts*, not of things – that is, it consists of things (objects) standing in certain relations to one another. These facts – the relations that exist between objects – are mirrored, pictured, by the relations between the symbols of a proposition. But if language is analysable into *atomic* propositions (as he had earlier insisted), then it looks as though there must be atomic *facts* corresponding to those atomic propositions. And just as atomic propositions are those that are incapable of being analysed any further, atomic facts are relations between *simple* rather than complex objects. Wittgenstein could produce no examples of either an atomic proposition or an atomic fact, nor could he say what a 'simple object' was, but he felt that the very possibility of analysis demanded that there be such things, providing the structure of both language and the world, which allowed the one to mirror the other.

> It does not go against our feeling, that *we* cannot analyse PRO-POSITIONS so far as to mention the elements by name: no, we feel that the world must consist of elements. And it appears as if that were identical with the proposition that the world must be what it is, it must be definite.

We can be indefinite and uncertain, but surely the world cannot be: 'The world has a fixed structure.' And this allows the possibility of language having a definite meaning: 'The demand for simple things *is* the demand for definiteness of sense.'

In the middle of this philosophically fruitful period, Wittgenstein received a letter from Russell, written in German and dated 10 May. Russell had, he told Wittgenstein, seen the notes dictated to Moore in Norway but had found them difficult to understand. 'I hope', he wrote, 'with all my heart that after the war you will explain everything to me orally.' 'Since the war began', he added, 'it has been impossible for me to think of philosophy.'

'I'm extremely sorry that you weren't able to understand Moore's notes', Wittgenstein replied:

> I feel that they're very hard to understand without further explanation, but I regard them essentially as definitive. And now I'm afraid that what I've written recently will be still more incomprehensible, and if I don't live to see the end of this war I must be prepared for all my work to go to nothing. – In that case you must get my manuscript printed whether anyone understands it or not.

'The problems are becoming more and more lapidary and general', he told Russell, 'and the method has changed drastically.' The book was to undergo a far more drastic change over the next two years, strangely enough in a way that was prefigured by the development of Pinsent's treatise. In a letter dated 6 April (which Wittgenstein would probably have received some time in May) Pinsent writes that his paper on philosophy has expanded from logic to 'ethics and philosophy in general'. The following year Wittgenstein's own work was to move in a similar direction.

The revitalization of Wittgenstein's work on logic coincided with a dramatic improvement in the position of the Central Powers on the Eastern Front. In March the plight of the Austro-Hungarians had looked desperate. The Russians were forcing them further back into the Carpathian mountains and threatening an incursion into Hungary itself. On 22 March the fortress town of Przemyśl fell, and it was clear that, if disaster were to be avoided, the Austrians would need the help of the superior strength and efficiency of their German allies. Throughout April preparations were thus made for a massive combined German and Austrian assault in Galicia, which on 1 May was launched under the leadership of the German General, von Mackensen. The place chosen to launch the offensive was an area between the localities of Gorlice and Tarnów. The success of the attack surprised even its planners, and a decisive breakthrough was achieved. Throughout the summer months of 1915 the German and Austrian forces swept through the Russian defences with remarkable ease, eventually advancing their position by some 300 miles. Przemyśl and Lemberg were retaken, and Lublin, Warsaw and Brest Litovsk were captured.

If Wittgenstein took any pleasure in the Gorlice–Tarnów break-through, there is no indication of it in his diary. Throughout the advance he remained at the workshop in Kraków, growing increasingly resentful of the fact. In Jolles, however, he had a correspondent who could always be relied upon to enthuse over a military success. On 25 March Jolles had written to lament the fall ('after brave resistence') of Przemyśl, and to hope that poor Galicia would be freed from the Russians in the spring. Throughout the campaign Jolles's letters read like a patriotic commentary on the news from the Eastern Front. 'It looks as if the Russian offensive in the Carpathians has ground to a halt', he wrote on 16 April; 'perhaps the occupied part of Galicia can now be successfully liberated!' On 4 May he wrote to say that he had heard a great victory was expected as a result of Mackensen's success: 'May poor Galicia soon be set free from the Russians!'

In the light of Mackensen's breakthrough, he wrote on 17 May, he could understand only too well Wittgenstein's urge to go to the Front. His wife was more concerned about Wittgenstein's safety and whether he was getting enough to eat. 'I write rarely', she explained on 8 April, 'because you yourself write so rarely and so stereotypically, always using the same few words – one has the feeling that you are hardly interested in what one has to write.' 'I am pleased', she added, 'that you are not going to the Front and will instead stay where you are.' In every letter she asked whether food was scarce and whether Wittgenstein needed anything. In his replies Wittgenstein spoke vaguely of the 'unpleasantness' with which he had to deal. 'What kind of unpleasantness?' Adele Jolles asked. 'We are sorry to hear that you have much to cope with, but that you bear it so courageously is splendid and pleases me most sincerely.'

In July he received a letter from Ficker, who was by this time himself in the Austrian army, serving in an Alpine regiment stationed at Brixen. The conditions under which he lived were frightful, Ficker complained: thirty-six men to a room, no chance to be alone at any time of the day or night – and it was likely to stay like that until September. He complained of sleeplessness and spiritual exhaustion; he was so weary he could hardly read or write. 'Sometimes, dear friend, it is as though my whole being were exhausted . . . So thoroughly have these circumstances already undermined my resistance.'

The tone sounded familiar. Wittgenstein replied with a piece of advice based on his own experience of a similar despair. 'I understand your sad news all too well', he wrote:

> You are living, as it were, in the dark and have not found the saving word. And if I, who am essentially so different from you, should offer some advice, it might seem asinine. However, I am going to venture it anyway. Are you acquainted with Tolstoi's *The Gospel in Brief*? At its time, this book virtually kept me alive. Would you buy the book and read it?! If you are not acquainted with it, then you cannot imagine what an effect it can have upon a person.

Perhaps surprisingly, this advice was enthusiastically received. 'God protect you!' Ficker replied. Yes, Wittgenstein was right, he *was* living in the dark: 'for no one had given me the word'. And Wittgenstein had not only given him the word, but also in such a way that he would never forget it: 'God protect you!'

Wittgenstein's letter to Ficker was written in hospital. As a result of an explosion at the workshop he had suffered a nervous shock and a few light injuries. After about a week in hospital he took a much needed three-week leave in Vienna. 'Three weeks' holiday', clucked Adele Jolles, 'after over a year's service and then after an injury and illness is really rather little.' It was, however, probably more than enough from his point of view.

By the time he returned to the repair unit, it had moved from Kraków. In the wake of the Gorlice–Tarnów breakthrough, it had been relocated to Sokal, north of Lemberg, and was housed in an artillery workshop train at the railway station there.

No notebooks have survived from Wittgenstein's time at Sokal, but there is reason to think that it was for him a comparatively happy period. He had at least one fairly close friend, a Dr Max Bieler, who was in charge of a Red Cross hospital train which stood next to the workshop train. Bieler first met Wittgenstein when he was invited to take his meals with the officers at the workshop. He recalls:

> Already during the first meal strikes my eye among the participants who were all officers, a lean and quick man, without military rank, of about twenty-five years. He ate little, drank little and did not smoke, while the rest of the table companions stuffed themselves

and were very noisy. I asked my table neighbour and he informed me that his name was Ludwig Wittgenstein. I was glad to find among the very young empty-headed career officers a man with a university culture and so sympathetic a man besides. I had the impression that he does not belong in this atmosphere; he was there because he must. I think the sympathy was mutual, because after the meal he invited me to visit his enclosure in the train. And so began our friendship, that lasted several months (almost a year) with daily hour-long conversations, without whisky or cigarettes. After a few days he proposed me to 'thou' him.

During the autumn of 1915 and throughout the following winter, when almost everything was in short supply and conditions at the Front were extremely harsh, the friendship between Bieler and Wittgenstein was of enormous comfort to them both. They had long and animated conversations on philosophical and metaphysical subjects, although, perhaps not surprisingly, these conversations were conducted on terms that were not quite equal. Wittgenstein once told Bieler that he would make a good disciple but that he was no prophet. 'I could say about him', writes Bieler, that: 'he had all the characteristics of a prophet, but none of a disciple.'

Militarily it was a quiet time, with the Russians having to regroup after the disaster of the previous summer, and the Central Powers content to hold their position while they concentrated on the Western Front. It was, evidently, a quiet time too for the repair unit. Wittgenstein, pleased with the results of his recent work on logic, was able to make a preliminary attempt to work it into a book. This, the first version of the *Tractatus*, has unfortunately not survived. We learn of its existence only in a letter to Russell dated 22 October 1915, in which he tells Russell that he is now in the process of writing the results of his work down in the form of a treatise. 'Whatever happens', he told Russell, 'I won't publish anything until you have seen it.' That, of course, could not happen until after the war:

But who knows whether I shall survive until then? If I don't survive, get my people to send you all my manuscripts: among them you'll find the final summary written in pencil on loose sheets of paper. It will perhaps cost you some trouble to understand it all, but don't let yourself be put off by that.

Russell's reply is dated 25 November. 'I am enormously pleased', he wrote, 'that you are writing a treatise which you want to publish.' He was impatient to see it, and told Wittgenstein that it was hardly necessary to wait until the end of the war. Wittgenstein could send it to America, to Ralph Perry at Harvard, who had, through Russell, already learnt of Wittgenstein's earlier theories of logic. Perry could then send it on to Russell who would publish it. 'How nice it will be when we finally see each other again!' Russell ended.

Frege, too, was told of Wittgenstein's treatise. On 28 November he wrote, in similar vein to Russell: 'I am pleased that you still have time and energy left for scientific work.' If Wittgenstein had followed Russell's suggestion, the work that would have been published in 1916 would have been, in many ways, similar to the work we now know as the *Tractatus*. It would, that is, have contained the Picture Theory of meaning, the metaphysics of 'logical atomism', the analysis of logic in terms of the twin notions of tautology and contradiction, the distinction between saying and showing (invoked to make the Theory of Types superfluous), and the method of Truth-Tables (used to show a logical proposition to be either a tautology or a contradiction). In other words, it would have contained almost everything the *Tractatus* now contains – *except* the remarks at the end of the book on ethics, aesthetics, the soul, and the meaning of life.

In a way, therefore, it would have been a completely different work.

The years during which the book underwent its final – and most important – transformation were years in which Wittgenstein and Russell were not in touch with one another. After the letter of 22 October 1915, Russell heard no more from Wittgenstein until February 1919, after Wittgenstein had been taken prisoner by the Italians. In his *Introduction to Mathematical Philosophy*, written during the final year of the war (while he himself was in prison, serving a sentence for having allegedly jeopardized Britain's relations with the United States), Russell raises the question of how 'tautology' should be defined, and appends the following footnote:

The importance of 'tautology' for a definition of mathematics was pointed out to me by my former pupil Ludwig Wittgenstein, who was working on the problem. I do not know whether he has solved it, or even whether he is alive or dead.

Communication with Pinsent also stopped for the last two years of the war. On 2 September 1915 Pinsent wrote to say that he had 'given up the study of that damned Law', and was now working for the government. During 1916 Pinsent managed to get three letters through – all written in German – the first of which emphasizes that: 'the war cannot change our personal relationships, it has nothing to do with them'. In these letters Pinsent tells Wittgenstein that he has now received some mechanical training and is employed as an engineer. The last letter Wittgenstein received from him is dated 14 September 1916.

The change in the conception of the book – and the accompanying transformation of Wittgenstein himself – came, then, at a time when he was cut off from his English friends. It is therefore not surprising that, after the war, he was doubtful whether his English friends would be able to understand him. What did they know – what could they know – of the circumstances that had produced the change in him?

An anticipation of the nature of this change can perhaps be seen in the discussions he had in Sokal with Bieler – discussions that, Bieler says, 'sometimes absorbed us so completely that we lost sight of place and time':

> I remember one comical incident. It was New Year's Eve 1915. The local Commandant had invited us all to the Officers' Mess for the New Year's celebrations. When supper was over, getting on for 10 o'clock, the two of us retired to Wittgenstein's room in order to resume yesterday's theme. At about 11 o'clock the officers from the train let us know that it was time to set off in order to arrive at the party in good time. Wittgenstein conveyed to them that they should simply go and we would follow immediately. We quickly forgot about the invitation and the time and continued our discussion until loud voices became audible outside. It was our comrades, returning merrily at 4 a.m. – and we thought it was not yet midnight. The next day we had to make our excuses to the local Commandant and pay him our New Year's compliments belatedly.

Such intensity suggests a wholehearted commitment on Wittgenstein's part. And yet the subject of these discussions was not logic: Wittgenstein did not attempt to teach Bieler, as he had earlier attempted to teach Pinsent, the results of his work. They talked instead of Tolstoy's *Gospel* and of Dostoevsky's *Brothers Karamazov*. The latter Wittgenstein read so often he knew whole passages of it by heart, particularly the speeches of the elder Zossima, who represented for him a powerful Christian ideal, a holy man who could 'see directly into the souls of other people'.

The period during which Wittgenstein and Bieler were together was one of the quietest times on the Eastern Front. It was, for Wittgenstein, a time of relative comfort. Although not an officer, he was in many ways treated like one. He was even provided with a servant – a young Russian boy from a nearby prisoner-of-war camp called Constantin. Bieler recalls: 'Constantin was a good boy and took care of Wittgenstein with great zeal. Wittgenstein treated him very well and in a short time the lean, frail, and dirty prisoner of war was transformed into the most fleshy and cleanest soldier of the whole garrison.'

This period of comparative serenity ended in March 1916, when the Russians, to relieve the pressure on France, launched an attack on the Baltic flank. At the same time, after over a year, a decision was reached by the Austrian authorities on Wittgenstein's status. It was decided that he could not retain the title or the uniform of an *Ingenieur*, but that he could be granted his long-expressed wish to be posted to the Front as an ordinary soldier. The decision came, says Bieler, as 'a heavy blow to us both'. Wittgenstein parted from him in the manner of one who did not expect to return alive:

> He took with him only what was absolutely necessary, leaving everything else behind and asking me to divide it among the troops. On this occasion he told me that he had had a house built beside a Norwegian fjord where he would sometimes take refuge in order to have peace for his work. He now wanted to make me a present of this house. I refused it and took in its place a Waterman's fountain pen.

One of the few personal possessions Wittgenstein packed was a copy of *The Brothers Karamazov*.

If he thought that he would not return from the Front alive, he knew with certainty that he could not return unchanged. In this sense the war really began for him in March 1916.

7
AT THE FRONT

Undoubtedly, it is the knowledge of death, and therewith
the consideration of the suffering and misery of life, that
give the strongest impulse to philosophical reflection and
metaphysical explanations of the world.
Schopenhauer, *The World as Will and Representation*

If Wittgenstein had spent the entire war behind the lines, the
Tractatus would have remained what it almost certainly was in its
first inception of 1915: a treatise on the nature of logic. The remarks in
it about ethics, aesthetics, the soul and the meaning of life have
their origin in precisely the 'impulse to philosophical reflection'
that Schopenhauer describes, an impulse that has as its stimulus a
knowledge of death, suffering and misery.

Towards the end of March 1916 Wittgenstein was posted, as he had
long wished, to a fighting unit on the Russian Front. He was assigned
to an artillery regiment attached to the Austrian Seventh Army,
stationed at the southernmost point of the Eastern Front, near the
Romanian border. In the few weeks that elapsed before his regiment
was moved up to the front line, he endeavoured to prepare himself,
psychologically and spiritually, to face death. 'God enlighten me.
God enlighten me. God enlighten my soul', he wrote on 29 March.
On the next day: 'Do your best. You cannot do more: and be
cheerful':

Help yourself and help others with all your strength. And at the same time be cheerful! But how much strength should one need for oneself and how much for the others? It is hard to live well!! But it is good to live well. However, not my, but Thy will be done.

When the long-awaited moment came, however, he fell ill and was told by his commanding officer that he may have to be left behind. 'If that happens', he wrote, 'I will kill myself.' When, on 15 April, he was told that he would, after all, be allowed to accompany his regiment, he prayed: 'If only I may be allowed to risk my life in some difficult assignment.' He counted the days until he would at last be in the line of fire, and, when the time came, prayed to God for courage. He noted that since he had been at the Front he had become completely asexual.

Once at the front line he asked to be assigned to that most dangerous of places, the observation post. This guaranteed that he would be the target of enemy fire. 'Was shot at', he recorded on 29 April. 'Thought of God. Thy will be done. God be with me.' The experience, he thought, brought him nearer to enlightenment. On 4 May he was told that he was to go on night-duty at the observation post. As shelling was heaviest at night, this was the most dangerous posting he could have been given. 'Only then', he wrote, 'will the war really begin for me':

And – maybe – even life. Perhaps the nearness of death will bring me the light of life. May God enlighten me. I am a worm, but through God I become a man. God be with me. Amen

During the following day in the observation post, he waited for the night's shelling with great anticipation. He felt 'like the prince in the enchanted castle'.

Now, during the day, everything is quiet, but in the night it must be *frightful*. Will I endure it?? Tonight will show. God be with me!!

The next day he reported that he had been in constant danger of his life, but through the grace of God he had survived. 'From time to time I was afraid. That is the fault of a false view of life.' Almost every night at his post he expected to die and prayed to God not to abandon him, to give him courage to look death squarely in the eye without fear. Only then could he be sure that he was living decently: 'Only death gives life its meaning.'

As on the *Goplana* Wittgenstein preferred being in a solitary and dangerous position to being in the company of his comrades. He needed as much, or more, strength from God to face them as he needed to face the enemy. They were 'a company of drunkards, a company of vile and stupid people':

> The men, with few exceptions, hate me because I am a volunteer. So I am nearly always surrounded by people that hate me. And this is the one thing that I still cannot bear. The people here are malicious and heartless. It is almost impossible to find a trace of humanity in them.

The struggle to stop himself from hating these people was, like the struggle against fear in the face of death, a test of his faith: 'The heart of a true believer understands everything.' So, he urged himself: 'Whenever you feel like hating them, try instead to understand them.' He tried, but it was obviously an effort:

> The people around me are not so much mean as *appallingly* limited. This makes it almost impossible to work with them, because they forever misunderstand. These people are not stupid, but limited. Within their circle they are clever enough. But they lack character and thereby breadth.

Finally, he decided that he did not *hate* them – but they disgusted him all the same.

Throughout these first few months at the Front, from March to May, Wittgenstein was able to write a little on logic. He continued with his theme of the nature of functions and propositions and the need to postulate the existence of simple objects. But he added this isolated and interesting remark about the 'modern conception of the world', which found its way unchanged into the *Tractatus* (6.371 and 6.372):

> The whole modern conception of the world is founded on the illusion that the so-called laws of nature are the explanations of natural phenomena.

Thus people today stop at the laws of nature, treating them as something inviolable, just as God and Fate were treated in past ages.

And in fact both are right and both wrong: though the view of the ancients is clearer in so far as they have a clear and acknowledged terminus, while the modern system tries to make it look as if *everything* were explained.

From Frege he received a postcard encouraging him to keep up his work on logic. 'Your desire not to allow your intellectual work to be abandoned', Frege wrote, 'I find very understandable.' He thanked Wittgenstein for the invitation to come to Vienna to discuss his work, but thought it doubtful whether he would be able to make it. He hoped, nevertheless, to be able to continue their scientific discussions in some way or other. Wittgenstein, however, was to write little on logic for the remainder of the war. And when Frege finally had a chance to read the *Tractatus*, he was unable, in Wittgenstein's eyes, to understand a word of it.

The fighting on the Eastern Front during the months of April and May was light, but in June Russia launched its long-expected major assault, known, after the general who planned and led it, as the 'Brusilov Offensive'. Thus began some of the heaviest fighting of the entire war. The Austrian Eleventh Army, to which Wittgenstein's regiment was attached, faced the brunt of the attack and suffered enormous casualties. It was at precisely this time that the nature of Wittgenstein's work changed.

On 11 June his reflections on the foundations of logic are interrupted with the question: 'What do I know about God and the purpose of life?' He answers with a list:

I know that this world exists.

That I am placed in it like my eye in its visual field.

That something about it is problematic, which we call its meaning.

That this meaning does not lie in it but outside it.

That life is the world.

That my will penetrates the world.

That my will is good or evil.

Therefore that good and evil are somehow connected with the meaning of the world.

The meaning of life, i.e. the meaning of the world, we can call God.

And connect with this the comparison of God to a father.

To pray is to think about the meaning of life.

I cannot bend the happenings of the world to my will: I am completely powerless.

I can only make myself independent of the world – and so in a certain sense master it – by renouncing any influence on happenings.

These remarks are not written in code, but presented as if they somehow belonged to the logical work that precedes them. And from this time on reflections of this sort dominate the notebook. It is as if the personal and the philosophical had become fused; ethics and logic – the two aspects of the 'duty to oneself' – had finally come together, not merely as two aspects of the same personal task, but as two parts of the same philosophical work.

In a notebook entry of 8 July, for example, we find: 'Fear in the face of death is the best sign of a false, i.e. a bad life' – not, this time, as a statement of a personal credo but as a contribution to philosophical thought.

At the beginning of the war, after he had received news that his brother Paul had been seriously wounded and assumed that he had lost his profession as a concert pianist, he wrote: 'How terrible! What philosophy will ever assist one to overcome a fact of this sort?' Now, it seems, having experienced the full horrors of the war for himself, he needed, not only a religious faith, but also a philosophy.

That is to say, he needed not only to *believe* in God – to pray to Him for strength and for enlightenment; he needed to *understand* what it was that he was believing in. When he prayed to God, what was he doing? To whom was he addressing his prayers? Himself? The world? Fate? His answer seems to be: all three:

To believe in a God means to understand the meaning of life.

To believe in God means to see that the facts of the world are not the end of the matter.

To believe in God means to see that life has a meaning.

The world is *given* me, i.e. my will enters the world completely from the outside as into something that is already there.

(As for what my will is, I don't know yet.)

However this may be, at any rate we *are* in a certain sense dependent, and what we are dependent on we can call God.

In this sense God would simply be fate, or, what is the same thing: The world – which is independent of our will.

I can make myself independent of fate.

There are two godheads: the world and my independent I.

. . . When my conscience upsets my equilibrium, then I am not in agreement with Something. But what is this? Is it *the world*?

Certainly it is correct to say: Conscience is the voice of God.

A little later on we read: 'How things stand, is God. God is, how things stand.' By 'how things stand' here, he means both how they stand *in the world* and how they stand in *oneself*. For the self is, as Weininger and Schopenhauer had said, a microcosm of the world.

These thoughts seem to have forced themselves upon him – almost to have taken him by surprise. On 7 July he recorded: 'Colossal exertions in the last month. Have thought a great deal on every possible subject. But curiously I cannot establish the connection with my mathematical modes of thought.' And on 2 August he remarked about his work – as though it had a life of its own – that it had 'broadened out from the foundations of logic to the essence of the world'.

The connection between Wittgenstein's thought on logic and his reflections on the meaning of life was to be found in the distinction he had made earlier between *saying* and *showing*. Logical form, he had said, cannot be expressed *within* language, for it is the form of language itself; it makes itself manifest in language – it has to be *shown*. Similarly, ethical and religious truths, though inexpressible, manifest themselves in life:

The solution to the problem of life is to be seen in the disappearance of the problem.

Isn't this the reason why men to whom the meaning of life had become clear after long doubting could not say what this meaning consisted in?

Thus: 'Ethics does not treat of the world. Ethics must be a condition of the world, like logic.' Just as to understand logical form one must

see language as a whole, so, to understand ethics, one must see the
world as a whole. When one tries to describe what one sees from such
a view, one inevitably talks nonsense (as Wittgenstein wrote about his
own attempts to do so: 'I am aware of the complete unclarity of all
these sentences'), but that such a view is attainable is undeniable:
'There are, indeed, things that cannot be put into words. They *make
themselves manifest*. They are what is mystical.'

In discussing this view of the world (the view that sees it as a limited
whole), Wittgenstein adopts the Latin phrase used by Spinoza: *sub
specie aeternitatis* ('under the form of eternity'). It is the view, not only
of ethics, but also of aesthetics:

> The work of art is the object seen *sub specie aeternitatis*; and the good
> life is the world seen *sub specie aeternitatis*. This is the connection
> between art and ethics.
>
> The usual way of looking at things sees objects as it were from the
> midst of them, the view *sub specie aeternitatis* from outside.
>
> In such a way that they have the whole world as background.

These remarks show the unmistakable influence of Schopenhauer.
In *The World as Will and Representation*, Schopenhauer discusses, in a
remarkably similar way, a form of contemplation in which we
relinquish 'the ordinary way of considering things', and 'no longer
consider the where, the when, the why, and the whither in things, but
simply the *what*':

> Further we do not let abstract thought, the concepts of reason, take
> possession of our consciousness, but, instead of all this, devote the
> whole power of our mind to perception, sink ourselves completely
> therein, and let our whole consciousness be filled by the calm
> contemplation of the natural object actually present, whether it be a
> landscape, a tree, a rock, a crag, a building, or anything else. We *lose*
> ourselves entirely in this object, to use a pregnant expression . . .
>
> It was this that was in Spinoza's mind when he wrote: *Mens aeterna
> est quatenus res sub specie aeternitatis* ['The mind is eternal in so far as it
> conceives things from the standpoint of eternity'].

Whether Wittgenstein was rereading Schopenhauer in 1916, or
whether he was remembering the passages that had impressed him in

his youth, there is no doubt that the remarks he wrote in that year have a distinctly Schopenhauerian feel. He even adopts Schopenhauer's jargon of *Wille* ('will') and *Vorstellung* ('representation' or, sometimes, 'idea'), as in:

As my idea is the world, in the same way my will is the world-will.

Wittgenstein's remarks on the will and the self are, in many ways, simply a restatement of Schopenhauer's 'Transcendental Idealism', with its dichotomy between the 'world as idea', the world of space and time, and the 'world as will', the *noumenal*, timeless, world of the self. The doctrine might be seen as the philosophical equivalent of the religious state of mind derided by Nietzsche, the morbid sensitivity to suffering which takes flight from reality into 'a merely "inner" world, a "real" world, an "eternal" world'. When this state of mind is made the basis of a philosophy it becomes solipsism, the view that *the* world and *my* world are one and the same thing. Thus we find Wittgenstein saying:

It is true: Man *is* the microcosm:
I am my world.

What distinguishes Wittgenstein's statement of the doctrine from Schopenhauer's is that in Wittgenstein's case it is accompanied by the proviso that, when put into words, the doctrine is, strictly speaking, nonsense: 'what the solipsist *means* is quite correct; only it cannot be *said*, but makes itself manifest'.

He had, he thought, reached a point where Schopenhauerian solipsism and Fregean realism were combined in the same point of view:

This is the way I have travelled: Idealism singles men out from the world as unique, solipsism singles me alone out, and at last I see that I too belong with the rest of the world, and so on the one side *nothing* is left over, and on the other side, as unique, *the world*. In this way idealism leads to realism if it is strictly thought out.

Frege, the thinker Wittgenstein credited with freeing him from his earlier Schopenhauerian idealism, was not, apparently, told of his relapse back into it. A card from Frege dated 24 June remarks again how pleased he is that Wittgenstein is capable of scientific work. 'I can hardly say the same for myself', he writes. His mind is occupied by the war and by the suffering of the people he knows who are engaged in it, one of whom had recently been injured for the second time, while another had been killed in Poland. Of the Brusilov Offensive he says nothing, but remarks how pleased he was at the recapture of Lemberg. In the next card, dated 2 July, he sympathizes with Wittgenstein for the latter's inability to work. He, too, he says, has been incapable of scientific work, but he hopes that after the war he and Wittgenstein can take up again their work on logical questions. On 29 July he again remarks on the low spirits evident from Wittgenstein's recent communications, and hopes to receive a card written in a better spirit soon, but: 'I am always pleased to receive a sign of life from you.'

Nothing in these cards indicates that he was made aware of the fundamental changes taking place in Wittgenstein's thought at this time – that he knew of the widening of Wittgenstein's concerns from the foundations of logic to the essence of the world, or of Wittgenstein's conviction that he had found the point at which solipsism and realism coincide.

Thoughts of Pinsent had never been far from Wittgenstein's mind during the writing of his book. On 26 July he recorded another letter from him. It was written in German and told Wittgenstein of the death of Pinsent's brother, who had been killed in France. 'The war cannot change our personal relationships', Pinsent insisted; 'it has nothing to do with them.' 'This kind, lovely letter', Wittgenstein wrote, 'has opened my eyes to the way in which I live in *exile* here. It may be a salutary exile, but I feel it now as an exile.'

By this time the Austrian forces had been driven back into the Carpathian mountains, pursued by the victorious Russians. The conditions were harsh – 'icy cold, rain and fog', Wittgenstein records. It was: 'a life full of torment':

> Terribly difficult not to lose oneself. For I am a weak person. But the spirit will help me. The best thing would be if I were already ill, then at least I would have a bit of peace.

But to avoid capture or death he had to keep on the move, pursued by the fire of the advancing Russians. 'Was shot at', he wrote on 24 July, 'and at every shot I winced with my whole being. I want so much to go on living.'

Under these circumstances, the question of the identity of the 'philosophical I', the self which is the bearer of moral values, was given a peculiar intensity. On the retreat through the Carpathian mountains Wittgenstein discovered, probably for the first time in his life, what it was like to lose sight of that self and to be overtaken by an instinctual, animal, will to stay alive, a state in which moral values were irrelevant:

> Yesterday I was shot at. I was scared! I was afraid of death. I now have such a desire to live. And it is difficult to give up life when one enjoys it. This is precisely what 'sin' is, the unreasoning life, a false view of life. From time to time I become an *animal*. Then I can think of nothing but eating, drinking and sleeping. Terrible! And then I suffer like an animal too, without the possibility of internal salvation. I am then at the mercy of my appetites and aversions. Then an authentic life is unthinkable.

For the next three weeks, his diary shows him remonstrating with himself about this tendency to sink into a life of sin. 'You know what you have to do to live happily', he told himself on 12 August. 'Why don't you do it? Because you are unreasonable. A bad life is an unreasonable life.' He prayed to God for strength in the struggle against his own weak nature.

Despite these self-admonitions, he in fact showed remarkable courage throughout the campaign. During the first few days of the Brusilov Offensive he was recommended for a decoration in recognition of his bravery in keeping to his post, despite several times being told to take cover. 'By this distinctive behaviour', the report states, 'he exercised a very calming effect on his comrades.' He was quickly promoted, first to *Vormeister* (a non-commissioned artillery rank similar to the British Lance-Bombardier) and then to *Korporal*. Finally, towards the end of August, when the Russian advance had ground to a halt, he was sent away to the regiment's headquarters in Olmütz (Olomouc), Moravia, to be trained as an officer.

Before going to Olmütz Wittgenstein had a period of leave in Vienna. There, he wrote in his diary, he felt depressed and lonely, the one cheerful piece of news being the fact that Loos was still alive. From Loos he received the name and address of a contact in Olmütz: an ex-student of Loos was, at the time, convalescing at his family home there after having been discharged from the army suffering from tuberculosis.

On 28 August Wittgenstein received a letter from Frege suggesting that they enter into a correspondence on logic. When Wittgenstein had enough time, Frege suggested, couldn't he write his thoughts on paper and send them to him? He would then attempt to respond to Wittgenstein's thoughts by letter. 'In this way', wrote Frege, 'perhaps a scientific communication between us could take place, and so at least provide some sort of substitute for a face-to-face discussion.' Wittgenstein appears not to have responded to this suggestion until after he had completed his book. Perhaps the offer came too late; for in the autumn of 1916 he found the discussion partner he needed to work out the new direction of his thoughts.

The student Loos mentioned was Paul Engelmann, a member of a group of young people which formed a self-consciously cultured oasis in what was otherwise a rather culturally barren outpost of the Austro-Hungarian empire. There was Fritz Zweig, a gifted pianist who later became first conductor at the Berlin State Opera House, his cousin Max Zweig, a law student and playwright, and Heinrich ('Heini') Groag, also a law student and later a successful barrister. Groag was, says Engelmann, 'one of the wittiest men I ever met'. Engelmann's brother, too, was a man of sharp wit – later to become famous in Vienna as the cartoonist 'Peter Eng' – although at this time he and Wittgenstein shared a mutual antipathy for one another. Engelmann himself was a disciple of both Adolf Loos and Karl Kraus. After his discharge from the army he devoted himself to assisting Kraus in his campaign against the war, helping to collect the newspaper cuttings that formed the material for Kraus's satirical anti-war propaganda.

Wittgenstein arrived in Olmütz some time in October 1916, and stayed there until shortly before Christmas. He wanted at first to lodge in the tower of Olmütz Town Hall, but upon being told by the watchman that it was not to let, he settled for a room in a tenement block on the outskirts of town. Shortly after moving in, he fell ill with enteritis, and was nursed back to health by Engelmann, with the help of Engelmann's mother, who cooked Wittgenstein light meals, which Engelmann would then deliver to the invalid. On the first occasion that he performed this act of kindness Engelmann spilt some soup on his way up to Wittgenstein's room. On his entering, Wittgenstein exclaimed: 'My dear friend, you are showering me with kindness', to which Engelmann, his coat bespattered, replied: 'I am afraid I have been showering myself.' It was exactly the sort of simple kindness and simple humour that Wittgenstein appreciated, and the scene stayed in his mind. When he was back at the Front he wrote to Engelmann: 'I often think of you . . . and of the time you brought me some soup. But that was your mother's fault as well as yours! And I shall never forget her either.'

Thanks to Engelmann's group of friends, Wittgenstein's time at Olmütz was a happy one. He joined in with their performances of Molière's *Malade imaginaire*, listened appreciatively to Fritz Zweig's piano recitals and, above all, he joined in with their conversations – about literature, music and religion. With Engelmann particularly he was able to discuss with a sympathetic and like-minded listener all the ideas that had come to him during the last six months at the Front. Sometimes, Engelmann recalls, these conversations would be conducted while he was accompanying Wittgenstein on his way back from Engelmann's house to his room on the outskirts of town. If they were still engrossed in discussion by the time they reached the tenement block, they would turn round and continue the conversation while Wittgenstein accompanied Engelmann back.

Engelmann was the closest friend Wittgenstein had had since leaving England. The friendship owed much to the fact that the two met each other at a time when both were experiencing a religious awakening which they each interpreted and analysed in a similar way. Engelmann puts it well when he says that it was his own spiritual predicament that:

> . . . enabled me to understand, from within as it were, his utterances that mystified everyone else. And it was this understanding on my part that made me indispensable to him at that time.

Wittgenstein himself used to say: 'If I can't manage to bring forth a proposition, along comes Engelmann with his forceps and pulls it out of me.'

The image brings to mind Russell's remark about dragging Wittgenstein's thoughts out of him with pincers. And, indeed, it is hard to resist comparing Engelmann and Russell with respect to the roles they played in Wittgenstein's life during the development of the *Tractatus*. Engelmann himself seems to have had the comparison in mind when he wrote that:

> In me Wittgenstein unexpectedly met a person, who, like many members of the younger generation, suffered acutely under the discrepancy between the world as it is and as it ought to be according to his lights, but who tended also to seek the source of that discrepancy within, rather than outside himself. This was an attitude which he had not encountered elsewhere and which, at the same time, was vital for any true understanding or meaningful discussion of his spiritual condition.

And of Russell's introduction to the book, he says:

> [It] may be considered one of the main reasons why the book, though recognized to this day as an event of decisive importance in the field of logic, has failed to make itself understood as a philosophical work in the wider sense. Wittgenstein must have been deeply hurt to see that even such outstanding men, who were also helpful friends of his, were incapable of understanding his purpose in writing the *Tractatus*.

To a certain extent, this is anachronistic. It shows, too, little awareness of the fact that the Wittgenstein Engelmann met in 1916 was not the same as the Wittgenstein Russell had met in 1911. Nor was his purpose in writing the *Tractatus* the same. Russell was not in touch with Wittgenstein at a time when his work 'broadened out from the foundations of logic to the essence of the world'; so far as Russell knew, his purpose in writing the book was to shed light on the nature of logic. Engelmann, one might say, would have been little use to Wittgenstein's development as a philosopher in 1911, when his preoccupations centred on the issues raised by Russell's Paradox.

Nevertheless, it remains true that in 1916 – just as in 1911 – Wittgenstein was fortunate to be in a situation in which he could have daily conversations with, and the almost undivided attention of, a kindred spirit.

It is noteworthy that there are no coded remarks in Wittgenstein's notebook for this time; Engelmann's presence made them unnecessary. There are, however, a number of philosophical remarks. In the main these are a continuation of the Schopenhauerian line of thought begun at the Front. It is likely, I think, that his protracted conversations with Engelmann helped Wittgenstein to formulate the connections between the mystical and the logical parts of the book. Certainly he discussed the book in depth with Engelmann, and from the latter's 'Observations on the *Tractatus*' included in his memoir it is clear that it had been firmly impressed upon him that: 'logic and mysticism have here sprung from the same root'. The central thread that links the logic and the mysticism – the idea of the unutterable truth that makes itself manifest – was an idea that came naturally to Engelmann. Indeed, he later supplied Wittgenstein with what both considered to be an excellent example: a poem by Uhland called 'Count Eberhard's Hawthorn'.

After spending Christmas in Vienna Wittgenstein returned to the Russia Front in January 1917, now an artillery officer attached to a division of the Austrian Third Army stationed just north of the Carpathian mountains. By now the Russians were in disarray and the Front was relatively quiet. He wrote to Engelmann that he was once again capable of work (unfortunately, the manuscripts from this period have not survived). In all probability the work he wrote at this time was concerned with the inexpressibility of ethical and aesthetic truths. In a letter dated 4 April 1917, Engelmann enclosed 'Count Eberhard's Hawthorn', Uhland's poem recounting the story of a soldier who, while on crusade, cuts a spray from a hawthorn bush; when he returns home he plants the sprig in his grounds, and in old age he sits beneath the shade of the fully grown hawthorn tree, which serves as a poignant reminder of his youth. The tale is told very simply, without adornment and without drawing any moral. And yet, as Engelmann says, 'the poem as a whole gives in 28 lines the picture of a life'. It is, he told Wittgenstein, 'a wonder of objectivity':

Almost all other poems (including the good ones) attempt to express the inexpressible, here that is not attempted, and precisely because of that it is achieved.

Wittgenstein agreed. The poem, he wrote to Engelmann, is indeed 'really magnificent':

> And this is how it is: if only you do not try to utter what is unutterable then *nothing* gets lost. But the unutterable will be – unutterably – *contained* in what has been uttered!

There was, at this time, some reason to think that the war might soon come to an end through a victory for the Central Powers. The government in Russia had collapsed; there had been a breakthrough for the Germans against the French on the Western Front; and the U-Boat campaign against the British seemed to be succeeding. So, at least, Frege thought. 'Let's hope for the best!' he wrote to Wittgenstein on 26 April, listing all these reasons for doing so.

During the quiet time that followed the Russian Revolution, Wittgenstein was given some leave in Vienna. There Frege wrote to him, apologizing for having to refuse his invitation to come to Vienna to discuss his work. 'The journey to Vienna and back again', he explained, 'is, under my present circumstances, too strenuous.' It was clear that if Wittgenstein wanted to discuss his work with Frege, he would have to go to Jena.

In the event, the collapse of the Tsarist government was to lead, initially, to renewed activity on the Eastern Front. The new Minister of War (and, from July, the new Prime Minister), Alexander Kerensky, was determined to continue the struggle, and in July the Russians launched the ill-fated offensive named after him. The will to prolong the war on the part of the ordinary soldiers had, however, by this time been dissipated, and the Russian advance soon ground to a halt. Wittgenstein was awarded the Silver Medal for Valour for his part in the stand made by the Austro-Hungarian forces in defence of their positions at Ldziany. In the counter-offensive that followed he took part in the advance along the line of the river Pruth which led, in August, to the capture of the city of Czernowitz (Chernovtsy) in the Ukraine.

The Russian war effort had by this time completely collapsed, and with it the Kerensky government. The war in the East had been won by the Central Powers. After coming to power with a slogan of 'Bread and Peace', it remained only for the new Bolshevik government to salvage whatever they could from their inevitable surrender.

Throughout the long drawn out negotiations that followed, Wittgenstein remained stationed in the Ukraine, and it was not until 3 March 1918, when Lenin and Trotsky finally gave their signatures to the draconian terms of the Treaty of Brest Litovsk, that he, along with the bulk of the Austro-Hungarian forces, was transferred to the Italian Front.

During these six months of effectively non-combatant service, he seems to have begun the work of arranging his philosophical remarks into something like the form they finally took in the *Tractatus*. The manuscript of an early version of the book (published as *Prototractatus*) appears to date from this time, and we have it from Engelmann that a typed copy of the book existed *before* Wittgenstein left for Italy. This cannot have been the final version, but it is clear that during the winter of 1917–18 the work was beginning to take its final shape.

During this time Wittgenstein was in communication with both Frege and Engelmann. Frege wrote cards expressing the by now customary wish that he and Wittgenstein would be able to meet to discuss logic after the war. Engelmann, who was at this time employed by the Wittgenstein family to make alterations to their house in the Neuwaldeggergasse, wrote on more personal matters. On 8 January 1918 he was bold enough to make an observation on Wittgenstein's spiritual condition. It was, he said, something he had wanted to say when the two met in Vienna during the Christmas vacation, but had neglected to do so. 'If in saying it, I do you an injustice, forgive me':

> It seemed to me as if you – in contrast to the time you spent in Olmütz, where I had not thought so – had no faith. I write this not in an attempt to influence you. But I ask you to consider what I say, and wish for you, that you do what is in your *true* best interests.

Wittgenstein's reply to this is remarkably forbearing. 'It is true', he wrote, 'that there is a difference between myself as I am now and as I was when we met in Olmütz. And, as far as I know, the difference is that I am now *slightly* more decent. By this I only mean that I am slightly clearer in my own mind about my lack of decency':

> If you tell me now I have no faith, you are *perfectly right*, only I did not have it before either. It is plain, isn't it, that when a man wants,

as it were, to invent a machine for becoming decent, such a man has no faith. But what am I to do? *I am clear about one thing*: I am far too bad to be able to theorize about myself; in fact I shall either remain a swine or else I shall improve, and that's that! Only let's cut out the transcendental twaddle when the whole thing is as plain as a sock on the jaw.

'I am sure you are quite right in all you say', the letter ends. Engelmann had, it seems, at one and the same time spoken twaddle and spoken the truth. It was a combination that Wittgenstein was also to attribute to his own words in the *Tractatus*, but which Russell, as a logician, was to find deeply unsatisfying.

On 1 February 1918 Wittgenstein was promoted *Leutnant*, and on 10 March he transferred to a mountain artillery regiment fighting on the Italian Front. His book now almost complete, he wrote to Frege on 25 March acknowledging the great debt his work owed to the elderly, and still much neglected, logician. Frege replied that he was astonished to read such an effusive acknowledgement:

Each of us, I think, has taken something from others in our intellectual work. If I have furthered your endeavours more than I thought I had, then I am very pleased to have done so.

In the preface to the final version of the book, Wittgenstein repeats that he is indebted 'to Frege's great works and to the writings of my friend Mr Bertrand Russell for much of the stimulation of my thoughts'.

Within a month of arriving in Italy Wittgenstein fell ill with the enteritis that had troubled him in Olmütz, and sent away to Engelmann for the medicine he had been given then – 'the *only one* that has ever helped me'. Engelmann was slow to reply, and when on 28 May he finally put pen to paper, it was to ask Wittgenstein whether he knew of any remedy for a weakness of the will! His letter crossed with a parcel of books sent by Wittgenstein: 'which you don't deserve as you are too lazy even to answer an urgent enquiry'.

In the meantime, Wittgenstein had spent some time in a military hospital in Bolzano, where he was presumably able to continue work on his book. A letter from Frege of 1 June remarks how pleased he is that Wittgenstein's work is coming to a conclusion, and that he hopes it will all soon be down on paper 'so that it doesn't get lost'.

On the same day Adele Jolles wrote to him in a slightly wounded tone, apologizing for bothering him with another letter when he was so contemptuous of letters and so reluctant to engage in a superficial exchange. The Jolles family were perhaps the first, but by no means the last, of Wittgenstein's friends to fall victim to the changes in him wrought by his experience of war.

By the time of the Austrian offensive of 15 June Wittgenstein was fit enough to take part, and was employed as an observer with the artillery attacking French, British and Italian troops in the Trentino mountains. Once again he was cited for his bravery. 'His exceptionally courageous behaviour, calmness, sang-froid, and heroism', ran the report, 'won the total admiration of the troops.' He was recommended for the Gold Medal for Valour, the Austrian equivalent of the Victoria Cross, but was awarded instead the Band of the Military Service Medal with Swords, it being decided that his action, though brave, had been insufficiently consequential to merit the top honour. The attack, which was to be the last in which Wittgenstein took part, and indeed the last of which the Austrian army was capable, was quickly beaten back. In July, after the retreat, he was given a long period of leave that lasted until the end of September.

It was not in Vienna, but at Wittgenstein's Uncle Paul's house in Hallein, near Salzburg, that what we now know as *Tractatus Logico-Philosophicus* received its final form. One day in the summer of 1918 Paul Wittgenstein came across his nephew unexpectedly at a railway station. He found him desperately unhappy and intent on committing suicide, but managed to persuade him to come to Hallein. There Wittgenstein finished his book.

The most likely cause of this suicidal wish is a letter from Mrs Ellen Pinsent, dated 6 July, written to inform Wittgenstein of the death of her son, David, who had been killed in an aeroplane accident on 8 May. He had been engaged in research on aerodynamics, and had died investigating the cause of a previous accident. 'I want to tell you', she wrote, 'how much he loved you and valued your friendship up to the last.' It was to David's memory that Wittgenstein dedicated the completed book. David was, he wrote to Mrs Pinsent, 'my first and my only friend':

I have indeed known many young men of my own age and have been on good terms with some, but only in him did I find a real friend, the hours I have spent with him have been the best in my life, he was to me a brother and a friend. Daily I have thought of him and have longed to see him again. God will bless him. If I live to see the end of the war I will come and see you and we will talk of David.

'One thing more,' he added. 'I have just finished the philosophical work on which I was already at work at Cambridge':

I had always hoped to be able to show it to him some time, and it will always be connected with him in my mind. I will dedicate it to David's memory. For he always took great interest in it, and it is to him I owe far the most part of the happy moods which made it possible for me to work.

This last, as we have seen, refers not only to the time they spent together in Cambridge, Iceland and Norway, but also to the letters that Pinsent wrote during the war, which were, at times, the only things capable of reviving Wittgenstein's spirits sufficiently to enable him to concentrate on philosophy.

Now, having finished the book – having solved the problems he had set out to solve – what struck him most forcibly was the relative unimportance of the task that he had achieved. 'The *truth* of the thoughts that are here communicated', he wrote in the preface, 'seems to me unassailable and definitive'; and he believed himself to have found, 'on all essential points', the solution to the problems of philosophy. But:

. . . if I am not mistaken in this belief, then the second thing in which the value of this work consists is that it shows how little is achieved when these problems are solved.

He chose as a motto for the book a quotation from Kürnberger: '. . . and anything a man knows, anything he has not merely heard rumbling and roaring, can be said in three words'. The quotation had been used before by Karl Kraus, and it is possible that Wittgenstein took it from Kraus, but it is equally likely he got it straight from Kürnberger (books by Kürnberger were among those sent by

Wittgenstein to Engelmann). In any case, it is extremely apt. The whole meaning of his book, he says in the preface, 'can be summed up as follows: What can be said at all can be said clearly; and whereof one cannot speak thereof one must be silent.'

In its final form, the book is a formidably compressed distillation of the work Wittgenstein had written since he first came to Cambridge in 1911. The remarks in it, selected from a series of perhaps seven manuscript volumes, are numbered to establish a hierarchy in which, say, remark 2.151 is an elaboration of 2.15, which in turn elaborates the point made in remark 2.1, and so on. Very few of the remarks are justified with an argument; each proposition is put forward, as Russell once put it, 'as if it were a Czar's ukase'. The Theory of Logic worked out in Norway before the war, the Picture Theory of Propositions developed during the first few months of the war, and the quasi-Schopenhauerian mysticism embraced during the second half of the war, are all allotted a place within the crystalline structure, and are each stated with the kind of finality that suggests they are all part of the same incontrovertible truth.

Central to the book in all its aspects is the distinction between showing and saying: it is at once the key to understanding the superfluity of the Theory of Types in logic and to realizing the inexpressibility of ethical truths. What the Theory of Types attempts to say can be shown only by a correct symbolism, and what one wants to say about ethics can be shown only by contemplating the world *sub specie aeternitatis*. Thus: 'There is indeed the inexpressible. This *shows* itself; it is the mystical.'

The famous last sentence of the book – 'Whereof one cannot speak, thereof one must be silent' – expresses both a logico-philosophical truth and an ethical precept.

To this extent, as Engelmann has pointed out, the book's central message is allied to the campaign of Karl Kraus to preserve the purity of language by exposing to ridicule the confused thought that stems from its misuse. The nonsense that results from trying to say what can only be shown is not only logically untenable, but ethically undesirable.

On completion of the book Wittgenstein evidently considered these ethical implications to be as important, if not more so, as its implications for logical theory. He wanted it published alongside the work of Kraus. And as soon as it was finished, he sent it to Kraus's publisher,

Jahoda, seemingly expecting the relevance of it to Kraus's work to be readily apparent. At the same time he wrote to Frege offering to send him a copy. In a letter of 12 September Frege says that he would indeed be pleased to see it. He could understand, he wrote, Wittgenstein's feeling that the work might prove fruitless: when one has forged a path up a steep mountain that no one has climbed before, there must be a doubt as to whether anyone else will have the desire to follow one up it. He knew that doubt himself. And yet he had confidence that his work had not all been in vain. In a later letter (15 October) he writes: 'May it be granted to you to see your work in print, and to me to read it!'

Engelmann, too, was promised a copy. Towards the end of September, immediately before he returned to Italy, Wittgenstein travelled to Olmütz, and it was then that Engelmann read the book for the first time. In a letter to Wittgenstein of 7 November he mentions that he often reads in it: 'and it gives me more and more joy, the more I understand it'.

At the end of September Wittgenstein returned to the Italian Front, and for the next month waited impatiently to hear from Jahoda. 'Still no reply from the publisher!' he wrote to Engelmann on 22 October:

> And I feel an insuperable repugnance against writing to him with a query. The devil knows what he is doing with my manuscript. Please be so *very* kind and look up the damned blighter some day when you are in Vienna, and then let me know the result!

A few days later he was informed that Jahoda could not publish the work, 'for technical reasons'. 'I would dearly like to know what Kraus said about it', he told Engelmann. 'If there were an opportunity for you to find out, I should be very glad. Perhaps Loos knows something about it.'

By the time Wittgenstein returned to Italy, the Austro-Hungarian Empire was beginning to break up. The allegiance of the Czechs, the Poles, the Croats and the Hungarians that made up the bulk of its army was no longer given to the Habsburg Empire (in so far as it ever had been), but to the various national states, the creation of which had been promised to them not only by the Allies, but by the Habsburg Emperor himself. After the final Allied breakthrough of 30 October, before any armistice had been signed, large numbers of the men formed themselves into groups of compatriots and simply turned their back on the war, making their way home instead to help found their new nations. Austrian officers frequently found that they had no control whatsoever over the troops that were still nominally under their command. One casualty of this situation was Wittgenstein's brother, Kurt, who in October or November shot himself when the men under him refused to obey his orders.

The Austrians could do nothing but sue for peace, a process which the Italians, presented with a golden opportunity to collect booty and win back territory, were in no mind to hurry. On 29 October an Austrian delegation, carrying a flag of truce, approached the Italians but was sent back because it lacked the proper credentials. It was not until five days later that an armistice was finally signed. In the meantime the Italians had taken about 7000 guns and about 500,000 prisoners – Wittgenstein among them.

Upon capture, he was taken to a prisoner-of-war camp in Como. There he met two fellow officers, who were to remain valuable friends in the years to come: the sculptor Michael Drobil and the teacher Ludwig Hänsel. A story told by Hermine Wittgenstein relates that Drobil had assumed from his ragged and unassuming appearance that Wittgenstein was from a humble background. One day their conversation turned to a portrait by Klimt of a certain Fräulein Wittgenstein. To Drobil's amazement, Wittgenstein referred to the painting as 'the portrait of my sister'. He stared in disbelief: 'Then you're a Wittgenstein are you?'

Wittgenstein got to know Hänsel after attending a class on logic that Hänsel was giving to prisoners who hoped upon release to train as teachers. This led to regular discussions between them, during which Wittgenstein led Hänsel through the elements of symbolic logic and explained the ideas of the *Tractatus* to him. They also read Kant's *Critique of Pure Reason* together.

In January 1919 Wittgenstein (together with Hänsel and Drobil) was transferred to another camp, in Cassino. There they were to remain, as bargaining material for the Italians, until August.

It was while he was held at Cassino that Wittgenstein made the decision that, on return to Vienna, he would train as an elementary school teacher. According to the writer Franz Parak, however, with whom Wittgenstein enjoyed a brief friendship at the prisoner-of-war camp, Wittgenstein would most have liked to have become a priest 'and to have read the Bible with the children'.*

In February Wittgenstein was able to write a card to Russell. 'I am prisoner in Italy since November', he told him, 'and hope I may communicate with you after a three years interruption. I have done lots of logical work which I am dying to let you know before publishing it.'

The card somehow managed to reach Russell at Garsington Manor, where he was staying as a guest of Ottoline Morrell and endeavouring to finish *The Analysis of Mind*, which had been started in Brixton Prison the previous year.

Russell had had, in his way, almost as difficult a time as Wittgenstein. At forty-two, he was too old to fight, but given his implacable opposition to the war he would not have volunteered anyway. His opposition to the war had caused him to be sacked from his lectureship by Trinity College, and had brought him briefly into an uneasy and emotionally fraught collaboration with D. H. Lawrence, which, when it ended, left him with a much firmer distaste for the irrational and impulsive sides of human nature than he had had hitherto.

He had campaigned tirelessly against conscription and published numerous political essays, one of which brought against him the charge of prejudicing relations between Britain and the United States. For this he was imprisoned for six months. To the public he was now better known as a political campaigner than as a philosopher/mathematician. *Principles of Social Reconstruction* and *Roads to Freedom* enjoyed a far wider readership than had *Principles of Mathematics* and *Principia Mathematica.* In prison, however, he returned to philosophical work, writing the *Introduction to Mathematical Philosophy* and beginning *The Analysis of Mind.* Now, in temporary retirement from public controversy and taking advantage of the peaceful surroundings offered at Garsington to reorientate himself back into philosophical thought,

---

*From Parak's point of view, the friendship was all too brief. Parak, who was seven years younger than Wittgenstein, formed a respect for Wittgenstein that bordered on worship. He hung on to Wittgenstein's every word, hoping, as he says in his memoir, to drink in as much as possible of Wittgenstein's superior knowledge and wisdom. After a time Wittgenstein tired of this and began to withdraw, 'like a mimosa', from Parak's attachment. Parak, he said, reminded him of his mother.

he was only too pleased to re-establish communication with Wittgenstein. He dashed off two cards on successive days:

> Most thankful to hear you are still alive. Please write on Logic, when possible. I hope it will not be long now before a talk will be possible. I too have very much to say about philosophy, etc. [2.3.19]

> Very glad to hear from you – had been anxious for a long time. I shall be interested to learn what you have done in Logic. I hope before long it may be possible to hear all about it. Shall be glad of further news – about your health etc. [3.3.19]

'You can't imagine how glad I was to receive your cards!' Wittgenstein replied, adding that, unless Russell were prepared to travel to Cassino, there was no hope of their meeting 'before long'. He could not write on logic, as he was allowed only two cards a week, but he explained the essential point: 'I've written a book which will be published as soon as I get home. I think I have solved our problems finally.' A few days later he was able, after all, to expand on this, when, thanks to a student who was on his way back to Austria, he had the opportunity to post a full-length letter. 'I've written a book called "Logisch-Philosophische Abhandlung" containing all my work of the last six years', he explained:

> I believe I've solved our problems finally. This may sound arrogant but I can't help believing it. I finished the book in August 1918 and two months after was made Prigioniere. I've got the manuscript here with me. I wish I could copy it out for you; but it's pretty long and I would have no safe way of sending it to you. In fact you would not understand it without a previous explanation as it's written in quite short remarks. (This of course means that *nobody* will understand it; although I believe, it's all as clear as crystal. But it upsets all our theory of truth, of classes, of numbers and all the rest.) I will publish it as soon as I get home.

He repeated that he expected to be in the camp for some time. But, he asked speculatively: 'I suppose it would be impossible for you to come and see me here?'

. . . or perhaps you think it's colossal cheek of me even to think of such a thing. But if you were on the other end of the world and I *could* come to you I would do it.

In fact, it was impossible for Russell to visit him at Cassino, although, as it turned out, Wittgenstein himself was given an opportunity to leave the camp. Through a relative with connections in the Vatican, strings were pulled to get him released by the Italians. He was to be examined by a doctor and declared medically unfit to stand prolonged confinement. Wittgenstein, however, rejected such privileged treatment, and at the examination insisted vehemently that he was in perfect health.

Russell also pulled strings, and through Keynes (who was at this time with the British delegation at the Versailles Peace Conference) managed to get permission for Wittgenstein to receive books and to be excepted from the rule allowing him only two postcards a week, so that he could engage in learned correspondence. These privileges Wittgenstein did not refuse. They made it possible for him both to send his manuscript to Russell and to receive Russell's newly published book, *Introduction to Mathematical Philosophy*, which Russell regarded as having been influenced by his reading of Wittgenstein's *Notes on Logic*.*

To Wittgenstein, however, the book was confirmation of his suspicion that Russell would not be able to understand his latest work. 'I should never have believed', he wrote after reading it, 'that the stuff I dictated to Moore in Norway six years ago would have passed over you so completely without trace':

> In short, I'm now afraid that it might be very difficult for me to reach any understanding with you. And the small remaining hope that my manuscript might mean something to you has completely vanished . . . *Now* more than ever I'm burning to see it in print. It's galling to have to lug the completed work round in captivity and to see how nonsense has a clear field outside! And it's equally galling to think that no one will understand it even if it does get printed!

Russell's reply is remarkably conciliatory. 'It is true', he wrote, 'that

---

* For the footnote acknowledging his debt, see p. 134.

what you dictated to Moore was not intelligible to me, and he would give me no help.' About his book he explained:

> Throughout the war I did not think about philosophy, until, last summer, I found myself in prison, and beguiled my leisure by writing a popular text-book, which was all I could do under the circumstances. Now I am back at philosophy, and more in the mood to understand.

'Don't be discouraged', he urged; 'you will be understood in the end.'

By the summer of 1919 the three people Wittgenstein most hoped and expected to understand his work – Engelmann, Russell and Frege – had each received a copy. Even on the assumption (confirmed in a later letter to Russell) that this left Wittgenstein himself without a copy, it is something of a mystery how he managed to make three copies of the book.

In a letter of 6 April, Engelmann paid his own tribute to the book with a friendly parody of its system of numbering:

> No writing between the lines!
> 1. Dear Mr Wittgenstein, I am very pleased to hear,
> 2. through your family, that you are well. I
> 3. hope that you do not take it badly that I have
> 4. not written to you for so long, but I had so
> 5. much to write that I preferred to leave it to
> 6. a reunion that I hope will be soon. But I must
> 7. now thank you with all my heart for your
> 8. manuscript, a copy of which I received some time
> 9. ago from your sister. I think I now, on the
> 10. whole, understand it, at least with me you have
> 11. entirely fulfilled your purpose of providing
> 12. somebody some enjoyment through the book; I am
> 13. certain of the truth of your thoughts and
> 14. discern their meaning. Best wishes,
> 15. yours sincerely, Paul Engelmann

Engelmann evidently enjoyed this, so much so that he repeated the format in his next letter of 15 August, written to explain to Wittgenstein why he had so far been unable to obtain a copy of Frege's

Grundgesetze der Arithmetik, which Wittgenstein had asked him to send.

There are some indications that it was Frege's response to the book that Wittgenstein most eagerly awaited. If so, the disappointment must have been all the more great when he received Frege's reactions.

Frege's first impressions are contained in a letter written on 28 June. He begins by apologizing for the late response, and for the fact that, as he had had much to do, he had had little time to read Wittgenstein's manuscript and could therefore offer no firm judgement on it. Almost the whole of his letter is concerned with doubts about the precision of Wittgenstein's language:

> Right at the beginning I come across the expressions 'is the case' and 'fact' and I suspect that *is the case* and *is a fact* are the same. The world is everything that is the case and the world is the collection of facts. Is not every fact the case and is not that which is the case a fact? Is it not the same if I say, A is a fact, as if I say, A is the case? Why then this double expression? . . . Now comes a third expression: 'What is the case, a fact, is the existence of *Sachverhalte*.' I take this to mean that every fact is the existence of a *Sachverhalt*, so that another fact is the existence of another *Sachverhalt*. Couldn't one delete the words 'existence of' and say 'Every fact is a *Sachverhalt*, every other fact is another *Sachverhalt*'. Could one perhaps also say 'Every *Sachverhalt* is the existence of a fact?'

'You see', Frege wrote, 'from the very beginning I find myself entangled in doubt as to what you want to say, and so make no proper headway.' He was unsure what Wittgenstein meant by the terms *Tatsache*, *Sachverhalt* and *Sachlage*, and would need, he said, examples to clarify the terminology. Are there *Sachverhalte* that do not exist? Is every collection of objects a *Sachverhalt*?★ Frege's letter must have been a bitter disappointment to Wittgenstein. There is nothing in it to indicate that Frege got past the first page; his questions all relate to the

---

★I have kept the German words here, because for the English reader Frege's confusion is compounded by differences of translation. Ogden translates *Sachverhalt* as 'atomic fact', and *Sachlage* as 'state of affairs'; Pears and McGuinness have 'state of affairs' for *Sachverhalt* and 'situation' for *Sachlage*. Ogden's translation has the merit, at least, of making it clear – as Wittgenstein had to explain to both Frege and Russell – that *Sachverhalte* are what correspond to (true) atomic propositions, and are therefore the constituent parts of *Tatsachen* (facts).

first ten or so propositions in the book, and are all concerned with terminology rather than substance. Of Wittgenstein's Theory of Symbolism and its implications for the understanding of logic, Frege obviously had no grasp at all; still less could he be expected to understand the ethical implications of the book.

Despondently, Wittgenstein pinned his hopes on Russell. In a letter of 19 August he told Russell of Frege's response to the book: 'I gather he doesn't understand a word of it':

> So my only hope is to see *you* soon and explain all to you, for it is VERY hard not to be understood by a single soul!

There were indeed reasons for hoping that Russell might, after all, be brought to an understanding of the book. His initial reactions to it were both more comprehending and more favourable than those of Frege. He had at least managed to read the whole book – 'twice carefully' so he told Wittgenstein. And he had, moreover, formed *some* idea (even if mistaken) of what it was about. 'I am convinced', he wrote on 13 August, 'you are right in your main contention, that logical props are tautologies, which are not true in the sense that substantial props are true.'

In fact, this was not the main contention of the book – at least as Wittgenstein understood it. But, nevertheless, it showed that Russell had understood what Wittgenstein was trying to say about logic. This was, however, Wittgenstein explained in his letter of 19 August, only a 'corollary' to his main contention:

> The main point is the theory of what can be expressed (gesagt) by props – i.e. by language – (and, which comes to the same, what can be *thought*) and what can not be expressed by props, but only shown (gezeigt); which, I believe, is the cardinal problem of philosophy.

This links, I believe, with what Wittgenstein had meant earlier when he said that *Introduction to Mathematical Philosophy* showed that the notes he had dictated to Moore had completely 'passed over' Russell. For though Russell had borrowed Wittgenstein's notion of tautology, he had made no use in the book of the distinction between saying and showing, the distinction that the notes to Moore had introduced. It was not that Russell did not understand the distinction, but rather that he thought it obscure and unnecessary. He later called it 'a curious kind of logical mysticism', and thought that, in logic at least, it could be dispensed with by introducing a higher level language (a 'meta-language') to say the things that could not be said using the original 'object-language'.

To his letter Russell appended a list of questions and doubts about the book. Like Frege, he wanted to know what the difference was between *Tatsache* and *Sachverhalt*. Wittgenstein gave the same answer he had given Frege:

> Sachverhalt is, what corresponds to an Elementarsatz (elementary proposition) if it is true. Tatsache is what corresponds to the logical product of elementary props when this product is true.

Most of the other queries raised by Russell in some way or other arise from his reluctance to accept the idea that some things – logical form, for instance – cannot be expressed in language but have to be shown. Russell objected, for example, to Wittgenstein's summary dismissal of the Theory of Types in proposition 3.331: 'The theory of types, in my view', he told Wittgenstein, 'is a theory of correct symbolism: (a) a simple symbol must not be used to express anything complex; (b) more generally, a symbol must have the same structure as its meaning.' 'That's exactly what one can't say', Wittgenstein replied:

> You cannot prescribe to a symbol what it *may* be used to express. All that a symbol CAN express, it MAY express. This is a short answer but it is true!

In two other replies to points raised by Russell Wittgenstein hammered home the same message:

> . . . Just think that, what you want to *say* by the apparent prop 'there are two things' is *shown* by there being two names which have different meanings.

> . . . 'It is necessary to be given the prop that all elementary props are given.' This is not necessary, because it is even *impossible*. There is no such prop! That all elementary props are given is SHOWN by there being none having an elementary sense which is not given.

Although these questions and answers relate to specific points of logical theory, not very far behind them lies a more general and more important difference. It is no coincidence that Russell's insistence on the applicability of meta-languages abolishes the sphere of the mystical, while Wittgenstein's insistence on the impossibility of saying what can only be shown preserves it.

What was perhaps Russell's gravest doubt, however, remained unanswered. This concerned Wittgenstein's brief discussion of mathematics, and particularly his abrupt dismissal of Set Theory. 'The theory of classes', he writes in proposition 6.031, 'is completely superfluous in mathematics.' As this cuts at the root of everything Russell had achieved in mathematics, he quite naturally found it perturbing:

> If you said classes were superfluous in *logic* I would imagine that I understood you, by supposing a distinction between logic and mathematics; but when you say they are unnecessary in *mathematics* I am puzzled.

To this Wittgenstein said only that it would require a lengthy answer, and: 'you know how difficult it is for me to write on logic'.

Of the final sections of the book, Russell had little to comment: 'I agree with what you say about induction, causality, etc.; at least I can find no ground for disagreeing.' On the remarks on ethics, aesthetics, the soul and the meaning of life, he said nothing.

'*I am sure you are right in thinking the book of first-class importance*', he concluded. 'But in places it is obscure through brevity':

> I have a most intense desire to see you, to talk it over, as well as simply because I want to see you. But I can't get abroad as yet. Probably you will be free to come to England before I am free to go abroad. – I will send back your MS when I know where to send it, but I am hoping you will soon be at liberty.

The letter was sufficiently encouraging to prompt Wittgenstein to seek a meeting as soon as possible. 'I should like to come to England', he wrote, 'but you can imagine it's rather awkward for a German to travel to England now.' The best thing would be to meet in some neutral country – say, Holland or Switzerland. And *soon*. 'The day after tomorrow', he told Russell, 'we shall probably leave the Campo Concentramento and go home. Thank God!'

He was released two days later, on 21 August 1919.

II
1919–28

8

THE UNPRINTABLE
TRUTH

Like many war veterans before and since, Wittgenstein found it almost insuperably difficult to adjust to peace-time conditions. He had been a soldier for five years, and the experience had left an indelible stamp upon his personality. He continued to wear his uniform for many years after the war, as though it had become a part of his identity, an essential part, without which he would be lost. It was also perhaps a symbol of his feeling – which persisted for the rest of his life – that he belonged to a past age. For it was the uniform of a force that no longer existed. Austria-Hungary was no more, and the country he returned to in the summer of 1919 was itself undergoing a painful process of adjustment. Vienna, once the imperial centre of a dynasty controlling the lives of fifty million subjects of mixed race, was now the capital of a small, impoverished and insignificant Alpine republic of little more than six million, mostly German, inhabitants.

The parts of the empire in which Wittgenstein himself had fought to defend what had been his homeland were now absorbed into foreign states. Lemberg and Kraków were now in the new state of Poland; the area around the Trentino mountains had been claimed by Italy; and Olmütz, that last outpost of Austro-Hungarian culture, was now in Czechoslovakia – itself a hybrid creation of 'self-determination' – of which Paul Engelmann had become a reluctant citizen. (The problems encountered by Engelmann in obtaining a Czechoslovakian passport kept him from visiting Wittgenstein in Vienna for many months.) To many Austrians, the whole *raison d'être* of their separate identity had been destroyed, and in 1919 the majority voted for *Anschluss* with Germany. If they were to be nothing more than a German state, it was felt, then surely they had better be part of the fatherland. That option was denied them by the Allies, who also, through the war reparations demanded by the Treaties of Versailles and St Germain, ensured that the German people of both German states would remain poor, resentful and revengeful throughout the inter-war period.

Wittgenstein had entered the war hoping it would change him, and this it had. He had undergone four years of active service and a year of incarceration; he had faced death, experienced a religious awakening, taken responsibility for the lives of others, and endured long periods of close confinement in the company of the sort of people he would not previously have shared a railway carriage with. All this had made him a different person – had given him a new identity. In a sense, he was not returning to anything in 1919: everything had changed, and he could no more slip back into the life he had left in 1914 than he could revert to being the 'little Wittgenstein' that the Jolles had known in Berlin. He was faced with the task of re-creating himself – of finding a new role for the person that had been forged by the experiences of the last five years.

His family were dismayed by the changes they saw in him. They could not understand why he wanted to train to become a teacher in elementary schools. Hadn't Bertrand Russell himself acknowledged his philosophic genius, and stated that the next big step in philosophy would come from him? Why did he now want to waste that genius on the uneducated poor? It was, his sister Hermine remarked, like somebody wanting to use a precision instrument to open crates. To this, Wittgenstein replied:

> You remind me of somebody who is looking out through a closed window and cannot explain to himself the strange movements of a passer-by. He cannot tell what sort of storm is raging out there or that this person might only be managing with difficulty to stay on his feet.

Of course, it might be thought that the most natural step for the person in Wittgenstein's analogy to take would be to come in out of the storm. But this Wittgenstein could not do. The hardship suffered during the war was not experienced by him as something from which he sought refuge, but as the very thing that gave his life meaning. To shelter from the storm in the comfort and security which his family's wealth and his own education could provide would be to sacrifice everything he had gained from struggling with adversity. It would be to give up climbing mountains in order to live on a plateau.

It was essential to Wittgenstein, not only that he should not use the privileges of his inherited wealth, but that he could not do so. On his arrival home from the war he was one of the wealthiest men in Europe, owing to his father's financial astuteness in transferring the family's wealth, before the war, into American bonds. But within a month of returning, he had disposed of his entire estate. To the concern of his family, and the astonishment of the family accountant, he insisted that his entire inheritance should be made over to his sisters, Helene and Hermine, and his brother Paul (Gretl, it was decided, was already too wealthy to be included). Other members of the family, among them his Uncle Paul Wittgenstein, could not understand how they could have accepted the money. Couldn't they at least have secretly put some of it aside in case he should later come to regret his decision? These people, writes Hermine, could not know that it was precisely that possibility that troubled him:

> A hundred times he wanted to assure himself that there was no possibility of any money still belonging to him in any shape or form. To the despair of the notary carrying out the transfer, he returned to this point again and again.

Eventually the notary was persuaded to execute Wittgenstein's wishes to the letter. 'So', he sighed, 'you want to commit financial suicide!'

In September 1919, after ridding himself of his wealth and having enrolled at the Lehrerbildungsanhalt in the Kundmanngasse, Wittgenstein took another step towards independence from his privileged background, moving out of the family home in the Neuwaldegger-gasse and taking lodgings in Untere Viaduktgasse, a street in Vienna's Third District within easy walking distance of the college.*

This period was one of great suffering for Wittgenstein, and on more than one occasion during these months he contemplated taking

---

* He was in these lodgings scarcely more than a month, but his time there has become the subject of a heated controversy following claims made by the writer William Warren Bartley III. See pp. 581–6.

his own life. He was exhausted and disorientated. 'I'm not quite normal yet', he wrote to Russell soon after his return; and to Engelmann: 'I am not very well (i.e. as far as my state of mind is concerned).' He asked both Russell and Engelmann to come and see him as soon as they could, but neither could manage the trip. Engelmann was having problems obtaining a Czechoslovakian passport, and Russell was engaged on a course of lectures at the London School of Economics (the material of which formed the basis for *The Analysis of Mind*), which would keep him in England until the Christmas vacation. Besides, there was a real possibility that Russell would not be given permission to leave the country – 'for as you may know', he wrote to Wittgenstein, 'I have fallen out with the Government'. He nevertheless suggested that they try to meet at The Hague at Christmas: 'I could manage a week, if the government will let me go.'

The frustration of not being able to reunite with either Engelmann or Russell undoubtedly added to the emotional strain Wittgenstein was suffering. He had the feeling of losing all his old friends and being unable to make any new ones. The meeting he had most looked forward to during the last five years had been denied him by the death of 'dear David' (so he wrote to Mrs Pinsent), and other eagerly anticipated meetings were either frustrated or turned out to be a bitter disappointment. He looked up Adolf Loos, but was, he told Engelmann, 'horrified and nauseated':

> He has become infected with the most virulent bogus intellectualism! He gave me a pamphlet about a proposed 'fine arts office', in which he speaks about a sin against the Holy Ghost. This surely is the limit! I was already a bit depressed when I went to see Loos, but that was the last straw!

Nor was he – a thirty-year-old war veteran – likely to make many friends among the teenagers with whom he attended lectures at the teacher training college. 'I can no longer behave like a grammar-school boy', he wrote to Engelmann, 'and – funny as it sounds – the humiliation is *so* great for me that often I think I can hardly bear it!' He complained in similar spirit to Russell:

> The benches are full of boys of 17 and 18 and I've reached 30. That leads to some very funny situations – and many *very* unpleasant ones too. I often feel miserable!

Though he was embarking on a new career and a new life, and in many ways was deliberately severing the ties that bound him to his family background, he needed to establish some continuity between the person he was before the war and the person he had become. Before he started his course at the Lehrerbildungsanhalt, he spent about ten days living at the Hochreit, in order, as he put it to Engelmann, 'to find something of myself again if I can'.

His family connections, and the ambivalence with which he regarded them, provoked one of the unpleasant situations at college he mentions to Russell. His teacher asked him whether he was related to *the* Wittgensteins, the rich Wittgensteins. He replied that he was. Was he *closely* related? the teacher persisted. To this, Wittgenstein felt compelled to lie: 'Not very.'

The defeat and impoverishment of his home country, the death of his most beloved friend, the frustration at not being able to re-establish old friendships and the strain of putting his whole life on a new footing might themselves be sufficient to account for Wittgenstein's suicidal state during the autumn of 1919. But perhaps the most important cause of his depression was his failure to find a publisher for the *Tractatus* – or even a single person who understood it.

He had, he thought, completed a book that provided a definitive and unassailably true solution to the problems of philosophy. How, then, could he have anticipated such difficulty in finding someone willing to publish it? Even after it had been rejected by Jahoda, Wittgenstein could write confidently from the prison camp at Cassino: 'My book will be published as soon as I get home.'

Within a few days of his return, he took the book to the Viennese offices of Wilhelm Braumüller, the publishers of Otto Weininger's *Sex and Character*. Braumüller, he told Russell, 'naturally neither knows my name nor understands anything about philosophy [and] requires the judgment of some expert in order to be sure that the book is really worth printing':

For this purpose he wanted to apply to one of the people he relies on here (probably a professor of philosophy). So I told him that no one here would be able to form a judgment on the book, but that *you* would perhaps be kind enough to write him a brief assessment of the value of the work, and if this happened to be favourable that would be enough to induce him to publish it. The publisher's address is: Wilhelm Braumüller, XI Servitengasse 5, Vienna. Now please write him a few words – as much as your conscience will allow you to.

After receiving Russell's testimonial, Braumüller offered to publish the book on condition that Wittgenstein himself paid for the printing and paper. By the time the offer was made he had no money to pay such costs, but even if he had he would still have refused. 'I consider it indecent', he said, 'to force a work upon the world – to which the publisher belongs – in this way. The writing was *my* affair; but the world must accept it in the normal manner.'

While waiting for Braumüller's decision, he received a letter from Frege – a late reply to Wittgenstein's last letter from Cassino, and to a further letter which Wittgenstein had written since his return to Vienna. Frege was still far from satisfied with the clarity of Wittgenstein's use of the word *Sachverhalt*:

> You now write: 'What corresponds to an elementary proposition, if it is true, is the existence of a *Sachverhalt*.' Here you do not explain the expression '*Sachverhalt*', but the whole expression 'the existence of a *Sachverhalt*'.

He was further perturbed by what Wittgenstein had written about the purpose of the book. 'This book will perhaps only be understood by those who have themselves already thought the thoughts which are expressed in it', Wittgenstein had written in the preface (he must also have written something similar to Frege). 'It is therefore not a textbook. Its object would be attained if it afforded pleasure to one who read it with understanding.' This Frege found strange:

> The pleasure of reading your book can therefore no longer be aroused by the content which is already known, but only by the peculiar form given to it by the author. The book thereby becomes an artistic rather than a scientific achievement; what is said in it takes second place to the way in which it is said.

He was encouraged, however, by one sentence in Wittgenstein's letter. Responding to Frege's remarks about the identical meanings of his propositions, 'The world is everything that is the case', and 'The world is the totality of facts', Wittgenstein wrote: 'The sense of both propositions is one and the same, but not the ideas that *I* associated with them when I wrote them.' Here Frege was (or thought he was) on home ground, and agreed wholeheartedly with Wittgenstein's point, the more so because it touched on a thought that was dear to him at this time. In order to make Wittgenstein's point, he argued, it was necessary to distinguish a proposition from its sense, thus opening up the possibility that two propositions could have the same sense and yet differ in the ideas associated with them. 'The actual sense of a proposition', he wrote to Wittgenstein, 'is the same for everybody; but the ideas which a person associates with the proposition belong to him alone . . . No one can have another's ideas.'

It was a theme Frege had dealt with in an article he had recently published, a copy of which he enclosed with his letter to Wittgenstein. The article was called '*Der Gedanke*' ('The Thought'), and was published in the journal *Beiträgen zur Philosophie des Deutschen Idealismus*. Though exasperated by Frege's laboured attempts to clarify the meaning of his book ('He doesn't understand a single word of my work', he wrote to Russell after receiving Frege's letter, 'and I'm thoroughly exhausted from giving what are purely and simply explanations'), Wittgenstein seized the opportunity to offer his work to another potentially sympathetic publisher. After rejecting Braumüller's offer to publish it if he would pay for the printing, he asked Frege to investigate the possibility of having it published in the same journal that had published Frege's article.

Frege's reply was not greatly encouraging. He could, he told Wittgenstein, write to the editor of the journal and tell him: 'that I have learnt to know you as a thinker to be taken thoroughly seriously'. But: 'Of the treatise itself I can offer no judgement, not because I am not in agreement with its contents, but rather because the content is too unclear to me.' He could ask the editor if he wished to see Wittgenstein's book, but: 'I hardly think that this would lead to anything.' The book would take up about fifty printed pages, nearly the whole journal, and: 'There seems to me not a chance that the editor would give up a whole edition to a single, still unknown writer.'

If, however, Wittgenstein were prepared to split the book into sections, its publication in a periodical would be more feasible (and, one gathers, would receive more support from Frege himself):

You write in your preface that the truth of the thoughts communicated seems to you unassailable and definitive. Now could not one
of these thoughts, in which the solution to a philosophical problem
is contained, itself provide the subject for an article and thus the
whole book be divided into as many parts as the number of
philosophical problems with which it deals?

This would have the merit, argued Frege, of not frightening the
reader away from the book because of its length. And furthermore: 'If
the first article, which would have to lay the foundations, met with
approval, it would be easier to find a place in the periodical for the rest
of the treatise.'

It would also, he thought, help to make Wittgenstein's work
clearer. After reading the preface, he told Wittgenstein, one did not
really know what to make of the first proposition. One expected to see
a question, to have a problem outlined, to which the book would
address itself. Instead, one came across a bald assertion, without being
given the grounds for it. Wouldn't it be better to make clear to which
problems the book was supposed to provide a definitive solution?

'Don't take these remarks badly', Frege ended; 'they are made with
good intentions.'

Wittgenstein would have nothing to do with Frege's suggestion. To
divide the book up in the manner recommended would be, in his
opinion, to 'mutilate it from beginning to end and, in a word, make
another work out of it'. As Frege had remarked earlier, the form in
which Wittgenstein's thoughts were expressed was essential to the
nature of the work. After receiving Frege's letter he abandoned the
attempt to have it published in *Beiträgen zur Philosophie des Deutschen
Idealismus*.

Reasoning, perhaps, that if the book was too literary for a philosophical journal he would try a literary journal instead, Wittgenstein
next thought of von Ficker and *Der Brenner*. By coincidence, the day
on which he was about to go to see Loos to get Ficker's address, a letter
from Ficker arrived telling him that *Der Brenner* would indeed continue to be published and asking him if he would like to be sent a copy.
Immediately, Wittgenstein wrote a long letter to Ficker, explaining
the history of his book. 'About a year ago', he wrote, 'I finished a
philosophical work on which I had worked for the previous seven
years':

It is quite strictly speaking the presentation of a system. And this presentation is *extremely* compressed since I have only retained in it that which really occurred to me – and how it occurred to me.

Immediately after finishing the work, he continued, he wanted to find a publisher: 'And therein lies a great difficulty':

The work is very small, only about sixty pages long. Who writes sixty-page brochures about philosophical matters? . . . [only] those certain, totally hopeless hacks who have neither the mind of the great, nor the erudition of the professors, and yet would like to have something printed at any price. Therefore such products are usually printed privately. But I simply cannot mix my life's work – for that is what it is – among these writings.

He then told Ficker of the unsatisfactory responses he had so far had from the publishers of, respectively, Kraus, Weininger and Frege. Finally, he got to the point: 'it occurred to me whether *you* might be inclined to take the poor thing into your protection'. If Ficker thought its publication in *Der Brenner* conceivable, Wittgenstein would send him the manuscript. 'Until then I should only like to say this about it':

The work is strictly philosophical and at the same time literary, but there is no babbling in it.

Ficker replied with a mixture of encouragement and caution. 'Why hadn't you thought of me immediately?' he asked. 'For you could well imagine that I would take a completely different, i.e. a deeper, interest in your work than a publisher who had only his commercial interests in mind.' Strangely, his letter then dwelt at length on the need for him to keep *his* commercial interests in mind. He had, he said, previously published *Der Brenner* for love, not money. But this could not continue; times were hard, he had a wife and children to support, and printing costs were prohibitively high. In the difficult financial climate that prevailed in Austria after the war, publishing was a risky business, and he had to ensure that he did not take more chances than were necessary. Nevertheless, with the proviso that 'strictly scientific works are not really our field' (and with the awareness that he was still somewhat in Wittgenstein's debt for the benefactions of 1914), he asked to see Wittgenstein's manuscript: 'Rest assured, dear Mr Wittgenstein, that I will do my best to meet your wishes.'

Wittgenstein was sufficiently encouraged by this to send Ficker the manuscript. 'I am pinning my hopes on you', he wrote in the accompanying letter, which also provides one of the most direct statements we have of how he wished his book to be understood. He needed to say *something* about it, he told Ficker: 'For you won't – I really believe – get too much out of reading it. Because you won't understand it; the content will be strange to you':

> In reality, it isn't strange to you, for the point of the book is ethical. I once wanted to give a few words in the foreword which now actually are not in it, which, however, I'll write to you now because they might be a key for you: I wanted to write that my work consists of two parts: of the one which is here, and of everything which I have *not* written. And precisely this second part is the important one. For the Ethical is delimited from within, as it were, by my book; and I'm convinced that, *strictly* speaking, it can ONLY be delimited in this way. In brief, I think: All of that which *many* are *babbling* today, I have defined in my book by remaining silent about it. Therefore the book will, unless I'm quite wrong, have much to say which you want to say yourself, but perhaps you won't notice that it is said in it. For the time being, I'd recommend that you read the *foreword* and the *conclusion* since these express the point most directly.

If this was intended to convince Ficker that the message of the *Tractatus* was, despite appearances, consonant with the aims of *Der Brenner*, it was misjudged. Wittgenstein was asking Ficker to accept that what he wanted to say about ethics had best be said by remaining silent – and, by implication, that much of what Ficker published in *Der Brenner* was mere 'babbling'. His letter was hardly calculated, either, to reassure Ficker's financial worries. A book in which the most important part has been left out could not be expected to be a very attractive proposition to a publisher with a concerned eye to his own solvency.

Ficker's response was cool. He could not give a definite answer, he wrote on 18 November, but there was a possibility that he would not be able to publish Wittgenstein's work. It was, at that moment, in the hands of his friend and colleague, who, as he had explained in the previous letter, was responsible for the financial affairs of the publishing house. The opinion of this colleague was that the work was too specialized to appear in *Der Brenner* – although that was not necessarily his last word on the subject. Nevertheless, Ficker had approached Rilke for advice on where an alternative publisher might be found. Finally, could he show the book to a philosophy professor? He knew someone at Innsbruck University who was familiar with the work of Russell and who was interested to read what Wittgenstein had written. Who knows, he might even be able to help find a publisher for it.

The letter threw Wittgenstein into a state of despondency. 'Do you remember', he wrote to Russell, 'how you were always pressing me to publish something? And now when I should like to, it can't be managed. The devil take it!' To Ficker he replied: 'Your letter, naturally, wasn't pleasant for me, although I wasn't really surprised by your answer. I don't know where I can get my work accepted either. If I were only somewhere else than in this lousy world!' Yes, Ficker could show the book to a professor if he liked, but showing a philosophical work to a professor of philosophy would be like casting pearls before swine – 'At any rate he won't understand a word of it':

And now, only *one* more request: Make it short and sweet with me. Tell me 'no' quickly, rather then too slowly; that is Austrian delicacy which my nerves are not strong enough to withstand, at the moment.

Alarmed by this note of despair, Ficker wired a telegram: 'Don't worry. Treatise will appear whatever the circumstances. Letter follows.' Much relieved, Wittgenstein replied that he would rather Ficker accepted the book because he considered it worth publishing than because he wanted to do a favour. He nevertheless seemed inclined to accept the offer: 'I think I can say that if you print Dallago, Haecker, etc., *then* you can also print *my* book.' The next letter he received, however, reinforced any doubts he may still have had. Ficker wrote that he was still hoping something would come of Rilke's attempt to find a publisher. But if not, so moved was he by the bitterness and distress evident in Wittgenstein's previous letter, he had decided – even if it meant risking everything he had – to see to the publication of Wittgenstein's work himself. Rather that than disappoint the trust Wittgenstein had placed in him. (By the way, he added, if it did come to that was it absolutely necessary to include the decimal numbers?)

This, obviously, would not do. 'I couldn't accept the responsibility', Wittgenstein wrote to him, 'of a person's (whoever's) livelihood being placed in jeopardy by publishing my book.' Ficker hadn't betrayed his trust:

> . . . for my trust, or rather, simply my hope, was only directed to your perspicacity that the treatise is not junk – unless I am deceiving myself – but not to the fact that you would accept it, without thinking something of it, just *out of kindness toward me and against your interests*.

And, yes, the decimals were absolutely necessary: 'because they alone give the book lucidity and clarity and it would be an incomprehensible jumble without them'. The book had to be published as it was, and for the reason that it was perceived to be worth publishing. Nothing else would do. If Rilke could somehow arrange that, he would be very pleased, but: 'if that isn't possible, we can just forget about it'.

It is difficult to know how much trouble Rilke went to on Wittgenstein's behalf. In a letter from Berne, dated 12 November 1919, he asks Ficker whether his own publisher, Insel-Verlag, might be suitable, and further suggests Otto Reichl, the publisher of Count Keyserling. Nothing came of either suggestion, and no further correspondence on the subject survives.

By this time Wittgenstein was sick to death of the whole business. 'Is there a *Krampus* who fetches evil publishers?' he asked Ficker; and on 16 November he wrote to Engelmann:

> Just how far I have gone downhill you can see from the fact that I have on several occasions contemplated taking my own life. Not from my despair about my own badness but for purely external reasons.

Wittgenstein's despair was alleviated to some extent when, in November, he left his lodgings in Untere Viaduktgasse and moved in with the Sjögren family at their home in St Veitgasse, in Vienna's

Thirteenth District. The Sjögrens were lifelong friends of the Wittgenstein family; the father, Arvid Sjögren, had been a director of a steelworks belonging to the Wittgenstein group, and the mother, Mima, now widowed, was a particularly close friend of Wittgenstein's sister Hermine. Mima was having problems bringing up her three sons alone, and it was thought by the Wittgenstein family that Wittgenstein, by acting as the man of the house, might be able to help her. If he refused to enjoy the benefits of living with his own family, perhaps he could be induced to share the responsibilities of caring for another. This, it was thought, might have a calming effect on him.

To a certain extent, it worked. Wittgenstein's time with the Sjögrens was, in the context of perhaps the most desperately unhappy year of his life, comparatively pleasant. 'Normal human beings are a balm to me', he wrote to Engelmann, 'and a torment at the same time.' With the middle son, Arvid, in particular, he formed a close friendship, and indeed became a sort of father figure to him. Arvid Sjögren was a big, clumsy, gruff boy – a 'bear of a man', he was later called – who continued to look to Wittgenstein for moral guidance throughout most of his life. Under Wittgenstein's influence he abandoned all thought of studying at university and trained instead as a mechanic. In this sense he was, perhaps, Wittgenstein's first disciple, the forerunner of the bright young undergraduates at Cambridge of the 1930s and 1940s who similarly chose to learn an honest trade rather than pursuing the kind of careers for which their education and privileged backgrounds had prepared them.

Throughout November Wittgenstein and Russell exchanged letters in connection with their proposed meeting at The Hague in December; there were dates to arrange, bureaucratic hurdles to overcome, and, in Wittgenstein's case at least, money to raise to finance the trip. 'It is terrible to think of your having to earn a living', Russell wrote to him, after hearing that he had given all his money away, 'but I am not surprised by your action. I am much poorer too. They say Holland is very expensive but I suppose we can endure a week of it without going bankrupt.' To pay Wittgenstein's expenses, Russell bought some furniture and books that Wittgenstein had left behind in a dealer's shop in Cambridge before his trip to Norway. It included the furniture he had chosen so painstakingly in the autumn of 1912. Russell paid £100; it was, he says in his autobiography, the best bargain he ever made.

Russell arrived at The Hague on 10 December, accompanied by his

new lover and future wife, Dora Black. They booked into the Hotal
Twee Steden. 'Come here as quick as you can after your arrival in The
Hague', Russell wrote to Wittgenstein; 'I am impatient to see you –
We will find some way to get your book published – in England if
necessary.' Wittgenstein arrived a few days later, accompanied by
Arvid Sjögren (remembered by Dora Russell as: 'a vague, shadowy
figure who spoke little, even at mealtimes'). For Russell and Wittgenstein, the week was taken up with intense discussion of Wittgenstein's
book. Wittgenstein was, Russell wrote to Colette on 12 December, 'so
full of logic that I can hardly get him to talk about anything personal'.
Wittgenstein didn't want to waste a moment of their time together.
He would rise early and hammer at Russell's door until he woke, and
then discuss logic without interruption for hours on end. They went
through the book line by line. The discussions were fruitful: Russell
came to think even more highly of the book than he had before, while
Wittgenstein had the euphoric feeling that, at last, somebody understood it.

Not that Russell agreed with it entirely. In particular, he refused to
accept Wittgenstein's view that any assertion about the world as a
whole was meaningless. To Russell, the proposition: 'There are at
least three things in the world' was both meaningful and true. During
discussion of this point Russell took a sheet of white paper and made
three blobs of ink on it: 'I besought him to admit that, since there were
these three blobs, there must be at least three things in the world; but
he refused resolutely':

> He would admit there were three blobs on the page, because that
> was a finite assertion, but he would not admit that anything at all
> could be said about the world as a whole.

'This part of his doctrine', Russell insisted, 'is to my mind definitely
mistaken.'

Related to this was Russell's refusal to accept what Wittgenstein had
earlier told him was the 'main contention' of the book: the doctrine
that what cannot be said by propositions *can* be shown. To Russell this
remained an unappealingly mystical notion. He was surprised, he
wrote to Ottoline, to find that Wittgenstein had become a complete
mystic. 'He has penetrated deep into mystical ways of thought and

feeling, but I think (though he wouldn't agree) that what he likes best in mysticism is its power to make him stop thinking.'

He was nonetheless sufficiently impressed by the Theory of Logic in the book to offer to write an introduction, based on their conversation at The Hague, which would attempt to explain the most difficult parts of the book. With an introduction by Russell, now a best-selling author, the publication of the book was almost guaranteed. Wittgenstein returned to Vienna in jubilant mood. 'I enjoyed our time together *very* much', he wrote to Russell on 8 January 1920, 'and I have the feeling (haven't you too?) that we did a great deal of real work during that week.' To Ficker, he wrote: 'The book is now a much smaller risk for a publisher, or perhaps even none at all, since Russell's name is very well known and ensures a quite special group of readers for the book':

> By this I naturally don't mean that it will thus come into the right hands; but at any rate, favourable circumstances are less excluded.

Ficker, who did not reply for over two weeks, was evidently still not convinced that the book would be anything other than a financial liability. 'With or without Russell', he wrote on 16 January, 'the publication of your treatise is, under the present circumstances, a risk that *no* publisher in Austria today can afford to take.' He advised Wittgenstein to have the book published in English first and then – if the opportunity arose – in German.

Anticipating he would have no success with Ficker, Wittgenstein had already made appoaches to another publisher. Through Engelmann, he obtained a recommendation from a Dr Heller to the Leipzig publishing house, Reclam, who, after learning of Russell's introduction, were only too willing to consider the book.

Wittgenstein at once took the manuscript from Ficker and sent it to Reclam, and throughout February and March waited impatiently for Russell's introduction to arrive. When it did, he was immediately disappointed. 'There's so much of it that I'm not in agreement with', he told Russell, 'both where you're critical of me and also where you're simply trying to elucidate my point of view.' He nevertheless had it translated into German, in preparation for its printing, but this only made matters worse: 'All the refinement of your English style', he wrote to Russell, 'was, obviously, lost in the translation and what remained was superficiality and misunderstanding.' He sent the introduction to Reclam but told them it was not for publication; it was to serve only for the publisher's own orientation with regard to the work. As a consequence Reclam, as Wittgenstein had anticipated, rejected the book. He comforted himself with the following argument, which, he told Russell, 'seems to me unanswerable':

> Either my piece is a work of the highest rank, or it is not a work of the highest rank. In the latter (and more probable) case I myself am in favour of it not being printed. And in the former case it's a matter of indifference whether it's printed twenty or a hundred years sooner or later. After all, who asks whether the Critique of Pure Reason, for example, was written in 17x or y.

Russell was at this time visiting Soviet Russia with a Labour Party delegation, and did not see Wittgenstein's letter until his return in June. He reacted with remarkable generosity. 'I don't care twopence about the introduction, but I shall be really sorry if your book isn't printed. May I try, in that case, to have it printed in England?' Yes, Wittgenstein replied, '*you can do what you like with it*'. He himself had given up trying: 'But if you feel like getting it printed, it is entirely at your disposal.'

The comforting argument he had earlier offered Russell did not prevent Wittgenstein from sinking into a deep depression after Reclam's rejection. At the end of May he wrote to Engelmann: 'I have continually thought of taking my own life, and the idea still haunts me sometimes. *I have sunk to the lowest point.* May you never be in that position! Shall I ever be able to raise myself up again? Well, we shall see.'

He was, by this time, living on his own again. At the beginning of April he moved out of the Sjögrens' home and into lodgings once more, this time in Rasumofskygasse, which, like his earlier lodgings, was in Vienna's Third District. 'This change of home was accompanied by operations which I can never remember without a sinking feeling', he told Engelmann. In fact, he fled the house after it became apparent that Mrs Sjögren was in love with him.*

---

* So it was believed, anyway, by certain members of the Sjögren and Wittgenstein families, who (according to Brian McGuinness, op. cit. p. 285) thereafter avoided inviting Mima and Wittgenstein to the same occasions.

Wittgenstein's letters to Russell, and especially to Engelmann, during this period, show him to be desperately, suicidally, depressed. The severity of self-accusation contained in them is extreme even for Wittgenstein, who was always harsh on himself. He attributes his miserableness to his own 'baseness and rottenness', and talks of being afraid that: 'the devil will come and take me one day'.*

For both Wittgenstein and Engelmann, religion was inseparable from an awareness of one's own failings. Indeed, for Engelmann, such awareness was central to the religious outlook:

> If I am unhappy and know that my unhappiness reflects a gross discrepancy between myself and life as it is, I solved nothing; I shall be on the wrong track and I shall never find a way out of the chaos of my emotions and thoughts so long as I have not achieved the supreme and crucial insight that that discrepancy is not the fault of life as it is, but of myself as I am . . .
>
> The person who has achieved this insight and holds on to it, and who will try again and again to live up to it, is religious.

On this view, to be unhappy *is* to find fault with oneself: one's misery can only be the consequence of one's own 'baseness and rottenness'; to be religious is to recognize one's own unworthiness and to take responsibility for correcting it.

This was a theme that dominated the conversations and the correspondence between Wittgenstein and Engelmann, as, for example, in the set of remarks on religion that Engelmann sent Wittgenstein in January:

> Before Christ, people experienced God (or Gods) as something outside themselves.
>
> Since Christ, people (not all, but those who have learnt to see through him) see God as something in themselves. So that one can say that, through Christ, God has been drawn into mankind . . .

---

*Since the publication of Bartley's book it has become natural to interpret these self-admonitions as being in some way connected with the alleged 'Prater episodes'. If there is any connection, however, Engelmann himself was unaware of it. In a diary entry written after Wittgenstein's death, he remarks that he is often asked about Wittgenstein's homosexuality, but can say nothing about it – he and Wittgenstein did not discuss such things.

. . . Through Christ God has become man.

Lucifer *wanted* to become God and was not.

Christ *became* God without wanting to.

So the wicked thing is to *want* pleasure without deserving it.

If, however, one *does* right, without wanting pleasure, so joy comes of its own accord.

When Wittgenstein came to comment on these remarks, he did not dispute the truth of them, but only the adequacy of their expression. 'They are still not clear enough', he wrote. 'It must be possible, I believe, to say all these things much more adequately. (Or, not at all, which is even more likely).' Even if their most perfect expression should turn out to be silence, then, they are nonetheless true.

Wittgenstein regarded Engelmann as 'someone who understands man'. When, after the attempt to be published by Reclam had come to nothing, he was feeling emotionally and spiritually demoralized, he felt an urgent need to talk with him. And when, at the end of May, he reached his 'lowest point' and continually thought of suicide, it was to Engelmann he turned for support. He received it in the form of a long letter about Engelmann's own experience. Engelmann wrote that he had recently been worried about his motives for his own work – whether they were decent and honest motives. He had taken some time off to be alone in the countryside, to think about it. The first few days were unsatisfactory:

> But then I did something about which I can tell *you*, because you know me well enough not to regard it as a piece of stupidity. That is, I took down a kind of 'confession', in which I tried to recall the series of events in my life, in as much detail as is possible in the space of an hour. With each event I tried to make clear to myself how I should have behaved. By means of such a general over-view [*Übersicht*] the confused picture was much simplified.
>
> The next day, on the basis of this newly-gained insight, I revised my plans and intentions for the future.

'I don't know at all', he wrote, 'whether something similar would be good or necessary for you now; but perhaps my telling you this would help you now to find something.'

'Concerning what you write about thoughts of suicide,' Engelmann added, 'my thoughts are as follows':

Behind such thoughts, just as in others, there can probably lie something of a noble motive. But that this motive shows itself in *this* way, that it takes the form of a contemplation of suicide, is certainly wrong. Suicide is certainly a mistake. So long as a person lives, he is never completely lost. What drives a man to suicide is, however, the fear that he is completely lost. This fear is, in view of what has already been said, ungrounded. In this fear a person does the worst thing he can do, he deprives himself of the time in which it would be possible for him to escape being lost.

'You undoubtedly know all this better than I', wrote Engelmann, excusing himself for appearing to have something to teach Wittgenstein, 'but one sometimes forgets what one knows.'

Wittgenstein himself was later to use, more than once, the technique of preparing a confession in order to clarify his own life. On this occasion, however, it was not the advice that did him good, but simply reading about Engelmann's own efforts. 'Many thanks for your kind letter', he wrote on 21 June, 'which has given me much pleasure and thereby perhaps helped me a little, although as far as the merits of my case are concerned I am beyond any outside help':

In fact I am in a state of mind that is terrible to me. I have been through it several times before: it is the state of *not being able to get over a particular fact*. It is a pitiable state, I know. But there is only one remedy that I can see, and that is of course to come to terms with that fact. But this is just like what happens when a man who can't swim has fallen into the water and flails about with his hands and feet and feels that he *cannot* keep his head above water. That is the position I am in now. I know that to kill oneself is always a dirty thing to do. Surely one *cannot* will one's own destruction, and anybody who has visualized what is in practice involved in the act of suicide knows that suicide is always a *rushing of one's own defences*. But nothing is worse than to be forced to take oneself by surprise. Of course it all boils down to the fact that I have no faith!

Unfortunately, there is no possible way of knowing what fact he is here talking about. Certainly, it is some fact about himself, and something for which he felt the only remedy to be religious faith.

Without such faith, his life was unendurable. He was in the position of wishing himself dead, but unable to bring himself to suicide. As he put it to Russell: 'The best for me, perhaps, would be if I could lie down one evening and not wake up again.'

'But perhaps there is something better left for me', he added parenthetically. The letter was written on 7 July, the day he received his teaching certificate: perhaps in teaching, it is implied, he would find something worth living for.

Wittgenstein had completed his course at the Lehrerbildungsanhalt satisfactorily, but not without misgivings. The best thing about it, he told Engelmann, was that on teaching practice he was able to read fairy-tales to the children: 'It pleases them and relieves the strain on me.' It was the 'one good thing in my life just now'.

He received help and encouragement from his friend from the prisoner-of-war camp, Ludwig Hänsel, himself a teacher, and a figure well known in Viennese educational circles. On at least one occasion he considered giving the course up, because, he told Hänsel, of the bad relations between himself and his fellow men. Hänsel, perceptively, attributed this to Wittgenstein's chronic sensitivity. 'There is no wall between you and your fellow men', he wrote. 'I have a thicker crust around me.'

At the Lehrerbildungsanhalt Wittgenstein would have been taught in accordance with the principles of the School Reform Movement, which was, under the leadership of the education minister, Otto Glöckel, attempting to reshape the education of the new, post-war, republic of Austria. It was a movement fired with secular, republican and socialist ideals, and it had attracted the good will, and even the participation, of a good number of well known Austrian intellectuals. It was not, however, a movement with which Wittgenstein himself could readily identify. It was not the idea of fitting pupils to live in a democracy that had inspired him to become a teacher, such social and political motives being alien to the fundamentally religious morality that he shared with Engelmann.

Hänsel, too, was a religious man, and for that very reason at odds with the School Reform Movement. He was to become a leading light in a Conservative-Catholic organization called *Der Bund Neuland*, which sought to reform education while maintaining, and indeed increasing, the influence of the Catholic Church. Wittgenstein no more identified himself with this movement, however, than he did with the Glöckel programme. In the struggle between clericals and socialists that dominated the public life of post-war Austria, Wittgenstein occupied an ambivalent position. He shared with the socialists a dislike of the Catholic establishment and a general egalitarianism, while firmly rejecting their secularism and their faith in social and political change. In the politically turbulent and increasingly polarized world of the 1920s, however, such ambivalence and aloofness would always be liable to be misunderstood: to conservative clericals, his contempt for convention was sufficient to establish him as a socialist; to socialists, on the other hand, his individualism and fundamentally religious outlook identified him as a clerical reactionary.

Wittgenstein, then, was trained within the Glöckel programme while distancing himself from some of its objectives. He felt sufficiently uncertain of his standing at the college to ask Hänsel what he had heard said of him by the lecturers there. The entire faculty, Hänsel reported, were united in their praise of him; he was regarded as a serious, capable student-teacher, who knew just what he was doing. The teachers of all his classes – educational theory, natural history, handwriting and music – were all pleased with his work. 'The professor of psychology said with great self-satisfaction that he was very pleased with the noble Lord Wittgenstein.'

Throughout his year as a student-teacher Wittgenstein saw Hänsel regularly, sometimes in the company of their fellow prisoner of war, Michael Drobil. With Hänsel he discussed not only educational matters, but also philosophy. As a learned *Hofrat Direktor*, Hänsel maintained a keen interest in the subject, and in his lifetime published some twenty articles on philosophical subjects (mostly ethics). In a letter of 23 May we find him providing Wittgenstein with a summary of the three kinds of object (actual, ideal and real) distinguished by the 'Critical Realist' O. Külpe, in his book *Die Realisierung*. What, precisely, Wittgenstein's interest in this might have been must remain a mystery, since Külpe is nowhere referred to again. However, further evidence of Wittgenstein's preoccupation at this time with the competing metaphysics of idealism and realism is provided by a letter from Frege – the last Frege is known to have written to Wittgenstein – dated 3 April.

Frege was evidently responding to criticisms Wittgenstein had made of his essay 'The Thought', in which Wittgenstein had spoken of 'deep grounds' for idealism. 'Of course I don't take exception to your frankness', Frege began:

> But I would like to know what deep grounds for idealism you think I have not grasped. I take it that you yourself do not hold the idealist theory of knowledge to be true. So, I think, you recognise that there can, after all, be no deep grounds for this idealism. The grounds for it can then only be apparent grounds, not logical ones.

The rest of this long letter is taken up with an analysis by Frege of the lack of clarity of the *Tractatus*. This time he concentrates solely on the first proposition: 'The world is everything that is the case.' Assuming, he argues, that the 'is' in this statement is the 'is of identity', and further assuming that it is meant to convey information and not simply to provide a definition of 'the world', then, in order for it to mean anything, there must be some way of identifying the sense of 'the world' and that of the phrase 'everything that is the case' *independently* of the statement of their identity. How is this to be done? 'I would be glad', he wrote, 'if you, by answering my questions, could facilitate my understanding of the results of your thinking.'

This is the last preserved communication between the two. Frege died four years later, presumably no nearer to understanding a word of the famous book inspired by his own work. The 'deep grounds' for idealism which Wittgenstein perceived are undoubtedly connected with the account of the world which he gives in propositions 5.6– 5.641 of the *Tractatus*. 'The world is *my* world', 'I am my world. (The microcosm.)', and yet I am not *in* my world: 'The subject does not belong to the world; rather it is a limit of the world.' Thus, solipsism, 'when its implications are followed out strictly', coincides with pure realism: 'The self of solipsism shrinks to a point without extension, and there remains the reality co-ordinated with it.' The realism of Frege is thus seen to coincide with the idealism of Schopenhauer and the solipsism of Weininger.

It is a view that gives a philosophical underpinning to the religious individualism adopted by Wittgenstein and Engelmann. I *am* my world, so if I am unhappy about the world, the *only* way in which I can do anything decisive about it is to change myself. 'The world of the happy man is a different one from that of the unhappy man.'

Nevertheless, in a sense Frege was right to find the metaphysics of this view unintelligible. On Wittgenstein's own theory, its expression in words can lead only to nonsense. And yet, though he was unable to explain it to Frege, unable to convince Russell of its truth, and unable to find a publisher for its expression as the outcome of a Theory of Logical Symbolism, Wittgenstein remained firmly convinced of its unassailability. Though he had suffered greatly from 'external' causes in the last year – the death of Pinsent, the defeat of the Habsburg Empire, the problems of publishing his book – he looked only to an 'internal' solution. What, in the final analysis, did it matter if his book remained unpublished? By far the most important thing was to 'settle accounts with himself'.

Thus in the summer, after completing his training as a teacher and after abandoning his book to Russell, he concentrated on what was, to him, the most immediate task: the struggle to overcome his own unhappiness, to combat the 'devils within' that pulled him away from the 'world of the happy man'. To this end he spent the summer working as a gardener at the Klosterneuburg Monastery, just outside Vienna. Working solidly the whole day through seemed to act as a kind of therapy. 'In the evening when the work is done,' he told Engelmann, 'I am tired, and then I do not feel unhappy.' It was a job to which he could bring his customary competence with practical, manual tasks. One day the Abbot of the monastery passed him while he was at work and commented: 'So I see that intelligence counts for something in gardening too.'

However, the therapy was only partially successful. 'External' causes of suffering continued to confine Wittgenstein to the 'world of the unhappy man'. 'Every day I think of Pinsent', he wrote to Russell in August. 'He took half my life away with him. The devil will take the other half.' As the summer vacation drew to an end, and his new life as a primary school teacher beckoned, he had, he told Engelmann, 'grim forebodings' about his future life:

For unless all the devils in hell pull the other way, my life is bound to become very sad if not impossible.

9

'AN ENTIRELY '
RURAL AFFAIR'

Though not inspired with the reforming zeal of the adherents to Glöckel's programme, Wittgenstein entered the teaching profession with a still more idealistic set of intentions, and a rather romantic, Tolstoyan conception of what it would be like to live and work among the rural poor.

In keeping with his general ethical *Weltanschauung*, he sought, not to improve their external conditions, but to better them 'internally'. He wanted to develop their intellects by teaching them mathematics, to extend their cultural awareness by introducing them to the great classics of the German language, and to improve their souls by reading the Bible with them. It was not his aim to take them away from their poverty; nor did he see education as a means to equip them for a 'better' life in the city. He wanted, rather, to impress upon them the value of intellectual attainment for its own sake – just as, conversely, he would later impress upon Cambridge undergraduates the inherent value of manual work.

The ideal that emerges from his teaching, whether in the Austrian countryside or at Cambridge University, is a Ruskinian one of honest toil combined with a refined intelligence, a deep cultural appreciation and a devout seriousness; a meagre income, but a rich inner life.

It was important to him to work in an area of rural poverty. However, as was customary for graduates of the Lehrerbildungsanhalt, he was sent to do his probationary teaching year at a school in Maria Schultz am Semmering, a small, pleasant and relatively prosperous town, famous as a pilgrim centre, in the countryside south of Vienna. After a brief inspection of the place, he decided it would not do. He explained to the astonished headmaster that he had noticed the town had a park with a fountain: 'That is not for me, I want an entirely rural affair.' In that case, the headmaster suggested, he should go to Trattenbach, a village the other side of the neighbouring hills. Wittgenstein at once set off on the ninety-minute hike and found, much to his delight, exactly the sort of place he had in mind.

Trattenbach was small and poor. Those of its villagers who had jobs were employed either at the local textile factory or on the neighbouring farms. Life for these villagers was difficult, especially in the deprived years of the 1920s. Wittgenstein was, however (initially, at any rate), enchanted with the place. Soon after his arrival he wrote to Russell, who was then in China at the start of his year's visiting lectureship at the University of Peking, giving his address proudly as 'LW Schoolmaster Trattenbach', and revelling in the obscurity of his new position:

> I am to be an elementary-school teacher in a tiny village called Trattenbach. It's in the mountains, about four hours' journey south of Vienna. It must be the first time that the schoolmaster at Trattenbach has ever corresponded with a professor in Peking.

To Engelmann, a month later, he was even more enthusiastic. He described Trattenbach as 'a beautiful and tiny place' and reported himself to be 'happy in my work at school'. But, he added darkly, 'I do need it badly, or else all the devils in hell break loose inside me.'

His letters to Hänsel during these first few months are written in a similarly cheerful spirit. He relied upon Hänsel to supply him with reading books for his pupils, and would send him requests to order multiple copies of, for example, Grimm's stories, *Gulliver's Travels*, Lessing's fables and Tolstoy's legends. Hänsel visited him regularly at the weekends, as did Arvid Sjögren, Moritz Nähe (the Wittgenstein family photographer) and Michael Drobil. These visits tended, however, to emphasize the already obvious differences between Wittgenstein and the villagers, including his own colleagues, and it was not long before he became the subject of rumour and speculation. One of his colleagues, Georg Berger, once came across Wittgenstein and Hänsel sitting together in the school office. Wittgenstein immediately demanded to know what was being said about him in the village.

Berger hesitated, but on being pressed told Wittgenstein: 'the villagers take you to be a rich baron'.

Berger omitted to use the word, but it was certainly as an *eccentric* aristocrat that Wittgenstein was regarded. '*Fremd*' (strange) was the word most often used by the villagers to describe him. Why, they asked, should a man of such wealth and culture choose to live among the poor, especially when he showed such little sympathy for their way of life and clearly preferred the company of his refined Viennese friends? Why should he live such a meagre existence?

At first Wittgenstein had lodged in a small room in the local guest-house, 'Zum braunen Hirschen', but he quickly found the noise of the dance music coming from below too much for him, and left. He then made a bed for himself in the school kitchen. There, according to Berger (who was, one suspects, one of the chief sources of the stories told by the villagers about Wittgenstein), he would sit for hours by the kitchen window, watching the stars.

He soon established himself as an energetic, enthusiastic but rather strict schoolmaster. In many ways, as his sister Hermine writes, he was a born teacher:

> He is interested in everything himself and he knows how to pick the most important aspects of anything and make them clear to others. I myself had the opportunity of watching Ludwig teach on a number of occasions, as he devoted some afternoons to the boys in my occupational school. It was a marvellous treat for all of us. He did not simply lecture, but tried to lead the boys to the correct solution by means of questions. On one occasion he had them inventing a steam engine, on another designing a tower on the blackboard, and on yet another depicting moving human figures. The interest which he aroused was enormous. Even the ungifted and usually inattentive among the boys came up with astonishingly good answers, and they were positively climbing over each other in their eagerness to be given a chance to answer or to demonstrate a point.

Despite his misgivings about the School Reform Movement, it was among the reformers, such as Putre and Wilhelm Kundt, the District School Superintendent, that Wittgenstein found most encouragement and support during his career as a teacher. His teaching methods shared some of the basic principles of the Reform Movement, the most important of which was that a child should not be taught simply to repeat what it has been told, but should instead be encouraged to think through problems for itself. Thus practical exercises played a large part in his teaching. The children were taught anatomy by assembling the skeleton of a cat, astronomy by gazing at the sky at night, botany by identifying plants on walks in the countryside, architecture by identifying building styles during an excursion to Vienna. And so on. With everything he taught, Wittgenstein attempted to arouse in the children the same curiosity and questioning spirit that he himself brought to everything in which he took an interest.

This naturally worked better with some children than with others. Wittgenstein achieved especially good results with some of the boys that he taught, and with a select group of his favourite pupils, mainly boys, he gave extra tuition outside school hours. To these children, he became a sort of father figure.

However, to those children who were not gifted, or whose interest failed to be aroused by his enthusiasm, he became not a figure of fatherly kindness, but a tyrant. The emphasis he placed on the teaching of mathematics led him to devote the first two hours of each morning to the subject. He believed that it was never too early to begin algebra, and taught mathematics at a far higher level than was expected of his age group. For some of his pupils, the girls especially, the first two hours of the day were remembered with horror for years afterwards. One of them, Anna Brenner, recalls:

During the arithmetic lesson we that had algebra had to sit in the first row. My friend Anna Völkerer and I one day decided not to give any answers. Wittgenstein asked: 'What do you have?' To the question what is three times six Anna said: 'I don't know.' He asked me how many metres there were in a kilometre. I said nothing and received a box on my ears. Later Wittgenstein said: 'If you don't know I'll take a child from the youngest class in the school who will know.' After the lesson Wittgenstein took me into the office and asked: 'Is it that you don't want to [do arithmetic] or is it that you can't?' I said 'Yes, I want to.' Wittgenstein said to me: 'You are a good student, but as for arithmetic . . . Or are you ill? Do you have a headache?' Then I lied, 'Yes!' 'Then', said Wittgenstein, 'please,

please Brenner, can you forgive me?' While he said this he held up
his hands in prayer. I immediately felt my lie to be a great disgrace.

As this account illustrates, one respect in which Wittgenstein's
methods differed sharply from those recommended by Glöckel's
reforms was in his use of corporal punishment. Another girl who was
weak at mathematics remembers that one day Wittgenstein pulled her
hair so hard that when she later combed it a lot of it fell out. The
reminiscences of his former pupils abound with stories of the
'*Ohrfeige*' (ear-boxing) and '*Haareziehen*' (hair-pulling) they received
at his hands.

As news of this brutality reached the children's parents it contributed to a growing feeling against him. It was not that the villagers
disapproved of corporal punishment, nor that such methods of discipline were at all unusual, despite Glöckel's recommendations.
However, though it was accepted that an unruly boy should have his
ears boxed if he misbehaved, it was not expected that a girl who could
not grasp algebra should receive the same treatment. Indeed, it was
not expected that she *should* grasp algebra.

The villagers (including some of his own colleagues) were, in any
case, disposed to take a dislike to this aristocratic and eccentric
stranger, whose odd behaviour sometimes amused and sometimes
alarmed them. Anecdotes about his *Fremdheit* were told and retold,
until he became a kind of village legend. There is the story, for
example, of how he once got together with two of his colleagues to
play a Mozart trio – himself on clarinet, Georg Berger playing the
viola part on a violin and the headmaster, Rupert Köllner, playing the
piano part. Berger recalls:

Again and again we had to start from the beginning, Wittgenstein
not tiring at all. Finally we were given a break! The headmaster,
Rupert Köllner, and I were then so unintentionally inconsiderate as
to play by heart some dance tune. Wittgenstein reacted angrily:
'*Krautsalat! Krautsalat!*' he cried. He then packed up and went.

Another story concerns the time he attended a catechism at the local
Catholic Church. He listened carefully to the questions put to the
children by the priest, with the Dean in attendance, and then said
suddenly, and very audibly: 'Nonsense!'

But the greatest wonder – and the story for which he was most remembered by the village – concerns the time he repaired the steam engine in the local factory, using an apparently miraculous method. The story is told here by Frau Bichlmayer, the wife of one of Wittgenstein's colleagues, who herself worked at the factory:

> I was in the office when the engine went dead and the factory had to stand idle. In those days we were dependent on steam. And then a lot of engineers came, who couldn't get it to go. Back at home I told my husband what had happened and my husband then told the story in the school office and the teacher Wittgenstein said to him: 'Could I see it, could you obtain permission for me to take a look at it?' Then my husband spoke to the director who said yes, he could come straight away . . . so then he came with my husband and went straight down into the engine room and walked around, saying nothing, just looking around. And then he said: 'Can I have four men?' The director said: yes, and four came, two locksmiths and two others. Each had to take a hammer and then Wittgenstein gave each of the men a number and a different place. As I called they had to hammer their particular spot in sequence: one, four, three, two . . .
>
> In this way they cured the machine of its fault.

For this 'miracle' Wittgenstein was rewarded with some linen, which he at first refused, and then accepted on behalf of the poorer children in his school.

The villagers' gratitude for this miracle, however, did not outweigh their growing mistrust of his *Fremdheit*, and throughout the autumn term relations between him and them gradually deteriorated. During this term his sister Hermine kept a watchful and motherly eye on the progress of his new career. She had to do this indirectly, through Hänsel, because, while Wittgenstein welcomed visits from his Viennese friends, his family were under strict instructions not to see him or to offer him any help. Food parcels were returned unopened, and letters left unanswered.

Hänsel was able to reassure Hermine that, though under some strain, Wittgenstein had got through the first term reasonably well. On 13 December, she wrote to him with obvious relief:

I am indeed very grateful to you for your kind letter. Firstly it reassured me about the anguish Ludwig has endured through the Trattenbachers and their curiosity; his letters of that time give a very encouraging impression and with his laconic way of writing they are doubly reassuring. Secondly, I greatly appreciate everything you say about my brother, although it is, in fact, nothing other than what I myself think. Of course, it is true what you say, though it is not easy having a saint for a brother, and after the English expression: 'I had rather be a live dog than a dead philosopher' I would like to add: I would (often) rather have a happy *person* for a brother than an unhappy *saint*.

Ironically, just a few weeks after this letter, on 2 January 1921, Wittgenstein wrote to Engelmann berating himself for not having chosen the heavenly course:

I was sorry not to have seen you at Christmas. It struck me as rather funny that you should want to hide from *me*, for the following reason: I have been morally dead for more than a year! From that you can judge for yourself whether I am fine or not. I am one of those cases which perhaps are not all that rare today: I had a task, did not do it, and now the failure is wrecking my life. I ought to have done something positive with my life, to have become a star in the sky. Instead of which I remained stuck on earth, and now I am gradually fading out. My life has really become meaningless and so it consists only of futile episodes. The people around me do not notice this and would not understand; but I know that I have a fundamental deficiency. Be glad of it, if you don't understand what I am writing here.

In the event, Engelmann did not understand. If Wittgenstein felt he had an unfinished task to accomplish, he replied, why did he not do it now – or at least at some future time when he was ready to do so? Furthermore, it was surely wrong for him to talk of a *fundamental* deficiency; as they had discussed before, no one is so lost that their position is irrevocable. This time, however, Engelmann's letter struck the wrong note. 'I cannot at present analyse my state in a letter', Wittgenstein wrote to him. 'I don't think – by the way – that you quite understand it . . . a visit from you would not suit me in the near future. Just now we would hardly know what to do with one another.'

For the time being, at least, Engelmann's place as the person to whom Wittgenstein turned for an understanding of his inner life had been taken by Hänsel. In his memoir of Wittgenstein, Hänsel writes: 'One night, while he was a teacher, he had the feeling that he had been called but had refused.' This perhaps explains Wittgenstein's mention to Engelmann of a task, the fulfilment of which would have brought him to the heavens, but the neglect of which condemned him to remain earth-bound.*

---

* This connects also with a dream quoted by Bartley (from where we do not know), which he says came to Wittgenstein 'possibly in early December 1920'. The dream is as follows:

> I was a priest. In the front hall of my house there was an altar; to the right of the altar a stairway led off. It was a grand stairway carpeted in red, rather like that at the Alleegasse. At the foot of the altar, and partly covering it, was an oriental carpet. And certain other religious objects and regalia were placed on and beside the altar. One of these was a rod of precious metal.
>
> But a theft had occurred. A thief entered from the left and stole the rod. This had to be reported to the police, who sent a representative who wanted a description of the rod. For instance, of what sort of metal was it made? I could not say; I could not even say whether it was of silver or of gold. The police officer questioned whether the rod had ever existed in the first place. I then began to examine the other parts and fittings of the altar and noticed that the carpet was a prayer rug. My eyes began to focus on the border of the rug. The border was lighter in colour than the beautiful centre. In a curious way it seemed to be faded. It was, nonetheless, still strong and firm.

This is the part of Bartley's book that most strongly indicates that in writing it he had access to a manuscript of Wittgenstein's. Bartley not only quotes the dream as though it were described by Wittgenstein himself; he also gives interpretations of it suggested by both Wittgenstein and 'some other party, possibly Hänsel'. Furthermore, unlike the 'Prater episodes', Bartley's information – the content of the dream, its timing, and even the interpretations given of it by Hänsel and Wittgenstein – connects plausibly with information from other sources. Bartley even gives us Wittgenstein's reaction to Hänsel's interpretation (which connects the symbolism of the dream to images taken from the Old Testament):

> It puzzled Wittgenstein to think that *if* such an interpretation were to be attached to the dream, it would be *his* dream.

This reaction, too, is very plausible. According to Bartley, Wittgenstein himself was inclined to interpret the dream in alchemical terms. The rod is at once a phallic symbol (his 'base self') and a symbol of alchemical transformation (the base metal

Or, to be more specific, stuck in Trattenbach. During the spring and summer terms of 1921 Wittgenstein's earlier delight with Trattenbach gradually turned to disgust, as his attempts to educate the village children above the customary expectations met with increasing misunderstanding and resistance from the parents, from the children themselves (those of them who felt unable to meet Wittgenstein's high expectations) and from his own colleagues.

In March he received from Russell a reply to his enthusiastic letter of September. 'I wonder how you like being an elementary schoolteacher', Russell wrote, 'and how you get on with the boys':

It is honest work, perhaps as honest as there is, and everybody now a-days is engaged in some form of humbug, which you escape from.

Russell himself was in good humour, enjoying Peking, and revelling in the occasional affront he caused to (British) conventional morality by openly living 'in sin' with Dora Black. 'I like China and the Chinese', he told Wittgenstein:

They are lazy, good-natured, fond of laughter, very like nice children – They are very kind and nice to me – All the nations set upon them and say they mustn't be allowed to enjoy life in their own way – They will be forced to develop an army and navy, to dig up their coal and smelt their iron, whereas what they want to do is to make verses and paint pictures (very beautiful) and make strange music, exquisite but almost inaudible, on many stringed instruments with green tassels. Miss Black and I live in a Chinese house, built around a courtyard, I send you a picture of me at the

---

changing into gold or silver), a transformation of which Wittgenstein is unable to convince his conscience, represented by the doubting police.

Thus, if we may be allowed to conflate Wittgenstein's letter to Engelmann, Hänsel's reminiscence and the dream quoted by Bartley, we arrive at a convincing account of the profound change in his temperamental state that is evident during the Christmas holiday period of 1921. Because he could not convince himself that the transformation in himself that he so desired could actually take place, he refused to follow what he regarded as a call to become a priest. The refusal could be explained only by a 'fundamental deficiency', for otherwise the longed-for transformation would surely be possible. He really *was* base metal; he *had* to remain stuck on earth.

door of my study. My students are all Bolsheviks, because that is the fashion. They are amazed with me for not being more of a Bolshevik myself. They are not advanced enough for mathematical logic. I lecture to them on Psychology, Philosophy, Politics and Einstein. Once in a while I have them to an evening party and they set off fire-works in the courtyard. They like this better than lectures.

Wittgenstein at once let Russell know that his earlier enchantment with Trattenbach had given way to disgust for its inhabitants. 'I am sorry you find the people in your neighbourhood so disagreeable', Russell replied. 'I don't think average human nature is up to much anywhere, and I dare say wherever you were you would find your neighbours equally obnoxious.' No, insisted Wittgenstein, 'here they are much more good-for-nothing and irresponsible than elsewhere'. Russell remained unconvinced:

> I am very sorry you find the people of Trattenbach so trying. But I refuse to believe they are worse than the rest of the human race: my logical instinct revolts against the notion.

'You are right', Wittgenstein at last conceded; 'the Trattenbachers are not uniquely worse than the rest of the human race':

> But Trattenbach is a particularly insignificant place in Austria and the *Austrians* have sunk so miserably low since the war that it's too dismal to talk about. That's what it is.

Russell had told Wittgenstein that he had left the manuscript of the *Tractatus* in England with Dorothy Wrinch, a friend of his, 'a good mathematician and a student of mathematical logic', with instructions to try and get it printed. 'I am determined to get your manuscript published', he affirmed, 'and if it has not been achieved during my absence, I will take the matter in hand as soon as I return.'

Apart from this encouraging news, the one bright spot in Wittgenstein's life during the summer term of 1921 was his relationship with one of his pupils, a boy from one of the poorest families in the village, called Karl Gruber. Gruber was a gifted boy who responded well to Wittgenstein's methods. Like many of Wittgenstein's pupils, he initially found algebra difficult. 'I could not grasp', he recalled later, 'how one could calculate using letters of the alphabet.' However, after receiving from Wittgenstein a box on the ears, he began to knuckle down: 'Soon I was the best at algebra in the class.' At the end of the summer term, he was due to leave the school and start work at the local factory. Wittgenstein was determined to do all he could to continue the boy's education. On 5 July he wrote to Hänsel explaining Gruber's position and asking for advice. Given that his parents could not afford to send him to a boarding school, what could be done? Might a free or a cheap place be found for him in one of the middle schools in Vienna? 'It would in my opinion', he wrote, 'be a great pity for the lad if he could not develop himself further.' Hänsel replied suggesting the possibility of the Calasanzverein, a Catholic establishment in Vienna which took on poor students. In the meantime, however, it was decided that Wittgenstein himself should continue to give the boy lessons, even after he had left the school, and that Hänsel should act as his occasional examiner, testing him to see that he reached the standard required to enter one of the Gymnasiums in Vienna.

In the summer vacation Wittgenstein travelled to Norway with Arvid Sjögren. It was the first time he had been there since 1914, and during the visit he was finally able to see the house that had been built for him in his absence. They left with very little money, and had to spend a night *en route* in a Salvation Army hostel in Hamburg. It was, as he explained in a letter to Hänsel, a working holiday: 'I work from early in the morning until the evening in a kind of carpentry workshop and together with Arvid make crates. In that way I earn myself a heap of money.' As ever, though, the reward he sought for his hard work was peace of mind. 'I think it is very good that I made this journey', he told Hänsel.

Shortly after his return to Trattenbach, Wittgenstein learnt from Russell that his book, finally, was to be published. Russell had returned from China with Dora Black in August, the latter six months pregnant, and his first two months back in England were taken up with arrangements to secure the legitimacy of his child. In China he had been in boat-burning mood, writing to Trinity to resign from the lectureship he had been offered ('because', he later said, 'I was living in open sin') and arranging a divorce from his wife, Alys. But the imminent arrival of a possible heir to the earldom impelled him to take steps towards respectability. He received his decree absolute from Alys on 21 September, married Dora six days later, and the baby, John Conrad, the future 4th Earl Russell, was born on 16 November.

Having taken the necessary steps to ensure that his son would inherit his title, Russell was able to turn his attention to arranging the publication of Wittgenstein's book. Through his friend C. K. Ogden he secured its publication in English in a series of monographs produced by Kegan Paul called The International Library of Psychology, Philosophy and Scientific Method, of which Ogden had recently been made editor. The book was still perceived as a financial liability, but a tolerable one. 'As they can't drop less than £50 on doing it I think it very satisfactory to have got it accepted', Ogden wrote to Russell on 5 November, 'though of course if they did a second edition soon and the price of printing went suddenly down they might get their costs back.'

Independently of these negotiations, Russell's friend Dorothy Wrinch had, while Russell was still in China, secured the book's acceptance in a German periodical called *Annalen der Naturphilosophie*, edited by Wilhelm Ostwald. Russell, knowing how Wittgenstein felt about the piece in its German translation, had left his introduction to the book with Miss Wrinch on the assumption that she would try English publishers. However, after having it rejected by Cambridge University Press, Miss Wrinch – considering, no doubt correctly, that this was her only chance of success – had approached the editors of three German periodicals. Only from Ostwald had she received a positive reply, and then only because of Russell's introduction. 'In any other case I should have declined to accept the article', Ostwald wrote to her on 21 February:

> But I have such an extremely high regard for Mr Bertrand Russell, both for his researches and for his personality, that I will gladly publish Mr Wittgenstein's article in my *Annalen der Naturphilosophie*: Mr Bertrand Russell's Introduction will be particularly welcome.

On 5 November, having received the proofs from Ostwald and a promise from Ogden that it would appear in the Kegan Paul series, Russell wrote to Wittgenstein to let him know what was happening.

He told him Ostwald would publish his introduction: 'I am sorry, as I am afraid you won't like that, but as you will see from his letter, it can't be helped.'

In a phrase which possibly shocked Wittgenstein, Russell told him: 'As for me, I am now married to Miss Black, and expecting a child in a few days':

We have bought this house [31 Sydney Street, London], and got your furniture from Cambridge, which we like very much. The child will probably be born in your bed.

He urged Wittgenstein to come to England, offering to pay his expenses as further recompense for the furniture: 'Your things are worth much more than I paid for them, and I will pay you more whenever you like. I didn't know when I bought them how much I was getting.' In a later letter he calculated that he owed Wittgenstein a further £200: 'I don't see why I should swindle you because Jolley understated the value of your things.'

Wittgenstein replied on 28 November: 'I must admit I am pleased my stuff is going to be printed', he wrote. 'Even though Ostwald is an utter charlatan':

As long as he doesn't tamper with it! Are you going to read the proofs? If so, please take care that he prints it exactly as I have it. He is quite capable of altering the work to suit his own taste – putting it into his idiotic spelling, for example. What pleases me most is that the whole thing is going to appear in England.

Russell evidently had little time to read the proofs carefully, and in any case the book had already gone to print before he received them. The proofs were therefore left uncorrected. Far from altering the work to suit his own taste, Ostwald – without, apparently, any interest in or concern for the meaning of the work he was publishing – simply had it printed exactly as it was in typescript. Thus one finds, for example – besides many more ordinary misprints – typewriter symbols where one would expect to find symbols of Russellian logic: '!' for the Sheffer stroke; '/' for the negation sign (and occasionally also for the Sheffer stroke); and the capital letter C for material implication.

Wittgenstein was not consulted by Ostwald at any stage in the publication; nor was he sent any offprints. On being told by Russell that it was finally in print, he had to write to Hänsel to ask him to search for a copy of *Annalen der Naturphilosophie* in the Viennese bookshops. The search was unsuccessful, and it was not until April of the following year, when he was sent a copy by Ogden, that Wittgenstein finally saw how his work had been printed. He was horrified. He regarded it, so he told Engelmann, as a 'pirated edition', and it was not until the English edition appeared, in 1922, that he considered his work to have been properly published.

The wheels for the English edition were set in motion by Russell when, on 6 December, he wrote to Ogden again, sending him Wittgenstein's letter of 28 November:

Enclosed from Wittgenstein gives all the authority needed for going ahead, so you can tell the publishers it is all right . . . I am much relieved that W. takes the whole affair sanely.

During the winter months of 1921–2, using an offprint of Ostwald's edition, the book was translated into English by Frank Ramsey, then an eighteen-year-old undergraduate at King's, who was a friend of Ogden's and was already recognized as a mathematician of outstanding promise.

Wittgenstein received Ramsey's translation towards the end of March, together with a questionnaire asking for his opinion on particular points that had puzzled both Ogden and Ramsey. In some cases, these puzzles were the outcome of Ostwald's careless printing of the German text; in others, they were due to a faulty understanding of Wittgenstein's intended meaning. Which was which was impossible for Wittgenstein to tell, as he had still not seen a copy of Ostwald's edition. Indeed, he was, by now, doubtful that Ostwald had even printed it – or that he would.

The task of correcting the translation was therefore long and difficult, but by 23 April Wittgenstein had completed a detailed list of comments and suggestions, which he sent to Ogden. In the main his suggestions were motivated by a desire to make the English as natural as possible, and to relax the literalness of Ramsey's translation. Not only was he forced to define particular German words and phrases; he also had to explain what *he* had meant by them and then find an English expression that captured the same meaning and tone. Thus, to a certain extent, the English version is not simply a translation from the German, but a reformulation of Wittgenstein's ideas.

The first question Ogden had raised concerned the title. Ostwald had published it under Wittgenstein's German title, *Logisch-Philosophische Abhandlung*, which, when translated literally, produces the rather awkward. 'Logico-Philosophical Treatise'. Russell had suggested 'Philosophical Logic' as an alternative, while Moore – in a conscious echo of Spinoza's *Tractatus Theologico-Politicus* – had put forward 'Tractatus Logico-Philosophicus' as 'obvious and ideal'. It was not, of course, a title that would reassure the public of the book's accessibility, and Ogden felt slightly uneasy about it. 'As a selling title, he told Russell, '*Philosophical Logic* is better, if it conveys the right impression.'

The matter was settled by Wittgenstein. 'I think the Latin one is better than the present title', he told Ogden:

> For although 'Tractatus logico-philosophicus' isn't *ideal* still it has something like the right meaning, whereas 'Philosophic logic' is wrong. In fact I don't know what it means! There is no such thing as philosophic logic. (Unless one says that as the whole book is nonsense the title might as well be nonsense too.)

The suggestions and comments made by Wittgenstein were given careful consideration by Ogden (who, in his correspondence with Wittgenstein, emerges as the most scrupulous and accommodating editor an author could wish for), and the text was altered in the light of them. By May, work on the English text was more or less complete.

One problem remained. At the time of preparing the typescript Wittgenstein had written a series of supplementary remarks, which were, with one exception, not included in the final text. These supplementary remarks were numbered, and the exception was No. 72, which was intended to be proposition 4.0141, an elaboration of the preceding remark comparing the pictorial relation between language and the world with the relation between a musical thought, a gramophone record and a musical score. However, in Ostwald's edition proposition 4.0141 reads, rather bizarrely: '*(Siehe Ergänzung Nr. 72)*'. He had evidently either lost or never received the supplementary list, and presumably found this no more unintelligible than the other propositions in the book. It was left for Ogden to query Ramsey's translation: '(See Supplement No. 72)'. 'What is this?' asked Ogden. 'There is presumably some mistake.'

In his reply, Wittgenstein explained about the supplements and provided Ogden with a translation of the one he had intended to include in the book. This raised in Ogden's mind the intriguing possibility that there might be more supplements to elucidate and expand what was, after all, a rather difficult – and short – book.

Wittgenstein refused to send any more. 'There can be no thought of printing them', he told Ogden. 'The supplements are exactly what must *not* be printed. Besides THEY REALLY CONTAIN NO ELUCIDATIONS AT ALL, but are still less clear than the rest of my props':

> As to the shortness of the book I am *awfully sorry for it; but what can I do?* If you were to squeeze me like a lemon you would get nothing more out of me. To let you print the Ergänzungen would be no remedy. It would be just as if you had gone to a joiner and ordered a table and he had made the table too short and now would sell you the shavings and sawdust and other rubbish along with the table to make up for its shortness. (Rather than print the Ergänzungen to make the book fatter leave a dozen white sheets for the reader to swear into when he has purchased the book and can't understand it.)

In June, when the book was ready to print, Wittgenstein was sent by Ogden a declaration to sign giving Kegan Paul all publication rights of the book, 'In consideration of their issuing it in German and English in the "International Library of Psychology & Philosophy" under the title *Tractatus Logico-Philosophicus*'. Under the terms of this contract, Wittgenstein was paid nothing for the rights of the book and entitled to no royalties from its sales. When, in 1933, a reprint was planned, he attempted to persuade Kegan Paul to pay him a royalty, but they did not respond, which is why he took his later work to a different publisher. At the time, however, he was less concerned with payment than with ensuring that Ellen Pinsent, David's mother, should be sent a complimentary copy. With every letter he wrote to Ogden during the final stages of publication, he asked him to trace Mrs Pinsent and to make sure she received a copy.

The proofs were ready in July, and Wittgenstein returned them, duly corrected, in the first week of August. The publishers seem to have wanted to print some details of Wittgenstein's biography and the peculiar circumstances in which the book was written, mentioning the prison camp at Monte Cassino, and so on. To this Wittgenstein responded with scathing contempt. 'As to your note about the Italian monastery etc. etc.', he wrote to Ogden on 4 August, 'do as you please':

> . . . only I can't for my life see the point of it. Why should the general reviewer know my age? Is it as much as to say: You can't expect more of a young chap especially when he writes a book in such a noise as must have been on the Austrian front? If I knew that the general reviewer believed in astrology I would suggest to print the date and hour of my birth in front of the book that he might set *the horoscope* for me. (26/IV 1889, 6 p.m.)

By the time the book was published, Wittgenstein had left Trattenbach. He had hinted to Russell as early as 23 October that this was to be his last year there, 'because I don't get on here even with the other teachers', and from then on his life in Trattenbach became progressively more difficult. He was determined to raise the sights of at least the more able of his students, and the private lessons he was giving Karl Gruber were extended to include also some of his better pupils from his new class. These included Emmerich Koderhold and Oskar Fuchs. From the parents of all three he encountered resistance. When he wanted to take Fuchs to Vienna to see a play, he was refused, Fuchs's mother not wishing to entrust her boy to 'that crazy fellow'. When he suggested to Koderhold's father that his son had the ability to attend a grammar school in Vienna, and should do so, he was told that it was out of the question; the boy was needed to help run the farm. His biggest disappointment, however, was with Karl Gruber, the most talented of his students. Every day after school, from four o'clock until half past seven, Wittgenstein conducted Gruber through an intensive study, concentrating on Latin, mathematics, geography and history. From time to time Gruber's progress was examined by Hänsel, especially in Latin, the subject Wittgenstein felt least qualified to teach. The plan was to see Gruber through a grammar school in Vienna. While attending school Gruber was to live with Hermine, and herein lay a difficulty: 'I would have felt it as a humiliation', Gruber later explained:

I didn't want to beg for alms and would have felt myself to be receiving charity. I would have come there as a 'poor chap' and would have had to say thank you for every bit of bread.

Perhaps for this reason, or perhaps simply because he had been worn down by the effort of studying for three and a half hours every day while working at the local factory, receiving nothing but discouragement from his family, Gruber told Wittgenstein he did not want to continue with his lessons. On 16 February 1921 Wittgenstein wrote to Hänsel: 'Today I had a conversation with Gruber who came to me to bring some books back. It turns out that he has no enthusiasm to go on with his studies . . . Of course he has no conception of where he is now heading. i.e. he does not know how bad a step he is taking. But how should he know. Sad! Sad!'

'I wish you didn't have to work so hard at elementary teaching', Russell wrote to him on 7 February; 'it must be very dreary.' Wittgenstein replied that he had indeed felt very depressed lately, but not because he found teaching in an elementary school repugnant: 'On the contrary!'

But it is *hard* to have to be a teacher in this country where the people are so completely and utterly hopeless. In this place I do not have a soul with whom I can exchange a single reasonable word. God knows how I will be able to stand it for much longer!

Russell had written of how he 'liked China much better than Europe': 'the people are more civilized – I keep wishing I were back there'. Yes, Wittgenstein replied, 'I can well believe that you found it more pleasant in China than in England, although in England it is doubtless a thousand times better than here.'

In his correspondence with Ogden, also, there are some indications that he was already beginning to look towards England, in order to be with at least a few people to whom he could talk. In his letters he frequently asks after, and asks to be remembered to, his old friends at Cambridge – Johnson and Keynes in particular.

Throughout the summer term he looked forward with great anticipation and pleasure to a proposed meeting with Russell, who was planning to visit the Continent to stay with his brother and wife at their home in Switzerland. Originally, the plan was for Wittgenstein to join the Russells there, but this was changed in favour of meeting for an over-night stay in Innsbruck. The tone of the letters that were exchanged to make this arrangement is warm and friendly, and gives no hint of the differences between the two that were to emerge. They exchanged comments on the baleful situation of Europe, told each other how much they were looking forward to their meeting, and Wittgenstein asked affectionately after Russell's wife and baby ('The little boy is lovely', Russell replied. 'At first he looked exactly like Kant, but now he looks more like a baby.')

And yet the meeting proved to be a great disappointment on both sides, and was, in fact, the last time the two met as friends. According to Dora Russell, it was the 'circumstances of the time' that made it a 'troubled meeting'. Inflation in Austria was then at its height, and: 'The whole place was full of ghouls and vultures, tourists profiting by the cheap currency to have a good time at the Austrians' expense':

> We all tramped the streets trying to find rooms in which to stay; Wittgenstein was in an agony of wounded pride at the state of his country and his inability to show some sort of hospitality.

Eventually, they took a single room, the Russells occupying the bed while Wittgenstein slept on the couch. 'But the hotel had a terrace, where it was pleasant enough to sit while Bertie discussed how to get Wittgenstein to England.' She strenuously denies that they quarrelled on this occasion: 'Wittgenstein was never easy, but I think any differences must have been over their philosophical ideas.'

Russell himself, however, remembers the differences as religious. Wittgenstein was, he said, 'much pained by the fact of my not being a Christian', and was at the time: 'at the height of his mystic ardour'. He: 'assured me with great earnestness that it is better to be good than clever', but was, nevertheless (Russell seems to see an amusing paradox here), 'terrified of wasps and, because of bugs, unable to stay another night in lodgings we had found in Innsbruck'.

In later life Russell gave the impression that, after their meeting at Innsbruck, Wittgenstein considered him too wicked to associate with, and so abandoned all contact. Russell enjoyed being thought wicked, and this is no doubt the aspect of the meeting that stayed freshest in his memory. Wittgenstein did, indeed, disapprove of his sexual mores, and had before their meeting in Innsbruck attempted to steer him in the direction of religious contemplation by suggesting he read Lessing's *Religiösen Streitschriften* (a suggestion Russell did not take up). But it is not true that Wittgenstein avoided all contact with Russell after they had met at Innsbruck; he wrote at least two letters to him in the months following the meeting, each of which begins: 'I have heard nothing from you for a long time.'

The indications are, then, that it was Russell who broke off communication. Perhaps the truth is that he found Wittgenstein's religious earnestness too tiresome to tolerate. For, if it is true that Wittgenstein was at the 'height of his mystic ardour', it is equally true that Russell was at the height of his atheist acerbity. Gone was the Ottoline-inspired transcendentalism of 'The Essence of Religion' and 'Mysticism and Logic'; in its place was a fierce anti-Christianity, which, in his now familiar role as a public speaker and a popular writer, he never lost an opportunity to express.

There is, too, the related, and perhaps still deeper, difference upon which Engelmann places so much emphasis: the difference between trying to improve the world, and seeking only to improve oneself. And, again, it is not just that Wittgenstein had become more introspective and individualistic, but that Russell had become much less so. The war had made him a socialist, and had convinced him of the urgent need to change the way the world was governed; questions of personal morality were subordinated by him to the overriding public concern to make the world a safer place. There is a story told by Engelmann which illustrates this difference in its starkest form, and which must surely refer to the meeting at Innsbruck:

> When, in the 'twenties, Russell wanted to establish, or join, a 'World Organization for Peace and Freedom' or something similar, Wittgenstein rebuked him so severely, that Russell said to him: 'Well, I suppose *you* would rather establish a World Organization for War and Slavery', to which Wittgenstein passionately assented: 'Yes, rather that, rather that!'

If this is true, then it may well have been Russell who regarded Wittgenstein as too wicked to associate with. For there can be no more complete repudiation of the ethical view upon which he based the rest of his life's activities.

In any case, Russell made no further attempt to communicate with

Wittgenstein or to persuade him to come to England. If Wittgenstein was to escape the 'odiousness and baseness' of the Austrian peasantry, it would not be through his old teacher at Cambridge.

That Wittgenstein's spell as an elementary school teacher in Trattenbach had not been a success was due in large measure to his very devotion to the task. His high expectations and his stern means of enforcing them had baffled and frightened all but a minority of his pupils; he had aroused the hostility of their parents and had failed to get on even with his own colleagues. And, as he had been forced to admit by Russell, there was nothing uniquely evil about the people at Trattenbach – he was very likely to encounter the same reaction elsewhere.

There are some indications that, if he could have found something better to do, he would have left school-teaching altogether. As well as talking to Russell about returning to England, he also discussed the possibility with Engelmann of a 'flight to Russia'. What he would have done in either place, he did not know. Certainly not philosophy – he had said all he had to say about *that* in his book.

In the event, September 1922 saw him starting at a new school in the same area as Trattenbach, this time a secondary school in a village called Hassbach. He did so without any great hopes. Before he started there he reported to Engelmann that he had formed 'a very disagreeable impression of the new environment there (teachers, parish priest, etc.)'. These people, he said, 'are not human *at all* but loathsome worms'. It had perhaps been thought that he would find it easier to get on with secondary school teachers, but in fact he found their pretence to 'specialized learning' utterly unbearable, and soon wished to return to an elementary school. He stayed barely a month.

In November he started at a primary school in Puchberg, a pleasant village in the Schneeberg mountains, now a popular skiing resort. Again, he found it difficult to discern any humanity in the people around him; in fact, he told Russell, they were not really people at all, but one-quarter animal and three-quarters human.

He had not been at Puchberg long before he at last received finished copies of the *Tractatus*. He wrote to Ogden on 15 November: 'They really look nice. I wish their contents were half as good as their external appearance.' He wondered whether Johnson – the first two volumes of whose three-volume work on logic had also recently been published – would buy it: 'I should like to know what *he* thinks about it. If you see him please give him my love.'

There was, naturally, no one at Puchberg with whom he could discuss philosophy, but he did, at least, find someone with whom he could share his passion for music in Rudolf Koder, a very talented pianist, who taught music at the school. On hearing Koder playing the 'Moonlight' Sonata, Wittgenstein walked into the music room and introduced himself. From then on the two would meet almost every afternoon to play duets for clarinet and piano – the clarinet sonatas by Brahms and Labor, and arrangements of the clarinet quintets of Brahms and Mozart.

Later, they were joined in these musical sessions by a local coal-miner called Heinrich Postl, a member of the village choir. Postl, who became a good friend and a kind of protégé of Wittgenstein's, was later employed as a porter and caretaker by the Wittgenstein family. Wittgenstein gave him copies of some of his favourite books – Tolstoy's *Gospel in Brief* and Hebel's *Schatzkästlein* – and sought to impress upon him his own moral teaching. Thus, when Postl once remarked that he wished to improve the world, Wittgenstein replied: 'Just improve yourself; that is the only thing you *can* do to better the world.'

Aside from Koder and Postl, Wittgenstein made few friends among the staff and villagers at Puchberg. As at Trattenbach, his teaching inspired a few of his pupils to heights they otherwise would not have attained, and antagonized the parents because of the disruption caused to their work at home.

While Wittgenstein was struggling to teach primary school children, the *Tractatus* was becoming the subject of much attention within the academic community. At Vienna University the mathematician Hans Hahn gave a seminar on the book in 1922, and it later attracted the attention also of a group of philosophers led by Moritz Schlick – the group that evolved into the famous Vienna Circle of Logical Positivists. In Cambridge, too, the *Tractatus* became the centre of discussion for a small but influential group of dons and students. The first public discussion of the book in Cambridge was probably in January 1923, when Richard Braithwaite addressed the Moral Science Club on the subject of 'Wittgenstein's logic as expounded in his *Tractatus Logico-Philosophicus*'.

For a time, Wittgenstein's only contact at Cambridge remained

Ogden, who in March sent Wittgenstein his recently published book *The Meaning of Meaning*, written jointly with the poet and literary critic I. A. Richards. Ogden regarded the book as providing a causal solution to the problem of meaning addressed by Wittgenstein in the *Tractatus*. Wittgenstein regarded it as an irrelevance. 'I think I ought to confess to you frankly', he wrote, 'that I believe you have not *caught the problems* which – for instance – I was at in my book (whether or not I have given the correct solution).' In a letter to Russell of 7 April, he went further:

> A short time ago I received 'The Meaning of Meaning'. It has surely also been sent to you. Is it not a miserable book?! Philosophy is not as easy as that! From this one sees how easy it is to write a thick book. The worst thing is the introduction of Professor Postgate Litt.D.F.B.A. etc. etc. I have seldom read anything so foolish.

It was the second letter Wittgenstein had written to Russell since their ill-starred meeting at Innsbruck, and he was impatient for a reply. 'Write to me sometime', he pleaded, 'how everything's going with you and what your baby's up to; whether he is already studying logic fluently.'

Russell appears not to have replied. Wittgenstein's categoric dismissal of Ogden's work possibly irritated him, since he himself saw little to criticize in the book. It was, in many ways, simply a restatement of what he himself had already said in *The Analysis of Mind*. Shortly afterwards, Wittgenstein was shocked to read in *The Nation* a favourable review by Russell of the book, describing it as 'undoubtedly important'. From Frank Ramsey he learnt that Russell 'does not really think *The Meaning of Meaning* important, but he wants to help Ogden by encouraging the sale of it' – an explanation certain to have increased Wittgenstein's disapproval, and to have confirmed him in his growing belief that Russell was no longer *serious*. In the 1930s Wittgenstein once or twice attempted (unsuccessfully) to interest Russell in the philosophical work that he was then doing, but he never again addressed Russell warmly, as a friend.

Increasingly isolated as he was ('To my great shame', he wrote to Engelmann, 'I must confess that the number of people to whom I can talk is constantly diminishing'), Wittgenstein *needed* friends. When, through Ogden, he was sent Keynes's 'Reconstruction in Europe' –

published as a special supplement to the *Manchester Guardian* – he tried
writing directly to Keynes to thank him. 'I should have preferred to
have got a line from you personally', he told him, 'saying how you are
getting on, etc':

> Or, are you too busy to write letters? I don't suppose you are. Do
> you ever see Johnson? If so, please give him my love. I should so
> much like to hear from him too (*not* about my book but about
> himself).
>   So do write to me sometime, if you will condescend to do such a
> thing.

It took Keynes over a year to reply. 'Did Keynes write to me?'
Wittgenstein asked Ogden on 27 March 1923. 'If so, please tell him it
hasn't reached me.' He even gave Ogden his Puchberg address
again – despite having given it him twice before – just in case
Keynes's letter had been misdirected.

It was Keynes who could (and eventually did) persuade Wittgenstein to return to England. In the meantime, contact with Cambridge
was kept up through a friend of Keynes's, a fellow Apostle and
member of King's College: Frank Ramsey.

Of the people at Cambridge who studied the *Tractatus* in its first year
of publication, Ramsey was undoubtedly the most perceptive.
Though still an undergraduate (in 1923 he was still just nineteen years
old), he was commissioned to write a review of Wittgenstein's work
for the philosophical journal, *Mind*. The review remains to this day
one of the most reliable expositions, and one of the most penetrating
criticisms, of the work. It begins in Russellian vein:

> This is a most important book containing original ideas on a large
> range of topics, forming a coherent system, which whether or not it
> be, as the author claims, in essentials the final solution of the
> problems dealt with, is of extraordinary interest and deserves the
> attention of all philosophers.

But Ramsey then goes on to take issue with some of the misunderstandings contained in Russell's introduction – for example, Russell's
misconception that Wittgenstein was concerned with the possibility of

a 'logically perfect language' – and to give a fuller and more reliable exposition of the main lines of the book.

When Wittgenstein heard from Ogden that Ramsey intended to visit Vienna in the summer vacation of 1923, he wrote to Ramsey himself, inviting him to Puchberg. Ramsey gratefully accepted, and arrived on 17 September, not quite knowing what to expect. He stayed about two weeks, during which time Wittgenstein devoted about five hours a day – from when he finished school at two o'clock in the afternoon until seven in the evening – to going through the *Tractatus* line by line with him. 'It is most illuminating', Ramsey wrote to Ogden; 'he seems to enjoy this and we get on about a page an hour':

> He is very interested in it, although he says that his mind is no longer flexible and he can never write another book. He teaches in the village school from 8 to 12 or 1. He is very poor and seems to lead a dreary life having only one friend here, and being regarded by most of his colleagues as a little mad.

In going through the book in such detail, Wittgenstein made some corrections and changes to the text which were incorporated in later editions. For both Wittgenstein and Ramsey, it was important that Ramsey should understand the book thoroughly, in every last detail. Wittgenstein was concerned lest Ramsey should forget everything when he returned to England – as Moore had appeared to have done when he came to Norway in 1914. 'It's terrible', Ramsey wrote to his mother, 'when he says "Is that clear" and I say "no" and he says "Damn it's *horrid* to go through that again."'

Ramsey intended to make Wittgenstein's work the basis for a theory of higher mathematics. When they had finished going through the book, he wrote, 'I shall try to pump him for ideas for its further development which I shall attempt':

> He says he himself will do nothing more, not because he is bored, but because his mind is no longer flexible. He says no one can do more than 5 or 10 years work at philosophy. (His book took 7.) And he is sure Russell will do nothing more important.

Wittgenstein seemed to support Ramsey's plan, at least to the extent of agreeing that *something* should take the place of Russell's *Principia*

Mathematica. He struck Ramsey as 'a little annoyed' that Russell was planning a new edition of *Principia*: 'because he thought that he had shown R that it was so wrong that a new edition would be futile. It must be done altogether afresh.'

As for Wittgenstein's present living conditions, Ramsey was somewhat dismayed:

> He is very poor, at least he lives very economically. He has one *tiny* room whitewashed, containing a bed, washstand, small table and one hard chair and that is all there is room for. His evening meal which I shared last night is rather unpleasant coarse bread, butter and cocoa.

He was, however, impressed by Wittgenstein's youthful appearance and his athletic vigour. 'In explaining his philosophy he is excited and makes vigorous gestures but relieves the tension by a charming laugh.' He was inclined to think that Wittgenstein 'exaggerates his own verbal inspiration', but of his genius he had no doubt:

> He is great. I used to think Moore a great man but beside W!

From Wittgenstein's point of view, the discussions with Ramsey provided a stimulating and pleasant – if strenuous – change from his normal routine, and also a welcome link with Cambridge. He told Ramsey that he was likely to leave Puchberg at the end of the school year, but had no firm idea of what he would do after that – perhaps find a job as a gardener, or perhaps come to England to look for work. He asked Ramsey to investigate whether he was entitled to receive a BA degree from Cambridge on the basis of the six terms he had spent with Russell before the war, with perhaps the *Tractatus* being accepted as a BA thesis.

On Ramsey's return to Cambridge for the Michaelmas term, he and Wittgenstein entered into a warm and friendly correspondence. In one of his first letters Ramsey explained (what he had found out from Keynes) that the regulations governing the eligibility of Cambridge degrees had changed. It was no longer possible to obtain a BA degree by keeping six terms' residence and submitting a thesis. If Wittgenstein wanted a degree he would have to come back to Cambridge for at least another year and then submit a thesis. In this way he could hope to obtain a Ph.D.

Through Ramsey, Keynes tried to entice Wittgenstein to England by offering him £50 to pay his expenses. He at first tried to make this offer anonymously, but, on being asked directly, Ramsey had to admit: 'the £50 belong to Keynes':

> He asked me not to say so straight away because he was afraid you might be less likely to take it from him than from an unknown source, as he has never written to you. I can't understand why he hasn't written, nor can he explain, he says he must have some 'complex' about it. He *speaks of you with warm affection and very much wants to see you again.*

Ramsey even wrote to Wittgenstein's nephew, Thomas Stonborough (whom he had got to know at Cambridge), to convince him of the same point: 'Keynes very much wants to see L.W. again and his offer of £50 is really better evidence of that, than his failure to answer letters is of the contrary. He speaks of L.W. with considerable affection.'

This marks the beginning of a long campaign to persuade Wittgenstein, first to visit England for a summer holiday, and then to abandon teaching and resume philosophical work at Cambridge. Ramsey did his best to allay Wittgenstein's fears about entering Cambridge society after such a long absence – an absence in which he had changed a great deal and had lived, to a large extent, away from any kind of society. On 20 December he wrote that he could quite understand this fear, 'but you mustn't give it any weight':

> I could get lodgings in Cambridge and you need not see more of people than you like or feel able to. I can see that staying with people might be difficult as you would inevitably be with them a lot, *but if you lived by yourself you could come into society gradually.*
>
> I don't want you to take this as endorsing your fear of boring or annoying people, for I know *I myself want to see you awfully*, but I just want to say that if you have such a fear surely it would be all right if you were not staying with anyone but lived alone first.

As Ramsey realized later, this line of attack was fruitless – the last thing Wittgenstein wanted was to live *alone* in England. But in any case, by February 1924 he gave up trying to persuade Wittgenstein to come to England for the summer and instead told him of his plan to go to Vienna.

Ramsey had for some time been interested in the prospect of being psychoanalysed. Originally this had been because of the emotional turmoil occasioned by an 'unhappy passion' for a married woman. In the Lent term of 1924 he returned to the idea after suffering from depression. This, together with a desire to have a break from Cambridge before he started his intended academic career, culminated in the decision to spend six months in Vienna. His choice of Vienna was not simply dictated by his desire to undergo psychoanalysis, but was also influenced by the fact that, while there, he could see Wittgenstein regularly to discuss his work.

In connection with his own work, he had recently been to see Russell to help him with the new edition of *Principia Mathematica*. Russell gave him the manuscript of the revisions that he intended to include in the new edition, in order for him to comment on them. What criticisms Ramsey made are unrecorded. The new introduction states merely that 'the authors' (referring to Russell and Whitehead, although in fact Russell alone was responsible for the changes) were 'under great obligations' to Ramsey.

To Wittgenstein, however, Ramsey was quite scathing of the project:

> You are quite right that it is of no importance; all it really amounts to is a clever proof of mathematical induction without using the axiom of reducibility. There are no fundamental changes, identity as it used to be. I felt he was too old: he seemed to understand and say 'yes' to each separate thing, but it made no impression so that 3 minutes afterwards he talked on his old lines. Of all your work he seems now to accept only this: that it is nonsense to put an adjective where a substantive ought to be which helps in his theory of types.

The new edition, indeed, seemed to please no one. While Wittgenstein and Ramsey thought it paid too little attention to Wittgenstein's criticisms, Whitehead considered it too Wittgensteinian and published a paper dissenting from the new ideas that Russell had included.

*

Ramsey went to Vienna in March. He travelled with Thomas Stonborough, and on the journey was briefed by him on some salient facts about the Wittgenstein family – that three of Wittgenstein's brothers had committed suicide, and that three sisters and a fourth brother remained, all of whom lived in Vienna. Having met Thomas Stonborough, it must have become apparent to Ramsey that his assessment of Wittgenstein as 'very poor' would have to be slightly amended. In Paris he was introduced to Jerome Stonborough, Thomas's father, who, he told his mother, 'looked just a prosperous American'.

In Vienna Ramsey saw for himself the scale of the Wittgenstein family wealth when he made the acquaintance of Margarete, who was at this time living in the Schönborn Palace: 'She must be collossally wealthy.' He was invited to a dinner party at the palace the following Saturday: 'As far as I could make out the party consisted of Wittgensteins, mostly female, professors, and friends of Tommy, the son, mostly male. So there was a good majority of males.' Music was provided by a professional string quartet, who played first Haydn and then Beethoven. Ramsey preferred the Haydn, but was told that this gave him away – 'what I didn't mind as I couldn't avoid it sooner or later'. After dinner he talked to Paul Wittgenstein – 'a brother, who is a celebrated pianist who lost an arm in the war and now plays with one hand. Lionel had heard of him without connecting him with Ludwig' – and was invited out to lunch by Paul and Hermine.

Having met the family, Ramsey had a better understanding of the completely self-inflicted nature of Wittgenstein's situation. He wrote to Keynes to explain that it was probably no good 'trying to get him to live any pleasanter life, or stop the ridiculous waste of his energy and brain':

I only see this clearly now because I have got to know one of his sisters and met the rest of the family. They are very rich and extremely anxious to give him money or do anything for him in any way, and he rejects all their advances; even Christmas presents or presents of invalid's food, when he is ill, he sends back. And this is not because they aren't on good terms but because he won't have any money he hasn't earned except for some very specific purpose like to come and see you again. I think he teaches to earn money and would only stop teaching if he had some other way of earning which was preferable. And it would have to be really earning, he wouldn't accept any job which seemed in the least to be wangled for him. It is an awful pity.

He even put forward the basis of a psychological explanation: 'it seems to be the result of a terribly strict upbringing. Three of his brothers committed suicide – they were made to work so hard by their father: at one time the eight children had twenty-six private tutors; and their mother took no interest in them.'

At the end of his first week in Vienna, Ramsey travelled to Puchberg to spend a day with Wittgenstein. His mind was chiefly on his psychoanalysis, and he had not intended to talk to Wittgenstein about his work on the foundations of mathematics. It appears, however, that he made some effort to do so, but found Wittgenstein's response disappointing. 'Wittgenstein seemed to me tired', he wrote to his mother, 'though not ill; but it isn't really any good talking to him about work, he won't listen. If you suggest a question he won't listen to your answer but starts thinking of one for himself. And it is such hard work for him like pushing something too heavy uphill.'

After his visit to Puchberg, Ramsey wrote to Keynes underlining the importance of getting Wittgenstein out of the hostile environment in which he had placed himself:

. . . if he were got away from his surroundings and were not so tired, and had me to stimulate him, he might do some more very good work; and he might conceivably have come to England with that in view. But while he is teaching here I don't think he will do anything, his thinking is so obviously frightfully uphill work as if he were worn out. If I am here during his summer holiday I might try to stimulate him then.

It appears Wittgenstein had asked Ramsey to write to Keynes explaining his attitude to visiting England, convinced that he could not express the matter adequately in English, and that Keynes wouldn't understand it if he wrote in German. Wittgenstein, Ramsey explained, had severe misgivings about coming to England to renew old acquaintances. He felt he could no longer talk to Russell, and the quarrel with Moore had remained unhealed; there remained only Keynes and Hardy. He wanted very much to get to know Keynes again, but only if he could renew their old intimacy; he did not want to come to England and see Keynes only occasionally and establish only a superficial acquaintanceship. He had changed so much since the war, he felt, that unless he spent a lot of time with Keynes, Keynes would never understand him.

He would therefore be prepared to come to England *if* Keynes were prepared to invite him to stay as a guest in his country home, and were willing to spend a great deal of time getting to know him again.

Ramsey ended his explanation of this with a warning:

> I'm afraid I think you would find it difficult and exhausting. Though I like him very much I doubt if I could enjoy him for more than a day or two, unless I had my great interest in his work, which provides the mainstay of our conversation.

But, he added, 'I should be pleased if you did get him to come and see you, as it might possibly get him out of this groove.'

For the time being, Keynes did not respond to the suggestion that he should invite Wittgenstein to spend the summer with him in the country; he possibly considered the demands involved too great. He had, however – on 29 March, apparently before seeing Ramsey's letter – finally replied to Wittgenstein's letter of the previous year. He explained the long delay as being caused by his desire to understand the *Tractatus* before he wrote: 'yet my mind is now so far from fundamental questions that it is impossible for me to get clear about such matters':

> I still do not know what to say about your book, except that I feel certain it is a work of extraordinary importance and genius. Right or wrong, it dominates all fundamental discussions at Cambridge since it was written.

He sent Wittgenstein some of his recent books, including *The Economic Consequences of the Peace*, and urged him to come to England, stressing: 'I would do anything in my power which could make it easier for you to do further work.'

This last statement, for the moment at least, struck the wrong note. It was not that Wittgenstein wanted to resume philosophical work, but that he wanted badly to re-establish old friendships. He replied only in July, writing half in English, half in German, and insisting there was nothing that could be done to enable him to return to philosophy:

> . . . because I myself no longer have any strong inner drive towards that sort of activity. Everything that I really *had* to say, I have said, and so the spring has run dry. That sounds queer, but it's how things are.

On the other hand, he told Keynes, if he had any work to do in England, even sweeping the streets or cleaning boots, 'I would come over with great pleasure'. Without such a job, the only thing that would make it worthwhile for him to come would be if Keynes were prepared to see him on something more than a casual basis. It would be nice, he said, to see Keynes again, but: 'staying in rooms and having tea with you every other day or so would not be *nice enough*'. It would be necessary, for the reasons that Ramsey had already outlined, for them to work hard at establishing an intimate relationship:

> We haven't met since 11 years. I don't know if you have changed during that time, but *I* certainly have tremendously. I am sorry to say I am no better than I was, but I am *different*. And therefore if we shall meet you may find that the man who has come to see you isn't really the one you meant to invite. There is no doubt that, even if we *can* make ourselves understood to one another, a chat or two will *not* be sufficient for the purpose, and that the result of our meeting will be disappointment and disgust on your side and disgust and despair on mine.

As it was, no such complications arose, because no such invitation was forthcoming. Wittgenstein spent the summer in Vienna.

He had already decided that the summer term of 1924 would be his last at Puchberg, although he appears to have been relatively happy at this time. When Ramsey visited him in May he reported to his mother that Wittgenstein seemed more cheerful: 'he has spent weeks preparing the skeleton of a cat for his children, which he seemed to enjoy'. 'But', he wrote, 'he is no good for my work.'

Ramsey's respect for Wittgenstein had not diminished in any way. Later, he was to write:

We really live in a great time for thinking, with Einstein, Freud and
Wittgenstein all alive (and all living in Germany or Austria, those
foes of civilisation!).

But although he stayed in Austria throughout the summer, he made
little effort to see much of Wittgenstein. When Ogden wrote to him
asking for the corrections to the text of the *Tractatus* made during the
discussions of the previous year, he replied that he wouldn't be seeing
Wittgenstein again until September, shortly before his return to
England. Ogden apparently wanted the material in case a new edition
should be published, but at the time this looked an unlikely prospect.
Ramsey's letter ends: 'I'm sorry so few have sold.'

Ramsey spent the summer completing his course in psychoanalysis
and working on his dissertation. While still in Vienna he received the
news that, at the extraordinarily early age of twenty-one, he was to
become a Fellow of King's College upon his return to Cambridge.
Before he left he made only one more visit to Wittgenstein. He told
him beforehand: 'I don't much want to talk about mathematics as I
haven't been doing much lately.'

This was, in all probability, a polite way of saying that, so long as
Wittgenstein continued 'this ridiculous waste of his energy and brain',
he was likely to remain 'no good' for Ramsey's work.

In what was to be his last attempt to raise the sights of the children of
rural Austria, and to withstand the hostility of their parents and of his
fellow teachers, Wittgenstein, in September 1924, started at yet
another village school, this time at Otterthal, a neighbouring village of
Trattenbach.

Given his experience of Trattenbach, it is perhaps surprising that he
should have chosen to return to the Wechsel mountains. But there was
some hope that he would enjoy better relations with his colleagues.
So, at least, Hermine thought. Almost as soon as Wittgenstein moved
to Otterthal, she wrote to Hänsel asking if he had any plans to visit her
brother. 'I would, naturally,' she said, 'be very happy if someone
could tell me how Ludwig is getting on there, I mean how relations
with the school are':

It *cannot*, I think, be completely without friction, since his teaching
programme is so different from that of the other teachers, but at

least one might hope that the friction should not result in his being *ground to dust*.

The head of the school in Otterthal was Josef Putre, whom Wittgenstein had befriended while at Trattenbach. Putre was a socialist and an enthusiastic proponent of Glöckel's School Reform Movement, and in his first two years of teaching Wittgenstein had often turned to him for advice.

There were, of course, differences of opinion between himself and Putre, particularly concerning the role of religion in education. While Putre discouraged praying in schools, Wittgenstein prayed with his pupils every day. When Putre once remarked that he was against paying lip-service to the Catholic faith, and considered it meaningless, Wittgenstein replied: 'People kiss each other; that too is done with the lips.'

Despite his friendship with Putre, Wittgenstein knew within a month that he would find it no easier at Otterthal than he had at Trattenbach. 'It's not going well here', he wrote to Hänsel in October, 'and perhaps now my teaching career is coming to an end':

It is too difficult for me. Not one but a dozen forces are against me, and what am I?

It was while at Otterthal, however, that Wittgenstein produced what is arguably his most lasting contribution to educational reform in Austria – a contribution that is, furthermore, fully in line with the principles of Glöckel's programme. That is his *Wörterbuch für Volksschulen*, a spelling dictionary for use in elementary schools. The origin of his desire to publish such a book seems to lie in his asking Hänsel to enquire into the cost of dictionaries for use in schools. In the letter to Hänsel quoted above, he says:

I had never thought the dictionaries would be so frightfully expensive. I think, if I live long enough, I will produce a small dictionary for elementary schools. It appears to me to be an urgent need.

The need for such a dictionary was well recognized by the authorities. There were at the time only two dictionaries available, both of them designed for the task of teaching students to spell. One was too big and too expensive to be used by children at the kind of rural schools at which Wittgenstein taught. The other was too small and badly put together, containing many foreign words which the children were unlikely ever to use, and omitting many words commonly mis-spelt by children. At Puchberg Wittgenstein had overcome this difficulty by getting his pupils to produce their own dictionaries. During German lessons and PE lessons when the weather prevented them from going outside, Wittgenstein wrote words on the blackboard and had the children copy them into their own vocabulary books. These vocabulary books were then sewn together and bound with cardboard covers to produce the finished dictionary.

In discussing this solution to the problem in the preface to the published dictionary, Wittgenstein remarks:

> He who works at the practical level is able to understand the difficulties of this work. Because the result should be that each student receives a clean and, if at all possible, correct copy of the dictionary, and in order to reach that goal the teacher has to control almost every word each student has written. (It is not enough to take samples. I do not even want to talk about the demands on discipline.)

Although he comments on the astonishing improvement of spelling which resulted ('The orthographic conscience had been awakened!'), he clearly had no desire to repeat what had obviously been an arduous and trying task. The *Wörterbuch* was envisaged as a more practical solution to the problem, both for himself and for other teachers in the same position.

In contrast to the *Tractatus*, the publication of the dictionary was achieved quickly and without any great problems. In November 1924, Wittgenstein contacted his former principal at the Lehrerbildungsanhalt, Dr Latzke, to inform him of the plan. Latzke contacted the Viennese publishing house of Hölder-Pichler-Tempsky, who on 13 November wrote to Wittgenstein to say that they would be willing to publish the dictionary. The manuscript was delivered during the Christmas vacation of 1924, and Wittgenstein was sent the proofs the following February.

Wittgenstein's preface is dated 22 April 1925. In it he explains the need for such a dictionary and the considerations that dictated the selection of words and their arrangement. He makes clear that these considerations are based on his own experience as a teacher. 'No word is too common to be entered,' he says, 'since I have experienced that *wo* has been written with the "h" that indicates a long vowel, and *was* with "ss".' It is clear from the preface that Wittgenstein intended his dictionary specifically to meet the needs of elementary schools in rural Austria. Thus, while some perfectly good German words have been omitted because they are not used in Austria, some Austrian dialectical expressions have been included. Dialect is also used to explain distinctions which Wittgenstein's experience had shown were often confused, such as the difference between *das* and *dass*, and the distinction between the accusative *ihn* and the dative *ihm*.

Before the publishers could go ahead with printing the book, they needed assurance that it would be recommended for use in the schools for which it was intended. They therefore submitted it for approval to the provincial board of education for Lower Austria. The report for the board was written by District School Inspector Eduard Buxbaum. In his report, dated 15 May, Buxbaum agrees with Wittgenstein about the need for such a dictionary, and goes so far as to describe this need as 'the most pressing question at the present time'. He also agrees with Wittgenstein's emphasis on words which belong to 'the common everyday vocabulary'. He finds fault, however, with Wittgenstein's selection of words, criticizing him for omitting such common words as *Bibliothek* (library), *Brücke* (bridge), *Buche* (beech tree) etc., and also takes exception to Wittgenstein's preface. Dictating a dictionary to students is, Buxbaum remarks, a strange way to control their spelling. It would have been better, he felt, to have dictated the correct spelling of words only after the children had used those words for themselves. He also finds fault with Wittgenstein's own use of the German language: 'By no means should the mistake of writing "*eine mehrmonatliche Arbeit*" instead of saying "*eine Arbeit von viele Monaten*" ["a work of several months"] creep into the German language, not even into the preface.'

Buxbaum concludes:

One can express the opinion that the dictionary will be a somewhat useful educational tool for the upper classes of elementary schools and of the Bürgerschulen after the cited shortcomings have been removed. It is the opinion of the undersigned that no board of education will find the dictionary in its present form recommendable.

After Wittgenstein's preface was omitted and the words which Buxbaum had mentioned were included, the book received its required official approval. In November, a contract between Wittgenstein and the publisher was drawn up, under the terms of which Wittgenstein received 10 per cent of the wholesale price for each copy sold and ten free copies. The book was published in 1926 and enjoyed a limited success. (It was not reprinted, however, until 1977, by which time its interest was confined to Wittgensteinian scholarship.)

As we have seen, soon after he arrived in Otterthal, Wittgenstein became convinced that he would not for very much longer be able to withstand the pressures of trying to teach in a hostile environment. In February 1925 he wrote to Engelmann:

I suffer much from the human, or rather inhuman, beings with whom I live – in short it is all as usual!

As before, Wittgenstein found an enthusiastic response from a small group of boys who became his favourites. These formed a special group who stayed behind after school for extra tuition and who were known to Wittgenstein by their Christian names. They were taken by Wittgenstein on outings to Vienna and on walks through the local countryside, and were educated to a standard far beyond what was expected in the kind of rural elementary school that they attended. And, as before, their commitment to their education, and Wittgenstein's commitment to them, aroused the hostility of the parents, who turned down Wittgenstein's suggestions that their children should continue their education at a grammar school. Again, the girls proved more resistant to Wittgenstein's methods, and resented having their hair pulled and their ears boxed because they were unable or unwilling to meet Wittgenstein's unrealistically high expectations, especially in mathematics.

In short, indeed, it was all as usual.

Engelmann, too, was finding life in post-war Europe difficult. Like Wittgenstein, he felt himself to belong to an earlier epoch, but unlike Wittgenstein, he characterized that epoch as essentially *Jewish*. In his memoir, he talks of the 'Austrian-Jewish spirit' and of the 'Viennese-Jewish' culture, which was the inheritance of both himself and Wittgenstein. Wittgenstein, as we shall see, saw it differently. But for both, in their different ways, an awareness of their Jewishness was heightened as the epidemic of European anti-Semitism became ever more virulent. In Engelmann's case, this resulted in his becoming a Zionist and looking to the creation of Israel for a new homeland to replace the one destroyed by the First World War. Though never at any time attracted to Zionism (the religious associations of Palestine would always, for him, have had more to do with the New Testament than the Old), Wittgenstein found something to cheer in Engelmann's desire to settle in the Holy Land. 'That you want to go to Palestine', he wrote, 'is the one piece of news that makes your letter cheering and hopeful for me':

> This may be the right thing to do and may have a spiritual effect. I might want to join you. Would you take me with you?*

Shortly after his letter to Engelmann, Wittgenstein received, completely unexpectedly, a letter from Eccles, his friend in Manchester, from whom he had heard nothing since the war (unlike Pinsent, Russell and Keynes, Eccles was not the sort to exchange friendly letters with a member of an enemy army). Eccles's letter was to provide the catalyst Wittgenstein needed to persuade him to visit England. On 10 March he replied with obvious pleasure at the renewal in contact:

> Dear Eccles,
> I was more than pleased to hear from you, for some reason or other I was convinced that you either were killed in the war, or if alive, that you would hate Germans and Austrians so much that you would have no more intercourse with me.
> . . . I wish I could see you again before long, but when and where we can meet God knows. Perhaps we might manage to meet during the summer vacation, but I haven't got much time and *no* money to

---

* Engelmann eventually left Europe for Tel Aviv in 1934 and remained there (after 1948 as an Israeli citizen) until his death in 1963. Nothing more was mentioned of the idea that Wittgenstein should join him.

come to England as I have given *all* my money away, about 6 years ago. Last summer I should have come to England to see a friend of mine Mr Keynes (whose name you might know) in Cambridge. He would have paid my expenses, but I resolved after all not to come, because I was so much afraid that the long time and the great events (external and internal) that lie between us would prevent us from understanding one another. However now – or at least *to-day* I feel as if I might still be able to make myself understood by my old friends and if I get any opportunity I might – w.w.p. come and see you at Manchester.

In a later letter, of 7 May, he accepts Eccles's invitation to stay at his home in Manchester, while stressing the point that had prevented him from staying with Keynes the previous summer (the fact that Keynes had not actually invited him seems to have been dismissed by Wittgenstein as irrelevant):

England may not have changed since 1913 but *I* have. However, it is no use writing to you about that as I couldn't explain to you the exact nature of the change (though I perfectly understand it). You will see it for yourself when I get there. I should like to come about the end of August.

In July, Wittgenstein wrote to Keynes about his projected visit to England, saying that his mind was not quite made up whether to go or not, and hinting that the final decision depended on Keynes: 'I should rather like to, if I could also see *you* during my stay (about the middle of August). Now please let me know FRANKLY if you have the slightest wish to see me.' Keynes evidently replied encouragingly, and even sent Wittgenstein £10 for the journey. Before he left Wittgenstein wrote: 'I'm awfully curious how we are going to get on with one another. It will be exactly like a dream.'

Wittgenstein arrived in England on 18 August, and stayed with Keynes in his country home in Lewes, Sussex before travelling to Manchester to see Eccles. Despite his earlier insistence to Russell that it was better to be good than to be clever, the experience of exchanging the company of rural peasants for that of some of the finest minds in Europe was delightful to him. From Lewes he wrote to Engelmann:

I know that brilliance – the riches of the spirit – is not the ultimate good, and yet I wish now that I could die in a moment of brilliance.

When he went to Manchester, both Eccles and his wife were surprised at the great change in him. They went to the railway station to meet him, and found in the place of the immaculately dressed young man, the 'favourite of the ladies' they had known before the war, a rather shabby figure dressed in what appeared to them to be a Boy Scout uniform. The appearance of eccentricity was compounded by Wittgenstein's giving Eccles the (false) impression that he had not yet seen a copy of the *Tractatus*. He asked Mrs Eccles to obtain a copy, and after she had tried in vain to buy one from the booksellers in Manchester, Eccles borrowed one from the university library. 'It was during this period', Eccles states confidently, but mistakenly, in his memoir, 'that he obtained his first copy of the English edition of his *Tractatus*.' Evidently, Wittgenstein very much wanted Eccles to see the book, but was too embarrassed to admit that as the reason for their determined search.

At the end of his stay in England Wittgenstein went to Cambridge, where he was finally reunited with Johnson. 'Tell Wittgenstein', Johnson wrote to Keynes on 24 August, 'that I shall be very pleased to see him once more; but I must bargain that we don't talk on the foundations of Logic, as I am no longer equal to having my roots dug up.' He also met with Ramsey, with whom, however, it appears he quarrelled so fiercely that the two did not resume communication until two years later.

Despite his argument with Ramsey, Wittgenstein's trip was a success. It had served the useful purpose of re-establishing contacts with old friends – contacts he intended to make use of in the likely event that life at Otterthal would become unbearable. 'In case of need I shall probably go to England', as he put it to Engelmann. In letters to both Engelmann and Eccles at the beginning of the new school term in September, he speaks of *trying once again* with his 'old job', as though this coming year were to be his very last attempt at teaching in rural schools. 'However', he told Eccles, 'I don't feel so miserable now, as I have decided to come to you if the worst came to worst, which it certainly will sooner or later.' In October he wrote to Keynes in similar vein, saying he would remain a teacher, 'as long as I feel that the troubles into which I get that way, may do me any good':

If one has toothache it is good to put a hot-water bottle on your face, but it will only be effective, as long as the heat of the bottle gives you some pain. I will chuck the bottle when I find that it no longer gives me the particular kind of pain which will do my character any good. That is, if people here don't turn me out before that time.

'If I leave off teaching', he added, 'I will probably come to England and look for a job there, because I am convinced that I cannot find anything at all possible in *this* country. In this case I will want your help.'

In the event, the worst did come to the worst, and Wittgenstein had to chuck the hot-water bottle perhaps even sooner than he had anticipated. He left Otterthal and gave up teaching altogether very suddenly, in April 1926. The event which precipitated this was much talked about at the time, and was known to the villagers in Otterthal and the surrounding area as '*Der Vorfall Haidbauer*' ('The Haidbauer Case').

Josef Haidbauer was an eleven-year-old pupil of Wittgenstein's whose father had died and whose mother worked as a live-in maid for a local farmer named Piribauer. Haidbauer was a pale, sickly child who was to die of leukaemia at the age of fourteen. He was not the rebellious type, but possibly rather slow and reticent in giving answers in class. One day, Wittgenstein's impatience got the better of him, and he struck Haidbauer two or three times on the head, causing the boy to collapse. On the question of whether Wittgenstein struck the boy with undue force – whether he ill-treated the child – a fellow pupil, August Riegler, has (with dubious logic) commented:

It cannot be said that Wittgenstein ill-treated the child. If Haidbauer's punishment was ill-treatment, then 80 per cent of Wittgenstein's punishments were ill-treatments.

On seeing the boy collapse, Wittgenstein panicked. He sent his class home, carried the boy to the headmaster's room to await attention from the local doctor (who was based in nearby Kirchberg) and then hurriedly left the school.

On his way out he had the misfortune to run into Herr Piribauer, who, it seems, had been sent for by one of the children. Piribauer is remembered in the village as a quarrelsome man who harboured a deep-seated grudge against Wittgenstein. His own daughter, Hermine, had often been on the wrong side of Wittgenstein's temper, and had once been hit so hard that she bled behind the ears. Piribauer recalls that when he met Wittgenstein in the corridor, he had worked himself up into a fierce rage: 'I called him all the names under the sun. I told him he wasn't a teacher, he was an animal-trainer! And that I was going to fetch the police right away!' Piribauer hurried to the police station to have Wittgenstein arrested, but was frustrated to find that the single officer who manned the station was away. The following day he renewed the attempt, but was informed by the headmaster that Wittgenstein had disappeared in the night.

On 28 April 1926 Wittgenstein handed in his resignation to Wilhelm Kundt, one of the District School Inspectors. Kundt had, naturally, been told of the 'Haidbauer Case', but reassured Wittgenstein that nothing much would come of it. Kundt placed great value on Wittgenstein's ability as a teacher, and did not want to lose him. He advised him to take a holiday to calm his nerves, and then to decide whether he really wished to give up teaching. Wittgenstein, however, was resolute. Nothing would persuade him to stay on. At the hearing which followed, he was, as Kundt had anticipated, cleared of misconduct. But he had, by then, despaired of accomplishing anything more as a teacher in the Austrian countryside.

The Haidbauer incident was not, of course, the cause of this despair, but simply the event that finally triggered its inevitable culmination in Wittgenstein's resignation. The despair itself had deeper roots. Shortly before the incident, Wittgenstein had met August Wolf, an applicant for the post of headmaster at Otterthal, and had told him:

I can only advise you to withdraw your application. The people here are so narrow-minded that nothing can be achieved.

10
OUT OF THE
WILDERNESS

The most natural thing for Wittgenstein to have done in 1926, after things had come to a head in Otterthal, might have been to avail himself of Keynes's hospitality and return to England. In fact, it was over a year before he once more got in touch with Keynes. He had, he then explained, postponed writing until he had got over the great troubles he had experienced.

Although he had expected to leave Otterthal, and to abandon his career as a teacher, the manner in which he did so left Wittgenstein completely devastated. The trial had been a great humiliation, the more so because, in defending himself against charges of brutality, he had felt the need to lie about the extent of corporal punishment he had administered in the classroom. The sense of moral failure this left him with haunted him for over a decade, and led eventually, as we shall see, to his taking drastic steps to purge himself of the burden of guilt.

In this state he could not contemplate returning to England. Nor, for the moment, did he feel able to return to Vienna. He considered, instead, a complete retreat from worldly troubles. Shortly after his retirement from teaching, he called at a monastery to enquire about the possibility of his becoming a monk. It was an idea that occurred to him at various times in his life, often during periods of great despair. On this occasion he was told by an obviously perceptive Father Superior that he would not find what he expected, and that he was, in any case, led by motives which the order could not welcome. As an alternative, he found work as a gardener with the monk-hospitallers in Hütteldorf, just outside Vienna, camping for three months in the tool-shed of their garden. As it had six years earlier, gardening proved an effective therapy, and at the end of the summer he felt able to return to Vienna to face society.

On 3 June 1926, while he was still working as a gardener, his mother, who had been ill for some time, died at the family home in the Alleegasse, leaving Hermine as the acknowledged head of the family. Whether or not this made it easier for Wittgenstein to return to Vienna, or whether his mother's death influenced him in any way, is impossible to say. But it is striking that from this time on there is a profound change in his attitude to his family. The family Christmas celebrations, which in 1914 had filled him with such dread and produced in him such confusion, were now looked forward to by him with delight. Every Christmas from now until the *Anschluss* of 1938 made it impossible for him to leave England, we find him taking part in the proceedings with enthusiasm – distributing gifts to his nieces and nephews, and joining in with the festive singing and dining with no hint that this compromised his integrity.

Wittgenstein's return to Vienna in the summer of 1926, then, appears to mark the end of an estrangement from his family that goes back at least to 1913, when his father died. On his return, he was offered a kind of work-therapy which, unlike his work as a gardener, would impose upon him the obligation to work with others, and help to bring him back into society. It would, furthermore, allow him an opportunity to put into practice his strongly held views on architectural aesthetics. He was asked by his sister Gretl and by Paul Engelmann to become Engelmann's partner in the design and construction of Gretl's new house.

Engelmann had already carried out some work for the Wittgenstein family. He had worked on the renovation of the family house in Neuwaldeggergasse, and had built for Paul Wittgenstein a room in the Alleegasse for the exhibition of his collection of porcelain. Towards the end of 1925 he was approached by Gretl to be the architect for a new town-house to be built on a plot of land she had bought in one of Vienna's least fashionable areas, on Kundmanngasse, in Vienna's Third District (next to the teacher training college Wittgenstein had attended). Wittgenstein's interest in the project was quickly aroused, and during his last year at Otterthal, whenever he returned to Vienna, he would discuss it with Gretl and Engelmann with great intensity and concern, so that it seemed to Engelmann that Wittgenstein understood Gretl's wishes better than he did himself.

The early plans were drawn up by Engelmann during Wittgenstein's last term of teaching, but after he had left Otterthal, it seemed natural to invite him to join him as a partner in the project. From then on, says Engelmann: 'he and not I was the architect, and although the ground plans were ready before he joined the project, I consider the result to be his and not my achievement'.

The final plan is dated 13 November 1926 and is stamped: 'P. Engelmann & L. Wittgenstein Architects'. Though he never had any architectural training, and was involved only in this one architectural job, there are signs that Wittgenstein began to take this designation seriously, and to see in architecture a new vocation, a new way of re-creating himself. For years he was listed in the Vienna city directory as a professional architect, and his letters of the time are written on notepaper headed: 'Paul Engelmann & Ludwig Wittgenstein Architects, Wien III. Parkgasse 18'. Perhaps, though, this is no more than another statement of his personal independence – an insistence on his status as a freelance professional and a denial that his architectural work for his sister was a mere sinecure.

His role in the design of the house was concerned chiefly with the design of the windows, doors, window-locks and radiators. This is not as marginal as it may at first appear, for it is precisely these details that lend what is otherwise a rather plain, even ugly, house its distinctive beauty. The complete lack of any external decoration gives a stark appearance, which is alleviated only by the graceful proportion and meticulous execution of the features designed by Wittgenstein.

The details are thus everything, and Wittgenstein supervised their construction with an almost fanatical exactitude. When a locksmith asked: 'Tell me, Herr Ingenieur, does a millimetre here or there really matter so much to you?' Wittgenstein roared 'Yes!' before the man had finished speaking. During discussions with the engineering firm responsible for the high glass doors which Wittgenstein had designed, the engineer handling the negotiations broke down in tears, despairing of ever executing the commission in accordance with Wittgenstein's standards. The apparently simple radiators took a year to deliver because no one in Austria could build the sort of thing Wittgenstein had in mind. Castings of individual parts were obtained from abroad, and even then whole batches were rejected as unusable. But, as Hermine Wittgenstein recalls:

Perhaps the most telling proof of Ludwig's relentlessness when it came to getting the proportions exactly right is the fact that he had the ceiling of one of the rooms, which was almost big enough to be a hall, raised by three centimetres, just when it was almost time to start cleaning the complete house.

Gretl was able to move into the house at the end of 1928. According to Hermine, it fitted her like a glove; the house was an extension of Gretl's personality, 'just as from childhood onwards everything surrounding her had to be original and grand'. For herself, however, Hermine had reservations:

. . . even though I admired the house very much, I always knew that I neither wanted to, nor could, live in it myself. It seemed indeed to be much more a dwelling for the gods than for a small mortal like me, and at first I even had to overcome a faint inner opposition to this 'house embodied logic' as I called it, to this perfection and monumentality.

It is easy to understand this slight abhorrence. The house was designed with little regard to the comforts of ordinary mortals. The qualities of clarity, rigour and precision which characterize it are indeed those one looks for in a system of logic rather than in a dwelling place. In designing the interior Wittgenstein made extraordinarily few concessions to domestic comfort. Carpets, chandeliers and curtains were strictly rejected. The floors were of dark polished stone, the walls and ceilings painted a light ochre, the metal of the windows, the door handles and the radiators was left unpainted, and the rooms were lit with naked light-bulbs.

In part because of this stark monumentality, and also in part because of the sad fate of Austria itself, the house – which had taken so much time, energy and money to build – has had an unfortunate history. Less then a year after Gretl moved in, the Great Crash of 1929 (though it did not by any means leave her destitute) forced her to lay off many of the staff she needed to run the house as it had been intended to be run, and she took to entertaining, not in the hall, but in the kitchen. Nine years later, after the *Anschluss*, she fled from the Nazis to live in New York, leaving the house empty and in the care of the sole remaining servant. In 1945, after the Russians occupied Vienna, the house was used as a barracks for Russian soldiers and as a stable for their horses. Gretl moved back in 1947 and lived there until her death in 1958, when the house became the property of her son, Thomas Stonborough. Sharing Hermine's reservations about its suitability as a home, Stonborough left it empty for many years before finally, in 1971, selling it to a developer for demolition. It was saved from this fate only by a campaign to have it declared a national monument by the Vienna Landmark Commission, and now survives as a home for the Cultural Department of the Bulgarian Embassy in Vienna, though its interior has been extensively altered to suit its new purpose. Were Wittgenstein to see it in its present state – room dividers removed to form L-shaped rooms, walls and radiators painted white, the hall carpeted and wood-panelled, and so on – it is quite possible he would have preferred it to have been demolished.

Through working for Gretl, Wittgenstein was brought back into Viennese society and, eventually, back into philosophy. While the Kundmanngasse house was being built, Gretl and her family continued to occupy the first floor of the Schönborn Palace. Her eldest son, Thomas, had recently returned from Cambridge and was now reading for a Ph.D. at the University of Vienna. At Cambridge he had met a Swiss girl by the name of Marguerite Respinger and had invited her to Vienna. With her, Wittgenstein began a relationship which he at least came to regard as a preliminary to marriage, and which was to last until 1931. She was, as far as anybody knows, the only woman with whom he fell in love.

Marguerite was a lively, artistic young lady from a wealthy background, with no interest in philosophy and little of the devout seriousness that Wittgenstein usually made a prerequisite for friendship. Her relationship with Wittgenstein was, presumably, encouraged by Gretl, although some of his other friends and relations were bemused and rather less than pleased by it. She first met Wittgenstein when, after an accident at the building site, he had hurt his foot and was staying with Gretl's family to convalesce. She was part of a group of young people – which included Thomas Stonborough and the Sjögren brothers, Talle and Arvid – which gathered round his bed to listen to him read. He read something from the Swiss writer Johann Peter Hebel, and, she reports: 'I felt again at home and moved by

hearing it read with such deep understanding.' Much to the displeasure – and, perhaps, jealousy – of Arvid Sjögren, Wittgenstein's
attention was drawn to her. On a similar occasion he asked his
audience what they would like him to read, directing his question in
particular to Marguerite. 'It doesn't matter what you read', Arvid
commented sourly, 'she won't understand it.'

Despite Sjögren's disapproval, Wittgenstein and Marguerite began
to see each other almost daily. While she was in Vienna, Marguerite
attended the art school, and after her lessons would go to the Kundmanngasse building site to meet Wittgenstein. They would then go
together to the cinema to see a Western, and eat together at a café a
simple meal consisting of eggs, bread and butter and a glass of milk. It
was not quite the style to which she was accustomed. And it required a
certain degree of courage for a respectable and fashionable young lady
like herself to be seen out with a man dressed, as Wittgenstein
invariably was, in a jacket worn at the elbows, an open-neck shirt,
baggy trousers and heavy boots. He was, moreover, nearly twice her
age. She would on occasion prefer the company of younger, more
fashionable, men like Thomas Stonborough and Talle Sjögren. This
both puzzled and angered Wittgenstein. 'Why', he would demand, 'do
you want to go out with a young thing like Thomas Stonborough?'

To their respective friends a much more puzzling question was why
Wittgenstein and Marguerite would want to go out with one another.
Arvid Sjögren was not the only close friend of Wittgenstein's who
could not get on with her. Another was Paul Engelmann, whom
Marguerite disliked in her turn. He was, she says, 'the sort of Jew one
didn't like'. 'One' could presumably put up with the Wittgensteins
because of their immense wealth, their integration into Viennese
society and because they were neither religiously nor fully 'racially'
Jewish. But Engelmann was simply *too* Jewish. It may or may not be a
coincidence that Wittgenstein's friendship with Engelmann deteriorated at the time that his relationship with Marguerite developed, and
that during the time he was in love with her Wittgenstein's attitude to
his own Jewishness underwent a profound change.

The relationship was apparently encouraged by Gretl because she
considered that Marguerite's company would have a calming and
'normalizing' influence on her brother. This may have been true, and
indeed it may have been Marguerite's very lack of intellectual depth
that enabled her to exert this influence. Wittgenstein explicitly asked

her *not* to try and penetrate his inner world of thought – a request with which she was more than happy to oblige.

Marguerite was used as the model for a bust which Wittgenstein sculpted at this time. The bust, executed in the studios of Michael Drobil, is not exactly a portrait of Marguerite, for although Wittgenstein's interest was primarily in the attitude and expression of the face, it was not her actual expression that he was attempting to capture, but one that he himself was interested in creating. One is reminded – as so often when describing Wittgenstein in love – of what Weininger says in *Sex and Character*:

> Love of a woman is possible only when it does not consider her real qualities, and so is able to replace the actual physical reality by a different and quite imaginary reality.

When the bust was finished it was given to Gretl and displayed in the Kundmanngasse house – an appropriate home for it, for aesthetically it is of a piece with the house. Wittgenstein said of his excursion into architecture:

> . . . the house I built for Gretl is the product of a decidedly sensitive ear and *good* manners, an expression of great *understanding* (of a culture, etc.). But *primordial* life, wild life striving to erupt into the open – that is lacking. And so you could say it isn't *healthy*.

One could say of his sculpture, too, that it lacks 'primordial life'. It thus falls short, on Wittgenstein's own terms, of being a great work of art. For: 'Within all great art there is a WILD animal: *tamed*.' Wittgenstein himself considered the bust as no more than a clarification of Drobil's work.

Even in music, the art for which Wittgenstein had the greatest feeling, he showed above all a great understanding, rather than manifesting 'wild life striving to erupt into the open'. When he played music with others, as he did frequently during this time in Vienna, his interest was in getting it right, in using his acutely sensitive ear to impose upon his fellow musicians an extraordinary exactitude of expression. One could even say that he was not interested in creating music, but in re-creating it. When he played, he was not expressing himself, his own primordial life, but the thoughts, the life, of others.

To this extent, he was probably right to regard himself not as creative, but as reproductive.

Despite Wittgenstein's interest in, and sensitivity to, the other arts, it was only in philosophy that his creativity could really be awakened. Only then, as Russell had long ago noticed, does one see in him 'wild life striving to erupt into the open'.

It was while he was working on Gretl's house that Wittgenstein was brought back to the activity in which he could best express his peculiar genius. Again, Gretl acted as social catalyst, when she brought Wittgenstein into contact with Moritz Schlick, Professor of Philosophy at the University of Vienna.

In bringing these two together Gretl succeeded where Schlick himself had, on more than one occasion over a number of years, failed. He had arrived in Vienna in 1922, the year that the *Tractatus* was published, and was one of the first people in Vienna to read it and to understand its value. In the summer of 1924, after meeting Frank Ramsey at Gretl's house, he wrote to Wittgenstein, addressing his letter to Puchberg:

> As an admirer of your *Tractatus Logico-Philosophicus* I have long intended to get in touch with you. My professorial and other duties are responsible for the fact that I have again and again put off carrying out my intention, though nearly five semesters have passed since I was called to Vienna. Every winter semester I have regular meetings with colleagues and gifted students who are interested in the foundations of logic and mathematics and your name has often been mentioned in this group, particularly since my mathematical colleague Professor Reidemaster reported on your work in a lecture which made a great impression on us all. So there are a number of people here – I am one myself – who are convinced of the importance and correctness of your fundamental ideas and who feel a strong desire to play some part in making your views more widely known.

In the letter Schlick suggested that he should like to visit Wittgenstein in Puchberg. Wittgenstein had, in fact, by this time moved to Otterthal, but the letter eventually found him there, and in his reply he welcomed the possibility of a visit from Schlick. Schlick wrote back quickly, announcing again his intention of coming, but it was not until April 1926, fifteen months later, that he, accompanied by a few chosen pupils, finally made the trip to Otterthal. Schlick's wife has described the spirit in which her husband undertook the journey: 'It was as if he were preparing to go on holy pilgrimage, while he explained to me, almost with awesome reverence, that W. was one of the greatest geniuses on earth.' On arriving in Otterthal the pilgrims were deeply disappointed to be told that Wittgenstein had resigned his post and had left teaching.

Thus Schlick was overjoyed when, in February 1927, he received Gretl's letter inviting him to dinner to meet Wittgenstein. 'Again', says Mrs Schlick, 'I observed with interest the reverential attitude of the pilgrim.' Schlick had, in the meantime, sent Wittgenstein some of his work and had proposed that Wittgenstein join him and some others in discussions on logical problems. In her letter of invitation Gretl responded to this proposal on Wittgenstein's behalf. She told Schlick:

He asks me to give you his warmest regards and to make his excuses to you, since he feels quite unable to concentrate on logical problems as well as doing his present work, which demands all his energies. He could certainly not have a meeting with a number of people. He feels that if it were with you alone, dear Professor Schlick, he might be able to discuss such matters. It would then become apparent, he thinks, whether he is at present at all capable of being of use to you in this connection.

After meeting Wittgenstein, his wife recalls, Schlick 'returned in an ecstatic state, saying little, and I felt I should not ask questions'. The next day Wittgenstein told Engelmann: 'Each of us thought the other must be mad.' Soon after this, Wittgenstein and Schlick began to meet regularly for discussions. According to Engelmann: 'Wittgenstein found Schlick a distinguished and understanding partner in discussion, all the more so because he appreciated Schlick's highly cultured personality.' But Wittgenstein could not be persuaded to attend meetings of Schlick's 'Circle', a group of philosophers and mathematicians, united in their positivist approach to philosophical problems and their scientific *Weltanschauung*, who met on Thursday evenings to discuss the foundations of mathematics and science, and who later evolved into the Vienna Circle. Wittgenstein told Schlick that he could talk only with somebody who 'holds his hand'.

Nevertheless, by the summer of 1927 Wittgenstein was meeting regularly with a group which met on Monday evenings and which included, in addition to himself and Schlick, a few carefully chosen members of Schlick's Circle. These included Friedrich Waismann, Rudolf Carnap and Herbert Feigl. The success of these meetings depended upon Schlick's sensitive handling of the situation. Carnap recalls that:

> Before the first meeting Schlick admonished us urgently not to start a discussion of the kind to which we were accustomed in the Circle, because Wittgenstein did not want such a thing under any circumstances. We should even be cautious in asking questions, because Wittgenstein was very sensitive and easily disturbed by a direct question. The best approach, Schlick said, would be to let Wittgenstein talk and then ask only very cautiously for the necessary elucidations.

To persuade Wittgenstein to attend these meetings Schlick had to assure him that the discussion would not have to be philosophical; he could discuss whatever he liked. Sometimes, to the surprise of his audience, Wittgenstein would turn his back on them and read poetry. In particular – as if to emphasize to them, as he had earlier explained to von Ficker, that what he had *not* said in the *Tractatus* was more important than what he had – he read them the poems of Rabindranath Tagore, an Indian poet much in vogue in Vienna at that time, whose poems express a mystical outlook diametrically opposed to that of the members of Schlick's Circle. It soon became apparent to Carnap, Feigl and Waismann that the author of *Tractatus Logico-Philosophicus* was not the positivist they had expected. 'Earlier', writes Carnap:

> when we were reading Wittgenstein's book in the Circle, I had erroneously believed that his attitude toward metaphysics was similar to ours. I had not paid sufficient attention to the statements in his book about the mystical, because his feelings and thoughts in this area were too divergent from mine. Only personal contact with him helped me to see more clearly his attitude at this point.

To the positivists, clarity went hand in hand with the scientific method, and, to Carnap in particular, it was a shock to realize that the author of the book they regarded as the very paradigm of philosophical precision and clarity was so determinedly unscientific in both temperament and method:

> His point of view and his attitude toward people and problems, even theoretical problems, were much more similar to those of a creative artist than to those of a scientist; one might almost say, similar to those of a religious prophet or a seer. When he started to formulate his view on some specific philosophical problem, we often felt the internal struggle that occurred in him at that very moment, a struggle by which he tried to penetrate from darkness to light under an intense and painful strain, which was even visible on his most expressive face. When finally, sometimes after a prolonged arduous effort, his answer came forth, his statement stood before us like a newly created piece of art or a divine revelation. Not that he asserted his views dogmatically . . . But the impression he made on us was as if insight came to him as through a divine inspiration, so that we could not help feeling that any sober rational comment or analysis of it would be a profanation.

In contrast to the members of the Circle, who considered the discussions of doubts and objections the best way of testing an idea, Wittgenstein, Carnap recalls, 'tolerated no critical examination by others, once the insight had been gained by an act of inspiration':

> I sometimes had the impression that the deliberately rational and unemotional attitude of the scientist and likewise any ideas which had the flavour of 'enlightenment' were repugnant to Wittgenstein.

Despite these differences in temperament and concerns, Wittgenstein and the members of Schlick's Circle were able to have a number of profitable discussions on philosophical issues, one focus of interest being provided by a recent paper of Frank Ramsey's, 'The Foundations of Mathematics', which Ramsey had delivered as a lecture to the London Mathematical Society in November 1925, and which had been published in the Society's *Proceedings*.

This marked the beginning of Ramsey's campaign to use the work of Wittgenstein on logic to restore the credibility of Frege and Russell's logicist approach to the foundations of mathematics. Until his untimely death in 1930, at the age of twenty-six, it was Ramsey's overriding and abiding aim to repair the theoretical holes in Russell's *Principia* and thus to re-establish the dominance of the logicist school of thought and to nip in the bud the more radical alternative proposed by the increasingly influential intuitionist school led by the Dutch mathematician L. E. J. Brouwer. Broadly speaking, the difference is that, whereas Russell wanted to show that all mathematics could be reduced to logic and thus provide a rigorous logical foundation for all the theorems accepted by pure mathematicians, Brouwer – starting from a fundamentally different conception of both mathematics and logic – wanted to *reconstruct* mathematics in such a way that only those theorems provable from within his system were to be accepted. The rest, which included a good number of well-established theorems, would have to be abandoned as unproven.

Ramsey wanted to use the *Tractatus* theory of propositions to show that mathematics consists of tautologies (in Wittgenstein's sense), and thus that the propositions of mathematics are simply logical propositions. This is not Wittgenstein's own view. In the *Tractatus* he distinguishes between logical and mathematical propositions: only the former are tautologies; the latter are 'equations' (*TLP* 6.22).

Ramsey's aim was thus to show that equations *are* tautologies. At the centre of this attempt was a Definition of Identity which, using a specially defined logical function $Q(x, y)$ as a substitute for the expression $x = y$, tries, in effect, to assert that $x = y$ is either a tautology (if x and y have the same value) or a contradiction (if x and y have different values). Upon this definition was built a Theory of Functions which Ramsey hoped to use to demonstrate the tautologous nature of mathematics. 'Only so', he thought, 'can we preserve it [mathematics] from the Bolshevik menace of Brouwer and Weyl.'

The paper came to Wittgenstein's attention through Schlick, who had been sent a copy by Ramsey. (Ramsey had not sent it to Wittgenstein himself, because of their quarrel in the summer of 1925.) Wittgenstein evidently read the paper very thoroughly. On 2 July 1927 he wrote to Ramsey criticizing his Definition of Identity at length, and expressing the view that all such theories (those that claim expressions of identity to be either tautologous or contradictory) would not do.

Wittgenstein himself – as Russell had discovered to his consternation in 1919 – had no stake at all in the enterprise of founding mathematics on logic. Indeed, he considered the enterprise misguided. 'The way out of all these troubles', he told Ramsey, 'is to see that neither "Q(x, y)", although it is a very interesting function, nor any propositional function whatever, can be substituted for "x = y".'

Ramsey replied to Wittgenstein's objections twice – once through Schlick, and again directly to Wittgenstein. The gist of his defence was that he had not intended to provide a *Definition* of Identity, but merely a substitute function which was defined in such a way that it did the job of identity statements within his theory and gave him the logical result he wanted.

The exchange is interesting as an illustration of the differences between Wittgenstein and Ramsey, and of what Wittgenstein may have meant when he described Ramsey as a 'bourgeois' thinker. For whereas Wittgenstein's objection attempts to go straight to the heart of the matter, and to demonstrate that Ramsey's whole enterprise of reconstructing Russellian foundations of mathematics was *philosophically* misguided, Ramsey's reply is concerned only with the logical and mathematical question of whether his function will do the task for which it was designed. Thus, according to Wittgenstein, Ramsey was 'bourgeois' in the sense that:

> . . . he thought with the aim of clearing up the affairs of some particular community. He did not reflect on the essence of the state – or at least he did not like doing so – but on how *this* state might reasonably be organized. The idea that this state might not be the only possible one in part disquieted him and in part bored him. He wanted to get down as quickly as possible to reflecting on the foundations – of *this* state. This was what he was good at and what really interested him; whereas real philosophical reflection disturbed him until he put its result (if it had one) to one side and declared it trivial.

The political metaphor, of course, alludes to Ramsey's remark about the 'Bolshevik menace' of Brouwer, and it might be thought that, in his use of this metaphor, Wittgenstein is equating 'real philosophical reflection' with Bolshevism. This is not so. Wittgenstein was not interested in organizing the affairs of *this* state (Russellian logicism), but neither was he interested in replacing it with another (Brouwer's intuitionism). 'The philosopher is not a citizen of *any* community of ideas', he wrote. 'That is what makes him into a philosopher.'

It was possibly this exchange with Ramsey that prompted Wittgenstein, at last, to write to Keynes. It was the first time he had written since he left teaching ('I couldn't stand the hot-water bottle any longer', he explained). He wrote to thank Keynes for his book, *A Short View of Russia*, and to tell him that he expected the house on which he was working to be finished in November of that year (1927), and that he would then like to visit England, 'if anybody there should care to see me'.

'About your book', Wittgenstein wrote, 'I forgot to say that I liked it. It shows that you know that there are more things between heaven and earth etc.'

This strange reason for liking a survey of Soviet Russia is explained by the fact that in it Keynes emphasizes that it is as a new religion, not as an economic innovation, that Soviet Marxism is to be admired. The economic aspects of Leninism he dismisses as: 'a doctrine which sets up as its bible, above and beyond criticism, an obsolete economic textbook, which I know to be not only scientifically erroneous but without interest or application for the modern world'. But the religious fervour accompanying this doctrine he found impressive:

> . . . many, in this age without religion, are bound to feel a strong emotional curiosity towards any religion which is really new and not merely a recrudescence of the old ones and has proved its motive force; and all the more when this new thing comes out of Russia, the beautiful and foolish youngest son of the European family, with hair on his head, nearer both to the earth and to heaven than his bald brothers in the West – who, having been born two centuries later, has been able to pick up the middle-aged disillusionment of the rest of the family before he had lost the genius of youth or become addicted to comfort and to habits. I sympathise with those who seek for something good in Soviet Russia.

The Soviet faith is characterized by Keynes as having in common with Christianity an exalted attitude towards the common man. But, in contrast to Christianity, there is something in it:

. . . which may, in a changed form and a new setting, contribute something to the true religion of the future, if there be any true religion – *Leninism is absolutely, defiantly non-supernatural, and its emotional and ethical essence centres about the individual's and the community's attitude towards the Love of Money*.

It is not difficult to see how such passages would have earned Wittgenstein's approval, nor how the faith which Keynes describes would have earned his respect and, potentially, his allegiance. Keynes's book, which was written after a brief visit to the Soviet Union, contrasts sharply with Russell's *The Practice and Theory of Bolshevism*, which was published after his own visit in 1920. Russell's book expressed nothing but loathing for the Soviet régime. He, too, draws a parallel with Christianity, but uses precisely that parallel to express his contempt:

> One who believes as I do, that free intellect is the chief engine of human progress, cannot but be fundamentally opposed to Bolshevism as much as to the Church of Rome. The hopes which inspire communism are, in the main, as admirable as those instilled by the Sermon on the Mount, but they are held as fanatically and are as likely to do as much harm.

Wittgenstein's own interest in Soviet Russia dates from soon after the publication of Russell's book – almost as though he thought that if Russell hated it so much there must be something good about it. Since 1922 (when he wrote to Paul Engelmann about 'the idea of a possible flight to Russia which we talked about'), Wittgenstein had been one of those who, in Keynes's words, 'seek for something good in Soviet Russia', and he continued to be attracted to the idea of living and working in the Soviet Union until 1937, when political circumstances made it impossible for him to do so.

Although Keynes proclaims himself a non-believer, in presenting Soviet Marxism as a faith in which there are fervently held religious *attitudes* (towards, for example, the value of the common man and the evils of money-love) but no supernatural *beliefs*, he has, I think, provided an important clue as to what Wittgenstein hoped to find in Soviet Russia.

Wittgenstein's suggestion to Keynes that the Kundmanngasse house would be finished by November 1927 was, for reasons already explained, hopelessly optimistic, and it was not until a year later that he was able to consider the proposed trip to England.

In the meantime he had an opportunity to see and hear for himself the 'Bolshevik menace' that had so disturbed Ramsey. In March 1928 Brouwer came to Vienna to deliver a lecture entitled 'Mathematics, Science and Language', which Wittgenstein attended, together with Waismann and Feigl. After it the three spent a few hours together in a café, and, reports Feigl:

> . . . it was fascinating to behold the change that had come over Wittgenstein that evening . . . he became extremely voluble and began sketching ideas that were the beginnings of his later writings . . . that evening marked the return of Wittgenstein to strong philosophical interest and activities.

It would be wrong to infer from Feigl's report that Wittgenstein underwent a sudden conversion to Brouwerian intuitionism – although there can be no doubt that hearing Brouwer was a tremendous stimulus to him and may well have planted a seed that developed during the following years. There is no evidence in Wittgenstein's earlier work that he was at all aware of Brouwer's ideas, and it may be that Ramsey's reference to him in his 1925 paper was the first he had heard of Brouwer. But references to Brouwer *do* crop up from 1929 onwards – so much so, that when Russell was called upon to report on Wittgenstein's work in 1930 he detected what he obviously considered to be an unhealthy influence:

> . . . he has a lot of stuff about infinity, which is always in danger of becoming what Brouwer has said, and has to be pulled up short whenever this danger becomes apparent.

It is likely, however, that Wittgenstein's excitement after the lecture had as much to do with his disagreements with Brouwer as with his agreement. There is much in the lecture that conflicts with Wittgenstein's own views, both in his early and in his later work. In particular, the Kantian notion of a 'basic mathematical intuition', which forms the philosophical foundation of intuitionism, was something with which Wittgenstein never had any sympathy, at any time in his life. In fact, if anything, his opposition to it strengthened as time went on, until in his 1939 lectures on the foundations of mathematics he told his audience bluntly: 'Intuitionism is all bosh – entirely.'

Nevertheless, there are in Brouwer's outlook certain elements that would have chimed with Wittgenstein's own, especially in his disagreements with the view propounded by Russell and Ramsey. These go deeper than the particular point noted by Russell – that Wittgenstein appeared to accept Brouwer's rejection of the notion of an infinite series in extension – and constitute a philosophical *attitude* that is fundamentally at variance with the 'bourgeois' mentality of Russell and Ramsey. On a general level one could say that Brouwer's philosophical position belongs to the tradition of continental anti-rationalist thought which one associates, for example, with Schopenhauer, and for which Wittgenstein – as Carnap discovered to his surprise – had a great deal of sympathy. (During this period Wittgenstein surprised Carnap by defending Schopenhauer against the criticism of Schlick.) The Vienna Circle, like Russell and Ramsey, placed themselves in a position that would have nothing to do with this anti-rationalist tradition.

More particularly, there are elements in Brouwer's disagreements with Russell's logicism that would have struck a sympathetic chord in Wittgenstein. Brouwer rejected the idea that mathematics either could or needed to be grounded in logic. He further rejected the notion that consistency proofs were essential in mathematics. He also rejected the 'objectivity' of mathematics in the sense that it is usually understood – i.e. for Brouwer, there is no mind-independent mathematical reality about which mathematicians make discoveries. The mathematician, on Brouwer's view, is not a discoverer but a creator: mathematics is not a body of facts but a construction of the human mind.

With all these points Wittgenstein was in agreement, and his later work can be seen as a development of these thoughts into an area that took him far away from the logical atomism of the *Tractatus*. If this development brought him no nearer to intuitionism, it perhaps helped to crystallize his many disagreements, in general and in detail, with the logicist approach to mathematics propounded by Russell and Ramsey – an approach which had guided, even if it had not dictated, the view he had expounded in the *Tractatus*.

Brouwer's lecture may not have persuaded Wittgenstein that the

Tractatus was mistaken, but it may have convinced him that his book was not, after all, the final word on the subject. There might, indeed, be more to be said.

Thus, in the autumn of 1928, when the house was finished and his thoughts turned once more to visiting England, he could, after all, contemplate returning to philosophical work. Not that such an intention is evident from the letters he wrote Keynes. In November he sent Keynes photographs of the house – 'à la Corbusier', as Keynes inaccurately described it in a letter to his wife, Lydia Lopokova – and announced his desire to visit England in December, implying a short, holiday, visit. He 'wants to stay with me here in about a fortnight', Keynes wrote. 'Am I strong enough? Perhaps if I do not work between now and then, I shall be.'

In the event, illness kept Wittgenstein in Vienna throughout December, and when, at the beginning of January, he was finally able to come to England, it was (as Keynes discovered with no apparent great surprise) not to enjoy a holiday in Lewes, nor to look for work sweeping the streets, but to return to Cambridge and work with Ramsey on philosophy.

III
1929–41

11

THE SECOND COMING

'Well, God has arrived. I met him on the 5.15 train.'
Thus was Wittgenstein's return to Cambridge announced by Keynes in a letter to Lydia Lopokova, dated 18 January 1929. Wittgenstein had been back in England just a few hours, and had already informed Keynes of his plan 'to stay in Cambridge permanently':

> Meanwhile we have had tea and now I retire to my study to write to you. I see that the fatigue is going to be crushing. But I must not let him talk to me for more than two or three hours a day.

For Wittgenstein, the experience of returning to a university that had remained largely unchanged throughout the years that had brought such a fundamental transformation in himself – and, moreover, of being greeted by some of the very people he had left in 1913 – was strange, almost eerie. It was, he wrote in his diary, 'as though time had gone backwards'. 'I do not know what awaits me', but whatever it would turn out to be: 'It will prove something! If time doesn't run out':

> At the moment I am wandering about with great restlessness, but around what point of equilibrium I do not know.

Upon his arrival there was an attempt, orchestrated by Keynes, to welcome Wittgenstein back into the Apostolic fold. On Wittgenstein's second day back in England, Keynes held a special supper meeting of the Apostles to celebrate his return. Among those attending were Richard Braithwaite, Frank Ramsey, George Rylands, George Thomson, Alister Watson, Anthony Blunt and Julian Bell – the cream of the current generation of Cambridge intelligentsia. At the meeting Wittgenstein was elected an honorary member (in Apostolic language: an 'Angel'), a gesture of forgiveness by the Society for his attitude towards them in 1912. At a subsequent meeting he was formally 'declared to be absolved from his excommunication at the appropriate time'.

The reason for this unprecedented humility on the part of the Society was that, in his absence, Wittgenstein had become an almost legendary figure among the Cambridge élite, and the *Tractatus* the centre of fashionable intellectual discussion.

But if the Apostles had hoped to claim this 'God' for their own, they were to be disappointed. Wittgenstein attended a few of their meetings, and at dinner parties at Keynes's house in Gordon Square he came into contact with a few members of what might be regarded as their London branch: the Bloomsbury group. But there was little common ground between the peculiarly English, self-consciously 'civilized', aestheticism of Bloomsbury and the Apostles, and Wittgenstein's rigorously ascetic sensibility and occasionally ruthless honesty. There was shock on both sides. Leonard Woolf recalls that he was once appalled by Wittgenstein's 'brutally rude' treatment of Lydia Keynes at lunch. At another lunch, Wittgenstein walked out, shocked at the frank discussion of sex in the presence of ladies. Clearly, the atmosphere of Bloomsbury was not one in which he felt at home. Frances Partridge describes how, in contrast to the Bells, Stracheys and Stephens with whom she mixed, Wittgenstein seemed unable or unwilling to discuss serious matters with members of the opposite sex: 'in mixed company his conversation was often trivial in the extreme, and larded with feeble jokes accompanied by a wintry smile'.

It is possible that at one of Keynes's parties Wittgenstein and Virginia Woolf may have met; if so, neither seems to have made much impression on the other. After Virginia Woolf's death Wittgenstein spoke to Rush Rhees about the effects of her background. She grew up, he said, in a family in which the measure of a person's worth was his distinction in some form of writing or in art, music, science or politics, and she had consequently never asked herself whether there might be other 'achievements'. This could be based on personal acquaintance, but it could equally well be based on hearsay. There are no references to Wittgenstein in Virginia Woolf's diaries, and only a few incidental mentions of him in her letters. In one of these, in a letter to Clive Bell written a few months after Wittgenstein's arrival in Cambridge, she mentions him in connection with Bell's son, Julian:

> . . . Julian, Maynard says, is undoubtedly the most important undergraduate at Kings, and may even get a Fellowship, and Maynard seems highly impressed with him altogether, and his poetry – Julian by the way says he tackled Maynard about Wittgenstein but was worsted.

The reference is interesting only for the fact that it was Julian Bell who was to provide, in a lengthy Drydenesque satire published in Anthony Blunt's student magazine, *The Venture*, a kind of Bloomsbury riposte to what some began to regard as the uncivilized savagery of Wittgenstein's domineering, argumentative style.

In the poem Bell seeks to defend the Bloomsbury creed that 'value is known and found in states of mind' against the *Tractatus* view that such statements are nonsense. Surely, Bell argues, Wittgenstein breaks his own rules:

> For he talks nonsense, numerous statements makes,
> Forever his own vow of silence breaks:
> Ethics, aesthetics, talks of day and night,
> And calls things good or bad, and wrong or right.

Not only does Wittgenstein talk of these things, about which he insists one must be silent; he dominates *all* talk of them:

> . . . who, on any issue, ever saw
> Ludwig refrain from laying down the law?
> In every company he shouts us down,
> And stops our sentence stuttering his own;
> Unceasing argues, harsh, irate and loud,
> Sure that he's right, and of his rightness proud,
> Such faults are common, shared by all in part,
> But Wittgenstein pontificates on Art.

The poem was written as an epistle to a fellow Apostle, Richard Braithwaite, and expressed the view of many of the young Apostolic aesthetes – 'these Julian Bells', as Wittgenstein contemptuously called them – among whom it was greatly enjoyed. When it was published, Fania Pascal says: 'the kindest people enjoyed a laugh; it released accumulated tension, resentment, even fear. For no one could ever turn the tables on Wittgenstein and pay him back in kind.'

If Wittgenstein did not turn his back on the Apostles altogether, this was chiefly because among its members was Frank Ramsey.

During his first year back at Cambridge, Ramsey was not only Wittgenstein's most valued partner in philosophical discussion, but also his closest friend. For the first two weeks after his arrival he lived with the Ramseys at their home in Mortimer Road. Ramsey's wife, Lettice, soon became a close friend and confidante – a woman who, 'at last has succeeded in soothing the fierceness of the savage hunter', as Keynes put it. She had the kind of robust sense of humour and earthy honesty that could make him relax, and gain his trust. With her alone he felt able to discuss his love for Marguerite, although, from a letter by Frances Partridge to her husband Ralph, it appears the confidence was not strictly kept:

> We have seen a lot of Wittgenstein; he confides in Lettice that he is in love with a Viennese lady, but he feels marriage to be sacred, and can't speak of it lightly.

What is surprising here is, not that he could not speak lightly of marriage, but that he could speak of it at all. He was at this time writing regularly and frequently, sometimes daily, to Marguerite, but it was not until about two years later that she realized he intended to make her his wife, and when she did, she beat a hasty retreat. Though flattered by his attention, and over-awed by the strength of his personality, Marguerite did not see in Wittgenstein the qualities she wished for in a husband. He was too austere, too demanding (and, one suspects, just a little too Jewish). Besides, when he made clear his intentions, he also made clear that he had a Platonic, childless, marriage in mind – and that was not for her.

During his first two terms at Cambridge, Wittgenstein's official status was that of an 'Advanced Student' reading for a Ph.D., with

Ramsey, seventeen years his junior, as his supervisor. In practice, he and Ramsey met as equals working on similar, or related, problems, and looking to each other for criticism, guidance and inspiration. Several times a week they would meet for many hours at a time to discuss the foundations of mathematics and the nature of logic. These meetings were described by Wittgenstein in his diary as 'delightful discussions': 'There is something playful about them and they are, I believe, pursued in a good spirit.' There was, he wrote, something almost erotic about them:

> There is nothing more pleasant to me than when someone takes my thoughts out of my mouth, and then, so to speak, spreads them out in the open.

'I don't like taking walks through the fields of science alone', he added.

Ramsey's role in these discussions was akin to that of any other supervisor: to raise objections to what Wittgenstein said. In the preface to the *Investigations*, Wittgenstein says that he was helped by Ramsey's criticism – 'to a degree which I am hardly able to estimate' – to realize the mistakes of the *Tractatus*. In a diary entry of the time, however, he took a less generous view:

> A good objection helps one forward, a shallow objection, even if it is valid, is wearisome. Ramsey's objections are of this kind. The objection does not seize the matter by its root, where the life is, but so far outside that nothing can be rectified, even if it is wrong. A good objection helps directly towards a solution, a shallow one must first be overcome and can, from then on, be left to one side. Just as a tree bends at a knot in the trunk in order to grow on.

Despite their enormous respect for each other, there were great differences, intellectual and temperamental, between Ramsey and Wittgenstein. Ramsey was a mathematician, dissatisfied with the logical foundations of his subject, who wanted to reconstruct mathematics on sound principles. Wittgenstein was not interested in reconstructing mathematics; his interest lay in extracting the philosophical root from which confusion about mathematics grew. Thus, while Ramsey could look to Wittgenstein for inspiration and Wittgenstein in Ramsey for criticism, frustrations between the two were inevitable. Ramsey once told Wittgenstein bluntly: 'I don't like your method of arguing', while Wittgenstein wrote of Ramsey, in a remark already quoted, that he was a 'bourgeois thinker' who was disturbed by *real* philosophical reflection 'until he put its result (if it had one) to one side and declared it trivial'.

A 'non-bourgeois' thinker whose profound influence on Wittgenstein's development dates from this first year back at Cambridge was Piero Sraffa. Sraffa was a brilliant Italian economist (of a broadly Marxist persuasion), and a close friend of Antonio Gramsci, the imprisoned Italian Communist leader. After jeopardizing his career in his home country by publishing an attack on Mussolini's policies, Sraffa was invited by Keynes to come to King's to pursue his work, and a lectureship in economics at Cambridge was created specially for him. Upon being introduced by Keynes, he and Wittgenstein became close friends, and Wittgenstein would arrange to meet him at least once a week for discussions. These meetings he came to value even more than those with Ramsey. In the preface to the *Investigations* he says of Sraffa's criticism: 'I am indebted to *this* stimulus for the most consequential ideas of this book.'

This is a large claim, and – considering their widely differing intellectual preoccupations – a puzzling one. But it is precisely because Sraffa's criticisms did not concern details (because, one might say, he was not a philosopher or a mathematician) that they could be so consequential. Unlike Ramsey, Sraffa had the power to force Wittgenstein to revise, not this or that point, but his whole perspective. One anecdote that illustrates this was told by Wittgenstein to both Malcolm and von Wright, and has since been retold many times. It concerns a conversation in which Wittgenstein insisted that a proposition and that which it describes must have the same 'logical form' (or 'grammar', depending on the version of the story). To this idea. Sraffa made a Neapolitan gesture of brushing his chin with his fingertips, asking: 'What is the logical form of *that*?' This, according to the story, broke the hold on Wittgenstein of the Tractarian idea that a proposition must be a 'picture' of the reality it describes.

The importance of this anecdote is not that it explains why Wittgenstein abandoned the Picture Theory of meaning (for it does not), but that it is a good example of the way in which Sraffa could make Wittgenstein see things anew, from a fresh perpective. Wittgenstein told many of his friends that his discussions with Sraffa made him feel like a tree from which all branches had been cut. The metaphor is carefully chosen: cutting dead branches away allows new, more vigorous ones to grow (whereas Ramsey's objections left the dead wood in place, forcing the tree to distort itself around it).

Wittgenstein once remarked to Rush Rhees that the most important thing he gained from talking to Sraffa was an 'anthropological' way of looking at philosophical problems. This remark goes some way to explain why Sraffa is credited as having had such an important influence. One of the most striking ways in which Wittgenstein's later work differs from the *Tractatus* is in its 'anthropological' approach. That is, whereas the *Tractatus* deals with language in isolation from the circumstances in which it is used, the *Investigations* repeatedly emphasizes the importance of the 'stream of life' which gives linguistic utterances their meaning: a 'language-game' cannot be described without mentioning their activities and the way of life of the 'tribe' that plays it. If this change of perspective derives from Sraffa, then his influence on the later work is indeed of the most fundamental importance. But in this case, it must have taken a few years for that influence to bear fruit, for this 'anthropological' feature of Wittgenstein's philosophical method does not begin to emerge until about 1932.

Apart from Ramsey and Sraffa, Wittgenstein had little to do with the college dons at Cambridge. After the first few weeks his relations with Keynes were confined largely to business matters, and although Keynes became an invaluable ally whenever Wittgenstein needed anything sorted out with the authorities, he was not a close friend. This, one gathers, was a role that Keynes was quite happy to fit into;

being Wittgenstein's *friend* demanded more time and energy than he was able, or prepared, to give.

G. E. Moore happened to be on the same train from London as Wittgenstein when Wittgenstein first arrived, and immediately their friendship, broken since Wittgenstein's wild letter to Moore in 1914, was resumed. Moore, who was by this time Professor of Philosophy at Cambridge, took responsibility for arranging the grants that enabled Wittgenstein to continue his work; other than this, however, their friendship was personal, rather than philosophical. Though he admired Moore's exactitude of expression, and would occasionally make use of it to find the precise word he wanted to make a particular point, Wittgenstein had little respect for him as an original philosopher. 'Moore?' – he once said – 'he shows you how far a man can go who has absolutely no intelligence whatever.'

Similarly with the, by now elderly, logician W. E. Johnson – another figure from his earlier Cambridge period – Wittgenstein maintained an affectionate friendship, despite the intellectual distance that existed between the two. Wittgenstein admired Johnson as a pianist more than as a logician, and would regularly attend his Sunday afternoon 'at homes' to listen to him play. For his part, though he liked and admired Wittgenstein, Johnson considered his return a 'disaster for Cambridge'. Wittgenstein was, he said, 'a man who is quite incapable of carrying on a discussion'.

Though he was approaching his fortieth birthday, Wittgenstein drew his circle of friends largely from the younger generation at Cambridge – from the undergraduates (of the non-Apostolic kind) who attended the Moral Science Club. It was in the 'sons of the English middle class' who made up this student philosophy society, according to Fania Pascal, that Wittgenstein found the two features he required in a disciple: childlike innocence and first-class brains. This may be so, but it is also true, I think, that Wittgenstein simply found he had more in common with the younger generation. He was, in a sense, very young himself. He even looked young, and at forty was frequently mistaken for an undergraduate himself. But more than this, he had the intellectual freshness and suppleness of youth. 'The mind', he told Drury, 'gets stiff long before the body does'; and in this sense he was still an adolescent. There was, that is, very little in his mental outlook that had become inflexible. He had returned to Cambridge prepared to overhaul all the conclusions he had reached up to now – prepared not only to consider new ways of thinking, but even new ways of life. Thus he was still as unformed, as unsettled into any particular pattern of life, as any undergraduate.

Many who had heard of Wittgenstein as the author of *Tractatus Logico-Philosophicus* imagined him to be an old and dignified German academic, and were unprepared for the youthfully aggressive and animated figure they encountered at meetings of the Moral Science Club. S. K. Bose, for example, who subsequently became one of the circle of Wittgenstein's friends and admirers, recalls:

> My first encounter with Wittgenstein was at a meeting of the Moral Science Club at which I read a paper on 'The nature of moral judgement'. It was a rather largely attended meeting and some people were squatting on the carpet. Among them was a stranger to all of us (except, of course, Professor Moore and one other senior member possibly present). After I had read the paper, the stranger raised some questions and objections in that downright fashion (but never unkind way) which one learned later to associate with Wittgenstein. I have never been able to live down the shame I felt when I learnt, some time later, who my interlocutor had been, and realised how supercilious I had been in dealing with the questions and objections he raised.

Wittgenstein came to dominate the discussions of the Moral Science Club so completely that C. D. Broad, the Professor of Moral Philosophy, stopped attending. He was not prepared, he later said, 'to spend hours every week in a thick atmosphere of cigarette-smoke, while Wittgenstein punctually went through his hoops and the faithful as punctually "wondered with a foolish look of praise"'.

Desmond Lee, another member of Wittgenstein's undergraduate circle of friends, has likened Wittgenstein, in his preference for discussions with younger men, and in the often numbing effect he had on them, to Socrates. Both, he points out, had an almost hypnotic influence on those who fell under their spell. Lee himself was freed from this spell when he left Cambridge, and, though deeply influenced by Wittgenstein, cannot correctly be described as a disciple. His contemporary, Maurice Drury, however, became the first, and perhaps the most perfect, example of the young disciples described by Fania Pascal.

After first meeting Wittgenstein in 1929, almost every major decision in Drury's life was made under his influence. He had originally intended, upon leaving Cambridge, to be ordained as an Anglican priest. 'Don't think I ridicule this for one minute', Wittgenstein remarked upon being told of the plan, 'but I can't approve; no, I can't approve. I would be afraid that one day that collar would choke you.' This was on the second, or possibly the third, occasion on which they had met. On the next, Wittgenstein returned to the theme: 'Just think, Drury, what it would mean to have to preach a sermon every week; you couldn't do it.' After a year at theological college, Drury agreed, and, prompted by Wittgenstein, took a job instead among 'ordinary people'. He worked on projects to help the unemployed, first in Newcastle and then in South Wales, after which, again prompted by Wittgenstein, he trained as a doctor. After the war he specialized in psychiatry (a branch of medicine suggested by Wittgenstein), and from 1947 until his death in 1976 worked at St Patrick's Hospital, Dublin, first as Resident Psychiatrist and then as Senior Consultant Psychiatrist. His collection of essays on philosophical problems in psychiatry, *The Danger of Words*, was published in 1973; though much neglected, it is perhaps, in its tone and its concerns, the most truly Wittgensteinian work published by any of Wittgenstein's students. 'Why do I now bring these papers together?' he asks in the preface, and answers:

> For one reason only. The author of these writings was at one time a pupil of Ludwig Wittgenstein. Now it is well known that Wittgenstein encouraged his pupils (those at least whom he considered had no great originality in philosophical ability) to turn from academic philosophy to the active study and practice of some particular avocation. In my own case he urged me to turn to the study of medicine, not that I should make no use of what he had taught me, but rather that on no account should I 'give up thinking'. I therefore hesitantly put these essays forward as an illustration of the influence that Wittgenstein had on the thought of one who was confronted by problems which had both an immediate practical difficulty to contend with, as well as a deeper philosophical perplexity to ponder over.

Similarly, shortly before his death, Drury published his notes of conversations with Wittgenstein to counteract the effect of 'well-meaning commentators', who 'make it appear that his writings were now easily assimilable into the very intellectual milieu they were largely a warning against'. These notes provide – perhaps more than any other secondary source – information on the spiritual and moral attitudes that informed Wittgenstein's life and work. Drury is the first, but by no means the last, disciple to illustrate that there is an important aspect of Wittgenstein's influence that is not, and cannot be, covered in the large body of academic literature which Wittgenstein's work has inspired. The line of apostolic succession, one might say, extends far beyond the confines of academic philosophy.

One of Wittgenstein's closest undergraduate friends, indeed, was a man who had no interest in philosophy whatever. Gilbert Pattisson met Wittgenstein on the train coming back from Vienna after the Easter break of 1929, and for over ten years the two enjoyed an affectionate, and strictly non-philosophical, friendship, which came to an end during the troubled years of the Second World War, when Wittgenstein began to suspect Pattisson of taking a jingoistic attitude towards the war. Pattisson was (indeed is) a genial, witty and rather worldly character, quite unlike the innocent and over-shy disciples described by Pascal. On completing his studies at Cambridge (with a minimum of academic effort and commitment), he became a chartered accountant in the City of London and led the kind of comfortable life for which his class, upbringing and education had prepared him. With him Wittgenstein could indulge the taste for what Frances Partridge had described as trivia and feeble humour, but which Wittgenstein himself called simply 'nonsense'. To have someone with whom he could 'talk nonsense to by the yard' was, he said, a deep-seated need.

At Cambridge, Pattisson and Wittgenstein would read together magazines like the *Tatler*, delighting in their rich supply of 'nonsense', and enjoying particularly the ludicrous advertisements that used to appear in such journals. They were avid readers, too, of the 'Letters from a satisfied customer' which used to be displayed in the windows of Burton's, 'The Tailor of Taste', and to which Pattisson and Wittgenstein would give exaggerated attention during their shopping trips to buy Wittgenstein's clothes. (It may have seemed to most people that Wittgenstein always wore the same things – an open-neck shirt, grey flannel trousers and heavy shoes; in fact, these items were chosen with meticulous care.)

After Pattison left Cambridge, he and Wittgenstein would meet whenever Wittgenstein passed through London (as he did frequently on his way to and from Vienna) to go through what Wittgenstein described as their 'ritual'. This consisted of tea at Lyons followed by a film at one of the big cinemas in Leicester Square. Before arriving in London, Wittgenstein would send Pattisson a card letting him know when he was arriving, so that Pattisson could make the necessary arrangements – i.e. search the *Evening Standard* for a cinema that was showing a 'good' film. In Wittgenstein's sense this meant an American film, preferably a Western, or, later, a musical or a romantic comedy, but always one without any artistic or intellectual pretensions. It was understood that Pattisson's work in the City would take second place to this ritual: 'I hope you won't be busybodying in your office', Wittgenstein wrote once, after Pattisson had pleaded pressure of work. 'Remember, even Bismarck could be replaced.'

Wittgenstein's correspondence with Pattisson consists almost entirely of 'nonsense'. In nearly every letter he makes some use of the English adjective 'bloody', which, for some reason, he found inexhaustibly funny. He would begin his letters 'Dear Old Blood' and end them 'Yours bloodily' or 'Yours in bloodiness'. Pattisson would send him photographs cut out from magazines, which he called his 'paintings', and to which Wittgenstein would respond with exaggeratedly solemn appreciation: 'I would have known it to be a Pattisson immediately without the signature. There is that bloodiness in it which has never before been expressed by the brush.' In reply, Wittgenstein would send 'portraits', photographs of distinguished looking middle-aged men, ripped out of newspaper advertisements for self-improvement courses. 'My latest photo', he announced, enclosing one such picture. 'The previous one expressed fatherly kindness only; this one expresses triumph.'

Throughout the correspondence there is a gentle ridicule of the language of the advertiser, the absurdity of the style being invoked simply by using it as though it were the normal way for two friends to write to each other. Sending Wittgenstein a (genuine) photograph of himself, Pattisson writes on the back: 'On the other side is pictured one of our 47/6 suits.' 'Somehow or other', Wittgenstein writes at the end of one letter, 'one instinctively feels that Two Steeples No. 83

Quality Sock is a real man's sock. It's a sock of taste – dressy, fashionable, comfortable.' In a postscript to another, he writes:

> You may through my generosity one of these days get a free sample of Glostora the famous hair oil, may your hair always retain that gloss which is so characteristic for well groomed gentlemen.

Some of the jokes contained in Wittgenstein's letters to Pattisson are, indeed, astonishingly feeble. Enclosing an address that ends 'W.C.1', he draws an arrow to the 'W.C.' and writes: 'This doesn't mean "Lavatory".' And on the back of a postcard of Christ Church Cathedral, Dublin, he writes: 'If I remember rightly this Cathedral was built, partly at least, by the Normans. Of course, it's a long time ago & my memory isn't what it was then.'

Within a few months of being at Cambridge, then, Wittgenstein established a fairly wide circle of friendships, which, to some extent, showed his fears of entering back into society to have been misplaced. And yet he continued to feel a foreigner at Cambridge, to feel the lack of someone like Paul Engelmann or Ludwig Hänsel – someone with whom he could discuss his innermost thoughts and feelings in his own language, and with the certainty that he would be understood. Perhaps for this reason, as soon as he returned to Cambridge, he reverted to a practice he had not kept since the *Tractatus* had been published: he began to make personal, diary-like entries in his note-books. As before, these were separated from his philosophical remarks by being written in the code he had used as a child. In one of the earliest entries, he remarks how strange it was: 'That for so many years I have never felt the slightest need to make notebook entries', and reflects on the genesis of the habit. In Berlin, when he began to write down thoughts about himself, it had arisen out of a need to preserve something of himself. It had been an important step, and though there was in it something of vanity and imitation (of Keller and Pepys), yet it still fulfilled a genuine requirement; it provided a substitute for a person in whom he could confide.

  Wittgenstein could not fully confide in the people at Cambridge because, given the linguistic and cultural differences of which he was far more acutely conscious than they perhaps realized, he could not feel entirely sure that he would be understood. Whenever a misunderstanding arose he was inclined to attribute it to those differences. 'What a statement seems to imply to me it doesn't to you', he wrote to Ramsey after one such misunderstanding. 'If you should ever live amongst foreign people for any length of time & be dependent upon them you will understand my difficulty.'

His feeling that he was dependent upon people to whom he could not make himself understood caused him intense suffering, particularly where money was involved. In May 1929 he wrote a long letter to Keynes attempting to explain these anxieties. 'Please try to understand it before you criticize it', he pleaded, adding: 'To write in a foreign language makes it more difficult.' He had become convinced (with, as we have seen, some justification) that Keynes had grown tired of his conversation. '*Now please don't think that I mind that!*' he wrote. 'Why shouldn't you be tired of me, I don't believe for a moment that I can be entertaining or interesting to you.' What pained him was the fear that Keynes might think he cultivated his friendship in order to receive financial assistance; in his anxiety about this, and about being misunderstood when he spoke in English, he invented a completely fictitious confirmation of this fear:

> In the beginning of this term I came to see you and wanted to return you some money you had lent me. And in my clumsy way of speaking I prefaced the act of returning it by saying 'Oh first I want money' meaning 'first I want to settle the money business' or some such phrase. But you naturally misunderstood me and consequently made a face in which I could read a whole story. And what followed this, I mean our conversation about the society [the Apostles], showed me what amount of negative feeling you had accumulated in you against me.

He was, however, probably right in thinking that Keynes saw himself as his benefactor rather than his friend. But, he insisted, 'I don't accept benefactions except from my friends. (That's why I accepted your help three years ago in Sussex.)' He ended: 'Please don't answer this letter unless you can write a short and kind answer. I did not write it to get explanations from you but to inform you about how I think. So if you can't give me a kind answer in three lines, no answer will please me best.' Keynes's reply to this is a masterpiece of tact and sensitivity:

Dear Ludwig,

What a maniac you are! Of course there is not a particle of truth in anything you say about money. It never crossed my mind at the beginning of this term that you wanted anything from me except to cash a cheque or something of that kind. I have never supposed it possible that you could want any money from me except in circumstances in which I should feel it appropriate to give it. When I mentioned your finances in my note the other day, it was because I had heard that you were bothered with heavy unexpected fees and I wanted, if this was so, to examine a possibility which I think I suggested to you when you first came up, namely that some help might conceivably be got out of Trinity. I had considered whether it could be a good thing for me to do anything myself, and had decided on the whole better not.

No – it was not 'an undertone of grudge' that made me speak rather crossly when we last met; it was just fatigue or impatience with the difficulty, almost impossibility, when one has a conversation about something affecting you personally, of being successful in conveying true impressions into your mind and keeping false ones out. And then you go away and invent an explanation so remote from anything then in my consciousness that it never occurred to me to guard against it!

The truth is that I alternate between loving and enjoying you and your conversation and having my nerves worn to death by it. It's no new thing! I always have – any time these twenty years. But 'grudge' 'unkindness' – if only you could look into my heart, you'd see something quite different.

Without committing himself to the strains of a more intimate friendship with Wittgenstein, Keynes managed to smooth things over to the extent of allowing Wittgenstein to accept his help in good conscience – of becoming a *friendly* benefactor, whose help was offered, and therefore accepted, in the right spirit.

Without some sort of financial assistance, Wittgenstein would not have been able to continue his philosophical work. By the end of his second term, whatever savings he had (presumably from his earnings as an architect) were insufficient to pay his college fees and leave anything for him to live on. Keynes's suggestion that he apply for a research grant from Trinity was taken up, but there were, inevitably, complications. These arose from the fact that the college found it hard to understand why someone from as wealthy a background as Wittgenstein should need a grant of this kind. Did he have any other source of money? he was asked by Sir James Butler, the Tutor in Trinity. He answered, no. Didn't he have any relations who could help? He answered, yes. 'Now as it somehow appears as if I tried to conceal something', he wrote to Moore after this interview, 'will you please accept my written declaration that: not only I have a number of wealthy relations, but also they would give me money if I asked them to, BUT THAT I WILL NOT ASK THEM FOR A PENNY.' His attitude, as he explained in another letter to Moore, was this:

> I propose to do some work, and I have a vague idea, that the College in some cases encourages such work by means of research grants, fellowships, etc. That's to say, I turn out some sort of goods and *if* the College has any use for these goods, I would like the College to enable me to produce them, as long as it *has* a use for them, and as long as I *can* produce them.

His application for a grant was given fulsome support by Frank Ramsey, who in his role as Wittgenstein's supervisor wrote to Moore urging the necessity of such assistance. 'In my opinion', he wrote, 'Mr Wittgenstein is a philosophic genius of a different order from anyone else I know':

> This is partly owing to his great gift for seeing what is essential in a problem and partly to his overwhelming intellectual vigour, to the intensity of thought with which he pursues a question to the bottom and never rests content with mere possible hypothesis. From his work more than that of any other man I hope for a solution of the difficulties that perplex me both in philosophy generally and in the foundations of Mathematics in particular. It seems to be, therefore, peculiarly fortunate that he should have returned to research.

Ramsey's report on the 'goods' that Wittgenstein had produced so far is, however, tantalizingly brief:

> During the last two terms I have been in close touch with his work and he seems to me to have made remarkable progress. He began

7 *Right:* Margarete Wittgenstein, painted by Gustav Klimt, on the occasion of her wedding to Jerome Stonborough, 1905

8 *Below:* The Technische Hochschule in Charlottenburg, Berlin

9 *Bottom:* The family at the dinner table in the Hochreit. From left to right: the housemaid Rosalie Hermann, Hermine, Grandmother Kalmus, Paul, Margarete, Ludwig

Wittgenstein & myself with a kite of his
Taken at Glossop whilst I was on
the kite-flying job.
It shows the house "The Grouse Inn"
where we stayed.

11 & 12 *Above:* With Eccles at the Kite-Flying Station in Glossop

10 *Left:* Ludwig Wittgenstein, aged about eighteen

13 *Top:* On the river in Cambridge. On the left, with his arms resting on the top of the seat, is John Maynard Keynes; standing on the right, with the flowered hat and long scarf, is Virginia Woolf; to the left of her, dressed in blazer, white trousers and cravat, is Rupert Brooke

14 *Above:* Members of the Moral Science Club, Cambridge, *c.* 1913. In the front row, third from left, is James Ward; to the right of him, Bertrand Russell; next to Russell is W. E. Johnson; in the second row, on the far right, is McTaggart; and third from the right, G. E. Moore

15 *Right:* David Pinsent

16–18 Postcards from
Norway, 1913

SHJOLDEN

19 & 20 Postcard to Eccles

Dear Eccles,
Enclosed please
find a Check
for 23 Norwegian
kroner = ~ 23/.
& a bill from Goodall
You would
highly oblige
me by paying
the amount to
Goodalls.
Yours ever L.W.

Remember me to Mrs Eccles

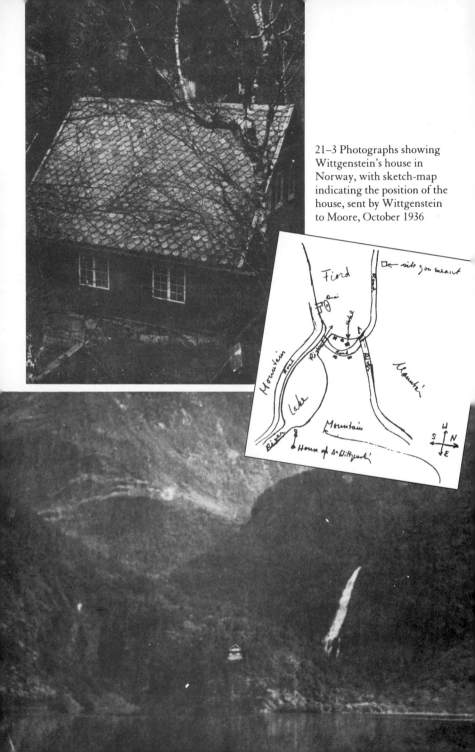

21–3 Photographs showing Wittgenstein's house in Norway, with sketch-map indicating the position of the house, sent by Wittgenstein to Moore, October 1936

with certain questions in the analysis of propositions which have now led him to problems about infinity which lie at the root of current controversies on the foundation of Mathematics. At first I was afraid that lack of mathematical knowledge and facility would prove a serious handicap to his working in this field. But the progress he had made has already convinced me that this is not so, and that here too he will probably do work of the first importance.

'He is now working very hard', Ramsey adds, 'and, so far as I can judge he is getting on well. For him to be interrupted by lack of money would be a great misfortune for philosophy.'

Perhaps in order to further convince the authorities, Wittgenstein was hurriedly awarded a Ph.D. for his 'thesis', the *Tractatus*, a work that had been in print for seven years and was already regarded by many as a philosophical classic. The examiners were Moore and Russell, the latter having to be somewhat reluctantly dragged up to Cambridge from his school in Sussex. He had had no contact with Wittgenstein since their meeting in Innsbruck in 1922, and was naturally apprehensive. 'I think', he wrote to Moore, 'that unless Wittgenstein has changed his opinion of me, he will not much like to have me as an Examiner. The last time we met he was so much pained by the fact of my not being a Christian that he has avoided me ever since; I do not know whether pain on this account has grown less, but he must still dislike me, as he has never communicated with me since. I do not want him to run out of the room in the middle of the Viva, which I feel is the sort of thing he might do.'

The Viva was set for 18 June 1929, and was conducted with an air of farcical ritual. As Russell walked into the examination room with Moore, he smiled and said: 'I have never known anything so absurd in my life.' The examination began with a chat between old friends. Then Russell, relishing the absurdity of the situation, said to Moore: 'Go on, you've got to ask him some questions – you're the professor.' There followed a short discussion in which Russell advanced his view that Wittgenstein was inconsistent in claiming to have expressed unassailable truths by means of meaningless propositions. He was, of course, unable to convince Wittgenstein, who brought the proceedings to an end by clapping each of his examiners on the shoulder and remarking consolingly: 'Don't worry, I know you'll never understand it.'

In his examiner's report, Moore stated: 'It is my personal opinion that Mr Wittgenstein's thesis is a work of genius; but, be that as it may, it is certainly well up to the standard required for the Cambridge degree of Doctor of Philosophy.'

The day after he received his Ph.D., Wittgenstein was awarded a grant of £100 by Trinity College – £50 for the summer, and £50 for the following Michaelmas term.

Wittgenstein spent the early part of the summer vacation in Cambridge, living as a lodger with Maurice Dobb and his wife at Frostlake Cottage, Malting House Lane. To this period belongs a brief and uneasy friendship with the renowned literary critic F. R. Leavis. They met at one of Johnson's 'at homes', and would occasionally take long walks together. Wittgenstein admired Leavis's personality more than his work; indeed, one might almost say he liked Leavis in spite of his work. He once greeted Leavis with the words: 'Give up literary criticism!' – a piece of advice in which Leavis, with striking misjudgement, saw only the bad influence of Bloomsbury, supposing Wittgenstein to have accepted 'Keynes, his friends and their protégés; as 'the cultural élite they took themselves to be'.

Wittgenstein was, Leavis recalls, working desperately hard at this time, and was chronically short of sleep. On one occasion, when they were out walking together until after midnight, Wittgenstein was so exhausted that on their way back to Malting House Lane he could hardly walk without the support of Leavis's arm. When they finally reached Frostlake Cottage Leavis implored him to go to bed at once. 'You don't understand', Wittgenstein replied. 'When I'm engaged on a piece of work I'm always afraid I shall die before I've finished it. So I make a fair copy of the day's work, and give it to Frank Ramsey for safe-keeping. I haven't made today's copy.'

The work that he was then engaged in writing was the paper entitled 'Some Remarks on Logical Form', which has the distinction of being the only piece of philosophical writing he published after the *Tractatus*. It was printed in the conference proceedings of the 1929 Annual Joint Session of the Aristotelian Society and the Mind Association, the most important of the British conferences of professional philosophers, which that year was held in Nottingham between 12 and 15 July. It is a mark of how quickly his thought was developing at this time, however, that almost as soon as he had sent it off to be printed he disowned it as worthless, and, at the meeting of which it supposedly forms part of the proceedings, read something quite different – a paper on the concept of infinity in mathematics, which has, consequently, been lost to posterity.

'Some Remarks on Logical Form' is nonetheless interesting as a record of a transitory phase in the development of Wittgenstein's philosophy – a phase in which the logical edifice of the *Tractatus*, though crumbling, had not yet been demolished altogether. The paper can be seen as an attempt to answer criticisms made by Frank Ramsey of Wittgenstein's discussion of colour-exclusion in the *Tractatus*. Ramsey's objections were first raised in his review of the *Tractatus*; no doubt they had been explored further in discussions between the two in the first two terms of 1929.

In proposition 6.375 of the *Tractatus* Wittgenstein had insisted: 'Just as the only necessity that exists is *logical* necessity, so too the only impossibility that exists is *logical* impossibility', and had gone on in the following proposition to apply this to the impossibility of something's being, say, both red and blue:

> . . . the simultaneous presence of two colours at the same place in the visual field is impossible, in fact, logically impossible, since it is ruled out by the logical structure of colour.

The problem here is that, if this is so, then the statement 'This is red' cannot be an atomic proposition. In the *Tractatus* it is claimed that atomic propositions are logically independent of one another, with 'This is red' quite clearly *not* being independent of 'This is blue': the truth of one implies the falsehood of the other. Thus, ascriptions of colour have to be complex, susceptible to further analysis. In the *Tractatus* Wittgenstein had appealed to the analysis of colour in terms of the velocities of particles as a way out of this difficulty. Thus, the impossibility of something's being both red and blue appears as the following contradiction: 'a particle cannot have two velocities at the same time; that is to say, it cannot be in two places at the same time'. But, as Ramsey insisted, even at this level of analysis the problem reappears:

> . . . even supposing that the physicist thus provides an analysis of what we mean by 'red', Mr Wittgenstein is only reducing the

difficulty to that of the *necessary* properties of space, time, and matter or the ether. He explicitly makes it depend on the *impossibility* of a particle being in two places at the same time.

And it is still hard to see, says Ramsey, how this can be a matter of logic rather than of physics.

Ramsey's remarks thus presented Wittgenstein with a challenge: he must either show how the properties of space, time and matter can appear as *logical* necessities, or provide an alternative account of colour-exclusion. In 'Some Remarks on Logical Form', Wittgenstein chose the latter.

He now abandons the claim that atomic propositions are independent; the truth of one can indeed imply the falsity of another, and 'This is both red and blue' is, therefore, 'ruled out'. But if this is so, then there is something seriously amiss with the analysis of the rules of logical form that was offered in the *Tractatus*. For, by the *Tractatus* rules, such constructions are ruled out only if they can be analysed into forms such as 'p and not-p', which can be shown to be contradictory by the Truth-Table Method. The paper therefore ends on a problematic note:

> It is, of course, a deficiency of our notation that it does not prevent the formation of such nonsensical constructions, and a perfect notation will have to exclude such structures by definite rules of syntax . . . Such rules, however, cannot be laid down until we have actually reached the ultimate analysis of the phenomena in question. This, we all know, has not yet been achieved.

In the work written during the following year Wittgenstein made some attempt to provide 'the ultimate analysis of the phenomena in question', and for this short period his work became, as he described it, a kind of phenomenology. Prompted by his discussions with Sraffa, however, he soon gave up the attempt to repair the structure of the *Tractatus*, and abandoned altogether the idea that there *had* to be a commonality of structure between the world and language. Indeed, the point at which he abandoned it is perhaps the point at which he decided he could not read this paper before the conference. For the paper does not present the solution to the problem raised by Ramsey so much as an admission that, within the terms of the *Tractatus*, Wittgenstein had no solution.

Having decided to speak instead on the concept of infinity in mathematics, he wrote to Russell asking him to attend – 'as your presence would improve the discussion immensely and perhaps would be the only thing making it worth while at all'. It was the first and only time in his career that Wittgenstein attended such a confer-ence, and, as he explained to Russell, he had no great hopes for it: 'I fear that whatever one says to them will either fall flat or arouse irrelevant troubles in their minds.' What he had to say about infinity would, he feared, 'be all Chinese to them'.

The Oxford philosopher, John Mabbott, recalls that when he arrived in Nottingham to attend the conference he met at the student hostel a youngish man with a rucksack, shorts and open-neck shirt. Never having seen Wittgenstein before, he assumed that this was a student on vacation who did not know his hostel had been given over to those attending the conference. 'I'm afraid there is a gathering of philosophers going on in here', he said kindly. Wittgenstein replied darkly: 'I too.'

In the event, Russell did not attend, and the conference served only to confirm Wittgenstein's contempt for such gatherings. One positive consequence of the meeting, however, was that he struck up a friendship with Gilbert Ryle, who had, as Ryle writes in his auto-biographical notes, 'for some time been a mystified admirer'. Accord-ing to Wittgenstein it was the serious and interested expression on Ryle's face during Wittgenstein's paper that attracted his attention, and compelled him to make Ryle's acquaintance. Later, Ryle became convinced that Wittgenstein's influence on his students was de-trimental, and Wittgenstein that Ryle was not, after all, *serious*. But throughout the 1930s the two enjoyed a cordial relationship, and occasionally accompanied each other on walking holidays. Their conversation on these walks was as likely to touch on films as on philosophy, Ryle stoutly resisting Wittgenstein's contention that, not only had a good British film never been made, but such a thing was an impossibility – almost, one might say (subject to further analysis), a *logical* impossibility.

Wittgenstein's conviction that his paper on infinity would be 'all Chinese' to the philosophers gathered at Nottingham is a typical expression of a recurrent feeling that whatever he said would be liable to be misunderstood. He was, he felt, surrounded by people unable to understand him. Even Ramsey was unable to follow him in his radical departures from the theory of the *Tractatus*. In September we find him complaining in his diary about Ramsey's lack of originality, his inability to see things afresh, as though he had come across the problems for the first time. On 6 October, at the beginning of the Michaelmas term, he recorded a dream that is a kind of allegory of his situation, or at least of how he felt about his position:

> This morning I dreamt: I had a long time ago commissioned someone to make me a water-wheel and now I no longer wanted it but he was still working on it. The wheel lay there and it was bad; it was notched all around, perhaps in order to put the blades in (as in the motor of a steam turbine). He explained to me what a tiresome task it was, and I thought: I had ordered a straightforward paddle-wheel, which would have been simple to make. The thought tormented me that the man was too stupid to explain to him or to make a better wheel, and that I could do nothing but leave him to it. I thought: I have to live with people to whom I cannot make myself understood. – That is a thought that I actually do have often. At the same time with the feeling that it is my own fault.

'The situation of the man, who so senselessly and badly worked on the waterwheel', he adds, 'was my own in Manchester when I made what were, with hindsight, fruitless attempts at the construction of a gas turbine.' But more than that, the dream is a picture of his present intellectual situation now that the *Tractatus* had been proved inadequate. There it lay: ineptly constructed and inadequate for the task, and *still* the man (himself or Ramsey?) was tinkering with it, performing the tiresome and pointless feat of making it still more elaborate, when what was really needed was a completely different, and simpler, kind of wheel.

In November Wittgenstein accepted an invitation from C. K. Ogden, the translator of the *Tractatus*, to deliver a paper to 'The Heretics', a society similar to the Apostles but less élitist and more concerned with science. The society had previously been addressed by such luminaries as H. G. Wells, Bertrand Russell and Virginia Woolf (*Mr Bennett and Mrs Brown* is based on Virginia Woolf's address to the Heretics). This time he chose not to speak 'Chinese', but rather to use the opportunity to try and correct the most prevalent and serious misunderstanding of the *Tractatus*: the idea that it is a work written in a positivist, anti-metaphysical spirit.

In what was to be the only 'popular' lecture he ever gave in his life, Wittgenstein chose to speak on ethics. In it he reiterated the view of the *Tractatus* that any attempt to say anything about the subject-matter of ethics would lead to nonsense, but tried to make clearer the fact that his own attitude to this was radically different from that of a positivist anti-metaphysician:

> My whole tendency and I believe the tendency of all men who ever tried to write or talk on Ethics or Religion was to run against the boundaries of language. This running against the walls of our cage is perfectly, absolutely hopeless. Ethics so far as it springs from the desire to say something about the meaning of life, the absolute good, the absolute valuable, can be no science. What it says does not add to our knowledge in any sense. But it is a document of a tendency in the human mind which I personally cannot help respecting deeply and I would not for my life ridicule it.

He also gave some examples from his own experience of this tendency to 'run against the walls of our cage':

> I will describe this experience in order, if possible, to make you recall the same or similar experiences, so that we may have a common ground for our investigation. I believe the best way of describing it is to say that when I have it I wonder at the existence of the world. And I am then inclined to use such phrases as 'how extraordinary that anything should exist' or 'how extraordinary that the world should exist'. I will mention another experience straight away which I also know and which others of you might be acquainted with: it is, what one might call, the experience of feeling absolutely safe. I mean the state of mind in which one is inclined to say 'I am safe, nothing can injure me whatever happens.'

He went on to show that the things one is inclined to say after such experiences are a misuse of language – they mean nothing. And yet the experiences themselves 'seem to those who have had them, for instance to me, to have in some sense an intrinsic, absolute value'. They cannot be captured by factual language precisely because their value lies beyond the world of facts. In a notebook of the time

Wittgenstein wrote a sentence which he did not include in the lecture, but which crystallizes his attitude perfectly: 'What is good is also divine. Queer as it sounds, that sums up my ethics.'

What is perhaps most striking about this lecture, however, is that it is not about ethics at all, as the term is usually understood. That is to say, there is no mention in it of moral problems, or of how those problems are to be analysed and understood. For Wittgenstein's thoughts on ethics in that sense, we have to turn to his diaries and the records of his conversations.

There is no doubt that, though he regarded ethics as a realm in which nothing was sayable, Wittgenstein did indeed think and say a great deal about moral problems. In fact, his life might be said to have been dominated by a moral struggle – the struggle to be *anständig* (decent), which for him meant, above all, overcoming the temptations presented by his pride and vanity to be dishonest.

It is not true, as some of his friends have insisted, that Wittgenstein was so honest that he was incapable of telling a lie. Nor is it true that he had no trace of the vanity of which he was always accusing himself. Of course, to say this is not to claim that he was, by ordinary standards, either dishonest or vain. He most certainly was not. But there were, equally certainly, occasions on which his concern to impress people overcame his concern to speak the strict truth. In his diary he says of himself:

> What others think of me always occupies me to an extraordinary extent. I am often concerned to make a good impression. I.e. I very frequently think about the impression I make on others and it is pleasant if I think that it is good, and unpleasant if not.

And though, in stating this, he is only remarking on something that is platitudinously true of all of us, yet he is also drawing attention to what he felt to be the biggest barrier between himself and *Anständigkeit* – namely, his vanity.

An impression Wittgenstein quite often made, and which no doubt appealed to his vanity, was of being aristocratic. F. R. Leavis, for example, once overheard him remark: 'In my father's house there were seven grand pianos', and immediately wondered whether he was related to the Princess Wittgenstein who figures in the annals of music. It was, in fact, widely believed in Cambridge that he was of the princely German family, the Sayn-Wittgensteins. Though Wittgen-

stein did not positively encourage this misapprehension, remarks such as the one quoted by Leavis (which is, incidentally, of doubtful truth, there being only three or four grand pianos at the house in the Alleegasse) would have done nothing to correct it. Opinions vary as to what degree of concealment there was about his true background.*
Perhaps the most important fact is that Wittgenstein himself felt that he was hiding something – felt that he was allowing people to think of him as an aristocrat when in fact he was a Jew. In December he reported a complex dream, which might be seen as an expression of this anxiety:

A strange dream:

I see in an illustrated newspaper a photograph of Vertsagt, who is a much talked about hero of the day. The picture shows him in his car. People talk about his disgraceful deeds; Hänsel is standing next to me and also someone else, someone who resembles my brother Kurt. The latter says that Vertsag [sic] is a Jew but has enjoyed the upbringing of a rich Scottish Lord. Now he is a workers' leader (*Arbeiterführer*). He has not changed his name because it is not the custom there. It is new to me that Vertsagt, which I pronounce with the stress on the first syllable, is a Jew, and I see that his name is simply *verzagt* [German for 'faint-hearted']. It doesn't strike me that it is written with 'ts' which I see printed a little bolder than the other letters. I think: must there be a Jew behind every indecency? Now Hänsel and I are on the terrace of a house, perhaps the big log-cabin on the Hochreit, and along the street comes Vertsag in his motor-car; he has an angry face, slightly reddish fair hair and a similarly coloured moustache (he does not look Jewish). He opens fire with a machine-gun at a cyclist behind him who writhes with pain and is mercilessly gunned to the ground with several shots. Vertsag has driven past, and now comes a young, poor-looking girl on a cycle and she too is shot at by Vertsag as he drives on. And these shots, when they hit her breast make a bubbling sound like an almost-empty kettle over a flame. I felt sorry for the girl and thought that it could only happen in Austria that this girl would find no help and compassion; that the people would look on as she suffers and is

---

* Bartley claims that Wittgenstein once pleaded with a cousin who was living in England not to reveal his partly Jewish descent, while most of his friends insist he did nothing at all to hide the truth about his origins.

killed. I myself am afraid to help her because I am afraid of being shot by Vertsag. I go towards her, but try and hide behind a board.

Then I wake up. I must add that in the conversation with Hänsel, first in the presence of the other person and then after he had left us, I am embarrassed and do not want to say that I myself am descended from Jews or that the case of Vertsag is my own case too.

Wittgenstein's waking reflections on the dream have to do mostly with the name of its central character. He thought, strangely, that it was spelt *pferzagt* (which means nothing) and also that it was Hungarian: 'The name had for me something evil, spiteful and very masculine about it.'

But more pertinent perhaps is his very first thought: that the case of Vertsagt is also his own – that of a man who is regarded as a hero and has the looks and upbringing of an aristocrat, but is actually a Jew and a scoundrel. And, what is worse, that he felt too embarrassed, too *verzagt*, to confess it. This feeling of cowardice haunted him for many years, and led him eventually, seven years after this dream, to make a formal confession of the extent of his Jewish background.

What is most disturbing about the dream, however, is Wittgenstein's use of Nazi slogans to express his own internal anxieties. Is a Jew behind every indecency? The question might have come out of *Mein Kampf*, so redolent is it of the Nazi picture of the deceitful, parasitic Jew hiding his real intentions and his real nature as he spreads his poison among the German peoples. Thankfully, the period during which Wittgenstein was inclined to adopt this image (or something not so very different from it) to describe and analyse his own *Unanständigkeit* is mercifully brief. It reaches its climax in a series of remarks about Jewishness written in 1931, and after that comes abruptly to an end.

One question which naturally arises out of the dream is not discussed by Wittgenstein: is Vertsagt's shooting of the innocent girl a symbol of his own corrupting influence on Marguerite? There is, of course, no way of answering the question, but there are, I think, reasons for thinking that his plans to marry Marguerite prompted him to make yet deeper and more strenuous efforts to cleanse himself of his own impurities, to unearth all the unpleasant and dishonest sides to his nature that he preferred to keep hidden, in readiness for his commitment to the 'sacred' act he mentioned to Lettice Ramsey.

12

THE 'VERIFICATIONIST PHASE'

Towards the end of 1929 Wittgenstein might have gained some hint of Marguerite's ambivalence about their relationship, and of her doubts about marrying him, when, shortly after he arrived in Vienna to spend Christmas with her and with his family, she announced that she no longer wished to kiss him. Her feelings for him, she explained, were not of the appropriate kind. Wittgenstein did not take the hint. In his diary notes he does not pause to reflect on *her* feelings, but dwells, rather, on his own. He found it painful, he admitted, but at the same time he was not unhappy about it. For, really, everything depended on his spiritual state rather than on the satisfaction of his sensual desires. 'For if the spirit does not abandon me, then nothing that happens is dirty and petty.' 'I will, however', he added, 'have to stand on tiptoe a great deal if I do not want to go under.' The problem, as he saw it, was not to win her over but to conquer his own desires. 'I am a beast and am still not unhappy about it', he wrote on Christmas Day. 'I am in danger of becoming still more superficial. May God prevent it!'

As a technique for avoiding this tendency, or perhaps in order to reveal it, he conceived the idea of writing an autobiography. And here again, *everything* depended on the spirit. On 28 December he wrote:

The spirit in which one can write the truth about oneself can take the most varied forms; from the most decent to the most indecent. And accordingly it is very desirable or very wrong for it to be written. Indeed, among the true autobiographies that one might write there are all the gradations from the highest to the lowest. I for instance cannot write my biography on a higher plane than I exist on. And by the very fact of writing it I do not *necessarily* enhance myself; I *may* thereby even make myself dirtier than I was in the first place. Something inside me speaks in favour of my writing my biography, and in fact I would like some time to spread out my life clearly, in order to have it clearly in front of me, and for others too. Not so much to put it on trial as to produce, in any case, clarity and truth.

Nothing came of this plan, although for the next two or three years he continued to make notes that attempted to expose the 'naked truth' about himself and to reflect upon the nature of a worthwhile autobiography.

Any autobiography he might have written would almost certainly have had more in common with St Augustine's *Confessions* than with, say, Bertrand Russell's *Autobiography*. The writing of it would, that is, have been fundamentally a spiritual act. He considered *Confessions* to be possibly 'the most serious book ever written'. He was particularly fond of quoting a passage from Book I, which reads: 'Yet woe betide those who are silent about you! For even those who are most gifted with speech cannot find words to describe you', but which Wittgenstein, in discussing it with Drury, preferred to render: 'And woe to those who say nothing concerning thee just because the chatterboxes talk a lot of nonsense.'

In conversation with Waismann and Schlick the text was translated even more freely: 'What, you swine, you want not to talk nonsense! Go ahead and talk nonsense, it does not matter!' These free translations, even if they fail to capture Augustine's intended meaning, certainly capture Wittgenstein's view. One should put a stop to the nonsense of chatterboxes, but that does not mean that one should refuse to talk nonsense oneself. Everything, as always, depends on the spirit in which one does it.

To Waismann and Schlick he repeated the general lines of his lecture on ethics: ethics is an attempt to say something that cannot be said, a running up against the limits of language. 'I think it is definitely important to put an end to all the claptrap about ethics – whether intuitive knowledge exists, whether values exist, whether the good is definable.' On the other hand, it is equally important to see that *something* was indicated by the inclination to talk nonsense. He could imagine, he said, what Heidegger, for example, means by anxiety and being (in such statements as: 'That in the face of which one has anxiety is Being-in-the-world as such'), and he sympathized too with Kierkegaard's talk of 'this unknown something with which the Reason collides when inspired by its paradoxical passion'.

St Augustine, Heidegger, Kierkegaard – these are not names one expects to hear mentioned in conversations with the Vienna Circle – except as targets of abuse. Heidegger's work, for example, was used frequently by logical positivists to provide examples of the sort of thing they meant by metaphysical nonsense – the sort of thing they intended to condemn to the philosophical scrapheap.

While Wittgenstein had been in Cambridge, the Circle had formed itself into a self-consciously cohesive group and had made the anti-metaphysical stance that united them the basis for a kind of manifesto, which was published under the title, *Die Wissenschaftliche Weltauffassung: Der Wiener Kreis* ('*The Scientific View of the World: The Vienna Circle*'). The book was prepared and published as a gesture of gratitude to Schlick, who was acknowledged as the leader of the group and who had that year rejected an offer to go to Berlin in order to stay with his friends and colleagues in Vienna. On hearing of the project, Wittgenstein wrote to Waismann to express his disapproval:

> Just because Schlick is no ordinary man, people owe it to him to take care not to let their 'good intentions' make him and the Vienna school which he leads ridiculous by boastfulness. When I say 'boastfulness' I mean any kind of self-satisfied posturing. 'Renunciation of metaphysics!' As if that were something new! What the Vienna school has achieved, it ought to show not say . . . The master should be known by his work.

Apart from an outline of the central tenets of the Circle's doctrine, their manifesto also contained an announcement of a forthcoming book by Waismann entitled *Logik, Sprache, Philosophie*, which was then described as an introduction to the ideas of the *Tractatus*. Despite his misgivings about the manifesto, Wittgenstein agreed to co-operate with the book and to meet regularly with Waismann to explain his ideas.

The discussions were held at Schlick's house. Waismann took fairly complete notes of what Wittgenstein said, partly to use for his

projected book and partly in order to keep the other members of
the Vienna Circle (whom Wittgenstein refused to meet) informed
about Wittgenstein's latest thoughts. These members then quoted
Wittgenstein's ideas in their own papers at philosophical conferences
etc. In this way Wittgenstein established a reputation as an influential
but somewhat shadowy contributor to Austrian philosophical debate.
Among some Austrian philosophers there was even speculation that
this 'Dr Wittgenstein', about whom they heard a great deal but of
whom they saw nothing, was no more than a figment of Schlick's
imagination, a mythological character invented as a figurehead for the
Circle.

What neither Schlick nor Waismann – still less the other members
of the Circle – appreciated in 1929 was how quickly and radically
Wittgenstein's ideas were moving away from those of the *Tractatus*. In
the ensuing years the conception of Waismann's book was forced to
undergo fundamental changes: from its intended beginnings as an
exposition of the ideas of the *Tractatus*, it became first a summary of
Wittgenstein's modifications of those ideas, and then, finally, a statement of Wittgenstein's entirely new thoughts. After it had reached this
final manifestation, Wittgenstein withdrew his co-operation, and the
book was never published.★

In his discussions with Schlick and Waismann during the Christmas
vacation, Wittgenstein outlined some of the ways in which his views
had changed since he had written the *Tractatus*. He explained to them
his conviction that the *Tractatus* account of elementary propositions
was mistaken, and had to be abandoned – and, with it, his earlier view
of logical inference:

> . . . at that time I thought that all inference was based on tauto-
> logical form. At that time I had not seen that an inference can also
> have the form: This man is 2m tall, therefore he is not 3m tall.

'What was wrong about my conception', he told them, 'was that I
believed that the syntax of logical constants could be laid down

---

★ At least, it was never published in either Waismann's or Wittgenstein's lifetime.
In 1965 it appeared in English as *The Principles of Linguistic Philosophy*, but by then
the posthumous publication of Wittgenstein's own work had made it more or less
obsolete.

without paying attention to the inner connection of propositions.' He now realized, though, that the rules for the logical constants form only a part of 'a more comprehensive syntax about which I did not yet know anything at the time'. His philosophical task now lay in describing this more complicated syntax, and in making clear the role of 'internal connections' in inference.

His thoughts on *how* he was to accomplish this task were, at this time, in a state of flux, changing from one week to the next, and even from one day to the next. A feature of these conversations is how often Wittgenstein begins his remarks with comments like 'I used to believe . . .', 'I have to correct my account . . .', 'I was wrong when I presented the matter in this way . . .', referring, not to positions he had taken in the *Tractatus*, but to views he had expressed earlier in the year, or, perhaps, earlier in the week.

As an example of what he meant by 'syntax' and of the internal connections it established, he imagined someone's saying: 'There is a circle. Its length is 3cm and its width is 2cm.' To this, he says, we could only reply: 'Indeed! What do you mean by a circle then?' In other words, the possibility of a circle that is longer than it is wide is ruled out by what we mean by the word 'circle'. These rules are provided by the syntax, or, as Wittgenstein also says, the 'grammar' of our language, which in this case establishes an 'internal connection' between something's being a circle and its having only *one* radius.

The syntax of geometrical terms prohibits, *a priori*, the existence of such circles, just as the syntax of our colour words rules out the possibility of a thing's being both red and blue. The internal connections set up by these different grammars allow the kind of inferences that had eluded analysis in terms of the tautologies of the *Tractatus*, because each of them forms a *system*:

> Once I wrote [*TLP* 2.1512], 'A proposition is laid against reality like a ruler . . .' I now prefer to say that a *system of propositions* is laid against reality like a ruler. What I mean by this is the following. If I lay a ruler against a spatial object, I lay *all the graduating lines* against it at the same time.

If we measure an object to be ten inches, we can also infer immediately that it is *not* eleven inches etc.

In describing the syntax of these systems of propositions, Wittgenstein was coming close to, as Ramsey had put it, outlining certain
'*necessary* properties of space, time, and matter'. Was he, then, in some
sense, doing physics? No, he replies, physics is concerned with
determining the *truth* or *falsity* of states of affairs; he was concerned
with distinguishing *sense* from *nonsense*. 'This circle is 3 cm long and
2 cm wide' is not false, but nonsensical. The properties of space, time
and matter that he was concerned with were not the subject of a
physical investigation, but, as he was inclined to put it at this time, a
phenomenological analysis. 'Physics', he said, 'does not yield a description of the structure of phenomenological states of affairs. In
phenomenology it is always a matter of possibility, i.e. of sense, not of
truth and falsity.'

This way of putting things had, for Schlick, an uncomfortably
Kantian ring. It almost sounded as if Wittgenstein were attempting, à
la *The Critique of Pure Reason*, to describe the general and necessary
features of the 'structure of appearance', and was being led along the
road that led to Husserl. With Husserl's phenomenology in mind, he
asked Wittgenstein: 'What answer can one give to a philosopher who
believes that the statements of phenomenology are synthetic *a priori*
judgements?' To this Wittgenstein replied enigmatically: 'I would
reply that it is indeed possible to make up words, but I cannot associate
a thought with them.' In a remark written at about this time he is more
explicit: his view that there are indeed grammatical rules that are not
replaceable by tautologies (e.g. arithmetical equations) 'explains – I
believe – what Kant means when he insists that $7 + 5 = 12$ is not an
analytic proposition, but synthetic *a priori*'. In other words, his answer
is the familiar one that his investigations *show* what Kant and the
Kantians have tried to *say*.

Though disturbed by this pseudo-Kantian strain in Wittgenstein's
new reflections, Schlick and (therefore) the other members of the
Vienna Circle took comparatively little notice of it. More congenial to
the empiricist tenor of their thinking was another point expressed by
Wittgenstein in the course of these conversations. This was that, if a
proposition is to have a meaning, if it is to say something, we must
have some idea of what would be the case if it were true. And therefore
we must have some means of establishing its truth or falsity. This
became known to the Vienna Circle as 'Wittgenstein's Principle of
Verification', and so enthusiastically was it adopted by the members of

the Circle that it has been regarded ever since as the very essence of logical positivism. In English it received its best-known and most strident statement in A. J. Ayer's *Language, Truth and Logic* (a title inspired – if that is the word – by Waismann's *Logik, Sprache, Philosophie*), which was published in 1936 and was written after Ayer had spent some time in Vienna sitting in on meetings of the Circle.

The principle is expressed in the slogan: The sense of a proposition is its means of verification; and it was explained by Wittgenstein to Schlick and Waismann as follows:

> If I say, for example, 'Up there on the cupboard there is a book', how do I set about verifying it? Is it sufficient if I glance at it, or if I look at it from different sides, or if I take it into my hands, touch it, open it, turn over its leaves, and so forth? There are two conceptions here. One of them says that however I set about it, I shall never be able to verify the proposition completely. A proposition always keeps a back-door open, as it were. Whatever we do, we are never sure that we are not mistaken.
>
> The other conception, the one I want to hold, says, 'No, if I can never verify the sense of a proposition completely, then I cannot have meant anything by the proposition either. Then the proposition signifies nothing whatsoever.'
>
> In order to determine the sense of a proposition, I should have to know a very specific procedure for when to count the proposition as verified.

Later, Wittgenstein denied that he had ever intended this principle to be the foundation of a Theory of Meaning, and distanced himself from the dogmatic application of it by the logical positivists. He told a meeting of the Moral Science Club in Cambridge:

> I used at one time to say that, in order to get clear how a sentence is used, it was a good idea to ask oneself the question: 'How would one try to verify such an assertion?' But that's just one way among others of getting clear about the use of a word or sentence. For example, another question which it is often very useful to ask oneself is: 'How is this word learned?' 'How would one set about teaching a child to use this word?' But some people have turned this

suggestion about asking for the verification into a dogma – as if I'd been advancing a theory about meaning.

When, in the early 1930s, he was asked by G. F. Stout about his views on verification, Wittgenstein told the following parable, the point of which seems to be that discovering that a sentence has no means of verification is to understand something important about it, but not to discover that there is nothing in it to understand:

> Imagine that there is a town in which the policemen are required to obtain information from each inhabitant, e.g. his age, where he came from, and what work he does. A record is kept of this information and some use is made of it. Occasionally when a policeman questions an inhabitant he discovers that the latter does not do any work. The policeman enters this fact on the record, because this too is a useful piece of information about the man!

And yet, despite these later disavowals, throughout 1930 – in his conversations with Schlick and Waismann, in a list of 'Theses' dictated to Waismann, and in his own notebooks – we find the principle expressed by Wittgenstein in formulations that sound every bit as dogmatic as those of the Vienna Circle and of Ayer: 'The sense of a proposition is the way it is verified', 'How a proposition is verified is what it says . . . The verification is not *one* token of the truth, it is *the* sense of the proposition', and so on. We can, it seems, talk of a 'Verificationist Phase' of Wittgenstein's thought. But only if we distance the verification principle from the logical empiricism of Schlick, Carnap, Ayer etc, and place it within the more Kantian framework of Wittgenstein's 'phenomenological', or 'grammatical', investigations.

In the new year of 1930 Wittgenstein returned to Cambridge to find that Frank Ramsey was seriously ill. He had suffered a spell of severe jaundice and had been admitted to Guy's Hospital for an operation to discover the cause. After the operation his condition became critical, and it became apparent that he was dying. Frances Partridge, a close friend of the Ramseys, has described how, the evening before Frank Ramsey's death, she visited his ward and was surprised to find

Wittgenstein sitting in a small room that opened off the ward a few feet from Frank's bed:

> Wittgenstein's kindness, and also his personal grief, were somehow apparent beneath a light, almost jocose tone which I myself found off-putting. Frank had had another operation from which he had not yet come round properly, and Lettice had had no supper, so the three of us set off to search for some, and eventually found sausage rolls and sherry in the station buffet. Then Wittgenstein went off and Lettice and I returned to our furnace.

Ramsey died at three o'clock the following morning, on 19 January. He was twenty-six years old.

The following day Wittgenstein gave his first lecture. He had been invited to give a course of lectures at the end of the previous term by Richard Braithwaite, on behalf of the Moral Science Faculty. Braithwaite asked him under what title the course should be announced. After a long silence Wittgenstein replied: 'The subject of the lectures would be philosophy. What else can be the title of the lectures but Philosophy.' And, under this uniquely general title, they were so listed for the rest of Wittgenstein's lecturing career.

During the Lent term of 1930 he gave an hour's lecture in the Arts School lecture room each week, followed later in the week by a two-hour discussion held in a room in Clare College lent by R. E. Priestley (later Sir Raymond Priestley), the explorer. Subsequently he abandoned the formality of the lecture room altogether and held both lecture and discussion in Priestley's rooms, until 1931, when he acquired a set of rooms of his own in Trinity.

His lecture style has often been described, and seems to have been quite different from that of any other university lecturer: he lectured without notes, and often appeared to be simply standing in front of his audience, thinking aloud. Occasionally he would stop, saying, 'Just a minute, let me think!' and sit down for a few minutes, staring at his upturned hand. Sometimes the lecture would restart in response to a question from a particularly brave member of the class. Often he would curse his own stupidity, saying: 'What a damn fool I am!' or exclaim vehemently: 'This is as difficult as hell!' Attending the lectures were about fifteen people, mostly undergraduates but including also a few dons, most notably G. E. Moore, who sat in the only armchair available (the others sat on deckchairs) smoking his pipe and taking copious notes. Wittgenstein's impassioned and syncopated performances left a memorable impression on all who heard him, and are vividly described by I. A. Richards (the co-author, with C. K. Ogden, of *The Meaning of Meaning*) in his poem, 'The Strayed Poet':

Your voice and his I heard in those Non-Lectures
– Hammock chairs sprawled skew-wise all about;
Moore in the armchair bent on writing it all out –
Each soul agog for any word of yours.

Few could long withstand your haggard beauty,
Disdainful lips, wide eyes bright-lit with scorn,
Furrowed brow, square smile, sorrow-born
World-abandoning devotion to your duty.

Such the torment felt, the spell-bound listeners
Watched and waited for the words to come,
Held and bit their breath while you were dumb,
Anguished, helpless, for the hidden prisoners.

Poke the fire again! Open the window!
Shut it! – patient pacing unavailing,
Barren the revelations on the ceiling –
Dash back again to agitate a cinder.

'O it's so clear! It's absolutely clear!'
Tense nerves crisp tenser then throughout the school;
Pencils are poised: 'Oh, I'm a bloody fool!
A damn'd fool!' – So: however it appear.

Not that the Master isn't pedagogic:
Thought-free brows grow pearly as they gaze
Hearts bleed with him. But – should you want a blaze,
Try prompting! Who is the next will drop a brick?

Window re-opened, fire attack't again,
(Leave, but leave what's out, long since, alone!)
Great calm; A sentence started; then the groan
Arrests the pencil leads. Round back to the refrain.

Richards's title is apt; Wittgenstein's lecturing style, and indeed his writing style, was curiously at odds with his subject-matter, as though a poet had somehow strayed into the analysis of the foundations of mathematics and the Theory of Meaning. He himself once wrote: 'I think I summed up my attitude to philosophy when I said: philosophy ought really to be written as a *poetic composition*.'

In these lectures Wittgenstein outlined his conception of philosophy as 'the attempt to be rid of a particular kind of puzzlement', i.e. 'puzzles of *language*'. The method it employs is that of spelling out the features of the grammar of our language: grammar tells us what makes sense and what does not — it 'lets us do some things with language and not others; it fixes the degree of freedom'. The colour octahedron is an example of grammar, in this sense, because it tells us that, though we can speak of a greenish blue, we cannot speak of a greenish red. It therefore concerns, not truth, but possibility. Geometry is also in this sense a part of grammar. 'Grammar is a mirror of reality.'

In explaining his view of the 'internal relations' established by grammar, Wittgenstein explicitly contrasts it with the causal view of meaning adopted by Ogden and Richards in *The Meaning of Meaning* and by Russell in *The Analysis of Mind*. A causal relation is *external*. In Russell's view, for example, words are used with the intention of causing certain sensations and/or images, and a word is used correctly 'when the average hearer will be affected by it in the way intended'. To Wittgenstein, this talk of cause and effect misses the point. In his notes he ridiculed Russell's account by the following analogy: 'If I wanted to eat an apple, and someone punched me in the stomach, taking away my appetite, then it was this punch that I originally wanted.'

At the end of term the question again arose of how to provide Wittgenstein with funds necessary for him to pursue his work. The grant made by Trinity the previous summer was all but spent, and the college council apparently had doubts as to whether it was worthwhile renewing it. On 9 March, therefore, Moore wrote to Russell at his school in Petersfield to ask him if he would be prepared to look at the work which Wittgenstein was doing, and report to the college on its value:

. . . for there seems to be no other way of ensuring him sufficient income to continue his work, unless the Council do make him a grant; and I am afraid there is very little chance that they will do so, unless they can get favourable reports from experts in the subject; and you are, of course, by far the most competent person to make one.

As Moore had anticipated, Russell was not very enthusiastic. 'I do not see how I can refuse', he replied:

At the same time, since it involves arguing with him, you are right that it will require a great deal of work. I do not know anything more fatiguing than disagreeing with him in an argument.

The following weekend Wittgenstein visited Russell at Beacon Hill School and tried to explain the work that he had been doing. 'Of course we couldn't get very far in two days', he wrote to Moore, 'but he seemed to understand a little bit of it.' He arranged to see Russell again after the Easter vacation, in order to give him a synopsis of the work that he had done since returning to Cambridge. Thus Wittgenstein's Easter vacation in Vienna was taken up with the task of dictating selected remarks from his manuscripts to a typist. 'It is a terrible bit of work and I feel wretched doing it', he complained to Moore.

The result of this work was the typescript that has now been published as *Philosophical Remarks*. It is usually referred to as a 'transitional' work – transitional, that is, between the *Tractatus* and *Philosophical Investigations* – and it is perhaps the only work that can be so-called without confusion. It does indeed represent a very transitory phase in Wittgenstein's philosophical development, a phase in which he sought to replace the Theory of Meaning in the *Tractatus* with the pseudo-Kantian project of 'phenomenological analysis' outlined in his discussions with Schlick and Waismann. This project, as we shall see, was soon abandoned – and with it the insistence on the Verification Principle as the criterion for meaningfulness. As it stands, *Philosophical Remarks* is the most verificationist, and at the same time the most phenomenological, of all his writings. It uses the tools adopted by the Vienna Circle for a task diametrically opposed to their own.

Upon his return from Vienna towards the end of April, Wittgenstein visited Russell at his home in Cornwall to show him the manuscript. From Russell's point of view it was not a convenient time. His wife Dora was seven months pregnant with the child of another man (Griffen Barry, the American journalist); his daughter Kate was ill with chickenpox; and his son John had gone down with measles. His marriage was falling apart amid mutual infidelities, and he was working desperately hard, writing the popular journalism, the lectures and potboiling books that paid for his financially draining experiment in educational reform. The pressures on him at this time were such that colleagues at Beacon Hill School seriously considered that he was going insane.

In these troubled circumstances Wittgenstein stayed for a day and a half, after which the beleaguered Russell made a rather tired attempt to summarize Wittgenstein's work in a letter to Moore:

> Unfortunately I have been ill and have therefore been unable to get on with it as fast as I hoped. I think, however, that in the course of conversation with him I got a fairly good idea of what he is at. He uses the words 'space' and 'grammar' in peculiar senses, which are more or less connected with each other. He holds that if it is significant to say 'This is red', it cannot be significant to say 'This is loud'. There is one 'space' of colours and another 'space' of sounds. These 'spaces' are apparently given a priori in the Kantian sense, or at least not perhaps exactly that, but something not so very different. Mistakes of grammar result from confusing 'spaces'. Then he has a lot of stuff about infinity, which is always in danger of becoming what Brouwer has said, and has to be pulled up short whenever this danger becomes apparent. His theories are certainly important and certainly very original. Whether they are true, I do not know; I devoutly hope not, as they make mathematics and logic almost incredibly difficult.

'Would you mind telling me whether this letter could possibly suffice for the Council?' he pleaded with Moore. 'The reason I ask is that I have at the moment so much to do that the effort involved in reading Wittgenstein's stuff thoroughly is almost more than I can face. I will, however, push on with it if you think it is really necessary.' Moore did not consider it necessary, although, unfortunately for Russell, he did not think the letter would suffice as a report to the Council. Russell accordingly rewrote his letter in, as he put it, 'grander language, which the Council will be able to understand', and this was then accepted as a report on Wittgenstein's work, and Wittgenstein was duly awarded a grant for £100. 'I find I can only understand Wittgenstein when I am in good health', Russell explained to Moore, 'which I am not at the present moment.'

Given the litany of Russell's troubles at this time, it is surprising that he coped as well as he did with the rigours of examining Wittgenstein's work. For his part, Wittgenstein was a harsh critic of Russell's predicament. He loathed Russell's popular works: *The Conquest of Happiness* was a 'vomative'; *What I Believe* was 'absolutely not a "harmless thing"'. And when, during a discussion at Cambridge, someone was inclined to defend Russell's views on marriage, sex and 'free love' (expressed in *Marriage and Morals*), Wittgenstein replied:

> If a person tells me he has been to the worst places I have no right to judge him, but if he tells me it was his superior wisdom that enabled him to go there, then I know he is a fraud.

On his arrival back in Cambridge on 25 April, Wittgenstein had reported in his diary the state of progress in his own, more restrained, love life:

> Arrived back in Cambridge after the Easter vacation. In Vienna often with Marguerite. Easter Sunday with her in Neuwaldegg. For three hours we kissed each other a great deal and it was very nice.

After the Easter term Wittgenstein returned to Vienna to spend the summer with his family and Marguerite. He lived on the family estate, the Hochreit, but not in the large house, preferring the woodman's cottage, where he had the peace, quiet and unencumbered surroundings that he needed for his work. He received the £50 grant from Trinity College designed to see him through the summer, but, as he wrote to Moore: 'My life is now very economical, in fact as long as I'm here there is no possibility of spending any money.' One of the few breaks he allowed himself from this work was to write nonsense to Gilbert Pattisson:

> Dear Gil (old beast),
> You have a goal of ambition; of course you have; otherwise you'd be a mere drifter, with the spirit of a mouse rather than of man. You are not content to stay where you are. You want something more

out of life. You deserve a better position & larger earnings for the
benefit of yourself & those who are (or will be) dependent on you.

How, you may ask, can I lift myself out of the ranks of the ill
paid?? To think about these and other problems I have retired to the
above address which is a country place about 3 hours journey from
Vienna. I have purchased a new big writing book of which I enclose
the label & am doing a good deal of work. I also enclose my photo
which has been taken recently. The top of my head has been
removed as I don't want it for philosophising. I have found
pelmanism the most useful method for the organisation of thought.
The little gray books have made it possible to 'card-index' my
mind.

Early in the summer Wittgenstein met with Schlick and Waismann
at Schlick's house in Vienna, primarily to prepare a lecture that
Waismann would deliver at the coming conference on the Theory of
Knowledge in the exact sciences to be held in Königsberg in September. Waismann's lecture, 'The Nature of Mathematics: Wittgenstein's
Standpoint', would be the fourth in a series covering the main schools
of thought on the subject of the foundations of mathematics (the
others in the series were: Carnap on logicism, Heyting on intuitionism
and von Neumann on formalism). The central point of this lecture was
the application of the Verification Principle to mathematics to form
the basic rule: 'The meaning of a mathematical concept is the mode of
its use and the sense of a mathematical proposition is the method of its
verification.' In the event, Waismann's lecture, and all other contribu-
tions to the conference, were overshadowed by the announcement
there of Gödel's famous Incompleteness Proof.*

---

* Gödel's first and second Incompleteness Theorems state: (1) that within any
consistent formal system, there will be a sentence that can neither be proved true
nor proved false; and (2) that the consistency of a formal system of arithmetic
cannot be proved *within* that system. The first (often known simply as Gödel's
Theorem) is widely believed to show that Russell's ambition in *Principia Mathematica*, of deriving all mathematics from within a single system of logic is, in
principle, unrealizable. Whether Wittgenstein accepted this interpretation of
Gödel's result is a moot point. His comments on Gödel's Proof (see *Remarks on the
Foundations of Mathematics*, Appendix to Part I) appear at first sight, to one trained in
mathematical logic, quite amazingly primitive. The best, and most sympathetic,
discussion of these remarks that I know of is S. G. Shanker's 'Wittgenstein's
Remarks on the Significance of Gödel's Theorem', in *Gödel's Theorem in Focus*, ed.
S. G. Shanker (Croom Helm, 1988), pp. 155–256.

During the summer, Wittgenstein also dictated to Waismann a list of 'Theses', presumably as a preliminary to the proposed joint book. These theses are for the most part a restatement of the doctrines of the *Tractatus*, but they include also a number of 'elucidations' on the subject of verification. Here the Verification Principle is stated in its most general and direct form: 'The sense of a proposition is the way it is verified', and is elucidated in the following way:

A proposition cannot say more than is established by means of the method of its verification. If I say 'My friend is angry' and establish this in virtue of his displaying a certain perceptible behaviour, I only mean that he displays that behaviour. And if I mean more by it, I cannot specify what that extra consists in. A proposition says only what it does say and nothing that goes beyond that.

Almost as soon as these theses were written, Wittgenstein became dissatisfied with their formulation, which he came to regard as sharing the mistaken dogmatism of the *Tractatus*. Indeed, Wittgenstein was developing a conception of philosophy without any theses at all. This, in fact, is implied by the remarks about philosophy in the *Tractatus*, especially proposition 6.53:

The correct method in philosophy would really be the following: to say nothing except what can be said, i.e. propositions of natural science – i.e. something that has nothing to do with philosophy – and then, whenever someone else wanted to say something metaphysical, to demonstrate to him that he had failed to give a meaning to certain signs in his propositions. Although it would not be satisfying to the other person – he would not have the feeling that we were teaching him philosophy – this method would be the only strictly correct one.

However, the *Tractatus* itself, with its numbered propositions, notoriously fails to adhere to this method. Insisting that these propositions are not really propositions at all, but 'pseudo-propositions' or 'elucidations', is an obviously unsatisfactory evasion of this central difficulty. And, clearly, a similar difficulty would attend the Theses being compiled by Waismann. Philosophical clarity must be elucidated in some other way than by the assertion of doctrines. In 1930, at the very time that Waismann was preparing his presentation of Wittgenstein's 'Theses', Wittgenstein wrote: 'If one tried to advance theses in philosophy, it would never be possible to debate them, because everyone would agree to them.'

Instead of teaching doctrines and developing theories, Wittgenstein came to think, a philosopher should demonstrate a technique, a method of achieving clarity. The crystallization of this realization and its implications brought him to, as he put it to Drury, 'a real resting place'. 'I know that my method is right', he told Drury. 'My father was a business man, and I am a business man: I want my philosophy to be businesslike, to get something done, to get something settled.' The 'transitional phase' in Wittgenstein's philosophy comes to an end with this.

13
THE FOG CLEARS

By the time he returned to Cambridge in the autumn of 1930, Wittgenstein had reached the resting place he had mentioned to Drury. He had, that is, arrived at a clear conception of the correct *method* in philosophy. His lectures for the Michaelmas term began on an apocalyptic note: 'The nimbus of philosophy has been lost', he announced:

> For we now have a method of doing philosophy, and can speak of skilful philosophers. Compare the difference between alchemy and chemistry: chemistry has a method and we can speak of skilful chemists.

The analogy of the transition from alchemy to chemistry is, in part, misleading. It is not that Wittgenstein thought he had replaced a mystical pseudo-science with a genuine science, but rather that he had penetrated beyond the cloudiness and the mystique of philosophy (its 'nimbus') and discovered that behind it lies *nothing*. Philosophy cannot be transformed into a science, because it has nothing to find out. Its puzzles are the consequence of a misuse, a misunderstanding, of grammar, and require, not solution, but dissolution. And the method of dissolving these problems consists not in constructing new theories, but in assembling reminders of things we already know:

> What we find out in philosophy is trivial; it does not teach us new facts, only science does that. But the proper synopsis of these trivialities is enormously difficult, and has immense importance. Philosophy is in fact the synopsis of trivialities.

In philosophy we are not, like the scientist, building a house. Nor are we even laying the foundations of a house. We are merely 'tidying up a room'.

This humbling of the 'Queen of the Sciences' is an occasion for both triumph and despair; it signals the loss of innocence that is a symptom of a more general cultural decay:

> . . . once a method has been found the opportunities for the expression of personality are correspondingly restricted. The tendency of our age is to restrict such opportunities; this is characteristic of an age of declining culture or without culture. A great man need be no less great in such periods, but philosophy is now being reduced to a matter of skill and the philosopher's nimbus is disappearing.

This remark, like much else that Wittgenstein said and wrote at this time, shows the influence of Oswald Spengler's *Decline of the West* (1918; English edition 1926). Spengler believed that a civilization was an atrophied culture. When a culture declines, what was a living organism rigidifies into a dead, mechanical, structure. Thus a period in which the arts flourish is overtaken by one in which physics, mathematics and mechanics dominate. This general view, especially as applied to the decline of Western European culture during the late nineteenth and early twentieth centuries, chimed perfectly with Wittgenstein's own cultural pessimism. One day, arriving at Drury's rooms looking terribly distressed, he explained that he had seen what amounts to a pictorial representation of Spengler's theory:

> I was walking about in Cambridge and passed a bookshop, and in the window were portraits of Russell, Freud and Einstein. A little further on, in a music shop, I saw portraits of Beethoven, Schubert and Chopin. Comparing these portraits I felt intensely the terrible degeneration that had come over the human spirit in the course of only a hundred years.

In an age in which the scientists have taken over, the great personality – Weininger's 'Genius' – can have no place in the mainstream of life; he is forced into solitude. He can only potter about tidying up his room, and distance himself from all the house-building going on around him.

*

During the Michaelmas term of 1930 Wittgenstein wrote several drafts of a foreword for a book – not the book he was working on with Waismann, but the typescript he had shown Russell earlier in the year. In each draft he tried to make explicit the spirit in which he was writing, and to distance his work from that of scientists and scientific philosophers: to make clear, as it were, that he was working from within the confines of his own tidy little room.

But here he came up against a familiar dilemma: to whom was he thus explaining his attitude? Those who understood it would surely see it reflected in his work, while those who did not would not understand his explanation of it either. It was a dilemma he discussed with himself in his notebooks: 'Telling someone something he does not understand is pointless, even if you add that he will not understand it. (That so often happens with someone you love.)':

> If you have a room which you do not want certain people to get into, put a lock on it for which they do not have the key. But there is no point in talking to them about it, unless of course you want them to admire the room from outside!
>
> The honourable thing to do is to put a lock on the door which will be noticed only by those who can open it, not by the rest.

'But', he added, 'it's proper to say that I think the book has nothing to do with the progressive civilization of Europe and America. And that while its spirit may be possible only in the surroundings of this civilization, they have different objectives.' In an early draft of the foreword he talks explicitly about his own work in relation to that of Western scientists:

> It is all one to me whether or not the typical western scientist understands or appreciates my work, since he will not in any case understand the spirit in which I write. Our civilization is charac-terised by the word 'progress'. Progress is its form rather than making progress one of its features. Typically it constructs. It is occupied with building an ever more complicated structure. And even clarity is sought only as a means to this end, not as an end in itself. For me on the contrary clarity, perspicuity are valuable in themselves.
>
> I am not interested in constructing a building, so much as in

having a perspicuous view of the foundations of possible buildings.

So I am not aiming at the same target as the scientists and my way of thinking is different from theirs.

In the final draft there is no mention of science or scientists. Wittgenstein talks instead of the spirit 'which informs the vast stream of European and American civilization in which all of us stand', and insists that the spirit of his work is different. But the same effect is achieved by striking a religious note:

> I would like to say 'This book is written to the glory of God', but nowadays that would be chicanery, that is, it would not be rightly understood. It means the book is written in good will, and in so far as it is not so written, but out of vanity, etc., the author would wish to see it condemned. He cannot free it of these impurities further than he himself is free of them.

Again and again in his lectures Wittgenstein tried to explain that he was not offering any philosophical *theory*; he was offering only the means to escape any *need* of such a theory. The syntax, the grammar, of our thought could not be, as he had earlier thought, delineated or revealed by analysis – phenomenological or otherwise. 'Philosophical analysis', he said, 'does not tell us anything new about thought (and if it did it would not interest us).' The rules of grammar could not be justified, nor even described, by philosophy. Philosophy could not consist, for example, of a list of 'fundamental' rules of the sort that determine the 'depth-grammar' (to use Chomsky's term) of our language:

> We never arrive at fundamental propositions in the course of our investigation; we get to the boundary of language which stops us from asking further questions. We don't get to the bottom of things, but reach a point where we can go no further, where we cannot ask further questions.

The 'internal relations' which are established by grammar cannot be further examined or justified; we can only give examples of where rules are used correctly and where they are used incorrectly, and say:

'Look – don't you see the rule?' For example, the relation between a musical score and a performance cannot be grasped causally (as though we find, mysteriously, that a certain score *causes* us to play in a certain way), nor can the rules that connect the two be exhaustively described – for, given a certain interpretation, *any* playing can be made to accord with a score. Eventually, we just have to '*see* the rule in the relations between playing and score'. If we cannot see it, no amount of explanation is going to make it comprehensible; if we can, then there comes a point at which explanations are superfluous – we do not need any kind of 'fundamental' explanation.

Wittgenstein's insistence on this point marks the turning point between his 'transitional' phase and his mature later philosophy. The later developments of his method, for example his use of 'language-games', are of less decisive importance. These developments are of an heuristic nature: they reflect the different ways in which Wittgenstein tried to make people see certain connections and differences – to see their way out of philosophical dilemmas. But the really decisive moment came when he began to take literally the idea of the *Tractatus* that the philosopher has nothing to *say*, but only something to *show*, and applied that idea with complete rigour, abandoning altogether the attempt to say something with 'pseudo-propositions'.

This emphasis on *seeing* connections links Wittgenstein's later philosophy with Spengler's *Decline of the West*, and at the same time provides the key to understanding the connection between his cultural pessimism and the themes of his later work. In *The Decline of the West* Spengler distinguishes between the Principle of Form (*Gestalt*) and the Principle of Law: with the former went history, poetry and life; with the latter went physics, mathematics and death. And on the basis of this distinction he announces a general methodological principle: 'The means whereby to identify dead forms is Mathematical Law. The means whereby to understand living forms is Analogy.' Thus Spengler was concerned to understand history, not on the basis of a series of laws, but rather through seeing analogies between different cultural epochs. What he was concerned above all to combat was a conception of history as 'natural science in disguise' – the 'taking of spiritual-political events, as they become visible day by day on the surface at their face value, and arranging them on a scheme of "causes" and "effects"'. He argued for a conception of history that saw the historian's job, not as gathering facts and providing explanations, but as perceiving the significance of events by seeing the morphological (or, as Spengler preferred to say, physiognomic) relations between them.

Spengler's notion of a physiognomic method of history was, as he acknowledges, inspired by Goethe's notion of a morphological study of nature, as exemplified in Goethe's poem *Die Metamorphose der Pflanze*, which follows the development of the plant-form from the leaf through a series of intermediate forms. Just as Goethe studied 'the Destiny in Nature and not the Causality', Spengler says, 'so here we shall develop the form-language of human history'. Goethe's morphology had as its motivation a disgust with the mechanism of Newtonian science; he wanted to replace this dead, mechanical, study with a discipline that sought to 'recognize living forms *as such*, to see in context their visible and tangible parts, to perceive them as *manifestations* of something within'.

Wittgenstein's philosophical method, which replaces theory with 'the synopsis of trivialities', is in this same tradition. 'What I give', he once said in a lecture, 'is the morphology of the use of an expression.' In *Logik, Sprache, Philosophie*, the work on which he collaborated with Waismann, the connection is made explicit:

Our thought here marches with certain views of Goethe's which he expressed in the *Metamorphosis of Plants*. We are in the habit, whenever we perceive similarities, of seeking some common origin for them. The urge to follow such phenomena back to their origin in the past expresses itself in a certain style of thinking. This recognizes, so to speak, only a single scheme for such similarities, namely the arrangement as a series in time. (And that is presumably bound up with the uniqueness of the causal schema). But Goethe's view shows that this is not the only possible form of conception. His conception of the original plant implies no hypothesis about the temporal development of the vegetable kingdom such as that of Darwin. What then *is* the problem solved by this idea? It is the problem of synoptic presentation. Goethe's aphorism 'All the organs of plants are leaves transformed' offers us a plan in which we may group the organs of plants according to their similarities as if around some natural centre. We see the original form of the leaf changing into similar and cognate forms, into the leaves of the calyx, the leaves of the petal, into organs that are half petals, half stamens, and so on. We follow this sensuous transformation of the type by linking up the leaf through intermediate forms with the other organs of the plant.

That is precisely what we are doing here. We are collating one form of language with its environment, or transforming it in imagination so as to gain a view of the whole of space in which the structure of our language has its being.

Explicit statements of what Wittgenstein is trying to accomplish in his philosophical work are rare, and it is perhaps not surprising that, as Drury has put it, 'well-meaning commentators' have made it appear that Wittgenstein's writings 'were now easily assimilable into the very intellectual milieu they were largely a warning against'. But, after all, when we see somebody tidying a room, we do not usually hear them keeping up a commentary all the while explaining what they are doing and why they are doing it – they simply get on with the job. And it was, on the whole, with this strictly 'business-like' attitude that Wittgenstein pursued his own work.

At the end of the Michaelmas term of 1930 Wittgenstein was awarded a five-year fellowship of Trinity College, the typescript that he had shown to Russell earlier in the year (published after his death as *Philosophical Remarks*) being accepted as a fellowship dissertation, with Russell and Hardy acting as examiners. The award put an end, for the time being, to the problem of funding his philosophical work, and gave him the opportunity of working out the consequences of his new method in the secure knowledge that there was indeed a demand for the 'goods' he intended to provide. Replying to congratulations sent by Keynes, he wrote: 'Yes, this fellowship business is very gratifying. Let's hope that my brains will be fertile for some time yet. God knows if they will!'

Wittgenstein's attack on theory dominates his discussions with Schlick and Waismann during the Christmas vacation of 1930. '*For me*', he told them, 'a theory is without value. A theory gives me nothing.' In understanding ethics, aesthetics, religion, mathematics and philosophy, theories were of no use. Schlick had, that year, published a book on ethics in which, in discussing theological ethics, he had distinguished two conceptions of the essence of the good: according to the first, the good is good because it is what God wants; according to the second, God wants the good because it is good. The second, Schlick said, was the more profound. On the contrary, Wittgenstein insisted, the first is: 'For it cuts off the way to any explanation "why" it is good, while the second is the shallow, rationalist one, which proceeds "as if" you could give reasons for what is good':

> The first conception says clearly that the essence of the good has nothing to do with facts and hence cannot be explained by any proposition. If there is any proposition expressing precisely what I think, it is the proposition 'What God commands, that is good'.

Similarly, the way to any explanation of aesthetic value must be cut off. What is valuable in a Beethoven sonata? The sequence of notes? The feelings Beethoven had when he was composing it? The state of mind produced by listening to it? 'I would reply', said Wittgenstein, 'that whatever I was told, I would reject, and that not because the explanation was false but because it was an *explanation*':

> If I were told anything that was a *theory*, I would say, No, no! That does not interest me – it would not be the exact thing I was looking for.

Likewise the truth, the value, of religion can have nothing to do with the *words* used. There need, in fact, be no words at all. 'Is talking essential to religion?' he asked:

> I can well imagine a religion in which there are no doctrinal propositions, in which there is thus no talking. Obviously the essence of religion cannot have anything to do with the fact that there is talking, or rather: when people talk, then this itself is part of a religious act and not a theory. Thus it also does not matter at all if the words used are true or false or nonsense.
>
> In religion talking is not *metaphorical* either; for otherwise it would have to be possible to say the same things in prose.

'If you and I are to live religious lives, it mustn't be that we talk a lot about religion', he had earlier told Drury, 'but that our manner of life is different.' After he had abandoned any possibility of constructing a philosophical theory, this remark points to the central theme of his later work. Goethe's phrase from *Faust*, '*Am Anfang war die Tat*' ('In the beginning was the deed'), might, as he suggested, serve as a motto for the whole of his later philosophy.

The deed, the activity, is primary, and does not receive its rationale or its justification from any theory we may have of it. This is as true with regard to language and mathematics as it is with regard to ethics, aesthetics and religion. 'As long as I can play the game, I can play it, and everything is all right', he told Waismann and Schlick:

> The following is a question I constantly discuss with Moore: Can only logical analysis explain what we mean by the propositions of ordinary language? Moore is inclined to think so. Are people therefore ignorant of what they mean when they say 'Today the sky is clearer than yesterday'? Do we have to wait for logical analysis here? What a hellish idea!

Of course we do not have to wait: 'I must, of course, be able to understand a proposition without knowing its analysis.'

The greater part of his discussions with Waismann and Schlick that vacation was taken up with an explanation of how this principle applies to the philosophy of mathematics. So long as we can use mathematical symbols correctly – so long as we can apply the rules – no 'theory' of mathematics is necessary; a final, fundamental, justification of those rules is neither possible nor desirable. This means that the whole debate about the 'foundations' of mathematics rests on a misconception. It might be wondered why, given his Spenglerian conviction of the superiority of music and the arts over mathematics and the sciences, Wittgenstein troubled himself so much over this particular branch of philosophy. But it should be remembered that it was precisely this philosophical fog that drew him into philosophy in the first place, and that to dispel it remained for much of his life the primary aim of his philosophical work.

It was the contradictions in Frege's logic discovered by Russell that had first excited Wittgenstein's philosophical enthusiasm, and to resolve those contradictions had seemed, in 1911, the fundamental task of philosophy. He now wanted to declare such contradictions trivial, to declare that, once the fog had cleared and these sorts of problems had lost their nimbus, it could be seen that the real problem was not the contradictions themselves, but the imperfect vision that made them look like important and interesting dilemmas. You set up a game and discover that two rules can, in certain cases, contradict one another. So what? 'What do we do in such a case? Very simple – we introduce a new rule and the conflict is resolved.'

They had seemed interesting and important because it had been assumed that Frege and Russell were not just setting up a game, but revealing the foundations of mathematics; if their systems of logic were contradictory, then it looked as if the whole of mathematics were resting on an insecure base and needed to be steadied. But this, Wittgenstein insists, is a mistaken view of the matter. We no more need Frege's and Russell's logic to use mathematics with confidence than we need Moore's analysis to be able to use our ordinary language.

Thus the 'metamathematics' developed by the formalist mathematician David Hilbert is unnecessary.* Hilbert endeavoured to construct a 'meta-theory' of mathematics, seeking to lay a provably consistent foundation for arithmetic. But the theory he has constructed, said Wittgenstein, is not metamathematics, but mathematics: 'It is another calculus, just like any other one.' It offers a series of rules and proofs, when what is needed is a clear *view*. 'A proof cannot dispel the fog':

> If I am unclear about the nature of mathematics, no proof can help me. And if I am clear about the nature of mathematics, then the question about its consistency cannot arise at all.

The moral here, as always, is: '*You cannot gain a fundamental understanding of mathematics by waiting for a theory.*' The understanding of one game cannot depend upon the construction of another. The analogy with games that is invoked so frequently in these discussions prefigures the later development of the 'language-game' technique, and replaces the earlier talk of 'systems of propositions'. The point of the analogy is that it is obvious that there can be no question of a *justification* for a game: if one can play it, one understands it. And

---

*Hilbert's formalist approach to the foundations of mathematics was announced in a lecture entitled 'On the Foundations of Logic and Arithmetic', delivered to the Third International Congress of Mathematicians in Heidelberg in 1904, and developed in a series of papers published in the 1920s. Two of the most important are reprinted in English translations in Jean van Heijenoort, ed., *From Frege to Gödel: A Source Book in Mathematical Logic* (Harvard, 1967).

similarly for grammar, or syntax: 'A rule of syntax corresponds to a configuration of a game . . . Syntax cannot be justified.'

But, asked Waismann, couldn't there be a theory of a game? There is, for example, a theory of chess, which tells us whether a certain series of moves is possible or not – whether, for instance, one can checkmate the king in eight moves from a given position. 'If, then, there is a theory of chess', he added, 'I do not see why there should not be a theory of the game of arithmetic, either, and why we should not use the propositions of this theory to learn something substantial about the possibilities of this game. This theory is Hilbert's meta-mathematics.'

No, replies Wittgenstein, the so-called 'theory of chess' is itself a calculus, a game. The fact that it uses words and symbols instead of actual chess pieces should not mislead us: 'the demonstration that I can get there in eight moves consists in my actually getting there in the symbolism, hence in doing with signs what, on a chess-board, I do with chessmen . . . and we agree, don't we?, that pushing little pieces of wood across a board is something inessential'. The fact that in algebra we use letters to calculate, rather than actual numbers, does not make algebra the theory of arithmetic; it is simply another calculus.

After the fog had cleared there could be, for Wittgenstein, no question of meta-theories, of theories of games. There were only games and their players, rules and their applications: 'We cannot lay down a rule for the application of another rule.' To connect two things we do not always need a third: 'Things must connect directly, without a rope, i.e. they must already stand in a connection with one another, like the links of a chain.' The connection between a word and its meaning is to be found, not in a theory, but in a practice, in the *use* of the word. And the direct connection between a rule and its application, between the word and the deed, cannot be elucidated with another rule; it must be *seen*: 'Here *seeing* matters essentially: as long as you do not see the new system, you have not got it.' Wittgenstein's abandonment of theory was not, as Russell thought, a rejection of serious thinking, of the attempt to understand, but the adoption of a different notion of what it is to understand – a notion that, like that of Spengler and Goethe before him, stresses the importance and the necessity of 'the understanding that consists in seeing connections'.

14
A NEW BEGINNING

For Wittgenstein, everything depended on the spirit. This is as true of his philosophy as it is of his personal relationships. What distinguished his rejection of metaphysics from that of the logical positivists, for example, was, above all else, the spirit in which it was done. In the forewords he had written in the Michaelmas term of 1930 he had tried to make the spirit of his work explicit. In 1931, he considered another possibility, a way of *showing* what he had previously tried to say. 'I think now', he wrote, 'that the right thing would be to begin my book with remarks about metaphysics as a kind of magic':

> But in doing this I must neither speak in defence of magic nor ridicule it.
>
> What it is that is deep about magic would be kept. –
>
> In this context, in fact, keeping magic out has itself the character of magic.
>
> For when I began in my earlier book to talk about the '*world*' (and not about this tree or this table), was I trying to do anything except conjure up something of a higher order by my words?

He was dissatisfied by these remarks, and wrote '*S*' (for '*schlecht*' = 'bad') by the side of them. But they are nonetheless revealing of his intentions. Given that he could not now, as he had in the *Tractatus*, attempt to 'conjure up' something of a higher order with words, with a theory, he wanted, as it were, to *point* to it. Just as speech is not essential in religion, so words cannot be essential to revealing what is true, or deep, in metaphysics.

Indeed, what is deep in metaphysics, as in magic, is its expression of a fundamentally religious feeling – the desire to run up against the limits of our language, which Wittgenstein had spoken of in connection with ethics, the desire to transcend the boundaries of reason and to take Kierkegaard's 'leap of faith'. This desire in all its manifestations was something for which Wittgenstein had the deepest respect, whether in the philosophies of Kierkegaard and Heidegger, the *Confessions* of St Augustine, the prayers of Dr Johnson, or the devotion of monastic orders. Nor was his respect confined to its Christian forms. *All* religions are wonderful, he told Drury: 'even those of the most primitive tribes. The ways in which people express their religious feelings differ enormously.'

What Wittgenstein felt was 'deep' about magic was precisely that it is a primitive expression of religious feeling. In connection with this, he had long wanted to read *The Golden Bough*, Sir James Frazer's monumental account of primitive ritual and magic, and in 1931 Drury borrowed the first volume from the Cambridge Union library. There are thirteen volumes in all, but Wittgenstein and Drury, though they read it together for some weeks, never got beyond a little way into the first volume, so frequent were Wittgenstein's interruptions to explain his disagreements with Frazer's approach. Nothing could have been more calculated to arouse his ire than Frazer's treatment of magical rituals as though they were early forms of science. The savage who sticks a pin in an effigy of his enemy does so, according to Frazer, because he has formed the mistaken scientific hypothesis that this will injure his opponent. This, on Wittgenstein's view, was to 'explain' something deep by reducing it to something incomparably more shallow. 'What narrowness of life we find in Frazer!' he exclaimed. 'And as a result: how impossible for him to understand a different way of life from the English one of his time!'

> Frazer cannot imagine a priest who is not basically an English parson of our times with all his stupidity and feebleness . . .
>
> Frazer is much more savage than most of his savages, for these savages will not be so far from any understanding of spiritual matters as an Englishman of the twentieth century. His explanations of the observances are much cruder than the sense of the observances themselves.

The wealth of facts which Frazer had collected about these rituals would, Wittgenstein thought, be more instructive if they were presented without any kind of theoretical gloss and arranged in such a way that their relationships with each other – and with our own rituals – could be *shown*. We might then say, as Goethe had said of the plant-forms he had described in *Metamorphose der Pflanze*: '*Und so deutet das Chor auf ein geheimes Gesetz*' ('And all this points to some unknown law'):

> I can set out this law in an hypothesis of evolution, or again, in analogy with the schema of a plant I can give it the schema of a religious ceremony, but I can also do it just by arranging the factual material so that we can easily pass from one part to another and have a clear view of it – showing it in a perspicuous way.
>
> For us the conception of a perspicuous presentation is fundamental. It indicates the form in which we write of things, the way in which we see things. (A kind of Weltanschauung that seems to be typical of our time. Spengler.)
>
> This perspicuous presentation makes possible that understanding which consists just in the fact that we 'see the connections'.

A *morphology* of magic rituals would, then, preserve what was deep about them, without either ridiculing or defending them. It would, in this way, have 'the character of magic'. Similarly, Wittgenstein hoped, his new method of philosophy would preserve what was to be respected in the old metaphysical theories, and would itself have the character of metaphysics, without attempting the conjuring tricks of the *Tractatus*.

There is an analogy here, too, with Wittgenstein's projected autobiography. This, too, he intended, would reveal his essential nature without any kind of explanation, justification or defence. He took it for granted that what would be revealed would be an 'unheroic', perhaps even an 'ugly', nature. But he was concerned above all that, in laying his real character bare, he should not deny it, make light of it, or, in some perverse way, take pride in it:

> If I may explain in a simile: If a street loafer were to write his biography, the danger would be that he would either
>> (a) deny that his nature was what it is,

or (b) would find some reason to be proud of it,

or (c) present the matter as though this – that he has such a nature – were of no consequence.

In the first case he lies, in the second he mimics a trait of the natural aristocrat, that pride which is a vitium splendidum and which he cannot really have any more than a crippled body can have natural grace. In the third case he makes as it were the gesture of social democracy, placing culture above the bodily qualities – but this is deception as well. He is what he is, and this is important and means something but is no reason for pride, on the other hand it is always the object of his self-respect. And I can accept the other's aristocratic pride and his contempt for my nature, for in this I am only taking account of what my nature is and of the other man as part of the environment of my nature – the world with this perhaps ugly object, my person, as its centre.

As Rush Rhees has pointed out, there is something Weiningerian about Wittgenstein's conception of writing an autobiography, a conception that sees it almost as a spiritual duty. 'Putting together a complete autobiography', Weininger writes in Sex and Character, 'when the need to do this originates in the man himself, is always the sign of a superior human being':

> For in the really faithful memory the root of piety lies. A man of real character, faced with the proposal or demand that he abandon his past for some material advantage or his health, would reject it, even if the prospect were of the greatest treasures in the world or of happiness itself.

It is in 1931, the year in which his planned autobiography received its greatest attention, that references to Weininger and Weiningerian reflections abound in Wittgenstein's notebooks and conversations. He recommended Sex and Character to his undergraduate friends, Lee and Drury, and to Moore. Their response was understandably cool. The work that had excited the imagination of pre-war Vienna looked, in the cold light of post-war Cambridge, simply bizarre. Wittgenstein was forced to explain. 'I can quite imagine that you don't admire Weininger very much', he wrote to Moore on 28 August, 'what with that beastly translation and the fact that W. must feel very foreign to you':

It is true that he is fantastic but he is great and fantastic. It isn't necessary or rather not possible to agree with him but the greatness lies in that with which we disagree. It is his enormous mistake which is great. I.e. roughly speaking if you add a ~ to the whole book it says an important truth.

What he meant by this elliptical remark remains obscure. On the subject of Weininger's central theme that women and femininity were the sources of all evil, Wittgenstein admitted to Drury: 'How wrong he was, my God he was wrong.' But this hardly reveals the important truth obtained by negating the whole book. The negation of an absurdity is not an important truth, but a platitude ('Women are *not* the source of all evil'). Perhaps he meant that Weininger had captured the essential characteristics of Man and Woman but charged the wrong suspect. In his dream about 'Vertsagt', after all, it is the woman who is the victim, while the perpetrator of the crime is a man whose very name has something disagreeably 'masculine' about it.

Certainly in his autobiographical notes there is nothing to suggest that he considered his 'unheroic', 'ugly' nature to be attributable to any supposed feminine traits.

There are, however, several remarks that indicate that he was inclined to accept a Weiningerian conception of Jewishness, and that he considered at least some of his less heroic characteristics to have something to do with his Jewish ancestry. Like Weininger, Wittgenstein was prepared to extend the concept of Jewishness beyond the confines of such ancestry. Rousseau's character, for example, he thought 'has something Jewish about it'. And, like Weininger, he saw some affinity between the characteristics of a Jew and those of an Englishman. Thus: 'Mendelssohn is not a peak, but a plateau. His Englishness'; 'Tragedy is something un-Jewish. Mendelssohn is, I suppose, the most untragic of composers.'

But – and in this he is also following Weininger – it is clear that for most of the time when he talks of 'Jews' he is thinking of a particular racial group. Indeed, what is most shocking about Wittgenstein's remarks on Jewishness is his use of the language – indeed, the slogans – of racial anti-Semitism. The echo that really disturbs is not that of *Sex and Character*, but that of *Mein Kampf*. Many of Hitler's most outrageous suggestions – his characterization of the Jew as a parasite 'who like a noxious bacillus keeps spreading as soon as a favourable medium invites him', his claim that the Jews' contribution to culture has been entirely derivative, that 'the Jew lacks those qualities which distinguish the races that are creative and hence culturally blessed', and, furthermore, that this contribution has been restricted to an *intellectual* refinement of another's culture ('since the Jew . . . was never in possession of a culture of his own, the foundations of his intellectual work were always provided by others') – this whole litany of lamentable nonsense finds a parallel in Wittgenstein's remarks of 1931.

Were they not written by Wittgenstein, many of his pronouncements on the nature of Jews would be understood as nothing more than the rantings of a fascist anti-Semite. 'It has sometimes been said', begins one such remark, 'that the Jews' secretive and cunning nature is a result of their long persecution':

> That is certainly untrue; on the other hand it is certain that they continue to exist despite this persecution only because they have an inclination towards such secretiveness. As we may say that this or that animal has escaped extinction only because of its capacity or ability to conceal itself. Of course I do not mean this as a reason for commending such a capacity, not by any means.

'They' escape extinction only because they avoid detection? And therefore they are, of necessity, secretive and cunning? This is anti-Semitic paranoia in its most undiluted form – the fear of, and distaste for, the devious 'Jew in our midst'. So is Wittgenstein's adoption of the metaphor of illness. 'Look on this tumour as a perfectly normal part of your body!' he imagines somebody suggesting, and counters with the question: 'Can one do that, to order? Do I have the power to decide at will to have, or not to have, an ideal conception of my body?' He goes on to relate this Hitlerian metaphor to the position of European Jews:

> Within the history of the peoples of Europe the history of the Jews is not treated as their intervention in European affairs would actually merit, because within this history they are experienced as a sort of disease, and anomaly, and no one wants to put a disease on the same level as normal life [and no one wants to speak of a disease as if it had the same rights as healthy bodily processes (even painful ones)].

We may say: people can only regard this tumour as a natural part of their body if their whole feeling for the body changes (if the whole national feeling for the body changes). Otherwise the best they can do is *put up with* it.

You can expect an individual man to display this sort of tolerance, or else to disregard such things; but you cannot expect this of a nation, because it is precisely not disregarding such things that makes it a nation. I.e. there is a contradiction in expecting someone *both* to retain his former aesthetic feeling for the body and *also* to make the tumour welcome.

Those who seek to drive out the 'noxious bacillus' in their midst, he comes close to suggesting, are right to do so. Or, at least, one cannot expect them – as a nation – to do otherwise.

It goes without saying that this metaphor makes no sense without a racial notion of Jewishness. The Jew, however 'assimilated', will never be a German or an Austrian, because he is not of the same 'body': he is experienced by that body as a growth, a disease. The metaphor is particularly apt to describe the fears of Austrian anti-Semites, because it implies that the more assimilated the Jews become, the more dangerous becomes the disease they represent to the otherwise healthy Aryan nation. Thus it is quite wrong to equate the anti-Semitism implied by Wittgenstein's remarks with the 'Jewish self-hatred' of Karl Kraus. The traits which Kraus disliked, and which he took to be Jewish (acquisitiveness etc.), he attributed not to any racial inheritance but to the social and religious isolation of the Jews. What he attacked primarily was the 'ghetto-mentality' of the Jews; far from wanting to keep Jew and non-Jew separate, and regarding the Jew as a 'tumour' on the body of the German people, he campaigned tirelessly for the complete assimilation of Jews: 'Through dissolution to salvation!'

From this perspective Kraus was far better placed than Wittgenstein to understand the horror of Nazi propaganda – and, one might add, more perceptive in recognizing its intellectual precedents. Wittgenstein, of course, could see that the Nazis were a barbarous 'set of gangsters', as he once described them to Drury, but at the time he was recommending Spengler's *Decline of the West* to Drury as a book that might teach him something about the age in which they were living, Kraus was drawing attention to the affinities between Spengler and the

Nazis, commenting that Spengler understood the *Untergangsters* of the West – and that they understood him.

Though alarming, Wittgenstein's use of the slogans of racist anti-Semitism does not, of course, establish any affinity between himself and the Nazis. His remarks on Jewishness were fundamentally intro-spective. They represent a turning inwards of the sense of cultural decay and the desire for a New Order (which is the path that leads from Spengler to Hitler) to his own internal state. It is as though, for a brief time (after 1931 there are, thankfully, no more remarks about Jewishness in his notebooks), he was attracted to using the then current language of anti-Semitism as a kind of metaphor for himself (just as, in the dream of Vertsagt, the image of the Jew that was propagated by the Nazis – an image of a cunning and deceptive scoundrel who hides behind a cloak of respectability while commit-ting the most dreadful crimes – found a ready response in his fears about his own 'real' nature). And just as many Europeans, particularly Germans, felt a need for a New Order to replace their 'rotten culture', so Wittgenstein strived for a new beginning in his life. His autobio-graphical notes were essentially confessional, and 'a confession', he wrote in 1931, 'has to be a part of your new life'. Before he could begin anew, he had to take stock of the old.

What is perhaps most ironic is that, just as Wittgenstein was beginning to develop an entirely new method for tackling philo-sophical problems – a method that has no precedent in the entire tradition of Western philosophy (unless one finds a place for Goethe and Spengler in that tradition) – he should be inclined to assess his own philosophical contribution within the framework of the absurd charge that the Jew was incapable of original thought. 'It is typical for a Jewish mind', he wrote, 'to understand someone else's work better than [that person] understands it himself.' His own work, for example, was essentially a clarification of other people's ideas:

Amongst Jews 'genius' is found only in the holy man. Even the greatest of Jewish thinkers is no more than talented. (Myself for instance.) I think there is some truth in my idea that I really only think reproductively. I don't believe I have ever *invented* a line of thinking. I have always taken one over from someone else. I have simply straightaway seized on it with enthusiasm for my work of clarification. That is how Boltzmann, Hertz, Schopenhauer, Frege,

Russell, Kraus, Loos, Weininger, Spengler, Sraffa have influenced me. Can one take the case of Breuer and Freud as an example of Jewish reproductiveness? – What I invent are new *similes*.

This belittling of his own achievement may have been a way of guarding himself from his own pride – from believing that he really was, as he once lightheartedly described himself in a letter to Pattisson, 'the greatest philosopher that ever lived'. He was acutely aware of the dangers of false pride. 'Often, when I have had a picture well framed or have hung it in the right surroundings', he wrote, 'I have caught myself feeling as proud as if I had painted it myself.' And it was against the background of such pride that he felt forced to remind himself of his limitations, of his 'Jewishness':

> The Jew must see to it that, in a literal sense, 'all things are as nothing to him'. But this is particularly hard for him, since in a sense he has nothing that is particularly his. It is much harder to accept poverty willingly when you *have* to be poor than when you might also be rich.
>
> It might be said (rightly or wrongly) that the Jewish mind does not have the power to produce even the tiniest flower or blade of grass that has grown in the soil of another's mind and to put it into a comprehensive picture. We aren't pointing to a fault when we say this and everything is all right as long as what is being done is quite clear. It is only when the nature of a Jewish work is confused with that of a non-Jewish work that there is any danger, especially when the author of the Jewish work falls into the confusion himself, as he so easily may. (Doesn't he look as proud as though he had produced the milk himself?)

So long as he lived, Wittgenstein never ceased to struggle against his own pride, and to express doubts about his philosophical achievement and his own moral decency. After 1931, however, he dropped the language of anti-Semitism as a means of expressing those doubts.

Wittgenstein's remarks on Jewishness, like his projected autobiography, were essentially confessional, and both seem in some way linked to the 'sacred' union he had planned for himself and

Marguerite. They coincide with the year in which his intention to marry Marguerite was pursued with its greatest earnestness.

Early in the summer he invited Marguerite to Norway, to prepare, as he thought, for their future life together. He intended, however, that they should spend their time separately, each taking advantage of the isolation to engage in serious contemplation, so that they would be spiritually ready for the new life that was to come.

Accordingly, while he stayed in his own house, he arranged lodgings for Marguerite at the farmhouse of Anna Rebni, a tough seventy-year-old woman who lived with her hundred-year-old mother. During the two weeks she spent there, Marguerite saw very little of Wittgenstein. When she arrived at the farmhouse, she unpacked her bags to find a Bible which Wittgenstein had slipped in there, together with a letter, significantly tucked into Corinthians I 13 – St Paul's discourse on the nature and virtue of love. It was a heavy hint that she did not take. Instead of meditating, praying and reading the Bible – which is how Wittgenstein spent much of his time – she did what Pinsent had done in 1913, and made the best she could of what little Skjolden had to offer in the way of entertainment. She took walks around the farm, went swimming in the fjord, got to know the villagers and learnt a little Norwegian. After two weeks she left for Rome to attend her sister's wedding, determined that the one man she was *not* going to marry was Ludwig Wittgenstein. Not only did she feel she could never rise to meet the demands a life with Wittgenstein would present; also, and equally important, she knew Wittgenstein would never be able to give her the sort of life she wanted. He had made it clear, for example, that he had absolutely no intention of having children, thinking that to do so would simply be to bring another person into a life of misery.

For some of his time in Norway, Wittgenstein was joined by Gilbert Pattisson, whose visit overlapped by about a week that of Marguerite, and who no doubt did something to lighten Wittgenstein's mood during the three weeks that he was there – although, as usual, Pattisson found it necessary to get away from Wittgenstein from time to time, taking himself to Oslo for a night to 'paint the town red'.

The visit to Norway may have put an end to any idea there might have been of Wittgenstein's marrying Marguerite, but it did not (or not immediately) result in a breaking off of friendship. For three weeks during the late summer of 1931 they saw each other almost every day at the Hochreit, where Wittgenstein stayed, as before, at the woodman's cottage on the edge of the estate, while Marguerite was a guest of Gretl's at the family residence. In a volume of reminiscences written for her grandchildren, she comments, in a phrase that recalls the role of David Pinsent: 'My presence brought him the peace which he needed while he was nurturing his ideas.'

At the Hochreit Wittgenstein worked on the completion of his book, which at this time had the working title of *Philosophical Grammar*, a title he admitted might have the smell of a textbook, 'but that doesn't matter, for behind it there is the book'.

Wittgenstein had a peculiarly laborious method of editing his work. He began by writing remarks into small notebooks. He then selected what he considered to be the best of these remarks and wrote them out, perhaps in a different order, into large manuscript volumes. From these he made a further selection, which he dictated to a typist. The resultant typescript was then used as the basis for a further selection, sometimes by cutting it up and rearranging it – and then the whole process was started again. Though this process continued for more than twenty years, it never culminated in an arrangement with which Wittgenstein was fully satisfied, and so his literary executors have had to publish either what they consider to be the most satisfactory of the various manuscripts and typescripts (*Philosophical Remarks*, *Philosophical Investigations*, *Remarks on the Philosophy of Psychology*), or a selection from them (or rearrangement of them) made by the executors themselves (*Philosophical Grammar*, *Remarks on the Foundations of Mathematics*, *Culture and Value*, *Zettel*). These we now know as the works of the later Wittgenstein, though in truth not one of them can be regarded as a completed work.

For this frustrating circumstance we can blame the fastidiousness about publication that had so infuriated Russell in 1913, and was soon to exasperate even further the unfortunate Friedrich Waismann. For in 1931, as Wittgenstein was just beginning to formulate some sort of satisfactory presentation of his new thought, Waismann was under the impression that his own presentation of Wittgenstein's ideas, the book that had been announced in 1929 under the title of *Logik, Sprache, Philosophie*, was nearing completion. On 10 September Schlick wrote to Waismann from California, commenting that he assumed the book would be ready for publication soon and that it would appear in print by the time he returned to Vienna the following Easter.

Waismann, however, had seen little of Wittgenstein that summer. Shortly before the end of the vacation, Wittgenstein met him in Vienna to present him with the latest typescripts to have been culled from his recent work. They discussed the changes in the proposed book that would have to be made in the light of this new work, and, on the basis of these discussions, Waismann rewrote his 'Theses' and sent the new version to Schlick. Wittgenstein, meanwhile, was becoming increasingly concerned that Waismann might misrepresent his new thoughts. In November he wrote to Schlick about 'this Waismann thing', and apologized for keeping him waiting for a final edition. He stressed that he wanted to honour his obligations to Schlick, but: 'For the thing itself I have no enthusiasm. I am convinced that Waismann would present *many* things in a form *completely* different to what I regard as correct.'

The central problem was that the book as originally conceived was now redundant. Wittgenstein's ideas had changed so fundamentally that he could no longer present them in a form that was essentially an updated version of the *Tractatus*. 'There are', he told Schlick, '*very, very* many statements in the book with which I now disagree!' The *Tractatus* talk about 'elementary propositions' and 'objects' had, he said, been shown to be erroneous, and there was no point in publishing a work that simply repeated the old mistakes. The *Tractatus* analysis of the proposition must be replaced by a 'perspicuous representation' of grammar which would throw overboard 'all the dogmatic things that I said about "objects", "elementary propositions" etc.'

Wittgenstein next met Waismann during the Christmas vacation of 1931, and it was then that he made clear to him his view that the whole conception of the book would have to be changed. He explained the implications of his new thinking for the status of philosophical theses:

> If there were theses in philosophy, they would have to be such that they do not give rise to disputes. For they would have to be put in such a way that everyone would say, Oh yes, that is of course obvious. As long as there is a possibility of having different opinions and disputing about a question, this indicates that things have not yet been expressed clearly enough. Once a perfectly clear

formulation – ultimate clarity – has been reached, there can be no second thoughts or reluctance any more, for these always arise from the feeling that something has now been asserted, and I do not yet know whether I should admit it or not. If, however, you make the grammar clear to yourself, if you proceed by very short steps in such a way that every single step becomes perfectly obvious and natural, no dispute whatsoever can arise. Controversy always arises through leaving out or failing to state clearly certain steps, so that the impression is given that a claim has been made that could be disputed.

About the *Tractatus*, he told Waismann that in it he had 'still proceeded dogmatically . . . I saw something from far away and in a very indefinite manner, and I wanted to elicit from it as much as possible.' 'But', he added firmly, 'a rehash of such theses is no longer justified.' He insisted that notes taken by Waismann of this discussion should be sent to Schlick in California, and that Waismann should inform Schlick of the change in plan and explain the reasons for it.

When Wittgenstein returned to Cambridge in the new year of 1932 he wrote to Schlick asking whether he had received Waismann's notes, and whether he could 'make head or tail of it'. Schlick evidently thought he could, for he persisted in encouraging Waismann to continue with the project. Like Wittgenstein, Waismann did so for Schlick's sake. For 'the thing' itself, we can assume that he had no more enthusiasm than Wittgenstein. The following Easter, his already unenviable position was made even more difficult when Wittgenstein proposed a new procedure: instead of Waismann receiving material for the book directly from Wittgenstein, he was to be dependent on Schlick for typescripts that Wittgenstein would send to him. Wittgenstein had, in other words, completely lost faith in Waismann as a communicator of his ideas; Waismann was no longer, for example, given the responsibility of presenting Wittgenstein's new ideas to the members of the Vienna Circle.

Almost all of Wittgenstein's energies were by now devoted to producing his own presentation of his new thoughts. He experimented with many different formulations – numbered remarks, numbered paragraphs, an annotated table of contents etc. In his lectures, as though to orientate himself within the Western tradition, he went through C. D.

Broad's taxonomy of philosophical styles and theories, given in Broad's own series of undergraduate lectures, 'Elements of Philosophy'. The method of Hume and Descartes, he rejected, but said of Kant's critical method: 'This is the right sort of approach.' With regard to the distinction between the deductive and dialectical methods of speculative philosophy – the first represented by Descartes, the second by Hegel – he came down, with reservations, on the side of Hegel:

> . . . the dialectical method is very sound and a way in which we do work. But it should not try to find, from two propositions, a and b, a further more complex proposition, as Broad's description implied. Its object should be to find out where the ambiguities in our language are.

Of Broad's three 'theories of truth' – the Correspondence Theory, the Coherence Theory and the Pragmatic Theory – he was dismissive: 'Philosophy is not a choice between different "theories"':

> We can say that the word ['truth'] has at least three different meanings; but it is mistaken to assume that any one of these theories can give the whole grammar of how we use the word, or endeavour to fit into a single theory cases which do not seem to agree with it.

What replaces theory is *grammar*. During this series of lectures Moore made a spirited attempt to insist that Wittgenstein was using the word 'grammar' in a rather odd sense. He presented to Wittgenstein's class a paper distinguishing what he took to be the usual meaning from its Wittgensteinian use. Thus, he argued, the sentence: 'Three men was working' is incontrovertibly a misuse of grammar, but it is not clear that: 'Different colours cannot be in the same place in a visual field at the same time' commits a similar transgression. If this latter is also called a misuse of grammar, then 'grammar' must mean something different in each case. No, replied Wittgenstein. 'The right expression is "It does not have sense to say . . ."' Both kinds of rules were rules in the same sense. 'It is just that some have been the subject of philosophical discussion and some have not':

Grammatical rules are all of the same kind, but it is not the same mistake if a man breaks one as if he breaks another. If he uses 'was' instead of 'were' it causes no confusion; but in the other example the analogy with physical space (c.f. two people in the *same* chair) does cause confusion. When we say we can't think of two colours in the same place, we make the mistake of thinking that this is a proposition, though it is not; and we would never try to say it if we were not misled by an analogy. It is misleading to use the word 'can't' because it suggests a wrong analogy. We should say, 'It has no sense to say . . .'

The grammatical mistakes of philosophers, then, differed from the ordinary mistakes mentioned by Moore only in being more pernicious. To study these mistakes was, therefore, pointless – indeed, it was worse than that, and could only do harm; the point was not to study them, but to free oneself from them. Thus, to one of his students, Karl Britton, Wittgenstein insisted that he *could* not take philosophy seriously so long as he was reading for a degree in the subject. He urged him to give up the degree and do something else. When Britton refused, Wittgenstein only hoped that it would not kill his interest in philosophy.

Similarly, he urged Britton, as he urged most of his students, to avoid becoming a teacher of philosophy. There was only one thing worse, and that was becoming a journalist. Britton should do a real job, and work with ordinary people. Academic life was detestable. When he returned from London, he told Britton, he would overhear one undergraduate talking to another, saying, 'Oh, really!' and know that he was back in Cambridge. The gossip of his bedmaker in college was much preferable to the insincere cleverness of high table.

Maurice Drury had already taken Wittgenstein's advice, and was working with a group of unemployed shipbuilders in Newcastle. As the project neared its completion, however, he was tempted into applying for a post as a lecturer in philosophy at Armstrong College, Newcastle. In the event, the post was given to Dorothy Emmett, and Drury went to South Wales to help run a communal market garden for unemployed miners. 'You owe a great debt to Miss Emmett', Wittgenstein insisted; 'she saved you from becoming a professional philosopher.'

Despite this contempt for the profession, Wittgenstein kept a jealous and watchful eye on the use to which his ideas were put by academic philosophers, and in the summer of 1932 was involved in what amounts to a *Prioritätstreit* with Rudolf Carnap. It was occasioned by an article by Carnap entitled '*Die physikalische Sprache als Universalsprache der Wissenschaft*', which was published in *Erkenntnis*, the journal of the Vienna Circle (it was later published in English, as *The Unity of Science*). The article is an argument for 'physicalism' – the view that *all* statements, in so far as they are worthy of inclusion into a scientific study, are ultimately reducible to the language of physics, whether the science concerned treats of physical, biological, psychological or social phenomena. It is indebted, as Carnap acknowledges, to the views of Otto Neurath, the most rigorously positivist of the Vienna Circle philosophers.

Wittgenstein, however, was convinced that Carnap had used the ideas he himself had expressed in conversations with the Vienna Circle, and had done so without proper acknowledgement. In August 1932, in two letters to Schlick and again in a letter to Carnap himself, Wittgenstein insists that his annoyance at Carnap's article is a purely ethical and personal matter, and is in no way to do with a concern to establish his authorship of the thoughts published by Carnap, or with his anxiety about his reputation within the academic community. On 8 August he wrote to Schlick:

> . . . from the bottom of my heart it is all the same to me what the professional philosophers of today think of me; for it is not for them that I am writing.

And yet his point was that the ideas published under Carnap's name – about, for example, ostensive definition and the nature of hypotheses – were properly speaking *his* ideas. Carnap took them, he alleged, from records of his conversations with Waismann. When Carnap replied that his central argument was concerned with *physicalism*, about which Wittgenstein had said nothing, Wittgenstein objected that the basic idea was to be found in the *Tractatus*: 'That I had not dealt with the question of "physicalism" is untrue (only not under that – horrible – name), and [I did so] with the brevity with which the whole of the *Tractatus* is written.'

With the publication of Carnap's article Wittgenstein's philosophical conversations with Waismann finally came to an end. Their last recorded discussion, indeed, is taken up with an attempt by Wittgenstein to refute Carnap's suggestion that his (Carnap's) conception of a hypothesis was taken from Poincaré, rather than from Wittgenstein himself. After that, Waismann was not to be trusted with privileged access to Wittgenstein's new ideas.

Wittgenstein's growing distrust of Waismann, and his pique at what he saw as Carnap's impertinence, coincided with renewed efforts on his part to compose a publishable presentation of his work.

During his sojourn at the Hochreit during the summer of 1932, he dictated to a typist a large selection of remarks from the eight manuscript volumes he had written during the previous two years. (In the letter to Schlick of 8 August he mentions that he is spending up to seven hours a day in dictation.) The result was what has become known to Wittgenstein scholars as 'the Big Typescript'. This, more than any of the other typescripts left by Wittgenstein, presents the appearance of a finished book, complete with chapter headings and a table of contents, and forms the basis of what has been published as *Philosophical Grammar*. It is, however, by no means identical with the published text.

In particular, an interesting chapter entitled 'Philosophy' has been omitted from the published version. 'All that philosophy can do', he says there, 'is to destroy idols.' 'And', he adds, in a swipe at the Vienna Circle, 'that means not making any new ones – say out of "the absence of idols".' It is not in practical life that we encounter philosophical problems, he stresses, but, rather, when we are misled by certain analogies in language to ask things like 'What is time?', 'What is a number?' etc. These questions are insoluble, not because of their depth and profundity, but rather because they are nonsensical – a misuse of language. Thus:

> The real discovery is the one that makes me capable of stopping doing philosophy when I want to – the one that gives philosophy peace, so that it is no longer tormented by questions which bring *itself* in question. – Instead, we now demonstrate a method, by examples; and the series of examples can be broken off. – Problems are solved (difficulties eliminated), not a *single* problem . . . 'But then we will never come to the end of our job!' Of course not, because it has no end.

This conception of philosophy, which sees it as a task of clarification that has no end, and only an arbitrary beginning, makes it almost impossible to imagine how a satisfactory book on philosophy *can* be written. It is no wonder that Wittgenstein used to quote with approval Schopenhauer's dictum that a book on philosophy, with a beginning and an end, is a sort of contradiction. And it comes as no surprise that, almost as soon as he had finished dictating the Big Typescript, he began to make extensive revisions to it. The section he revised least, however, was that on the philosophy of mathematics (hence the complete reproduction of those chapters in *Philosophical Grammar*). It is unfortunate that his work in that area has not received the same attention as have his remarks on language.

Not only did Wittgenstein himself regard his work on mathematics as his most important contribution to philosophy; it is also in this work that it is most apparent how radically his philosophical perspective differs from that of the professional philosophy of the twentieth century. It is here that we can see most clearly the truth of his conviction that he was working against the stream of modern civilization. For the target at which his remarks are aimed is not a particular view of mathematics that has been held by this or that philosopher; it is, rather, a conception of the subject that is held almost universally among working mathematicians, and that has, moreover, been dominant throughout our entire culture for more than a century – the view, that is, that sees mathematics as a *science*.

'Confusions in these matters', he writes in the Big Typescript, 'are entirely the result of treating mathematics as a kind of natural science':

> And this is connected with the fact that mathematics has detached itself from natural science; for, as long as it is done in immediate connection with physics, it is clear that *it* isn't a natural science. (Similarly, you can't mistake a broom for part of the furnishing of a room as long as you use it to clean the furniture.)

Wittgenstein's philosophy of mathematics is not a contribution to the debate on the foundations of the subject that was fought during the first half of this century by the opposing camps of logicists (led by Frege and Russell), formalists (led by Hilbert) and intuitionists (led by Brouwer and Weyl). It is, instead, an attempt to undermine the whole basis of this debate – to undermine the idea that mathematics *needs* foundations. All the branches of mathematics that were inspired by this search for 'foundations' – Set Theory, Proof Theory, Quantificational Logic, Recursive Function Theory, etc. – he regarded as based on a philosophical confusion. Thus:

Philosophical clarity will have the same effect on the growth of mathematics as sunlight has on the growth of potato shoots. (In a dark cellar they grow yards long.)

Wittgenstein knew, of course, that with regard to mathematics, if not with regard to his entire philosophical enterprise, he was tilting at windmills. 'Nothing seems to me less likely', he wrote, 'than that a scientist or mathematician who reads me should be seriously influenced in the way he works.' If, as he repeatedly emphasized, he was not writing for professional philosophers, still less was he writing for professional mathematicians.

15
FRANCIS

Wittgenstein's quixotic assault on the status of pure mathematics reached a peak during the academic year of 1932–3. During this year he gave two sets of lectures, one entitled 'Philosophy', and the other 'Philosophy for Mathematicians'. In the second of these he attempted to combat what he regarded as the baleful influence on undergraduate mathematicians of the textbooks that were used to teach them. He would read out extracts from Hardy's *Pure Mathematics* (the standard university text at that time) and use them to illustrate the philosophical fog that he believed surrounded the whole discipline of pure mathematics – a fog he thought could be dispelled only by uprooting the many commonly held assumptions about mathematics that are so deeply embedded as to be very rarely examined.

The first of these is that mathematics stands upon the logical foundations given to it by Cantor, Frege and Russell, among others. He began his lectures with a straightforward statement of his position on this question. 'Is there a substratum on which mathematics rests?' he asked rhetorically:

> Is logic the foundation of mathematics? In my view mathematical logic is simply part of mathematics. Russell's calculus is not fundamental; it is just another calculus. There is nothing wrong with a science before the foundations are laid.

Another of these assumptions is the idea that mathematics is concerned with the discovery of *facts* that are in some way objectively true (about something or other). *What* they are true of, and in what this objectivity consists, has, of course, been the subject-matter of the philosophy of mathematics since the time of Plato, and philosophers have traditionally been divided between those who say that mathematical statements are true about the *physical* world (empiricists) and those who, feeling this view does not do justice to the inexorability of mathematics, claim that they are true of the *mathematical* world – Plato's eternal world of ideas or forms (hence, Platonists). To this division Kant added a third view, which is that mathematical statements are true of the 'form of our intuition', and this was roughly the view of Brouwer and the intuitionist school. But, for Wittgenstein, the whole idea that mathematics is concerned with the discovery of truths is a mistake that has arisen with the growth of pure mathematics and the separation of mathematics from physical science (the unused broom being mistaken for part of the furniture). If, says Wittgenstein, we looked on mathematics as a series of *techniques* (for calculating, measuring etc.), then the question of what it was *about* simply would not arise.

The view of mathematics that Wittgenstein is attacking is stated very succinctly in a lecture given by Hardy, which was published in *Mind* in 1929 under the title 'Mathematical Proof'. Hardy – who appears to have regarded his excursion into philosophy as a kind of light relief from the serious business of his work as a mathematician – states unequivocally:

> . . . no philosophy can possibly be sympathetic to a mathematician which does not admit, in one manner or another, the immutable and unconditional validity of mathematical truth. Mathematical theorems are true or false; their truth or falsity is absolute and independent of our knowledge of them. In *some* sense, mathematical truth is part of objective reality . . . [mathematical propositions] are in one sense or another, however elusive and sophisticated that sense may be, theorems concerning reality . . . They are not creations of our minds.

Both the tone and the content of this lecture infuriated Wittgenstein. He told his class:

> The talk of mathematicians becomes absurd when they leave mathematics, for example, Hardy's description of mathematics as not being a creation of our minds. He conceived philosophy as a decoration, an atmosphere, around the hard realities of mathematics

and science. These disciplines, on the one hand, and philosophy on the other, are thought of as being like the necessities and decoration of a room. Hardy is thinking of philosophical opinions. I conceive of philosophy as an activity of clearing up thought.

In relation to mathematics, Wittgenstein had, at this time, a fairly clear idea of the way in which he wanted to present this activity of clarification; it was in the presentation of his more general philosophical position that he was still feeling his way towards a satisfactory formulation. Philosophy was, for him, like mathematics, a series of techniques. But whereas the mathematical techniques already existed, and his role consisted in persuading his audience to see them as techniques (and not as true or false propositions), the philosophical techniques he wished to advance were of his own creation, and were still in their infancy.

In the series of lectures entitled 'Philosophy', Wittgenstein introduced a technique that was to become increasingly central to his philosophical method: the technique of inventing what he called 'language-games'. This is the method of inventing imaginary situations in which language is used for some tightly defined practical purpose. It may be a few words or phrases from our own language or an entirely fictitious language, but what is essential is that, in picturing the situation, the language cannot be described without mentioning the *use* to which it is put. The technique is a kind of therapy, the purpose of which is to free ourselves from the philosophical confusions that result from considering language in isolation from its place in the 'stream of life'.

As examples of the sort of thinking he was attempting to liberate his audience from, Wittgenstein mentioned his own earlier work and that of Russell. Both, he said, had been misled, by concentrating on *one* type of language, the assertoric sentence, into trying to analyse the whole of language as though it consisted of nothing but that type, or as though the other uses of language could be analysed as variations on that basic theme. Thus, they had arrived at an unworkable notion – the 'atomic proposition':

> Russell and I both expected to find the first elements, or 'individuals', and thus the possible atomic propositions, by logical analysis . . . And we were both at fault for giving no examples of atomic propositions or of individuals. We both in different ways

pushed the question of examples aside. We should not have said 'We can't give them because analysis has not gone far enough, but we'll get there in time.'

He and Russell had had too rigid a notion of proposition, and the purpose of the language-game method was, so to speak, to loosen such notions. For example, he asked his audience to consider the language-game of teaching a child language by pointing to things and pronouncing the words for them. Where in this game, he asked, does the use of a proposition start? If we say to a child: 'Book', and he brings us a book, has he learnt a proposition? Or has he learnt propositions only when there is a question of truth and falsity? But then, still, one word – for example, the word: 'Six' in answer to the question: 'How many chairs?' – might be true or false. And is it, therefore, a proposition? It does not matter, Wittgenstein implies, how we answer these questions; what matters is that we see how arbitrary *any* answers to them would be, and thus how 'fluid' our concepts are – too fluid to be forced into the kind of analysis once advocated by Russell and himself:

I have wanted to show by means of language-games the vague way in which we use 'language', 'proposition', 'sentence'. There are many things, such as orders, which we may or may not call propositions and not only one game can be called language. Language-games are a clue to the understanding of logic. Since what we call a proposition is more or less arbitrary, what we call logic plays a different role from that which Russell and Frege supposed.

Among those attending these lectures was a twenty-year-old undergraduate student of mathematics, then in his third year at Trinity, who was soon to become the most important person in Wittgenstein's life – his constant companion, his trusted confidant, and, even, his most valued collaborator in philosophical work.

Francis Skinner had come up to Cambridge from St Paul's in 1930, and was recognized as one of the most promising mathematicians of his year. By his second year at Cambridge, however, his mathematical work had begun to take second place to his interest in Wittgenstein. He became utterly, uncritically and almost obsessively devoted to Wittgenstein. What it was about him that attracted Wittgenstein, we can only guess. He is remembered by all who knew him as shy, unassuming, good-looking and, above all, extraordinarily gentle. But attracted Wittgenstein certainly was. As with Pinsent and Marguerite, Skinner's mere presence seemed to provide Wittgenstein with the peace he needed to conduct his work. In 1932 Wittgenstein left a note concerning the work he was then endeavouring to finish which suggests that he himself regarded Skinner's relation to that work as parallel to Pinsent's to the *Tractatus*:

> In the event of my death before the completion or publication of this book my notes should be published as fragments under the title 'Philosophical Remarks' and with the dedication: 'To Francis Skinner'.

Skinner's letters were kept by Wittgenstein, and were found among his possessions after his death, and from them we can reconstruct something of how the relationship developed. (Wittgenstein's letters to Skinner were retrieved by Wittgenstein after Skinner's death and were, presumably, burnt.) The first letter to survive is dated 26 December 1932, and is written to thank Wittgenstein for a Christmas tree he had given. Two days later Skinner writes: 'I am glad to read that you think about me. I think about you a lot.'

But it was not until the Easter break of 1933 that they became 'Francis' and 'Ludwig' to each other, and that Skinner began to express himself in terms that suggest he was writing – albeit nervously and self-consciously – to a beloved. On 25 March, while on holiday in Guernsey, he wrote:

> Dear Ludwig,
> I have thought about you a lot since we left last Saturday. I hope I think about you in the right way. When we were talking about the case which your sister gave you, I smiled several times, and you said you could see it wasn't a kind smile. Sometimes when I am thinking about you, I have smiled in the same sort of way. I always knew it was wrong to smile, because immediately afterwards I tried to put it out of my mind, but I didn't know how unkind it was.
> . . . I am staying for a few days on an island in the Channel, where some of the people speak French. I remember when I once asked if you could speak French, you told me you were taught when you were young by a lady who stayed in your house who was very nice indeed. When I thought about this this morning, I hoped that you

would be pleased if you knew how much I enjoyed remembering things like this you have told me.

Francis

We must assume that Wittgenstein found the childlike simplicity – one might almost say simple-mindedness – revealed in this letter endearing. Certainly Skinner's letters show nothing of the 'cleverness' that Wittgenstein so disliked in many of the students and dons at Cambridge. He was not the type to be overheard saying 'Oh, really!' Neither do his letters show any trace of egotism. In his devotion to Wittgenstein (which he maintained for the rest of his tragically short life), Skinner surrendered his own will almost entirely. Everything else took second place. His sister has recalled that when she and her mother came to Trinity to meet Francis, they would be met by him rushing down the stairs and hushing them with: 'I'm busy. I've got Dr Wittgenstein here. We're working. Come back later.'

Skinner is the most perfect example of the childlike innocence and first-class brains that Fania Pascal has described as the prerequisites of Wittgensteinian disciplehood. He came from a family steeped in the value of academic achievement. His father was a physicist at Chelsea Polytechnic, and his two elder sisters had both been at Cambridge before him, the first to study classics, the second, mathematics. It was expected – indeed, regarded as inevitable – that Francis would pursue an academic career. Had it not been for Wittgenstein's intervention, he would almost certainly have done so.

So complete was Skinner's absorption in Wittgenstein during his final year as an undergraduate that when, in the summer of 1933, he graduated with a first-class degree in mathematics and was awarded a postgraduate scholarship, his family had the impression that this was to allow him to continue working with Wittgenstein. In fact, the award was given by Trinity with the intention that he should use it to pursue mathematical research.

It had by this time become difficult for Skinner to endure the long summer vacations that Wittgenstein spent away from Cambridge. At the end of the summer he wrote: 'I feel much further away from you, and am longing to be nearer you again.' He sent Wittgenstein a series of picture postcards depicting scenes of his home town of Letchworth in Hertfordshire. On the front of the cards he scribbled remarks which were ostensibly designed to explain a little about the town, but which in fact are much more revealing of Skinner's own frame of mind, showing that, with Wittgenstein hundreds of miles away, Letchworth was the very last place on earth he wished to be.

On a card showing Howard Corner, he explained that the 'Garden City' of Letchworth had been founded by Sir Ebenezer Howard, who had wanted everyone to have the chance of living in the country. 'The result', he wrote, 'is something incredibly depressing and bloody (for me, at any rate).' On a card showing the Broadway: 'This is the road to the town & station. There is a row of houses one side. They always make me feel very miserable.' On a photograph of the Spirella Works: 'This is the largest factory in Letchworth . . . the garden looks to me quite uninteresting and dead always.' The last two cards show Leys Avenue – 'a very dull and depressing street. All the people are disagreeably dressed and have such mean expressions on their faces' – and East Cheap – 'an absurd name . . . When I'm in these streets I feel surrounded by gossip.'

His relationship with Wittgenstein was to provide him with some sort of escape from this 'dead' and 'dull' existence, and eventually – much to the consternation of his family – a release from their expectations. It was also to provide him with a new set of expectations, to which he zealously conformed. For the three years of his postgraduate scholarship he worked assiduously with Wittgenstein on the preparation of his work for publication, and when the time came he abandoned academic life altogether for a job that Wittgenstein considered more suitable for him.

Wittgenstein's advice to his friends and students to leave academia was based on his conviction that its atmosphere was too rarefied to sustain proper life. There is no oxygen in Cambridge, he told Drury. It didn't matter for him – he manufactured his own. But for people dependent on the air around them, it was important to get away, into a healthier environment. His ideal was a job in the medical profession. He had already nudged Marguerite in this direction, and she was at this time training to become a nurse in Berne, a project in which Wittgenstein took a great personal interest. Their relationship had lost any trace of romantic involvement, and Marguerite had fallen in love with Talle Sjögren, but Wittgenstein would still occasionally travel to Berne to see how Marguerite was getting on in her training.

Now, in the summer of 1933, after the completion of his project working with unemployed miners in South Wales, Drury decided he, too, wanted to train as a nurse. He was told, however, that with his education he would be more useful if he trained as a doctor. Upon being told of this, Wittgenstein immediately took the matter into his own hands. He arranged for Keynes and Gilbert Pattisson to lend Drury the necessary funds, and sent a telegram to Drury urging him: 'Come to Cambridge at once.' Drury was hardly out of the train before Wittgenstein announced: 'Now there is to be no more argument about this: it has all been settled already, you are to start work as a medical student at once.' He was later to say that, of all his students, it was in his influence on Drury's career that he could take most pride and satisfaction.

On more than one occasion Wittgenstein himself thought seriously of training to be a doctor, and of escaping the 'deadness' of academic philosophy. He might be able to generate oxygen – but what was the point of providing lungs for a corpse? He knew, of course, that a great many philosophers wanted to know his latest thoughts, for by 1933 it was widely known, particularly in Cambridge and Vienna, that he had radically changed his position since the publication of the *Tractatus*. He resolutely refused to accept that it was for *them* – for the 'philosophic journalists' – that he was preparing his new work, but still he could not bear to see his oxygen being recycled by them. In March 1933, he had been pained to see an article by Richard Braithwaite in a collection entitled *Cambridge University Studies*, in which Braithwaite outlined the impression that various philosophers, including Wittgenstein, had made upon him. The fact that Braithwaite might have been regarded as presenting Wittgenstein's present views prompted Wittgenstein to write a letter to *Mind* disclaiming all responsibility for the views that had been attributed to him: 'Part of [Braithwaite's] statements can be taken to be inaccurate representations of my views', he wrote; 'others again clearly contradict them.' He ended:

That which is retarding the publication of my work, the difficulty of presenting it in a clear and coherent form, *a fortiori* prevents me from stating my views within the space of a letter. So the reader must suspend his judgement about them.

The same edition of *Mind* carries a contrite apology from Braithwaite, which ends, however, with a sting in its tail: 'The extent to which I have misrepresented Dr Wittgenstein cannot be judged until the appearance of the book which we are all eagerly awaiting.'

16

LANGUAGE-GAMES:
The Blue and Brown Books

After Wittgenstein's return to Cambridge for the academic year of 1933–4, Wittgenstein and Skinner were rarely to be seen apart: they both had rooms in college; they walked together, talked together, and whatever social life they had (chiefly going to the cinema to watch Westerns and musicals) was shared. Above all, perhaps, they worked together.

Wittgenstein began the term, as he had the previous year, by giving two sets of lectures, one entitled 'Philosophy', and the other 'Philosophy for Mathematicians'. The second set, much to his dismay, proved particularly popular, between thirty and forty people turning up – far too many for the kind of informal lectures he wanted to deliver. After three or four weeks he amazed his audience by telling them that he could no longer continue to lecture in this way, and that he proposed instead to dictate his lectures to a small group of students, so that they could be copied and handed out to the others. The idea, as he later put it to Russell, was that the students would then 'have something to take home with them, in their hands if not in their brains'. The select group included his five favourite students – Skinner, Louis Goodstein, H. M. S. Coxeter, Margaret Masterman and Alice Ambrose. The duplicated set of notes was bound in blue paper covers and has been known ever since as 'The Blue Book'.

This was the first publication in any form of Wittgenstein's new method of philosophy, and as such it created great interest. Further copies were made and distributed, and the book reached a far wider audience than Wittgenstein had expected – much wider, indeed, than he would have wished. By the late 1930s, for example, it had been distributed among many members of the philosophy faculty of Oxford. The *Blue Book* was thus responsible for introducing into philosophic discourse the notion of a 'language-game' and the technique, based upon it, for dissolving philosophical confusion.

In many ways the *Blue Book* can be regarded as an early prototype for subsequent presentations of Wittgenstein's later philosophy. Like all future attempts to arrange his work in coherent form (including the *Brown Book* and *Philosophical Investigations*), it begins with 'one of the great sources of philosophical bewilderment' – i.e. the tendency to be misled by substantives to look for something that corresponds to them. Thus, we ask: 'What is time?', 'What is meaning?', 'What is knowledge?', 'What is a thought?', 'What are numbers?' etc., and expect to be able to answer these questions by naming some *thing*. The technique of language-games was designed to break the hold of this tendency:

> I shall in the future again and again draw your attention to what I shall call language games. These are ways of using signs simpler than those in which we use the signs of our highly complicated everyday language. Language games are the forms of language with which a child begins to make use of words. The study of language games is the study of primitive forms of language or primitive languages. If we want to study the problems of truth and falsehood, of the agreement and disagreement of propositions with reality, of the nature of assertion, assumption, and question, we shall with great advantage look at primitive forms of language in which these forms of thinking appear without the confusing background of highly complicated processes of thought. When we look at such simple forms of language the mental mist which seems to enshroud our ordinary use of language disappears. We see activities, reactions, which are clear-cut and transparent.

Connected with the inclination to look for a substance corresponding to a substantive is the idea that, for any given concept, there is an 'essence' – something that is common to all the things subsumed under a general term. Thus, for example, in the Platonic dialogues, Socrates seeks to answer philosophical questions such as: 'What is knowledge?' by looking for something that all examples of knowledge have in common. (In connection with this, Wittgenstein once said that his method could be summed up by saying that it was the exact opposite of that of Socrates.) In the *Blue Book* Wittgenstein seeks to replace this notion of *essence* with the more flexible idea of *family resemblances*:

> We are inclined to think that there must be something in common to all games, say, and that this common property is the justification for applying the general term 'game' to the various games; whereas games form a *family* the members of which have family likenesses. Some of them have the same nose, others the same eyebrows and others again the same way of walking; and these likenesses overlap.

The search for essences is, Wittgenstein states, an example of 'the craving for generality' that springs from our preoccupation with the method of science:

> Philosophers constantly see the method of science before their eyes, and are irresistibly tempted to ask and answer questions in the way science does. This tendency is the real source of metaphysics, and leads the philosopher into complete darkness.

Wittgenstein's avoidance of this tendency – his complete refusal to announce any general conclusions – is perhaps the main feature that makes his work difficult to understand, for without having the moral pointed out, so to speak, it is often difficult to see the point of his remarks. As he himself once explained at the beginning of a series of lectures: 'What we say will be easy, but to know why we say it will be very difficult.'

During the Christmas vacation of 1933 Skinner wrote to Wittgenstein every few days, telling him how much he missed him, how often he thought about him and how much he was longing to see him again. Every last moment he had spent with Wittgenstein was recalled with fond affection:

> After I stopped waving my handkerchief to you I walked through Folkestone and took the train at 8.28 back to London. I thought about you and how wonderful it had been when we said goodbye

. . . I loved very much seeing you off. I miss you a great deal and think about you a lot.

With love,
Francis

At the family Christmas at the Alleegasse, Marguerite (who continued to spend Christmas in Vienna as the guest of Gretl) caused something of a sensation by announcing her engagement to Talle Sjögren. Encouraged by Gretl, but in the face of disapproval from her father, Marguerite decided on an extremely short engagement, and she and Talle were married on New Year's Eve. Her father, at least, was a safe distance away in Switzerland. Wittgenstein was not. Recalling her wedding day, she writes:

My despair reached its zenith when Ludwig came to see me on the Sunday morning, an hour before my wedding. 'You are taking a boat, the sea will be rough, remain always attached to me so that you don't capsize', he said to me. Until that moment I hadn't realised his deep attachment nor perhaps his great deception. For years I had been like soft putty in his hands which he had worked to shape into a better being. He had been like a Samaritan who gives new life to someone who is failing.

It is hard to believe that she had not appreciated until that day how deep was Wittgenstein's attachment to her. It is characteristic, however, of many of his friendships that she should have felt his involvement in her life to have had a fundamentally *ethical* purpose. 'He conjured up a vision of a better you', as Fania Pascal has put it. It was, after all, partly because she did not want to live with this kind of moral pressure that Marguerite had chosen to marry someone else.

For most of 1934 Wittgenstein continued to work on three different, but related, projects, which attempted to solve the problem he had described in his letter to *Mind* – that of presenting his philosophical method 'in a clear and coherent form'. At Cambridge, as well as dictating the *Blue Book*, he also made copious revisions to the Big Typescript – 'pottering about with it', as he put it to Russell. (The results of this 'pottering about' have been incorporated into the first part of *Philosophical Grammar*). In Vienna he continued to co-operate (albeit with increasing reluctance and with ever-growing misgivings) with the scheme to publish a book with Waismann. In the Easter vacation of 1934, this scheme took a new turn: it was now proposed that Waismann and Wittgenstein should be co-authors, with Wittgenstein providing the raw material and taking control of the form and structure, and Waismann being responsible for writing it up in a clear and coherent way. Waismann, that is to say, was given what Wittgenstein himself regarded as the most difficult part of the job.

With each new arrangement Waismann's position seemed to get worse. By August he was complaining to Schlick about the difficulties of writing a book with Wittgenstein:

> He has the great gift of always seeing things as if for the first time. But it shows, I think, how difficult collaborative work with him is, since he is always following up the inspiration of the moment and demolishing what he has previously sketched out . . . all one sees is that the structure is being demolished bit by bit and that everything is gradually taking on an entirely different appearance, so that one almost gets the feeling that it doesn't matter at all how the thoughts are put together since in the end nothing is left as it was.

Wittgenstein's habit of following up the inspiration of the moment applied not only to his work, but also to his life. In 1934, despite the fact that he was then involved in two projects to prepare a book for publication (*Logik, Sprache, Philosophie* in Vienna, and *Philosophical Grammar* in England), he conceived the idea of giving up academic life altogether and going, with Skinner, to live in Russia, where they would both seek work as manual labourers. Skinner's family was naturally apprehensive about the idea, but for Skinner himself it had the inestimable advantage that he would be with Wittgenstein all the time. He had begun to regard being with Wittgenstein almost as a necessity; away from Wittgenstein nothing looked the same or felt the same. 'If I am with you', he wrote during the Easter vacation, 'I can feel everything deeply.' It was a constant theme of his letters:

> I thought of you a lot. I longed to have you with me. The night was very wonderful and the stars looked particularly beautiful. I longed to be able to feel everything in the way I would feel it if I was with you. [25.3.34]

I long to be with you in any open space. I think of you a lot and how wonderful our walks have been. I look forward *enormously* to our tour next week. Yesterday I got your Easter card which was very lovely. I thought the houses in the street on the other card looked very beautiful. I should like to have looked at them with you. [4.4.34]

Skinner also stressed in his letters the *moral* necessity of having Wittgenstein by his side, as though without Wittgenstein's guidance he would fall into the hands of the devil. The most remarkable instance of this occurs in a letter written on 24 July 1934, the day after Skinner had waved goodbye to Wittgenstein at Boulogne. The letter begins with the by now customary remarks about how 'wonderful and sweet' it had been waving goodbye; he then goes on to describe how sinful he became as soon as he had been left alone in Boulogne. He had visited a casino, lost ten francs and then, despite his best resolutions, had been tempted to return, this time winning fifty francs. Disgusted with himself, he vowed to return to England on the afternoon boat, but when the time came to leave he was drawn once more into the casino. By this time, he was a lost soul:

I started off again by playing very carefully and keeping myself very restrained. Then I began to lose slightly and I suddenly lost my restraint and care and played more and more recklessly. I became quite feverishly excited and unable to control myself. Altogether I lost about 150 francs. I first lost all the French money which I had with me, about 80 francs, and then I changed a 10/- note into French money and lost it all and then I changed all the loose English silver I had and lost it all. I then left the Casino at about 5 o'clock. When I got out into the fresh air I suddenly felt in what a horrible unnatural and loathesome way I had been acting since I had begun to gamble. It seemed dreadful that I should have felt such eagerness to win money. I suddenly realised in what a mean filthy state of degradation I had fallen. I felt physically stirred up and excited in my body. I walked about the streets for a time in a wretched state of mind. I felt I understood why gamblers often committed suicide for the feeling of degradation is so awful. I felt a most terrible philistine. I felt I had been destroying myself. I then returned to the Hotel and washed myself all over.

Skinner is no Dostoevsky, and his depiction of his own moral depravity has a curiously unconvincing ring, but the effect he is trying to achieve is surely something like that of the Russian novels he knew Wittgenstein to have admired. His tale, with its evocation of desperate suicidal guilt, seems to point inexorably towards the necessity of redemptive religion. Indeed, he goes on to describe how, after washing his hands, he sought out the church in Boulogne that he had visited with Wittgenstein. Inside the church: 'I thought of you a lot. I felt comforted by the Church though I was hardly able to look at it at all.' He adds: 'I felt I would be a terrible rascal and be utterly unworthy of your love if I wrote without saying anything.'

The religious theme is renewed a few weeks later, on 11 August, when Skinner writes quoting the passage from *Anna Karenina* where the almost suicidal Levin says: 'I cannot live without knowing what I am.' The passage ends: 'But Levin did not hang himself, or shoot himself, but lived and struggled on.' 'When I read this last sentence', Skinner tells Wittgenstein, in a phrase that echoes many of Wittgenstein's own, 'I suddenly realised I was reading something terrific':

> I suddenly seemed to understand what all I had been reading meant. I went on reading the following chapters and it all seemed written with enormous truth. I felt as if I was reading the chapters of the Bible. I didn't understand it all but I felt it was religion. I wanted very much to tell you this.

Skinner and Wittgenstein had, by this time, begun to take Russian lessons together in preparation for their impending visit to the Soviet Union. Their teacher was Fania Pascal, the wife of the Marxist intellectual and Communist Party member Roy Pascal. In discussing Wittgenstein's motives for wanting to go to Russia, Mrs Pascal remarks: 'To my mind, his feeling for Russia would have had at all times more to do with Tolstoy's moral teachings, with Dostoyevsky's spiritual insights, than with any political or social matters.' The tone and content of Skinner's letters seems to confirm this. And yet it was not the Russia of Tolstoy and Dostoevsky that Wittgenstein and Skinner wanted to visit, and in which they planned to find work; it was the Russia of Stalin's Five Year Plans. And neither of them could possibly have been so politically naïve or so ill-informed as not to recognize any difference between the two.

Wittgenstein probably struck Pascal as 'an old-time conservative' because of his hostility to Marxism. But many of Wittgenstein's other friends received a very different impression. George Thomson, for example, who knew Wittgenstein well during the 1930s, speaks of Wittgenstein's 'growing political awareness' during those years, and says that, although he did not discuss politics very often with Wittgenstein, he did so 'enough to show that he kept himself informed about current events. He was alive to the evils of unemployment and fascism and the growing danger of war.' Thomson adds, in relation to Wittgenstein's attitude to Marxism: 'He was opposed to it in theory, but supported it in practice.' This chimes with a remark Wittgenstein once made to Rowland Hutt (a close friend of Skinner's who came to know Wittgenstein in 1934): 'I am a communist, *at heart.*' It should be remembered, too, that many of Wittgenstein's friends of this period, and particularly the friends on whom he relied for information about the Soviet Union, were Marxists. In addition to George Thomson, there were Piero Sraffa, whose opinion Wittgenstein valued above all others on questions of politics, Nicholas Bachtin and Maurice Dobb. There is no doubt that during the political upheavals of the mid-1930s Wittgenstein's sympathies were with the working class and the unemployed, and that his allegiance, broadly speaking, was with the Left.

However, it remains true that Russia's attraction for Wittgenstein had little or nothing to do with Marxism as a political and economic theory, and much to do with the sort of life he believed was being led in the Soviet Union. This emerged during a conversation which Wittgenstein and Skinner had with Maurice Drury in the summer of 1934, when they spent a summer holiday at Drury's brother's cottage in Connemara, on the west coast of Ireland. On their arrival Drury prepared for them a rather elaborate meal consisting of roast chicken followed by suet pudding and treacle. Wittgenstein expressed his disapproval, insisting that while they were staying at Connemara they should eat nothing but porridge for breakfast, vegetables for lunch and a boiled egg in the evening. When the subject of Russia came up, Skinner announced that he wanted to do something 'fiery', a way of thinking that struck Wittgenstein as dangerous. 'I think', said Drury, 'Francis means that he doesn't want to take the treacle with him.' Wittgenstein was delighted. 'Oh, that is an excellent expression: I understand what that means entirely. No, we don't want to take the treacle with us.'

Presumably, for Wittgenstein, the life of a manual labourer in Russia was the epitome of a life without treacle. During the following year, to give Skinner some taste of what that would be like, he arranged for Skinner, together with Rowland Hutt, to spend six weeks working on a farm during the winter months. Wittgenstein himself came out one morning at six o'clock on a cold February day to help with the work.

During the year 1934–5 Wittgenstein dictated what is now known as the *Brown Book*. This, unlike the *Blue Book*, was not a substitute for a series of lectures, but rather an attempt by Wittgenstein to formulate the results of his own work for his own sake. It was dictated to Skinner and Alice Ambrose, who sat with Wittgenstein for between two and four hours a day for four days a week. The *Brown Book* is divided into two parts, corresponding, roughly, to the method and its application. Part I, introducing the method of language-games, reads almost like a textbook. After an introductory paragraph describing St Augustine's account of 'How, as a boy, he learned to talk', it consists of seventy-two numbered 'exercises', many of which invite the reader to, for example:

> Imagine a people in whose language there is no such form of sentence as 'the book is in the drawer' or 'water is in the glass', but wherever we should use these forms they say, 'The book can be taken out of the drawer', 'The water can be taken out of the glass'. [p. 100]

> Imagine a tribe in whose language there is an expression corresponding to our 'He has done so and so', and another expression corresponding to our 'He can do so and so', this latter expression, however, being used only where its use is justified by the same fact which would also justify the former expression. [p. 103]

> Imagine that human beings or animals were used as reading machines; assume that in order to become reading machines they need a particular training. [p. 120]

The book is difficult to read because the *point* of imagining these various situations is very rarely spelt out. Wittgenstein simply leads the reader through a series of progressively more complicated language-games, occasionally pausing to remark on various features of the games he is describing. When he does make the point of these remarks explicit, he claims it is to ward off thoughts that may give rise to philosophical puzzlement. It is as though the book was intended to serve as a text in a course designed to nip in the bud any latent philosophizing. Thus we are first introduced to a language which contains just four nouns – 'cube', 'brick', 'slab' and 'column' – and which is used in a building 'game' (one builder shouts, 'Brick!' and another brings him a brick). In subsequent games this proto-language is supplemented by the addition first of numerals, and then of proper nouns, the words 'this' and 'there', questions and answers, and finally colour words. So far, no philosophical moral has been drawn other than that, in understanding how these various languages are used, it is not necessary to postulate the existence of mental images; all the games could be played with or without such images. The unspoken point of this is to loosen the hold of the idea that mental images are an essential concomitant to any meaningful use of language.

It is not until we have been led through another series of language-games, which introduce, first, the notion of an infinite series, and then the notions of 'past', 'present' and 'future', that Wittgenstein explicitly mentions the relevance of all this to philosophical problems. After describing a series of language-games with more or less primitive means of distinguishing one time of day from another, he contrasts these with our own language, which permits the construction of such questions as: 'Where does the present go when it becomes past, and where is the past?' 'Here', he says, 'is one of the most fertile sources of philosophic puzzlement.' To a reader studying the *Brown Book* as a work of philosophy, this statement, the only mention of philosophy in the first thirty pages of the book, comes as something of a relief. Such questions, he states, arise because we are misled by our symbolism into certain analogies (in this case, the analogy between a past event and a *thing*, the analogy between our saying 'Something has happened' and 'Something came towards me'). Similarly: 'We are inclined to say that both "now" and "six o'clock" refer to points in time. This use of words produces a puzzlement which one might express in the question: "What is the 'now'?" – for it is a moment of time and yet it can't be said to be either the "moment at which I speak" or "the moment at which the clock strikes", etc., etc.' Here, in relation to what is essentially St Augustine's problem of time, Wittgenstein finally spells out the point of his procedure:

> Our answer is: the function of the word 'now' is entirely different from that of a specification of time – This can easily be seen if we look at the role this word really plays in our usage of language, but it is obscured when instead of looking at the *whole language game*, we only look at the contexts, the phrases of language in which the word is used.

There is no indication that Wittgenstein considered publishing the *Brown Book*. On 31 July 1935 he wrote to Schlick describing it as a document which shows 'the way in which I think the whole stuff should be handled'. Perhaps, as he was then planning to leave philosophy altogether to take up manual work in Russia, it represents an attempt to present the results of his seven years' work in philosophy in a way that would enable someone else (perhaps Waismann) to make use of them.

It is unlikely, however, that he would ever have been satisfied with the attempts of another to represent his thought faithfully. Again and again attempts were made by others to present his ideas, and again and again he reacted angrily, accusing whoever used his ideas of plagiarism if they did not acknowledge their debt, or misrepresentation if they did. During the dictation of the *Brown Book*, it was the turn of Alice Ambrose to encounter his wrath on this point. She planned to publish in *Mind* an article entitled 'Finitism in Mathematics', in which she would present what she took to be Wittgenstein's view on the matter. The article annoyed Wittgenstein intensely, and he tried hard to persuade her not to publish it. When she and G. E. Moore, who was then editor of the journal, refused to succumb to this pressure, he abruptly ended any association with her. In the letter to Schlick mentioned above, however, he blames not her, but the academics who encouraged her to go ahead with the article. The fault lay primarily, he thought, with the curiosity of academic philosophers to know what his new work was all about before he felt able to publish his results himself. Reluctant as he was to cast pearls before swine, he was nonetheless determined they should not be offered counterfeits.

17

JOINING THE RANKS

In his letter to Schlick of 31 July 1935, Wittgenstein wrote that he would probably not be coming to Austria that summer:

At the beginning of September I want to travel to Russia & will either stay there or, after about two weeks, return to England. What, in that case, I will do in England is still completely uncertain, but I will probably not continue in philosophy.

Throughout the summer of 1935 he made preparations for his impending visit to Russia. He met regularly with those of his friends, many of them members of the Communist Party, who had been to Russia or who might be able to inform him about conditions there. Possibly he hoped, too, that they could put him in contact with people who could help to find work there for himself and Skinner. Among these friends were Maurice Dobb, Nicholas Bachtin, Piero Sraffa and George Thomson. The impression they received was that Wittgenstein wanted to settle in Russia as a manual worker, or possibly to take up medicine, but in any case to abandon philosophy. At a meeting with George Thomson in the Fellows' garden at Trinity he explained that, since he was giving up philosophical work, he had to decide what to do with his notebooks. Should he leave them somewhere or should he destroy them? He talked at length to Thomson about his philosophy, expressing doubts about its worth. It was only after urgent appeals by Thomson that he agreed not to destroy his notebooks, but to deposit them instead in the college library.

Wittgenstein was not the only one at Cambridge then seeking in

Soviet Russia an alternative to the countries of Western Europe, menaced as those countries were by the growth of fascism and the problems of mass unemployment. The summer of 1935 was the time when Marxism became, for the undergraduates at Cambridge, the most important intellectual force in the university, and when many students and dons visited the Soviet Union in the spirit of pilgrimage. It was then that Anthony Blunt and Michael Straight made their celebrated journey to Russia, which led to the formation of the so-called 'Cambridge Spy Ring', and that the Cambridge Communist Cell, founded a few years earlier by Maurice Dobb, David Hayden-Guest and John Cornford, expanded to include most of the intellectual élite at Cambridge, including many of the younger members of the Apostles.

Despite the fact that Wittgenstein was never at any time a Marxist, he was perceived as a sympathetic figure by the students who formed the core of the Cambridge Communist Party, many of whom (Hayden-Guest, Cornford, Maurice Cornforth etc.) attended his lectures. But Wittgenstein's reasons for wanting to visit Russia were very different. His perception of the decline of the countries of Western Europe was always more Spenglerian than Marxian, and, as we have remarked earlier, it is likely that he was extremely attracted to the portrait of life in the Soviet Union drawn by Keynes in his *Short View of Russia* – a portrait which, while deprecating Marxism as an economic theory, applauded its practice in Russia as a new religion, in which there were no supernatural beliefs but, rather, deeply held religious attitudes.

Perhaps because of this, Wittgenstein felt he might be understood by Keynes. 'I am sure that you partly understand my reasons for wanting to go to Russia', he wrote to him on 6 July, 'and I admit that they are partly bad and even childish reasons but it is true also that behind all that there are deep and even good reasons.' Keynes, in fact, disapproved of Wittgenstein's plan, but despite this did all he could to help Wittgenstein overcome the suspicions of the Soviet authorities. Wittgenstein had had a meeting at the Russian Embassy with an official called Vinogradoff, who, he told Keynes, was 'exceedingly careful in our conversation . . . He of course knew as well as anyone that recommendations might help me but it was quite clear that he wasn't going to help me get any.' Characteristically, Keynes went straight to the top, and provided Wittgenstein with an introduction to

Ivan Maisky, the Russian Ambassador in London: 'May I venture to introduce to you Dr Ludwig Wittgenstein . . . who is a distinguished philosopher [and] a very old and intimate friend of mine . . . I should be extremely grateful for anything you could do for him.' He added: 'I must leave it to him to tell you his reasons for wanting to go to Russia. He is not a member of the Communist Party, but has strong sympathies with the way of life which he believes the new regime in Russia stands for.'

At his meeting with Maisky, Wittgenstein took great pains to appear both respectable and respectful. Keynes had warned him that, while Maisky was a Communist, that did not mean he would not wish to be addressed as 'Your Excellency', nor that he had any less respect than any other high bourgeois official for standards of formality and politeness. Wittgenstein took the advice to heart. The meeting was one of the few occasions in his life when he wore a tie, and he used the phrase 'Your Excellency' as often as he could. Indeed, as he later told Gilbert Pattisson, he was so anxious to show respect to the ambassador that he made a great show of wiping his shoes well on the mat – on the way *out* of the room. After the meeting Wittgenstein reported to Keynes that Maisky was: 'definitely nice and in the end promised to send me some addresses of people in Russia of whom I might get useful information. He did not think that it was utterly hopeless for me to try to get permission to settle in Russia though he too didn't think it was likely.'

Apart from these – not very encouraging – meetings at the Russian Embassy, Wittgenstein also tried to make contacts through the Society for Cultural Relations with the Soviet Union (SCR). The SCR was founded in 1924 and was (indeed, is) an organization dedicated to improving cultural links between Britain and the Soviet Union. It organizes lectures, discussions and exhibitions, and publishes its own magazine, the *Anglo-Soviet Journal*, each issue of which in the 1930s carried an advertisement for the tours of Russia organized by *Intourist*, the Soviet travel company ('For the experience of a lifetime visit USSR' etc.). Because (unlike its companion organization, the Society of Friends of Soviet Russia) its aims were cultural rather than political, the SCR numbered among its members many non-Communists such as Charles Trevelyan and, indeed, Keynes himself. By 1935, however, it was dominated by much the same people (Hayden–Guest, Pat Sloan etc.) as the Society of Friends. On 19 August Wittgenstein went to the offices of the SCR to meet with Miss Hilda Browning, its Vice-Chairman. The following day he reported to Gilbert Pattisson:

> My interview with Miss B. went off better than I had expected. At least I got one useful piece of information: – that my only chance of getting a permission to settle in R. is to go there as a tourist & talk to officials; & that all I can do at this end is to try to get letters of introduction. Also Miss B. told me that she would give me such letters to two places. This is, on the whole, better than nothing. It doesn't however settle anything & I'm as much in the dark as ever, not only about what they'll let me do but also about what I want to do. It is shameful, but I change my mind about it every two hours. I see what a perfect ass I am, at bottom & feel rather rotten.

The two places to which he had secured an introduction were the Institute of the North and the Institute of National Minorities. These were both educational institutes dedicated to improving the level of literacy among the ethnic minorities in the Soviet Union. Though considering this 'better than nothing', Wittgenstein did not particularly want a teaching job. But, as he had been told by Keynes, he was likely to get permission to settle in the Soviet Union only if he received an invitation from a Soviet organization: 'If you were a qualified technician of a sort likely to be useful to them', Keynes wrote to him, 'that might not be difficult. But, without some such qualification, which might very well be a medical qualification, it would be difficult.' Wittgenstein, who throughout his life harboured a desire to become a doctor, considered the possibility of studying medicine in England with the intention of practising in Russia, and even secured from Keynes a promise to finance his medical training. What he really wanted, however, was to be allowed to settle in Russia as a manual worker. But, as became increasingly clear to him, it was extremely unlikely that he would receive an invitation from a Soviet organization to do that. The one thing that was not in short supply in Soviet Russia was unskilled labour.

By the time he left for Leningrad, on 7 September, all Wittgenstein had managed to obtain were the introductions from Hilda Browning and a few names and addresses of people living in Moscow. He was seen off at Hay's Wharf in London by Gilbert Pattisson, Francis being too ill to make the trip. It was understood, however, that he was looking for work on Francis's behalf as well as his own. On the same boat was Dr George Sacks, who has recalled that he and his wife sat opposite Wittgenstein at meal-times. Next to Wittgenstein sat an American Greek Orthodox priest. Wittgenstein, who seemed depressed and preoccupied, sat staring into space, not speaking to anyone, until one day he introduced himself to the priest by sticking up his hand and exclaiming: 'Wittgenstein!' to which the priest replied by saying his own name. For the rest of the journey he was silent.

He arrived in Leningrad on 12 September, and for the next two weeks his pocket diary is full of the names and addresses of the many people he contacted in an effort to secure an offer of employment. In Leningrad he visited, as well as the Institute of the North, the university professor of philosophy, Mrs Tatiana Gornstein, and offered to give a philosophy course at Leningrad University. At Moscow he met Sophia Janovskaya, the professor of mathematical logic, with whom he struck up a friendship that lasted through correspondence long after he had returned to England. He was attracted to her by the forthrightness of her speech. Upon meeting him for the first time, she exclaimed: 'What, not the great Wittgenstein?' and during a conversation on philosophy she told him quite simply: 'You ought to read more Hegel.' From their discussions of philosophy, Professor Janovskaya received the (surely false) impression that Wittgenstein was interested in dialectical materialism and the development of Soviet philosophic thought. It was apparently through Janovskaya that Wittgenstein was offered first a chair in philosophy at Kazan University, and then a teaching post in philosophy at the University of Moscow.

In Moscow Wittgenstein also met two or three times with Pat Sloan, the British Communist who was then working as a Soviet trade union organizer (a period of his life recalled in the book *Russia Without Illusions*, 1938). It seems quite likely that these meetings centred on Wittgenstein's continuing hopes to work in some manual capacity. If so, they were apparently unsuccessful. George Sacks recalls that in Moscow: 'we [he and his wife] heard that Wittgenstein wanted to work on a collective farm, but the Russians told him his own work was a useful contribution and he ought to go back to Cambridge'.

On 17 September, while still in Moscow, Wittgenstein received a letter from Francis urging him to stay as long as it took to find work. 'I wish I could be with you and see things with you', he wrote. 'But I feel it is as though I was with you.' From this letter it appears that Wittgenstein and Skinner were planning to spend the following academic year preparing the *Brown Book* for publication, prior, presumably, to their settling in the Soviet Union. This makes sense in that the coming academic year, 1935–6, was to be the final year of both Skinner's three-year postgraduate scholarship and Wittgenstein's five-year fellowship at Trinity. 'I think a lot about the work which we are going to do next year', Francis told him. 'I feel that the spirit of the method which you used last year is so good':

> Everything, I feel, is absolutely simple and yet it's all full of light. I feel it will be very good to go on with it and get it ready for publication. I feel that the method is so valuable. I hope very much we shall be able to get on with it. We will do our best.

'I'd like to say again', he added, 'that I hope you will stay longer in Moscow than the time you arranged for if you feel there is any chance that you might learn more. It would be valuable for both of us.'

Wittgenstein evidently saw no reason to extend his stay. His visit had served only to confirm what he had been told before he left: that he was welcome to enter the Soviet Union as a teacher, but unwelcome as a worker on a collective farm. On the Sunday before he left he wrote a postcard to Pattisson asking to be met in London:

> My dear Gilbert!
> Tomorrow evening I shall leave Moskow (I am staying in the rooms which Napoleon had in 1812). The day after tomorrow my boat sails from Leningrad & I can only hope that Neptune will have a heart when he sees me. My boat is due in London on Sunday 29th [September]. Could you either meet the boat or leave a message for me at my Palace (usually called 'Strand Palace')? I'm certainly looking forward to seeing your old and bloody face again. Ever in blood.
>
>   Ludwig
>
> P.S. If the censor reads this it serves him right!

After his return to England Wittgenstein very rarely discussed his trip to Russia. He sent Francis to deliver a report to Fania Pascal, which told her of his meeting with Mrs Janovskaya and his offer of an academic job at Kazan, and concluded with a statement that: 'He had taken no decisions about his future.' What the report did not provide were any of Wittgenstein's impressions of Soviet Russia – any hint of whether he liked or disliked what he had seen. On this he remained, apart from one or two isolated comments, completely silent. The reason he gave friends for this silence was that he did not wish his name to be used, as Russell had allowed *his* name to be used (after the publication of *Theory and Practice of Bolshevism*), to support anti-Soviet propaganda.

This suggests that, had he been open about his impression of the Soviet Union, he would have drawn an unflattering picture. An important clue to his attitude perhaps lies in his remark to Gilbert Pattisson that living in Russia was rather like being a private in the army. It was difficult, he told Pattisson, for 'people of our upbringing' to live there because of the degree of petty dishonesty that was necessary even to survive. If Wittgenstein thought of life in Russia as comparable to his experience on the *Goplana* during the First World War, it is perhaps not surprising that he showed so little inclination to settle there after he returned from his brief visit.

He nevertheless repeatedly expressed his sympathy for the Soviet régime and his belief that, as material conditions for ordinary Soviet citizens were improving, the régime was strong and unlikely to collapse. He spoke admiringly of the educational system in Russia, remarking that he had never seen people so eager to learn and so attentive to what they were being told. But perhaps his most important reason for sympathizing with Stalin's régime was that there was in Russia so little unemployment. 'The important thing', he once said to Rush Rhees, 'is that the people have *work*.' When the regimentation of life in Russia was mentioned – when it was pointed out that, although they were employed, the workers there had no freedom to leave or change their jobs – Wittgenstein was not impressed. 'Tyranny', he told Rhees with a shrug of his shoulders, 'doesn't make me feel indignant.' The suggestion that 'rule by bureaucracy' was bringing class distinctions in Russia, however, did arouse his indignation: 'If anything could destroy my sympathy with the Russian regime, it would be the growth of class distinctions.'

For two years after his return from Russia Wittgenstein toyed with the idea of taking up the teaching post in Moscow that he had been offered. During this time he continued to correspond with Sophia

Janovskaya, and when he went away to Norway he arranged with Fania Pascal for Janovskaya to be sent insulin for her diabetes. As late as June 1937 he remarked in a letter to Engelmann: 'perhaps I shall go to Russia'. Shortly after this, however, the offer of a post was withdrawn, because (according to Piero Sraffa) by this time all Germans (including Austrians) had become suspect in Russia.

Nevertheless, even after the show trials of 1936, the worsening of relations between Russia and the West and the Nazi-Soviet Pact of 1939, Wittgenstein continued to express his sympathy with the Soviet régime – so much so that he was taken by some of his students at Cambridge to be a 'Stalinist'. This label is, of course, nonsense. But at a time when most people saw only the tyranny of Stalin's rule, Wittgenstein emphasized the problems with which Stalin had to deal and the scale of his achievement in dealing with them. On the eve of the Second World War he asserted to Drury that England and France between them would not be able to defeat Hitler's Germany; they would need the support of Russia. He told Drury: 'People have accused Stalin of having betrayed the Russian Revolution. But they have no idea of the problems that Stalin had to deal with; and the dangers he saw threatening Russia.' He immediately added, as though it were somehow relevant: 'I was looking at a picture of the British Cabinet and I thought to myself, "a lot of wealthy old men".' This remark recalls Keynes's characterization of Russia as 'the beautiful and foolish youngest son of the European family, with hair on his head, nearer to both the earth and to heaven than his bald brothers in the West'. Wittgenstein's reasons for wanting to live in Russia, both the 'bad and even childish' reasons and the 'deep and even good' ones, had much to do, I think, with his desire to dissociate himself from the old men of the West, and from the disintegrating and decaying culture of Western Europe.

It is also, of course, one more manifestation of his perennial desire to join the ranks. The Soviet authorities knew, just as the Austrian authorities had in 1915, that he would be more use to them as an officer than as a private; and Wittgenstein himself realized that he could not really tolerate life among the 'petty dishonesty' of the ordinary soldiers. Yet he continued to wish it could be otherwise.

When, in the autumn of 1935, Wittgenstein began the final year of his fellowship at Trinity, he still had little idea of what he would do after it had expired. Perhaps he would go to Russia – perhaps, like Rowland Hutt, get a job among 'ordinary people'; or perhaps, as Skinner had wanted, he would concentrate on preparing the *Brown Book* for publication. One thing seemed sure: he would not continue to lecture at Cambridge.

His lectures during this last year centred on the theme of 'Sense Data and Private Experience'. In these lectures he tried to combat the philosopher's temptation to think that, when we experience something (when we see something, feel pain etc.), there is some thing, a sense datum, that is the primary content of our experience. He took his examples, however, not from philosophers but from ordinary speech. And when he quoted from literature, it was not from the great philosophical works, nor from the philosophical journal *Mind*, but from Street & Smith's *Detective Story Magazine*.

He began one lecture by reading a passage from Street & Smith in which the narrator, a detective, is alone on the deck of a ship in the middle of the night, with no sound except the ticking of the ship's clock. The detective muses to himself: 'A clock is a bewildering instrument at best: measuring a fragment of infinity: measuring something which does not exist perhaps.' Wittgenstein told his class that it is much more revealing and important when you find this sort of confusion in something said 'in a silly detective story' than it is when you find it in something said 'by a silly philosopher':

Here you might say 'obviously a clock is not a bewildering instrument at all'. – If in some situation it strikes you as a bewildering instrument, and you can then bring yourself round to saying that of course it is not bewildering – then this is the way to solve a philosophical problem.

The clock becomes a bewildering instrument here because he says about it 'it measures a fragment of infinity, measuring something which does not exist perhaps'. What makes the clock bewildering is that he introduces a sort of entity which he then can't see, and it seems like a ghost.

The connection between this and what we were saying about sense data: What is bewildering is the introduction of something we might call 'intangible'. It seems as though there is nothing intangible about the chair or the table, but there is about the fleeting personal experience.

A recurrent theme of Wittgenstein's lectures for that year was his concern to uphold, against philosophers, our ordinary perception of the world. When a philosopher raises doubts, about time or about mental states, that do not occur to the ordinary man, this is not because the philosopher has more insight than the ordinary man, but because, in a way, he has less; he is subject to temptations to misunderstand that do not occur to the non-philosopher:

> We have the feeling that the ordinary man, if he talks of 'good', of 'number' etc., does not really understand what he is talking about. I see something queer about perception and he talks about it as if it were not queer at all. Should we say he knows what he is talking about or not?
>
> You can say both. Suppose people are playing chess. I see queer problems when I look into the rules and scrutinise them. But Smith and Brown play chess with no difficulty. Do they understand the game? Well, they play it.

The passage is redolent of Wittgenstein's own doubts about his status as a philosopher, his weariness of 'seeing queer problems' and his desire to start playing the game rather than scrutinizing its rules. His thoughts turned again to the idea of training as a doctor. Drury was at this time preparing for his first MB examination at Dublin, and Wittgenstein wrote asking him to make enquiries about the possibility of his entering the medical school there, his training presumably to be paid for by Keynes. He suggested to Drury that the two of them might practise together as psychiatrists. Wittgenstein felt that he might have a special talent for this branch of medicine, and was particularly interested in Freudian psychoanalysis. That year he sent Drury, as a birthday present, Freud's *Interpretation of Dreams*, telling Drury that when he first read it he said to himself: 'Here at last is a psychologist who has something to say.'

Wittgenstein's feeling that he would have made a good psychiatrist seems to rest on a belief that his style of philosophizing and Freudian psychoanalysis required a similar gift. Not, of course, that they are the same technique. Wittgenstein reacted angrily when his philosophical method was dubbed 'therapeutic positivism' and compared with psychoanalysis. When, for example, A. J. Ayer drew the comparison in an article in the *Listener*, he received from Wittgenstein a strongly worded letter of rebuke. However, Wittgenstein was inclined to see some sort of connection between his work and Freud's. He once described himself to Rhees as a 'disciple of Freud', and at various times summed up the achievements of both himself and Freud in strikingly similar phrases. 'It's all excellent similes', he said in a lecture of Freud's work; and of his own contribution to philosophy: 'What I invent are new *similes*.' This ability to form a synoptic view by constructing illuminating similes and metaphors was, it appears, what he wished to contribute to psychiatric medicine.

As the year wore on, however, Wittgenstein's interest in training as a doctor or in getting any other sort of job declined in favour of the idea of finishing his book. At the end of the year, as his fellowship was coming to an end, Wittgenstein discussed the possibilities open to him with a number of his favourite students. The latest of these was the postgraduate student Rush Rhees. Rhees had arrived in Cambridge in September 1935 to study under G. E. Moore, after having studied philosophy previously at Edinburgh, Göttingen and Innsbruck. He had, at first, been put off attending Wittgenstein's lectures by the mannerisms of Wittgenstein's students, but in February 1936 he overcame these misgivings and attended all the remaining lectures of that year. He became one of Wittgenstein's closest friends, and remained so until Wittgenstein's death. In June 1936 Wittgenstein invited Rhees to tea and discussed with him the question of whether he should try to get a job of some sort, or go somewhere by himself and spend his time working on his book. He told Rhees: 'I still have a little money. And I could live and work by myself as long as that lasts.'

This latter idea held sway, and when Wittgenstein and Skinner visited Drury in Dublin later that June, the issue of training as a psychiatrist was not raised. What perhaps clinched the decision was news of the death of Moritz Schlick. Wittgenstein was in Dublin when he heard that Schlick had been murdered – shot on the steps of Vienna University by a mentally deranged student. The fact that the student later became a member of the Nazi Party gave rise to rumours that the killing had a political motive, although the evidence suggests that the student had a more personal grudge against Schlick, who had rejected his doctoral thesis. Upon hearing the news, Wittgenstein immediately wrote to Friedrich Waismann:

Dear Mr Waismann,
The death of Schlick is indeed a great misfortune. Both you and I
have lost much. I do not know how I should express my sympathy,
which as you know, I really feel, to his wife and children. If it is
possible for you, you would do me a great kindness if you contact
Mrs Schlick or one of the children and tell them that I think of them
with warm sympathy but I do not know what I should write to
them. Should it be impossible for you (externally or internally) to
convey this message, please let me know.

> With kind sympathy and regards
> Yours
> Ludwig Wittgenstein

Schlick's death finally put an end to any idea there might still have
been to fulfil the plans made in 1929 for Waismann and Wittgenstein to
co-operate together on a book. With Waismann's exasperation at
Wittgenstein's constant changes of mind, and Wittgenstein's distrust
of Waismann's understanding of him, only their mutual respect for
Schlick, and Schlick's encouragement to persist with the project, had
provided even a slender hope of completion. After Schlick's death
Waismann decided to work without Wittgenstein, and signed a
contract to finish the book himself and have it published under his own
name. The book reached the galley-proof stage in 1939, but was then
withdrawn.

Wittgenstein, meanwhile, decided to do as he had done in 1913 – to go
to Norway, where he could live alone without any distractions and
bring his work to completion. It is possible that his decision was made
in the wake of Schlick's death, but possible too that it was prompted
by the more personal reason of needing to get away from the
'distraction' of his relationship with Francis, whose three-year postgraduate studentship ended at the same time as Wittgenstein's
fellowship.

Until the summer of 1936 it seems to have been understood that
whatever Wittgenstein and Francis would do – train as doctors, go to
Russia, work with 'ordinary' people or work on Wittgenstein's
book – they would do together. So, at least, it was understood by
Francis. It is doubtful, however, whether Wittgenstein ever took
Francis seriously as a philosophical collaborator; he was useful to

dictate ideas to, especially when, as in the case of the *Blue* and *Brown Books*, the dictation was done in English. But for the *discussion* of ideas, the clarification of thoughts, Francis was no use; his awed respect for Wittgenstein paralysed him and got in the way of his making any useful contribution. 'Sometimes', Wittgenstein told Drury, 'his silence infuriates me and I shout at him, "Say something, Francis!"' 'But', he added, 'Francis isn't a thinker. You know Rodin's statue called *The Thinker*; it struck me the other day that I couldn't imagine Francis in that attitude.'

For similar reasons Wittgenstein discouraged Francis from going on with academic work. 'He would never be happy in academic life', he decided, and Francis, as always, accepted his decision. It was not, however, the view of Francis's family, nor that of many of his friends. Louis Goodstein, for example, who was Francis's contemporary at both St Paul's and Cambridge and who later became Professor of Mathematical Logic at Leicester University, thought that Francis might have had a promising career as a professional mathematician. He was one of the first people to be told by Francis of his decision to abandon mathematics, and he disapproved strongly, seeing in the decision only the unfortunate influence of Wittgenstein's own dislike of academic life. So, too, did Francis's family. His mother particularly came to dislike deeply the influence that Wittgenstein was exerting on her son. She reacted with great consternation both to the plan to settle in Russia and to the idea that Francis should abandon his potentially brilliant academic career. His sister, Priscilla Truscott, was equally incredulous. 'Why?' she demanded. '*Why?*'

For Francis, however, the only person whose opinion mattered was Wittgenstein, and he resolutely adhered to Wittgenstein's decision, even when that meant living away from Wittgenstein himself and working in a job which made little use of his talents and in which he felt exploited. It was not to train as a doctor, but as a factory mechanic, that Skinner left university, and not alongside Wittgenstein, but on his own. The idea that he might train as a doctor was impractical: his parents could not afford to see him through medical studies, and Keynes's promise to finance Wittgenstein's medical training did not extend to Francis. Francis volunteered to fight in the Spanish Civil War alongside the International Brigade, but was turned down because of his physical disability. (Francis, whose health was always precarious, was lame in one leg as a result of the osteomyelitis from which he suffered as a young boy and from which he was always subject to renewed attacks.)

Wittgenstein's (and therefore Skinner's) second choice of career after medicine was that of a mechanic. And so in the summer of 1936 Francis was taken on as a two-year apprentice mechanic at the Cambridge Instrument Company. For most of the time he was employed in making mainscrews, a repetitive and tiring task that he neither enjoyed nor found at all interesting; it was simply a drudge which he put up with for Wittgenstein's sake. Fania Pascal, however, believes that Skinner was happier among working people than among people of his own class. The working people were, she says, kinder and less self-conscious. This is perhaps true, although for the first few years at the factory Francis spent little time socializing with his colleagues. His evenings were spent either alone or with friends from the university – the Bachtins, Rowland Hutt and Pascal herself. What he wanted more than anything else was to live and work together with Wittgenstein, and this he had been denied by Wittgenstein himself.

Francis did not have a Weiningerian conception of love; he did not believe that love needed a separation, a certain distance, to preserve it. Wittgenstein, on the other hand, probably shared Weininger's view. While in Norway he recorded in his diary that he realized how unique Francis was – that he really appreciated him – only when he was away from him. And thus it was, perhaps, precisely to get away from him that he decided to go to Norway.

Before he left for Norway Wittgenstein took a holiday in France with Gilbert Pattisson, the two touring the Bordeaux region together in a car. Pattisson was one of the relatively few people with whom Wittgenstein could relax and enjoy himself. For Pattisson's part, however, Wittgenstein's company could be a little too heavy. He accordingly insisted, as he had before in 1931, on spending at least a few nights of the holiday away from Wittgenstein at a fashionable resort, where he could indulge himself in unfettered luxury – wining, dining and gambling. On the one occasion when Wittgenstein accompanied Pattisson in the pleasures of gambling, he showed himself to be a novice in the art of wasting money. They went together to the Casino Royan, where they played roulette, a game obviously new to Wittgenstein. He studied the game carefully before remarking to Pattisson, incredulously: 'I don't see how you *can* win!' Sometimes, it seems, there is more point in scrutinizing the rules than in playing the game.

18

CONFESSIONS

Wittgenstein's leaving for Norway in August 1936 is strongly reminiscent of his earlier departure in October 1913. In both cases he was leaving for an indefinite period to accomplish a definite task – the preparation of a final formulation of his philosophical remarks. In both cases, too, he was leaving behind someone he loved.

The difference is that in 1913 Pinsent had had no wish to accompany him. It is doubtful whether Pinsent ever realized how much Wittgenstein was in love with him, and almost certain that he did not return that love. He was 'thankful' for his 'acquaintance' with Wittgenstein, but not in any way dependent upon it. In October 1913 Pinsent's training as a lawyer figured much larger in his concerns than his friendship with Wittgenstein, a break from whom possibly came to him as something of a relief.

For Francis, however, his relationship with Wittgenstein was the very centre of his life: if asked, he would have dropped everything to go and live with him in Norway. 'When I got your letter', he wrote just a few weeks after they were separated, 'I wished I could come and help you clean your room.' His life in Cambridge without Wittgenstein was lonely and dreary. He no longer got on well with his family, he could no longer participate in Wittgenstein's work, and, though he persevered with it for Wittgenstein's sake, he disliked his job at the factory. As he had no doubt been asked by Wittgenstein to do, he gave regular reports of his work. They sound far from enthusiastic: 'My work goes on all right. I am working at mainscrews' (21.8.36); 'My work is going on all right. I am almost reaching the end of making the mainscrews. Last week I had to do some hand tool work on them, which was difficult at first. I am now polishing them up ready to be nickelled' (1.9.36); 'I have an order for 200 draught and pressure gauges. I wish there weren't going to be so many' (14.10.36). Eventually, after a discussion with Rowland Hutt about his position at the factory, even the mild and compliant Francis was moved to express his dissatisfaction:

> I don't feel clear about my relation to the firm. I don't feel clear whether I am getting work which makes full use of me. It seems to me (and Hutt agrees with me) that there is a line to be drawn between being favoured exceptionally and letting them do anything with you. For instance the foreman said to me that if I had been going to be there five years he could have advanced me very quickly, but as I was only going to be there two years and the firm knew anyhow I would not ever be much use to them, it was very different.

He tried, he said, to remember what Wittgenstein had told him about being 'hopeful, grateful & thoughtful', but in such circumstances it was not easy. He does not say so, but one can imagine him thinking that in such a position he had little to hope for, nothing to be grateful for and nothing to occupy his thoughts except that he would rather be with Wittgenstein. His conversation with Hutt, he told Wittgenstein, 'made me feel how much I wished I could have you here to talk with you'. Time and again in his letters he emphasizes that: 'I think of you a lot with great love.' Wittgenstein's side of this correspondence has not survived, but the form of these declarations of love sometimes suggests that they were written to reassure doubts that Wittgenstein might have expressed: 'My feelings for you haven't changed at all. This is the honest truth. I think of you a lot and with great love.'

It is likely that the advice to stay 'hopeful, grateful & thoughtful' was all that Francis received in the way of sympathetic understanding from Wittgenstein. In Norway, Wittgenstein gave more thought to himself and to his work – the two, as ever, being inextricably linked – than he did to Francis. And, as in 1913–14, and again in 1931, being alone in Norway proved conducive to thinking seriously about both logic and his sins.

'I do believe that it was the right thing for me to come here thank God', he wrote to Moore in October. 'I can't imagine that I could have worked anywhere as I do here. It's the quiet and, perhaps, the wonderful scenery; I mean, its quiet seriousness.' To the news that both Moore and Rhees were finding it difficult to write anything, Wittgenstein replied that this was a good sign: 'One can't drink wine while it ferments, but that it's fermenting shows that it isn't dishwater'. 'You see', he added, 'I still make beautiful similes.'

Wittgenstein sent Moore a map, showing his hut in relation to the fjord, the neighbouring mountains and the nearest village. The point was to illustrate that it was impossible for him to get to the village without rowing. In clement weather this was not too bad, but by October it was wet and cold. He wrote to Pattisson: 'The weather has changed from marvellous to rotten. It rains like hell now. Two days ago we had our first snow.' Pattisson responded by sending Wittgenstein a sou'wester, with which Wittgenstein was very pleased. Recalling the 'Letters from a Satisfied Customer', he wrote: ' "Both fit and style are perfect" as they always write to Mr Burton, the tailor of taste.'

He had taken with him a copy of the *Brown Book*, with the intention of using it as the basic material out of which to construct a final version of his book. For over a month, he worked on a revision of it, translating it from English into German and rewriting it as he went along. At the beginning of November he gave this up, writing, in heavy strokes: '*Dieser ganze "Versuch einer Umarbeitung" vom (Anfang) bis hierher ist nichts wert*' ('This whole attempt at a revision, from the beginning right up to here, is worthless'). He explained in a letter to Moore that when he read through what he had written so far he found it all, 'or nearly all, boring and artificial':

For having the English version before me had cramped my thinking. I therefore decided to start all over again and not to let my thoughts be guided by anything but themselves. – I found it difficult the first day or two but then it became easy. And so I'm writing now a new version and I hope I'm not wrong in saying that it's somewhat better than the last.

This new version became the final formulation of the opening of Wittgenstein's book. It forms, roughly, paragraphs 1–188 of the published text of *Philosophical Investigations* (about a quarter of the book), and is the only section of Wittgenstein's later work with which he was fully satisfied – the only part he never later attempted to revise or rearrange, or indicate that he would *wish* to revise if he had time.

To a large extent it follows the arrangement of the *Brown Book*, beginning with St Augustine's account of how he learnt to talk, using that to introduce the notion of a language-game and then proceeding to a discussion of following a rule. In this final version, however, the passage from Augustine's *Confessions* is actually quoted, and the point of beginning with that passage is spelt out more clearly:

> These words, it seems to me, give us a particular picture of the essence of human language. It is this: the individual words in language name objects – sentences are combinations of such names. – In this picture of language we find the roots of the following idea: Every word has a meaning. This meaning is cor-related with the word. It is the object for which the word stands.

The rest of the book was to examine the implications of this idea and the traps into which it led philosophers, and to suggest routes out of those traps. These routes all begin by dislodging the (pre-philosophical) picture of language expressed by Augustine, which gives rise to the philosophical idea mentioned above. In this way, Wittgenstein hoped to dig out philosophical confusion by its pre-philosophical roots.

The quotation from St Augustine is not given, as is sometimes thought, to present a *theory* of language, which Wittgenstein will then show to be false. *Confessions*, after all, is not (primarily, at least) a philosophical work, but a religious autobiography, and in the passage quoted Augustine is not *theorizing*, but is describing how he learnt to talk. And this is precisely why it is appropriate for presenting the target of Wittgenstein's philosophical enterprise. Though it expresses no theory, what is contained in Augustine's account is a *picture*. And, for Wittgenstein, *all* philosophical theories are rooted in just such a picture, and must be uprooted by the introduction of a new picture, a new metaphor:

> A simile that has been absorbed into the forms of our language produces a false appearance and this disquiets us.

A *picture* held us captive. And we could not get outside it, for it lay in our language and language seemed to repeat it to us inexorably.

The final version of the beginning of Wittgenstein's book differs from the *Brown Book* in that, rather than simply leading the reader through a series of language-games without any explanation, he pauses now and again to elucidate his procedure and to guard against some possible misunderstandings of it:

Our clear and simple language-games are not preparatory studies of a future regularization of language – as it were first approximations, ignoring friction and air-resistance. The language-games are set up as *objects of comparison* which are meant to throw light on the facts of our language by way not only of similarities, but also of dissimilarities.

It is not our aim to refine or complete the system of rules for the use of our words in unheard-of ways.

For the clarity that we are aiming at is indeed *complete* clarity. But this simply means that the philosophical problems should *completely* disappear. The real discovery is the one that makes me capable of stopping doing philosophy when I want to. – The one that gives philosophy peace, so that it is no longer tormented by questions which bring *itself* in question. – Instead we now demonstrate a method, by examples; and the series of examples can be broken off. – Problems are solved (difficulties eliminated), not a *single* problem.

Anticipating a natural reaction to his conception of philosophy and its method, he asks: 'Where does our investigation get its importance from, since it seems only to destroy everything interesting, that is, all that is great and important? (As it were all the buildings, leaving behind only bits of stone and rubble.)' He answers: 'What we are destroying is nothing but houses of cards and we are clearing up the ground of language on which they stand.' And, changing the metaphor, but keeping to the same point:

The results of philosophy are the uncovering of one or other piece of plain nonsense and of bumps that the understanding has got by running its head up against the limits of language. These bumps make us see the value of the discovery.

Whether such explanations would mean anything to people who have not themselves experienced such 'bumps' remains doubtful. But then, the method was not developed for such people, just as Freudian analysis was not developed for the psychologically unconcerned. *Philosophical Investigations* – more, perhaps, than any other philosophical classic – makes demands, not just on the reader's intelligence, but on his *involvement*. Other great philosophical works – Schopenhauer's *World and Representation*, say – can be read with interest and entertainment by someone who 'wants to know what Schopenhauer said'. But if *Philosophical Investigations* is read in this spirit it will very quickly become boring, and a chore to read, not because it is intellectually difficult, but because it will be practically impossible to gather what Wittgenstein is 'saying'. For, in truth, he is not *saying* anything; he is presenting a technique for the unravelling of confusions. Unless these are *your* confusions, the book will be of very little interest.

Connected with the degree of personal involvement required to make sense of it, there is another reason why it seems appropriate to begin the book with a quotation from St Augustine's *Confessions*. And that is that, for Wittgenstein, *all* philosophy, in so far as it is pursued honestly and decently, begins with a confession. He often remarked that the problem of writing good philosophy and of thinking well about philosophical problems was one of the will more than of the intellect – the will to resist the temptation to misunderstand, the will to resist superficiality. What gets in the way of genuine understanding is often not one's lack of intelligence, but the presence of one's pride. Thus: 'The edifice of your pride has to be dismantled. And that is terribly hard work.' The self-scrutiny demanded by such a dismantling of one's pride is necessary, not only to be a decent person, but also to write decent philosophy. 'If anyone is unwilling to descend into himself, because this is too painful, he will remain superficial in his writing':

> Lying to oneself about oneself, deceiving yourself about the pretence in your own state of will, must have a harmful influence on [one's] style; for the result will be that you cannot tell what is genuine in the style and what is false . . .

24 *Top:* With the family at the Hochreit

25 *Above:* Ludwig, Helene and Paul at the Hochreit

26 & 27 *Below:* Wittgenstein's military identity card during the First World War

28 *Bottom:* Wittgenstein's room in the guest-house 'Zum Braunen Hirschen', Trattenbach

30 Frank Ramsey

29 Wittgenstein with his pupils in Puchberg am Schneeberg

31 *Left:* Wittgenstein, 1925

32 & 33 *Below and right:* Examples of a window-catch and door-handle designed by Wittgenstein for his sister's house in the Kundmanngasse

34 *Bottom:* The Kundmanngasse house

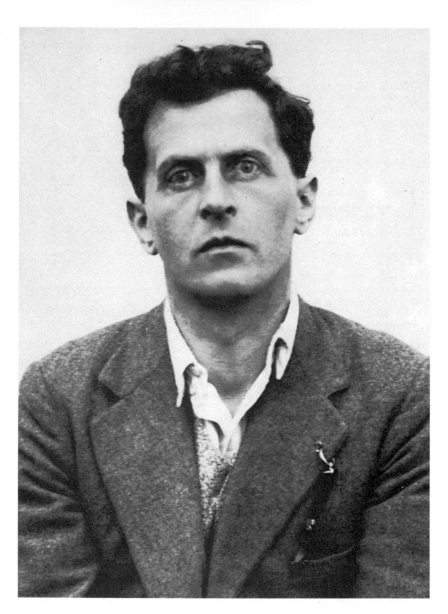

35 & 36 Portraits of Wittgenstein: *above* on being awarded a scholarship from Trinity College, 1929; *right* the Fellowship Portrait, 1930

37 & 38 Postcard to Gilbert Pattisson from Vienna: 'Dear old Blood, I'm sure you'll be interested to see me as I walk with a sister & a friend of mine [Margarete Stonborough and Arvid Sjögren] in an exhibition of bloody modern houses. Don't I look enterprising?! You can gather from this picture that we had very hot weather but not that there was a terrific thunderstorm half an hour after this was taken. I am, old god, yours in bloodyness Ludwig'

If I perform to myself, then it's this that the style expresses. And then the style cannot be my own. If you are unwilling to know what you are, your writing is a form of deceit.

It is no coincidence that Wittgenstein wrote the set of remarks with which he remained most satisfied at a time when he was most ruthlessly honest about himself – when he made the most intense efforts to 'descend into himself' and admit to those occasions on which his pride had forced him to be deceitful.

During the months in which he prepared the final formulation of the beginning of his book, Wittgenstein also prepared a confession, describing the times in his life when he had been weak and dishonest. His intention was to read the confession out to members of his family and to a number of his closest friends. He presumably felt that to admit the deceit to himself was not enough; properly to 'dismantle the pride' that had given rise to his weakness would involve confession to other people. It was, for him, a matter of the utmost importance, and accordingly, in November 1936, he wrote to, among others, Maurice Drury, G. E. Moore, Paul Engelmann, Fania Pascal and, of course, Francis Skinner, telling them that he *had* to meet them some time during the Christmas period. The only one of these letters to survive is the one to Moore, although we can guess that the others were broadly similar. He told Moore that, besides his work, 'all sorts of things have been happening inside me (I mean in my mind)':

I won't write about them now, but when I come to Cambridge, as I intend to do for a few days about the New Year, I hope to God I shall be able to talk to you about them; and I shall then want your advice and your help in some very difficult and serious matters.

To Francis he must have been a little more direct, telling him that what he had in mind was to make a confession. In a letter of 6 December, we find Francis promising: 'Whatever you say to me can't make any difference to my love for you. I am terribly rotten in every way myself.' What was of more importance for Francis was that he would, at last, be seeing Wittgenstein again: 'I think of you a lot and of our love for each other. This keeps me going and gives me cheerfulness and helps me to get over despondency.' Three days later he repeated the promise: 'Whatever you have to tell me about yourself can't make any difference to my love for you . . . There won't be any question of my forgiving you as I am a much worse person than you are. I think of you a lot and love you always.'

Wittgenstein spent Christmas in Vienna, and delivered the confession to Engelmann, some members of his family and, probably, to some other friends as well (surely, one would think, Hänsel must have been included). None of these people left any record of what the confession contained. When Engelmann published his letters from Wittgenstein he omitted the one that mentioned the confession; in all probability, he destroyed it. In the New Year Wittgenstein visited Cambridge and made his confession to G. E. Moore, Maurice Drury, Fania Pascal, Rowland Hutt and Francis.

Moore, Drury and Francis died without revealing the secret of what the confession contained, and we therefore have only the recollections of Pascal and Hutt to depend on. How the others reacted to the confession we do not know, although Pascal most likely captures the spirit of Drury's and Moore's responses when she remarks that, without being told, she knows they: 'listened patiently, said little, but showed friendly participation, implying by manner and look that there was no need for him to make this confession, but if he thought he should, well and good, so be it'. According to Drury, however, he did not *listen* to the confession, but read it. Drury adds that Moore had already read it, and, according to Wittgenstein, had seemed very distressed at having to do so. Other than this, Drury says nothing in his memoir about the confession. As for Francis, Pascal is no doubt correct in speculating: 'He would have sat transfixed, profoundly affected, his eyes undeviatingly on Wittgenstein.'

For both Rowland Hutt and Fania Pascal, listening to the confession was an uncomfortable experience. In Hutt's case the discomfort was simply embarrassment at having to sit in a Lyons café while opposite him sat Wittgenstein reciting his sins in a loud and clear voice. Fania Pascal, on the other hand, was exasperated by the whole thing. Wittgenstein had phoned at an inconvenient moment to ask whether he could come and see her. When she asked if it was urgent she was told firmly that it was, and could not wait. 'If ever a thing could wait', she thought, facing him across the table, 'it is a confession of this kind and made in this manner.' The stiff and remote way in which he delivered his confession made it impossible for her to react with sympathy. At one point she cried out: 'What is it? You want to be perfect?' '*Of course* I want to be perfect', he thundered.

Fania Pascal remembers two of the 'sins' confessed to by Wittgenstein. As well as these, there were a number of more minor sins, which elude her memory. Some of these have been remembered by Rowland Hutt. One concerned the death of an American acquaintance of Wittgenstein's. Upon being told by a mutual friend of this death, Wittgenstein reacted in a way that was appropriate to hearing sorrowful news. This was disingenuous of him, because, in fact, it was not news to him at all; he had already heard of the death. Another concerned an incident in the First World War. Wittgenstein had been told by his commanding officer to carry some bombs across an unsteady plank which bridged a stream. He had, at first, been too afraid to do it. He eventually overcame his fear, but his initial cowardice had haunted him ever since. Yet another concerned the fact that, although most people would have taken him to be a virgin, he was not so: as a young man he had had sexual relations with a woman. Wittgenstein did not use the words 'virgin' or 'sexual relations', but Hutt is in no doubt this is what he meant. The actual words used by Wittgenstein have eluded his memory. They were, he thinks, something like: 'Most people would think that I have had no relationship with women, but I have.'

The first of the 'sins' that Fania Pascal does remember was that Wittgenstein had allowed most people who knew him to believe that he was three-quarters Aryan and one-quarter Jewish, whereas, in fact, the reverse was the case. That is to say, of Wittgenstein's grandparents, three were of Jewish descent. Under the Nuremberg Laws, this made Wittgenstein himself a Jew, and Pascal is surely right in linking this confession with the existence of Nazi Germany. What Wittgenstein did not tell her, but what she subsequently discovered, was that not one of his 'Jewish' grandparents was actually a Jew. Two were baptized as Protestants, and the third as a Roman Catholic. 'Some Jew', she remarks.

So far, all these 'crimes' are sins of omission: they concern only cases in which Wittgenstein *failed* to do something, or declined to correct a misleading impression. The final, and most painful, sin concerns an actual untruth told by Wittgenstein. At this stage in the confession, Pascal recalls, 'he had to keep a firmer control on himself, telling in a clipped way of the cowardly and shameful manner in which he had behaved'. Her account of this confession, however, gives a strangely distorted impression of the incident she describes:

> During the short period when he was teaching at a village school in Austria, he hit a little girl in his class and hurt her (my memory is, without details, of a physically violent act). When she ran to the headmaster to complain, Wittgenstein denied he had done it. The event stood out as a crisis of his early manhood. It may have been this that made him give up teaching, perhaps made him realise that he ought to live as a solitary.

This is distorted in a number of ways. First, Wittgenstein was in his late thirties when the incident at Otterthal occurred, which is surely a little old to be described as 'early manhood'. More important, Pascal seems to have had no idea that physically violent acts were, by all accounts, a not infrequent occurrence in Wittgenstein's classes, nor that Wittgenstein actually stood trial before a court to answer charges of violence. It is possible that Wittgenstein did not tell her these things – that he used the isolated incident as a symbol of his misdemeanours at Otterthal. But it is also possible – and I think not unlikely – that Pascal's memory is at fault. She was, after all, in no mood to listen to Wittgenstein's confession, and was further alienated by his manner while delivering it. Rowland Hutt remembers the confession, not as concerning a denial made to a headmaster about an isolated incident, but rather as an admission to having told lies in a court case. Put like this, it both squares better with the accounts given by the Otterthal villagers and explains better why the deception so haunted Wittgenstein.

There is no doubt that of all the deceptions confessed to by Wittgenstein, his behaviour at Otterthal was felt to be the greatest burden, and he went to much greater lengths than Pascal and Hutt could have known to relieve himself of it. In the same year in which he made his confessions, Wittgenstein astounded the villagers of Otterthal by appearing at their doorsteps to apologize personally to the children whom he had physically hurt. He visited at least four of these children (and possibly more), begging their pardon for his ill-conduct towards them. Some of them responded generously, as the Otterthal villager Georg Stangel recalls:

I myself was not a pupil of Wittgenstein's, but I was present when shortly before the war Wittgenstein visited my father's house to apologise to my brother and my father. Wittgenstein came at midday, at about 1 o'clock, into the kitchen and asked me where Ignaz is. I called my brother, my father was also present. Wittgenstein said that he wanted to apologise if he had done him an injustice. Ignaz said that he had no need to apologise, he had learnt well from Wittgenstein. Wittgenstein stayed for about half an hour and mentioned that he also wanted to go to Gansterer and Goldberg to beg their pardon in a similar way.

But at the home of Mr Piribauer, who had instigated the action against Wittgenstein, he received a less generous response. There he made his apologies to Piribauer's daughter Hermine, who bore a deep-seated grudge against him for the times he had pulled her by the ears and by the hair in such a violent fashion that, on occasion, her ears had bled and her hair had come out. To Wittgenstein's plea for pardon, the girl responded only with a disdainful, 'Ja, ja.'

One can imagine how humiliating this must have been for Wittgenstein. And it might almost seem that the point of humbling himself in this way was precisely that: to punish himself. But this, I think, would be to misunderstand the purpose of his confessions and apologies. The point was not to *hurt* his pride, as a form of punishment; it was to *dismantle* it – to remove a barrier, as it were, that stood in the way of honest and decent thought. If he felt he had wronged the children of Otterthal, then he ought to apologize to them. The thought might have occurred to anyone, but most people would entertain the idea and then dismiss it for various reasons: it happened a long time ago; the villagers would not understand such an apology, and would think it very strange; the journey to Otterthal is difficult in winter; it would be painful and humiliating to offer such an apology and, given the other reasons, not worth the trouble; and so on. But to find these reasons compelling, as, I think, most of us would, is in the end to submit to cowardice. And this, above all else, is what Wittgenstein was steadfastly determined not to do. He did not, that is, go to Otterthal to *seek* pain and humiliation, but rather with the determination to go through with his apology despite it.

In reflecting upon the effects of his confession he wrote:

Last year with God's help I pulled myself together and made a confession. This brought me into more settled waters, into a better relation with people, and to a greater seriousness. But now it is as though I had spent all that, and I am not far from where I was before. I am cowardly beyond measure. If I do not correct this, I shall again drift entirely into those waters through which I was moving then.

Wittgenstein regarded his confessions as a kind of surgery, an operation to remove cowardice. Characteristically, he regarded the infection as malignant and in need of continued treatment. It was characteristic, too, for him to regard a mere physical injury as trivial by comparison. Soon after he returned to Norway in the New Year of 1937 he suffered an accident and broke one of his ribs. Whereas his moral condition had been a matter of urgency, this was simply brushed aside with a joke. He told Pattisson: 'I thought of having it removed & of having a wife made of it, but they tell me that the art of making women out of ribs has been lost.'

If the confessions had any effect on Francis, it was possibly that of emboldening him to speak his mind a bit more freely – to reveal some of the things *he* had kept hidden. 'I feel it is wrong to hide things from you', he wrote in March 1937, 'even though I do so because I am ashamed of myself.' But in his case, it was not past deeds that he revealed, but present feelings, and in particular the feeling that he did not want to be in Cambridge working at the factory, but with Wittgenstein, and preferably working with him: 'I sometimes wish that we could do some work together, any sort of work. I feel you are part of my life.' What worried him was not his own moral state (and certainly not Wittgenstein's), but their relationship – his fear that they were growing apart or that they might be forced apart by circumstances:

I think a lot about our relation. Are we going to act independently of each other, will I be able to act independently of you? What will happen if there is a war? Or if we are permanently separated? I am so terribly deficient in courage. I long for you often. I do feel you are near me in whatever state of mind I am in, and would feel so even if I did something very bad. I am always your old heart. I love to think about you.

It was painful for Francis to think that he was no longer involved in Wittgenstein's work — to recognize that he was no longer in any sense Wittgenstein's collaborator. In May he wrote: 'I don't think I have ever understood your present work thoroughly, and I think it would be good for me to try and understand it better.' The letter contains a report of a meeting with Sraffa, from which, he said, he had 'learnt a lot and it had done me good'. Sraffa had: 'talked in a very nice way about working men'. But, as a working man himself, Francis was beginning to find, to his great consternation, that the problems of philosophy seemed rather remote to him now:

> I have been trying to think lately about what use philosophy is to me now. I don't want to lose my intellectual conscience. I want to make some use of all those years I spent learning philosophy. I don't want now just to have been made a cleverer person. I want to keep in mind the importance of trying to use words correctly . . . I think also I ought not to forget that philosophical problems are really important problems to me.

This letter, dated 27 May, was written to Wittgenstein in Vienna. His work in Norway during the spring of 1937 had gone badly — 'partly', he told Moore, 'because I've been troubled about myself a lot', and he spent the summer, first with his family, and then in East Road with Francis. At Cambridge he undertook work that, presumably, Francis *could* help him with: he dictated a typescript of the remarks, written the previous winter, that now form the first 188 paragraphs of *Philosophical Investigations*. On 10 August he left again for Norway.

That Wittgenstein returned to Norway full of trepidation is apparent from his diary entries of this period. On the ship to Skjolden he notes that he has managed to write a little, but that his mind is not 'wholeheartedly' on his work. A few days later he describes himself as: 'vain, thoughtless, anxious' — anxious, that is, about living alone. 'Am afraid I will be depressed and not able to work':

> I would now like to live with somebody. To see a human face in the morning. — On the other hand, I have now become so *soft*, that it

would perhaps be good for me to have to live alone. Am now extraordinarily contemptible.

'I have the feeling', he writes, 'that I would not be completely without ideas, but that the solitude will depress me, that I will not be able to work. I am afraid that in my house all my thoughts will be killed off, that there a spirit of despondency will take complete possession of me.' But where else could he work? The idea of living in Skjolden but not in his house disturbed him, and in Cambridge, 'I could *teach*, but not write as well.' The following day he was: 'unhappy, helpless and thoughtless', and it occurred to him: 'how unique and irreplaceable Francis is. And yet how little I realise this when I am with him':

> Am completely ensnared in pettiness. Am irritable, think only of myself, that my life is wretched, and at the same time I have no idea of how wretched it is.

He could not face moving back into his house. His room, which before had seemed charming, now struck him as alien and unfriendly. He took lodgings instead with Anna Rebni, but in so doing he had to wrestle with his conscience. It struck him as 'weird' (*unheimlich*) that he should live with her and leave his own house standing empty: 'I am ashamed to have this house and not to live in it. It is, however, strange that this shame should be such a powerful feeling.' After a night at Rebni's house, he wrote that he felt strange being there: 'I do not know whether I have either a right or any good reason to live here. I have neither any real need for solitude nor any overpowering urge to work.' He felt weak at the knees. 'Is it the climate?? – It is terrible how easily I am overcome by anxiety [*die Sorge*].' He thought of moving back to his own house, 'but I am frightened of the sadness that can overcome me there'. It is difficult, he wrote, to walk uphill, and one does it only reluctantly. He himself felt too weak to make the effort. He was, for a day or two, inclined to think that the trouble was physical rather than psychological. 'Am now really ill', he wrote on 22 August, 'abdominal pains and temperature.' The following evening, however, he recorded that his temperature was normal, but that he felt as tired as ever. It was not until 26 August that he recorded the first sign of recovery: he was able once more to look at the Norwegian scenery with pleasure. He had that day received two letters ('showered with gifts' as he put it) – one from Francis and another from Drury, 'both stirringly lovely'. On the same day he finally – a year after he had first gone to live in Norway – wrote to Francis to invite him to join him. 'May it go well. And may it be given to me to be halfway decent.'

Francis accepted the invitation with alacrity. On 23 August he had written: 'You said in one of your letters "I wish I had you here". Would I be of any help to you if I could come to see you? You know I would come and would love to come.' Now: 'I would love very much to come and see you. I definitely think it would do me good. I'm quite sure of it.' Owing, however, to a blister on his leg that had to be operated on, it was not until the third week of September that he was able to travel.

During this time Wittgenstein gradually recovered his mental stability and his ability to work, and was able to move back into his house. 'The way to solve the problem you see in life', he wrote on 27 August, 'is to live in a way that will make what is problematic disappear':

> The fact that life is problematic shows that the shape of your life does not fit into life's mould. So you must change the way you live and, once your life does fit into the mould, what is problematic will disappear.
>
> But don't we have the feeling that someone who sees no problem in life is blind to something important, even to the most important thing of all? Don't I feel like saying that a man like that is just living aimlessly – blindly, like a mole, and that if only he could see, he would see the problem?
>
> Or shouldn't I say rather: a man who lives rightly won't experience the problem as *sorrow*, so for him it will be a bright halo round his life, not a dubious background.

In these terms Wittgenstein saw himself as neither blind, nor one who lives rightly. He felt the problem of life as a problem, as sorrow. Inevitably, he identified the problem as himself: 'I conduct myself badly and have mean and shabby feelings and thoughts' (26.8.37); 'I am a coward, that I notice again and again, on all sorts of occasions' (2.9.37); 'Am irreligious, but with *Angst*' (7.9.37). The 'but' in the last sentence seems to have been some reassurance, as though if he felt his lack of faith with anxiety, that at least proved that he was not living blindly – it gave him at least the possibility of living 'with a bright halo round his life'. On 4 September he wrote:

Christianity is not a doctrine, not, I mean, a theory about what has happened and will happen to the human soul, but a description of something that actually takes place in human life. For 'consciousness of sin' is a real event and so are despair and salvation through faith. Those who speak of such things (Bunyan for instance) are simply describing what has happened to them, whatever gloss anyone may want to put on it.

It was, as ever, the God within himself that he sought – the transformation of his own despair into faith. He chastized himself when, during the violent storms of the following few days, he found himself tempted to curse God. It was, he told himself, 'just wicked and superstitious'.

By 11 September Wittgenstein's ability to work had revived sufficiently for him to start writing into one of his large manuscript volumes (rather than his notebooks), but he was frightened, he said, that he would write 'in a stilted and bad style'. He found he could just about manage to work, but he could find no pleasure in so doing: 'It's as though my work had been drained of its juice', he wrote on 17 September.

The following day he travelled to Bergen to meet Francis. He felt, he wrote, very sensual: in the night, when he could not sleep, he had sensual fantasies. A year ago he had been much more decent – more *serious*. After Francis had arrived at the house, Wittgenstein was 'sensual, susceptible, indecent' with him: 'Lay with him two or three times. Always at first with the feeling that there was nothing wrong in it, *then* with shame. Have also been unjust, edgy and insincere towards him, and also cruel.' Whether this was the only occasion on which he and Francis were sexually intimate, we do not know. It is certainly the only occasion mentioned in his coded remarks. What is striking is the juxtaposition of his account of their lying together with observations of his lovelessness towards Francis. Or perhaps what he is expressing is his *fear* of becoming loveless, as though he expected to find that Weininger was right when he wrote: 'physical contact with the beloved object, in which the sexual impulse is awakened . . . suffices to kill love on the spot'.

During the ten days or so that Francis stayed at Wittgenstein's house there is only one coded remark: 'Am very impatient!' (25.9.37) On 1 October, the day that Francis left, however, he wrote:

> The last 5 days were nice: he settled into the life here and did everything with love and kindness, and I was, thank God, not impatient, and truly I had no reason to be, except for my own rotten nature. Yesterday I accompanied him as far as Sogndal; returned today to my hut. Somewhat depressed, also tired.

For Francis, of course, the sensuality and the intimacy of their first night together in Wittgenstein's house had no Weiningerian connotations. He could give himself over to his 'susceptibility' to Wittgenstein without any fear of losing his love. In an undated letter, for example, he writes: 'I often remember all the things we have done together in the past and also the things we did here in Cambridge. This makes me long for you sometimes very violently'; and his letters immediately after his visit to Norway are repetitious in their affirmation of how 'wonderful' the visit had been:

> I think *constantly* of you and of the wonderful time I have had with you. It was wonderful that it was possible. It was so lovely being with you and living in the house with you. It was a wonderful gift to us. I hope it will do me a lot of good. [undated]

> I am often thinking now how good I felt when I was with you and how wonderful it was being with you and looking at the landscape with you. You were most wonderfully good to me. It has done me a lot of good being with you . . . It was wonderful being with you. [14.10.37]

During his stay, Francis had helped Wittgenstein clean his room, just as he had longed to do a year earlier. Wittgenstein's horror of uncleanliness impelled him to adopt a particularly rigorous method of cleaning his floor: he would throw wet tea-leaves over it, to soak up the dirt, and then sweep them up. He performed this task frequently wherever he stayed, and resolutely refused to have a carpet in any room that he lived in for any length of time. When Francis returned to his flat in East Road he adopted this fastidiousness as a sort of memento of his stay:

> I'm thinking of you a lot. I also think often how lovely it was cleaning your room with you. When I got back I decided I wouldn't put my carpet down even though it had been beaten because I know I can't keep it properly clean. I now have to sweep my room. I like to do it because it reminds me of when I was with you. I'm glad I learnt how to do it properly then.

Francis also put on Wittgenstein's mantle when he attended a meeting of the Moral Science Club. In his report of the meeting he eschews the modest and mild tone of almost all his other recorded utterances, and displays an uncharacteristic fierceness, borrowed, one suspects, from Wittgenstein:

> Prof. Moore wasn't present and Braithwaite took the chair. The paper was on ethics. I must say I thought Braithwaite was most revolting in the discussion. He took away all the seriousness from it. He never talked as if he had any responsibility for the discussion, or as if the discussion had a serious purpose. There was constant laughter throughout the discussion, a good deal of it provoked by him. I wouldn't have minded if what he had said had just been bad but I hated his lack of seriousness. This prevents anything useful and valuable coming from the discussion.

In his diary Wittgenstein describes this as a 'lovely letter from Fr.':

> He writes . . . how miserably bad the discussion was under Braithwaite's chairmanship. It is dreadful. But I wouldn't know what to do about it, for the other people are not serious enough either. Also, I would be *too cowardly* to do anything decisive.

In another letter, Francis mentions, in a similarly disapproving manner, Fania Pascal's lectures on 'Modern Europe', a course on current events that she had agreed to give to the Workers' Educational Association. Here Wittgenstein did attempt a decisive intervention: he wrote Pascal what she describes as a 'harsh and hectoring' letter, which 'caused the greatest explosion of fury on my part, a fury that rankled the more since I would not dare to express it to him'. Wittgenstein wrote that she must on no account give the course – that it was wrong for her, it was evil and damaging. *Why* he thought this, and what exactly the letter said, we will never know; Pascal tore it up in a fit of anger.

The first of Francis's letters did not reach Wittgenstein until about two weeks after Francis had left Skjolden. This, though not an extraordinarily long delay, was enough to confirm his fears. On 16 October he wrote: 'Have not heard from Francis for about 12 days and am rather worried, because he has not yet written from England. God, how much misery and wretchedness there is in this world.' The next day he received the first letter: 'Am relieved and gladdened. God may help us.'

In the meantime, he had received a short visit from Ludwig Hänsel's son, Hermann: 'He made a *good* impression. I have no *very* close relationship with him, because he is rough-grained [*grobkörnig*] and I am not entirely suited to rough-grained people.' But, though the grain was rough, the wood was good, Hänsel, 'who is much more decent than I', showed him what a shabby person he was: 'how worried I am that something will corrupt me; how *annoyed* if the slightest thing is ruined'. He worried that he might lose his energy for work, his imagination. Images of decay impressed themselves upon him:

[I] just took some apples out of a paper bag where they had been lying for a long time. I had to cut half off many of them and throw it away. Afterwards when I was copying out a sentence I had written, the second half of which was bad, I at once saw it as a half-rotten apple.

And was there not, he asked himself, something feminine about this way of thinking, whereby: 'Everything that comes my way becomes a picture for me of what I am thinking about at the time.' It was as though, in Weininger's terms, he had relapsed into thinking in henids rather than in concepts.

Throughout November and December, his last two months in Norway, Wittgenstein's diary is full of the fears, anxieties and unpleasant thoughts that assailed him. He thought about illness and death – his own, his friends' and his family's. He worried that something would happen to him before he could leave. He fretted about his relationship with Anna Rebni, and about what he would do after he had left Norway. Would his book be finished by then? Would he be able to work on his own again, or should he go somewhere where he could be with someone – perhaps to Dublin, to Drury?

He worried, too, about his sensuality and his ability to love. He recorded the occasions on which he masturbated, sometimes with shame, and sometimes with bewildered doubt: 'How bad is it? I don't know. I guess it is bad, but I have no reason to think so.' Was his ability to love, with a clean and pure heart, threatened by the sexual desire manifested in his urge to masturbate?

Think of my earlier love, or infatuation, for Marguerite and of my love for Francis. It is a bad sign for me that my feelings for M could go so completely cold. To be sure, there is a difference here; but still *my coldheartedness* remains. May I be forgiven; i.e., may it be possible for me, to be sincere and loving. [1.12.37]

Masturbated last night. Pangs of conscience. But also the conviction that I am too weak to withstand the urge and the temptation if they and the images which accompany them offer themselves to me without my being able to take refuge in others. Yet only *yesterday evening* I was reflecting on the need to lead a pure life. (I was thinking of Marguerite and Francis.) [2.12.37]

Throughout all these worries, anxieties and fears, he tried to work on his book. During these months he wrote most of the remarks that now form Part I of *Remarks on the Foundations of Mathematics*, although at the time of writing he intended them to form the second half of the work he had written the previous year. The remarks are an application of the method described in the earlier work to the problems in the philosophy of mathematics, trying to show that these problems arise out of 'the bewitchment of our intelligence by means of language'. In particular, he uses his 'anthropological' method in an attempt to dissolve the way of thinking that gave rise to the logicism of Frege and Russell. By imagining tribes with conventions or ways of reasoning different to our own, and by constructing metaphors different to ones commonly employed, he tries to weaken the hold of certain analogies, certain 'similes that have been absorbed into the forms of our language'. He attacks, for example, the Platonism that regards logical propositions as analogous to factual propositions. 'Isn't there a truth corresponding to logical inference?' he makes his interlocutor ask. 'Isn't it *true* that this follows from that?' Well, replies Wittgenstein, what would happen if we made a different inference? How would we get into conflict with the truth?

> How should we get into conflict with truth, if our footrules were made of very soft rubber instead of wood and steel? – 'Well, we shouldn't get to know the correct measurement of the table.' – You mean: we should not get, or could not be sure of getting, *that* measurement which we get with our rigid rulers.

The point here is that the criteria for correct or incorrect reasoning are not provided by some external realm of Platonic truths, but, rather, by ourselves, by 'a *convention*, or a *use*, and perhaps our practical requirements'. The convention of using rigid rulers rather than floppy ones is not *truer*; it is simply more useful.

Wittgenstein also attacks the simile that lies at the heart of logicism: the analogy between a mathematical proof and a logical argument. In a logical argument, connections are made between various (empirical) propositions, with the intention of establishing the truth of a conclusion: All men are mortal; Socrates is a man; *therefore* Socrates is mortal. The result of a mathematical proof, on the other hand, is never the truth of an empirical proposition, but the establishing of a generally applicable *rule*. In this particular assault, Wittgenstein had to show the disanalogy between mathematical and empirical propositions, but his remarks on this point are less than completely satisfying. Occasionally his own dissatisfaction is acknowledged in the body of the text: 'I am merely – in an unskilful fashion – pointing to the *fundamental* difference, together with an apparent similarity, between the roles of an arithmetical proposition and an empirical proposition.' He was never happy with his presentation of this point, or with his treatment of other issues in the philosophy of mathematics, and over the next six years was to attempt to improve on it again and again.

Wittgenstein was dissatisfied with this work as he was writing it. In his diary he criticizes it often, and severely. The style, he says repeatedly, is bad, too uncertain, and he has constantly to cross out and change what he has written: 'I am nervous when writing and all my thoughts are short of breath. And I feel constantly that I cannot *completely* justify the expression. That it tastes bad.' This is indicative of his own nervousness, and of the fact that he got so little sleep and had been so long without seeing the sun. The weather was upsetting him; it was too cold. The fjord was already completely frozen, and the lake was beginning to ice over as well. He could no longer row, but had to walk across the ice, and this, too, worried him. He began to count the days until he could leave to go to Vienna for Christmas. Of course, he could leave at any time, but would this be right?

> I would like to flee, but that would be wrong and I simply can't do it. On the other hand, perhaps I could – I could pack *tomorrow* and leave the next day. But would I want to? Would it be right? Is it not right to stick it out here? Sure. I would leave tomorrow with a *bad* feeling. 'Stick it out', a voice says to me. There is also some vanity in this desire to stick it out, but something better as well. – The only cogent reason to leave here any earlier or at once would be that now I could perhaps work better somewhere else. For it is a fact that the pressure I am under at the moment makes it almost impossible for me to work and perhaps in a few more days really impossible.

When, during the following few days, he was able to work again, he thanked God for a gift he did not deserve. He always felt, he wrote, what a truly devout person never feels – that God was responsible for what he was: 'It is the opposite of piety. Again and again I want to say: "God, if you do not help me, what can I do?"' And although this attitude accords with what the Bible teaches, it is not that of a truly devout man, for such a one would assume responsibility for himself. 'You must *strive*', he urged himself; 'never mind God.'

Despite these urgings, he remained 'sensual, weak and mean', and subject to all the old anxieties – that he would not be able to leave because something would happen to him, that he would become ill or have an accident on the way home. He was troubled, too, by all the problems of spending the winter in Norway that Russell had pointed out in 1913: 'The ever-changing, difficult weather, cold, snow, sheet ice, etc., and the darkness and my exhaustion make everything very difficult.' He was sent, of course, encouragement and loving concern from Francis:

I'm sorry you are having storms. Please be very careful about going across the lake. I will be thinking about you a great deal. I love to remember our time together in Norway. It does me good to think about it.

But when his last night in Norway came, on 10 December, he greeted it with some relief, writing that it was perfectly possible that he would never return.

On the ship to Bergen Wittgenstein wrote of Christ's Resurrection and of what inclined even him to believe in it. If Christ did not rise from the dead, he reasoned, then he decomposed in the grave like any other man. '*He is dead and decomposed.*' He had to repeat and underline the thought to appreciate its awfulness. For if that were the case, then Christ was a teacher like any other, 'and can no longer *help*; and once more we are orphaned and alone. So we have to content ourselves with wisdom and speculation.' And if that is all we have, then: 'We are in a sort of hell where we can do nothing but dream, roofed in, as it were, and cut off from heaven.' If he wanted to be saved, to be redeemed, then wisdom was not enough; he needed faith:

And faith is faith in what is needed by my *heart*, my *soul*, not my speculative intelligence. For it is my soul with its passions, as it were with its flesh and blood, that has to be saved, not my abstract mind. Perhaps we can say: Only *love* can believe the Resurrection. Or: it is *love* that believes the Resurrection. We might say: Redeeming love believes even in the Resurrection; holds fast even to the Resurrection.

Ultimately, then, perhaps what he needed to do to escape the hell of being alone was to love; if he could do this, then he could overcome his doubts, believe in the Resurrection, and thus be saved. Or, perhaps, it was that he needed first to *be* loved, by God:

What combats doubts is, as it were, *redemption*. Holding fast to *this* must be holding fast to that belief. So what that means is: first you must be redeemed and hold on to your redemption – then you will see that you are holding fast to this belief.

First, you must be redeemed: 'Then *everything* will be different and it will be "no wonder" if you can do things that you cannot do now.' Such as: believing in the Resurrection. So, it seems, belief in the Resurrection is necessary for salvation, but salvation is needed to believe in the Resurrection. Who is to break the vicious circle: himself or God?

As he escaped the hell of being alone in Norway, Wittgenstein seemed to be saying that his escape from the wider hell, from the greater aloneness, was God's responsibility.

He could confess his sins, but it was not for him to forgive them.

19

FINIS AUSTRIAE

In December 1937, just as in July 1914, Wittgenstein arrived back in Austria from Norway at a critical moment in his country's history. As the earlier crisis had led to the end of the Habsburg Empire, so the present crisis was to lead to the end of Austria itself.

That Hitler had both the intention and the means to incorporate Austria into his German *Reich* should, in December 1937, have been no surprise to anyone who cared to think about it. *Mein Kampf* had been in print since 1925, and on its very first page Hitler declares: 'German-Austria must return to the great German mother country . . . One blood demands one Reich.' And, a few pages later: 'in my earliest youth I came to the basic insight which has never left me, but only became more profound: *That Germanism could be safeguarded only by the destruction of Austria.*' After the failure of the attempted Nazi *Putsch* of 1934, Hitler had been pursuing this policy of the destruction of Austria by 'legal' means, and in the treaty for the 'Normalization of Relations between Austria and Germany' of July 1936, Austria had acknowledged itself to be a 'German State', and the Austrian Chancellor, Schuschnigg, had had to admit into his cabinet two Nazi members of the 'Nationalist Opposition'. Hitler's subsequent repudiation of the Versailles Treaty, his rearmament campaign, and the unwillingness of Britain, France, Russia and Italy to intervene made it inevitable that this Nazi opposition would one day govern Austria, not as an independent country, but as part of Nazi Germany.

With very few exceptions, the large Jewish population of Vienna were slow to realize – or, perhaps, reluctant to admit to themselves – the likely consequences of the impending *Anschluss*. Even those who admitted its inevitability could not bring themselves to believe its possible repercussions. Surely, it was urged, the Nuremberg Laws couldn't be enforced in Austria. The Jewish population was too well assimilated into the mainstream of Austrian life: there were too many Jews in high places, too many marriages between Jew and non-Jew, too many loyal Austrian citizens who just happened to have Jewish forebears. How could these laws be applied in a country in which the distinction between Aryan and non-Aryan had become so blurred?

So, at least, it was reasoned by Hermine Wittgenstein. Writing her memoirs, in 1945, she found it inconceivable that she could have been so naïve – 'but', she adds, 'cleverer people than I also regarded the threatening political events with the same obtuseness'. No doubt in the light of what was to follow, the Christmas of 1937 is remembered by her in particularly rosy terms. She describes how delighted she was that all four of her brothers and sisters, together with members of their own families, were present (by this time she and Ludwig were the only childless members of the family, while Helene was the head of a large extended family of her own, the mother of four and the grandmother of eight), and how they, together with pupils and ex-pupils from the school at which she taught, sang carols, talked of old times, laughed and joked, and, most ironically, gathered around the Christmas tree to sing the Austrian national anthem. 'When, at midnight, the feast had to come to an end, we were all of one mind that it had been the most lovely Christmas ever, and we were already talking of the Christmas we would have next year.'

In Wittgenstein's diary-notes of the time there is none of this sentimental *Gemütlichkeit*. But neither is there any mention of political events. It is impossible to believe, however, that he was as naïve about the situation as his sister. Admittedly, his only source of information during his stay in Norway was the *Illustrated London News*, which he had sent to him by Fania Pascal; on the other hand, it should be remembered that he had been in Cambridge twice during the last year, and there would have had the inestimable benefit of Piero Sraffa's informed political analysis and judgement. His confession of his non-Aryan origins in January was made, I believe, with awareness both of the terms of the Nuremberg Laws and of the possibility of their future application to Austrian citizens.

Nevertheless, in his diary he does not discuss politics. He writes, instead, of himself – of his mental and physical exhaustion after his trying time in Norway, and of how difficult he finds it to converse with the people he is with, how he can hardly speak to them, his mind is so befogged, and of how *unnecessary* he feels himself to be there. He writes also of Freud:

> Freud's idea: In madness the lock is not destroyed, only altered; the old key can no longer unlock it, but it could be opened by a differently constructed key.

Perhaps here, too, he is writing about himself, and a feeling that if only he could find a new key, he could unlock the doors to his own prison, and then '*everything* will be different'.

In the first week of January he confined himself to bed, suffering from gallbladder trouble, although scarcely believing that that was really why he felt so tired and weak. In bed he reflected on his sensuality and dwelt on his feelings for Francis. It was often the case, he wrote, that when he was unwell he was open to sensual thoughts and susceptible to sensual desires. He thought of Francis with sensual desires, 'and that is bad, but that's what it's like now'. He worried that it had been so long since he had heard from Francis, and, as always, was inclined to think the worst – to consider, for example, the possibility that Francis had died: 'Thought: it would be good and right if he had died, and thereby taken my "folly" away.' This dark, solipsistic, thought is immediately retracted, although only in part: 'Although, there again, I only *half* mean that.'

This qualification is, if anything, still more shocking. After giving the matter a second thought, was he really still even *half-way* inclined to think that the death of Francis would be a good thing?

'I am cold and wrapped up in myself', he wrote, reflecting on the fact that he did not feel himself to be in any loving relationship with anyone in Vienna. He was inclined to think that the comfortable life at the Alleegasse was bad for him, but where else was he to go? The solitude of his house in Norway had proved unendurable, and he had no wish to reenter academic life at Cambridge. Again, Dublin presented itself as an attractive alternative. There he could be with Drury, and perhaps even join Drury in training to be a psychiatrist. Everything was in flux; he did not know what he would do any more than he knew where he wanted to live. Of one thing, however, he was sure: that he needed to be with someone with whom he could talk.*

Wittgenstein arrived in Dublin on 8 February, and moved into Drury's old flat in Chelmsford Road. On his second day there he described himself as: 'irreligious, ill-tempered, gloomy'. He was in the 'hateful situation' of being incapable of work, of not knowing what he should do, of having to simply vegetate and wait. He was, he said, still inclined to *lie*: 'Again and again I see that I cannot resolve to speak the truth about myself. Or that I admit it to myself only for a moment and then forget about it.' His vanity, his cowardice, his fear of the truth, prompted him to keep hidden things about himself that he did not want to acknowledge: 'until I am no longer *clever* enough to find them'. Two days later he was beginning to regret that he had come to Dublin, where he could apparently do nothing; 'on the other hand I will have to wait, because nothing is still very clear'. During these first few weeks in Dublin he wrote very little philosophy; his philosophical thoughts had, so to speak, been lulled to sleep: 'It is entirely as though my talent lies in a kind of half-slumber.'

While his philosophical thoughts slept, his ideas of becoming a psychiatrist awoke. He asked Drury to arrange for him to visit St Patrick's Hospital so that he could meet patients who were seriously mentally ill. This was, he told Drury, a matter of great interest to him. After the visit he wrote (in English): 'See the sane man in the maniac! (and the mad man in yourself.)', and for the next few weeks he went two or three times a week to visit some of the long-stay patients. He remained, however, uncertain as to what, if anything, it might lead to.

Drury was at this time in his final year of training as a doctor, and was spending his period of residence in the City of Dublin Hospital. He told Wittgenstein that, when working in the casualty department,

---

* The fact that Wittgenstein chose to be with Drury rather than Francis demands explanation. Unfortunately, however, we are forced to speculate on the point; in his diary he does not even consider the idea that he should go to Cambridge to be with Francis. Perhaps it was not Francis, but Cambridge, that he was avoiding, or perhaps he was attracted to Dublin by the possibility that there he might train as a doctor. But in the light of the remarks already quoted there must also be a possibility that his desire for Francis, and Francis's almost overwhelming desire for him, made Cambridge unattractive – that he considered the sensuality between himself and Francis incompatible with the change he wished to see in himself.

he was disturbed by his clumsiness, and wondered whether he had made a mistake in taking up medicine. Wittgenstein, whatever ambivalence he felt about his own plans to take up medicine, was quick to quash Drury's doubts. The next day Drury received a letter from him which stated emphatically: 'You didn't make a mistake because there was nothing at the time you knew or ought to have known that you overlooked.' He urged Drury: 'Don't think about yourself, but think about others':

> Look at people's sufferings, physical and mental, you have them close at hand, and this ought to be a good remedy for your troubles. Another way is to take a rest whenever you ought to take one and collect yourself. (Not with me because I wouldn't rest you.) . . . Look at your patients more closely as human beings in trouble and enjoy more the opportunity you have to say 'good night' to so many people. This alone is a gift from heaven which many people would envy you. And this sort of thing ought to heal your frayed soul, I believe. It won't rest it; but when you are healthily tired you can just take a rest. I think in some sense you don't look at people's faces closely enough.

The letter ends: 'I wish you good thoughts but chiefly good feelings.'

The first mention in Wittgenstein's diary of the crisis facing Austria during the early months of 1938 occurs on 16 February. 'Can't work', he then wrote:

> Think a great deal of a possible change of my nationality. Read in today's paper that a further compulsory rapprochement between Austria and Germany has taken place – But I don't know what I should really do.

It was on that day that the Nazi leader of the 'Nationalist Opposition', Dr Arthur Seyss-Inquart, was appointed the Austrian Minister of the Interior, and the significance of the Berchtesgaden meeting between Hitler and Schuschnigg became apparent to the world.

This meeting had been held on 12 February, and had initially been celebrated in Austria as a sign of more cordial relations between the two countries. It was only later realized that in this 'friendly discussion' Hitler had demanded of Schuschnigg that Nazi ministers be appointed in charge of the Austrian police, army and financial affairs, and had threatened: 'You will either fulfill my demands in three days, or I will order the march into Austria.' On 15 February *The Times* reported:

> If Herr Hitler's suggestion that Dr von Seyss-Inquart should be made Austrian Minister of the Interior with control of the Austrian police were granted, it would in the general view of anti-Nazis in Austria mean that before long the words 'finis Austriae' would be written across the map of Europe.

The following day the paper commented drily on the fact that, immediately after taking his ministerial oath, Seyss-Inquart left Vienna for Berlin: 'That the first act of the Minister of the Interior is to pay a visit to a foreign country is a fair indication of the unusual situation in which Austria finds itself after the Hitler–Schuschnigg meeting.'

During the following few weeks Wittgenstein kept a close watch on developments. Every evening he asked Drury: 'Any news?', to which, presumably, Drury responded by telling Wittgenstein what had been reported that day. Reading Drury's recollections, however, one wonders which newspapers he read. His account of the days leading up to the *Anschluss* is, to say the least, somewhat strange. He writes that on the evening of 10 March he told Wittgenstein that all the papers reported that Hitler was poised to invade Austria. Wittgenstein replied, with quite breath-taking naïvety: 'That is a ridiculous rumour. Hitler doesn't want Austria. Austria would be no use to him at all.' The next evening, according to Drury, he had to tell him that Hitler had indeed taken over Austria. He asked Wittgenstein if his sisters would be in any danger. Again Wittgenstein replied with quite extraordinary insouciance: 'They are too much respected, no one would dare to touch them.'

From this account one might think that Wittgenstein had forgotten what he had read in the papers on 16 February – that he knew nothing about the threat to Austria, that he was entirely ignorant about the nature of the Nazi régime, and that he was unconcerned about the safety of his family. All this is quite assuredly false, and one can only think that he gave this misleading impression to Drury because he did not wish to add to Drury's burdens. That Drury was inclined to accept Wittgenstein's responses at face value perhaps says much about his unquestioning attitude towards Wittgenstein, and about his own political naïvety. It is also possible, I think, that Wittgenstein, who tended to compartmentalize his friendships, did not think it worth discussing these matters with Drury. With Drury he discussed religious questions; it was Keynes, Sraffa and Pattisson upon whom he relied for discussion of political and worldly affairs.

However, even on its own account – without, that is, bringing to it anything else we might know or suspect about Wittgenstein's awareness of events – Drury's story is a little puzzling. For if he told Wittgenstein the news every evening, he would, for example, have told him on 9 March about Schuschnigg's announcement that he was to hold a plebiscite asking the Austrian people to vote for or against an independent Austria. It was this announcement that prompted Hitler, on the following day, to move his forces up to the Austrian border in readiness for an invasion. Now if Wittgenstein reacted to this latter piece of news by denying that Hitler wanted Austria, what did he (or Drury for that matter) think was the point of Schuschnigg's plebiscite? Why should Austria's independence have needed reaffirming? Independence from whom?

Furthermore, the day after the troops had gathered on the border was not the day on which Hitler took over Austria, but rather the day on which Schuschnigg resigned and Seyss-Inquart became Chancellor. Hitler and the German troops did not cross the border until the day after that, 12 March, when they were invited by the new Chancellor, and it was then that the *Anschluss* was formally effected. This might be seen as a quibble, but the events of these three days are etched clearly into the minds of all who lived through them, and for Wittgenstein, if not for Drury, the change in the state of affairs on each of these days would have been of momentous importance. On 10 March Austria was an independent state under Schuschnigg; on the 11th it was an independent state under Nazi rule; and on the 12th it was part of Nazi Germany. To an Austrian family of Jewish descent the difference between the second and third days was decisive: it marked the difference between being an Austrian citizen and a German Jew.

On the day of the *Anschluss* Wittgenstein wrote in his diary: 'What I hear about Austria disturbs me. Am unclear what I should do, whether to go to Vienna or not. Think chiefly of Francis and that I do not want to leave him.' Despite his assurances to Drury, Wittgenstein was extremely concerned about the safety of his family. His first reaction was to go immediately to Vienna to be with them; what stopped him was his fear that, if he did so, he would never see Francis again. He nevertheless wrote to his family offering to come to Vienna if they needed him.

The only letter that survives from the correspondence between Wittgenstein and Sraffa is a long analysis of Wittgenstein's position following the *Anschluss*, which was written by Sraffa on 14 March, the day of Hitler's triumphant procession through Vienna. It demonstrates clearly the calibre of informed political opinion and advice that was open to Wittgenstein through Sraffa, and shows that Wittgenstein must have written to him straight away for advice on the possible consequences of his leaving for Vienna.

The letter begins:

> Before trying to discuss, probably in a confused way, I want to give a clear answer to your question. If, as you say, it is of 'vital importance' for you to be able to leave Austria and return to England, there is no doubt – *you must not go to Vienna.*

Sraffa pointed out that the Austrian frontier would be closed to the exit of Austrians, and that, though these restrictions might soon be lifted, there was every chance that, were he to go to Vienna, Wittgenstein would not be allowed out for a long time. 'You are aware no doubt that now you are a German citizen', Sraffa continued:

> Your Austrian passport will certainly be withdrawn as soon as you enter Austria: and then you will have to apply for a German passport, which may be granted if and when the Gestapo is satisfied that you deserve it . . .
>
> As to the possibility of war, I do not know: it may happen at any moment, or we may have one or two more years of 'peace'. I really have no idea. But I should not gamble on the likelihood of 6 months' peace.

Wittgenstein must also have asked Sraffa whether it would help his situation if he were to become a lecturer at Cambridge, for he goes on:

If however you decided in spite of all to go back to Vienna, I think: a) it would certainly increase your chance of being allowed out of Austria if you were a lecturer in Cambridge; b) there would be no difficulty in your entering England, once you are let out of Austria (of Germany, I should say); c) *before* leaving Ireland or England you should have your passport changed with a German one, at a German Consulate: I suppose they will begin to do so in a very short time; and you are more likely to get the exchange effected here than in Vienna; and, if you go with a German passport, you are more likely (though not at all certain) to be let out again.

'You must be careful', Sraffa warned, 'about various things':

1) if you go to Austria, you must have made up your mind not to say that you are of Jewish descent, or they are sure to refuse you a passport;
2) you must not say that you have money in England, for when you are there they could compel you to hand it over to the Reichsbank;
3) if you are approached, in Dublin or Cambridge, by the German Consulate, for registration, or change of passport, be careful how you answer, for a rash word might prevent your ever going back to Vienna;
4) take great care how you write home, stick to purely personal affairs, for letters are certainly censored.

With regard to the question of a change of nationality, Sraffa advised that, if Wittgenstein had made up his mind to apply for Irish citizenship, then he should do so before his Austrian passport was taken away from him, for it would be easier as an Austrian than as a German. On the other hand:

In the present circumstances I should not have qualms about British nationality if that is the only one which you can acquire without waiting for another ten years' residence: also you have friends in England who could help you to get it: and certainly a Cambridge job would enable you to get it quickly.

Sraffa, who was leaving for Italy the following Friday, invited Wittgenstein to come to Cambridge to discuss the matter if he could make it before then, but warned: 'afterwards letters will be forwarded to me in Italy, so take care what you say, that you may be writing to the Italian censor'. He ends: 'Excuse this confused letter', forcing one to wonder what levels of clarity and precision he reached in the rest of his correspondence.

'You are aware no doubt that now you are a German citizen.' On the day that Sraffa wrote these dreaded words, Wittgenstein's diary shows him to be wrestling with precisely this awareness:

> I am now in an extraordinarily difficult situation. Through the incorporation of Austria into the German Reich I have become a German citizen. That is for me a frightful circumstance, for I am now subject to a power that I do not in any sense recognise.

Two days later, he was, 'in my *head* and with my mouth', decided upon the loss of his Austrian nationality and resigned to the thought of emigrating for several years: 'it can't be any different. But the thought of leaving my people alone is dreadful.'

Upon receiving Sraffa's letter Wittgenstein immediately left Dublin for Cambridge to discuss the situation with him. On 18 March he reported in his diary:

> Sraffa advised me yesterday that I should, for the time being, not go to Vienna under any circumstances, for I could not now help my people and in all probability would not be allowed to leave Austria. I am not *fully* clear what I should do, but, for the time being, I think Sraffa is right.

Following this conversation with Sraffa, Wittgenstein decided upon a course of action. First, he would secure an academic job at Cambridge, and then apply for British citizenship. In connection with both aims he immediately wrote to Keynes for help. He began by explaining to Keynes the situation – that by the annexation of Austria he had become a German citizen, and, by the Nuremberg Laws, a German Jew: 'The same, of course, applies to my brother and sisters (not to their children, *they* count as Aryans).' 'I must say', he added, 'that the idea of becoming (or being) a German citizen, even apart from all the nasty consequences, is APPALLING to me. (This may be foolish, but it just is so.)' He outlined Sraffa's arguments against his going to Vienna – that his Austrian passport would be taken away from him, that, as a Jew, he would not be issued with a new passport, and that, therefore, he would be unable to leave Austria or ever again get a job. Presented with the choice of being a German Jew or a British university lecturer, he was forced, with some reluctance, to choose the latter:

> The thought of acquiring British citizenship had *occurred* to me before; but I have always rejected it on the ground: that I do not wish to become a sham-english-man (I think you will understand what I mean). The situation has however entirely changed for me now. For now I have to choose between two new nationalities, one of which deprives me of *everything*, while the other, at least, would allow me to work in a country in which I have spent on and off the greater part of my adult life, have made my greatest friends and have done my best work.
>
> . . . As to getting a job at Cambridge you may remember that I was an 'assistant faculty lecturer' for 5 years . . . Now it is for *this* that I shall apply, for there is no other job vacant. I had, in fact, thought of doing so anyway; though not now, but perhaps next autumn. But it would be important now for me to get a job *as quickly as possible*; for a) it would help me in becoming naturalised and b) if I failed in this and *had* to become a 'German' I would have more chance to be allowed out of Austria again on visiting my people if I had a JOB in England.

On Sraffa's advice Wittgenstein asked Keynes for an introduction to a solicitor – 'one who is an expert in this kind of thing' – to help with his application for naturalization. 'I want to add that I'm in no sort of financial difficulties. I shall have about 300 or 400 £ and can therefore easily hold out for another year or so.'

Keynes's reply to this letter has not survived, but it is clear that he did what he could to secure Wittgenstein a place at the university, and to help him in his application for British citizenship. Wittgenstein, however, was typically anxious that Keynes might have misunderstood his situation, and sent Keynes's letter to Pattisson, asking him to 'smell' it. Above all, he was concerned that Keynes might present him to the university authorities and to the Home Office as a member of that most wretched of species, the impoverished refugee. He was therefore suspicious of Keynes's suggestion that he might be eligible for a grant from the Academic Assistance Council. This, he told Pattisson, 'is a body who helps people, say refugees, who have no money, & accepting there [*sic*] assistance would not only not be quite fair of me but also place me in an *entirely* wrong category'. So nervous was he on this point that he was inclined to doubt whether he should use Keynes's introduction to a solicitor:

> I have a *vague* fear that this introduction, if slightly wrongly worded, might make things more awkward for me; it may, for instance, represent me as a *refugee* of sorts & stress a wrong aspect of the business.

His anxieties proved to be unfounded. The university responded quickly, and he was given a lecturing post starting from the beginning of the following term.

Of great concern to Wittgenstein throughout the long wait for his British passport was the situation of his family. It was difficult for him to know how much danger they were in, and he was not reassured when, soon after the *Anschluss*, he received this note (written in English):

> My dear Ludwig,
> Not a day passes but that Mining and I talk about you; our loving thoughts are always with you. Please do not worry about us, we are quite well really and in best spirits and ever so happy to be here. To see you again will be our greatest joy.
>
> > Lovingly yours,
> > · Helene

In his diary Wittgenstein dismissed this (no doubt correctly) as: 'reassuring *sounding* news from Vienna. Obviously written for the censor.'

In fact, both Helene and Hermine were slow to appreciate the danger they were in, and when realization finally came they panicked. Hermine recalls how, one morning soon after the *Anschluss*, Paul announced, with terror in his voice: 'We count as Jews!' Hermine could understand why this should strike such fear into Paul's heart.

His career as a concert pianist mattered a great deal to him, and as a Jew he would not be allowed to perform; besides, he liked to go for long walks in the country, and all those signs proclaiming '*Juden verboten*' must make his walks a good deal less pleasant. But for herself, the fact that she counted as a Jew under German law seemed to mean very little. She spent most of her life inside her own four walls, and apart from the fact that a few people who used to greet her in public might no longer do so, her life would surely go on much the same.

At first Paul tried to get reassurances that the family would be treated as Aryans, on the grounds that they had always been loyal and patriotic citizens, and had accomplished much for their country. To this end he and Gretl (who, as an American citizen, was in no personal danger) travelled to Berlin to negotiate with the Nazi authorities. Their appeal came to nothing. Unless they could produce evidence of a second Aryan grandparent, they were told, they would remain Jews.

Another branch of the family, the descendants of Wittgenstein's Aunt Milly, made efforts to establish the Aryan credentials of Hermann Christian Wittgenstein. In the Berlin archives a report survives written by Brigitte Zwiauer, Milly's granddaughter, pleading Hermann Christian's case. It is addressed to the *Reichstelle für Sippenforschung* ('Department for Genealogical Research', the Nazi ministry responsible for determining who was and who was not Aryan), and states that Hermann Christian is known in the family to be the illegitimate son of a member of the princely family of Waldeck. Zwiauer admits that there is no direct proof of this, but stresses that there is also no proof to the contrary; that, although Hermann Christian was brought up in the Jewish community, there is no evidence that he was actually the son of a Jew. As indirect proof of his Aryan origins, she encloses a photograph of the eleven children of Hermann and Fanny. 'That these children descend from two fully Jewish parents', she argues, 'appears to us biologically impossible.' The report points out that Hermann chose the middle name 'Christian' for himself, and was known as an anti-Semite who, in adult life, avoided association with the Jewish community and did not allow his offspring to marry Jews. The report is dated 29 September 1938, but its plea was ignored until nearly a year later, when the Nazis saw some advantage to themselves in accepting it.

Hermine, Gretl and Helene would have nothing to do with this report. As far as they were concerned, Hermann Christian was the son

of Moses Maier, and if that meant that, under German law, they were
regarded as Jews, then so be it. Paul would probably have gone along
with whatever steps were necessary to escape the consequences of
being a Jew in the German *Reich*. As it was, he saw no hope of being
reclassified and therefore sought only to leave Greater Germany as
soon as he could. He urged Hermine and Helene to do the same – to
leave everything behind and go to Switzerland. When a house is
burning down, he argued, the sensible thing to do is to jump out of the
window and forget about one's possessions inside. Hermine, however, could not bring herself to leave her friends, her family and her
beloved Hochreit, and neither could Helene face leaving her children
and grandchildren. Both refused to go. In July 1938, after many harsh
words had been exchanged, Paul left his sisters in Austria and went to
Switzerland alone.

Helene and Hermine left Vienna to spend the summer at the
Hochreit, still convinced that their status as Jews would not place them
in any danger. They were shaken out of this conviction by Gretl, who
in September came to the Hochreit and told them that outside
Germany it was widely believed by those who were well informed
that war would break out at any moment (this being the time of the
Czechoslovakia crisis), and that it was also known that the Jews in
Germany would be rounded up and placed in concentration camps,
where they would be insufficiently fed and treated very badly. Gretl
urged Hermine and Helene to leave Austria.

By this time, however, it was no longer possible for German Jews to
enter Switzerland, and some other plan had to be devised. Upon
Gretl's suggestion, Hermine agreed to buy Yugoslav passports for
herself and Helene from a Jewish lawyer in Vienna. She apparently
believed that this was the way in which the Yugoslav government
conferred nationality, for she says she had no idea that what they were
buying were false passports until Arvid Sjögren, who travelled to
Yugoslavia on their behalf to collect them, reported that they had been
produced in a workshop specializing in forged documents.

Nevertheless, Hermine went ahead with the plan and travelled to
Munich herself to obtain visas for Switzerland using the false passports. Soon afterwards, the police began to investigate this particular
source of forgeries, and before they could begin their flight to Switzerland Hermine and Helene were arrested, together with Gretl and
Arvid. They each spent two nights in prison, except Gretl, who was

detained a further night. At the subsequent trial Gretl did everything she could to present herself as solely responsible for the whole fiasco, a claim that was accepted by the magistrate, although according to Hermine their best defence was their appearance and their manner of speech. Appearing before the court was not a collection of the grubby, smelly, kaftan-wearing Jews described in *Mein Kampf*, but proud members of a famous and wealthy high-bourgeois Austrian family. All four were cleared of the charges brought against them.

How much Wittgenstein himself knew of this story is impossible to say. Enough, anyway, for him to be sick with worry about his sisters' situation. In a letter to Moore of October 1938 he speaks of 'the great nervous strain of the last month or two', and attributes it to the fact that: 'My people in Vienna are in great trouble.' The wait for his British passport became almost unendurable, as he longed to be able to use it to travel to Vienna to do whatever he could to help his sisters. In the midst of all this anxiety, the sight of Neville Chamberlain returning from Munich proclaiming 'Peace in our time' was too much to bear. He sent Gilbert Pattisson one of the postcards printed to celebrate Chamberlain's 'success'. Beneath a picture of Chamberlain and his wife the legend reads: 'The Pilgrim of Peace. Bravo! Mr Chamberlain.' On the back Wittgenstein wrote: 'In case you want an Emetic, there it is.'

In the winter of 1938–9 the Reichsbank began to make enquiries about the huge amounts of foreign currency held by the Wittgenstein family. Under Nazi law the Reichsbank was empowered to compel the family to hand this money over to them. Owing to the complicated arrangement under which the wealth was held, however, it was difficult for them to get their hands on it. This circumstance suggested to Gretl another possibility of securing the safety of her sisters: they would agree to hand over the foreign currency in return for a written declaration that Hermine and Helene would be treated as Aryans.

So began a long series of negotiations between the authorities in Berlin and the Wittgensteins, which culminated in the Nazis agreeing to accept the report prepared by Brigitte Zwiauer the previous year in return for the transfer of the Wittgensteins' foreign currency. The negotiations were complicated by the disagreement between Paul and the rest of the family. Paul, who by this time had left Switzerland and was living in America, was against doing a deal with the Nazis in order to satisfy his sisters' perverse desire to stay in Austria. It would be wrong, he argued, to help the Nazis by placing in their hands such a large fortune. (Hermine attributes this latter argument to Paul's advisors, who, she points out, were, without exception, Jews – as though only a Jew would think such a consideration relevant.)

These wrangles continued throughout the spring of 1939, with Gretl travelling between New York, Berlin and Vienna, trying to come to an agreement that suited all parties, and the matter was still unsettled when Wittgenstein finally received his British passport on 2 June 1939. Barely a month later, he used it to travel to Berlin, Vienna and New York, with the aim of helping Gretl to reach a settlement. It was not, as Hermine says, the sort of thing to which her brother was suited, either by experience or by temperament. Furthermore (though she does not point this out), the irony of bribing the Nazis to accept a lie about the very thing to which he had confessed just two years previously can hardly have escaped him. He nevertheless entered into the negotiations with all the considerable precision and tenacity at his disposal. 'And if', Hermine adds, 'he did not achieve in New York what he had had in mind, then the blame was really not his.' It was, she implies elsewhere, Paul's.

Despite Paul's objections, the result of these negotiations was that a great deal of the family wealth was transferred from Switzerland to the Reichsbank, and the *Reichstelle für Sippenforschung* issued a formal declaration to its Viennese office that Hermann Christian Wittgenstein was, without qualification, *deutschblütig*. Consequently, in August 1939, Hermine and Helene, and all the other grandchildren of Hermann Christian, received certificates stating that they were *Mischlinge* (of mixed Jewish blood) rather than Jews. Later, in February 1940, the Berlin authorities went further, and issued a proclamation that the regulations covering *Mischlinge* were not applicable to the descendants of Hermann Christian Wittgenstein, and that 'their racial classification under the Reich Citizenship Law [the Nuremberg Laws] presents no further difficulties'. Hermine and Helene were thus able to survive the war relatively untroubled.

20

THE RELUCTANT
PROFESSOR

Whether Wittgenstein would ever have returned to Cambridge had it not been for the *Anschluss*, one cannot say. His attempts to find a niche in life outside academia had, however, been at best inconclusive. Though he sometimes talked of finding a job among 'ordinary' people, as he had encouraged Skinner and Hutt to do, he seems to have made little effort to do so. His plans to work in Russia and/or to train as a doctor, though pursued with greater purpose, never crystallized into a firm and unequivocable intention. He would, perhaps, have continued to try and find the peace of mind and concentration he required to finish his book, perhaps in Dublin with Drury or in Norway by himself. But his savings, of £300 or £400, would not have lasted a lifetime. Eventually, he would have had to have found some paid employment. That is, as he had put it to Moore in 1930, he would have had to have found someone who had a use for the sort of goods he produced. And the place where these goods were in most demand was, inevitably, in academic life, and particularly in Cambridge. It is, therefore, perfectly possible that at some time or other he would have applied for a lectureship. What one can say with certainty, however, is that if it had not been for the *Anschluss*, this would not have been as early as April 1938.

This is not only because Wittgenstein was then not eager to return to teaching, but also because he was apprehensive about his relationship with Francis. As indicated by his diary entries in the New Year, he was deeply concerned about the sensuality that existed between himself and Francis, and anxious whether, on his part at least, such sensual desires were compatible with true love. He would have preferred to have loved Francis at a distance, away from the temptation of his sensual 'susceptibility'. And yet, his fear of losing Francis altogether had now brought him back to Cambridge, and more firmly than ever into the sphere of that temptation.

Upon his return he moved into Francis's lodgings above the grocer's shop on East Road, and for over a year they lived, as Francis had always wished them to live, as a couple. Their period as collaborators on Wittgenstein's work had long come to an end. While Wittgenstein lectured and continued to work on his book, Francis worked at the factory. There are no letters from Francis during this period, and no relevant remarks among Wittgenstein's coded diary-notes, so we do not know how or why their relationship deteriorated during this year. All we know is that by 1939 it had deteriorated, and that for the following two years it was only Francis's undyingly faithful, perhaps even clinging, love for Wittgenstein that kept it going. Wittgenstein's love for Francis, it seems, did not – perhaps could not – survive the physical closeness that he at once craved and feared.

Among his students at this time, Wittgenstein found a new generation of disciples. In order to keep his class down to a size with which he felt comfortable, he did not announce his lectures in the usual way in the *Cambridge University Recorder*. Instead, John Wisdom, Moore and Braithwaite were asked to tell those students they thought would be interested about the classes. No more than about ten students attended. Among this select band were Rush Rhees, Yorick Smythies, James Taylor, Casimir Lewy and Theodore Redpath. The class was small enough for them all to get to know Wittgenstein fairly well, although it was Rhees, Taylor and Smythies that became particularly close friends during this period.

The classes were held in Taylor's rooms. Taylor, about whom almost nothing is mentioned in the published memoirs, was a Canadian, a graduate of Toronto University, who had come to Cambridge to study under G. E. Moore and, through Moore, became a friend of Wittgenstein's. After the war he was offered a lectureship in philosophy at an Australian university, but died in a pub brawl in Brisbane while on his way to take up the post. Smythies is one of those mysterious figures who are referred to repeatedly in the published texts, but about whom little is ever said. He was a devoted disciple of Wittgenstein's and a truly Wittgensteinian character in the sense that, though he never became a professional philosopher, he never ceased to think seriously and deeply about philosophical problems. He remained a close friend of Wittgenstein's for the rest of Wittgenstein's life. When he left Cambridge he became a librarian at Oxford. In later life he suffered from paranoid schizophrenia and became a patient of Maurice Drury. He died in tragic circumstances in 1981. Regarding such people, one is reminded of the fact that those whom Wittgenstein influenced most strongly, particularly in the 1930s (one thinks of Drury, Skinner and Hutt, as well as Smythies), did not enter academic life. There is therefore a large and important aspect of Wittgenstein's influence that is not, and cannot be, reflected in the large body of academic literature that Wittgenstein's work has inspired. The only one of these to have published anything is Maurice Drury, whose collection of essays on philosophical and psychological issues, *The Danger of Words*, though it has been almost completely ignored in the secondary literature, is, in its attitudes and concerns, more truly Wittgensteinian than almost any other secondary text.

On vacation from his final year's training as a doctor, Drury managed to attend one of the lectures in Wittgenstein's new course. During this lecture Wittgenstein told one of the students to stop making notes:

> If you write these spontaneous remarks down, some day someone may publish them as my considered opinions. I don't want that done. For I am talking now freely as my ideas come, but all this will need a lot more thought and better expression.

Fortunately, this request was ignored, and notes from these lectures have indeed been published.*

These lectures are unique among Wittgenstein's corpus. Their subject-matter alone would make them so, for they are concerned, not with mathematics or philosophy generally, but with aesthetics and religious belief. This difference is less radical than it might appear, for Wittgenstein brings to his discussion of these subjects many of the same examples that he used in other contexts – Cantor's Diagonal Proof, Freud's confusion between cause and reason and so on – so that

---

* See *Lectures and Conversations on Aesthetics, Psychology and Religious Belief*, ed. Cyril Barrett (Blackwell, 1978).

his discussion of aesthetics, for example, looks not so very different from his discussions of the philosophy of mathematics or the philosophy of psychology. What distinguishes these lectures is their tone. Precisely because he was speaking in a spontaneous and unguarded manner, they provide one of the most unambiguous statements of his purpose in philosophy, and of how this purpose connects with his personal *Weltanschauung*. Through them, it is made even clearer that his target was not merely, as he had put it in the *Blue Book*, the damage that is done when philosophers 'see the method of science before their eyes and are irresistibly tempted to ask and answer questions in the way that science does'; it was, more generally, the wretched effect that the worship of science and the scientific method has had upon our whole culture. Aesthetics and religious belief are two examples – for Wittgenstein, of course, crucially important examples – of areas of thought and life in which the scientific method is not appropriate, and in which efforts to make it so lead to distortion, superficiality and confusion.

Wittgenstein told his audience that what he was doing was 'persuading people to change their style of thinking'. He was, he said, 'making propaganda' for one style of thinking as opposed to another. 'I am honestly disgusted with the other', he added. The 'other' he identified as the worship of science, and he therefore spent some time in these lectures execrating what he considered to be powerful and damaging forms of evangelism for this worship – the popular scientific works of the time, such as Jeans's *The Mysterious Universe*:

> Jeans has written a book called *The Mysterious Universe* and I loathe it and call it misleading. Take the title . . . I might say the title *The Mysterious Universe* includes a kind of idol worship, the idol being Science and the Scientist.

In discussing aesthetics, Wittgenstein was not attempting to contribute to the philosophical discipline that goes by that name. The very idea that there could be such a discipline was a consequence, or perhaps a symptom, of the 'other'. He was, instead, trying to rescue questions of artistic appreciation from that discipline, particularly from the idea that there could be a kind of science of aesthetics:

You might think Aesthetics is a science telling us what's beautiful – almost too ridiculous for words. I suppose it ought to include also what sort of coffee tastes well.

When Rhees asked Wittgenstein about his 'theory' of deterioration (referring to one of Wittgenstein's examples, which was the deterioration of the German musical tradition), Wittgenstein reacted with horror to the word: 'Do you think I have a theory? Do you think I'm saying what deterioration is? What I do is describe different things called deterioration.'

Rather than trying to answer the traditional questions of aesthetics ('What is beauty?' etc.), Wittgenstein gives a succession of examples to show that artistic appreciation does not consist (as one might think from reading some philosophical discussions of aesthetics) in standing before a painting and saying: 'That is beautiful.' Appreciation takes a bewildering variety of forms, which differ from culture to culture, and quite often will not consist in *saying* anything. Appreciation will be *shown*, by actions as often as by words, by certain gestures of disgust or satisfaction, by the way we read a work of poetry or play a piece of music, by how often we read or listen to the same piece, and how we do so. These different forms of appreciation do not have any one thing in common that one can isolate in answer to the question: 'What is artistic appreciation?' They are, rather, linked by a complicated series of 'family resemblances'. Thus:

It is not only difficult to describe what appreciation consists in, but impossible. To describe what it consists in we would have to describe the whole environment.

Above all, in seeking to answer the why and how of aesthetic understanding, we are not looking for a *causal* explanation. There is no science of aesthetics, and neither can the results of some other science, such as physics, or some pseudo-science, such as psychology, be brought to bear on these questions. Wittgenstein quotes two kinds of explanation from the work of Freud, which illustrate, respectively, the kind of reductive account that he thought should be avoided at all costs, and the other 'style of thinking' that he was trying to promote.

The first comes from *The Interpretation of Dreams*, and concerns Freud's 'explanation' of what his patient had described to him as a pretty dream. In retelling the dream Freud puts certain words in capitals to indicate – with a nod and a wink, as it were – the sexual allusions:

> She was descending from a height . . . She was holding a BIG BRANCH in her hand; actually it was like a tree, covered over with RED BLOSSOMS . . . Then she saw, after she had got down, a manservant who was combing a similar tree, that is to say he was using a PIECE OF WOOD to drag out some THICK TUFTS OF HAIR that were hanging down from it like moss.

And so on. Later in the dream the woman comes across people taking branches and throwing them into the road where they lay (LAY) about. She asks whether she might also take one – that is, explains Freud, whether she might pull one down, i.e. masturbate (in German, the phrase 'to pull one down' is equivalent to the English 'to toss oneself off'). Freud adds: 'The dreamer quite lost her liking for this pretty dream after it had been interpreted.'

Wittgenstein's response to this is to say that Freud has cheated his patient: 'I would say to the patient: "Do these associations make the dream not beautiful? It was beautiful. Why shouldn't it be?"' Freud's reduction of the pretty elements of the dream to bawdy innuendo has a certain charm, a certain fascination, but it is wrong to say that Freud has shown what the dream is *really* about. Wittgenstein compared it to the statement: 'If we boil Redpath at 200 degrees C. all that is left when the water vapour is gone is some ashes, etc. This is all Redpath really is.' Saying this, he says, might have a certain charm, 'but it would be misleading to say the least'.

The sort of Freudian explanations that Wittgenstein mentioned with approval are those contained in *Jokes and their Relation to the Unconscious*. Wittgenstein does not give any examples, but perhaps a simple one will suffice. In the early part of the book, Freud discusses a joke in Heine's *Reisebilder*. One of Heine's characters, a humble lottery-agent, in boasting about his relations with Baron Rothschild, remarks: 'He treated me quite as his equal – quite familionairely'. The reason this makes us laugh, Freud claims, is not only that it is a clever abbreviation of the thought that Rothschild treated the man as his equal, quite familiarly, so far as a millionaire can, but also because it brings out a suppressed subsidiary thought: that there is actually something rather unpleasant about being treated with a rich man's condescension.

If we are inclined to accept this sort of explanation, Wittgenstein asks, on what grounds do we do so?

'If it is not causal how do you know it's correct?' You say: 'Yes, that's right.' Freud transforms the joke into a different form which is recognised by us as an expression of the chain of ideas which led us from one end to another of a joke. An entirely new account of a correct explanation. Not one agreeing with experience but one accepted.

It was essential to this form of explanation, he stressed, that: 'You have to give the explanation that is accepted. This is the whole point of the explanation.' And this is precisely the sort of explanation one wants in aesthetics: not one that establishes a *cause* for something's being beautiful, or for our regarding something as beautiful, but rather one that, by showing connections we had not thought of previously, *shows* what is beautiful about it – shows why, for example, a certain piece of music or a certain play, poem etc. is correctly regarded as a great work.

In his lectures Wittgenstein gave some examples from his own experience of what happens when one begins to understand the greatness of an artistic work. He had, he said, read the work of Friedrich Klopstock, the eighteenth-century poet, and initially failed to see anything in it. Then he realized that the way to read him was to stress his metre abnormally:

When I read his poems in this new way, I said: 'Ah-ha, now I know why he did this.' What had happened? I had read this kind of stuff and had been moderately bored, but when I read it in this particular way, intensely, I smiled, said: 'This is *grand*, etc. But I might not have said anything. The important fact was that I read it again and again. When I read these poems I made gestures and facial expressions which were what would be called gestures of approval. But the important thing was that I read the poems entirely differently, more intensely, and said to others: 'Look! This is how they should be read.'

Another example he might have given was *The King of the Dark Chamber* by the Indian poet, Rabindranath Tagore. Wittgenstein had first read this play, in a German translation (it was originally written in Bengali), in 1921, when Tagore was at the height of his fame and enormously popular in Europe, particularly in Germany and Austria. He had then written to Engelmann that, despite its great wisdom, the play had failed to make a deep impression on him. He was not *moved*:

> It seems to me as if all that wisdom has come out of the ice box; I should not be surprised to learn that he got it all second-hand by reading and listening (exactly as so many among us acquire their knowledge of Christian wisdom) rather than from his own genuine *feeling*. Perhaps I don't understand his tone; to me it does not ring like the tone of a man possessed by the truth. (*Like for instance Ibsen's tone.*) It is possible, however, that here the translation leaves a chasm which I cannot bridge. I read *with interest* throughout, but without being gripped. That does not seem to be a good sign. For this is a subject that could have gripped me – or have I become so deadened that nothing will touch me any longer? A possibility, no doubt.
>
> – Again, I do not feel for a single moment that here is a drama taking place. I merely understand the allegory in an abstract way.

Just a few months after this, he wrote to Hänsel saying that he had been rereading Tagore, 'and this time with much *more* pleasure'. 'I now believe', he told Hänsel, 'that there is *indeed* something grand here.' *The King of the Dark Chamber* subsequently became one of his favourite books, one of those he habitually gave or lent to his friends. And at about the time of his lectures on aesthetics he reread the play together with Yorick Smythies, this time in an English translation made by Tagore himself. Again, it seems, the translation left a chasm, and in order to overcome this – in order to, as it were, defrost the text – Smythies and Wittgenstein prepared their own translation. Among Smythies's papers was found a typed copy of their version of Act II of the play, headed:

> THE KING OF THE DARK CHAMBER, by Rabindranath Tagor [*sic*] *translated from* the English of Rabindranath Tagor *into* English used by L. Wittgenstein and Yorick Smythies, *by* L. Wittgenstein and Yorick Smythies.

Almost all the changes introduced by Smythies and Wittgenstein involve substituting modern, idiomatic words and phrases for Tagore's old-fashioned 'poetic' diction. Thus, where Tagore has 'chamber', they have 'room' (except in the title), and where Tagore wrote: 'He has no dearth of rooms', they write: 'He's not short of rooms', and so on.

The play is an allegory of religious awakening, and it echoes many of Wittgenstein's own thoughts on the subject. The King of the title is never seen by his subjects, some of whom doubt his existence, while others believe that he is so ugly he dare not reveal himself. Others, such as the maidservant Surangama, are so devoted to the King and so worshipful that they do not ask to *see* him; they *know* him to be a being without comparison to other mortals. Only these people, who have completely overcome their own pride in subjection to their master, have a sense of when the King is approaching and when he is present. The play concerns the awakening – or, one might say, the humbling, the subjugation – of the King's wife, Sudarshana. She is shown first as a proud Queen, bemoaning the cruelty of her husband, whom she can meet only in a room that is kept forever dark. She longs to see him, to know whether he is handsome, and out of that longing falls in love with another king, whom she meets in the world outside and mistakes for her husband. Only when she has been brought by this mistake to complete despair, when she feels utterly humiliated and degraded and has cast away her pride, can she be reconciled with her real husband, before whom she now bows with total servility. Only, that is, when Queen Sudarshana is brought down to the level of the servant Surangama can she become enlightened. The play ends with her realization that *everything* of any real value is conferred upon her by the King, who can now say to her: 'Come, come with me now, come outside – *into the light!*'

The part of the play translated by Wittgenstein and Smythies is a conversation between Surangama and Sudarshana in which the servant tries to explain to the Queen how she became so completely devoted to the King, though she has never seen him, and though he caused her to suffer greatly when he banished her father from the kingdom. When the King exiled her father, the Queen asks, didn't Surangama feel bitterly oppressed? 'It made me furious', the servant replies:

I was on the road to ruin and destruction: when that road was closed to me, I seemed left without any support, without help or shelter. I raved and raged like a wild animal in a cage – I wanted, in my powerless anger, to tear everyone to pieces.

'But how did you become devoted to the King who had done all this?' Sudarshana asks. When did this change of feeling take place? 'I couldn't tell you', comes the reply:

I don't know myself. A day came when all the rebel in me knew itself beaten, and then my whole nature bowed down in humble resignation in the dust. And then I saw . . . I saw that he was as incomparable in beauty as he was in terror. I was saved, I was rescued.

Wittgenstein's translation of Tagore might fruitfully be read in conjunction with his lectures on religious belief, for in those passages he translated, Tagore expresses Wittgenstein's own religious ideal. That is, like Surangama, Wittgenstein did not wish to see God or to find reasons for His existence. He thought that if he could overcome *himself* – if a day came when his whole nature 'bowed down in humble resignation in the dust' – then God would, as it were, come to him; he would then be saved.

In his lectures on religious belief he concentrates only on the first part of this conviction – the denial of the necessity to have reasons for religious beliefs. In their rejection of the relevance of the scientific mode of thought, these lectures are of a piece with those on aesthetics. They might also be seen as an elaboration of his remark to Drury: 'Russell and the parsons between them have done infinite harm, infinite harm.' Why pair Russell and the parsons in the one condemnation? Because both have encouraged the idea that a philosophical justification for religious beliefs is necessary for those beliefs to be given any credence. Both the atheist, who scorns religion because he has found no *evidence* for its tenets, and the believer, who attempts to *prove* the existence of God, have fallen victim to the 'other' – to the idol-worship of the scientific style of thinking. Religious beliefs are not analogous to scientific theories, and should not be accepted or rejected using the same evidential criteria.

The kind of experience that can make a man religious, Wittgenstein insists, is not at all like the experience of drawing a conclusion from an experiment, or of extrapolating from a collection of data. He takes as an example someone who dreams of the Last Judgement, and now says he knows what it will be like:

> Suppose someone said: 'This is poor evidence.' I would say: 'If you want to compare it with the evidence for it's raining to-morrow it is no evidence at all.' He may make it sound as if by stretching the point you may call it evidence. But it may be more than ridiculous as evidence. But now, would I be prepared to say: 'You are basing your belief on extremely slender evidence, to put it mildly?' Why should I regard this dream as evidence – measuring its validity as though I were measuring the validity of the evidence for meteorological events?
>
> If you compare it with anything in Science which we call evidence, you can't credit that anyone could soberly argue: 'Well, I had this dream . . . therefore . . . Last Judgement.' You might say: 'For a blunder, that's too big.' If you suddenly wrote numbers down on the blackboard, and then said: 'Now, I'm going to add', and then said: '2 and 21 is 13', etc. I'd say: 'This is no blunder.'

On the question of how we *are* to accept or reject religious beliefs, and of what we are to believe about such things as the existence of God, the Last Judgement, the immortality of the soul etc., Wittgenstein is, in these lectures, non-committal:

> Suppose someone said: 'What do you believe, Wittgenstein? Are you a sceptic? Do you know whether you will survive death?' I would really, this is a fact, say 'I can't say. I don't know', because I haven't any clear idea what I'm saying when I'm saying 'I don't cease to exist', etc.

It is clear from remarks he wrote elsewhere, however (for example in his remarks written on the boat to Bergen and quoted earlier), that he thought that if he could come to believe in God and the Resurrection – if he could even come to attach some *meaning* to the expression of those beliefs – then it would not be because he had found any evidence, but rather because he had been redeemed.

Still there is a persistent and nagging doubt about how Wittgenstein expected, or hoped, this redemption to come about – whether, so to speak, it was in his hands or God's.

On this central question *The King of the Dark Chamber* is, like Wittgenstein, ambiguous. After Sudarshana has been saved, she remarks to the King: 'You are not beautiful, my lord – you stand beyond all comparisons!' To which the King replies: 'That which can be comparable with me lies within yourself.' 'If this be so', says Sudarshana, 'then that too is beyond comparison':

> Your love lives in me – you are mirrored in that love, and you see your face reflected in me: nothing of this is mine, it is all yours.

And yet elsewhere in the play, it is the King who holds up the mirror. Those who think he is ugly, we are told, do so because they fashion the King after the image of themselves they see reflected there. And so, one wants to ask, is 'that which lies beyond all comparisons' within us or not? What do we need to do in order to see it – polish up the mirror that is our self so that *it* can be reflected, or look with open eyes at the mirror and see it reflected *in ourselves*? Perhaps here we run up against the limits of meaningful language, and go beyond the applicability of the Law of Excluded Middle and the Law of Contradiction.* 'It', perhaps, both is and is not within us, and to find it we must both search within ourselves and recognize our dependence on something, some power, outside ourselves.

Perhaps the difference between allowing 'it' to be reflected in us and finding it in the reflection of us is not as great as it seems. In both cases we must remove the dirt that obscures the reflection. In this respect Wittgenstein laboured hard, polishing off the slightest speck, determined not to let himself get away with the smallest misdemeanour. In October 1938, for example, he wrote to George Thomson's mother-in-law earnestly apologizing for a transgression of quite extraordinary inconsequence:

> Dear Mrs Stewart,
> I must apologise for an untruth I told you today in Miss Pate's

---

* The Law of Excluded Middle states that either a proposition or its denial must be true; the Law of Contradiction states that *both* cannot be true.

office. I said that I had seen Mrs Thomson recently in Birmingham; & only when I came home this evening it occurred to me that this wasn't true at all. I stayed with the Bachtin's a few weeks ago in Birmingham & I *tried* to see Mrs Thomson & we had a talk on the phone; but I wasn't able to see her. When I talked to you this afternoon what was in my head was that I had seen Mrs Thomson at your house before she went to Birmingham. Please forgive my stupidity.

Yours sincerely,
L. Wittgenstein

In the context of his search for redemption through the dismantling of his pride, Wittgenstein's philosophical work occupies a curiously ambivalent place. On the one hand it is undoubtedly informed by the same attitudes that directed that search. On the other hand, it was itself the greatest source of his pride. Though he tried repeatedly to exclude from his work any question of pride, and to write, as he put it, 'to the glory of God' rather than out of vanity, yet we find again and again that it was to his philosophical work more than to anything else that he brought what Russell called his 'pride of Lucifer'.

In the summer of 1938 he prepared for publication a typescript based on the work he had written in Norway. This typescript constitutes the very earliest version of *Philosophical Investigations*. 'For more than one reason', he wrote in the preface:

what I publish here will have points of contact with what other people are writing today. – If my remarks do not bear a stamp which marks them as mine, – I do not wish to lay any further claim to them as my property.

And yet, that they were his property was enormously important to him, and that Carnap, Braithwaite, Waismann, Ambrose and others had published ideas derivative of them was precisely the reason he was now prepared to go into print. In a later preface he admitted as much:

I was obliged to learn that my results (which I had communicated in lectures, typescripts and discussions), variously misunderstood, more or less angled or watered down, were in circulation. This stung my vanity and I had difficulty in quieting it.

But if pride gave birth to his desire to publish, it also prevented his doing so. In September the book was offered to Cambridge University Press, who agreed to publish the German original with a parallel English translation. About a month later, however, the Press was told that Wittgenstein was now uncertain about the publication of his book, and the project had been, for the time being, shelved.

There were two reasons for Wittgenstein's doubts. One, the most important, was that he became increasingly dissatisfied with the second half of the book, which dealt with the philosophy of mathematics. The other was concerned with the problems in translating his work.

On Moore's recommendation, Wittgenstein asked Rush Rhees to undertake the translation. It was a formidable task – not because Wittgenstein's German is difficult (in the way that, for example, Kant's German is difficult), but rather because Wittgenstein's language has the singularly rare quality of being both colloquial and painstakingly precise.

Rhees laboured on the translation throughout the Michaelmas term of 1938. During this time he met with Wittgenstein regularly to discuss the problems that arose. In January 1939 he had to leave Cambridge to visit the United States, and so left a typescript of his work with Wittgenstein. Wittgenstein, who was never easily pleased with any attempt by others to represent his thoughts, was horrified at what he saw.

By this time the question of having a decent English edition of his work had acquired an importance outside his plans to publish. He had by then decided to apply for the post of Professor of Philosophy, which had become vacant on G. E. Moore's resignation, and he wanted to submit the translated portion of his book in support of his application. He was, in any case, convinced that he would not be elected, partly because one of the other applicants was John Wisdom, whom he felt sure would get it, and partly because one of the electors was R. G. Collingwood of Oxford, a man who was sure to disapprove of Wittgenstein's work. More than compensating for these two disadvantages, however, was the fact that also among the electors was John Maynard Keynes. Wittgenstein hurriedly attempted to improve on Rhees's translation in time for Keynes to read through the English version. 'I needn't say the whole thing is absurd', he wrote to Moore, 'as he couldn't make head or tail of it if it were translated very well.'

Wittgenstein would probably have been awarded the chair with or without Keynes's support, and regardless of the quality of the translation. By 1939 he was recognized as the foremost philosophical genius of his time. 'To refuse the chair to Wittgenstein', said C. D. Broad, 'would be like refusing Einstein a chair of physics.' Broad himself was no great admirer of Wittgenstein's work; he was simply stating a fact.

On 11 February Wittgenstein was duly elected professor. It was, inevitably, an occasion for both expressing pride and condemning it. 'Having got the professorship is very flattering & all that', he wrote to Eccles, 'but it might have been very much better for me to have got a job opening and closing crossing gates. I don't get any kick out of my position (except what my vanity & stupidity sometimes gets).' This in turn helped with his application for British citizenship, and on 2 June 1939 he received his British passport. No matter how illiberal their policy on the admission of Austrian Jews, the British government could hardly refuse citizenship to the Professor of Philosophy at the University of Cambridge.

More serious than the problems with translation, as far as the publication of Wittgenstein's remarks was concerned, was his dissatisfaction with what he had written on the philosophy of mathematics. In the three terms of 1939 he devoted a series of lectures to the subject. They are, to a certain extent, similar in theme to the previous year's lectures on aesthetics and religious belief, only now it is Russell and the *logicians* who between them have done infinite harm, and mathematics that has to be rescued, from the clutches of philosophical theorists. The strategy of these lectures was, indeed, announced in the earlier lectures on aesthetics, when, in discussing Cantor's Diagonal Proof, he expressed his loathing of it and his view that it was only the 'charm' of such proofs (he presumably meant by this the fascination it exerts to be told that it is provable that there exists an infinite number of different infinite cardinalities) that gave them their interest. 'I would', he said, 'do my utmost to show the effects of this charm, and of the associations of "Mathematics"':

Being Mathematics . . . it looks incontrovertible and this gives it a still greater charm. If we explain the surrounding of the expression we see that the thing could have been expressed in an entirely different way. I can put it in a way in which it will lose its charm for a great number of people and certainly will lose its charm for me.

The aim, then, was to reinterpret mathematics – to redescribe it in such a way that the mathematical realm that appeared to have been opened up by Cantor's Proof was presented, not as a fascinating world awaiting the discovery of mathematicians, but as a swamp, a quagmire of philosophical confusions. The mathematician Hilbert had once said: 'No one is going to turn us out of the paradise which Cantor has created.' 'I would say', Wittgenstein told his class: 'I wouldn't dream of trying to drive anyone out of this paradise':

> I would do something quite different: I would try to show you that it is not a paradise – so that you'll leave of your own accord. I would say, 'You're welcome to this; just look about you.'

The lectures on mathematics form part of Wittgenstein's general attack on the idol-worship of science. Indeed, he perceived this particular campaign as the most important part of that struggle. 'There is no religious denomination', he once wrote, 'in which the misuse of metaphysical expressions has been responsible for so much sin as it has in mathematics.' The 'charm' exerted by the metaphysics of mathematics was even more potent than that exerted by such books as Jeans's *The Mysterious Universe*, and an even more powerful influence in the idolization of science, which was, Wittgenstein thought, the most significant symptom, and perhaps even a contributory cause, of the decay of our culture.

It was thus his task to destroy that metaphysics. A feature of these lectures is that, in attempting to accomplish that task, he does not, as he had earlier, discuss mathematics itself with any degree of technical sophistication. He does not, for example, as he had in 1932–3, read out extracts from Hardy's textbook *A Course of Pure Mathematics*; nor does he, as he had in *Philosophical Grammar*, subject particular proofs (such as Skolem's Proof of the Associative Law) to rigorous and detailed analysis. Technical details are eschewed altogether. When he discusses Russell's Paradox, for instance, he does so in a way that is, from a mathematical point of view, quite extraordinarily primitive:

> Take Russell's contradiction. There are concepts which we call predicates – 'man', 'chair', and 'wolf' are predicates, but 'Jack' and

'John' are not. Some predicates apply to themselves and others don't. For instance 'chair' is not a chair, 'wolf' is not a wolf, but 'predicate' is a predicate. You might say this is bosh. And in a sense it is.

This lack of sophistication has, I think, a propagandist purpose. Wittgenstein's use of casual, everyday, language in discussion of problems in mathematical logic, and his simple dismissal as 'bosh' of the terms in which those problems have been raised, serves as an antidote to the seriousness and earnestness with which they have been discussed by those who have fallen for their 'charm' (including, for example, himself, in 1911). But also, for the problems he wished to raise, technical details were irrelevant. 'All the puzzles I will discuss', he said in his first lecture, 'can be exemplified by the most elementary mathematics – in calculations which we learn from ages six to fifteen, or in what we easily might have learned, for example, Cantor's proof.'

This series of lectures was remarkable in having among its audience a man who was one of the ablest exponents of the view that Wittgenstein was attacking, and also one of the greatest mathematicians of the century: Alan Turing. During the Easter term of 1939, Turing too gave classes under the title, 'Foundations of Mathematics'. They could not have been more different from Wittgenstein's. Turing's course was an introduction to the discipline of mathematical logic, in which he took his students through the technique of proving mathematical theorems from within a strictly axiomatic system of logic. Lest it be thought that *his* lectures had anything to do with the 'foundations of mathematics' in this sense, Wittgenstein announced:

> Another idea might be that I was going to lecture on a particular branch of mathematics called 'the foundations of mathematics'. There is such a branch, dealt with in *Principia Mathematica*, etc. I am not going to lecture on this. I know nothing about it – I practically only know the first volume of *Principia Mathematica*.

That it was at one time thought (by both himself and Russell) that he would be responsible for rewriting sections of the *Principia*, he does not mention. His present series of lectures was relevant to that branch of mathematics only in the sense of trying to undermine the rationale for its existence – of trying to show that: 'The *mathematical* problems of what is called foundations are no more the foundations of mathematics for us than the painted rock is the support of the painted tower.'

The lectures often developed into a dialogue between Wittgenstein and Turing, with the former attacking and the latter defending the importance of mathematical logic. Indeed, the presence of Turing became so essential to the theme of the discussion that when he announced he would not be attending a certain lecture, Wittgenstein told the class that, therefore, that lecture would have to be 'somewhat parenthetical'.

Wittgenstein's technique was not to reinterpret certain particular proofs, but, rather, to redescribe the whole of mathematics in such a way that mathematical logic would appear as the philosophical aberration he believed it to be, and in a way that dissolved entirely the picture of mathematics as a science which discovers facts about mathematical objects (numbers, sets etc.). 'I shall try again and again', he said, 'to show that what is called a mathematical discovery had much better be called a mathematical invention.' There was, on his view, nothing for the mathematician to discover. A proof in mathematics does not establish the truth of a conclusion; it fixes, rather, the *meaning* of certain signs. The 'inexorability' of mathematics, therefore, does not consist in *certain knowledge* of mathematical truths, but in the fact that mathematical propositions are *grammatical*. To deny, for example, that two plus two equals four is not to disagree with a widely held view about a matter of fact; it is to show ignorance of the meanings of the terms involved. Wittgenstein presumably thought that if he could persuade Turing to see mathematics in this light, he could persuade anybody.

But Turing was not to be persuaded. For him, as for Russell and for most professional mathematicians, the beauty of mathematics, its very 'charm', lay precisely in its power to provide, in an otherwise uncertain world, unassailable truths. ('Irrefragability, thy name is mathematics!' as W. V. Quine once put it.) Asked at one point whether he understood what Wittgenstein was saying, Turing replied: 'I understand but I don't agree that it is simply a question of giving new meanings to words.' To this, Wittgenstein – somewhat bizarrely – commented:

Turing doesn't object to anything I say. He agrees with every word. He objects to the idea he thinks underlies it. He thinks we're undermining mathematics, introducing Bolshevism into mathematics. But not at all.

It was important to Wittgenstein's conception of his philosophical method that there could be no disagreements of opinion between himself and Turing. In his philosophy he was not advancing any theses, so how could there possibly be anything to disagree with? When Turing once used the phrase: 'I see your point', Wittgenstein reacted forcefully: 'I have no point.' If Turing was inclined to object to what Wittgenstein was saying, it could only be because he was using words in a different way to Wittgenstein – it *could* only be a question of giving meanings to words. Or, rather, it could only be a question of Turing's not understanding Wittgenstein's use of certain words. For example, Turing was inclined to say that there could be experiments in mathematics – that is, that we could pursue a mathematical investigation in the same spirit in which we might conduct an experiment in physics: 'We don't know how this might turn out, but let's see . . .' To Wittgenstein, this was quite impossible; the whole analogy between mathematics and physics was completely mistaken, and one of the most important sources of the confusions he was trying to unravel. But how was he to make this clear without opposing Turing's view with a view of his own? He had to: (a) get Turing to admit that they were both using the word 'experiment' in the same sense; and (b) get him to see that, in that sense, mathematicians do not make experiments.

Turing thinks that he and I are using the word 'experiment' in two different ways. But I want to show that this is wrong. That is to say, I think that if I could make myself clear, then Turing would give up saying that in mathematics we make experiments. If I could arrange in their proper order certain well-known facts, then it would become clear that Turing and I are not using the word 'experiment' differently.

You might say: 'How is it possible that there should be a misunderstanding so very hard to remove?'

It can be explained partly by a difference of education.

It might also be explained by the fact that Turing refused to leave his mathematician's paradise, or that he suspected Wittgenstein of

Bolshevism. What could not account for it, on Wittgenstein's view, was that there was here a substantive difference of opinion. 'Obviously', he told his class, 'the whole point is that I must not have an opinion.'

Wittgenstein, however, quite clearly did have very strong opinions – opinions that were, moreover, at variance with the conception of their subject held by most professional mathematicians. His suggestion that Turing suspected him of 'introducing Bolshevism into mathematics' is an allusion to Frank Ramsey's 1925 essay 'The Foundations of Mathematics', in which he had talked of rescuing mathematics from the 'Bolshevik menace' of Brouwer and Weyl, who, in their rejection of the Law of Excluded Middle, had regarded as illegitimate certain standard proofs in conventional analysis. To Turing, however, it must have seemed that Wittgenstein's Bolshevism was of a far more extreme sort. It was not, after all, the Law of Excluded Middle that Wittgenstein challenged, but the Principle of Contradiction.

All the conventional schools of thought on the foundations of mathematics – logicism, formalism and intuitionism – agree that if a system has a hidden contradiction in it, then it is to be rejected on the grounds of being inconsistent. Indeed, the whole point of providing mathematics with sound logical foundations was that Calculus, as traditionally understood, is manifestly inconsistent.

In his lectures, Wittgenstein ridiculed this concern for 'hidden contradictions', and it was to this that Turing voiced his most dogged and spirited dissent. Take the case of the Liar Paradox, Wittgenstein suggested:

> It is very queer in a way that this should have puzzled anyone – much more extraordinary than you might think: that this should be the thing to worry human beings. Because the thing works like this: if a man says 'I am lying' we say that it follows that he is not lying, from which it follows that he is lying and so on. Well, so what? You can go on like that until you are black in the face. Why not? It doesn't matter.

What was puzzling about this sort of paradox, Turing tried to explain, is 'that one usually uses a contradiction as a criterion for having done something wrong. But in this case one cannot find anything done wrong.' Yes, replied Wittgenstein, because nothing *has* been done wrong: 'One may say, "This can only be explained by a theory of types." But what is there which needs to be explained?'

Turing clearly needed to explain, not only why it was puzzling, but also why it *mattered*. The real harm of a system that contains a contradiction, he suggested, 'will not come in unless there is an application, in which case a bridge may fall down or something of the sort'. In the following lecture, he returned to the fray, and almost the entire lecture was taken up with a debate between the two on the importance of discovering 'hidden contradictions':

> *Turing*: You cannot be confident about applying your calculus until you know that there is no hidden contradiction in it.
>
> *Wittgenstein*: There seems to me to be an enormous mistake there. For your calculus gives certain results, and you want the bridge not to break down. I'd say things can go wrong in only two ways: either the bridge breaks down or you have made a mistake in your calculation – for example you multiplied wrongly. But you seem to think there may be a third thing wrong: the calculus is wrong.
>
> *Turing*: No. What I object to is the bridge falling down.
>
> *Wittgenstein*: But how do you know that it will fall down? Isn't that a question of physics? It may be that if one throws dice in order to calculate the bridge it will never fall down.
>
> *Turing*: If one takes Frege's symbolism and gives someone the technique of multiplying in it, then by using a Russell paradox he could get a wrong multiplication.
>
> *Wittgenstein*: This would come to doing something which we would not call multiplying. You give him a rule for multiplying and when he gets to a certain point he can go in either of two ways, one of which leads him all wrong.

'You seem to be saying', suggested Turing, 'that if one uses a little common sense, one will not get into trouble.' 'No', thundered Wittgenstein, 'that is NOT what I mean at all.' His point was rather that a contradiction cannot lead one astray because it leads nowhere at all. One cannot calculate wrongly with a contradiction, because one simply cannot use it to calculate. One can do nothing with contradictions, except waste time puzzling over them.

After two more lectures Turing stopped attending, convinced, no doubt, that if Wittgenstein would not admit a contradiction to be a fatal flaw in a system of mathematics, then there could be no common ground between them. It must indeed have taken a certain amount of courage to attend the classes as the single representative of all that Wittgenstein was attacking, surrounded by Wittgenstein's acolytes and having to discuss the issues in a way that was unfamiliar to him. Andrew Hodges, in his excellent biography of Turing, expresses surprise at what he sees as Turing's diffidence in these discussions, and gives as an example the fact that, despite long discussions about the nature of a 'rule' in mathematics, Turing never offered a definition in terms of Turing machines. But, surely, Turing realized that Wittgenstein would have dismissed such a definition as irrelevant; the discussion was conducted at a more fundamental level. Wittgenstein was attacking, not this or that definition, but the very motivation for providing such definitions.

With the certain exception of Alister Watson, and the possible exception of others, it is likely that many of those who attended these lectures did not fully grasp what was at stake in the arguments between Wittgenstein and Turing, nor fully understand how radically Wittgenstein's views broke with anything that had previously been said or written on the philosophy of mathematics. They were, on the whole, more interested in Wittgenstein than in mathematics. Norman Malcolm, for one, has said that, though he was aware that 'Wittgenstein was doing something important', he 'understood almost nothing of the lectures' until he restudied his notes ten years later.

Malcolm was then a doctoral student at Harvard, who had arrived in Cambridge in the Michaelmas term of 1938 to study with Moore, and quickly fell under the spell of Wittgenstein's personality. It is in his memoir that that personality is most memorably and (in the opinion of many who knew Wittgenstein) accurately described. Wittgenstein warmed to Malcolm's kindness and his human understanding, and during Malcolm's brief time at Cambridge the two became close friends. Upon Malcolm's return to the United States, he became, as well as a cherished correspondent, an invaluable supplier of Wittgenstein's favourite journal, Street & Smith's *Detective Story Magazine*, at a time when American magazines became unavailable in England.

Why Wittgenstein insisted – and insist he did; when Malcolm sent some other brand, Wittgenstein gently admonished him, asking why he had tried to be original instead of sticking to the 'good, old, tried out stuff' – on Street & Smith is a mystery: it was at this time practically indistinguishable from its more famous rival, *Black Mask*. Both published 'hard-boiled' detective stories written largely by the same group of writers, the most famous of which are: Carroll John Daly, Norbert Davis, Cornell Woolrich and Erle Stanley Gardner. Raymond Chandler published but one story in Street & Smith, a lesser known piece called 'No Crime in the Mountains', and Dashiell Hammett had, by this time, given up writing for the 'pulps' altogether.

In one respect, at least, the ethos of the hard-boiled detective coincides with Wittgenstein's own: they both, in their different ways, decry the importance of the 'science of logic', exemplified in the one case by *Principia Mathematica* and in the other by Sherlock Holmes. 'I am not the deducting, deducing book type of detective', explains Race Williams in a typical Street & Smith story:

> I'm a hard working, plugging sort of guy who can recognize a break when I see it and act at the same minute, at the same second or even split second if guns are brought into it.

This fast-acting, fast-shooting, honest sort of a guy bears an obvious similarity to movie cowboys, and it is probably no coincidence that the Western was Wittgenstein's favourite genre. By the late 1930s, however, his taste had broadened to include musicals. His favourite actresses, he told Malcolm, were Carmen Miranda and Betty Hutton. Exhausted and disgusted by his lectures, he would invariably go to see a 'flick' after them, accompanied by Malcolm, Smythies or one of his other friends from the class. He would always sit at the front of the cinema, where he could be totally immersed in the picture. He described the experience to Malcolm as 'like a shower bath', washing away his thoughts of the lecture.

It was the custom at that time to play the national anthem at the end of the film, at which point the audience was expected to rise to their feet and stand respectfully still. This was a ceremony that Wittgenstein could not abide, and he would dash out of the cinema before it could begin. He also found the movie newsreels, which used to be shown between films, unbearable. As war with Germany approached, and the newsreels became more and more patriotic and jingoistic, Wittgenstein's anger increased. Among his papers there is a draft of a letter addressed to their makers, accusing them of being 'master pupils of Goebbels'. It was at this time that his friendship with Gilbert Pattisson, of ten years' standing, came to an end, when he perceived in Pattisson's attitude to the war something he took to be jingoism. His friendship with Norman Malcolm was threatened by a similar issue. Passing a newspaper vendor's sign which announced the German government's accusation that the British had attempted to assassinate Hitler, Wittgenstein commented that he would not be surprised if it were true. Malcolm demurred. Such an act was, he said, incompatible with the British 'national character', Wittgenstein reacted angrily to this 'primitive' remark:

> . . . what is the use of studying philosophy if all that it does for you is to enable you to talk with some plausibility about some abstruse questions of logic, etc., & if it does not improve your thinking about the important questions of everyday life, if it does not make you more conscientious than any . . . journalist in the use of the DANGEROUS phrases such people use for their own ends.

The rift healed before Malcolm's return to the United States in February 1940, but for a time Wittgenstein ceased his habit of taking a walk with Malcolm before his lectures.

Wittgenstein had reason to be wary of the nationalist sentiment and anti-German feeling that was being whipped up in readiness for the coming war. On the day that war was declared, 3 September 1939, he and Skinner were in Wales, visiting Drury and staying in an hotel in Pontypridd. The following morning he was told to report to the local police station, his German name having aroused the suspicions of the hotel manageress. By this time he was a British national, and he had no trouble establishing the fact, but, as he said to Skinner and Drury, he would in future have to be very careful.

For the first two years of the war Wittgenstein was forced to remain a lecturer at Cambridge, despite strenuous efforts to find alternative work related to the war effort, such as joining the ambulance brigade. In September 1937, when things had been going badly with his work, he had urged himself to do something else. But: 'how should I find the strength to do something different now' he had asked, 'unless I were being forced, as in a war?' When war did come he found that, far from forcing him to do something else, it was preventing him from doing so. The doors to his doing something 'useful' were closed by his German name and Austrian background. While he continued to lecture and to work on the second half of his book, he longed to get away from Cambridge and to be, in some way or other, engaged in the struggle. 'I feel I will die slowly if I stay there', he told John Ryle. 'I would rather take a chance of dying quickly.'

He tried, unsuccessfully, to dissuade Malcolm from an academic career (Smythies, he felt sure, would never be offered an academic appointment anyway – he was 'too serious'). Couldn't Malcolm do some manual work instead? On a ranch or on a farm, say? Malcolm declined. He returned to Harvard, collected his Ph.D. and took up a teaching post at Princeton. In his letters Wittgenstein repeated his warnings. Congratulating Malcolm on his doctorate, he urged him to make good use of it and not to cheat himself or his students: 'Because, unless I'm very much mistaken, *that's* what will be expected from you.' Wishing him luck with his academic appointment, he stressed again that the temptation for Malcolm to cheat himself would be overwhelming: '*Only by a miracle* will you be able to do decent work in teaching philosophy.'

By the time war broke out, Skinner's period as an apprentice at the Cambridge Instrument Company had come to an end, and he seems to have made an attempt to return to theoretical work. In a letter dated 11 October 1939, written from Leeds, he mentions collaborating on a book (one assumes a mathematics textbook) with his old mathematics tutor, Ursell. The project was presumably abandoned (at least, I have been able to find no trace of such a book being published). In the letter Skinner says how difficult he now finds this sort of work, and mentions that he may soon return to Cambridge to look for a job. He also alludes to some sort of break between himself and Wittgenstein, a problem in their relationship, for which, characteristically, he assumes full blame:

> I feel very unhappy that I should have given you cause to write that you feel I'm away from you. It's a terrible thing that I have acted in a way that might loosen what is between us. It would be a catastrophe for me if anything happened to our relation. Please forgive me for what I have done.

What he had done he does not say, and no doubt did not know; he knew only that he was losing Wittgenstein's love. After his return to Cambridge, he and Wittgenstein lived separately – he in East Road, and Wittgenstein in his favoured set of rooms in Whewell's Court.

After Skinner's death Wittgenstein repeatedly chastized himself for having been unfaithful to him in the last two years of his life. It is a reasonable conjecture that this guilt is connected with Wittgenstein's feelings for a young working-class colleague of Skinner's called Keith Kirk. In 1939, Kirk, who was then nineteen, worked as an apprentice alongside Skinner, and they became friends when he began to ask Skinner questions about the mathematics and mechanics of the instruments they were using. Skinner, who was too reticent to be an adequate teacher, introduced Kirk to Wittgenstein, and from then on Wittgenstein gave Kirk regular lessons on physics, mathematics and mechanics to help him with the City and Guilds professional examinations for which he was then preparing.

To Kirk these lessons from a Cambridge professor were nothing but an unexpected and extremely welcome source of help, and a remarkable opportunity. From Wittgenstein's diary, however, it appears that he thought rather more of the relationship than one would expect:

> See K once or twice a week; but am doubtful whether the relationship is the right one. May it be genuinely good [13 June 1940]

> Occupied myself the *whole day* with thoughts of my relations with Kirk. For the most part, *very* insincere and fruitless. If I wrote these thoughts down, one would see how low and dishonest – how *indecent* they were [7 October 1940]

Throughout 1940 and the first half of 1941 Kirk came regularly to Wittgenstein's rooms in Trinity for his unpaid lessons. Wittgenstein taught without a textbook; instead, he would ask Kirk a series of questions that forced him to think through the problems from first principles. Thus, a lesson might begin with Wittgenstein asking Kirk what happens when water boils – What are bubbles? Why do they rise to the surface? and so on. The amount that Kirk learnt from these lessons therefore depended to a large extent on his own ability to think, and, as in Wittgenstein's philosophy classes, there would frequently be long silences. However, according to Kirk, what he learnt in these lessons has stayed with him ever since, and the style of thinking imparted to him by Wittgenstein has been of lasting benefit to him.

Kirk never had the slightest idea that Wittgenstein's feelings for him were anything other than those of a helpful teacher. After the lesson he would occasionally accompany Skinner and Wittgenstein to see a Western at the local cinema, but apart from that he saw little of Wittgenstein outside his periods of instruction.

The lessons came to an end in 1941, when Kirk was sent by the Ministry of War to work in Bournemouth on Air Ministry Research. The move put an end to his City and Guilds studies, but not immediately to his friendship with Wittgenstein. Wittgenstein did what he could to stay in touch. He once went down to Bournemouth to see how Kirk was getting on, and when Kirk came back to Cambridge Wittgenstein would invariably arrange to meet him.

It was during one of these latter visits that Wittgenstein called on Kirk in an extremely distraught state to tell him that Francis had been taken seriously ill with polio and had been admitted into hospital. A few days later, on 11 October 1941, Francis died.

Wittgenstein's initial reaction was one of delicate restraint. In letters to friends telling them of Francis's death, he managed a tone of quiet dignity. To Hutt, for example, he wrote:

My dear Ro[w]land,
I have to give you very terrible news.

Francis fell ill four days ago with poliomyelitis & died yesterday morning. He died without *any* pain or struggle *entirely* peacefully. I was with him. I think he has had one of the happiest lives I've known anyone to have, & also the most peaceful death.

I wish you good and kind thoughts.

As always,
Ludwig

By the time of the funeral, however, his restraint had gone. He has been described by Skinner's sister as behaving like a 'frightened wild animal' at the ceremony, and after it, she recalls, he refused to go to the house but was seen walking round Letchworth with Dr Burnaby, the tutor of Trinity, looking 'quite wild'. He would not, in any case, have been unreservedly welcome at the Skinner home. Skinner's family

were always mistrustful of the influence he had exerted on their
delicate boy, and his mother, who believed that his job at the
Cambridge Instrument Company had hastened Francis's death,
refused to speak to Wittgenstein at the funeral.

But Wittgenstein's guilt over Francis was entirely unconnected with
the way in which he had influenced him. It had to do with more
internal matters – with how Wittgenstein himself had felt towards
Francis during the last few years of his life. On 28 December 1941, he
wrote:

> Think a lot about Francis, but always only with remorse over my
> lovelessness; not with gratitude. His life and death seem only to
> accuse me, for I was in the last 2 years of his life very often loveless
> and, in my heart, unfaithful to him. If he had not been so bound-
> lessly gentle and true, I would have become *totally* loveless towards
> him.

Immediately after this passage he goes on to discuss his feelings for
Kirk: 'I see Keith often, and what this really means I don't know.
Deserved disappointment, anxiety, worry, inability to settle into a
pattern of life.' About seven years later, in July 1948, he wrote: 'Think
a great deal about the last time I was with Francis; about my odiousness towards him . . . I cannot see how I can ever in my life be freed
from this guilt.'

Wittgenstein's infatuation with Kirk – entirely unspoken, un-
acknowledged and unreciprocated as it was – exemplifies in its purest
form a feature that had characterized his earlier loves for Pinsent and
for Marguerite; namely, a certain indifference to the feelings of the
other person. That neither Pinsent nor Marguerite – and certainly not
Kirk – were in love with him seemed not to affect his love for them.
Indeed, it perhaps made his love easier to give, for the relationship
could be conducted safely, in the splendid isolation of his own
feelings. The philosophical solipsism to which he had at one time been
attracted, and against which much of his later work is addressed (he
characterized his later work as an attempt to show the fly the way out
of the fly-bottle), has its parallel in the emotional solipsism in which
his romantic attachments were conducted. With Francis that isolation
was threatened, and, in the face of that threat, Wittgenstein had
withdrawn, like the porcupines of Schopenhauer's fable, behind his
spiky exterior.

IV
1941–51

21

WAR WORK

For the first two years of war, a recurrent theme of conversation with Wittgenstein was his frustration at not being able to find work outside academic life. He found it intolerable to be teaching philosophy while a war was being fought, and wanted more than anything else to be able to contribute to the war effort. His chance to do so came through his friendship with the Oxford philosopher Gilbert Ryle. Gilbert's brother, John Ryle, was Regius Professor of Physic at Cambridge, but in 1940 he had returned to Guy's Hospital to help them prepare for the Blitz. In September 1941 Wittgenstein wrote to John Ryle asking to meet him at Guy's. Ryle invited him to lunch, and was immediately impressed. 'He is one of the world's famousest philosophers', he wrote to his wife. 'He wears an open green shirt and has a rather attractive face':

I was so interested that after years as a Trinity don, so far from getting tarred with the same brush as the others, he is overcome by the deadness of the place. He said to me 'I feel I will die slowly if I stay there. I would rather take a chance of dying quickly.' And so he wants to work at some humble manual job in a hospital as his war-work and will resign his chair if necessary, but doesn't want it talked about at all. And he wants the job to be in a blitzed area. The works department are prepared to take him as an odd job man under the older workmen who do all the running repairs all over the hospital. I think he realises that his mind works so differently to most people's that it would be stupid to try for any kind of war-work based on intelligence. I have written to him tonight to tell him about this job but am not trying to persuade him unduly.

Someday I must bring him and also one or two of the Canadians down to see you.

Wittgenstein clearly needed no undue persuasion, for a week or so after this letter was written he started work at Guy's. Not, however, as an odd-job man but as a dispensary porter.

John Ryle respected Wittgenstein's wish that his change of job from Professor of Philosophy at Cambridge to dispensary porter at Guy's Hospital should not be talked about, and does not seem to have mentioned to any of the staff at Guy's that the new porter was 'one of the world's famousest philosophers'. One indication of his discretion is that Humphrey Osmond, a good friend of Ryle's and the editor during the war of the in-house journal *Guy's Gazette* (and therefore always on the look-out for an interesting story), did not find out that Wittgenstein had been at Guy's until after the publication of Norman Malcolm's memoir in 1958. It is fortunate that Ryle kept his silence, for if the *Gazette* had run a 'Famous philosopher at Guy's' piece, there is no doubt that Wittgenstein would have reacted with the utmost rage.

While he was at Guy's, Wittgenstein lived and dined with the medical staff at Nuffield House. (This in itself would have been enough to distinguish him from the other porters in the hospital, because the non-medical staff usually lived outside the hospital grounds and dined separately from the doctors.) Shortly after his arrival at Nuffield House, he was enthusiastically greeted at dinner by the hospital haematologist, Dr R. L. Waterfield. Waterfield had been at Cambridge and had attended meetings of the Moral Science Club. Upon being recognized, Wittgenstein turned as white as a sheet and said: 'Good God, don't tell anybody who I am!' But whether through Waterfield or some other source – and despite the fact that *Guy's Gazette* never got hold of the story – many of the staff at Guy's knew perfectly well who Wittgenstein was. Everyone there who knew him at all knew him as 'Professor Wittgenstein'.

Wittgenstein's job as a porter was to deliver medicines from the dispensary to the wards, where, according to John Ryle's wife, Miriam, he advised the patients not to take them. His boss at the

pharmacy was Mr S. F. Izzard. When asked later if he remembered
Wittgenstein as a porter, Izzard replied: 'Yes, very well. He came and
worked here and after working here three weeks he came and explained how we should be running the place. You see, he was a man
who was used to thinking.' After a short while, he was switched to the
job of pharmacy technician in the manufacturing laboratory, where
one of his duties was to prepare Lassar's ointment for the derma-
tological department. When Drury visited Wittgenstein at Guy's, he
was told by a member of staff that no one before had produced Lassar's
ointment of such high quality.

Wittgenstein arrived at Guy's needing a friend. After the death of
Francis, and with the departure of Kirk for Bournemouth, he was
desperately lonely. He needed some sort of emotional contact. '*One
word* that comes from your heart', he had written to Rowland Hutt on
20 August 1941, 'would mean more to me than 3 pages out of your
head!' And on 27 November: 'I can't write about Francis, and what
you write about him, though in a sense true, somehow doesn't click
with *my* thoughts of him.' He told Hutt of his job at the dispensary,
how he earned twenty-eight shillings a week and of how hard the
work was. 'I hope my body'll be able to stick it. My soul is *very* tired,
& isn't at all in a good state; I mean, not at all as it should be.' 'Perhaps',
he added, 'when we see each other again it will help us in some
way.'

It was important for Wittgenstein that if he and Hutt did meet they
should do so for long enough for it to mean something. In subsequent
letters he stressed the importance of meeting on a Sunday, the only day
on which he was not working at the hospital:

> If, however, you *can't* come on a Sunday, a week day would have to
> do. In this case to come even half an hour too late would be unwise;
> for under the circs, it's quite easy for us to make a mess of things,
> but ever so undesirable!

'It is on the whole', he explained in another letter, 'not a good plan
for people like us to see each other *hurriedly*. If possible we should be
together leisurely.' After Hutt had shown some hesitation about the
proposed meeting, he was told by Wittgenstein to wait three months
before they tried to see each other:

As long as you find it difficult to say that you want to see me, as you write, why should you see me? I want to see people who want to see *me*; & if the time should come (& perhaps it will come soon) when nobody'll want to see me, I think I'll see nobody.

The fear that his body would not be able to cope with the work of a dispensary porter was a real one. He was, by now, fifty-two, and was beginning to look (and feel) *old*. 'When I finish work about 5', he told Hutt, 'I'm so tired I often can hardly move.' But if his body was weak, his spirit was, in the wake of Francis's death, almost broken. He spent Christmas with the Barbrooke family, who owned the grocery on East Road below Francis's flat. It was a melancholy occasion. On New Year's Eve, he wrote to Hutt:

I feel, on the whole, lonely & am afraid of the months & years to come! . . . I hope that you have some happiness & that you appreciate whatever you have of it more than I did.

In the New Year of 1942, John Ryle fulfilled the promise he had made to his wife and took Wittgenstein back to their home in Sussex, to meet her. Happily, the weekend is recorded in the diary of their son, Anthony, who was then fourteen years old. His first impressions were not entirely favourable:

Daddy and another Austrian (?) professor called Winkenstein (spelling?) arrived at 7.30. Daddy rather tired. Wink is awful strange – not a very good english speaker, keeps on saying 'I mean' and 'its "tolerable"' meaning intolerable.

By the end of the following day, although making a closer approximation to the spelling of Wittgenstein's name, Anthony was still far from being won over by his father's new friend:

In the morning Daddy, Margaret, goats, Tinker & I went for a walk. Frosty but sunny. Witkinstein spent the morning with the evacuees. He thinks we're terribly cruel to them.
We spent the afternoon argueing – he's an impossible person everytime you say anything he says 'No No, that's not the point.' It probably isn't his point, but it is ours. A tiring person to listen to.

After tea I showed him round the grounds and he entreated me to be kind to the miserable little children – he goes far too much to the other extreme – Mommy wants them to be good citizens, he wants them to be happy.

The Ryles rented a farmhouse in Sussex, and the 'miserable little children' were evacuees – two working-class boys from Portsmouth whom Mrs Ryle had taken on as a political statement. They joined a group of children she organized to knit gloves for the Russian Red Cross. Although she looked after these children well, she evidently maintained strict discipline among them. On occasions when John Ryle was at home, or when they had visitors, the Ryle family, to some extent, kept a certain distance from the evacuees – dining, for example, in separate rooms. While Wittgenstein was staying there, he insisted on showing his support and sympathy for the children by dining with them.

It is easy to see why Wittgenstein should have liked and respected John Ryle. Like Wittgenstein, Ryle fitted uneasily into academic life at Cambridge, and it is clear that he shared Wittgenstein's preference for the dangers of working in a blitzed hospital over the 'deadness' of Cambridge. While at Cambridge he had been politically active, and had stood in the 1940 election as a left-wing independent candidate. From 1938 onwards he had been active in getting Jewish doctors out of Austria and Germany (which is presumably why Wittgenstein is described by Anthony Ryle as 'another Austrian professor').

Ryle's kindness is remembered with warmth and gratitude by many of the staff who served at Guy's during the Blitz. Many of them were young and, unlike Ryle, who had served in the First World War, had had no experience of war. Humphrey Osmond's memories of the dangers of working at Guy's during the heavy bombing – and Ryle's inspiration in helping the staff to cope with those dangers – are typical:

The hospital had scores of firebombs dropped on it & at least a dozen exploded or unexploded bombs on its premises . . . Under the pressure of bombing & taking in many casualties the small staff left at Guy's itself knew each other pretty well . . . I used to firewatch on the roof at Guy's . . . We spent a lot of time gossiping & drinking tea . . . We used to camp out in the basement of Nuffield

House. Ryle was a wise & intelligent man, whose serenity, which
had been tempered in the trenches during WWI, was a great
support to those like myself who disliked being bombed.

In April Wittgenstein underwent an operation at Guy's to remove
the gall-stone that had been troubling him for a number of years. His
mistrust of English doctors (he was inclined to believe that both
Ramsey's death and Skinner's might have been avoided if they had
received proper medical care) impelled him to insist on remaining
conscious during the operation. Refusing a general anaesthetic, he had
mirrors placed in the operating theatre so that he could watch what
was happening. To help him through what was undoubtedly a painful
ordeal, John Ryle sat with him throughout the operation, holding his
hand.

Apart from Ryle, Wittgenstein's few friends at Guy's tended to be
technicians rather than doctors. One of these was Naomi Wilkinson, a
radiographer and a cousin of Ryle's. Miss Wilkinson used to organize
gramophone recitals at the hospital, at which Wittgenstein was a
regular attender. He took an intense interest in the choice of records,
and was often very critical of the selection. As a result of this common
interest in music, he and Miss Wilkinson became friends, and, as with
many of his friends, she was invited to join him for tea at Lyons. At
one of these teas she asked him how many people he thought
understood his philosophy. He pondered the question for a long time
before he replied: 'Two – and one of them is Gilbert Ryle.' He did not,
unfortunately, say who the second one was. And perhaps his choice of
Gilbert Ryle indicates nothing more than that, even in his fifties, he
had not entirely lost his childhood good manners – his inclination to
say things he thought would please the other person.

Naomi Wilkinson's gramophone recitals perhaps provided one of
the elements in a dream that Wittgenstein recorded while he was
working at Guy's:

Tonight I dreamt: my sister Gretl gave Louise Politzer a present: a
bag. I saw the bag in the dream, or rather just its steel lock, which
was very big and square and very finely constructed. It looked like
one of those complicated old padlocks one sometimes sees in
museums. In this lock there was, among other things, a mechanism
by which the words 'From your Gretl', or something similar, were

spoken through the key-hole. I thought about how intricate the mechanism of this device must be and whether it was a kind of gramophone and of what sort of material the records could be made, whether they were possibly made of steel.

Wittgenstein himself offers no interpretation of this dream, but given his preoccupation at this time with Freud's work, his previous use of the metaphor of a lock to describe Freud's central idea, and the fact that Gretl was the member of his family most closely associated with Freud, it is possible, I think, to regard this dream as being *about* the interpretation of dreams. Dreams seem to say something, and a skilful use of Freud's work will enable us to hear what they say (through, as it were, the key-hole of Freud's theories), but the mechanism that lies behind their saying something and the material from which dream symbols are constructed (the unconscious) is intricate and complicated, too complicated to be understood in terms of Freud's rather crude analogy with nineteenth-century mechanics.

Such, anyway, were the central themes of the discussions Wittgenstein had with Rhees in the summer of 1942. He went to Swansea to stay with Rhees, partly in order to recuperate from his gall-stone operation, and the two of them would take walks along the South Wales coastline, of which Wittgenstein was extremely fond. Rhees was at that time one of the very few people left alive whom Wittgenstein valued as a partner in philosophical discussion, but it is striking that, at a time when his philosophical work centred mainly on the philosophy of mathematics, his conversations with Rhees dealt with the nature of Freud's explanations in psychology.

There *is* a sense, he stressed, in which the images in a dream might be regarded as symbols, a sense in which we can speak of a dream language, even if the symbols are not understood by the dreamer. This can emerge when we discuss the dream with an interpreter and accept his interpretation. Similarly, when we draw apparently meaningless doodles and an analyst asks us questions and traces associations, we might come to an explanation of why we drew what we did: 'we may then refer to the doodling as a kind of writing, as using a kind of language, although it was not understood by anyone'. But it was important to Wittgenstein to dissociate this kind of explanation from those given in science. Explanations of dreams or doodles do not proceed by the application of laws, 'and to me the fact that there *aren't* actually any such laws seems important'. Freud's explanations have more in common with a mythology than with science; for example, Freud produces no evidence for his view that anxiety is always a repetition of the anxiety we felt at birth, and yet 'it is an idea which has a marked attraction':

It has the attraction which mythological explanations have, explanations which say that this is all a repetition of something that has happened before. And when people do accept or adopt this, then certain things seem clearer and easier for them.

Freud's explanations, then, are akin to the elucidations offered by Wittgenstein's own work. They provide, not a causal, mechanical theory, but:

. . . something which people are inclined to accept and which makes it easier for them to go certain ways: it makes certain ways of behaving and thinking natural for them. They have given up one way of thinking and adopted another.

It was in this respect that Wittgenstein described himself to Rhees at this time as a 'disciple' or 'follower' of Freud.

Wittgenstein's philosophical preoccupations throughout most of the Second World War centred on the philosophy of mathematics. Most of what he wrote at this time is an attempt to improve on the remarks written during his last months in Norway, and thus improve the section of the *Investigations* that was based on them. During the time he worked at Guy's he filled three notebooks with remarks on mathematics. They, and the manuscript volume compiled from them, have now been published and form Parts IV, V, VI and VII of *Remarks on the Foundations of Mathematics*.

Though in its general outlines it is of a piece with his earlier work on the subject, the assault on mathematical logic is expressed in more caustic terms. It is, perhaps, his most polemical work.

In his essay 'Mathematics and the Metaphysicians', Russell provides the most perfect summary of the target of Wittgenstein's polemic. 'One of the chief triumphs of modern mathematics', Russell writes, 'consists in having discovered what mathematics really is':

All pure mathematics – Arithmetic, Analysis, and Geometry – is built up by combinations of the primitive ideas of logic, and its propositions are deduced from the general axioms of logic, such as the syllogism and the other rules of inference . . . The subject of formal logic has thus shown itself to be identical with mathematics.

He goes on to discuss the problems of the infinitesimal, the infinite and continuity:

In our time, three men – Weierstrass, Dedekind, and Cantor – have not merely advanced the three problems, but have completely solved them. The solutions, for those acquainted with mathematics, are so clear as to leave no longer the slightest doubt or difficulty. This achievement is probably the greatest of which our age has to boast.

Wittgenstein's work is an attack on both the conception of mathematics that is outlined here, and also the attitude towards it that is revealed. 'Why do I want to take the trouble to work out what mathematics is?' he asks in one of the notebooks kept during his period at Guy's:

Because we have a mathematics, and a special conception of it, as it were an ideal of its position and function, – and this needs to be clearly worked out.
    It is my task, not to attack Russell's logic from within, but from without.
    That is to say: not to attack it mathematically – otherwise I should be doing mathematics – but its position, its office.

For Wittgenstein, formal logic had not shown itself to be identical with mathematics; to say it had: 'is almost as if one tried to say that cabinet-making consisted in glueing'. Nor has mathematical logic finally shown us what mathematics is. It has rather: 'completely deformed the thinking of mathematicians and of philosophers'. And the work of Weierstrass, Dedekind and Cantor, far from being the greatest achievement of our age, was, in relation to the rest of mathematics: 'a cancerous growth, seeming to have grown out of the normal body aimlessly and senselessly'.

In order to show that logic and mathematics are different techniques, and that the results in mathematical logic do not have the importance attributed to them by Russell (in understanding the concepts of infinity, continuity and the infinitesimal), Wittgenstein tries a number of tacks, including, for example, trying to show that the notions of infinity, continuity and the infinitesimal as actually used in mathematics and everyday life have not been clarified by the definitions of them given by Cantor, Dedekind and Weierstrass, but, rather, distorted.

But the centre of his attack consists in trying to show that the methods of proof that typify mathematics are disanalogous to those used in logic. A proof in logic consists in a series of propositions intended to establish the truth of a conclusion. What Wittgenstein wants to show is that a proof in mathematics consists rather in a series of *pictures* intended to establish the usefulness of a technique.

For example, he sees no reason why this picture:

$$\begin{matrix} \bigcirc & \bigcirc & \bigcirc & \bigcirc & \bigcirc \\ \bigcirc & \bigcirc & \bigcirc & \bigcirc & \bigcirc \\ \bigcirc & \bigcirc & \bigcirc & \bigcirc & \bigcirc \\ \bigcirc & \bigcirc & \bigcirc & \bigcirc & \bigcirc \end{matrix}$$

should not be regarded as a proof of the Commutative Law for multiplication – i.e.: $(a \times b) = (b \times a)$. For someone might, by looking at the picture first one way and then the other, see that (5×4) is equal to (4×5) and then come to use the principle of commutation in all other cases.

Here there is no question of propositions or conclusions, and consequently the question of what the commutative law, if true, is true *about* does not arise. And if this sort of picture, rather than the axiomatic systems of logic, were regarded as paradigmatic, then there would be no reason at all to think that mathematical logicians had, as Russell would have it, 'discovered what mathematics really is'. In their work on the 'foundations of mathematics' they had simply drawn a different sort of picture, and invented a different sort of technique.

But the point of emphasizing the role of pictures in mathematics is not simply to destroy a particular conception of the subject. It is also to substitute for it a conception of mathematical reasoning which stresses the role of 'seeing connections'. In order to grasp the principle of commutation from the picture above we need to see this:

as the same as this:

If we could not 'see the connection', the proof would not convince us of anything. The understanding of the proof, then, is a good, if rudimentary, example of the kind of understanding that forms the basis of Wittgenstein's *Weltanschauung*. Mathematical proofs, like his own philosophical remarks, should be seen as 'perspicuous representations', the point of which is to produce 'just that understanding which consists in seeing connections'.

In this way, curious though it sounds, proofs in pure mathematics are analogous to the explanations offered in Freudian psychoanalysis. And perhaps the clue to Wittgenstein's shift in concerns, from mathematics to psychology, lies in his finding Freud's 'patterns' more interesting than the 'pictures' of mathematicians.

It would, one suspects, have been something of relief for Wittgenstein to have been able to place the events of his own life into some kind of pattern.

'I no longer feel any hope for the future of my life', he wrote on 1 April 1942:

> It is as though I had before me nothing more than a long stretch of living death. I cannot imagine any future for me other than a ghastly one. Friendless and joyless.

A few days later:

> I suffer greatly from the fear of the complete isolation that threatens me now. I cannot see how I can bear this life. I see it as a life in which every day I have to fear the evening that brings me only dull sadness.

At Guy's he felt that he had to keep himself busy. 'If you can't find happiness in stillness', he told himself, 'find it in running!'

> But what if I am too tired to run? 'Don't talk of a collapse until you break down.'
> Like a cyclist I have to keep pedalling, to keep moving, in order not to fall down.

'My unhappiness is so complex', he wrote in May, 'that it is difficult to describe. But probably the main thing is still *loneliness*.'

After Skinner's death Kirk had returned to Bournemouth, and, as he had with Skinner, Wittgenstein began to fret about not receiving letters from him. On 27 May he noted:

> For ten days I've heard nothing more from K, even though I pressed him a week ago for news. I think that he has perhaps broken with me. A *tragic* thought!

In fact, Kirk married in Bournemouth, made a successful career for himself in mechanical engineering and never saw Wittgenstein again. But for Kirk there had been nothing to 'break' from. It had never occurred to him that Wittgenstein might be, in any sense, homosexual, or that their relationship was anything other than that between a teacher and a pupil.

As if acknowledging this, Wittgenstein wrote, in the same diary entry: 'I have suffered much, but I am apparently incapable of *learning* from my life. I suffer still *just* as I did many years ago. I have not become any stronger or wiser.'

Some comfort – some relief from this desperate loneliness – came from a friendship with a young colleague of his in the dispensary at Guy's, Roy Fouracre. It was, one gathers, principally Fouracre's warmth and jovial good humour that endeared him to Wittgenstein. Sometimes, Wittgenstein told Drury, he would be rushed or agitated and Roy would say to him, 'Steady, Prof.' This he liked.

Fouracre would visit Wittgenstein in his room on the third floor of Nuffield House. The room, like his rooms at Cambridge, was completely bare, and Fouracre was surprised to see no philosophy books at all, but only neat piles of detective magazines. Fouracre was at the time studying for a correspondence course in modern languages, and would often sit in Wittgenstein's room reading while Wittgenstein sat quite still and silent. During these times Wittgenstein would be preparing for the lectures that he gave in Cambridge every alternate weekend. On the other weekends Wittgenstein and Fouracre would go on outings, perhaps to the zoo or to Victoria Park in Hackney, where they would go rowing on the lake.

Like many who knew Wittgenstein well, Fouracre remembers his virtuoso whistling. He recalls Wittgenstein's ability to whistle whole movements of symphonies, his showpiece being Brahms's *St Anthony Variations*, and that when other people whistled something wrong, Wittgenstein would stop them and firmly tell them how it should go – something that didn't endear him to his fellow workers in the dispensary.

Fouracre's background could hardly have been more different to that of Skinner. Whereas Skinner had been brought up in a middle-class home in Letchworth and had been educated at public school and Cambridge, Fouracre lived in a council house in Hackney, East

London, and had started work at the age of fifteen. But their personal qualities were, in many ways, similar. Fania Pascal's description of Skinner:

> He could be cheerful and liked the company of others. Without guile of any kind, he was incapable of thinking evil of anyone. He could and did learn to be more practical, though alas, he would always be too unselfish, too self-effacing.

could serve equally as a description of Fouracre. Like Skinner, Fouracre was considerably younger than Wittgenstein – in his early twenties to Wittgenstein's fifty-two. And while it would be wrong to imply that Wittgenstein's friendship with Fouracre provided anything like a substitute for his love for Skinner, it is true that for the eighteen months they worked together Fouracre filled a role in Wittgenstein's life similar to that which Skinner had filled at Cambridge. That is, he provided Wittgenstein with some sort of *human* contact: he was, like Francis, someone whose mere presence had a reassuring effect.

In many of his later letters to Fouracre, Wittgenstein mentions Guy's with warmth and with some element, perhaps, of nostalgia:

> I'm sorry to hear the atmosphere at Guy's is getting worse. It's difficult to imagine. [8.6.49]

> I wonder what the job news are you write about. I suppose it isn't that they are errecting a huge statue of me in front of Nuffield House. Or is it? Of course, no monument of stone could really show what a wonderful person I am. [15.12.50]

Fouracre obviously replied to the last suggestion telling Wittgenstein that all the statues to him at Guy's had been pulled down. 'I'm glad to hear [it]', Wittgenstein wrote in his next letter, 'as long as it wasn't done in any disrespectful way!'

Of the medical staff at Guy's, the only person to have gained Wittgenstein's trust and friendship, apart from John Ryle, seems to have been Basil Reeve, a young doctor (then in his early thirties) with an interest in philosophy. When he heard from Reg Waterfield that the new member at the dining table (whom he had previously thought 'looked interesting and rather lost amongst the hospital physicians') was Ludwig Wittgenstein, he decided to try to make his acquaintance. He therefore started sitting next to Wittgenstein at dinner, and eventually a friendship developed between the two. The topic of conversation, however, hardly ever turned to philosophy, but would centre instead on art or architecture or music, or people Wittgenstein had known, or even Freudian interpretations of some of the medical conversation that went on at the dinner table. Later, it became centred on Reeve's own work, in which Wittgenstein began to take a keen interest.

Reeve was at Guy's working in the Medical Research Council's Clinical Research Unit with a colleague, Dr Grant. Early in the Blitz the laboratories of this unit were destroyed by bombing, and, unable to pursue their original studies, Grant and Reeve started studying the plentiful air-raid casualties that were being admitted to Guy's at this time. Their object was to try and familiarize themselves with the condition of 'wound shock', which would occur not only in battle casualties but in any condition of acute traumatic injury.

Grant and Reeve's initial problem was that, in spite of a detailed study of the scientific literature, there seemed to be no satisfactory way of defining clinically the condition of 'wound shock'. Some authors identified the condition on the basis of the presence of haemoconcentration (the development of an abnormally high concentration of red cells in the blood thought to be due to the leakage of plasma from the blood into the tissues), while others recognized it as a syndrome of low blood pressure, skin pallor and rapid pulse. Quite early on in the research, therefore, Grant recommended that the very concept of 'wound shock' should be abandoned and that detailed observations of casualties should be made without using the term. In January 1941 – ten months before Wittgenstein came to Guy's – Grant produced a memorandum on the observations required in cases of wound shock, outlining his objections to the concept:

Recent experience of air raid casualties shows that in spite of all the work already done, specially in the last war, but little is known about the nature and treatment of traumatic or wound shock. In the first place there is in practice a wide variation in the application of the diagnosis of 'shock'. We cannot yet foretell and we are often in doubt about treatment. Moreover, the lack of a common basis of diagnosis renders it impossible to assess the efficacy of the various methods of treatment adopted.

There is good ground, therefore, for the view that it would be better to avoid the diagnosis of 'shock' and to replace it by an accurate and complete record of a patient's state and progress together with the treatment given.

It is clear, I think, why Wittgenstein should find this radical approach to the problem interesting and important. Grant's way of dealing with the problem of 'shock' has an obvious parallel with Heinrich Hertz's way of dealing with the problems of 'force' in physics. In *The Principles of Mechanics* Hertz had proposed that, instead of giving a direct answer to the question: 'What is force?' the problem should be dealt with by restating Newtonian physics without using 'force' as a basic concept. Throughout his life, Wittgenstein regarded Hertz's solution to the problem as a perfect model of how philosophical confusion should be dispelled, and frequently cited – as a statement of his own aim in philosophy – the following sentence from Hertz's introduction to *The Principles of Mechanics*:

> When these painful contradictions are removed, the question as to the nature of force will not have been answered; but our minds, no longer vexed, will cease to ask illegitimate questions.

In a conscious echo of this sentence, Wittgenstein wrote:

> In my way of doing philosophy, its whole aim is to give an expression such a form that certain disquietudes disappear. (Hertz).

And we might say of Grant's proposal to avoid the diagnosis of 'shock' that its whole aim was to: 'give an expression such a form that certain disquietudes disappear'.

Grant's approach was not, however, universally well received – especially by the army. Colonel Whitby of the Army Blood Transfusion Service responded to Grant's report in the following letter to the Medical Research Council:

> Quite a lot of the preamble, and some of the discussion was devoted to a diatribe against the word 'Shock'. I do not feel that this point needs to be so heavily emphasised.

It is not justifiable to throw over the findings of the last war. These men were not fools . . . they at least established the fundamental fact that lowered blood pressure was a sign very constantly observed. Grant would throw over the whole of the valuable MRC literature of the last war because their records do not attain his standard of detail.

As Wittgenstein realized when he discussed the project with Reeve, the problem with the theories of wound shock formulated during the First World War was not primarily that their standard of detail was inadequate, but that they were operating with an unusable concept. It was precisely the 'diatribe against the word "Shock"' that most interested him. (Reeve remembers that when they came to write an annual report, Wittgenstein suggested printing the word 'shock' upside-down to emphasize its unusability.)

Because of the interest he showed in the project, Wittgenstein was introduced by Reeve to Dr Grant, who was immediately impressed by the acuteness and relevance of the many questions and suggestions he made concerning the investigations. During 1942, the heavy bombing of London, which had provided Grant's team with a steady supply of research material, began to peter out. The unit therefore began to search elsewhere for casualties suitable for their observations. On two occasions, stations of Bomber Command were visited and a number of instances of injury to air-crew, incurred in bombing raids, were observed. But to make progress in the research a more constant supply of injured people was needed, so arrangements were made for the unit to move to the Royal Victoria Infirmary, Newcastle, which admitted a large number of heavy industrial and road injuries to its wards. At the time this move was planned Wittgenstein told Reeve he would like to go with the Unit to Newcastle.

The Unit moved to Newcastle in November 1942. Grant's technician, however, refused to go, and remembering Wittgenstein's interest in the project, Grant offered him the post. By the spring of 1943, Fouracre had left Guy's to join the army, and there was, presumably, little else to keep Wittgenstein there. In April 1943 Grant wrote to Dr Herrald at the Medical Research Council office in London saying:

Professor Ludwig Wittgenstein, of whom I told you, joined the unit as Laboratory Assistant on the 29th April for a probationary period of one month. As I arranged with you, he will be paid at the rate of £4 a week.

As he was earning only twenty-eight shillings a week as a dispensary porter, this would have constituted a significant increase in income. When the probationary period of a month was up Grant wrote again to Herrald confirming the arrangement, adding: 'He is proving very useful.'

The change from a manual job to the more cerebral task of assisting the research unit was no doubt welcome to Wittgenstein, and not only because he was finding the physical demands of the work as a porter a little difficult. Just before he left Guy's, on 17 March, he wrote to Hutt about the value of thinking. 'I *imagine*', he wrote, 'that thinking a little more than you probably do would do you good. – I hope your family isn't keeping you from thinking!? If anyone does they act *very* foolishly.' Hutt had, by now, left Woolworth's and was to join the army. He had written to Wittgenstein about some trouble he had with his superiors. 'I imagine', Wittgenstein replied, 'that it's partly external & partly internal':

> I mean, they mayn't be as decent with you as you deserve, – but you *tend* to be unreliable. I.e. you tend to be alternatively cold, warm, & lukewarm; & you mustn't be surprised if people sometimes disregard your periods of warmth & treat you as if you could be cold & lukewarm only.

Before he left for Newcastle, Wittgenstein spent some time in Swansea with Rush Rhees. There he resumed the conversations he had the previous summer about Freud. Again, it was the idea that dream symbols form a kind of language that interested him – the fact that we naturally think that dreams *mean* something, even if we do not know *what* they mean. Analogously, he told Rhees of the five spires of Moscow Cathedral: 'On each of these there is a different sort of curving configuration. One gets the strong impression that these different shapes and arrangements must mean something.' The question at issue was the extent to which Freud's work is useful in enabling us to interpret dreams. He stressed that what was wanted was not an explanation but an interpretation. Thus a scientific theory of dreams – which might, for example, enable us to predict that a dreamer could be brought to recall certain memories after providing us with a description of a dream – would not even touch the problem. Freud's work is interesting precisely because it does not provide such a scientific treatment. What puzzles us about a dream is not its causality but its *significance*. We want the kind of explanation which 'changes the aspect' under which we see the images of a dream, so that they now make sense. Freud's idea that dreams are wish fulfilments is important because it 'points to the sort of interpretation that is wanted', but it is too general. Some dreams obviously are wish fulfilments – 'the sexual dreams of adults, for instance'. But it is strange that these are precisely the kind of dreams ignored by Freud:

> Freud very commonly gives what we might call a sexual interpretation. But it is interesting that among all the reports of dreams which he gives, there is not a single example of a straightforward sexual dream. Yet these are as common as rain.

This again is connected with Freud's determination to provide a *single* pattern for all dreams: all dreams must be, for him, expressions of longing, rather than, for example, expressions of fear. Freud, like philosophical theorists, had been seduced by the method of science and the 'craving for generality'. There is not one type of dream, and neither is there one way to interpret the symbols in a dream. Dream symbols do mean something – 'Obviously there are certain similarities with language' – but to understand them requires not some general theory of dreams, but the kind of multi-faceted skill that is involved, say, in the understanding of a piece of music.

In April Wittgenstein left Swansea to join Grant's research unit in Newcastle. The members of the unit, Basil Reeve, Dr Grant and Miss Helen Andrews, Grant's secretary, all lodged in the same house in Brandling Park, an area within walking distance of the hospital. The house belonged to a Mrs Moffat. Miss Andrews remembers the arrival of Wittgenstein:

> There was a vacant room at Mrs Moffat's so he joined us there. By this time we had settled in & adapted to our unusual surroundings, but Prof. W. did not easily fit in. He came down to breakfast in a bright & chatty mood, while we all shared a Manchester Guardian &

did not talk much. In the evening when we relaxed, he would not join us at dinner, but preferred to eat in his bedroom. Mrs Moffat, grumbling, put his meal on a tray & he came downstairs & fetched it. (I thought this was rude to Dr Grant.)

We had a sitting room with a good coal fire & he never spent an evening there with us. He went to a cinema almost every evening, but could not remember anything about the films when asked about them the following day. He just went to relax.

Not long after Wittgenstein's arrival, the members of the unit had to leave the house in Brandling Park, because of Mrs Moffat's ill health. They each found separate digs, but, recalls Miss Andrews, 'Prof. W. had difficulty in finding anywhere to live because as he had a foreign accent, looked a bit shabby & said he was a professor, most landladies were quite naturally suspicious.'

That Wittgenstein went every evening to see a film is an indication of how hard he worked at Newcastle, and how seriously he took the work. It is reminiscent of his remark to Drury:

> You think philosophy is difficult enough but I can tell you it is nothing to the difficulty of being a good architect. When I was building the house for my sister in Vienna I was so completely exhausted at the end of the day that all I could do was go to a 'flick' every night.

Another indication of this is that while at Newcastle he wrote no philosophy at all, whereas while he was at Guy's he filled three notebooks with remarks on the philosophy of mathematics. He did not confine himself to fulfilling his duties as a technician, but took an intense and active interest in the thinking behind the research. Although both Grant and Reeve benefited from discussing their ideas with Wittgenstein, and encouraged his interest in their work, they sometimes found his absorption in the research a little too intense. Miss Andrews remembers that, because the unit worked so hard, Grant would sometimes suggest that they all take a day off and go for a walk together along Hadrian's Wall. She noticed that Wittgenstein was never invited to accompany them on these communal walks, and asked Grant why he was left out. She was told that if he came with them it would defeat the purpose of the walk, because he: 'talked shop all the time'.

Although he was not invited on these 'rest-day' walks, both Grant and Reeve remember accompanying Wittgenstein on many other occasions on walks along the Roman wall. Usually the conversation centred on their research, but with Reeve in particular Wittgenstein would often discuss more personal matters. He talked to Reeve, for example, about his early childhood, mentioning that he did not talk until he was four years old. He told Reeve a childhood memory that he had also related to Drury, and which obviously had a great significance for him. In the lavatory of his home, he said, some plaster had fallen from the wall, and he always saw this pattern as a duck, but it frightened him: it had the appearance for him of those monsters that Bosch painted in his *Temptations of St Anthony*.

Reeve would at times ask Wittgenstein about philosophy, but Wittgenstein characteristically discouraged his interest in the subject. He emphasized to Reeve that, unlike his own subject of medicine, philosophy was absolutely useless, and that unless you were compelled to do it, there was no point in pursuing it. 'You do *decent* work in medicine', he told Reeve; 'be content with that.' 'In any case', he would add mischievously, 'you're too stupid.' It is interesting, however, that forty years later Reeve should say that he had been influenced in his thinking by Wittgenstein in two important ways: first, to keep in mind that things are as they are; and secondly, to seek illuminating comparisons to get an understanding of how they are.

Both these ideas are central to Wittgenstein's later philosophy. Wittgenstein, indeed, thought of using Bishop Butler's phrase: 'Everything is what it is, and not another thing' as a motto for *Philosophical Investigations*. And the importance of illuminating comparisons not only lies at the heart of Wittgenstein's central notion of: 'the understanding which consists in seeing connections', but was also regarded by Wittgenstein as characterizing his whole contribution to philosophy. Wittgenstein's conversations with Reeve, like his work in helping Grant and Reeve to clarify their ideas about 'shock', show that there are more ways of having a philosophical influence than by discussing philosophy. Wittgenstein imparted a way of thinking and understanding, not by saying what was distinctive about it, but by showing how it can be used to clarify one's ideas.

Both Grant and Reeve recall that Wittgenstein's influence played an important part in the thinking embodied in the introduction to the final report of the unit, which, significantly, did not use the word 'shock' in its main title, but was called, rather, *Observations on the General Effects of Injury in Man*. The main thread of argument is the same as that in Grant's original memorandum of January 1941, but the 'diatribe against the word "Shock"' is expressed in even stronger terms:

> In practice we found that the diagnosis of shock seemed to depend on the personal views of the individual making it rather than on generally accepted criteria. Unless we were acquainted with these views we did not know what to expect when called to the bedside. The label alone did not indicate what signs and symptoms the patient displayed, how ill he was or what treatment he required. The only common ground for diagnosis that we could detect was that the patient seemed *ill*. We were led, therefore, to discard the word 'shock' in its varying definitions. We have not since found it to be of any value in the study of injury; it has rather been a hindrance to unbiased observation and a cause of misunderstanding.

Whether this was written by Wittgenstein or not, it had an effect that he hoped his philosophical work would have – namely, it put an end to many misguided lines of research. The Report of the Medical Research Council for 1939–45 says of the work done under Grant:

> [It] threw grave doubt upon the value of attacking the 'shock' problem as if wound 'shock' were a single clinical and pathological entity. In consequence, several lines of investigation started for the Committee at the beginning of the war were abandoned.

It had the effect, in fact, that Wittgenstein had hoped for in his later work on the philosophy of mathematics – the effect that sunlight has on the growth of potato shoots.

The purpose of the research conducted by Grant and Reeve was not primarily to campaign against the use of the word 'shock' in diagnosing the effects of injury, but to uncover other, more fruitful, diagnoses and treatments than those derived from the research done in the First World War. For this they needed detailed observations of the effects of injuries. Wittgenstein's part in this practical aspect of the work was to cut frozen sections of tissue and stain them in order to detect the presence of, for example, fat. He apparently did this very well.

As well as this histological work, Wittgenstein was asked by Grant to assist in his investigations into Pulsus Paradoxus, a pulse pressure that varies with respiration, which often occurred in badly injured patients. In this he seems to have introduced a technological innovation by inventing a better apparatus for recording pulse pressure than the one they had. Both Grant and Reeve remember that this apparatus was innovatory, but neither could remember the details of it. The only description we have of this apparatus, therefore, is the one Drury gives when he describes the time he used his leave from the army to visit Wittgenstein in Newcastle:

> After the end of the campaign in North Africa I was posted back to England to prepare for the Normandy landing. Having a period of disembarkation leave, I travelled up to Newcastle to spend a few days with Wittgenstein . . . He took me to his room in the Research Department and showed me the apparatus which he himself had designed for his investigation. Dr Grant had asked him to investigate the relationship between breathing (depth and rate) and pulse (volume and rate). Wittgenstein had so arranged things that he could act as his own subject and obtain the necessary tracings on a revolving drum. He had made several improvements in the original apparatus, so much so that Dr Grant had said he wished Wittgenstein had been a physiologist and not a philosopher. In describing to me his results so far he made a characteristic remark: 'It is all very much more complicated than you would imagine at first sight.'

Drury's visit to Newcastle also provides us with a revealing conversation, showing an interesting change in Wittgenstein's attitude to sex. By 1943, it seems, far from accepting Weininger's view that sex and spirituality were incompatible, Wittgenstein was sympathetic to a view of the sexual act which saw it as an object of religious reverence. Drury relates that while he was staying in Newcastle with Wittgenstein, the two of them caught a train to Durham and took a walk by the river there. As they walked Drury talked to Wittgenstein about his experiences in Egypt, and especially about seeing the temples at Luxor. He told Wittgenstein that, although seeing the temples was a wonderful experience, he had been surprised and shocked to find on the wall of one of the temples a bas-relief of the god Horus, with an erect phallus, in the act of ejaculation and collecting the semen in a bowl. Wittgenstein responded to this story with an encouraging rejection of Drury's implied disapproval:

> Why in the world shouldn't they have regarded with awe and reverence that act by which the human race is perpetuated? Not every religion has to have St Augustine's attitude to sex.

When Wittgenstein had first moved to Newcastle, he had responded with an even more dismissive frankness to another remark of Drury's. Drury had written to him wishing him luck in his new work, and added that he hoped Wittgenstein would make lots of friends. Wittgenstein replied:

> It is obvious to me that you are becoming thoughtless and stupid. How could you imagine I would ever have 'lots of friends'?

Though harshly expressed, this was doubtless true. Wittgenstein's only friend at Newcastle seems to have been Basil Reeve. He got on well with Grant, and they shared an interest in music (Grant can remember Wittgenstein's enthusiastic agreement when he once mentioned that he disliked the opening of Beethoven's 'Emperor' Concerto), but there was little of the warmth of feeling – the simple human contact – that Wittgenstein had shared at Guy's with Roy Fouracre. Grant was too absorbed in his own work for that. Wittgenstein had complained to Fouracre about the lack of human contact his philosophical work at Cambridge provided, but at Newcastle, as his letters to Norman Malcolm show, he began to miss his Cambridge friends:

> I haven't heard from Smythies for many months. I know he is in Oxford but he doesn't write to me. – [Casimir] Lewy is still at Cambridge . . . Rhees is still lecturing at Swansea . . . I hope you'll see Moore & find him in good health. [11.9.43]

> I am feeling rather lonely here & may try to get to some place where I have someone to talk to. E.g. to Swansea where Rhees is a lecturer in philosophy. [7.12.43]

More important, perhaps, he began to miss the opportunity to pursue his own work. Absorption in Grant and Reeve's work was no longer enough:

> I too regret that for external & internal reasons I can't do philo-sophy, for that's the only work that's given me real satisfaction. No other work really bucks me up. I'm extremely busy now & my mind is kept occupied the whole time but at the end of the day I just feel tired & sad.

The 'internal reasons' were Wittgenstein's doubts about whether he was still capable of good work in philosophy. He used to say to Reeve, time and again: 'my brain has gone', and would often talk about his days in Norway in 1913 with a wistful longing: '*Then* my mind was on fire . . . but now it's gone.' The 'external reasons' were the demands of the job that he was doing in Newcastle, and rather unsatisfactory lodgings. He was also finding continued exposure to hospital regis-trars and house officers, with their outspoken and often ribald com-ments about their patients, more and more difficult to accept, and he required more and more help from Reeve in understanding the responses of young doctors to the stresses of their profession.

Perhaps as a consequence of these frustrations, together with the extra limitations on Reeve's time caused by the arrival in Newcastle of his wife and young baby, even Wittgenstein's relationship with Reeve began to deteriorate. Wittgenstein – ever a possessive friend – began to demand more of Reeve's time and attention while the demands of Reeve's work and home life limited the amount he could give. They eventually parted on bad terms. Wittgenstein's words of goodbye to Reeve were: 'You're not such a nice person as I had thought.' For his part, Reeve felt relieved that he would not have to go on giving Wittgenstein the emotional support he demanded.

Given Wittgenstein's frustrated yearning to return to philosophical work, and his worsening relationship with Reeve, it was probably a relief for him to hear that Grant and Reeve were leaving Newcastle. Their research had begun to emphasize the need for further study of the effects of blood loss and tissue damage, and this necessitated access to injuries of a more severe degree than were available in civil life. They therefore needed to conduct their research on the battlefield, and so, towards the end of 1943, arrangements were made to transfer them to Italy.

Grant's successor was Dr E. G. Bywaters, who, like Grant and Reeve, had previously carried out observations on air-raid casualties in London. Before he left, Grant wrote to Dr A. Landsborough Thomson at the Medical Research Council Head Office in London, telling him:

> Wittgenstein has agreed to continue as laboratory assistant in the meantime, but the duration of his stay will depend on how he gets on with Bywaters.

He urged him to keep Wittgenstein on as an employee of the Council, even if he decided to leave Newcastle:

> Wittgenstein has taken up laboratory work as a contribution to the war effort, as I told you he is Professor of Philosophy at Cambridge. If he decides that he cannot continue here after Reeve and I go, it seems a pity not to use him further . . . He has a first class brain and a surprising knowledge of physiology. He is an excellent man to discuss problems with. On the practical side, he has served us well as a laboratory assistant and in addition has by himself made new observations on man on the respiratory variations of blood pressure devising his own apparatus and experiments. He is not an easy man to deal with, but given suitable conditions, can be a helpful and stimulating colleague. I presume that after the war, he will return to his Chair at Cambridge.

Grant and Reeve finally left for Italy at the end of January 1944. Wittgenstein was, as we have seen, feeling lonely and depressed before Bywaters arrived, and although he continued to fulfil his duties as a technician with care and attention, he did not care to socialize. Bywaters remembers:

> He was reserved & rather withdrawn: when in conversation at coffee or teatime, philosophical subjects came up, he refused to be drawn. I was disappointed in this, but pleased with his meticulous & conscientious approach to the frozen sections of lung & other organs that he prepared for me. I remember him as an enigmatic,

non-communicating, perhaps rather depressed person who preferred the deck chair in his room to any social encounters.

Bywaters had been there only three weeks when he had to write to his head office asking for help in finding a new technician:

Professor Wittgenstein has been doing the histological work here for Dr Grant . . . He has now received a letter from Cambridge requesting him to spend the next three months or longer writing a treatise on his own subject (philosophy).

A week later, on 16 February, he wrote:

Professor Wittgenstein left us today: he has been called back to his Cambridge Chair to write a treatise on Philosophy, which has been in the air for the last year or so, but they now want it on paper.

So, on 16 February 1944, Wittgenstein left Newcastle and returned to Cambridge. The reference in Bywaters's letter to a treatise which has 'been in the air for the last year or so' but which 'they now want on paper' makes it plausible to assume that 'they' refers not to Cambridge University, but to Cambridge University Press.

In September 1943 Wittgenstein had approached the Press with a suggestion that they publish his new book, *Philosophical Investigations*, alongside his old book, the *Tractatus*. This idea had occurred to him earlier in the year, when he and Nicholas Bachtin had been reading the *Tractatus* together. He also mentioned the idea to Reeve, saying that he liked the idea of publishing a refutation of ideas in the *Tractatus* alongside the *Tractatus*. Cambridge University Press confirmed their acceptance of this offer on 14 January 1944, which ties in with Bywaters's first letter saying: 'He has now received a letter from Cambridge . . .' This plan, however, like the previous plan accepted by the University Press in 1938, was never carried out.

22
SWANSEA

Despite Bywaters's impression that Wittgenstein had had to leave the research unit at Newcastle because he had been 'called back to his Cambridge Chair', Wittgenstein was determined to avoid going back to Cambridge if at all possible. He wanted to finish his book before he resumed his duties as a professor, and for that purpose he considered Swansea a much better place. The thought of going to Swansea had occurred to him the previous December, after he had been told that Grant and Reeve would have to leave Newcastle in the new year. He wanted, as he had said in a letter to Malcolm, to be with someone with whom he could discuss philosophy, and Rhees was the obvious choice. 'I don't know if you remember Rhees', he wrote. 'You saw him in my lectures I believe. He was a pupil of Moore's & is an excellent man & has a real talent for philosophy, too.'

A week before he left Newcastle, however, it suddenly occurred to him that he might not be able to spend a long period working in Swansea. As he explained to Rhees, he was on leave of absence from his duties as a professor because he was doing 'important' war work:

> If, e.g., I leave here & try to find another job, say in a hospital, I have to let the general Board know & they have to approve the new job. Now if I come to Cambridge next week they'll want to know what I'm doing & I'll have to tell them that I want to do some philosophy for a couple of months. And in this case they can say: if you want to do philosophy you're not doing a war job & have to do your philosophy in Cambridge.

. . . I'm almost sure that I couldn't work at Cambridge now! I hope I'll be able to come to Swansea.

Wittgenstein's fears proved to be unfounded, and after spending a few weeks in Cambridge he was granted leave of absence to go to Swansea to work on his book. He left Cambridge in March 1944, and did not have to return until the following autumn.

The prospect of daily discussions with Rhees was not the only attraction of Swansea. Wittgenstein loved the Welsh coastline, and, perhaps more important, found the people in Swansea more congenial than those in Cambridge. 'The weather's foul', he was to tell Malcolm in 1945, 'but I enjoy not being in Cambridge':

I know quite a number of people here whom I like. I seem to find it more easy to get along with them here than in England. I feel much more often like smiling, e.g. when I walk in the street, or when I see children, etc.

Through an advertisement in a newspaper, Rhees found lodgings for him in the home of a Mrs Mann, who lived by the coast at Langland Bay. So ideal was this position that when Mrs Mann wrote to Wittgenstein explaining that she had changed her mind and could not, after all, take him in as a lodger, he refused to accept it and insisted on moving in regardless. He stayed with her throughout the spring of 1944, and she indeed proved to be a good landlady, taking good care of him throughout his periodic bouts of ill health.

Soon after he moved in with Mrs Mann he entered into a correspondence with Rowland Hutt which illustrates something of what Fania Pascal may have had in mind when she wrote that, if you had committed a murder, or if you were about to change your faith, Wittgenstein would be the best man to consult, but that for more ordinary anxieties and fears he could be dangerous: 'his remedies would be all too drastic, surgical. He would treat you for original sin.'

Hutt was at this time serving in the Royal Army Medical Corps and was dissatisfied with his position. He hoped to be given a commission and to be able to work in a laboratory or an operating theatre. Deeply depressed, he wrote to Wittgenstein complaining of his situation. Though he always encouraged any desire to take on a medical position, Wittgenstein treated Hutt's problem as one of the soul rather than one concerning his career. 'I hadn't a good impression from your letter', he wrote to Hutt on 17 March. 'Though it's very difficult for me to say what's wrong':

> I feel as though you were getting more and more slovenly. I'm not *blaming* you for it, & I'ld have no right to do so. But I've been thinking what's to be done about it. Seeing a psychologist – unless he is a very extraordinary *man* – won't get you far.

He was, in any case, inclined to doubt whether Hutt would be particularly good in an operating theatre: 'You've got to be rather quick there & resourceful, & I just don't know if you are.' But: 'One thing seems to me fairly clear: that you mustn't go on in a humiliating or demoralising position.' The central problem, as Wittgenstein saw it, was that of preserving Hutt's self-respect. If he couldn't get a commission, and if he was not prepared to make a good job of whatever he was doing, then he should apply to be sent, in whatever capacity he could, to a unit near the Front. There, Wittgenstein told him, 'you'll at least live some sort of *life*':

> I have extremely little courage myself, much less than you; but I have found that whenever, after a long struggle, I have screwed my courage up to do something I always felt *much* freer & happier after it.

'I know that you have a family', he wrote, anticipating the most obvious objection to the wisdom of this advice, 'but you won't be any use to your family if you're no use to yourself.' And if Lotte, Hutt's wife, did not see this now, 'she'll see it one day'.

This piece of advice, like others that Wittgenstein gave friends during the Second World War, is quite obviously based on his own experience of the Great War. For example, before he left to embark for 'D-Day' Maurice Drury came to Swansea to say goodbye to Wittgenstein, who left him with these words:

> If it ever happens that you get mixed up in hand-to-hand fighting, you must just stand aside and let yourself be massacred.

'I felt', writes Drury, 'that this advice was one that he had had to give himself in the previous war.' Similarly, when Norman Malcolm enlisted in the US Navy he was sent by Wittgenstein a 'foul copy' (presumably second-hand and a bit scruffy) of Gottfried Keller's novel *Hadlaub*. The advantage of its not being in pristine condition, Wittgenstein wrote, 'is that you can read it down in the engine-room without making it *more* dirty'. He obviously pictured Malcolm working in some manual capacity on a steam vessel similar to the *Goplana*. It is as though the war gave him the opportunity of vicariously reliving, through his younger friends, the intense and transforming events of 1914–18.

If he had been in Hutt's position, one feels, he would have had no hesitation in applying to be sent to the Front – just as he had in 1915.

But his advice to Hutt was also based on a more general attitude. 'I think', he told him, 'you must stop creeping & start *walking* again':

> When I talked of courage, by the way, I didn't mean, make a row with your superiors; particularly not when it's entirely useless & just shooting off your mouth. I meant: take a burden & try to *carry* it. I know that I've not any right to say this. I'm not much good at carrying burdens myself. But still it's all I've got to say; until perhaps I can see you.

Hutt wrote back showing no inclination to accept the advice and reporting that he had recently seen a psychologist. 'I wish I knew more about military matters', Wittgenstein replied with impatient irony:

> I can't understand, e.g., what a psychologist has to do with your medical category in the Army. Surely there's nothing wrong with you *mentally*! (Or if there is the psychologist won't know it.)

He repeated the outlines of his previous advice. If he couldn't get a commission, then the only thing for Hutt to do was: 'To do the job *which you've got really well*; so well that you don't lose your self-respect doing it':

> I don't know if you understand me. It is an intelligent thing to do to use whatever means one has to get a better, or more suitable job. *But* if those means fail then there comes a moment when it no longer

makes sense always to complain & to kick but when you've got to *settle down*. You're like a man who moves into a room & says 'Oh this is only temporary' & doesn't unpack his trunks. Now this is all right – for a time. But if he *can't* find a better place, or *can't* make up his mind to risk moving perhaps into another town altogether, then the thing to do is to unpack his trunks & settle down whether the room's good or not. For *anything's* better than to live in a state of waiting.

'This war *will* end', he insisted, '& the most important thing is what sort of person *you'll* be when it's over. That's to say: when it's over you ought to be a *man*. And you won't be if you don't train yourself now':

The first thing to do is: stop kicking when it's fruitless. It seems to me you ought either apply to be posted somewhere nearer the front & just *risk* it, or, if you don't want to do that, *sit down* where you are, don't think of moving but only of doing that work well which you've got *now*.

'I'll be quite frank with you', he added, with another suggestion that indicates he was perhaps projecting his own history on to Hutt's situation, '& say that I think it *might* be better for you not to be within reach of your family':

Your family is, of course, soothing, but it may also have a softening effect. And for certain sores you want to make the skin *harder*, not softer. I mean, I have an idea (perhaps it's as wrong as hell) that your family makes it more difficult, or impossible, for you to settle down & get down to your work without looking right or left. Also you should perhaps look a little more inside you, & this also is perhaps impossible with your family around. In case you show this letter to Lotte & she wildly disagrees with me I'll say this: maybe she wouldn't be a good wife if she didn't disagree, but that doesn't mean that what I tell you mayn't be *true*!

Still hankering after a commission, Hutt wrote telling Wittgenstein he had seen his commander and might do so again soon. 'It seems

to me', Wittgenstein replied, 'that you're alternatively living in unfounded hopes & in despair . . . To pester your Commander about a
commission now seems to me silly. *Nothing* has changed since you've
been refused!'

> You write: 'All these steps have made or will make my position here
> satisfactory, or at least a lot better.' This is all nonsense, & it makes
> me really sick to read it. The one step which can make things more
> satisfactory for you is a step that has to be taken inside you.
> (Though I won't say that getting away from your family mightn't
> help.)

The exchange on this subject ended in June, with Wittgenstein
having the last word. 'I wish you *luck* and *patience*!' he wrote in
conclusion, '& no more dealings with psychologists.'

By this time, Wittgenstein had moved out of Mrs Mann's house and
into the home of a Methodist minister, the Reverend Wynford
Morgan. On his first visit to the house Mrs Morgan, acting the
solicitous hostess, asked him whether he would like some tea, and also
whether he would like this and that other thing. Her husband called
out to her from another room: 'Do not ask; *give*.' It was a remark that
impressed Wittgenstein enormously, and he repeated it to his friends
on a number of occasions.

But in other respects Wittgenstein was less favourably impressed
with his host. He made fun of him for having his walls lined with
books that he never read, accusing him of having them there simply to
impress his flock. When Morgan asked Wittgenstein whether he
believed in God, he replied: 'Yes I do, but the difference between what
you believe and what I believe may be infinite.'

This remark does not, of course, refer to the difference between
Methodism and other forms of Christianity. Wittgenstein was no
more a Catholic than he was a Methodist. Of his friends who had
converted to Catholicism, he once remarked: 'I could not possibly
bring myself to believe all the things that they believe.' One of these
was Yorick Smythies, who wrote to Wittgenstein announcing his
conversion at the time that Wittgenstein was lodging with Reverend
Morgan. Wittgenstein was very concerned, the more so as he thought
he might have unwittingly been partly responsible for the conversion
by encouraging Smythies to read Kierkegaard. His reply to Smythies

was oblique: 'If someone tells me he has bought the outfit of a tightrope walker I am not impressed until I see what is done with it.'

The point of this analogy is clarified in one of his notebooks:

> An honest religious thinker is like a tightrope walker. He almost looks as though he were walking on nothing but air. His support is the slenderest imaginable. And yet it really is possible to walk on it.

Though he had the greatest admiration for those who could achieve this balancing act, Wittgenstein did not regard himself as one of them. He could not, for example, bring himself to believe in the literal truth of reported miracles:

> A miracle is, as it were, a gesture which God makes. As a man sits quietly and then makes an impressive gesture, God lets the world run on smoothly and then accompanies the words of a saint by a symbolic occurrence, a gesture of nature. It would be an instance if, when a saint has spoken, the trees around him bowed, as if in reverence. – Now, do I believe this happens? I don't.
>
> The only way for me to believe in a miracle in this sense would be to be impressed by an occurrence in this particular way. So that I should say e.g.: 'It was impossible to see these trees and not to feel that they were responding to the words.' Just as I might say 'It is impossible to see the face of this dog and not to see that he is alert and full of attention to what his master is doing.' And I can imagine that the mere report of the words and life of a saint can make someone believe the reports that the tree bowed. But I am not so impressed.

The belief in God which he acknowledged to Morgan did not take the form of subscribing to the truth of any particular doctrine, but rather that of adopting a religious attitude to life. As he once put it to Drury: 'I am not a religious man but I cannot help seeing every problem from a religious point of view.'

Next door to Morgan lived the Clement family, with whom Wittgenstein quickly made friends – a good example of his remark to Malcolm that he found it easier to get along with people in Swansea than in England. He particularly liked Mrs Clement, who invited him to have Sunday lunch with her family every week. 'Isn't she an angel?' he said of her to her husband one Sunday lunch-time. 'Is she?' replied Mr Clement. 'Damn it all, man! of course she is!' roared Wittgenstein.

In fact, he was so impressed by Mrs Clement that he wished to lodge in her house rather than with Morgan. The Clements had not until then taken lodgers, and had no great desire to do so, but, on being pressed, they assented to Wittgenstein's moving in. Wittgenstein's association with the Clements lasted for the next three years, and during his last years at Cambridge he would spend his vacations as a guest in their home.

The Clements had two daughters, Joan, aged eleven, and Barbara, aged nine, and while he was staying there Wittgenstein was treated almost as part of the family. Finding the name 'Wittgenstein' something of a mouthful, they all called him 'Vicky', although it was made clear that they were the only people allowed to do so. Unusually, Wittgenstein took his meals with the family while he was staying with the Clements. He also joined in with other aspects of family life. In particular, he enjoyed playing *Ludo* and *Snakes and Ladders* with the girls – so much so that on one occasion, when a game of *Snakes and Ladders* in which Wittgenstein was particularly absorbed had gone on for over two hours, the girls had to plead with him against his will to leave the game unresolved.

He took an active interest, too, in the education of the two girls. The elder, Joan, was at the time taking her scholarship examinations for the local grammar school. On the day that the results were announced, Wittgenstein came home to find her in tears. She had been told that she had failed. Wittgenstein was emphatic that this could not be so. 'Damn it all!' he said. 'We'll see about that!' With Joan and her mother following anxiously, Wittgenstein marched down to Joan's school to confront the teacher who had told her that she had failed. 'I am stunned that you say she failed', he told the teacher, 'and I can tell you on authority that she *must* have passed.' The somewhat intimidated teacher checked the records and discovered, much to everybody's relief, that there had indeed been a mistake and that Joan had gained enough marks to pass the examination. The teacher was denounced as an 'incompetent fool' by Wittgenstein, but although both his judgement and Joan's ability had been vindicated, Mrs Clement was ashamed to show her face again at the school.

Apart from his self-imposed family responsibilities and his almost daily walks with Rhees, Wittgenstein's time at Swansea was taken up largely with writing. He had taken with him the typescript of the 1938 version of the *Investigations*, and the notebooks and hard-back ledger volumes that he had written while he had been working at Guy's, and he set to work on a revision of the book which he hoped would be ready for the publishers by the time he had to return to Cambridge the following autumn.

For the first two months that he was in Swansea, the focus of his work was on the philosophy of mathematics. He resumed work on the notebook he had kept at Guy's and to which he had given the title 'Mathematics and Logic'. His chief preoccupation in this notebook is with the notion of following a rule. Part 1 of the 1938 version had ended with remarks concerning the confusions associated with this notion, and Part 2 began with an attempt to unravel these confusions as a preliminary to a discussion of issues in the philosophy of mathematics. In the reworked version of the *Investigations* which was published after his death, however, the discussion of following a rule is used instead as a preliminary to a discussion of issues in the philosophy of psychology. This change was effected in Swansea in the spring and summer months of 1944.

How quickly and radically Wittgenstein's interests shifted while he was at Swansea is illustrated by two incidents that are separated only by a few months. The first occurred soon after he had moved there, and is connected with a short biographical paragraph that John Wisdom was writing of Wittgenstein for inclusion in a biographical dictionary. Before publication, Wisdom sent the piece to Wittgenstein for his comments. Wittgenstein made only one change; he added a final sentence to the paragraph, which read: 'Wittgenstein's chief contribution has been in the philosophy of mathematics.' Two or three months later, when Wittgenstein was at work on the set of remarks which have since become known as the 'Private Language Argument', Rhees asked him: 'What about your work on mathematics?' Wittgenstein answered with a wave of his hand: 'Oh, someone else can do that.'

Of course, switching from the philosophy of mathematics to the philosophy of psychology and back again, using the problems in one area as analogies to illustrate points in the other, was something that Wittgenstein had done in his lectures, notebooks and conversations since the early 1930s. Neither was his interest in combating the idea that a private language is possible new in 1944: he had discussed it in his lectures as early as 1932. What is significant about the shift in 1944 is that it was permanent: Wittgenstein never again returned to the attempt to arrange his remarks on mathematics in a publishable form, and he spent the rest of his life arranging, rearranging and revising his thoughts on the philosophy of psychology. Moreover, this seemingly permanent shift came at a time when he seemed most anxious to complete the part of his book dedicated to the philosophy of mathematics.

The clue to this shift, I think, lies in Wittgenstein's changing conception of his book, and in particular in his recognition that his remarks on following a rule should serve, not as a preliminary to his discussion of mathematics, but rather as an overture to his investigations of both mathematical and psychological concepts. Despite his remark to Rhees that 'someone else can do that', and despite the fact that he never returned to his work on mathematics, Wittgenstein continued to regard his remarks on mathematics as belonging to his *Philosophical Investigations*. Thus the preface to the book, written in 1945, still lists 'the foundations of mathematics' as one of the subjects about which the book is concerned, and as late as 1949 he wrote in one of his notebooks:

> I want to call the enquiries into mathematics that belong to my Philosophical Investigations 'Beginnings of Mathematics'.

So the change should be considered first and foremost as a change in Wittgenstein's conception of the force of his remarks on following a rule. They now led, not in one direction, but in two, and after recognizing this fact Wittgenstein was more inclined to follow the line that led to the investigation of psychological concepts. Although he did not live long enough to retrace his steps and continue along the other branch of the forked road, he did not give up his idea that it was there to be followed. Thus the final remark of the *Investigations* – 'An investigation is possible in connexion with mathematics which is entirely analogous to our investigation of psychology' – ties in with his remark to Rhees. Although *he* had not drawn out all the implications of the first part of his book, it was still possible that it could be done by someone else.

In conversation with Rhees Wittgenstein once remarked that he could feel really active only when he changed his philosophical position and went on to develop something new. He gave as an example of this something that he considered to be an important change in his philosophical logic, concerning his view of the relation between 'grammatical' and 'material' propositions. Previously, he said, he had regarded this distinction to be fixed. But now he thought that the boundary between the two was fluid and susceptible to change. In truth, this appears as a change of emphasis rather than of opinion, for even in the 1938 version of the *Investigations* he had not treated the distinction as fixed. But neither had he particularly emphasized its fluidity. And it is this emphasis that dictated the course of his work in the summer of 1944.

The distinction between the two types of proposition lies at the heart of Wittgenstein's entire philosophy: in his thinking about psychology, mathematics, aesthetics and even religion, his central criticism of those with whom he disagrees is that they have confused a grammatical proposition with a material one, and have presented as a discovery something that should properly be seen as a grammatical (in Wittgenstein's rather odd sense of the word) innovation.

Thus, in his view, Freud did not discover the unconscious; rather, he introduced terms like 'unconscious thoughts' and 'unconscious motives' into our grammar of psychological description. Similarly, Georg Cantor did not discover the existence of an infinite number of infinite sets; he introduced a new meaning of the word 'infinite' such that it now makes sense to talk of a hierarchy of different infinities. The question to ask of such innovations is not whether these 'newly discovered' entities exist or not, but whether the additions they have made to our vocabulary and the changes they have introduced to our grammar are useful or not. (Wittgenstein's own view was that Freud's were and that Cantor's were not.)

Wittgenstein had many ways of characterizing grammatical propositions – 'self-evident propositions', 'concept-forming propositions', etc. – but one of the most important was in describing them as *rules*. In emphasizing the fluidity of the grammatical/material distinction, he was drawing attention to the fact that concept-formation – and thus the establishing of rules for what it does and does not make sense to say – is not something fixed by immutable laws of logical form (as he had thought in the *Tractatus*) but is something that is always linked with a custom, a practice. Thus, different customs or practices would presuppose different concepts from the ones *we* find useful. And this in turn would involve the acceptance of different rules (to determine what does and does not make sense) to the ones we, in fact, have adopted.

The concern with grammatical propositions was central to Wittgenstein's philosophy of mathematics because he wanted to show that the 'inexorability' of mathematics does not consist in certain knowledge of mathematical truths, but rather in the fact that mathematical propositions are grammatical. The certainty of '$2 + 2 = 4$' consists in the fact that we do not use it as a description but as a rule.

In his last writings on the philosophy of mathematics – as in his conversation with Rhees – Wittgenstein was increasingly concerned with the connection between rule-following and customs:

> The application of the concept of 'following a rule' presupposes a custom. Hence it would be nonsense to say: just once in the world someone followed a rule (or a signpost; played a game, uttered a sentence, or understood one; and so on).

This is such a general point that in the notebook from which the remark comes – written in 1944 – it is not obvious that Wittgenstein has mathematics in mind at all. And the connection between this point and Wittgenstein's argument against the possibility of a private language is obvious:

> I may give a new rule today, which has never been applied, and yet is understood. But would it be possible, if no rule had ever actually been applied?
>
> And if it is now said: 'Isn't it enough for there to be an imaginary application?' the answer is: No.

In this way it seemed perfectly natural to restructure the book so that the section on following a rule led not into the philosophy of mathematics but into the argument against the possibility of a private language. In the work that he did during this summer Wittgenstein extended Part I of the 1938 version of *Investigations* to about double its previous length, adding to it what are now considered to be the central parts of the book: the section on rule-following (paragraphs 189–242 of the published version), and the section on the 'privacy of experience' (the so-called 'Private Language Argument' in paragraphs 243–421).

In August he began to make what looks like an attempt at a final arrangement of the book, which he intended to have finished before he left Swansea in the autumn. Then, he told Hutt, 'I'll probably take on a war-job again.' In a later letter, of 3 September, he writes: 'What I'll do when I have to leave at the beginning of Oct. I don't yet know & I hope events will take the decision out of my hands.' With the Allies making swift progress through France, and the Russians advancing on Poland, it was by now clear that the war would end soon with a defeat for Germany. In this Wittgenstein saw no grounds for rejoicing. 'I'm pretty sure', he told Hutt, 'that the peace after this war will be more horrible than the war itself.'

Whether because he could not find a suitable war job, or because his leave of absence could not be extended, when the time came to leave Swansea, Wittgenstein was forced to return to Cambridge. He did so grudgingly, not least because his book remained unfinished. Before he left Swansea he had a typescript prepared of the parts he regarded as publishable. (This more or less corresponds to the final version up to paragraph 421.) Having given up hope of arranging to his satisfaction the section of the book he had previously considered the most important (that on the philosophy of mathematics), his one remaining hope was to complete his 'first volume': his analysis of psychological concepts.

23
THE DARKNESS OF
THIS TIME

In October 1944 Wittgenstein returned to Cambridge, frustrated at not having finished his book and not at all enthusiastic at the prospect of resuming his lecturing responsibilities.

Russell was also back in Cambridge, having spent the last six years living and working in America. There his life had become unbearable, owing to the hysteria and outrage whipped up against him by the more conservative elements in American society in response to his widely-publicized views on marriage, morals and religion, and he had gratefully accepted the invitation to a five-year lectureship in the quieter and calmer environment of Trinity College. He arrived, however, to find himself out of fashion with English academic philosophers, among whom Moore and Wittgenstein were now far more influential than Russell himself. He brought back with him the manuscript of his *History of Western Philosophy*, which, although it enjoyed a huge commercial success (it was for many years the main source of Russell's income), did not improve his reputation as a philosopher.

Although he maintained his admiration for the keenness of Russell's intellect, Wittgenstein detested the popular work that Russell had published since the 1920s. 'Russell's books should be bound in two colours', he once said to Drury:

. . . those dealing with mathematical logic in red – and all students of philosophy should read them; those dealing with ethics and politics in blue – and no one should be allowed to read them.

Russell, Wittgenstein thought, had achieved all he was ever likely to achieve. 'Russell isn't going to kill himself doing philosophy now', he told Malcolm, with a smile. And yet Malcolm recalls that, during the 1940s, on the rare occasions that Russell and Wittgenstein both attended the Moral Science Club, 'Wittgenstein was deferential to Russell in the discussion as I never knew him to be with anyone else.'

Russell, for his part, could see no merit whatever in Wittgenstein's later work. 'The earlier Wittgenstein', he said, 'was a man addicted to passionately intense thinking, profoundly aware of difficult problems of which I, like him, felt the importance, and possessed (or at least so I thought) of true philosophical genius':

> The later Wittgenstein, on the contrary, seems to have grown tired of serious thinking and to have invented a doctrine which would make such an activity unnecessary.

Not surprisingly, therefore, when the two remet in the autumn of 1944 (after a break of about fourteen years), there was little warmth between them. 'I've seen Russell', Wittgenstein wrote to Rhees after being back about a week; he 'somehow gave me a *bad* impression'. And after that he had little or nothing to do with his former teacher.

Russell's contempt for Wittgenstein's later work was undoubtedly heightened by (but not entirely attributable to) his personal pique at being left philosophically isolated. The philosophical problems with which he was chiefly concerned were no longer regarded as fundamental. Partly under Wittgenstein's influence, the Theory of Knowledge had been subordinated to the analysis of meaning. Thus, when *Human Knowledge: Its Scope and Limits* – a work which Russell conceived as a major statement of his philosophical position – was published in 1948, it was greeted with cool indifference. Russell's greatest contempt, therefore, was reserved for Wittgenstein's disciples:

> It is not an altogether pleasant experience to find oneself regarded as antiquated after having been, for a time, in the fashion. It is difficult to accept this experience gracefully. When Leibniz, in old age, heard the praises of Berkeley, he remarked: 'The young man in Ireland who disputes the reality of bodies seems neither to explain himself sufficiently nor to produce adequate arguments. I suspect him of

wishing to be known for his paradoxes.' I could not say quite the same of Wittgenstein, by whom I was superseded in the opinion of many British philosophers. It was not by paradoxes that he wished to be known, but by a suave evasion of paradoxes. He was a very singular man, and I doubt whether his disciples knew what manner of man he was.

Moore had not suffered in the same way, but although relations between him and Wittgenstein were still friendly, by 1944 he was too old and infirm wholeheartedly to welcome the arduous prospect of frequent and prolonged philosophical discussions with Wittgenstein. His wife therefore limited Wittgenstein's visits to one and a half hours, much to Wittgenstein's displeasure. 'Moore is as nice as always', he told Rhees:

I couldn't see him for long as we were interrupted by Mrs Moore. She told me later that Moore wasn't really as well as he seemed & that he mustn't have long conversations. I have good reason for believing that this, on the whole, is baloney. Moore has queer blackouts at times but then he's an oldish man. For his age he is obviously fit. Mrs Moore, however, doesn't like the idea of his seeing me. Perhaps she's afraid that I might criticise the book which was written about him &, generally, have a bad effect on his morale.

The book Wittgenstein mentions is *The Philosophy of G. E. Moore*, a collection of articles by a number of distinguished philosophers on various aspects of Moore's philosophy, edited by P. A. Schilpp and published in 1942. Moore agreed to the book's production, and wrote a short autobiographical piece specially for it. Wittgenstein strongly disapproved. 'I fear', he wrote to Moore after hearing about the book, 'that you may now be walking at the edge of that cliff at the bottom of which I see lots of scientists and philosophers lying dead, Russell amongst others.' When the book came out Moore was in the USA, and their meeting in the autumn of 1944 was thus the first opportunity Wittgenstein would have had since the book's publication to renew his criticism of it. Dorothy Moore's anxieties, therefore, were probably entirely justified.

In fact, Wittgenstein was wrong to blame her solely for the time regulation imposed on his meetings with Moore. Moore had suffered a stroke while in America, and his wife was acting on instructions from his doctor to forbid any kind of excitement or fatigue. She therefore limited his discussions with all his philosophical friends to one and a half hours. Wittgenstein, she says, was the only one of them who resented this: 'He did not realise how exhausting he could be, so much so that at least on one occasion Moore said to me beforehand "Don't let him stay too long."'

Wittgenstein, however, continued in his belief that Moore was being forced by his wife to cut short his conversations with him. Two years later he told Malcolm that he considered it unseemly that Moore, 'with his great love for truth', should be forced to break off a discussion before it had reached its proper end. He should discuss as long as he liked, and if he became very excited or tired and had a stroke and died – well, that would be a decent way to die: 'with his boots on'.

Nothing should come between a philosopher and his search for the truth. 'Thinking is sometimes easy, often difficult but at the same time thrilling', he wrote to Rhees:

> But when it's most important it's just disagreeable, that is when it threatens to rob one of one's pet notions & to leave one all bewildered & with a feeling of worthlessness. In these cases I & others shrink from thinking or can only get ourselves to think after a long sort of struggle. I believe that you too know this situation & I wish you *lots of courage*! though I haven't got it myself. We are all *sick* people.

His mind turned to the argument he had had with Malcolm at the beginning of the war, when Malcolm had talked about the British 'national character'. This was a case in point – an example of when, precisely because it is disagreeable, thinking clearly is most important. 'I then thought', he wrote to Malcolm:

> . . . what is the use of studying philosophy if all that it does for you is enable you to talk with some plausibility about some abstruse questions of logic, etc., & if it does not improve your thinking about the important questions of everyday life, if it does not make you more conscientious than any . . . journalist in the use of DANGEROUS phrases such people use for their own ends.

You see, I know that it's difficult to think well about 'certainty', 'probability', 'perception', etc. But it is, if possible, still more difficult to think, or try to think, really honestly about your life & other people's lives. And the trouble is that thinking about these things is not thrilling, but often downright nasty. And when it's nasty then it's most important.

Malcolm had not written for some time, and – perhaps thinking of his break with Russell in 1914 – Wittgenstein began to think that this was because Malcolm feared they would clash if they talked on serious non-philosophical subjects. 'Perhaps I was quite wrong', he wrote:

But anyway, if we live to see each other again let's not shirk digging. You can't think decently if you don't want to hurt yourself. I know all about it because I am a shirker.

In fact, the lapse in Malcolm's correspondence had nothing to do with the quarrel recalled by Wittgenstein, nor with his supposed feeling that they would not 'see eye to eye in very serious matters'. It had more to do with the demands of his job as an officer with the US Navy, which prevented his replying to Wittgenstein's letter until May 1945, when he wrote acknowledging that his remark about 'national character' had been foolish. Unfortunately for him, he arrived in Britain before his reply reached Wittgenstein. When his ship came into Southampton, Malcolm obtained leave to visit Wittgenstein in Cambridge. Wittgenstein had evidently interpreted his failure to reply as a sign that he was indeed a 'shirker', unwilling to dig deep. When Malcolm arrived at Whewell's Court Wittgenstein did not even greet him, but nodded grimly and invited him to sit down to a supper of powdered eggs. 'We sat in silence for a long time', recalls Malcolm. 'He was cold and severe the whole time. We were not in touch with one another at all.'

The day after this meeting Wittgenstein received Malcolm's letter and immediately wrote him a warm, conciliatory reply: 'Had I had it before I saw you it would have made getting into contact with you rather easier.' He suggested that they should, from now on, call each other by their Christian names. But it seems perfectly possible that, had Wittgenstein not received this acknowledgement from Malcolm of the foolishness of his remarks on 'national character', and of the need to 'dig deep', their friendship would have come to a close.

During the last year of the war, both in his attempts to finish his book and in his efforts to present his thoughts to an uncomprehending audience in his lectures, Wittgenstein felt himself to be struggling against superficiality and stupidity – his own as well as other people's – and everything else in his life was subordinated to that struggle. 'This war', he wrote to Hutt, 'I believe, has a *bad* effect on *all* of us. (It also seems to be gradually killing me, although I'm in good health.)'

One of the few people he regarded as an ally in this struggle was Rhees. When Rhees wrote to Wittgenstein about his own frustrations with teaching logic to uninterested students in Swansea, Wittgenstein responded with empathy and encouragement:

I'm sorry to hear about the depressing circumstances under which you are working. Please don't give in or despair! I know how immensely depressing things can look; &, of course, I'm the first man to think of running away, but I hope you'll pull yourself together. I wonder what lines for a logic course I recommended. Anyhow, there is nothing more difficult than to teach logic with any success when your students are all half asleep. (I've heard Braithwaite snore in my lectures.) Please go the *bloody rough* way! – I wish you *one moderately* intelligent & awake pupil to sweeten your labour!

. . . I repeat; Please go the bloody rough way! Complain, swear but go on. The students are stupid but they get something out of it.

He was dissatisfied with his own students. 'My class is exceedingly poor', he wrote to Rhees. 'I have so far 6 people, none of whom is really good.'

But a much bigger source of dissatisfaction was the fact that his book was still so far from completion. He told Rhees: 'I have no hope whatever to finish my book in the near future.' This engendered in him a feeling of worthlessness, exacerbated by the reading of other people's books:

I have recently been reading a fair amount; a history of the Mormons & two books of Newman's. The chief effect of this reading is to make me feel a little more my worthlessness. Though I'm aware of it only as a slumbering man is aware of certain noises going on around him which, however, don't wake him up.

His lectures dealt with the problems in the philosophy of psychology that he had concentrated on in Swansea the previous summer. He had thought of using as a text William James's *Principles of Psychology* – primarily to illustrate the conceptual confusions that he was concerned to combat – but, as he told Rhees, 'you were right; I didn't take James as my text but just talked out of my own head (or through my own hat)'. In fact, what he was doing in these lectures was thinking through the problems that he was concerned with in the section of the *Investigations* that he was then writing.

Those problems centred on the issue between those who assert and those who deny the existence of mental processes. Wittgenstein wanted to do neither; he wanted to show that both sides of the issue rest on a mistaken analogy:

How does the philosophical problem about mental processes and states and about behaviourism arise? – The first step is the one that altogether escapes notice. We talk of processes and states and leave their nature undecided. Sometime perhaps we shall know more about them – we think. But that is just what commits us to a particular way of looking at the matter. For we have a definite concept of what it means to learn to know a process better. (The decisive movement in the conjuring trick has been made, and it was the very one that we thought quite innocent.) – And now the analogy which was to make us understand our thoughts falls to pieces. So we have to deny the yet uncomprehended process in the yet unexplored medium. And now it looks as if we had denied mental processes. And naturally we don't want to deny them.

'What is your aim in philosophy?' he asks himself immediately after this passage, and answers: 'To show the fly the way out of the fly-bottle.' William James's textbook was used to provide examples of the sort of things that people are led to say when they are caught in this particular fly-bottle.

For example, when discussing the concept of 'the Self' James describes what happens when he tries to glance introspectively at his own 'Self of selves'. He records that what he is mostly conscious of during these attempts at introspection are motions of the head. So he concludes:

> . . . The 'Self of selves', when carefully examined, is found to consist mainly of the collection of these peculiar motions of the head or between the head and throat.

What this shows, according to Wittgenstein, is: 'not the meaning of the word "self" (so far as it means something like "person", "human being", "he himself", "I myself"), nor any analysis of such a thing, but the state of a philosopher's attention when he says the word "self" to himself and tries to analyse its meaning.' And, he adds, 'a good deal could be learned from this'.

Like his use of St Augustine to illustrate the confused picture of language that he wanted to combat, and his use of Russell to illustrate confusions in the philosophy of mathematics, Wittgenstein's use of James to provide examples of confusion in the philosophy of psychology implies no lack of respect. Just as he told Malcolm that he used the quotation from Augustine to begin the *Investigations* because: 'the conception must be important if so great a mind held it', so he cited James in his remarks on psychology precisely because he held him in high regard. One of the few books that he insisted Drury should read was James's *Varieties of Religious Experience*. Drury told him that he had already read it: 'I always enjoy reading anything of William James. He is such a human person.' Yes, Wittgenstein replied: 'That is what makes him a good philosopher; he was a real human being.'

During the Christmas vacation in Swansea, the prospect of finishing the book soon appeared brighter, and Wittgenstein returned to Trinity confident that the time for publication was near. The final version of the preface to the book is dated 'Cambridge, January 1945'.

In the preface he describes the book as 'the precipitate of philosophical investigations which have occupied me for the last sixteen years' (i.e. since his return to Cambridge in 1929), and says about his remarks:

> I make them public with doubtful misgivings. It is not impossible that it should fall to the lot of this work, in its poverty and in the

darkness of this time, to bring light into one brain or another – but, of course, it is not likely.

Evidently the 'doubtful misgivings' triumphed over the inclination to publish. Wittgenstein did not deliver his typescript to the publishers, but instead spent the rest of the year working on an extension to it that considerably expands his investigations into psychological concepts.

For this extension he selected remarks from the manuscript volumes he had written since 1931. He worked on this throughout the Lent and Easter terms of 1945, and by the summer he was ready to dictate the selection to a typist. On 13 June he wrote to Rhees:

> The Term's over & my thoughts travel in the direction of Swansea. I've been working fairly well since Easter. I am now dictating some stuff, remarks, some of which I want to embody in my first volume (if there'll ever be one). This business of dictating will take roughly another month or 6 weeks. After that I could leave Cambridge.

Two weeks later he was in more frustrated mood. His work, he told Malcolm, was 'going damn slowly. I wish I could get a volume ready for publishing by next autumn; but I probably shan't. I'm a bloody bad worker!'

In fact the work of dictating his remarks kept him in Cambridge until August. The typescript he had produced was not conceived by him as a final version of the book, but rather as something from which – together with the typescript he had produced in Swansea the previous year – a final version could be compiled. Nevertheless, he was now confident that a publishable version was in sight. 'I might publish by Christmas', he told Malcolm:

> Not that what I've produced is good, but it is now about as good as I can make it. I think when it'll be finished I ought to come into the open with it.

During the months of preparing this typescript, he became increasingly oppressed by the 'darkness of this time'. The final stages of the Second World War were accompanied by scenes of savagery and inhumanity on a scale previously unimaginable. In February the bombardment of Dresden by British and American air forces left the city almost completely devastated, and killed 130,000 civilians. In April Berlin fell to the Allies and Vienna to the Russians, with appalling casualties on both sides. Shortly before the German surrender of 7 May, pictures were released of the heaps of rotting corpses discovered by the Allies at the concentration camps at Belsen and Buchenwald. On 14 May Wittgenstein wrote to Hutt: 'The last 6 months have been more nauseating than what went before. I wish I could leave this country for a while & be alone somewhere as I was in Norway.' Cambridge, he said, 'gets on my nerves!'

In the British elections of July he voted for the Labour Party, and strongly urged his friends to do the same. It was important, he felt, to get rid of Churchill. He was convinced, as he put it to Malcolm, 'that this peace is only a truce':

> And the pretence that the complete stamping out of the 'aggressors' of this war will make this world a better place to live in, as a future war could, of course, only be started by them, stinks to high heaven &, in fact, promises a horrid future.

Thus, when the Japanese finally surrendered in August, the celebrations in the streets of Swansea did nothing to lift his spirits. 'We've had two VJ days', he wrote to Malcolm, '& I think there was much more noise than real joy.' In the aftermath of the war he could see only gloom. When Hutt was demobbed, Wittgenstein wrote to him wishing him 'lots of luck' – 'I really mean: strength to bear whatever comes.' He had, he told Hutt, been feeling unwell lately: 'partly because I'm having trouble with one of my kidneys, partly because whatever I read of the beastliness of the Allies in Germany & Japan makes me feel sick'.

In the context of reports of the chronic food shortages in Germany and Austria, and of the policy of the British army not to 'fraternize' with their conquered enemy, and – in the midst of this – of calls in the Press to *punish* the German people for the war, Wittgenstein was gratified to read in the *News Chronicle* an article by Victor Gollancz, calling for an end to 'self-righteousness in international affairs' and a determination to feed the German people: 'not because if we don't we ourselves may suffer, but simply because it is right to feed our starving neighbours'. After remarking on Gollancz's article to Rhees, he was lent Gollancz's earlier pamphlet, *What Buchenwald Really Means*. Writing as 'a Jew who believes in Christian ethics', Gollancz attacked the British Press for their reaction to the horrors of Buchenwald, and pointed out that it was wrong to hold *all* Germans responsible. He further attacked the whole concept of 'collective guilt' as a throwback to the Old Testament, from which the example of Christ ought to have liberated us.

Wittgenstein was powerfully struck by both the strengths and the weaknesses revealed by Gollancz in his call for a humane attitude towards the Germans. On 4 September he wrote to him praising him for his *News Chronicle* article. He was, he wrote, 'glad to see that someone, publicly and in a conspicuous place, called a devilry a devilry'. About the Buchenwald pamphlet, he told Gollancz:

> I am deeply in sympathy with your severe criticism (and it cannot be too severe) of the cruelty, meanness and vulgarity of the daily press and of the BBC. (Our cinema news reels are, if possible, more poisonous still.) It is because I strongly sympathise with your attitude to these evils that I think I ought to make what seems to me a serious criticism of your polemic against them.

Gollancz, he said, had weakened the impact of his criticism by embellishing it with subsidiary points, 'which, even if they are not weak and dubious, draw the reader's attention from the main issue, and make the polemic ineffectual'. If Gollancz wanted to be heard 'above the shouting of the daily press and the radio', he would do well to stick to the point:

> If you really want people to remove the dirt, don't talk to them about the philosophical issues of the value of life and happiness. This, if it does anything, will start academic chat.
> In writing about the wrong attitude of people towards the Buchenwald horrors, e.g., did you wish to convince only those who agree with you about the Old and New Testament? Even if they do, your lengthy quotations serve to sidetrack their attention from the one main point. If they don't – and an enormous number who might be seriously shaken by your argument do not – they will feel that all this rigmarole makes the whole article smell fishy. All the more so as they will not gladly give up their former views.

I will stop now. – If you ask me why, instead of criticising you, I don't write articles myself, I should answer that I lack the knowledge, the facility of expression and the time necessary for any decent and effective journalism. In fact, writing this letter of criticism to a man of your views and of your ability is the nearest approach to what is denied me, i.e., to write a good article myself.

The letter reveals Wittgenstein's sound appreciation of the art of polemic. The general outlines of his advice to Gollancz were repeated about a year later to Rush Rhees. Rhees had written an article in which he attacked Gilbert Ryle for the latter's enthusiastic review of Karl Popper's *The Open Society and its Enemies*, in which Popper tars Plato, Hegel and Marx with the same brush, accusing them all of being advocates of totalitarianism. Wittgenstein told Rhees he agreed with the tendency of his article, but criticized him for making too many gestures and not landing enough square blows:

Polemic, or the art of throwing eggs, is, as you well know, as highly skilled a job as, say, boxing . . . I'd love you to throw eggs at Ryle – but keep your face straight and throw them well! The difficulty is: not to make superfluous noises or gestures, which don't harm the other man but only yourself.

Gollancz, however, received Wittgenstein's advice with disdainful indifference. His reply (addressed to 'L. Wiltgenstein, Esq.') is brief and dismissive: 'Thank you for your letter, which I'm sure was very well meant.' Wittgenstein took the rebuff good-humouredly. 'Well, that's rich!' he said to Rhees with a smile, and threw Gollancz's note in the fire.

Despite his fears for the future of Europe, and his conviction that there would soon be another, even more horrible, war, Wittgenstein was able to spend the late summer of 1945 enjoying a holiday in Swansea. Or, at least, as he put it to Malcolm, 'enjoying my absence from Cambridge'.

'My book is gradually nearing its final form', he told Malcolm at the end of the summer:

. . . & if you're a good boy & come to Cambridge I'll let you read it. It'll probably disappoint you. And the truth is: it's pretty lousy. (Not that I could improve on it essentially if I tried for another 100 years.) This, however, doesn't worry me.

These last two sentences were not true; it did worry him that his book was not as good as he thought it ought to be, and he did think he could improve it. And it is for precisely these two reasons that it remained unpublished at the time of his death.

He dreaded going back to Cambridge to resume his professorial duties, and implored Malcolm to come to England soon, 'before I make up my mind to resign the absurd job of a prof. of philosophy. It is a kind of living death.'

The final version of what is now *Philosophical Investigations*, Part I, was prepared during the Michaelmas and Lent terms of 1945–6. From the typescript he had dictated during the summer he selected about 400 remarks to add to the work he had done in Swansea in 1944, and, after some rearrangement and renumbering, this produced the 693 numbered paragraphs of which the work now consists.

Thus, roughly speaking, the development of the book falls into three identifiable stages: paragraphs 1–188 constitute Part I of the 1938 version; paragraphs 189–421 were added in 1944; and paragraphs 421–693 form the extension added in 1945–6, which was in turn compiled from manuscripts dating from 1931–45.

This complicated patchwork is well described by Wittgenstein in his preface:

After several unsuccessful attempts to weld my results together into a whole, I realised that I should never succeed. The best that I could write would never be more than philosophical remarks; my thoughts were soon crippled if I tried to force them on in any single direction against their natural inclination. – And this was, of course, connected with the very nature of the investigation. For this compels us to travel over a wide field of thought criss-cross in every direction. – The philosophical remarks in this book are, as it were, a number of sketches of landscapes which were made in the course of these long and involved journeyings.

The same or almost the same points were always being approached afresh from different directions, and new sketches made. Very many of these were badly drawn or uncharacteristic, marked by all the defects of a weak draughtsman. And when they were rejected a number of tolerable ones were left, which now had to be arranged and sometimes cut down, so that if you looked at them you could get a picture of the landscape. Thus this book is really only an album.

Even now, there were sketches in this album that he was dissatisfied with, and he made no attempt to publish this final rearrangement. However, for the rest of his life he spoke of this typescript as 'my book', and went through it paragraph by paragraph with a number of his most trusted friends and students, so that when he died there would be at least a few people to whom his book was not totally unintelligible.

He was convinced his book would be fundamentally misunderstood – *especially* by academic philosophers – and this was undoubtedly another reason why the book remained unpublished in his lifetime. In a rewritten version of the preface he states: 'It is not without reluctance that I deliver this book to the public':

> It will fall into hands which are not for the most part those in which I like to imagine it. May it soon – this is what I wish for it – be completely forgotten by the philosophical journalists, and so be preserved for a better sort of reader.

Wittgenstein's hostility towards professional philosophy and his dislike of Cambridge remained constant throughout his academic career, but in the years of 'reconstruction in Europe' that followed the Second World War, they seemed to become fused with a kind of apocalyptic vision of the end of humanity. During the Easter vacation of 1946, he renewed the acquaintance of Karl Britton, previously a student of his, and now a lecturer in philosophy at Swansea University. One afternoon, during a long walk along the coast, Wittgenstein told Britton that he had become convinced that a new war was being planned, and that atomic weapons would put an end to everything: 'They mean to do it, they mean to do it.'

What links this apocalyptic anxiety with his hostility to academic philosophy is his detestation of the power of science in our age, which on the one hand encouraged the philosopher's 'craving for generality', and on the other produced the atomic bomb. In a curious sense, he even welcomed the bomb, if only the fear of it could do something to diminish the reverence with which society regarded scientific progress. At about the same time as his conversation with Britton, he wrote:

> The hysterical fear over the atom bomb now being experienced, or at any rate expressed, by the public almost suggests that at last something really salutary has been invented. The fright at least gives the impression of a really effective bitter medicine. I can't help thinking: if this didn't have something good about it the philistines wouldn't be making an outcry. But perhaps this too is a childish idea. Because really all I can mean is that the bomb offers a prospect of the end, the destruction, of an evil, – our disgusting soapy water science. And certainly that's not an unpleasant thought.

'The truly apocalyptic view of the world', he wrote, 'is that things do not repeat themselves.' The end might indeed come:

> It isn't absurd, e.g., to believe that the age of science and technology is the beginning of the end for humanity; that the idea of great progress is a delusion, along with the idea that the truth will ultimately be known; that there is nothing good or desirable about scientific knowledge and that mankind, in seeking it, is falling into a trap. It is by no means obvious that this is not how things are.

In either case, scientific progress would come to an end. But the most pessimistic view, for him, was one which foresaw the triumph of science and technology:

> Science and industry, and their progress, might turn out to be the most enduring thing in the modern world. Perhaps any speculation about a coming collapse of science and industry is, for the present and for a long time to come, nothing but a dream; perhaps science and industry, having caused infinite misery in the process, will unite the world – I mean condense it into a single unit, though one in which peace is the last thing that will find a home.
> Because science and industry do decide wars, or so it seems.

'The darkness of this time', therefore, is directly attributable to the worship of the false idol of science against which his own work had been directed since the early 1930s. Thus, his 'dream' of the coming collapse of science and industry was an anticipation of an age in which his type of thinking would be more generally accepted and understood. It is linked with his remark to Drury: 'My type of thinking is not wanted in this present age, I have to swim so strongly against the tide. Perhaps in a hundred years people will really want what I am writing.' And yet, if 'they' mean to do it, and the apocalyptic view is not absurd, then that time might never come. There never would be an age in which his type of thinking was wanted.

As Wittgenstein's political forebodings drew him closer to the Left, his identification of the worship of science as the greatest evil kept him at some distance from Marxism. Looking through Max Eastman's *Marxism: Is it Science?* (which he took from Rhees's bookshelves), he commented on Eastman's view that Marxism has to be made more scientific if it is to help revolution:

> In fact, nothing is more *conservative* than science. Science lays down railway tracks. And for scientists it is important that their work should move along those tracks.

He shared with the Communists a fierce dislike of the complacency of the British establishment, and he wanted to see some sort of revolution. But he wanted that revolution to be a rejection of the scientific *Weltanschauung* of our age, not an endorsement of it.

In any case, the extent to which he could identify himself with a party was limited by his conception of himself as a philosopher – one who in the ruthless search for truth would willingly abandon whatever 'pet notions' he had formed. At this time Rhees felt he ought to join the (Trotskyist) Revolutionary Communist Party, because, as he put it to Wittgenstein, 'I find more and more that I am in agreement with the chief points in their analysis and criticism of present society and with their objectives.' Wittgenstein was sympathetic, but tried to dissuade him on the grounds that his duties as a loyal party member would be incompatible with his duties as a philosopher. In doing philosophy, he insisted, you have got to be ready constantly to change the direction in which you are moving, and if you are thinking as a philosopher you cannot treat the ideas of Communism differently from others.

Ironically, at a time when his interest in political affairs was at its strongest, and his sympathies with the Left at their peak, he lost the opportunity to have discussions with the Marxist intellectual for whom he had the greatest respect. In May 1946 Piero Sraffa decided he no longer wished to have conversations with Wittgenstein, saying that he could no longer give his time and attention to the matters Wittgenstein wished to discuss. This came as a great blow to Wittgenstein. He pleaded with Sraffa to continue their weekly conversations, even if it meant staying away from philosophical subjects. 'I'll talk about anything', he told him. 'Yes', Sraffa replied, 'but in *your* way.'

Whether this was a contributory factor or not, throughout the summer term of 1946 Wittgenstein thought increasingly often of resigning his Chair and of leaving Cambridge. When he returned to Swansea for the summer vacation his dislike of both Cambridge and academic philosophy was at its peak. In Rhees's absence, Karl Britton had to face the fury of this distaste:

> One day in July . . . Wittgenstein rang me up and explained that his friend was away and that he wished me to take him out. However, he seemed, on the whole, very hostile. The journal *Mind* had just published two papers on 'Therapeutic Positivism' and (as I afterwards found out) this had much annoyed and upset him. With me he was angry too for going to the Joint Session of the Mind Association and the Aristotelian Society, the annual jamboree of philosophers: he took it as a sign of frivolity and of ulterior interests. He railed against professional philosophers, mourned the state of philosophy in England and asked: 'What can one man do alone?' When I told him that the next jamboree was to be held at Cambridge in 1947 and that I was to read a paper, he said: 'Very well, to me it is just as if you had told me that there will be bubonic plague in Cambridge next summer. I am very glad to know and I shall make sure to be in London.' (And so he was.)

Later that day Wittgenstein had tea at Britton's home. He was in a more genial mood, talking (in contrast to his dislike of London and Cambridge) of his liking for Swansea. He told Britton that he liked the North of England, too, recalling an occasion in Newcastle when he had asked the bus conductor where to get off for a certain cinema. The conductor at once told him that that particular cinema was showing a bad film, and he ought to go to another. This prompted a heated argument in the bus as to which film Wittgenstein ought to see and why. He liked that, he told Britton; it was the sort of thing that would have happened in Austria.

The final comparison is revealing, and perhaps partly accounts for the vehemence with which he, at this time, attacked what he called 'the disintegrating and putrefying English civilization'. Put simply: he was missing Vienna. He had not been there since before the *Anschluss*, and had had very little contact since then with his family and friends in Austria.

To be a professor was bad enough, but to be an English professor became, in the end, unbearable.

24
A CHANGE OF
ASPECT

Wittgenstein's pessimism about the fate of humanity was not caused by the catastrophic events that brought the Second World War to a close – as we have seen, it has a much longer history; but those events seemed to reinforce in him the certitude of a long-held conviction that mankind was headed for disaster. The mechanical means of killing people that had been employed, and the fearsome displays of technological might that had been witnessed – the fire-bombs at Dresden, the gas-ovens of the concentration camps, the atomic bombs unleashed on Japan – established powerfully and finally that 'science and industry do decide wars'. And this seemed further to convince him in his apocalyptic view that the end of mankind was the consequence of replacing the spirit with the machine, of turning away from God and placing our trust in scientific 'progress'.

His notebooks of the post-war years abound with reflections of this sort. A picture that intruded upon him, he wrote, was of our civiliz-ation, 'cheaply wrapped in cellophane, and isolated from everything great, from God, as it were'. The houses, cars and other trappings of our environment struck him as 'separating man from his origins, from what is lofty and eternal, etc'. It was as though life itself was coming to an end, suffocated by the trappings of our industrial age. And, of course, it was futile to expect to alter this course by pointing it out. Is this journey really necessary? One might ask the question, but it was hardly likely that, in response, mankind would say: 'On second thoughts, no.' Yet Wittgenstein continued in his work of undermining the way of thinking that, he thought, lay at the root of the whole

disaster. And in his disciples he had people who could continue this
work after his death. Not that he had any wish to found a school, or
anything of that sort. 'I am by no means sure', he wrote, 'that I
should prefer a continuation of my work by others to a change in the
way people live which would make all these questions superfluous.'

The problem could have only an existential, never a theoretical,
solution. What was required was a change of spirit: 'Wisdom is cold
and to that extent stupid. (Faith on the other hand is a passion.)' To
breathe again, it was no use merely thinking correctly; one had to
act – to, as it were, rip the cellophane away and reveal the living world
behind it. As he put it: ' "Wisdom is grey". Life on the other hand and
religion are full of colour.' The passion of religious faith was the only
thing capable of overcoming the deadness of theory:

> I believe that one of the things Christianity says is that sound
> doctrines are all useless. That you have to change your *life*. (Or the
> *direction* of your life.)
>
> It says that wisdom is all cold; and that you can no more use it for
> setting your life to rights than you can forge iron when it is *cold*.
>
> The point is that a sound doctrine need not *take hold* of you; you
> can follow it as you would a doctor's prescription. – But here you
> need something to move you and turn you in a new direction. –
> (I.e. this is how I understand it.) Once you have been turned round,
> you must *stay* turned round.
>
> Wisdom is passionless. But faith by contrast is what Kierkegaard
> calls a *passion*.

What Russell had long ago mistakenly identified with his own
theoretical passion was, in fact, the very repudiation of it: Wittgenstein's was a devoutly anti-theoretical passion. Russell's later remark
that Wittgenstein liked mysticism for its power to stop him thinking,
and his jibe that Wittgenstein had adopted a doctrine to make serious
thinking unnecessary, are in fact much nearer the mark, if we equate
'serious thinking' with the attempts to formulate a true theory.

Wittgenstein's ideal of '*primordial* life, wild life striving to erupt into
the open' – even though he rarely felt himself to live up to it – is a key
to understanding both the purpose of his work and the direction of his
life. In so far as he felt himself to be too theoretical, too 'wise', he felt
deadened. The need for passion, for religion, was not just something

he saw in the world around him; it was something he felt in himself. He felt himself to share exactly the faults characteristic of our age, and to need the same remedy: faith and love. And just as our age finds belief in God impossible, so he too found that he could not pray: 'it's as though my knees were stiff. I am afraid of dissolution (of my own dissolution), should I become soft.'

In love, too, though he felt a deep need for it, he often felt himself incapable, frightened. And, of course, frightened of its being taken away from him, all too conscious of its possible impermanence and of its uncertainty. In 1946 – and it probably came as some relief to find that he was, after all, still capable of loving someone – he fell in love with Ben Richards, an undergraduate student of medicine at Cambridge. Richards had what one by now perceives as the qualities that warmed Wittgenstein's heart: he was extraordinarily gentle, a little timid, perhaps even docile, but extremely kind, considerate and sensitive.

In his mood of deep despair after the Second World War, Wittgenstein found at least some solace in his love for Ben – even if, at times, it seemed that it offered this only to provide him with something else to worry about. 'I am very sad, very often sad', he wrote on 8 August 1946. 'I feel as though my life is now coming to an end':

> The *only* thing that my love for B. has done for me is this: it has driven the other small worries associated with my position and my work into the background.

The anxieties of being in love were perhaps the hardest to bear. And Ben was very young – nearly forty years younger than Wittgenstein. Wasn't it easy to imagine, he wrote on 12 August, that Ben would completely grow out of his love for him, 'just as a boy no longer remembers what he had felt as a young child'? And so, a few days later, when he was waiting impatiently for a letter from Ben, nothing struck him as more probable, indeed more natural, than that Ben had forsaken him. And yet, every morning, when he again found no letter from Ben, it seemed strange to him: 'I feel as though there was something I have not yet *realised*; as though I had to find some standpoint from which to see the truth more clearly.'

These accounts of the almost unbearable anguish Wittgenstein felt while waiting for a letter from his loved one strike a familiar chord. It

492   WITTGENSTEIN: THE DUTY OF GENIUS

was the same with Pinsent, and with Skinner, and even with Kirk. Yet in his love for Ben, there is a new note, a break with the solipsism of the past. On 14 August, he wrote – as though it had struck him for the first time:

It is the mark of a *true* love that one thinks of what the *other* person suffers. For he suffers too, is also a poor devil.

Perhaps the fly had at last found its way out of the fly-bottle. And, furthermore, discovered that life was not necessarily any better outside it. To expose oneself to the elements could even be dangerous. 'I feel', he wrote on 18 August, 'that my mental health is hanging on a thin thread':

It is of course the worry and anxiety about B. that have so worn me out. And yet that would not be the case if I were not so easily set aflame, 'highly inflammable'.

In former times, he reflected, people went into monasteries: 'Were they stupid or insensitive people? – Well, if people like that found they needed to take such measures in order to be able to go on living, the problem cannot have been an easy one!'

But if love, whether human or divine, was the solution to the problem, it was not one that could be taken; it had to be bestowed as a gift. Thus, to combat his anxieties about other philosophers publishing ideas derived from him, he would remind himself that his work was worthwhile only 'if a light shines on it from above':

And if that happens – why should I concern myself that the fruits of my labours should be stolen? If what I am writing really has some value, how could anyone steal the value from me? And if the light from above is lacking, I can't in any case be more than clever.

And in connection with his love for Ben, he wrote:

'For our desires conceal from us even what we desire. Blessings come from above in their own guises etc.' I say that to myself whenever I receive the love of B. For I well know that it is a great and rare gift; I know too that it is a rare jewel – and also that it is not entirely of the sort of which I had dreamed.

Of course, there were other reasons to get out of Cambridge. On the very day that he arrived back there from Swansea, on 30 September, Wittgenstein wrote:

> Everything about the place repels me. The stiffness, the artificiality, the self-satisfaction of the people. The university atmosphere nauseates me.

To Fouracre he wrote: 'What I miss most is someone I can talk nonsense to by the yard.' Fouracre was the only person at Guy's with whom he had maintained contact. In 1943, shortly after he had married, Fouracre had joined the army, and was sent to the Far East. He did not return home until February 1947. While he was away he was deeply missed by Wittgenstein, who wrote to him with remarkable frequency, urging him to: 'come home from that bl . . . Sumatra or wherever you are'. Not all these letters have survived, but the affection which Wittgenstein held for Fouracre is evident from those that have, including a series of six written in as many months – from August to December 1946 – every one of which ends with the exclamation: 'God bless you!' and includes a request for Fouracre to come home quickly.

The first of these six is dated August 1946, and mentions some heather which Wittgenstein picked for Fouracre and sent to him in the Far East. It describes the 'lousy' situation in Europe and ends: 'So when you'll come back you won't find anything marvellous. But I hope you'll come soon nevertheless. It'll save me a lot of trouble picking flowers & posting them to Sumatra!'

In their lightness of tone, and the preponderance in them of the kind of 'nonsense' that Wittgenstein enjoyed, these letters are reminiscent of those to Pattisson. There is hardly one of them that does not contain a joke or a playful remark:

> Sorry you don't get post regularly, & particularly my letters which are full of content. I mean, paper, ink, & air. – The mosquitos don't bite you because you're so nice – because you aren't – but because you're so bl . . . awful & its the blood they want. – I hope that the Dutch will soon take over for food & send you back! [7.10.46]

Why in hell you don't get my letters beats me! Do you think the Censor keeps them as souvenirs because they are so marvellous? I shouldn't be surprised! – Well, for God's sake finish your tours to South Sumatra & to Central Sumatra & take a plane (I don't mean the sort a joiner uses) & get home. [21.10.46]

I'm feeling far better now than I did at the beginning of term. I then felt very lousy & had queer attacks of exhaustion. Finally in despair I went to see a physician here in Cambridge . . . Well, he advised me this & that & in the end he mentioned that I might try a Vitamin B preparation . . . So, I took Vit. B. tablets without the slightest hope that they'd help, & to my great surprise they did help. I'm taking them regularly now & I haven't had any more attacks of exhaustion. In fact, when I'm all tanked up with Vit. B. I get so witty that the jokes get jammed & can't come out. Isn't that terrible? [9.11.46]

The kind of simple, uncomplicated, relationship he had with Fouracre remained for him a model of what was possible outside academic life. In his letter of 21 October he wrote:

I'm thinking every day of retiring from my job & taking on something else which might bring me into a more human contact with my fellow men. But what I'll do God Knows! for I'm already a pretty old codger.

The letter ends with the familiar refrain: 'I hope you'll come back from that bl . . . Sumatra.'

'Should I carry on teaching?' he asked himself at the beginning of November, after a meeting of the Moral Science Club, disgusted by the vanity and stupidity of his own performance there. The 'atmosphere', he wrote, was 'wretched'.

His dominance of these meetings was noted with disapproval by other philosophers at Cambridge (Broad and Russell, in particular), and by many of the visiting lecturers. On 26 October a clash took place that has since become famous, when Karl Popper addressed the club on the question: 'Are there Philosophical Problems?' Popper's chosen subject, and his manner of addressing it, was deliberately designed to provoke Wittgenstein (whom Popper thought denied the existence of philosophical problems). And provoke him it did, although exactly in what way has become lost in the mists of legend. Stories have been told that have Popper and Wittgenstein coming to blows with one another, each armed with a poker. In his autobiography Popper scotches this rumour, only to replace it with another tale, the details of which have in turn been challenged by some of those who were present at the time. According to Popper, he and Wittgenstein engaged in an animated exchange on the existence or otherwise of philosophical problems, and he gave as an example the question of the validity of moral rules. Wittgenstein, who had all the while been playing with a poker, then stood up, poker in hand, and demanded an example of a moral rule. 'Not to threaten visiting lecturers with pokers', Popper replied, whereupon Wittgenstein stormed out of the room. Russell was present at the meeting, and made it known that his sympathies were with Popper. An alternative account of the argument has Popper and Wittgenstein each accusing the other of confusing the issue, until Wittgenstein exasperatedly stormed out, with Russell calling after him: 'Wittgenstein, it is you who are creating all the confusion.'

Whatever happened, it did nothing to affect the fervent allegiance to Wittgenstein that was given by most of the young Cambridge philosophers at this time. Gilbert Ryle writes that on his occasional visits to the Moral Science Club he was disturbed to find that: 'veneration for Wittgenstein was so incontinent that mentions, for example, my mentions, of any other philosopher were greeted with jeers':

This contempt for thoughts other than Wittgenstein's seemed to me pedagogically disastrous for the students and unhealthy for Wittgenstein himself. It made me resolve, not indeed to be a philosophical polyglot, but to avoid being a monoglot; and most of all to avoid being one monoglot's echo, even though he was a genius and a friend.

Wittgenstein, Ryle thought, 'not only properly distinguished philosophical from exegetic problems but also, less properly, gave the impressions:

. . . first that he himself was proud not to have studied other philosophers – which he had done, though not much – and second, that he thought that people who did study them were academic and therefore unauthentic philosophers.

To a certain extent Ryle is writing here as an Oxford man (his criticisms are given in the context of extolling the virtues of the Oxford tutorial system), but what he says about Wittgenstein's attitude towards reading the great works of the past is perfectly true. 'As little philosophy as I have read', Wittgenstein wrote, 'I have certainly not read too little, *rather too much*. I see that whenever I read a philosophical book: it doesn't improve my thoughts at all, it makes them worse.'

This attitude would never have been tolerated at Oxford, where respect for things past is in general much stronger than at Cambridge, and where a training in philosophy is inseparable from a reading of the great works in the subject. It is almost inconceivable that a man who claimed proudly never to have read a word of Aristotle would have been given any tutorial responsibilities at all at Oxford, let alone be allowed to preside over the affairs of the department. From Wittgenstein's point of view, Oxford was a 'philosophical desert'.

The only time he is known to have addressed an audience of Oxford philosophers was in May 1947, when he accepted an invitation to speak to the Jowett Society. He was to reply to a paper presented by Oscar Wood, the undergraduate secretary of the society, on Descartes' '*Cogito, ergo sum*'. The meeting was held in Magdalen College and was unusually well attended. Mary Warnock, a contemporary of Wood's, noted in her diary: 'Practically every philosopher I'd ever seen was there.' Among the more notable philosophers present were Gilbert Ryle, J. O. Urmson, Isaiah Berlin and H. A. Prichard. In his reply to Wood's paper Wittgenstein ignored altogether the question of whether Descartes' argument was valid, and concentrated instead on bringing his own philosophical method to bear on the problem raised. To established Oxford orthodoxy, in the person of H. A. Prichard, this was an unwelcome novelty:

> *Wittgenstein*: If a man says to me, looking at the sky, 'I think it will rain, therefore I exist,' I do not understand him.
> *Prichard:* That's all very fine; what we want to know is: is the *cogito* valid or not?

Prichard – described by Mary Warnock in her diary as: 'extremely old and deaf with a terrible cough. Totally tactless' – several times interrupted Wittgenstein in an effort to get him to address the question of whether Descartes' *cogito* was a valid inference or not. And every time he did so, Wittgenstein avoided the question, implying that it was unimportant. What Descartes was concerned with, Prichard retorted, was far more important than any problem that Wittgenstein had discussed that evening. He then, in Mary Warnock's words, 'shuffled out in disgust'. He died about a week later.

Though the majority feeling at the meeting was that Pritchard had been unbearably rude, there was also a certain degree of sympathy with his objections, and a feeling, too, that Wittgenstein had treated Wood with unjustifiable disdain in not addressing his reply to the substance of Wood's paper. Wittgenstein's ahistorical, existential method of philosophizing could, in the context of respect for the great philosophers engendered at Oxford, readily be taken for arrogance.

The person indirectly responsible, as Wood's intermediary, for bringing Wittgenstein to Oxford on this occasion was Elizabeth Anscombe. Anscombe had been an undergraduate at St Hugh's, Oxford, and had come to Cambridge as a postgraduate student in 1942, when she began attending Wittgenstein's lectures. When Wittgenstein resumed lecturing in 1944, she was one of his most enthusiastic students. For her, Wittgenstein's therapeutic method was felt as a tremendous liberation, a 'medicine' that succeeded, where more theoretical methods had failed, in freeing her from philosophical confusion. 'For years', she writes, 'I would spend time, in cafés, for example, staring at objects saying to myself: "I see a packet. But what do I really see? How can I say that I see here anything more than a yellow expanse?"':

I always hated phenomenalism and felt trapped by it. I couldn't see my way out of it but I didn't believe it. It was no good pointing to difficulties about it, things which Russell found wrong with it, for example. The strength, the central nerve of it remained alive and raged achingly. It was only in Wittgenstein's classes in 1944 that I saw the nerve being extracted, the central thought 'I have got this, and I define "yellow" (say) as this' being effectively attacked.

In 1946–7 she was again in Oxford, having taken up a research fellowship at Somerville College, but she continued to go to Cambridge once a week to attend tutorials with Wittgenstein in the company of another student, W. A. Hijab. These tutorials, at the request of both Hijab and Anscombe, dealt with issues in the philosophy of religion. By the end of the year she had become one of Wittgenstein's closest friends and one of his most trusted students, an exception to his general dislike of academic women and especially of female philosophers. She became, in fact, an honorary male, addressed by him affectionately as 'old man'. 'Thank God we've got rid of the women!' he once said to her at a lecture, on finding, to his delight, that no (other) female students were in attendance.

Anscombe was, at this time, an enthusiastic admirer of Kafka, and in an effort to share her enthusiasm she lent Wittgenstein some of his novels to read. 'This man', said Wittgenstein, returning them, 'gives himself a great deal of trouble not writing about his trouble.' He recommended, by comparison, Weininger's *The Four Last Things* and *Sex and Character*. Weininger, he said, whatever his faults, was a man who really did write about his trouble.

This directness – this determination to strip away all inessentials and all pretence, to 'extract the root' – could be unsettling as well as inspiring, and Anscombe was fairly rare in finding it liberating. Iris Murdoch, who attended a few of Wittgenstein's last series of lectures, found both him and his setting 'very unnerving':

> His extraordinary directness of approach and the absence of any sort of paraphernalia were the things that unnerved people . . . with most people, you meet them in a framework, and there are certain conventions about how you talk to them and so on. There isn't a naked confrontation of personalities. But Wittgenstein always imposed this confrontation on all his relationships. I met him only twice and I didn't know him well and perhaps that's why I always thought of him, as a person, with awe and alarm.

The student for whom Wittgenstein had the greatest respect during this period was Georg Kreisel. Originally from Graz, Kreisel came to Trinity in 1942 as an undergraduate mathematician, and attended the lectures on the philosophy of mathematics that Wittgenstein gave during the war. In 1944 – when Kreisel was still only twenty-one – Wittgenstein shocked Rhees by declaring Kreisel to be the most able philosopher he had ever met who was also a mathematician. 'More able than Ramsey?' Rhees asked. 'Ramsey?!' replied Wittgenstein. 'Ramsey was a mathematician!'

Although he had not written on the philosophy of mathematics for over two years, during 1946 and 1947 Wittgenstein had regular discussions with Kreisel on the subject. Unusually, the tenor of these discussions was set by Kreisel rather than Wittgenstein, and when Wittgenstein's remarks on mathematics were published after his death, Kreisel expressed astonishment at their tendency. After reading *Remarks on the Foundations of Mathematics*, Kreisel wrote, he realized that the topics raised in the discussions he had had with Wittgenstein: 'were far from the centre of his interest though he never let me suspect it'.

Stimulated by his discussions with Kreisel, Wittgenstein, in his last year at Cambridge, added regular seminars on the philosophy of mathematics to his weekly classes on the philosophy of psychology. Kreisel, however, remembers the discussions as being of more value than the seminars. Wittgenstein's public performances, he said, he found 'tense and often incoherent'.

Kreisel was not the stuff of which disciples are made, and after leaving Cambridge he studied with Kurt Gödel and became a leading figure in the very branch of mathematics against which Wittgenstein's work is an assault: the 'cancerous growth' of mathematical logic. 'Wittgenstein's views on mathematical logic are not worth much', he later wrote, 'because he knew very little and what he knew was confined to the Frege–Russell line of goods.' When the *Blue and Brown Books* were published, his dismissal was couched in still stronger, perhaps even bitter, terms. 'As an introduction to the significant problems of traditional philosophy', he wrote in his review, 'the books are deplorable':

This is largely based on a personal reaction. I believe that early contact with Wittgenstein's outlook has hindered rather than helped me to establish a fruitful perspective on philosophy as a discipline in its own right.

Wittgenstein himself often felt that he had a bad influence on his students. 'The only seed I am likely to sow', he said, 'is a certain jargon.' People imitated his gestures, adopted his expressions, even wrote philosophy in a way that made use of his techniques – all, it seems, without understanding the point of his work.

He tried again and again to make this point clear. His last series of lectures began with an emphatic and unambiguous statement of their purpose: that of resolving the confusions to which the notion of psychology as the 'science of mental phenomena' gives rise:

> These lectures are on the philosophy of psychology. And it may seem odd that we should be going to discuss matters arising out of, and occurring in a science, seeing that we are not going to do the science of Psychology and we have no particular information about the sort of things that are found when the science is done. But there are questions, puzzles that naturally suggest themselves when we look at what psychologists may say, and what non-psychologists (and we) say.
>
> Psychology is often defined as the science of Mental Phenomena. This is a little queer, as we shall see: contrast it with physics as the science of physical phenomena. It is the word 'phenomena' which may be troublesome. We get the idea: on the one hand you have phenomena of one kind which do certain things, on the other, phenomena of another kind which do other things: so how do the two sorts of things compare? But perhaps it makes no sense to say that both do the sort of things the other does. 'The science of mental phenomena' – by this we mean what everybody means, namely, the science that deals with thinking, deciding, wishing, desiring, wondering . . . And an old puzzle comes up. The psychologist when he finds his correlations finds them by watching people doing things like screwing up their noses, getting rises in blood pressure, looking anxious, accepting this after S seconds, reflecting that after S plus 3 seconds, writing down 'No' on a piece of paper, and so on. So where is the science of mental phenomena? Answer: You observe your own mental happenings. How? By introspection. But if you observe, i.e., if you go about to observe your own mental happenings you alter them and create new ones: and the whole point of observing is that you should not do this – observing is supposed to be just the thing that avoids this. Then the science of mental phenomena has this puzzle: I can't observe the mental phenomena of others and I can't observe my own, in the proper sense of 'observe'. So where are we?

His answer to this last question is: in a fog, a set of confusions that cannot be resolved by the accumulation of more data – either by introspection or by behavioural analysis. Nor can they be resolved by a *theory* of thinking. The only thing capable of clearing the fog is a conceptual investigation, an analysis of the use of words like 'intention', 'willing', 'hope' etc., which shows that these words gain their meaning from a form of life, a 'language-game', quite different from that of describing and explaining physical phenomena.

The lectures for the first two terms covered roughly the same ground as that covered in the last third of *Investigations*, Part I: the question 'What is thinking?', the analysis of 'mental phenomena' and the investigation of particular psychological concepts such as 'intention', 'willing', 'understanding' and 'meaning'.

Wittgenstein had by now a good appreciation of the ways in which his approach to philosophical problems was liable to be misunderstood, and he devoted much time in these lectures to an attempt to describe his philosophical method. In addition, he gave a talk to the Moral Science Club on: 'what I believe philosophy is, or what the method of philosophy is' (as he put it in a letter to Moore asking him to attend). One common cause of confusion was that, though he began with a question ostensibly about a *phenomenon* ('What is thinking?'), he ended up with an investigation into the way we use *words* (like 'thinking').

In his second lecture he summed up the unease that many people feel about this procedure when he summarized what had been said in the previous session:

> Now let us go back to last day. You must remember I suggested (i) we want analysis. This wouldn't do unless it meant (ii) we want the definition of thinking. And then I made a fishy step. I suggested: Perhaps we really want the use of 'thinking'. 'But', you say, 'clearly, we don't want to know about the "use of words". And, in a sense, we clearly don't.

This is, we don't want to know about the use of words for its own sake. The point of describing the (real and imagined) use of words was to loosen the hold of the confused way of looking at things that is the product of the philosopher's 'impoverished diet' of examples:

> What I give is the morphology of the use of an expression. I show that it has kinds of uses of which you had not dreamed. In

philosophy one feels forced to look at a concept in a certain way. What I do is suggest, or even invent, other ways of looking at it. I suggest possibilities of which you had not previously thought. You thought that there was one possibility, or only two at most. But I made you think of others. Furthermore, I made you see that it was absurd to expect the concept to conform to those narrow possibilities. Thus your mental cramp is relieved, and you are free to look around the field of use of the expression and to describe the different kinds of uses of it.

Another problem with this method was that, in providing a richer diet of examples, Wittgenstein was in danger of leading his students through the trees without giving them a glimpse of the wood. As two of these students, D. A. T. Gasking and A. C. Jackson, recall, the difficulty in following the lectures: 'arose from the fact that it was hard to see where all this rather repetitive concrete detailed talk was leading to – how the examples were inter-connected and how all this bore on the problems which one was accustomed to put oneself in abstract terms'.

This problem, too, Wittgenstein was aware of. 'I am showing my pupils details of an immense landscape', he wrote, 'which they cannot possibly know their way around.' In his lectures he elaborated on the analogy:

In teaching you philosophy I'm like a guide showing you how to find your way round London. I have to take you through the city from north to south, from east to west, from Euston to the embankment and from Piccadilly to the Marble Arch. After I have taken you many journeys through the city, in all sorts of directions, we shall have passed through any given street a number of times – each time traversing the street as part of a different journey. At the end of this you will know London; you will be able to find your way about like a born Londoner. Of course, a good guide will take you through the more important streets more often than he takes you down side streets; a bad guide will do the opposite. In philosophy I'm a rather bad guide.

In his writing, too, Wittgenstein was concerned that he might be spending too much time traversing side streets. He was, he said, a long way from knowing 'what I do and don't need to discuss' in the book:

I still keep getting entangled in details without knowing whether I ought to be talking about such things at all; and I have the impression that I may be inspecting a large area only eventually to exclude it from consideration.

Although he referred to the typescript he had prepared the previous year as 'my book', he was deeply dissatisfied with it, particularly with the last third of it – the analysis of psychological concepts that had largely been drawn from earlier manuscripts. Nevertheless, one afternoon a week he met with Norman Malcolm (who was in Cambridge during Wittgenstein's last year, on a Guggenheim Fellowship), to discuss the book. He lent Malcolm a copy of the typescript with the idea that they should read it through together, paragraph by paragraph. The procedure, as Malcolm recalls it, was this:

Starting at the beginning of the work, Wittgenstein first read a sentence aloud in German, then translated it into English, then made some remarks to me about the meaning of it. He then went on to the next sentence; and so on. At the following meeting he started at the place where we had last stopped.

'The reason I am doing this', Wittgenstein explained, 'is so there will be at least one person who will understand my book when it is published.' This is slightly odd, in the sense that he had at this time no intention of publishing this typescript, and was already working on a reformulation of its final section. Contemporaneous with his discussions with Malcolm is a series of manuscript volumes from which he hoped to produce a more satisfactory presentation of his investigations into psychological concepts. Not that any time was wasted, for the style of their meetings had changed before they reached the last section of the book. Wittgenstein's form of 'discussion' proved to be too rigidly exegetical for Malcolm's taste; he wanted to discuss philosophical problems that were currently puzzling *him*. And so Wittgenstein gradually relaxed the procedure.

During the Michaelmas term of 1946, Wittgenstein's love for Ben Richards provided him with moments of happiness and prolonged periods of torment. 'All is happiness', he wrote on 8 October. 'I could not write like this now if I had not spent the last 2 weeks with B. And I

could not have spent them as I did if illness or some accident had
intervened.'

But the happiness was fragile — or, at least, he felt it to be so. 'In love
I have too little *faith* and too little *courage*', he wrote on 22 October:

> But I am easily hurt and afraid of being hurt, and to protect oneself
> in *this* way is the death of all love. For real love one needs *courage*.
> But this means one must also have the courage to make the break
> and renounce [one's love], in other words to endure a mortal
> wound. But I can only hope to be spared the worst.

'I do not have the courage or the strength and clarity to look the facts
of my life straight in the face', he wrote a few days later. One of these
facts, he thought, was that: 'B. has for me a *pre*-love [in German there
is a pun here: *Vorliebe* means a liking, a preference], something that can
not last':

> How it will fade I don't know of course. Nor do I know how some
> part of it might be preserved, alive, not pressed between the leaves
> of a book as a memento.

He felt sure that he would lose Ben, and that conviction made it
painful to carry on in the affair. It presented a 'frightful difficulty of my
life': 'I do not know whether and how I can bear to continue *this*
relationship with *this* prospect.'

Neither, however, could he bear the thought of ending the relationship: 'Whenever I imagine myself having made the break, the
loneliness terrifies me.' And in any case, was it not a great and
wonderful gift from the heavens, which it would be almost blasphem-
ous to throw away? The pain and suffering of either continuing or
ending the affair seemed more than he could possibly endure.

But, he insisted the following day: 'love is a *joy*. Perhaps a joy mixed
with pain, but a joy nevertheless.' And if it wasn't a joy, then it wasn't
love. 'In love I have to be able to rest secure.' As it was, his doubts
would give him no rest. That Ben was warm-hearted, he did not
doubt. 'But can you reject a warm heart?' The question immediately
prompted the central doubt: 'is it a heart that beats warmly for *me*?' He
quotes in English (and, therefore, presumably from Ben) the saying:
'I'll rather do anything than to hurt the soul of friendship', and

continues in English (but this time surely in his own words): 'I must know: he won't hurt *our friendship*.' Having fallen for Ben, he demanded, not just friendship, not just fondness, but love:

A person cannot come out of his skin. I cannot give up a demand that is anchored deep inside me, in my whole life. For *love* is bound up with nature; and if I became unnatural, the love would have to end. – Can I say: 'I will be reasonable and no longer demand it?' . . . I can say: Let him do as he pleases, – it will be different some day – *Love*, that is the pearl of great price that one holds to one's heart, that one would exchange for *nothing*, that one prizes above all else.* In fact it *shows* – if one has it – what great value *is*. One learns what it *means* to single out a precious metal from all others.

'The frightening thing is the uncertainty.' And in this uncertainty Wittgenstein's imagination tormented him with all manner of frightful possibilities. 'Trust in God', he told himself. But the whole point was that he was unable to trust in anything:

From where I am to a trust in God is a *long* way. Joyous hope and fear are close cousins. I can't have the one without its bordering on the other.

And there was, too, a doubt as to whether he had any right to fall in love. In doing so, was he not being unfaithful to the memory of Francis? 'Ask yourself this question', he wrote on 10 November:

. . . when you die who will mourn for you; and *how deep* will their mourning be? Who mourns for F., how deeply do I – who have more reason to mourn than anyone – mourn for him? Did he not deserve that someone should mourn him their whole life long? If anyone did, it was he.

Francis, however, was in God's hands: 'Here one would like to say: God will take care of him and give him what a bad person denies him.'

---

* A reference to Matthew 13:45–6: 'the Kingdom of heaven is like unto a merchant man, seeking goodly pearls, who, when he had found one pearl of great price went and sold all that he had, and bought it.' I'm grateful to Dr David McLintock for drawing my attention to this allusion.

His own life, though, was entirely in his own hands. An isolated phrase two days later simply notes: 'The fundamental insecurity of life.' The foundations might at any moment give way. 'Don't be too cowardly to put a person's friendship to the test', he urged. He had to know whether his relationship with Ben would stand up to the pressure put upon it: 'The walking-stick that looks pretty so long as one carries it, but bends as soon as you rest your weight upon it, is worth nothing.'

Better, surely, to walk without a stick than use one that could not be relied upon:

> Can you not be cheerful even without his love? Do you *have* to sink into despondency without this love? Can you not live without this prop? For that is the question: can you *not* walk upright without leaning on this staff? Or is it only that you cannot *resolve* to give it up. Or is it both? – You *mustn't* go on expecting letters that don't arrive.

In so far as it was used as a prop, the relationship was not worthy: 'It is not love that draws me to this prop, but the fact that I cannot stand securely on my own two feet alone.'

Without Ben, certainly, his life would be more lonely and miserable. But why not suffer? After all: 'Some men are ill their whole lives and the only happiness they know is that which comes from a few painless hours following a long period of intense suffering (a blessed sigh of relief)':

> Is it so unheard of for a person to suffer, e.g., that an elderly person is tired and lonely – yes even, that he becomes half-crazy?

Exhaustion, loneliness, madness – these were his lot, and he had to accept them: 'Only nothing theatrical. Of that you must guard against.'

The hardest feat was to love with hope, and not to despair if those hopes were not fulfilled: 'The belief in a benevolent father is actually the expression of just this life.'

To live like that would be a real solution, an achievement against which his philosophical work would pale into insignificance: 'What good does all my talent do me, if, at heart, I am unhappy? What help is it to me to solve philosophical problems, if I cannot settle the chief, most important thing?' And what real use were his lectures?

> My lectures are going well, they will never go better. But what effect do they leave behind? Am I helping anyone? Certainly no *more* than if I were a great actor playing out tragic roles for them. What they learn is not worth learning; and the personal impression I make does not serve them with anything. That's true for all of them, with, perhaps, one or two exceptions.

During the summer term of 1947 Wittgenstein resolved to give up lecturing. He told Georg von Wright that he would resign his professorship, and that, when he did, he would like to see von Wright as his successor.

The lectures that Wittgenstein gave in his last term are of particular interest, because they introduce the issues that were to preoccupy him for the next two years, and which found their final expression in the typescript that now forms Part II of *Philosophical Investigations*. It was in these lectures that he first introduced the famous ambiguous figure of the duck–rabbit:

Suppose I show it to a child. It says 'It's a duck' and then suddenly 'Oh, it's a rabbit.' So it recognises it as a rabbit. – This is an experience of recognition. So if you see me in the street and say 'Ah, Wittgenstein.' But you haven't an experience of recognition all the time. – The experience only comes at the moment of change from duck to rabbit and back. In between, the aspect is as it were dispositional.

The point about the figure is that it can be seen under more than one aspect: the same drawing can be seen as a duck and as a rabbit. And it is this phenomenon of *seeing-as* that interested Wittgenstein. In describing this sort of phenomenon, there is a great temptation to talk of psychological states as if they were objects of some kind. For example, we might say that when we see it now as a duck, now as a rabbit, the external figure – the drawing – has not changed; what has changed is our internal picture – our sense-datum. And if this idea were generalized, it would lead to the very theory of sensory experience that is the target of Wittgenstein's philosophy of psychology – the phenomenalist notion that the objects of our immediate experience are the private, shadowy entities that empiricists call sense-data. It is for fear of this kind of generalization that one of the first points Wittgenstein makes about aspect-seeing – in the lecture quoted above and in the *Investigations* – is that it is not typical; we do not see everything as something:

> It would have made as little sense for me to say 'Now I am seeing it as . . .' as to say at the sight of a knife and fork 'Now I am seeing this as a knife and fork.'

But although the experience of seeing-as is not typical of all perception, it is of particular importance to Wittgenstein, and not only because of the dangers of phenomenalism. It could be said of his philosophical method that its aim is to change the aspect under which certain things are seen – for example, to see a mathematical proof not as a sequence of propositions but as a picture, to see a mathematical formula not as a proposition but as a rule, to see first-person reports of psychological states ('I am in pain' etc.) not as descriptions but as expressions, and so on. The 'understanding that consists in seeing connections', one might say, is the understanding that results from a change of aspect.

As he acknowledges in the *Investigations*, Wittgenstein took the duck–rabbit figure from Joseph Jastrow's *Fact and Fable in Psychology* (1900), but his discussion of aspect-seeing owes far more to Wolfgang Köhler than it does to Jastrow. It is Köhler's *Gestalt Psychology* (1929), and especially the chapter on 'Sensory Organization', that Wittgenstein has in mind in much of his discussion. Many of the lectures began with Wittgenstein reading a short passage from the book.

To understand Wittgenstein's interest in Köhler, we have, I think, to understand their common inheritance from Goethe. For both Köhler and Wittgenstein the word 'Gestalt' had connotations of a way of understanding that had its origins in Goethe's morphological studies (of colour, plants and animals). And both, in very different ways, used this Goethean conception as a central plank in their thinking.

The German word 'Gestalt' usually means 'shape' or 'form'. Köhler, however, following Goethe, used it to mean something quite different:

> In the German language – at least since the time of Goethe, and especially in his own papers on natural science – the noun 'gestalt' has two meanings: besides the connotation of 'shape' or 'form' as a property of things, it has the meaning of a concrete individual and characteristic entity, existing as something detached and having a shape or form as one of its attributes. Following this tradition, in gestalttheorie the word 'gestalt' means any segregated whole.

This notion of a 'segregated whole', or, as Köhler often puts it, an 'organized whole', forms the basis of Köhler's anti-behaviourist psychology. As against the behaviourist's mechanical model of stimulus-response, Köhler uses what he calls a 'dynamic' model of human behaviour which emphasizes the active role of organization in perception. Our perceptions, says Köhler, are not of discrete stimuli but of organized Gestalten: we do not, for example, see three dots on a page; we form them into a triangle and see them as a whole, a Gestalt.

Köhler's programme for a 'dynamic' understanding of human psychology has a close parallel with Goethe's programme for a 'dynamic' understanding of nature. Just as Köhler is opposed to the mechanism implicit in behaviourism, so Goethe began his scientific studies in response to a desire to see an alternative to the mechanistic Newtonian science of his day.

Goethe's first venture in the morphological understanding of natural forms was his study of plants. His idea – developed on his 'Italian Journey' – was that plant-life could be studied systematically (but non-mechanically) if all plants could be seen under the aspect of a single *Gestalt*. For each type of natural phenomenon – for example, plants and animals – there was to be a single form, the *Urphänomen*, of which all instances of that type could be seen as metamorphoses. In the case of plants, this *Urphänomen* would be the *Urpflanze* (the 'original plant').

In Goethe's work, however, there is some confusion about the nature of this *Urpflanze*; at one time he regarded it as an actual plant that might one day be discovered:

> Here [in Italy] where, instead of being grown in pots or under glass as they are with us, plants are allowed to grow freely in the open fresh air and fulfil their natural destiny, they become more intelligible. Seeing such a variety of new and renewed forms, my old fancy suddenly came back to mind: Among this multitude might I not discover the *Urpflanze*? There certainly must be one. Otherwise, how could I reognize that this or that form was a plant if all were not built upon the same basic model?

A month later, however, he conceived it, not as something discoverable in nature, but as something created by himself and brought to nature as a measure of possibilities:

> The *Urpflanze* is going to be the strangest creature in the world, which Nature herself shall envy me. With this model and the key to it, it will be possible to go on for ever inventing plants and know that their existence is logical; that is to say, if they do not actually exist, they could.

The difference between these two conceptions is of fundamental importance. The first makes Goethe's morphology look like a spurious kind of pseudo-evolutionary theory – as though the task were a Darwinian one of finding a plant from which all others are (causally) derived. The second makes clear that the *Urpflanze* cannot be used to make any causal inferences; the task of morphology is not to discover empirical laws (of evolution etc.) but to present us with an *Übersicht* (a 'synoptic view') of the whole field of plant-life. It is this second conception that forms the connection between Goethe's work and Wittgenstein's.

39 *Below:* Wittgenstein and Francis Skinner in Cambridge

40 *Bottom:* Wittgenstein with his niece Marie Stockert (a daughter of Helene)

41 *Top left:* Postcard sent to Pattisson by Wittgenstein while on holiday in Tours, France, 1949

43 *Above:* Wittgenstein on holiday in France with Gilbert Pattisson, July 1936

42 *Left:* A typical bit of 'nonsense' sent by Wittgenstein to Gilbert Pattisson: 'My latest photo. The previous one expressed fatherly kindness only; this one expresses triumph'

44 & 45 *Below and right:* Wittgenstein's acerbic reaction to Chamberlain's diplomacy at Munich: 'In case you want an Emetic, there it is'

THE PILGRIM OF PEACE
BRAVO! MR. CHAMBERLAIN

TUCK'S POST CARD
CARTE POSTALE
(FOR ADDRESS ONLY)

In case you want
an Emetic, there it is.
tt
Ludwig

46 *Above:* Wittgenstein in the Fellows' Garden at Trinity, 1939 (taken by Norman Malcolm)

50 *Right:* Wittgenstein in
Swansea (taken by Ben
Richards)

47 *Left:* From
Wittgenstein's photo-
album: Francis Skinner;
and family and friends at
Christmas in Vienna

49 *Below:* Tommy
Mulkerrins outside his
tiny, crowded cottage in
Connemara, together
with his mother, aunt
and sisters

48 *Left:* The Kingstons' farmhouse in
Co. Wicklow, Ireland, where
Wittgenstein stayed in 1948

51 Wittgenstein and Ben Richards in London

52 *Right:* One of the last photographs taken of Wittgenstein, in the garden at the von Wrights' home in Cambridge; Wittgenstein had taken the sheet from his bed and draped it behind him

53 Wittgenstein on his death-bed

54 Wittgenstein's grave, St Giles, Cambridge

Goethe's morphology provided Wittgenstein with an example of a study that seeks to clarify without explaining the phenomena with which it deals. This type of study consists in seeing analogies. It is crucial, however, to Wittgenstein's understanding of this morphological technique, that the *Gestalten* that are used as *Urphänomene* (the *Urpflanze* etc.) are not themselves objects, any more than ideas or concepts are objects. We see or recognize a *Gestalt*, not in the sense that we see a physical object, but in the sense that we see or recognize a likeness. This distinction is centrally important, but because *Gestalt*, *Urphänomen*, *Urpflanze* etc. are all nouns, and we can talk of seeing and recognizing them, is easily lost sight of. Thus, in his discussion of aspect-seeing in the *Investigations*, Wittgenstein begins with a masterfully clear statement of the distinction:

> Two uses of the word 'see'.
> The one: 'What do you see there?' – 'I see this' (and then a description, a drawing, a copy). The other: 'I see a likeness between these two faces' – let the man I tell this to be seeing the faces as clearly as I do myself.
> The importance of this is the difference of category between the two 'objects' of sight.

This ambiguity of the word 'see' lies at the root of a disagreement that Goethe had with Schiller about the *Urpflanze* when Goethe tried to explain his conception:

> I explained to him with great vivacity the *Metamorphosis of Plants* and, with a few characteristic strokes of the pen, conjured up before his eyes a symbolical plant.

Schiller refused to regard this 'symbolical plant' as an object of vision:

> . . . when I had ended, he shook his head saying: This has nothing to do with *experience*, it is an idea.

But Goethe was unmoved, and insisted that what he was talking about was something he had seen:

Well, so much the better; it means that I have ideas without knowing it, and even *see them with my eyes* . . . if he takes for an idea what to me is an experience then there must, after all, prevail some mediation, some relationship between the two.

On Wittgenstein's view, both Goethe and Schiller could be said to be right: Schiller is right to insist that the *Urpflanze* belongs in the same category as ideas (rather than that of physical objects), and Goethe is right to insist that, in some sense, he sees it with his own eyes. The philosophical task is to explain how this can be so – to describe the phenomenon of seeing-as in such a way that it does not appear paradoxical that a *Gestalt* (an 'aspect', an 'organized whole') is at one and the same time an idea and an 'object' of vision.

The issues raised by Köhler's *Gestalt Psychology*, then, were central to Wittgenstein's concerns. Köhler's treatment of them, however, falls foul of the very conceptual confusions that Wittgenstein had been trying to dispel in his 'Private Language Argument'. These confusions begin with Köhler's description of a *Gestalt* as 'a concrete individual and characteristic entity, existing as something detached and *having* a shape or form as one of its attributes'. This already makes it sound as if what was being described was an object, a private object. And this is exactly the sort of object that Köhler needs for his theory of perception, because he wants to say that the 'organization' of an object of perception is as much a part of it as its colour and shape. This blurs the distinction between a physical object and a mental construct (an idea etc.), and results in a rather confused notion of a somewhat shadowy *thing*:

If you put the 'organisation' of a visual impression on a level with colours and shapes, you are proceeding from the idea of the visual impression as an inner object. Of course this makes this object into a chimera; a queerly shifting construction.

Wittgenstein was likewise unhappy about Köhler's use of the phrase 'visual reality' to describe what it is that changes when we 'organize' a perception in different ways. For example, we would not ordinarily see the number 4 in the following figure until it was pointed out to us:

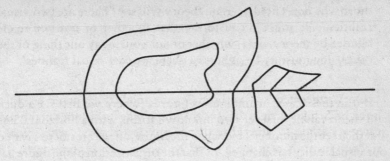

Köhler says about this:

> When I tell the reader that the number 4 is before him in the field, he will undoubtedly find it [see below]; but if he is not influenced by theoretical prejudices, he will confess that the form of the 4 did not exist as a visual reality at first and that, if it began to exist later on, that meant a transformation of visual reality.

In his lectures Wittgenstein ridiculed this passage as follows:

> Now Köhler said: 'you see two visual realities'. As opposed to what? To interpreting, presumably. How does he do this? [i.e., how is this established?] It won't do to ask people. Köhler never says it will; but he says 'If you're not blinded by theory you'll admit there are two visual realities.' But of course, he can't mean only that

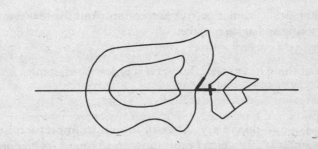

those who don't hold a certain theory will say 'There are two visual realities.' He must intend to say that whether or not you're (1) blinded by theory, or (2) whether or not you do say one thing or the other, you must, to be right, say 'there are two visual realities'.

But in these cases of ambiguous figures (where we first see a duck and then a rabbit, first see two unknown forms with a horizontal line and then see the number 4 hidden in the figure), if we are not to say that our visual reality has changed, or that the organization of the figure has changed, then what are we to say? What *has* changed? Typically, Wittgenstein wants to describe the process in such a way that this question does not arise. Like all cases of philosophical confusion, it is the question itself that misleads. 'It makes no sense to ask: "What has changed"', Wittgenstein told his class. 'And the answer: "the organisation has changed" makes no sense either.'

He did not, however, find it very easy to formulate a felicitous description of aspect-seeing that removed the confusions inherent in Köhler's description of it. Two years after these lectures he showed Drury the duck–rabbit picture and said to him: 'Now you try and say what is involved in seeing something as something. It is not easy. These thoughts I am now working on are as hard as granite.'

This strain perhaps shows in the paradoxical, and even contradictory, descriptions that were finally published in the *Investigations*:

The expression of a change of aspect is the expression of a new perception and at the same time of the perception's being unchanged.

'Seeing as . . .' is not part of perception. And for that reason it is like seeing and again not like.

On one thing he *was* clear: however it is described, it must not be by recourse to a 'private object':

. . . above all do not say 'After all my visual impression isn't the drawing: it is this which I can't show to anyone.' – Of course it is not the drawing, but neither is it anything of the same category, which I carry within myself.

He was also emphatic that the question to ask about changes of aspect was not: '*What* changes?' but: 'What *difference* does the change make?' Thus in his discussion of Köhler's example of the hidden 4, Wittgenstein replaces talk of 'a transformation of visual reality' with talk of the consequences of seeing the figure differently:

Köhler says that very few people would of their own accord see the figure 4 in the drawing

and that is certainly true. Now if some man deviates radically from the norm in his description of flat figures or when he copies them, what difference does it make between him and normal humans that he uses different 'units' in copying and describing? That is to say, how will such a one go on to differ from normal humans in yet other things?

In the case of a drawing, the consequence of seeing it differently might be that it is copied differently (someone might, for example, with the drawing above, start with the figure 4); in the case of a piece of music, hearing it differently might result in its being sung, played or whistled differently; in the case of a poem, it might be read differently. From these examples we can perhaps see that Wittgenstein's dictum: 'An "inner process" stands in need of outward criteria' (*PI*, I, 580) could have (and did have) a vastly different motivation from the superficially similar slogans of the behaviourists.

But this is especially clear when we consider that in the case of a philosophical *Weltanschauung* the consequence of a 'change of aspect' might be a change of *life*. In Wittgenstein's case, the consequence – the 'outward criteria' – that he earnestly hoped for was a culture which treated music, poetry, art and religion with the same respect and seriousness with which our present society treats science.

Was there any point in urging such a change of aspect?

> A philosopher says 'Look at things like this!' – but in the first place that doesn't ensure that people will look at things like that, and in the second place his admonition may come altogether too late; it's possible, moreover, that such an admonition can achieve nothing in any case and that the impetus for such a change in the way things are perceived has to originate somewhere else entirely.

But that this 'change in the way things are perceived' should happen somehow was crucially important to him. It was not true, as he and Engelmann had earlier insisted, that the discrepancy between how things are and how they ought to be always pointed to an internal change. It was impossible not to allow the external to encroach, to have an effect. And, somehow, one had to try and change things.

Or, at least, to change one's external surroundings. Wittgenstein was now convinced he had to get out of England. 'In this country', he wrote on 13 April, 'there is no more obvious reaction for people like me than misanthropy.' The fact that one could not possibly imagine a revolution taking place in England made it all the more depressing: 'It is as though one could say of this country: it has a damp, cold *spiritual* climate.' Ten days later:

> Cambridge grows more and more hateful to me. The disintegrating and putrefying English civilization. A country in which politics alternates between an evil purpose and *no* purpose.

'[I] feel myself to be an alien in the world', he wrote in July. 'If you have no ties to either mankind or to God, then you *are* an alien.'

As soon as the term was over he travelled to Swansea, where he was joined for two weeks by Ben. Though he had not yet formally resigned his Chair, he had resolved to leave England and to live alone.

His thoughts turned first to Norway, and then to Ireland. In August he went to Dublin to visit Drury, who had recently been appointed as a psychiatrist at St Patrick's Hospital in Dublin. Wittgenstein was intensely interested in the new post: 'I wouldn't be altogether surprised', he told Drury, 'if this work in psychiatry turned out to be the right thing for you. You at least know that "There are more things in heaven and earth" etc.' Drury lent him the book which was the basis of the treatment given at St Patrick's – Sargant and Slater's *Physical Methods of Treatment in Psychiatry* – to which Wittgenstein responded with a characteristic combination of an enthusiastic appreciation of the value of sound scientific technique together with an urgent reminder of its limitations:

> This is an excellent book. I like the spirit in which it is written. I am going to get Ben to read this book. I can quite understand that you would adopt the attitude 'Let's see now what these methods of treatment will accomplish.'
>
> I don't want for one moment to underestimate the importance of the work you are doing; but don't ever let yourself think that all human problems can be solved in this way.

At the end of August he returned to Cambridge, resolved to resign his Chair but still undecided whether to go to Norway or to Ireland. His plan was to spend about a month in Vienna and then, as he put it to von Wright:

> . . . go somewhere where I can be alone for a longish time and, if possible, to finish a part of my book . . . I haven't told the Cambridge authorities anything about it so far, as it's not absolutely certain. (Though just now I can't see how it can be avoided, I mean, my leaving Cambridge.)

'My mind just now is in *great* disorder', he told von Wright:

> It's partly due to this: that I dread seeing Vienna again after all that's happened and, in a way, I also dread chucking my job at Cambridge. But I'll get over it.

The thought of returning to a Vienna that he knew would be much altered for the worse was dreadful. And in this case the reality was

possibly even worse than the expectation. The city was still occupied
by the Russian army, who had for a time used the house Wittgenstein
had built for Gretl as a barracks and stables. The occupying army was
despised by the Austrians, and tales of brutality, rape and pillage were
common. Gretl's servant, who had loyally done her best to protect the
Kundmanngasse house, had herself received rough treatment from the
Russians. The whole situation would have been bleak and depressing.
Friedrich von Hayek, a distant cousin of Wittgenstein's, remembers
meeting him on a train on the way back from the visit. According to
Hayek: 'he was reacting to having encountered the Russians at Vienna
(as an army of occupation) in a manner which suggested that he had
met them in the flesh for the first time and that this had shattered all
his illusions'. Though entirely wrong in thinking that this was
Wittgenstein's first encounter with Russian people, Hayek's impression of his anger and disillusionment is no doubt correct. Indeed, it is
difficult to imagine any other reaction.

As soon as he returned from Vienna, Wittgenstein handed in his
resignation. He was told that he could take the Michaelmas term as
sabbatical leave. So, though he did not formally cease to be a professor
until the end of 1947, he was relieved of the burden both of giving
lectures and of living in Cambridge.

Before he left he spent a month preparing a typescript of his recent
work on the philosophy of psychology. This has now been published
as *Remarks on the Philosophy of Psychology*, Volume I. Wittgenstein had
it typed, however, not as a separate, publishable, work, but as material
to use in his attempt to revise the last third of *Philosophical Investigations*. 'It's mostly bad', he told von Wright, 'but I've got to have it in a
handy form, i.e. typewritten, because it may possibly give rise to
better thoughts when I read it'. He added:

I am in no way optimistic about my future, but as soon as I had
resigned I felt that it was the only natural thing to have done.

It is hard not to see, in his flight to Ireland and solitude, an attempt to
escape, not only Cambridge, lecturing and the English people, but,
even more painful, the torments of being close to his beloved. His
ostensible reason for being alone was to finish his book, but though he
wrote a good deal in the years that he spent in Ireland, it is difficult to
see in this work a concerted effort to bring it to completion. In this

work he was pursuing an entirely new line of thought, and the strongest impression one gets from it is of Wittgenstein 'philosophising for all he is worth' – of doing the 'only work that really bucks me up'.

25
IRELAND

Wittgenstein spent his first two weeks in Ireland living at Ross's Hotel in Dublin. Whenever Drury was free from hospital duties he and Wittgenstein went together to look at possible lodgings in or around Dublin. None could offer the solitariness and peace that was required, but the problem was temporarily solved by a friend of Drury's at St Patrick's, Robert McCullough. McCullough had been in the habit of spending his holidays at a farmhouse at Red Cross, in County Wicklow, which belonged to Richard and Jenny Kingston, and they had told him they were prepared to take in a permanent guest. This information was passed on to Wittgenstein, who immediately set off from Dublin to 'case the joint' (by this time, his vocabulary contained a liberal sprinkling of phrases borrowed from American detective fiction). He was enchanted by Wicklow. 'On my journey down in the bus', he told Drury on his return, 'I kept remarking to myself what a really beautiful country this is.'

Soon after moving into the Kingstons' farmhouse, however, he wrote to Rhees saying he felt 'cold and uncomfortable' there: 'I may, in a couple of months, move to a much more isolated place in the West of Ireland.' But after a few weeks he became much more acclimatized, and on Drury's first visit to Red Cross all seemed to be going well. Wittgenstein told him: 'Sometimes my ideas come so quickly that I feel as if my pen was being guided. I now see clearly that it was the right thing for me to give up the professorship. I could never have got this work done while I was in Cambridge.'

Being away from the 'disintegrating and putrefying English civilization' that Cambridge represented was undoubtedly one of the chief attractions of living in Ireland. When von Wright wrote to him about his hesitation in applying for the Cambridge Chair in Philosophy, Wittgenstein replied that he understood perfectly, and in fact had assumed von Wright would not apply, for: 'the prospect of becoming English, or a refugee in England, seemed to me anything but attractive in our time'.

When von Wright finally did apply, Wittgenstein's encouragement was tempered by a fearful warning:

> Cambridge is a dangerous place. Will you become superficial? smooth? If you don't you will have to suffer terribly. – The passage in your letter which makes me feel particularly uneasy is the one about your feeling enthusiasm at the thought of teaching at Cambridge. It seems to me: if you go to Cambridge you must go as a SOBER man. May my fears have no foundation, and may you not be tempted beyond your powers!

Apart from not being in Cambridge, the chief attraction of living at Red Cross was the beauty of the Wicklow countryside. The winter was mild, and Wittgenstein could go for a walk almost every day. 'There is nothing like the Welsh coast here', he wrote to Rhees, 'but the colours are most wonderful & make up for everything.' And to his sister, Helene, he wrote:

> The country here would not have so many attractions for me if the colours were not often so wonderful. I think it must be to do with the atmosphere, for not only the grass, but also the sky, the sea and even everything that is brown are all magnificent. – I feel a good deal better here than in Cambridge.

He took his notebook with him on his walks around Red Cross, and would often work outdoors. A neighbour of the Kingstons', who often saw Wittgenstein out on his favourite walk, reports that he once passed him sitting in a ditch, writing furiously, oblivious of anything going on around him. This is presumably one of those occasions when, as he told Drury, his ideas came so quickly that he felt as if his pen were being guided. He was, however, cautious in attributing too much importance to these moods of inspiration:

In a letter (to Goethe I think) Schiller writes of a 'poetic mood'. I think I know what he means, I believe I am familiar with it myself. It is a mood of receptivity to nature in which one's thoughts seem as vivid as nature itself. But it is strange that Schiller did not produce anything better (or so it seems to me) and so I am not entirely convinced that what I produce in such a mood is really worth anything. It may be that what gives my thoughts their lustre on these occasions is a light shining on them from behind. That they do not themselves glow.

He had taken with him both the typescript that is now *Philosophical Investigations*, Part I, and that which is now *Remarks on the Philosophy of Psychology*, Volume I. From these — together with the remarks he was writing at Red Cross — he hoped to put together a final version of the first part of his book. (The second part — that dealing with the philosophy of mathematics — could by now be considered an abandoned project.) He reported to all his friends that the work was going fairly well. There is, however, some indication that he was already inclined to leave the task of publishing to his literary executors. 'Heaven knows if I'll ever publish this work', he wrote to von Wright, 'but I should like you to look at it after my death if you survive me. There is a good deal of hard thinking in it.'

Wittgenstein was prevented from working as hard as he would have liked by ill health. Despite claiming to Rhees, on 5 February 1948, that: 'I am in very good bodily health', he was in fact suffering from painful attacks of indigestion. To combat this he would keep by his side as he worked a tin of 'Scragg's' charcoal biscuits. He had so much faith in this remedy (the Kingstons' children, Maude and Ken, remember him eating very little else) that he would frequently have to walk to Arklow to replenish his stock. The biscuits, however, did not appear to solve the problem: 'My work's going moderately well', he wrote to Malcolm in January, '& I think it might even go very well if I weren't suffering from some kind of indigestion which I don't seem to be able to shake off.'

Far worse (but perhaps in some way linked to his poor digestion) was his deteriorating nervous condition. On 3 February he wrote:

Feel unwell. Not physically, but mentally. Am frightened of the onset of insanity. God alone knows whether I am in danger.

If the nearness of Ben had been the cause of his mental instability during his last year at Cambridge, absence from him made him no more sane. On 5 February he reported to Malcolm: 'occasionally queer states of nervous instability about which I'll only say that they're rotten while they last & teach one to pray'. And on the same day he wrote to Rhees:

> My nerves, I'm afraid, often misbehave. Of course they're tired and old nerves. – My work, on the whole, goes fairly well. Again it's the work of an old man: for, though I am not really old, I have, somehow, an old soul. May it be granted to me that my body doesn't survive my soul!

'I often believe that I am on the straight road to insanity', he told von Wright a month later. 'It is difficult for me to imagine that my brain should stand the strain very long.'

He spent the following two weeks in a state of acute depression, unable to work and increasingly dissatisfied with his accommodation. He had originally been pleased with his hosts. 'They are very quiet', he had written to von Wright in December. 'I have my meals in my room and am very little disturbed.' But in March, Ken, the youngest of the family (he was then eleven years old), had a friend to stay. The two of them shared a bedroom, and would be up late at night talking and laughing together. When Wittgenstein banged furiously on the wall to tell them to be quiet, they took it as a joke. But Wittgenstein was truly at his wits' end. He sent a telegram to Drury in Dublin asking him to book a room at Ross's Hotel and to come and see him there, as a matter of urgency. Drury recalls: 'As soon as he had arrived I went down to see him. He looked distressed and agitated':

WITTGENSTEIN: It has come.
DRURY: I don't understand; what has happened?
WITTGENSTEIN: What I have always dreaded: that I would no longer be able to work. I have done no work at all for the past two weeks. And I can't sleep at nights. The people under my room sit up late talking and the continual murmur of voices is driving me crazy.

Drury prescribed some tablets to help Wittgenstein sleep, and told him that his brother's cottage on the west coast of Ireland was now empty, and that Wittgenstein was welcome to make use of it. There, at least, he would find peace and solitude.

Relieved, Wittgenstein returned to Red Cross to think it over. He spent Easter with the Kingstons, but was still unable to work, and therefore resolved to take up Drury's offer. His state of mind, however, improved considerably – as did his relations with the Kingstons – and shortly before he left he presented the children with a big, bright green Easter egg full of chocolates; on the day he left for the west coast, 28 April, he signed the visitors' book with the remark: 'Thank you for a very good time.'

There is no reason to see in the remark any irony or insincerity – it was no doubt a genuine expression of gratitude to the Kingstons. But the last two months, at least, of his stay at Red Cross could hardly be called 'a very good time', as is shown by the letter he wrote Rhees a week before he left:

> I often thought of you these days &, although this may sound awful, often thought; thank God I wrote to you not to come to see me at Easter. For the last 6 or 8 weeks have been a bad time for me. First I suffered terrible depressions, then I had a bad flu, & all the time I didn't know where to go from here. I am now gradually getting better & I intend leaving here next week & so go to Rosro in the West. This has great disadvantages (it's a 10 hours journey from Dublin) but there's nothing else I can do, so far as I can see. So, had you come, you'd have found me in a state of great tribulation. Wish me some strength, some courage, & luck! During the last month my work has hardly progressed at all, & only in the last few days I've been able to think a little (I mean about philosophy; for my brain, though dull, wasn't inactive, I wish it had been!).

Wittgenstein knew Rosro, the cottage in Connemara, from 1934, when he had spent a holiday there in the company of Francis Skinner and Maurice Drury. It stands facing the sea at the mouth of the Killary harbour, and the countryside around it is dominated by a range of mountains with peaks of extraordinary angularity, known as 'The Twelve Pins'. The cottage was built as a coastguard station, but fell into disuse after the First World War. During the early 1920s it remained unoccupied, used only by the IRA as a place to hide prisoners until, in 1927, it was bought by Maurice Drury's brother,

Miles, as a holiday cottage. There are a few neighbouring cottages, but it is many miles away from any shop, post office or any other village or town amenity. This isolation, though it had, as Wittgenstein anticipated, 'great disadvantages', was necessary if he were to enjoy the freedom from interruption he thought essential for his work.

On his arrival there Wittgenstein was met by Thomas Mulkerrins ('Tommy', as Wittgenstein, like everybody else in Killary, learnt to call him), an employee of the Drury family, who lived in a tiny cottage about half a mile away from Rosro and who was paid £3 a week to look after the Drurys' holiday home. (He supplemented this inconsiderable wage by gathering peat and fishing for mackerel.) Tommy had been told by Drury that Wittgenstein had suffered a nervous breakdown, and had been asked to help in whatever way he could. So every morning he walked down to Rosro to deliver milk and peat, and to check that Wittgenstein was all right. Wittgenstein found him (so he told Malcolm): 'quite nice & certainly better company than the people I stayed with in Co Wicklow'.

In conversation with Rhees, later, he was more critical, describing the whole Mulkerrins family as people ill disposed to do any work. He was shocked to see that Tommy's mother, though an excellent sempstress, went about in rags, and that though Tommy himself was a competent carpenter every chair in their cottage had a broken leg. In his diary, Tommy – 'the man upon whom I am totally dependent here' – is described simply as 'unreliable'.

Unreliable or not, Tommy was all he had. His immediate neighbours, the Mortimer family, considered him completely mad, and would have nothing to do with him. They even forbade him to walk on their land, on the grounds that he would frighten their sheep. He therefore had to take a long and circuitous route along the road if he wanted to walk on the hills behind Rosro. On one of these walks, the Mortimers saw him stop suddenly and, using his walking-stick as an implement, draw an outline figure (a duck–rabbit?) in the dirt on the track, which he stood staring at in complete absorption for a long time before resuming his walk. This confirmed their original assessment. So, too, did Wittgenstein's vehement outburst one night when the barking of the Mortimers' dog disturbed his concentration. He appeared to the Mortimers, in fact, in much the same way that he had earlier appeared to the villagers of rural Austria.

Tommy, too, thought Wittgenstein a little odd. But partly because of his loyalty to the Drury family (Miles Drury had once dived off a boat to save Tommy from drowning), and partly because he came to enjoy the company of 'the Professor', he was prepared to do what he could to make Wittgenstein's stay at Rosro as comfortable and as enjoyable as possible. He did his best, for example, to satisfy Wittgenstein's strict standards of cleanliness and hygiene. At Wittgenstein's suggestion, he brought with him every morning, not only the milk and peat, but also his own used tea-leaves. Every morning the leaves were sprinkled on the kitchen floor to absorb the dirt, and were then swept up. Tommy was also called upon to rid the cottage of 'slaters' (wood-lice). This he did by showering the whole cottage with a suffocating amount of disinfectant powder. Wittgenstein, who throughout his life had a dread of bugs of any kind, was pleased with the result, preferring the threat of suffocation to the sight of wood-lice.

Rosro cottage had two rooms, a bedroom and a kitchen, and it was in the latter that Wittgenstein spent most of his time. He did not, however, use the kitchen to prepare his meals. While at Rosro he lived almost entirely on tinned food ordered from a grocer's shop in Galway. Tommy was concerned about this diet. 'Tinned food will be the death of you', he once said. 'People live too long anyway', came the grim reply. Instead, Wittgenstein used the kitchen as a study, and when Tommy came in the morning he would often find him sitting at the kitchen table writing on to loose sheets of paper clipped together. Almost every day there would be a pile of rejected sheets, which it was Tommy's job to burn.

One morning when Tommy arrived at Rosro, he heard Wittgenstein's voice and, on entering the cottage, was surprised to find 'the Professor' alone. 'I thought you had company', he said. 'I did', Wittgenstein answered. 'I was talking to a very dear friend of mine – myself.' The remark is echoed in one of his notebooks of the period:

> Nearly all my writings are private conversations with myself. Things that I say to myself tête-à-tête.

Apart from the time he spent with Tommy, Wittgenstein's solitude at Rosro was interrupted only by a brief visit from Ben Richards, who spent a couple of weeks there in the summer of 1948. Together they went on Wittgenstein's favourite walks up the hills and along the coast, admiring the magnificently varied flora and fauna of the area.

Wittgenstein had taken a particular interest in the different kinds of birds that are to be seen at Killary. (Northern Divers, Cormorants, Curlews, Oyster Catchers, Puffins and Terns are all fairly common along that part of the west Ireland coast.) At first he used to ask Tommy to identify the birds for him. He would describe a bird he had seen, and Tommy would do his best to name it, although, as he freely admits: 'maybe it wasn't always the right name I gave him'. Having caught him out a few times, Wittgenstein relied instead on the illustrated handbooks sent to him by Drury.

In order to gain a better view of the sea-birds, Wittgenstein wanted to build a hut on one of the small islands off the Killary coast. He was eventually dissuaded from this by Tommy (whose job it would have been to construct it) on the grounds that a small wooden hut would not be strong enough to withstand the exposed conditions on the island. Instead, Tommy took Wittgenstein out in a rowing-boat; while Tommy rowed, Wittgenstein would either look out for sea-birds or sit silently in contemplation. Occasionally, while out in the boat, they would chat, Wittgenstein reminiscing about his time in Norway, when he would have to row across the fjord to fetch his supplies, and Tommy answering Wittgenstein's questions about the history of Killary.

Wittgenstein took an interest, too, in the more domestic birds, the robins and chaffinches, that used to come to the cottage in search of crumbs. He would encourage them by leaving food out for them, and eventually they grew so tame that they would come to him at the kitchen window, and eat off his hand. When he left Rosro he gave Tommy some money with which to buy food to provide for the birds, who had now come to expect a daily feed. By the time Tommy next visited the cottage, however, he found the birds' tameness had been their undoing. While waiting by the window to be fed, they had fallen easy prey to the local cats.

The way of life at Rosro, though strenuous, seems to have provided the necessary conditions for an improvement in Wittgenstein's mental and physical well-being. He had, as we have seen, arrived there in poor shape. 'I've had a bad time lately: soul, mind & body', he wrote to Malcolm on 30 April, a few days after he arrived. 'I felt exceedingly depressed for many weeks, then felt ill & now I'm weak & completely dull. I haven't done any work for 5–6 weeks.' But within a month, the solitude of the cottage, the beauty of the coastal scenery, the company of the birds and Tommy Mulkerrins's good-humoured (if not entirely dependable) support had effected a change for the better. Wittgenstein found himself once again able to work.

His biggest complaint about the way of life there was that he had to do all his own housework. This he found an infuriating nuisance, but, as he wrote to Malcolm's wife, Lee, 'it's undoubtedly a great blessing, too, because it keeps me sane, it forces me to live a regular life & is in general good for me although I curse it every day'.

The remoteness of Rosro was a problem only in so far as the scarcity of American pulp fiction was concerned. The nearest village was ten miles away, and the selection of books to be had there was so poor that, in the periods between his regular parcels of 'mags' from Norman Malcolm, Wittgenstein was forced to resort to reading Dorothy Sayers. This, he told Malcolm, 'was so bl . . . foul that it depressed me'. Malcolm's supply of the 'real thing' came as a relief: 'when I opened one of your mags it was like getting out of a stuffy room into the fresh air'.

By chance, however, he did manage to find at the village shop a paperback copy of his favourite detective novel, *Rendezvous with Fear* by Norbert Davis. He had read Davis's book during his last year at Cambridge, and had enjoyed it so much that he lent it to both Moore and Smythies (he later gave a copy to Ben Richards as well). Seeing it again, he couldn't resist the temptation to buy it and reread it, and having done so his regard for it increased even further: 'For though, as you know', he wrote to Malcolm, 'I've read hundreds of stories that amused me & that I liked reading, I think I've only read two perhaps that I'd call good stuff, & Davis's is one of them.' He asked Malcolm to try to find out more about Davis:

It may sound crazy, but when I recently re-read the story I liked it again so much that I thought I'd really like to write to the author and thank him. If this is nuts don't be surprised, for so am I.

Unfortunately, Malcolm reports: 'As I recall, I was unable to obtain any information about this author.' This is a pity, because by 1948 Norbert Davis was, in fact, in sore need of encouragement. He was, along with Dashiell Hammett and other *Black Mask* writers, one of the pioneers of the American 'hard-boiled' detective story. In the early 1930s he had given up a career as a lawyer to write detective stories, and then enjoyed ten years as a successful author. By the late 1940s, however, he had fallen on hard times. Shortly after Wittgenstein's letter to Malcolm, Davis wrote to Raymond Chandler saying that fourteen of his last fifteen stories had been rejected for publication, and asking Chandler to lend him $200. He died in poverty the following year, unaware of his rare (probably unique) distinction in having written a book which Wittgenstein liked sufficiently to want to write a letter of thanks to its author.

Wittgenstein's gratitude is, no doubt, partly accounted for by the scarcity of detective fiction in Connemara. But why should he have rated *Rendezvous with Fear* above all the other detective stories he had read (of which there was a great number)?

The answer perhaps lies in the humour of the novel, which is in fact its most striking feature. The detective in the story, Doan, is distinguished from such figures as Sam Spade and Philip Marlowe by his rather comically unprepossessing appearance: he is a short, fat man who is followed everywhere by an enormous, well-trained Great Dane called Carstairs. The feature of Davis's style that particularly impressed Raymond Chandler was the casual way in which he killed off his characters, and this is particularly evident in *Rendezvous with Fear*. For example, after setting the scene by describing the tourists at the Azteca, a hotel in South America, Davis introduces 'Garcia':

> All this was very boring to a man who, for the time being, was named Garcia. He sat and drank beer the general colour and consistency of warm vinegar, and glowered. He had a thin, yellowish face and a straggling black moustache, and he was cross-eyed. He should really have been more interested in the tourists coming from the Hotel Azteca, because in a short time one of them was going to shoot him dead. However, he didn't know that, and had you told him he would have laughed. He was a bad man.

When Doan shoots Bautiste Bonofile, another 'bad man', the romantic but naïve heroine, Jane, asks with concern: 'Is he hurt?' 'Not a bit', says Doan, 'he's just dead.'

'Humour is not a mood but a way of looking at the world',

Wittgenstein wrote while he was at Rosro. 'So if it is correct to say that humour was stamped out in Nazi Germany, that does not mean that people were not in good spirits, or anything of that sort, but something much deeper and more important.' To understand what that 'something' is, it would perhaps be instructive to look at humour as something strange and incomprehensible:

> Two people are laughing together, say at a joke. One of them has used certain somewhat unusual words and now they both break out into a sort of bleating. That might appear very extraordinary to a visitor coming from quite a different environment. Whereas we find it completely reasonable. (I recently witnessed this scene on a bus and was able to think myself into the position of someone to whom this would be unfamiliar. From that point of view it struck me as quite irrational, like the responses of an outlandish animal.)

Understanding humour, like understanding music, provides an analogy for Wittgenstein's conception of philosophical understanding. What is required for understanding here is not the discovery of facts, nor the drawing of logically valid inferences from accepted premises – nor, still less, the construction of *theories* – but, rather, the right point of view (from which to 'see' the joke, to hear the expression in the music or to see your way out of the philosophical fog). But how do we explain or teach what is meant by the 'right point of view'?

> So how do we explain to someone what 'understanding music' means? By specifying the images, kinaesthetic sensations, etc., experienced by someone who understands? *More likely*, by drawing attention to his expressive movements. – And we really ought to ask what function explanation has here. And what it means to speak of: understanding what it means to understand music. For some would say: to understand that means: to understand music itself. And in that case we should have to ask 'Well, can someone be taught to understand music?', for that is the only sort of teaching that could be called explaining music.
>   There is a certain *expression* proper to the appreciation of music, in listening, playing, and at other times too. Sometimes gestures form part of this expression, but sometimes it will just be a matter of how a man plays, or hums, the piece, now and again of the

comparisons he draws and the images with which he as it were illustrates the music. Someone who understands music will listen differently (e.g. with a different expression on his face), he will talk differently, from one who does not. But he will show that he understands a particular theme not just in manifestations that accompany his hearing or playing that theme but in his understanding for music in general.

Appreciating music is a manifestation of the life of mankind. How should we describe it to someone? Well, I suppose we should first have to describe *music*. Then we could describe how human beings react to it. But is that all we need do, or must we also teach him to understand it for himself? Well, getting him to understand and giving him an explanation that does not achieve this will be 'teaching him what understanding is' in *different* senses of that phrase. And again, teaching him to understand poetry or painting may contribute to teaching him what is involved in understanding music.

These remarks on understanding music – like those on humour quoted earlier – have been published in a collection of remarks 'which do not belong directly with his philosophical works although they are scattered amongst the philosophical texts' (editor's preface to *Culture and Value*). But their connection with Wittgenstein's philosophical work is more direct than this would suggest. One of his chief philosophical preoccupations while he was at Rosro was the problem of aspect-seeing. To discuss this problem he would often imagine people who were 'aspect-blind' (or, as he sometimes put it, 'gestalt-blind') – people who were unable to see something as something. His remarks on what it is like to be unable to see a joke, or unable to appreciate music, are not distinct from this philosophical preoccupation; they are part of it.

'What would a person who is blind towards these aspects be lacking?' Wittgenstein asks, and replies: 'It is not absurd to answer: the power of imagination.' But the imagination of individuals, though necessary, is not sufficient. What is further required for people to be alive to 'aspects' (and, therefore, for humour, music, poetry and painting to mean something) is a culture. The connection between Wittgenstein's philosophical concern with aspect-seeing and his cultural concerns is therefore simple and direct. It is made clear in the following sequence of remarks (written at Rosro, and, it should be added, occurring in Wittgenstein's *bona fide* philosophical work):

> What is lacking to anyone who doesn't understand the question which way the letter F is facing, where, for example, to paint a nose on? Or to anyone who doesn't find that a word loses something when it is repeated several times, namely, its meaning; or to someone who doesn't find that it then becomes a mere sound?
>
> *We* say: 'At first something like an image was there.'

> Is it that such a person is unable to appreciate a sentence, judge it, the way those who understand it can? Is it that for him the sentence is not alive (with all that implies)? Is it that the word does not have an aroma of meaning? And that therefore he will often react differently to a word than we do? – It *might* be that way.

> But if I hear a tune with understanding, doesn't something special go on in me – which does not go on if I hear it without understanding? And what? – No answer comes; or anything that occurs to me is insipid. I may indeed say: 'Now I've understood it', and perhaps talk about it, play it, compare it with others etc. *Signs* of understanding may accompany hearing.

> It is wrong to call understanding a process that accompanies hearing. (Of course its manifestation, expressive playing, cannot be called an accompaniment of hearing either.)

> For how can it be explained what 'expressive playing' is? Certainly not by anything that accompanies the playing. – What is needed for the explanation? One might say: a culture. – If someone is brought up in a particular culture – and then reacts to music in such-and-such a way, you can teach him the use of the phrase 'expressive playing'.

Seeing aspects, understanding music, poetry, painting and humour, are reactions that belong to, and can only survive within, a culture, a form of life:

> What is it like for people not to have the same sense of humour? They do not react properly to each other. It's as though there were a custom amongst certain people for one person to throw another a ball which he is supposed to catch and throw back; but

some people, instead of throwing it back, put it in their pocket.

Thus, if it is true that humour was stamped out in Nazi Germany, this would mean, not just that people were not in good spirits, but that the Nazis had been successful in destroying a whole way of life, a way of looking at the world and the set of reactions and customs that go with it. (It would mean that the Nazis had, so to speak, pocketed the ball.)

The philosophical difficulty about aspect-seeing arises from the *prima facie*, and puzzling, fact that, though the aspect changes, the thing that is seen does not; the same drawing is now a duck, and now a rabbit. Likewise, it is the same joke, poem, painting or piece of music that is now just an extraordinary, outlandish piece of behaviour, words on a page, splashes on canvas or an incoherent noise, and now (when it is understood) funny, moving, beautiful or wonderfully expressive: 'What is incomprehensible is that *nothing*, and yet *everything*, has changed.'

Wittgenstein's remark about philosophy – that it 'leaves everything as it is' – is often quoted. But it is less often realized that, in seeking to change nothing but the way we look at things, Wittgenstein was attempting to change *everything*. His pessimism about the effectiveness of his work is related to his conviction that the way we look at things is determined, not by our philosophical beliefs, but by our culture, by the way we are brought up. And in the face of this, as he once said to Karl Britton: 'What can one man do alone?'

> Tradition is not something a man can learn; not a thread he can pick up when he feels like it; any more than a man can choose his own ancestors.
>
> Someone lacking a tradition who would like to have one is like a man unhappily in love.

Wittgenstein had a tradition – one that he loved dearly: the German/Austrian literature, art and (especially) music of the nineteenth century. But he was acutely aware that, for the greater part of his life, this tradition was no longer alive. In this sense, he was not so much unhappily in love, as desperately bereaved. The physical isolation at Connemara that he felt necessary to pursue his work matches the sense of cultural isolation that pervades it.

*

Wittgenstein stayed at Rosro throughout the summer of 1948, from May to August. During these four months he wrote a great deal. But the demands of the life-style and his uncertain health combined to make him feel too weak to accomplish what he had set out to achieve. 'I get tired, bodily and mentally, very easily', he told von Wright. He was, he wrote in his diary, 'too soft, too weak, and so too lazy to achieve anything significant':

> The industry of great men is, among other things, a sign of their strength, quite apart from their inner wealth.

He was, in addition, plagued by attacks of melancholy that he was inclined to personify, as though haunted by a ghost. 'Don't let grief vex you', he wrote on 29 June:

> You should let it into your heart. Nor should you be afraid of madness. It comes to you perhaps as a friend and not as an enemy, and the only thing that is bad is your resistance. Let grief into your heart. Don't lock the door on it. Standing outside the door, in the mind, it is frightening, but in the *heart* it is not.

A little later, on 11 July, the ghost is identified:

> Think a great deal of the last time with Francis, of my odiousness towards him. I was at that time very unhappy; *but with a wicked heart*. I cannot see how I will ever in my life be freed from this guilt.

The psychological and physical strains of living alone in Rosro could not, he thought, be withstood for much longer. He found it almost inconceivable that he could stand to spend the winter there. 'But', he wrote on 17 July, 'I have decided to *try* and do so':

> I pray a good deal. But whether in the right spirit I do not know. – Without the blessings of C and B [Con Drury and Ben] I could not live here.

He asked Tommy whether he would consider having him as a guest for the winter. Tommy declined. His tiny, two-room, cottage was already over-crowded with himself, his mother and his sister. Wittgenstein also approached Mrs Phillips, the proprietor of nearby Kylemore House (now Kylemore Hotel), but was told that she took guests only during the summer. If he was to stay in Connemara, the only option open to him was to live alone at Rosro.

He left Connemara in August, travelling first to Dublin to visit Drury, and then to Uxbridge to stay with Ben at his family home. In September he left for Vienna to visit Hermine, who was seriously ill with cancer.

On his return he spent a couple of weeks at Cambridge dictating a typescript compiled from the work he had written in Ireland. This has now been published as *Remarks on the Philosophy of Psychology*, Volume II. But, like its predecessor, it was not conceived as a separate work, its intended – or, perhaps, ostensible – purpose being to provide, in a convenient form, a set of remarks to use in the revision of the *Investigations*.

By 16 October the work was completed, and Wittgenstein returned to Dublin, intending initially to go on to Rosro. From Vienna he had written to Tommy, asking him to have the cottage ready for his return. He had, however, as we have seen, serious misgivings about returning. And as Wittgenstein's doctor, Drury, too, was concerned about his spending the winter in a place where, if he fell ill, there would be no one to look after him, and no way of getting him medical attention. Moreover, Wittgenstein found that in the warm, comfortable, and above all quiet room that he occupied at the top of the Dublin hotel in which he was staying, he could work quite well. In the event, therefore, he spent the winter as a guest at Ross's Hotel.

Ross's Hotel was, in 1948, a large but not especially luxurious hotel on Parkgate Street, close to Phoenix Park. (It still stands, but is now extensively altered and has been renamed the Ashling Hotel.) It was known locally as a 'Protestant' hotel: many of the permanent guests there were Protestants, and it was used by Protestant clergymen when they came to Dublin to attend conferences and meetings. 'When I look at the faces of the clergy here in Dublin', Wittgenstein remarked to Drury, 'it seems to me that the Protestant ministers look less smug than the Roman priests. I suppose it is because they know they are such a small minority.'

Of more importance to him, however, was the fact that it was only a short walk away from the Zoological Gardens in Phoenix Park.

Through Drury he became a member of the Royal Zoological Society, which allowed him free access to the gardens and the right to have his meals in the members' room. While he was in Dublin he saw Drury almost every day: they would meet for lunch either at the members' room of the Zoological Gardens or at Bewley's Café in Grafton Street, where the waitress quickly became accustomed to Wittgenstein's unvarying diet, and would bring him an omelette and coffee without his having to order it. Drury also introduced him to the Botanical Gardens at Glasnevin, where the heated Palm House provided a warm and congenial place in which to work during the winter.

During the winter months in Dublin Wittgenstein worked with great intensity. 'I'm anxious to make hay during the very short period when the sun shines in my brain', he told Malcolm on 6 November. On one occasion, when he and Drury had planned to have lunch together, Drury arrived at the hotel to be told: 'Just wait a minute until I finish this.' Wittgenstein then continued to write for two hours without saying a word. When he finally finished he seemed quite unaware that it was now long past their lunch-time.

The work he wrote in Dublin has been published under the title *Last Writings on the Philosophy of Psychology*. The title has misled many into thinking that it is Wittgenstein's last work. It is not; it predates, for example, Part II of *Philosophical Investigations*, *On Certainty* and *Remarks on Colour*. It is, however, the last of the series of manuscript volumes, begun in Cambridge in 1946, in which he attempts to provide a better, more perspicuous, analysis of psychological concepts than that given in Part I of the *Investigations*. It is a continuation of his attempts to exhibit the multiplicity and complexity of psychological concepts (such as 'fear', 'hope', 'belief' etc.) in a way that exposes the barrenness and confusion of 'the philosopher's search for generality'. The work is full of fine distinctions, designed to show, among other things, the danger of assuming that all sentences in the indicative mode can be regarded as *descriptions*:

> I hear the words 'I am afraid'. I ask: 'In what connection did you say that? Was it a sigh from the bottom of your heart, was it a confession, was it self-observation . . . ?'

On one of their walks in Phoenix Park, Drury mentioned Hegel. 'Hegel seems to me to be always wanting to say that things which look different are really the same', Wittgenstein told him. 'Whereas my interest is in showing that things which look the same are really different.' He was thinking of using as a motto for his book the Earl of Kent's phrase from *King Lear* (Act I, scene iv): 'I'll teach you differences.'

His concern was to stress life's irreducible variety. The pleasure he derived from walking in the Zoological Gardens had much to do with his admiration for the immense variety of flowers, shrubs and trees and the multitude of different species of birds, reptiles and animals. A theory which attempted to impose a single scheme upon all this diversity was, predictably, anathema to him. Darwin had to be wrong: his theory 'hasn't the necessary multiplicity'.

The concepts with which Wittgenstein is particularly concerned in these 'Last Writings' are those of 'thinking' and 'seeing'. More particularly, his concern is with the relation between the two. Of central importance to his whole later work is the idea that there is a kind of seeing that is also a kind of thinking (or, at least, a kind of *understanding*): the seeing of connections. We *see* a connection in the same sense that we see an aspect, or a *Gestalt* To distinguish this sense of 'see' from that in which we see a physical object, and to describe the connections and the differences between this sense of 'see' and the concepts of 'thinking' and 'understanding', is the central task of the work written at Ross's Hotel.

'Now you try and say what is involved in seeing something as something', Wittgenstein challenged Drury; 'it is not easy. These thoughts I am now working on are as hard as granite.' In reply Drury quoted James Ward: '*Denken ist schwer*' ('Thinking is difficult'), a response which perhaps prompted the following notebook entry:

'Denken ist schwer' (Ward). What does this really mean? Why is it difficult? – It is almost like saying 'Looking is difficult.' Because looking intently is difficult. And it's possible to look intently without seeing anything, or to keep thinking you see something without being able to see clearly. Looking can tire you even when you don't see anything.

It was on the same day that Wittgenstein remarked to Drury: 'It is impossible for me to say one word in my book about all that music has meant in my life. How then can I hope to be understood?' The work that he was writing at the time, however, does contain a strong hint of this. For in drawing attention to the sense of 'seeing' (or 'hearing'), in the act of which we understand something, the paradigmatic example of music is never far from his thoughts:

> We say that someone has the 'eye of a painter' or 'the ear of a musician', but anyone lacking these qualities hardly suffers from a kind of blindness or deafness.

> We say that someone doesn't have a 'musical ear', and 'aspect-blindness' is (in a way) comparable to this inability to hear.

The example of understanding music was important to him, not only because of the immense importance of music in his own life, but also because it is clear that the meaning of a piece of music cannot be described by naming anything that the music 'stands for'. And in this way: 'Understanding a sentence is much more akin to understanding a theme in music than one may think.'

'I would like it if some day you were able to read what I am writing now', Wittgenstein told Drury. But the demands of Drury's job at St Patrick's, and his relative lack of acquaintance with the specific philosophical problems with which Wittgenstein was concerned, forbade any detailed discussion of Wittgenstein's work. Indeed, Drury recalls that it was Wittgenstein's express decision not to discuss philosophy with him: 'I think he felt that his own thinking was so much more developed than mine that there was a danger of swamping me and of my becoming nothing but a pale echo of himself.' Nor did Wittgenstein read through his current work with Ben Richards, who came to stay with him at Ross's Hotel for a week or two in November.

In December, however, Wittgenstein had a chance to discuss his work in detail, when he was joined at the hotel first by Elizabeth Anscombe, who stayed for the first two weeks of December, and then by Rush Rhees, who came to Dublin immediately after Anscombe to spend Christmas with Wittgenstein. Wittgenstein had already decided that Rhees should be the executor of his will, and also, perhaps, that Anscombe and Rhees should be two of his literary executors. In any case, with both of them he read through the work that he had written in the previous two months, and discussed his attempts to revise *Philosophical Investigations*, using this new material together with some of the remarks contained in the two typescripts he had prepared in the previous two years.

Rhees left Dublin on the first day of the new year, while Wittgenstein stayed on at Ross's Hotel hoping to continue his good run of work. Early in January, however, he fell ill with a complaint similar to that which had dogged him during the previous year. He described it to Malcolm as: 'some sort of infection of the intestines'. 'Of course it hasn't done my work any good', he added. 'I had to interrupt it completely for a week & after that it just crawled along, as I do when I take a walk these days.'

He felt tired, ill and old. He wondered whether this would be his last illness. He also felt isolated. 'Drury, I think, is growing more and more unfaithful', he wrote on 29 January. 'He has found friends with whom he can live more easily.' His doctor diagnosed him as suffering from nothing more serious than gastro-enteritis, but he was inclined to distrust the doctor, and ignored the prescribed treatment. On 11 February he reported 'great weakness and pain'. Mining, he had heard, was dying – 'a *great* loss for me and for everyone'. She had many and varied talents, he wrote, that were not exposed to the day, but hidden: 'like human innards *should* be'.

Throughout February he was still able to work, but not with anything like the intensity and industry of which he had been capable before Christmas. By the end of March even this limited capacity for work had deserted him, and for a few months after that he wrote nothing at all. During this fallow period he read a fair amount. Drury was a member of the Royal Dublin Society's library, and used to borrow books from there on Wittgenstein's behalf. He recalls that what Wittgenstein generally wanted to read was history – Macaulay's *Essays Critical and Historical*, Livy's account of the second Punic War, Morley's *Life of Cromwell*, Ségur's *L'Histoire de Napoléon* and Bismarck's *Gedanken und Erinnerungen*. They were, for the most part, books Wittgenstein had read before. In 1937, for example, he had written of the Macaulay essays:

[They] contain many excellent things; but his value judgements about people are tiresome and superfluous. One feels like saying to him: stop gesticulating! and just say what you have to say.

And in 1942 he had written to Rhees that he was reading Livy's account of Hannibal's invasion of Italy: 'this interests me immensely'. A favourite passage (so he told Drury) concerned the incident when, after the battle of Cannae, Hannibal has the battle-field searched for the bodies of the two consuls, in order that he could show his respect for them.

In his present state, he wrote in his diary, he would not try to work unless it came easily to him: 'for otherwise, even if I strive, nothing will come out'. At the beginning of March he was again joined at the hotel by Ben, who stayed for ten days: 'Nice time. Always loving.' But even while he enjoyed being with Ben he was conscious of the fact that he was unwell. He slept badly and was troubled by thoughts of the future: '*Do not know how it will turn out.*' A few days after Ben left, he wrote: 'Often it is as though my soul were dead.'

His conversations with Drury turned with increasing frequency to religious subjects. He contrasted Drury's 'Greek' religious ideas with his own thoughts, which were, he said, 'one hundred per cent Hebraic'. Drury had admired Origen's vision of a final restitution of all things, a restoration to their former glory of even Satan and the fallen angels, and commented sadly on its condemnation as a heresy. 'Of course it was rejected', Wittgenstein insisted:

> It would make nonsense of everything else. If what we do now is to make no difference in the end, then all the seriousness of life is done away with.

Wittgenstein's 'Hebraic' conception of religion was, Drury suggested, based on the sense of awe which one feels throughout the Bible. In illustration of this he quoted from Malachi: 'But who may abide the day of his coming and who shall stand when he appeareth?' (Mal. 3:2). This stopped Wittgenstein in his tracks: 'I think you have just said something very important. Much more important than you realize.'

Central to Wittgenstein's 'Hebraic' conception of religion (like that of his favourite English poet, Blake) is the strict separation of philosophy from religion: 'If Christianity is the truth then all the philosophy that is written about it is false.' In conversation with Drury he sharply distinguished the more philosophical St John's Gospel from the others: 'I can't understand the Fourth Gospel. When I read those long discourses, it seems to me as if a different person is speaking than in the synoptic Gospels.'

But what of St Paul? In 1937 he had written: 'The spring which flows gently and limpidly in the Gospels seems to have froth on it in Paul's Epistles.' He had then seen in St Paul, in contrast to the humility of the Gospels, 'something like pride or anger'. In the Gospels you find huts; in Paul a church: 'There all men are equal and God himself is a man; in Paul there is already something like a hierarchy; honours and official positions.' But now, he told Drury, he saw that he had been wrong: 'It is one and the same religion in both the Gospels and the Epistles.'

And yet, within his fundamentally ethical conception of religious faith, he still found the Pauline doctrine of predestination hard to embrace. For, like Origen's teaching, it seems to have the consequence that: 'what we do now is to make no difference in the end'. And if this is so, how can the seriousness of life be upheld?

In 1937 Wittgenstein had characterized the Pauline doctrine as one that could have arisen only from the most dreadful suffering: 'It's less a theory than a sigh, or a cry.' At his own 'level of devoutness' it could appear only as 'ugly nonsense, irreligiousness':

If it is a good and godly picture, then it is so for someone at a quite different level, who might use it in his life in a way completely different from anything that would be possible for me.

In 1949, he could no longer speak of it as 'irreligious'. But neither could he quite see how it could be used as a 'good and godly picture':

Suppose someone were taught: there is a being who, if you do such and such or live thus and thus, will take you to a place of everlasting torment after you die; most people end up there, a few get to a place of everlasting happiness. – This being has selected in advance those who are to go to the good place and, since only those who have lived a certain sort of life go to the place of torment, he has also arranged in advance for the rest to live like that.

What might be the effect of such a doctrine? Well, it does not mention punishment, but rather a sort of natural necessity. And if you were to present things to anyone in this light, he could only react with despair or incredulity to such a doctrine.

Teaching it could not constitute an ethical upbringing. If you wanted to bring someone up ethically while yet teaching him such a doctrine, you would have to teach it to him after having educated him ethically, representing it as a sort of incomprehensible mystery.

Though Wittgenstein had, as yet, no medical grounds for thinking so, he felt that his death might come soon. When Malcolm wrote asking about his financial situation, he replied that he had enough to live on for two years: 'What happens after that time I don't yet know. Maybe I won't live that long anyway.'

In April he left for Vienna to visit Mining on her death-bed. He stayed for three or four weeks, returning to Dublin on 16 May. From there he wrote to Malcolm that Mining was still alive, but that there was no hope of her recovering: 'While I was in Vienna I was hardly able to write at all. I felt so rotten myself.'

Soon after arriving back in Dublin, he went, on Drury's advice, to see the Professor of Medicine at Trinity College for a diagnosis of the intestine trouble and the general feeling of exhaustion that had dogged him since the beginning of the year. It was suspected that he might have a growth in his stomach, but after being admitted to hospital for a full investigation he was told that no such growth showed up on the X-ray, and the only findings made were that he had an atypical and unexplained anaemia. He was put on a treatment of iron and liver extract, and although he still found himself unable to concentrate on philosophy, his condition gradually improved.

He was anxious to overcome his anaemia quickly for two reasons. First, because he had at last decided to accept a long-standing invitation from Norman Malcolm to spend the summer at the Malcolms' home in Ithaca, USA (after first insisting in jest that, if he came, Malcolm was to introduce him to his favourite film star, Betty Hutton). He had booked a passage on the *Queen Mary*, sailing on 21 July. The second reason was that, before he left for America, he wanted to spend a few weeks in Cambridge preparing a final, polished typescript of the work with which he had been occupied since 1946.

During his period of recovery he remained in Dublin, and it was presumably during this time that he prepared the fair manuscript copy of what is now *Philosophical Investigations*, Part II. As a restful diversion from this work, Drury proposed giving him a record-player and some records of his choice. Wittgenstein declined. It would never do, he said; it would be like giving him a box of chocolates: 'I wouldn't know when to stop eating.' On the other hand, Drury himself, he said, ought to listen to music when he was tired after his work. And so the next morning he had a radio set delivered to Drury's rooms. Shortly after this Drury remarked on the great improvement of recording techniques evident in the records he heard on the radio. This elicited from Wittgenstein a typically Spenglerian reflection:

> It is so characteristic that, just when the mechanics of reproduction are so vastly improved, there are fewer and fewer people who know how the music should be played.

On 13 June, Drury and Wittgenstein listened together to a radio discussion between A. J. Ayer and Father Copleston on 'The Existence of God'. Ayer, Wittgenstein said, 'has something to say, but he is incredibly shallow'. Copleston, on the other hand, 'contributed nothing at all to the discussion'. To attempt to justify the beliefs of Christianity with philosophical arguments was entirely to miss the point.

A week later he left Dublin. One senses that, in packing his large pile of notebooks, manuscripts and typescripts, he was not only winding up his affairs in Dublin, but also bringing to a close his entire contribution to philosophy. He told Drury of a letter he had received from Ludwig Hänsel in which Hänsel had expressed the hope that Wittgenstein's work would go well, if it should be God's will. 'Now that is all I want', he said, 'if it should be God's will':

> Bach wrote on the title page of his *Orgelbüchlein*, 'To the glory of the most high God, and that my neighbour may be benefited thereby.' That is what I would have liked to say about my work.

The use of the past tense here is telling; it indicates that he now considered his work to be all but over.

He spent the month before his journey to the United States staying alternately with von Wright in Cambridge and with Ben Richards in Uxbridge. Von Wright had just finished his first year as Wittgenstein's successor as Professor of Philosophy of Cambridge, and was living in a rented house ('Strathaird') in Lady Margaret Road. During his stay there Wittgenstein occupied a separate apartment of two rooms and had his meals with the family (von Wright, his wife and their two children). 'There is one thing that I'm afraid of', he wrote to von Wright before he came to stay with him: 'I may not be able to discuss philosophy. Of course it's possible that things will have changed by then, but at present I'm quite incapable of even thinking of philosophical problems. My head is *completely* dull.'

His chief concern during these few weeks in Cambridge was to dictate to a typist the manuscript containing his final selection of the remarks written over the last three years, which now forms Part II of *Philosophical Investigations*. This is the last typescript that Wittgenstein is known to have prepared, and as such it represents the culmination of his attempts to arrange his remarks on psychological concepts into a publishable form.

It does not represent, however, the completion of that task: as he had told Elizabeth Anscombe in Dublin, he regarded this new selection as material to use in the revision of *Philosophical Investigations*, Part I. As he never carried out this work of revision himself, the book as we now have it has the rather unsatisfying two-part structure whereby the second 'part' is no more than material to be used in the revision of the first. Moreover, the work that was originally conceived of as the 'second part' – Wittgenstein's analysis of mathematical concepts – does not appear in the book at all. Wittgenstein's painstaking fastidiousness over the structure of his book has had the ironic result that his work has been published in a form very far removed from his original conception.

The longest section of this new typescript is that concerned with the problems of aspect-seeing, and is a distillation of the work, already discussed, that he had written on that topic over the previous three years. This section constitutes roughly half (thirty-six pages in the printed version) of the entire typescript. He told Rhees, however, that the section he was particularly satisfied with was that concerned with 'Moore's Paradox' (Section X). He was pleased, he said, to have condensed his many remarks on this paradox into such a relatively short section (three printed pages).

'Moore's Paradox' is the name Wittgenstein gave to the absurdity of stating a proposition and then saying that one does not believe it – for example: 'There is a fire in this room and I don't believe there is.' The title 'Moore's Paradox' is perhaps a misnomer: Wittgenstein believed, probably erroneously, that Moore had discovered this type of absurdity. (Indeed, he once remarked to Malcolm that its discovery was the only work of Moore's that had greatly impressed him.) The interest Wittgenstein took in the Paradox arises from the fact that, although anybody who uttered such a statement would ordinarily be taken to be contradicting themselves, it is not formally a contradiction. That is, the two statements: 'There is a fire in this room' and: 'RM does not believe there is a fire in this room' do not contradict one another.

Wittgenstein first came across the Paradox in a paper by Moore given to the Moral Science Club in October 1944. He immediately wrote to Moore urging him to publish his 'discovery' and explaining why he considered it so important:

> You have said something about the *logic* of assertion. Viz: It makes sense to say 'Let's suppose: p is the case and I don't believe that p is the case', whereas it makes *no* sense to assert 'I-p is the case and I don't believe that p is the case.' This *assertion* has to be ruled out and *is* ruled out by 'common sense', just as a contradiction is. And this just shows that logic isn't as simple as logicians think it is. In particular: that contradiction isn't the *unique* thing people think it is. It isn't the *only* logically inadmissible form and it is, under certain circumstances, admissible. And to show that seems to me the chief merit of your paper.

This was not how Moore himself saw it. He was inclined to say that, as the Paradox did not issue in formal contradiction, it was an absurdity for psychological, rather than logical, reasons. This Wittgenstein vigorously rejected:

> If I ask someone 'Is there a fire in the next room?' and he answers 'I believe there is' I can't say: 'Don't be irrelevant. I asked you about the fire not about your state of mind!'

Any investigation into what it does and does not make sense to assert was, for Wittgenstein, a part of logic, and to point out that, in this sense: 'logic isn't as simple as logicians think it is' was one of the chief concerns of his own investigations. It was an aspect of Wittgenstein's later work that was noted early by Bertrand Russell, who in his report to the Council of Trinity College of 1930 remarked that Wittgenstein's theories were 'novel, very original, and indubitably important'. But: 'Whether they are true, I do not know. As a logician, who likes simplicity, I should wish to think that they are not.'

'Moore's Paradox' interested Wittgenstein as an illustration that, contrary to the logician's desire for simplicity, the forms of our language cannot be squeezed without distortion into the pigeon-holes created for them by the categories of formal logic. The statement: 'I believe there is a fire in the next room' is used to assert, albeit hesitantly, that there is a fire in the next room; it is not used to assert a state of mind. ('Don't regard a hesitant assertion as an assertion of hesitancy.') This distinguishes it from the statements: 'I believed then that there was a fire in the next room'; and: 'He believes there is a fire in the next room' – both of which would ordinarily be taken to be about people's beliefs, rather than about fires. This feature of the logic of our language forbids us from constructing the convenient form: 'x believes/believed p' and thinking that the form remains unchanged whatever values are given to x and p: 'I believe there is a fire in the next room' is not the same kind of assertion as 'I believed there was a fire in the next room':

> 'But surely "I believed" must tell of just the same thing in the past as "I believe" in the present!' – Surely $\sqrt{-1}$ must mean just the same in relation to -1, as $\sqrt{1}$ means in relation to 1! This means nothing at all.

If we regard the form $\sqrt{x}$ as having a single meaning, whatever the value of x, we get into a hopeless tangle when we consider $\sqrt{-1}$. For, given our ordinary rules of multiplication, the square root of minus one can be neither a positive nor a negative number, and within the realm of 'real numbers' there is nothing left for it to be. And yet $\sqrt{-1}$ has a use: it is an essential notion in many important branches of pure and applied mathematics. But to give it a meaning it has been found necessary to construct different meanings of 'multiplication', 'square root' and even 'number' such that the square root of minus one is said to be, not a real number, but i, an 'imaginary number' (or, as it is sometimes called, an 'operator'). Given this revised framework, $i^2 = -1$, and the notion of the square root of minus one is not only unproblematic but is made the basis of a whole Theory of 'Complex

Numbers'. Wittgenstein was interested in the square root of minus one for exactly the same reason that he was interested in 'Moore's Paradox': it illustrates the fact that superficial similarities of form can disguise very important differences of meaning.

This latter idea is one of the main themes of the book, justifying Wittgenstein's suggestion to Drury that he might use the Earl of Kent's phrase: 'I'll teach you differences' as a motto, and it is particularly evident in the analysis of psychological concepts in *Philosophical Investigations*, Part II. Just as he wished to show that logic isn't as simple as logicians think it is, so he wished to show that psychological concepts and the sentences in which they are used, are not as uniform as philosophers and psychologists would wish them to be. In both cases the aim is to disencourage the 'craving for generality' – to encourage people to look before they think.

For example, the question: 'What does the sentence "I am afraid" mean?' does not have a single answer that would be adequate to cover all the occasions on which the sentence might be used. For, as in the case of the square roots of one and minus one, the differences between the various uses might be just as important as the similarities:

> We can imagine all sorts of things here, for example:
>
> 'No, no! I am afraid!'
> 'I am afraid. I am sorry to have to confess it.'
> 'I am still a bit afraid, but no longer as much as before.'
> 'At bottom I am afraid, though I won't confess it to myself.'
> 'I torment myself with all sorts of fears.'
> 'Now, just when I should be fearless, I am afraid!'
>
> To each of these sentences a special tone of voice is appropriate, and a different context. It would be possible to imagine people who as it were thought more definitely than we, and used different words where we use only one.

To understand what 'I am afraid' means on a particular occasion one might have to take into account the tone of voice and the context in which it is uttered. There is no reason to think that a general theory of fear would be much help here (still less a general theory of language). Far more to the point would be an alert and observant sensitivity to people's faces, voices and situations. This kind of sensitivity can be gained only by experience – by attentive looking and listening to the people around us. Once, when Wittgenstein and Drury were walking together in the west of Ireland, they came across a five-year-old girl sitting outside a cottage. 'Drury, just look at the expression on that child's face', Wittgenstein implored, adding: 'You don't take enough notice of people's faces; it is a fault you ought to try to correct.' It is a piece of advice that is implicitly embodied in his philosophy of psychology: 'An inner process stands in need of outward criteria.' But those outward criteria stand in need of careful attention.

What is 'internal' is not hidden from us. To observe someone's outward behaviour – if we understand them – is to observe their state of mind. The understanding required can be more or less refined. At a basic level: 'If I see someone writhing in pain with evident cause I do not think: all the same, his feelings are hidden from me.' But at a deeper level some people, and even whole cultures, will always be an enigma to us:

> It is important for our view of things that someone may feel concerning certain people that their inner life will always be a mystery to him. That he will never understand them. (English-women in the eyes of Europeans.)

This is because the commonality of experience required to interpret the 'imponderable evidence', the 'subtleties of glance, gesture and tone', will be missing. This idea is summed up in one of Wittgenstein's most striking aphorisms: 'If a lion could talk, we could not understand him.'

The abstractions and generalities, the laws and principles, that result from theorizing can, on Wittgenstein's view, only hinder our attempts towards a better understanding of this 'imponderable evidence'. But how, in the absence of theory, are we to better our understanding, to deepen our insight?

Take, for example, one of the hardest and one of the most important distinctions to make concerning our understanding of people: the distinction between a genuine and an affected expression of feeling:

> Is there such a thing as 'expert judgment' about the genuineness of expressions of feeling? – Even here there are those whose judgment is 'better' and those whose judgment is 'worse'.

Correcter prognoses will generally issue from the judgments of those with better knowledge of mankind.

Can one learn this knowledge? Yes; some can. Not, however, by taking a course in it, but through '*experience*'. – Can someone else be a man's teacher in this? Certainly. From time to time he gives him the right *tip*. – This is what 'learning' and 'teaching' are like here. – What one acquires here is not a technique; one learns correct judgments. There are also rules, but they do not form a system, and only experienced people can apply them right. Unlike calculating rules.

An example of such a teacher might be the figure of Father Zossima in Dostoevsky's *The Brothers Karamazov*:

It was said by many people about the elder Zossima that, by permitting everyone for so many years to come to bare their hearts and beg his advice and healing words, he had absorbed so many secrets, sorrows, and avowals into his soul that in the end he had acquired so fine a perception that he could tell at the first glance from the face of a stranger what he had come for, what he wanted and what kind of torment racked his conscience.

In describing Father Zossima, Dostoevsky is here describing Wittgenstein's ideal of psychological insight. When, after being persuaded by Wittgenstein to read *The Brothers Karamazov*, Drury reported that he had found the figure of Zossima very impressive, Wittgenstein replied: 'Yes, there really have been people like that, who could see directly into the souls of other people and advise them.'

Such people, Wittgenstein suggests, have more to teach us about understanding ourselves and other people than the experimental methods of the modern–day 'science' of psychology. This is not because the science is undeveloped but because the methods it employs are inappropriate to its task:

The confusion and barrenness of psychology is not to be explained by calling it a 'young science'; its state is not comparable with that of physics, for instance, in its beginnings. (Rather with that of certain branches of mathematics. Set Theory.) For in psychology there are experimental methods and *conceptual confusion*. (As in the other case conceptual confusion and methods of proof.) The existence of the experimental method makes us think we have the means of solving the problems which trouble us; though problem and method pass one another by.

Philosophical Investigations, Part II, ends with a suggestion of what the second volume of Wittgenstein's book might have contained:

> An investigation is possible in connexion with mathematics which is entirely analogous to our investigation of psychology. It is just as little a mathematical investigation as the other is a psychological one. It will not contain calculations, so it is not for example logistic. It might deserve the name of an investigation of the 'foundations of mathematics'.

By 12 July the work of dictating this typescript was finished, and Wittgenstein left Cambridge to spend the week remaining before his trip to the United States with Ben Richards in Uxbridge. During the remaining two years of his life, although he continued to write philosophy, he made no further attempt to restructure his book in the way that he had intended. *Philosophical Investigations* has therefore reached us in the somewhat transitory state in which it was left in the summer of 1949.

26
A CITIZEN OF
NO COMMUNITY

The last two years of Wittgenstein's life have about them something of the nature of an epilogue. The task of arranging his work
for publication, though not complete, was now over – at least for
him. He had by now accepted that his book – the work that had been
the centre of his life for nearly twenty years – would not appear in his
lifetime. The job of editing it and seeing to its posthumous publication
was in the hands of others. And in other ways, too, he was dependent
on other people in a way that he had not been since before the First
World War. He had no income, no home of his own, and little taste for
the solitariness and fierce independence that before he had craved. His
last two years were spent living as a guest of his friends and disciples –
with Malcolm in Ithaca, von Wright in Cambridge, and Elizabeth
Anscombe in Oxford.

But his motives for living with others were not primarily financial.
Indeed, there was actually no financial need for him to do so: as he had
earlier told Malcolm, he had enough money saved from his salary at
Cambridge to last another two years. The need to live with others was
partly emotional, partly physical (he was increasingly ill and in need of
attention), and also partly intellectual. So long as he lived, he wanted
to live as a philosopher, and though he now felt, for the most part,
unable to live alone and write, he did feel able to discuss philosophy.
Thus we find, to a much greater extent than hitherto, the stimulus for
his philosophical thinking being provided by the thoughts and problems of others. The work he wrote in his last two years, though
naturally in many ways of a piece with the *Investigations*, is in another
respect quite distinct from it; it is much more directed to the solution

of other people's problems. It has the character that he himself had earlier attributed to all his work – that of clarifying the work of others – and it is written much more consciously than his other work with a view to being useful. It is as though he wished to reward the hospitality of his hosts by availing t. em of his most prized possession: his philosophical talent.

In his exchange of letters with Malcolm before he left for the States, Wittgenstein returned again and again to the question of whether, in coming to Ithaca, he would be of any use to Malcolm philosophically. 'My mind is tired & stale', he wrote in April. 'I think I could discuss philosophy if I had someone here to discuss with, but alone I can't concentrate on it.' Two months later he wrote: 'I *know* you'd extend your hospitality to me even if I were *completely* dull & stupid, but *I* wouldn't want to be a mere dead weight in your house. I want to feel that I can at least give a *little* for so much kindness.'

He set sail on 21 July 1949, travelling on the *Queen Mary* across the Atlantic. 'My anaemia is as good as cured', he wrote before he left, insisting that it was unnecessary for Malcolm to meet him from the boat: 'Maybe, like in the films, I'll find a beautiful girl whom I meet on the boat & who will help me.' Malcolm was, nevertheless, there to meet him, and was surprised to find him apparently fit and strong, 'striding down the ramp with a pack on his back, a heavy suitcase in one hand, cane in the other'.

In some respects, at least, the Malcolms found him an undemanding guest. He insisted on eating bread and cheese at all meals, declaring that he did not care what he ate so long as it was always the same.

The Malcolms lived on the edge of the settled area around Ithaca, just outside the boundaries of the Cayuga Heights, and Wittgenstein often took long walks in the nearby countryside. He took a great interest in the unfamiliar flora of the area. Stuart Brown, a colleague of Malcolm's at Cornell University, remembers that, on one occasion at least, this unfamiliarity resulted in astonished disbelief:

Ordinarily, he would refuse the offer of a ride. But one afternoon, after it had begun to rain, I stopped to offer him a ride back to the Malcolms. He accepted gratefully, and once in the car asked me to identify for him the seed pods of a plant which he picked. 'Milkweed', I told him and pointed out the white sap for which the weed is named. He then asked me to describe the flowers of the plant. I failed so miserably that I at length stopped the car by a grown up field, walked out and picked him more plants, some with flowers and some with seeds. He looked in awe from flowers to seed pods and from seed pods to flowers. Suddenly he crumpled them up, threw them down on the floor of the car, and trampled them. 'Impossible!' he said.

Brown was one of a group of philosophers at Cornell with whom Wittgenstein held discussions. The others included Max Black, Willis Doney, John Nelson and Oets Bouwsma. 'I'm doing my old work here' was how he put it in a letter to Roy Fouracre.* He had, he said, often thought of Fouracre – 'particularly because I often thought I might take up my old work at Guy's or some such place, & now I'm such an old cripple that I couldn't possibly do the work I used to in the dispensary lab'. To Malcolm, too, he expressed an anxiety about what he was to do with the remainder of his life: 'When a person has only one thing in the world – namely a certain talent – what is he to do when he begins to lose that talent?'

In the meantime, there was plenty of demand and appreciation at Cornell for that talent. Together with Malcolm he attended a surprisingly large number of seminars and discussions. There were regular meetings with Brown, Bouwsma and Black, in which they discussed a variety of philosophical topics, seminars with Doney to read the *Tractatus*, and meetings with Bouwsma to discuss Frege's 'On Sense and Reference'. He also met with Nelson and Doney to discuss a problem about memory, an occasion remembered by Nelson as 'probably the most philosophically strenuous two hours I have ever spent':

Under the relentless probing and pushing of his enquiry my head felt almost as if it were ready to burst . . . There was no quarter

---

* Fouracre had finally returned from Sumatra in February 1947, and from then until Wittgenstein's death the two continued their friendship, meeting regularly both in London and in Cambridge. Whenever Wittgenstein was away he would write to Fouracre with the same regularity as he had when Fouracre was in the army. Letters survive written from Dublin, Vienna and Oxford, as well as Ithaca.

given – no sliding off the topic when it became difficult. I was absolutely exhausted when we concluded the discussion.

Nelson's reactions were typical. Though the topics of these meetings were usually suggested by others, the discussions were invariably dominated by Wittgenstein, who demanded from the participants a degree of absorption and attentive rigour to which they were unaccustomed. After one such discussion, Bouwsma asked Wittgenstein whether such evenings robbed him of his sleep. He said that they did not. 'But then', recalls Bouwsma:

. . . he added in all seriousness and with the kind of smile Dostoyevsky would suggest in such a circumstance: 'No but do you know, I think I may go nuts.'

Apart from Malcolm, Bouwsma was the person with whom Wittgenstein spent most time. He seemed to see in him the quality of seriousness that he considered essential in a discussion partner. Unlike the others, Bouwsma was the same age as Wittgenstein. He had been Malcolm's tutor at the University of Nebraska, and Malcolm was one of several students whom Bouwsma had encouraged to go to Cambridge to study with G. E. Moore. Bouwsma himself had been deeply influenced by Moore's work, having abandoned his earlier Hegelianism under the impact of Moore's refutations of idealism. Later, through another of his students, Alice Ambrose, he came across Wittgenstein's *Blue Book*, and made a close study of it.

After a few meetings at Malcolm's house in the company of others, Wittgenstein arranged to meet Bouwsma alone. It was then that the conversation quoted above took place. Wittgenstein had come to see Bouwsma primarily to ask him whether he thought their discussion had been 'any good' – did Bouwsma get anything out of it? 'I am a very vain person', he told him. 'The talk wasn't good. Intellectually, it may have been, but that isn't the point . . . My vanity, my vanity.' He discussed with Bouwsma his reasons for resigning his position at Cambridge:

First I wanted to finish my book . . . Second, why should I teach? What good is it for X to listen to me? Only the man who thinks gets any good out of it.

He made an exception of a few students, 'who had a certain obsession and were serious'. But most of them came to him because he was clever, 'and I am clever, but it's not important'.

What was important was that his teaching should have a good effect, and in this respect the students with whom he was most satisfied were those who had not become professional philosophers – Drury, for example, and Smythies, and those that had become mathematicians. Within professional philosophy he thought his teaching had done more harm than good. He compared it to Freud's teachings, which, like wine, had made people drunk. They did not know how to use the teaching soberly. 'Do you understand?' he asked. 'Oh yes', Bouwsma replied. 'They had found a formula.' 'Exactly.'

That evening Bouwsma took Wittgenstein in his car up to the top of the hill overlooking the town. The moon was up. 'If I had planned it', said Wittgenstein, 'I should never have made the sun at all':

See! How beautiful! The sun is too bright and too hot . . . And if there were only the moon there would be no reading and writing.

In addition to the other meetings mentioned, Wittgenstein had a number of private discussions with Malcolm. These are of special interest, because they provided the primary stimulus for the work which Wittgenstein produced in the last eighteen months of his life.

He had taken with him to Ithaca copies of both parts of *Philosophical Investigations*, so that he and Malcolm could read it through together. He told Malcolm that, though the book was not in a completely finished state, he did not now think that he could give the final polish to it in his lifetime. And, although he did not want to take it to a publisher in its unfinished state, he did want his friends to read and understand it. He therefore considered having it mimeographed and distributed among his friends with expressions of dissatisfaction, like: 'This is not quite right' or: 'This is fishy', written in parentheses after remarks that needed revision. Malcolm did not like the plan, and advised Wittgenstein against it; mimeograph copies, he thought, were an unfitting form of publication for a work of such importance.

A more time-consuming alternative would have been for Wittgenstein to go through the book paragraph by paragraph with each of his friends separately. This he seems to have made some attempt to do. Soon after arriving at Ithaca, he suggested that he and Malcolm should read through the book in this way – just as they had begun to do in Cambridge in 1946. Again, however, Malcolm found the procedure too confining, and after a few meetings the project was once more abandoned. Instead, they began a series of discussions on a philosophical issue that had more immediate relevance to Malcolm's own work.

The topic of these discussions was Moore's attempt to refute philosophical scepticism in his articles 'Proof of an External World' and 'A Defence of Common Sense'. Scepticism asserts that nothing about the external world can be known with certainty, not even that it is external. Moore's 'Proof of an External World' begins with an attempt to prove that some external objects at least can be shown with certainty to exist, his famous example being the existence of his own hands:

> I can prove now, for instance, that two human hands exist. How? By holding up my two hands, and saying, as I make a certain gesture with the right hand, 'Here is one hand', and adding, as I make a certain gesture with the left, 'and here is another.'

In 'A Defence of Common Sense' Moore provides a list of common-sense beliefs, all of which he claims to know with certainty to be true. These include: that a body exists which is Moore's body; that this body has been, throughout its existence, not far from the surface of the earth; that the earth had existed for many years before Moore was born; etc.

Not long before Wittgenstein's visit Malcolm had published an article criticizing Moore for incorrectly using the verb 'to know' in these claims to knowledge. Holding up a hand and saying: 'I know that this is a hand', or pointing to a tree and saying: 'I know for certain that this is a tree' is, Malcolm maintained, a senseless use of 'know'. Moore had written a spirited defence of his use of 'know' in a letter to Malcolm, and now Malcolm had the opportunity of finding out Wittgenstein's view of the matter; he was determined not to waste it.

In conversation with Malcolm, Wittgenstein insisted that: 'An expression has meaning only in the stream of life.' So whether or not Moore's statements were senseless depends on whether we can imagine an occasion on which they could sensibly be used: 'To understand a sentence is to be prepared for one of its uses. If we can't think of any use for it at all, then we don't understand it at all.' In this way:

> Instead of saying that Moore's statement 'I know that this is a tree' is a misuse of language, it is better to say that it has no clear meaning, and that Moore himself doesn't know how he is using it . . . It isn't even clear to him that he is not giving it an ordinary usage.

We could, Wittgenstein thought, imagine ordinary uses for some of Moore's statements more easily than for others: 'It isn't difficult to think of usages for "I know that this is a hand"; it is more difficult for "I know that the earth has existed for many years".'

Moore, of course, was not using his statements in an 'ordinary' way; he was using them to make a philosophical point. He was not informing his readers that he had two hands; he was attempting to refute philosophical scepticism. On this point Wittgenstein was quite clear that Moore had failed:

> When the sceptical philosophers say 'You don't know' and Moore replies 'I do know', his reply is quite useless, unless it is to assure them that he, Moore, doesn't feel any doubt whatever. But that is not what is at issue.

Wittgenstein's own view of scepticism remained that succinctly expressed in the *Tractatus*: 'Scepticism is *not* irrefutable, but obviously nonsensical, when it tries to raise doubts where no questions can be asked.' And it is in connection with this view of scepticism that he found something philosophically interesting about Moore's 'common-sense propositions'. They do not give examples of 'certain knowledge', but, rather, examples of cases in which doubt is nonsensical. If we could seriously doubt that Moore was holding up two hands, there would be no reason not to doubt anything else, including the trustworthiness of our senses. And in that case the whole framework in which we raise doubts and answer them would collapse: 'Certain propositions belong to my "frame of reference". If I had to give *them* up, I shouldn't be able to judge *anything*.' One such proposition might be the statement: 'That's a tree', said while standing in front of a tree:

If I walked over to the tree and could touch nothing I might lose confidence in everything my senses told me . . . Moore said 'I know that there's a tree', partly because of the feeling that if it turned out *not* to be a tree, he would have to 'give up'.

The idea that there are certain judgements (among them, some of Moore's statements of common sense) that belong to our frame of reference, and as such cannot sensibly be doubted, was developed by Wittgenstein in the work written during the eighteen months left of his life following his visit to the United States.★

At the beginning of the autumn term Malcolm took Wittgenstein along to a meeting of the graduate students of philosophy at Cornell University. His presence there, as John Nelson has recalled, had a tremendous impact. 'Just before the meeting was to get underway', Nelson writes, 'Malcolm appeared approaching down the corridor':

On his arm leaned a slight, older man, dressed in windjacket and old army trousers. If it had not been for his face, alight with intelligence, one might have taken him for some vagabond Malcolm had found along the road and decided to bring out of the cold.

. . . I leaned over to Gass and whispered, 'That's Wittgenstein.' Gass thought I was making a joke and said something like, 'Stop pulling my leg.' And then Malcolm and Wittgenstein entered. [Gregory] Vlastos was introduced and gave his paper and finished. Black, who was conducting this particular meeting, stood up and turned to his right and it became clear, to everyone's surprise . . . that he was about to address the shabby older man Malcolm had brought to the meeting. Then came the startling words; said Black, 'I wonder if you would be so kind, Professor Wittgenstein . . .' Well, when Black said 'Wittgenstein' a loud and instantaneous gasp went up from the assembled students. You must remember: 'Wittgenstein' was a mysterious and awesome name in the philosophical world of 1949, at Cornell in particular. The gasp that went up was just the gasp that would have gone up if Black had said 'I wonder if you would be so kind, Plato . . .'

★ This work has now been published as *On Certainty*.

Soon after this meeting Wittgenstein fell ill and was admitted to hospital for an examination. He had already booked his return passage to England in October, and was extremely frightened that he would have to remain in the United States as a result of the operation. He feared that, like Mining, he would be found to have cancer, and would be bed-ridden for the rest of his life. On the day before he went into hospital he said to Malcolm in a frenzy:

I don't want to die in America. I am a European – I want to die in Europe . . . What a fool I was to come.

The examination, however, did not find anything seriously wrong with him, and he recovered sufficiently well over the next two weeks to return to England as planned, arriving in London at the end of October. His original plan was to spend a few days in Cambridge with von Wright and then return to Ross's Hotel in Dublin. Soon after arriving in London, however, he fell ill once more, and it was not until 9 November that he was able to go to Cambridge, still too ill to contemplate the journey to Dublin.

Drury had once told Wittgenstein that if he ever needed to see a doctor when in Cambridge he should consult Dr Edward Bevan. Drury had got to know Bevan during the war, when they had been in the same unit in the army, and had been impressed by his ability. By a coincidence, Bevan was also von Wright's family doctor. Soon after his arrival at Cambridge, therefore, Wittgenstein was examined by Dr Bevan. The final diagnosis was given on 25 November: cancer of the prostate.

Wittgenstein was in no way shocked to learn that he had cancer. He was, however, shocked to hear that something could be done about it. Cancer of the prostate often responds well to hormone therapy, and Wittgenstein was therefore immediately prescribed oestrogen. He was told that, with the help of this hormone, he could reasonably hope to live for another six years. 'I am sorry that my life should be prolonged in this way', he wrote to Rhees: 'six months of this half-life would be plenty.'

A few days after he learnt that he had cancer he wrote to Helene, asking if it would be convenient for him to come to Vienna to stay in the family home in the Alleegasse. 'My health is very bad', he told her, 'and I can therefore do no work. In Vienna I hope to find peace . . . If I could have my old room in the Alleegasse (with the overhead light), that would be good.'

Having warned her that she would find him in bad health, and that he would have to spend part of each day in bed, he told her nothing more about the nature of his illness. He was determined that his family should not know that he had cancer. Before he left for Vienna he wrote to Malcolm imploring him not to let anyone know about his illness: 'This is of the greatest importance for me as I plan to go to Vienna for Christmas & not to let my family know about the real disease.'

He flew to Vienna on 24 December, and moved into his old room at the Alleegasse. With Hermine lying in bed dying of cancer, and with Wittgenstein himself having the unmistakable pallor of a man stricken with the same disease, it is unlikely that his family did not guess the real nature of his illness. Wittgenstein, however, continued with his attempts at concealment, sending a telegram to von Wright with the euphemistic message: 'ARRIVED VIENNA EXCELLENT HEALTH AND SPIRITS. NOTIFY FRIENDS.'

For the first month that he was there, Wittgenstein did no writing at all. He allowed himself the luxury of leading the kind of comfortable life for which the family home was so admirably equipped. At the Alleegasse he was well fed and well looked after, and even entertained. 'I haven't been to a concert so far', he wrote to von Wright:

> but I hear a fair amount of music. A friend of mine [Rudolf Koder] plays the piano to me (very beautifully) and one of my sisters and he play piano duets. The other day they played two string quartets by Schumann and a sonata written for 4 hands by Mozart.

'I'm very happy & being treated *very* well', he wrote to Dr Bevan. Bevan had written to him about Ben, and had obviously commented on Ben's timidity. 'He isn't so much *timid*', Wittgenstein explained, 'as *very* shy & *very* repressed, particularly before he knows someone *well*':

> I wish I knew how important it really is that he should get a job at *Barts*. He seems to regard it as important. But I wish he could get out of London! I have an idea Barts isn't good for him. I *don't* mean by this that he is in any danger of becoming superficial, or snobbish, or anything like that. There is no danger there. But I wish he could be with more simple & more kindly people with whom he could open up, or he will get more & more withdrawn.

To his doctor, Wittgenstein was prepared to dwell a little on the state of his health. It was, as one would expect (especially in an Austrian winter – 'we had – 15 C', he told Bevan), rather precarious:

> I had a rather nasty cold lately, accompanied by stomach troubles; I'm afraid I was on the verge of seeing a doctor & very worried about *that*, but it cleared up by itself & I'm almost as good as new again.

Of course, he could only really feel 'as good as new' in so far as he was capable of philosophizing. 'Colours spur us to philosophize. Perhaps that explains Goethe's passion for the theory of colours', he had written in 1948, and in January 1950 it was exactly with the intention of spurring himself to philosophize that he began reading Goethe's *Farbenlehre* ('Theory of Colour'). 'It's partly boring and repelling, but in some ways also very instructive and philosophically interesting', he told von Wright. Its chief merit, as he put it to Malcolm, was that it 'stimulates me to think'.

Eventually, it also stimulated him to write. A short series of twenty remarks inspired by reading Goethe's *Farbenlehre* have survived, presumably written during what was to be Wittgenstein's last visit to Vienna. They are now published as Part II of *On Colour*.

In them Wittgenstein connects Goethe's Theory of Colour, as he had earlier connected Goethe's other scientific work, with his own philosophical investigations. Contrary to Goethe himself, who regarded his theory as a successful refutation of Newton's Theory of Optics, Wittgenstein was clear that whatever interest the theory had, it was not as a contribution to physics. It was, rather, a *conceptual* investigation. From Wittgenstein's point of view this made it more, not less, interesting:

> I may find scientific questions interesting, but they never really grip me. Only conceptual and aesthetic questions do that. At bottom I am indifferent to the solution of scientific problems; but not of the other sort.

To be sure, Goethe's studies, like scientific investigations, were based on careful observations, but these observations do not enable us to construct explanatory laws. They do, however, enable us to clarify certain concepts. Take, for example, the proposition: 'Blending in white removes the colouredness from the colour; but blending in yellow does not.' What kind of proposition is this?

> As I mean it, it can't be a proposition of physics. Here the temptation to believe in a phenomenology, something midway between science and logic, is very great.

It can't be a proposition of physics, because its contrary is not false but meaningless: 'If someone didn't find it to be this way, it wouldn't be that he had experienced the contrary, but rather that we wouldn't understand him.' Therefore, to analyse this proposition (and others like it) is not to clarify a matter of fact, whether physical or phenomenological; it is to clarify certain concepts ('colour', 'colouredness', 'white' etc.). Thus:

> Phenomenological analysis (as e.g. Goethe would have it) is analysis of concepts and can neither agree with nor contradict physics.

On 11 February Hermine died. 'We had expected her end hourly for the last 3 days', Wittgenstein wrote to von Wright the next day. 'It wasn't a shock.'

His own health, meanwhile, continued to improve, and he was able to meet with Elizabeth Anscombe (who was in Vienna to improve her German in preparation for translating Wittgenstein's work) two or three times a week. Anscombe acted as a further stimulus to his attempts to recover his ability for philosophical work. At a meeting of the Austrian College Society in Alpbach, she had met Paul Feyerabend, who was then a student at the University of Vienna. She gave Feyerabend manuscripts of Wittgenstein's work and discussed them with him. Feyerabend was then a member of the Kraft Circle, an informal philosophy club founded by students at the university who were dissatisfied with the official course of lectures. It was exactly the kind of informal gathering at which Wittgenstein felt able to discuss philosophy publicly, and eventually he was persuaded to attend. Feyerabend recalls:

> Wittgenstein who took a long time to make up his mind and then appeared over an hour late gave a spirited performance and seemed

to prefer our disrespectful attitude to the fawning admiration he encountered elsewhere

This meeting of the Kraft Circle is probably the only public meeting of philosophers that Wittgenstein attended while he was in Vienna. His regular meetings with Anscombe, however, probably helped to 'spur him to philosophize'. As well as the twenty remarks on Goethe's theory of colour, there is also a series of sixty-five remarks which continue the topic of his conversations with Malcolm. These have now been published as the first sixty-five remarks of *On Certainty*. In them Wittgenstein insists that, like 'Moore's Paradox', Moore's 'Defence of Common Sense' is a contribution to logic. For: 'everything descriptive of a language-game is part of logic'.

The line of thought here is strikingly reminiscent of the *Tractatus* (as Wittgenstein himself later acknowledges: *On Certainty*, p. 321). The idea is that, if the contrary of a proposition makes sense, then that proposition can be regarded as an empirical hypothesis, its truth or falsity being dependent on the way things stand in the world. But if the contrary of a proposition does not make sense, then the proposition is not descriptive of the world but of our conceptual framework; it is then a part of logic.

Thus: 'Physical objects exist' is not an empirical proposition, for its contrary is not false but incomprehensible. Similarly, if Moore holds up two hands and our reaction is to say: 'Moore's hands don't exist', our statement could not be regarded as false but as unintelligible. But if this is so, then these 'framework propositions' do not describe a body of knowledge; they describe the way in which we understand the world. In this case, it makes no sense to claim, as Moore does, that you know them with certainty to be true:

If 'I know etc', is conceived as a grammatical proposition, of course the 'I' cannot be important. And it properly means 'There is no such thing as a doubt in this case' or 'The expression "I do not know" makes no sense in this case.' And of course it follows from this that 'I know' makes no sense either.

There is an important parallel between these remarks on Moore and the remarks on Goethe. In both cases Wittgenstein's concern is to point out that what look like experiential propositions should actually be seen as grammatical propositions, descriptive not of our experience but of the framework within which our experience can be described. In some ways his discussion of both is an application of a general truth enunciated in the *Investigations*:

> If language is to be a means of communication there must be agreement not only in definitions but also (queer as this may sound) in judgments. This seems to abolish logic but does not do so.

Such statements as: 'Blending in white removes the colouredness from the colour' and: 'The earth has existed for a long time' are examples of such judgements. Recognizing them as such does not abolish logic, but it does considerably expand and complicate it, in such a way as to include within its domain discussions, for example, of Goethe's Theory of Colour and of Moore's 'Defence of Common Sense'.

The work written in Vienna is no more than the beginning of these discussions. Compared to the work written in Dublin the previous year, it is dull stuff. It has none of the aphoristic compression of that work, nor does it contain any of the kind of startlingly imaginative metaphors that characterize Wittgenstein's best work. It does show, however, that, as Wittgenstein's health gradually recovered, so too did his capacity for philosophical writing.

Wittgenstein left Vienna on 23 March and returned to London, where he stayed for a week at the home of Rush Rhees's wife, Jean, in Goldhurst Terrace. Being back in England was, he wrote, 'woeful'. The order of the place was 'loathsome'. The people seemed dead; every spark of life was extinguished.

On 4 April he moved back to von Wright's house in Cambridge, where he found waiting for him an invitation from Oxford University to deliver the John Locke lectures for 1950. These are an annual series of prestigious and relatively well-paid lectures which are traditionally delivered by a distinguished visiting philosopher. Despite the financial rewards (he was offered £200 to give them), he was not tempted. He was told that there would be a large audience of over 200 students, and that there was not to be any discussion during the lectures. No two conditions could be more likely to put him off. He told Malcolm: 'I don't think I can give formal lectures to a large audience that would be any good.'

Concerned that Wittgenstein's money would soon run out, Malcolm approached the Rockefeller Foundation on his behalf. He told Wittgenstein that he had managed to interest a director of the foundation, Chadbourne Gilpatrick, in the possibility of awarding him a research grant. Wittgenstein's gratitude for this was tempered by a remarkable piece of fiercely honest self-assessment. There were, of course, reasons to accept the grant:

> The thought of being able to live where I like, of not having to be a burden or a nuisance to others, of doing philosophy when my nature inclines me to do it is, of course, pleasant for me.

But, he told Malcolm, he could not take the money unless the Rockefeller Foundation 'knew the complete truth about me':

> The truth is this. a) I have not been able to do any sustained good work since the beginning of March 1949. b) Even before that date I could not work well for more than 6 or 7 months a year. c) As I'm getting older my thoughts become markedly less forceful & crystallize more rarely & I get tired very much more easily. d) My health is in a somewhat labile state owing to a constant slight anaemia which inclines me to catch infections. This further diminishes the chance of my doing really good work. e) Though it's impossible for me to make any definite predictions, it seems to me likely that my mind will never again work as vigorously as it did, say, 14 months ago. f) I cannot promise to publish anything during my lifetime.

He asked Malcolm to show this letter to the foundation's directors. 'It is obviously impossible to accept a grant under false pretences, & you *may* unintentionally have presented my case in too rosy a light.' 'I believe', he added, 'that as long as I live & as often as the state of my mind permits it I will think about philosophical problems & try to write about them':

> I also believe that much of what I wrote in the past 15 or 20 years may be of interest to people when it's published. But it is, nevertheless, perfectly possible that all that I'm going to produce will be flat, uninspired & uninteresting.

When, eight months later, he was visited by Gilpatrick, Wittgenstein told him: 'in my present state of health & intellectual dullness I couldn't accept a grant'.

He attributed his 'intellectual dullness' in part to the oestrogens that he was taking to alleviate the symptoms of his cancer. While taking them he found the intense concentration required to write philosophy difficult to achieve. 'I'm doing some work', he told Malcolm, on 17 April, 'but I get stuck over simple things & almost all I write is pretty dull.'

The work in question forms Part III of *On Colour*, and is a continuation of the remarks on Goethe's *Farbenlehre* that he wrote in Vienna. In some ways it bears out Wittgenstein's own assessment of it: it is a repetitive and rather laboured attempt to clarify the 'logic of colour concepts', in particular the concepts of 'primary colour', 'transparency' and 'luminosity'. Wittgenstein's dissatisfaction with it is manifest: 'That which I am writing about so tediously, may be obvious to someone whose mind is less decrepit.' It does, however, contain a marvellously succinct dismissal of Goethe's remarks on the general characteristics of various colours:

One and the same musical theme has a different character in the minor than in the major, but it is completely wrong to speak of the character of the minor mode in general. (In Schubert the major often sounds more sorrowful than the minor.)

And in this way I think that it is worthless and of no use whatsoever for the understanding of painting to speak of the characteristics of the individual colours. When we do it, we are really thinking of special uses. That green as the colour of a tablecloth has this, red that effect, does not allow us to draw any conclusions as to their effect in a picture.

Imagine someone pointing to a spot in the iris in a face by Rembrandt and saying 'the wall in my room should be painted this colour'.

It was while he was staying with the von Wrights in April 1950 that the last photographs of Wittgenstein were taken. They show Wittgenstein and von Wright sitting together in folding chairs in front of a bed sheet. This odd arrangement was, as K. E. Tranøy (who took the photographs) remembers, Wittgenstein's own idea:

> In the late spring of 1950 we had tea with the von Wrights in the garden. It was a sunny day and I asked Wittgenstein if I could take a photograph of him. He said, yes, I could do that, if I would let him sit with his back to the lens. I had no objections and went to get my camera. In the meantime Wittgenstein had changed his mind. He now decided I was to take the picture in the style of a passport photograph, and von Wright was to sit next to him. Again I agreed, and Wittgenstein now walked off to get the sheet from his bed; he would not accept Elizabeth von Wright's offer of a fresh sheet from her closets. Wittgenstein draped the sheet, hanging it in front of the verandah, and pulled up two chairs.

On 25 April Wittgenstein left Cambridge to move into Elizabeth Anscombe's house in St John Street, Oxford. 'I like to stay with the von Wrights', he told Malcolm, 'but the two children are noisy & I need quiet.' At Anscombe's house he occupied a room on the second floor, the ground floor being occupied by Frank and Gillian Goodrich, and the first by Barry Pink. Soon after he moved in he told von Wright: 'The house isn't very noisy but not very quiet, either. I don't know yet how I shall get on. The lodgers seem all to be rather nice, and one of them even very nice.'

The 'very nice' one was Barry Pink, who was then attending art college. His interests were many and varied: 'Pink wants to sit on six stools at once', Wittgenstein once remarked, 'but he only has one arse.' Pink had long been a friend of Yorick Smythies, and, like Smythies and Anscombe, was a convert to Catholicism. He found in Wittgenstein someone willing and able to converse with him about the whole range of his interests – art, sculpture, stone-masonry, machine-construction and so on.

The two took walks together around Oxford, and for a time Pink became a confidant. They were able to discuss their thoughts, feelings and lives with a fair degree of frankness. They discussed, for example, the tendency to hide one's real nature. In connection with this, Pink asked Wittgenstein whether he thought his work as a philosopher, even his being a philosopher, had anything to do with his homosexuality. What was implied was that Wittgenstein's work as a philosopher may in some way have been a device to hide from his homosexuality. Wittgenstein dismissed the question with anger in his voice: 'Certainly not!'

Wittgenstein planned to spend the summer in Norway with Ben, who was then in his final year as a medical student at Bart's in London. In July, however, Ben failed his final qualifying exams, and so had to stay in London during the summer to study for the 'retake' in September. Their holiday was therefore postponed until the autumn, and Wittgenstein stayed in Oxford throughout the summer, devoting himself to a continuation of the remarks on colour that he had written in Cambridge.

In the same manuscript notebook as the remarks on colour is a series of remarks on Shakespeare, which have been published in *Culture and Value* (pp. 84–6). Wittgenstein had long been troubled by his inability to appreciate the greatness of Shakespeare. In 1946, for example, he had written:

> It is remarkable how hard we find it to believe something that we do not see the truth of for ourselves. When, for instance, I hear the expression of admiration for Shakespeare by distinguished men in the course of several centuries, I can never rid myself of the suspicion that praising him has been the conventional thing to do; though I have to tell myself that this is not how it is. It takes the authority of a Milton really to convince me. I take it for granted that he was incorruptible. – But I don't of course mean by this that I don't believe an enormous amount of praise to have been, and still to be, lavished on Shakespeare without understanding and for the wrong reasons by a thousand professors of literature.

One of the difficulties he had in accepting Shakespeare as a great poet was that he disliked many of Shakespeare's metaphors and similes: 'Shakespeare's similes are, *in the ordinary sense*, bad. So if they are all the same good – and I don't know whether they are or not – they must be a law to themselves.' An example he discussed with Ben was the use of a portcullis as a metaphor for teeth in Mowbray's speech in *Richard II*: 'Within my mouth you have engaol'd my tongue/ Doubly portcullis'd with my teeth and lips.'

A more fundamental difficulty was Wittgenstein's dislike of English culture in general: 'I believe that if one is to enjoy a writer one has to like the culture he belongs to as well. If one finds it indifferent or distasteful, one's admiration cools off.' This did not prevent Wittgenstein from admiring Blake or Dickens. The difference is that, in Shakespeare, Wittgenstein could not see a writer whom he could admire as a great human being:

> I could only stare in wonder at Shakespeare; never do anything with him . . .
>
> 'Beethoven's great heart' – nobody could speak of 'Shakespeare's great heart' . . .
>
> I do not think that Shakespeare would have been able to reflect on the 'lot of the poet'.
>
> Nor could he regard himself as a prophet or as a teacher of mankind.
>
> People stare at him in wonderment, almost as at a spectacular natural phenomenon. They do not have the feeling that this brings them into contact with a great *human being*. Rather with a phenomenon.

In Dickens, on the other hand, Wittgenstein did find an English writer whom he could respect for his 'good universal art' – in the Tolstoyan sense of art that is intelligible to everyone, and that espouses Christian virtues. He gave a pocket edition of *A Christmas Carol*, bound in green leather and plastered with cheerful 'Merry Xmas' stickers, to Fouracre as a belated Christmas present when Fouracre returned from Sumatra. The choice of book, of course, is significant. F. R. Leavis recalls that Wittgenstein knew *A Christmas Carol* practically by heart, and the book is, in fact, placed by Tolstoy in his treatise *What is Art?* in the very highest category of art 'flowing from the love of God'. It is thus a highly appropriate gift to make within a friendship that stands out in Wittgenstein's life as a rare example of his Tolstoyan respect for 'the common man', exemplified in a simple and straightforward affection for an ordinary working man.

In the late summer of 1950 Wittgenstein resumed his remarks on the philosophical significance of Moore's 'common-sense propositions'. This work now constitutes remarks 65–299 of *On Certainty*. In it Wittgenstein elaborates on the idea that Moore's statements have the peculiarity that their denial is not just false, but incomprehensible:

If Moore were to pronounce the opposite of those propositions which he declares certain, we should not just not share his opinion: we should regard him as demented.

Thus: 'if I make certain false statements, it becomes uncertain whether I understand them.' Moore gives us examples of such statements. Another example might be knowing where one lives:

> For months I have lived at address A, I have read the name of the street and the number of the house countless times, have received countless letters here and have given countless people the address. If I am wrong about it, the mistake is hardly less than if I were (wrongly) to believe I was writing Chinese and not German.
> If my friend were to imagine one day that he had been living for a long time past in such and such a place, etc. etc., I should not call this a mistake, but rather a mental disturbance, perhaps a transient one.

A mistake becomes, for us, a mental disturbance when it contradicts, not just this or that proposition which we believe to be true, but the whole framework within which we can give grounds for our beliefs. The only occasion Wittgenstein can think of in which it would be appropriate for Moore to assert: 'I know that I have not left the surface of the earth', would be one in which he is faced by people operating within a vastly different framework:

> I could imagine Moore being captured by a wild tribe, and their expressing the suspicion that he has come from somewhere between the earth and the moon. Moore tells them that he knows etc. but he can't give them the grounds for his certainty, because they have fantastic ideas of human ability to fly and know nothing about physics. This would be an occasion for making that statement.

But this example indicates that a different framework is not necessarily evidence of insanity. In 1950 it was absurd to suppose that someone might have been in outer space and returned to earth. We have now grown accustomed to the idea. Frameworks change, both between different cultures and within a culture between different times.

This, though, is not a point against Wittgenstein. On the contrary, he stresses that a framework itself cannot be justified or proven correct; it provides the limits within which justification and proof take place:

> Everything that I have seen or heard gives me the conviction that no man has ever been far from the earth. Nothing in my picture of the world speaks in favour of the opposite.
>
> But I did not get my picture of the world by satisfying myself of its correctness; nor do I have it because I am satisfied of its correctness. No: it is the inherited background against which I distinguish between true and false.

Frameworks change: what was once dismissed as absurd may now be accepted; hard and fast certainties become dislodged and abandoned. Nevertheless, we cannot make sense of anything without some sort of framework, and with any particular framework there has to be a distinction between propositions that, using that framework, describe the world, and those that describe the framework itself, though this distinction is not fixed at the same place for ever:

> . . . the river-bed of thoughts may shift. But I distinguish between the movements of the waters on the river-bed and the shift of the bed itself; though there is not a sharp division of the one from the other.

We do not, however, need to consider imaginary wild tribes to find examples of people with a world picture fundamentally different to our own:

> I believe that every human being has two parents; but Catholics believe that Jesus only had a human mother. And other people might believe that there are human beings with no parents, and give no credence to all the contrary evidence. Catholics believe as well that in certain circumstances a wafer completely changes its nature, and at the same time that all evidence proves the contrary. And so if Moore said 'I know that this is wine and not blood', Catholics would contradict him.

This remark was possibly prompted by a conversation about Transsubstantiation that Wittgenstein had with Anscombe about this time. He was, it seems, surprised to hear from Anscombe that it really was Catholic belief that 'in certain circumstances a wafer completely changes its nature'. It is presumably an example of what he had in mind when he remarked to Malcolm about Anscombe and Smythies: 'I could not possibly bring myself to believe all the things that they believe.' Such beliefs could find no place in his own world picture. His respect for Catholicism, however, prevented him from regarding them as mistakes or 'transient mental disturbances'.

'I have a world picture. Is it true or false? Above all it is the substratum of all my enquiring and asserting.' There is no reason why a religious faith should not provide this substratum, and why religious beliefs should not be part of 'the inherited background against which I distinguish between true and false'. But for this a thoroughgoing religious education and instruction may be necessary: 'Perhaps one could "convince someone that God exists" by means of a certain upbringing, by shaping his life in such and such a way.'

But what intelligibility can religious belief have in the absence of such an upbringing? Wittgenstein seems to have thought the concept of God can, in some cases (his own for example), be forced upon one by life:

Life can educate one to a belief in God. And experiences too are what bring this about; but I don't mean visions and other forms of experience which show us the 'existence of this being', but, e.g., sufferings of various sorts. These neither show us an object, nor do they give rise to conjectures about him. Experiences, thoughts, – life can force this concept on us.

So perhaps it is similar to the concept of 'object'.

Of course, in this case, the form that this faith takes is unlikely to be acceptance, or even comprehension, of the Catholic doctrines of the Virgin Conception and Transsubstantiation. What is forced upon one is, rather, a certain attitude:

The attitude that's in question is that of taking a certain matter seriously and then, beyond a certain point, no longer regarding it as serious, but maintaining that something else is even more important.

Someone may for instance say it's a grave matter that such and such a man should have died before he could complete a certain piece of work; and yet, in another sense, this is not what matters. At this point one uses the words 'in a deeper sense'. Actually I should like to say that in this case too the *words* you utter or what you think as you utter them are not what matters, so much as the difference they make at various points in your life. How do I know that two people mean the same when each says he believes in God? And the same goes for belief in the Trinity. A theology which insists on the use of *certain particular* words and phrases, and outlaws others, does not make anything clearer (Karl Barth). It gesticulates with words, as one might say, because it wants to say something and does not know how to express it. *Practice* gives the words their sense.

Wittgenstein's example in the second paragraph is not, of course, arbitrary. But if, as it implies, the completion of *Philosophical Investigations* before his death is not what matters, then what is this 'something else' that, 'in a deeper sense', is even more important?

The answer seems to be: his reconciliation with God. In the autumn Wittgenstein asked Anscombe if she could put him touch with a 'non-philosophical' priest. He did not want to discuss the finer points of Catholic doctrine; he wanted to be introduced to someone to whose life religious belief had made a practical difference. She introduced him to Father Conrad, the Dominican priest who had instructed Yorick Smythies during his conversion to Catholicism. Conrad came to Anscombe's house twice to talk to Wittgenstein. 'He wanted', Conrad recalls, 'to talk to a priest as a priest and did not wish to discuss philosophical problems':

He knew he was very ill and wanted to talk about God, I think with a view to coming back fully to his religion, but in fact we only had, I think, two conversations on God and the soul in rather general terms.

Anscombe, however, doubts that Wittgenstein wanted to see Conrad 'with a view to coming back fully to his religion', if by that Conrad means that Wittgenstein wanted to return to the Catholic

Church. And, given Wittgenstein's explicit statements that he could not believe certain doctrines of the Catholic Church, it seems reasonable to accept her doubt.

In September Ben successfully retook his final qualifying exams, leaving him free to join Wittgenstein on their postponed visit to Norway. In the first week of October, therefore, they set off on the long and difficult journey to Wittgenstein's remote hut by the side of the Sogne fjord.

To travel so far north at that time of the year might have been considered a foolhardy risk for Wittgenstein to take in his precarious state of health. It was, however, Ben's health that suffered from the cold. After they had been in Norway a short time he developed bronchitis and had to be moved from Wittgenstein's hut into a nursing home further up the fjord. They then moved into Anna Rebni's farmhouse, where they spent the remainder of their holiday.

Ben had taken with him a copy of J. L. Austin's recently published translation of Frege's *Foundations of Arithmetic*, and while in Norway he and Wittgenstein spent much time reading and discussing Frege's work. Wittgenstein began to think that he might, after all, be able to live alone once again in Norway and work on philosophy.

On his return to Oxford, he wrote to von Wright that, in spite of Ben's illness, 'we enjoyed our stay enormously':

> We had excellent weather the whole time and were surrounded by the greatest kindness. I decided then and there that I'd return to Norway to work there. I get no real quiet here. If all goes well I shall sail on Dec. 30th and go to Skjolden again. I don't think I'll be able to stay in my hut because the physical work I've got to do there is too heavy for me, but an old friend told me that she'd let me stay at her farmhouse. Of course I don't know whether I'm able any more to do decent work, but at least I'm giving myself a real chance. If I can't work there I can't work anywhere.

He even booked a passage on a steamer from Newcastle to Bergen for 30 December. Shortly before Christmas, however, he was told by Anna Rebni that she could not put him up after all. Wittgenstein was, in any case, in no fit state to make the journey. While visiting Dr Bevan to have an examination before his proposed trip to Norway, he had fallen ill in Bevan's house, and had to remain there for Christmas. None of this deterred him from his plan, however, and after Christmas he wrote to Arne Bolstad, another friend in Norway, asking him if he knew of a suitable place for him to live and work in isolation. This, too, came to nothing.

His plans to go to Norway thwarted, Wittgenstein tried another favoured refuge: a monastery. Father Conrad made arrangements on Wittgenstein's behalf for him to stay at a Blackfriars Priory in the Midlands, where he could live the life of a Brother, doing the house chores such as washing up and, most important, where he could be alone.

By January 1951, however, Wittgenstein's health made all these plans impractical. He needed constant medical attention. As his condition worsened, he had to travel to Cambridge with increasing frequency to see Dr Bevan. In addition to the hormones he was taking, he was also given X-ray treatment at Addenbrooke's Hospital.

He had a deep horror of the idea of dying in an English hospital, but Bevan promised him that, if necessary, he could spend his last days being looked after at Bevan's own home. At the beginning of February, Wittgenstein decided to accept his offer, and so moved to Cambridge, there to die in Bevan's home: 'Storeys End'.

27

STOREYS END

Wittgenstein arrived at the Bevans' home resigned to the fact that he would do no more work. He had written nothing since his visit to Norway, and now that he had been forced to give up the idea of living and working by the side of the Sogne fjord, his only wish was that these unproductive last months of his life should be few in number. 'I can't even *think* of work at present', he wrote to Malcolm, '& it doesn't matter, if only I don't live too long!'

Mrs Bevan was initially somewhat frightened of Wittgenstein, especially after their first meeting, which was something of an ordeal for her. Before Wittgenstein moved into their house, Dr Bevan had invited him for supper to introduce him to his wife. She had been warned by her husband that Wittgenstein was not one for small talk and that she should be careful not to say anything thoughtless. Playing it safe, she remained silent throughout most of the evening. But when Wittgenstein mentioned his visit to Ithaca, she chipped in cheerfully: 'How lucky for you to go to America!' She realized at once she had said the wrong thing. Wittgenstein fixed her with an intent stare: 'What do you mean, *lucky*?'

After Wittgenstein had been there a few days, however, she began to relax in his company, and eventually they became close friends. Not that he was a particularly easy guest:

He was very demanding and exacting although his tastes were very simple. It was *understood* that his bath would be ready, his meals on time and that the events of the day would run to a regular pattern.

It was also understood that Wittgenstein should pay for nothing while he was there – not even for the items on the shopping lists that he would leave lying on the table for Mrs Bevan to collect when she went out. These items would include food and books, and, of course, every month, Street & Smith's *Detective Story Magazine*.

When they had become friends, Wittgenstein and Mrs Bevan would, as part of the regular pattern of each day, walk to the local pub at six o'clock in the evening. Mrs Bevan remembers: 'We always ordered two ports, one I drank and the other one he poured with great amusement into the Aspidistra plant – this was the only dishonest act I ever knew him to do.' Conversation with Wittgenstein was, in spite of her first experience of him, surprisingly easy: 'It was remarkable that he never discussed or tried to discuss with me, subjects which I did not understand, so that in our relationship I never felt inferior or ignorant.' This is not to say, however, that the significance of all his remarks was always transparently clear; perhaps the most gnomic was his comment on Peter Geach, Elizabeth Anscombe's husband. When Mrs Bevan asked Wittgenstein what Geach was like, he replied solemnly: 'He reads Somerset Maugham.'

In February Wittgenstein wrote to Fouracre:

> I have been ill for some time, about 6 weeks, & have to spend part of the day in bed. I don't know when I'll come to London again. If there's no chance of it I'll let you know & you might be able to visit me here on a Sunday sometime.

He does not tell Fouracre that he has cancer, and as his condition deteriorated sharply soon after this letter was written, it is unlikely that Wittgenstein met Fouracre again in London. But the fact that it should even have been suggested at this stage illustrates how important to him his meetings with his ex-colleague at Guy's had become.

At the end of February it was decided that there was no further point in continuing Wittgenstein's hormone and X-ray treatment. This, even when accompanied by the information that he could not expect to live more than a few months, came as an enormous relief to him. He told Mrs Bevan: 'I am going to work now as I have never worked before.' Remarkably, he was right. During the two months left of his life Wittgenstein wrote over half (numbered paragraphs 300–676) of the remarks which now constitute *On Certainty*, and in doing so produced what many people regard as the most lucid writing to be found in any of his work.

The work picks up the threads of Wittgenstein's earlier discussions of Moore's 'Defence of Common Sense', but explores the issues in much greater depth, and expresses the ideas with much greater clarity and succinctness than hitherto. Even when he is chiding himself for his own lack of concentration, he does so with an amusingly apt simile: 'I do philosophy now like an old woman who is always mislaying something and having to look for it again: now her spectacles, now her keys.' Despite this self-deprecation, he was in no doubt that the work he was now writing would be of interest: 'I believe it might interest a philosopher, one who can think himself, to read my notes. For even if I have hit the mark only rarely, he would recognize what target I had been ceaselessly aiming at.'

The target he was aiming at was the point at which doubt becomes senseless – the target at which he believed Moore to have made an inaccurate shot. We cannot doubt everything, and this is true not only for practical reasons, like insufficient time or having better things to do; it is true for the intrinsic, logical reason that: 'A doubt without an end is not even a doubt.' But we do not reach that end with statements that begin: 'I know . . .' Such statements have a use only in the 'stream of life'; outside of it, they appear absurd:

> I am sitting with a philosopher in the garden; he says again and again 'I know that that's a tree', pointing to a tree that is near us. Someone else arrives and hears this, and I tell them: 'This fellow isn't insane. We are only doing philosophy.'

We reach the end of doubt, rather, in practice: 'Children do not learn that books exist, that armchairs exist, etc., etc., – they learn to fetch books, sit in armchairs, etc. etc.' Doubting is a rather special sort of practice, which can be learnt only after a lot of non-doubting behaviour has been acquired: 'Doubting and non-doubting behaviour. There is a first only if there is a second.' The thrust of Wittgenstein's remarks is to focus the attention of philosophers away from words, from sentences, and on to the occasions in which we use them, the contexts which give them their sense:

Am I not getting closer and closer to saying that in the end logic cannot be described? You must look at the practice of language, then you will see it.

His attitude is summed up by Goethe's line in Faust: '*Im Anfang war die Tat*' ('In the beginning was the deed'), which he quotes with approval, and which might, with some justification, be regarded as the motto of *On Certainty* – and, indeed, of the whole of Wittgenstein's later philosophy.

The last remark of *On Certainty* was written on 27 April, the day before Wittgenstein finally lost consciousness. The day before that was his sixty-second birthday. He knew it would be his last. When Mrs Bevan presented him with an electric blanket, saying as she gave it to him: 'Many happy returns', he stared hard at her and replied: 'There will be no returns.' He was taken violently ill the next night, after he and Mrs Bevan had returned from their nightly stroll to the pub. When told by Dr Bevan that he would live only a few more days, he exclaimed 'Good!' Mrs Bevan stayed with him the night of the 28th, and told him that his close friends in England would be coming the next day. Before losing consciousness he said to her: 'Tell them I've had a wonderful life.'

The next day Ben, Anscombe, Smythies and Drury were gathered at the Bevans' home to be with Wittgenstein at his death. Smythies had brought with him Father Conrad, but no one would decide whether Conrad should say the usual office for the dying and give conditional absolution, until Drury recollected Wittgenstein's remark that he hoped his Catholic friends prayed for him. This decided the matter, and they all went up to Wittgenstein's room and kneeled down while Conrad recited the proper prayers. Shortly after this, Dr Bevan pronounced him dead.

The next morning he was given a Catholic burial at St Giles's Church, Cambridge. The decision to do this was again prompted by a recollection of Drury's. He told the others:

I remember that Wittgenstein once told me of an incident in Tolstoy's life. When Tolstoy's brother died, Tolstoy, who was then a stern critic of the Russian Orthodox Church, sent for the parish priest and had his brother interred according to the

Orthodox rite. 'Now', said Wittgenstein, 'that is exactly what I should have done in a similar case.'

When Drury mentioned this, everyone agreed that all the usual Roman Catholic prayers should be said by a priest at the graveside, although Drury admits: 'I have been troubled ever since as to whether what we did then was right.' Drury does not expand on this, but the trouble perhaps stems from doubt as to whether the story about Tolstoy quite fits the occasion. For the point of the story is that, although not himself an adherent of the Orthodox Church, Tolstoy had the sensitivity to respect his brother's faith. But in Wittgenstein's case the position is reversed: it was Anscombe and Smythies, and not he, who adhered to the Catholic faith.

Wittgenstein was not a Catholic. He said on a number of occasions, both in conversation and in his writings, that he could not bring himself to believe the things that Catholics believe. Nor, more important, did he practise Catholicism. And yet there seems to be something appropriate in his funeral being attended by a religious ceremony. For, in a way that is centrally important but difficult to define, he had lived a devoutly religious life.

A few days before his death Wittgenstein was visited in Cambridge by Drury, and remarked to him: 'Isn't it curious that, although I know I have not long to live, I never find myself thinking about a "future life". All my interest is still on this life and the writing I am still able to do.' But if Wittgenstein did not think of a future life, he did think of how he might be judged. Shortly before his death he wrote:

God may say to me: 'I am judging you out of your own mouth. Your own actions have made you shudder with disgust when you have seen other people do them.'

The reconciliation with God that Wittgenstein sought was not that of being accepted back into the arms of the Catholic Church; it was a state of ethical seriousness and integrity that would survive the scrutiny of even that most stern of judges, his own conscience: 'the God who in my bosom dwells'.

APPENDIX:
BARTLEY'S WITTGENSTEIN AND
THE CODED REMARKS

One of the books that has done most to stimulate interest in Wittgenstein's life in recent years has been W. W. Bartley III's short study, *Wittgenstein*. This is an account of Wittgenstein's 'lost years', from 1919 to 1929, during which he abandoned philosophy and worked as an elementary school teacher in rural Austria. Bartley's chief interest in writing the book seems to have been to emphasize the philosophical relevance of this part of Wittgenstein's life, and, in particular, the influence on Wittgenstein's later philosophy of the educational theories of the Austrian School Reform Movement (the movement that shaped educational policy in Austria after the First World War).

Interest in Bartley's book, however, has tended to focus, not on his main themes, but almost exclusively on the sensational claims he makes towards the beginning of it about Wittgenstein's sexuality. The interest generated by these assertions is, in my opinion, disproportionate, but I feel obliged to say something about them. The question I was asked most during the writing of this book was: 'What are you going to do about Bartley?' – meaning: what response was I going to give in my book to Bartley's claims about Wittgenstein's homosexual promiscuity?

What are these claims? According to Bartley, while Wittgenstein was training as a school teacher and living on his own in lodgings in Vienna, he discovered an area in the nearby *Prater* (a large park in Vienna, analogous, perhaps, to Richmond Park in London), where 'rough young men were ready to cater to him sexually'. Once Wittgenstein had discovered this place, Bartley maintains:

> [he] found to his horror that he could scarcely keep away from it. Several nights each week he would break away from his rooms and make the quick walk to the Prater, possessed, as he put it to friends, by a demon he could

barely control. Wittgenstein found he much preferred the sort of rough blunt homosexual youth he could find strolling the paths and alleys of the Prater to those ostensibly more refined young men who frequented the Sirk Ecke in the Kärtnerstrasse and the neighbouring bars at the edge of the city. [*Wittgenstein*, p. 40]

In an 'Afterword', written in 1985 and published in a revised edition of his book, Bartley clears up one widespread misinterpretation of this passage. He had not, it seems, meant to imply that the 'rough young men' in question were prostitutes. But, cleared of this misunderstanding, he stands by the truth of what he says.

He does not, however, clear up the mystery of how he knows it to be true. Neither in this revised edition of the book nor in the original does he give any source for these claims. He says merely that his information is based on 'confidential reports from his [Wittgenstein's] friends'.

Ever since it appeared, this passage has been the subject of a heated and apparently unresolvable controversy. Many who knew Wittgenstein well felt outraged, and vented their anger in reviews and letters to periodicals pouring scorn on Bartley's book and swearing that his claims about Wittgenstein's sexuality were false – that they *had* to be false, since the Wittgenstein they knew could not have done such things.

On the other hand, many who did not know Wittgenstein but who had read his published correspondence and the memoirs of him written by his friends and students felt inclined to believe what Bartley said – felt, in fact, that Bartley had provided the key to Wittgenstein's tormented personality. A few (though not Bartley himself) even thought that these sexual encounters provided the key to understanding Wittgenstein's philosophy. Colin Wilson, for example, in his book *The Misfits: A Study of Sexual Outsiders* (the theme of which is the connection between genius and sexual perversion), states that it was only after he had read Bartley's book that he felt he understood Wittgenstein's work.

Many people, it seems, find it so natural to think of Wittgenstein as guiltily and promiscuously homosexual that they are inclined to accept Bartley's claims without any evidence. It somehow 'fits' with their image of Wittgenstein – so much so that the picture of Wittgenstein guiltily wandering the paths of the Prater in search of 'rough young homosexual youths' has become an indelible part of the public image of him. Wittgenstein is, I was once assured, the 'Joe Orton of philosophy'.

Another reason, I think, why Bartley's claims have been generally accepted is the widespread feeling that Wittgenstein's friends, and especially his literary executors, would not admit the truth of such things, even if they knew them to be true. There is, it is felt, a cover-up going on. One of

Wittgenstein's executors, Professor Elizabeth Anscombe, gave ammunition to that view when, in a letter to Paul Engelmann (published in the introduction to Engelmann's *Letters from Ludwig Wittgenstein with a Memoir*), she stated:

> If by pressing a button it could have been secured that people would not concern themselves with his personal life I should have pressed the button.

Further ammunition has been provided by the executors' attitude to the personal remarks that Wittgenstein wrote in his philosophical manuscripts – the so-called coded diaries.

These remarks were separated by Wittgenstein from his philosophical remarks by being written in a very simple code that he had learnt as a child (whereby $a = z$, $b = y$, $c = x$ etc.). The simplicity of the code, and the fact that Wittgenstein used it to write instructions concerning the publication of his work, suggest that he used it, not to disguise what he was saying from posterity, but, rather, to disguise it from someone who, say, happened to lean over his shoulder or who happened to see his manuscript volume lying on a table.

A collection of these remarks, the less personal of them, has been published under the title *Culture and Value*. The more personal remarks have remained unpublished. In the microfilm edition of Wittgenstein's complete manuscripts, these more personal remarks have been covered up with bits of paper.

All this has (a) increased people's curiosity about what the coded remarks contain; and (b) confirmed their view that the executors are hiding something. And this, in turn, has helped to create a climate of opinion favourable to the acceptance of Bartley's otherwise extraordinary allegations. 'Aha!' people have thought. 'So that's what Anscombe has been covering up all these years!'

Bartley himself has made use of this climate of opinion to defend himself against accusations of peddling falsehoods. In the aforementioned 'Afterword' (which is subtitled 'A Polemical Reply to my critics'), he alleges that the executors were bluffing when they expressed their outrage at his book. For all the time they:

> . . . had coded notebooks, in Wittgenstein's own hand, written in a very simple cipher and long since decoded and transcribed, corroborating my statements about his homosexuality.

Now this is actually not true. In the coded remarks Wittgenstein *does* discuss his love for, first David Pinsent, then Francis Skinner, and finally Ben Richards (this is over a period of some thirty years or so), and in that sense they do 'corroborate' his homosexuality. But they do nothing to corroborate *Bartley*'s statements about Wittgenstein's homosexuality. That is, there is not a word in them about going to the Prater in search of 'rough young men', nor is there anything to suggest that Wittgenstein engaged in promiscuous behaviour at any time in his life. Reading them, one would rather get the impression that he was incapable of such promiscuity, so troubled does he seem by even the slightest manifestation of sexual desire (homosexual or heterosexual).

Not many people would have been able to point this out, because few have ever seen the coded remarks. Indeed, the way Bartley himself talks of 'coded notebooks' suggests that his information, too, is second-hand – that he has not actually seen the sources he mentions. There simply *are* no coded notebooks. The coded remarks are not gathered together in two volumes (as Bartley appears to think), but are scattered throughout the eighty or so notebooks that constitute Wittgenstein's literary and philosophical *Nachlass*. This alleged 'corroboration', then, is entirely spurious.

Of the many attempts to refute Bartley, the most often quoted are those by Rush Rhees and J. J. Stonborough in *The Human World* (No. 14, Feb. 1972). They are, in my opinion, unsuccessful. Rhees, indeed, does not even attempt to refute Bartley in the ordinary sense of showing what Bartley says to be false. The gist of his argument is that, even if what Bartley says is true, it was 'foul' of him to repeat it. Stonborough's piece, stripped of its bombast, its heavy-handed irony and its moral indignation, contains only one, rather flimsy, argument: that if Wittgenstein had behaved as Bartley suggests, he would have been blackmailed. This argument is quite easily dealt with by Bartley in his 'Afterword'. By concentrating on the morality of Bartley's book, rather than on the veracity of his information, Rhees and Stonborough have, I believe, merely clouded the issue, and, inadvertently, let Bartley off the hook.

The only way in which Bartley's statements could be effectively refuted is by showing, either that the information he received was false, or that he had misinterpreted it. And before that can even be attempted, it is necessary to know what that information was. This, Bartley has resolutely refused to reveal.

Elsewhere in Bartley's book there are signs that, in writing it, he had access to a manuscript of Wittgenstein's dating from the years 1919–20. The most striking indication of this occurs on page 29 (of the revised edition), when he quotes a dream-report of Wittgenstein's and comments on Wittgenstein's own interpretation of the dream. I find it impossible to imagine how Bartley's information here could have come from any other source than a document written by Wittgenstein himself. If it strains credulity to think that Wittgenstein's friends supplied Bartley with accounts of his trips to the

Prater, it positively defies belief that they gave him reports of Wittgenstein's dreams, told in the first person.

Interestingly, in the aforementioned coded remarks, Wittgenstein does occasionally record and comment on his dreams (three examples can be found in this book, on pages 276, 279 and 436). And the discussion of the dream that Bartley quotes, though more elaborate than anything else that has been preserved, is entirely consistent with the interest that Wittgenstein showed at various times in Freud's techniques of interpreting dreams.

Thus, there is every reason to believe that the dream-reports that Bartley gives are real, and, therefore, a *prima facie* reason to think that Bartley had access to a manuscript, the existence of which is unknown to Wittgenstein's literary executors (indeed, which has been kept from them). The executors have no manuscripts belonging to the years 1919 and 1920, even though it is quite likely that there were some.

If this (admittedly highly speculative) hypothesis is correct, then this manuscript might also be the source for the alleged 'Prater episodes'. In correspondence with Bartley, I asked him directly whether there was such a manuscript or not. He neither confirmed nor rejected the suggestion; he said only that to reveal his source of information would be to betray a confidence, and that he was not prepared to be so dishonourable. I therefore regard the hypothesis as still awaiting falsification.

In writing this book, I have had unrestricted access to all the coded remarks in possession of the literary executors, and permission to quote any of them that I wish. I have chosen to quote virtually all the remarks that are in any way revealing of Wittgenstein's emotional, spiritual and sexual life. (Discretion, as Lytton Strachey once said, is not the better part of biography.) I have left nothing out that would lend support to the popular notion that Wittgenstein was tormented by his homosexuality, although I myself believe this to be a simplification that seriously misrepresents the truth.

What the coded remarks reveal is that Wittgenstein was uneasy, not about homosexuality, but about sexuality itself. Love, whether of a man or a woman, was something he treasured. He regarded it as a gift, almost as a divine gift. But, together with Weininger (whose *Sex and Character* spells out, I believe, many attitudes towards love and sex that are implicit in much that Wittgenstein said, wrote and did), he sharply differentiated love from sex. Sexual arousal, both homo- and heterosexual, troubled him enormously. He seemed to regard it as incompatible with the sort of person he wanted to be.

What the coded remarks also reveal is the extraordinary extent to which Wittgenstein's love life and his sexual life went on only in his imagination. This is most striking in the case of Keith Kirk (for whom Wittgenstein formed a brief obsession that he regarded as 'unfaithful' to his love for Francis

Skinner; see pages 426 to 428), but it is also evident in almost all of Wittgenstein's intimate relationships. Wittgenstein's perception of a relationship would often bear no relation at all to the perception of it held by the other person. If I had not met Keith Kirk, I would have been almost certain, from what I had read in the coded remarks, that he and Wittgenstein had had some kind of 'affair'. Having met Kirk, I am certain that whatever affair there was existed only in Wittgenstein's mind.

If I may be allowed a final twist to my speculations concerning Bartley: I believe it to be possible that his information came from coded remarks contained in a manuscript written between 1919 and 1920, but that he has been too hasty in inferring from those remarks that Wittgenstein engaged in sexually promiscuous behaviour. It would be entirely in keeping with what else we know about Wittgenstein that he did indeed find the 'rough, young, homosexual youths' that he discovered in the Prater fascinating, that he returned again and again to the spot from where he could see them, and that he recorded his fascination in diary form in his notebooks. But it would also be entirely in keeping with what we know that the youths themselves knew nothing at all about his fascination, and indeed were unaware of his existence. If Wittgenstein was 'sexually promiscuous' with street youths, it was, I believe, in the same sense that he was 'unfaithful' to Francis Skinner.

REFERENCES

Wittgenstein's manuscripts are kept in the Wren Library, Trinity College, Cambridge. They are cited here according to the numbers assigned them by Professor G. H. von Wright in his article 'The Wittgenstein Papers' (see *Wittgenstein*, Blackwell, 1982). In the text, the extracts have been given in English. Where this follows a previously published translation, I cite here only the published reference. Where it is my translation of an extract previously published (or quoted) only in German, I give the manuscript reference, together with a reference to the original publication. In cases where I have translated a previously unpublished extract, I give the manuscript reference, together with the original German text. I have followed this procedure also with some of the more important letters from Frege to Wittgenstein.

Wittgenstein's letters to Bertrand Russell, G. E. Moore, J. M. Keynes, W. Eccles, Paul Engelmann, Ludwig von Ficker, C. K. Ogden and G. H. von Wright have been published in the various editions of letters listed in the Bibliography. His letters to Ludwig Hänsel are published as an appendix in *Der Volksschullehrer Ludwig Wittgenstein*, by Konrad Wünsche. His letters to his sisters Hermine and Helene, and to his friends Roy Fouracre, Rowland Hutt, Gilbert Pattisson, Rush Rhees, Moritz Schlick and Friedrich Waismann are hitherto unpublished unless otherwise indicated, and remain in private hands.

The letters to Wittgenstein from Engelmann, Eccles, Gottlob Frege, von Ficker, Hänsel, Adele and Stanislav Jolles, Ogden, David Pinsent and Russell are held by the Brenner Archive, Innsbruck. Those from Francis Skinner are in private hands.

The letters from Russell to Lady Ottoline Morrell are held by the Humanities Research Center, University of Texas, and have been extensively quoted in at least three previous publications: *The Life of Bertrand Russell*, by Ronald W. Clark; *Wittgenstein: A Life*, by Brian McGuinness; and 'The Early

Wittgenstein and the Middle Russell', by Kenneth Blackwell (in *Perspectives on the Philosophy of Wittgenstein*, ed. Irving Block).

The letters between Drs Grant, Bywater, Herrald and Landsborough Thomson quoted in Chapter 21 are held by the Medical Research Council (MRC) Library, London. Records of the interviews with Adolf Hübner quoted in Chapter 9 are held by the Wittgenstein Documentation Centre in Kirchberg, Lower Austria.

In the notes that follow, *Recollections of Wittgenstein*, ed. Rush Rhees, is abbreviated as *Recollections*; Ludwig Wittgenstein as 'LW'; and his co-correspondents as follows:

PE	Paul Engelmann
WE	W. Eccles
GF	Gottlob Frege
LF	Ludwig von Ficker
RF	Roy Fouracre
LH	Ludwig Hänsel
RH	Rowland Hutt
AJ	Adele Jolles
SJ	Stanislav Jolles
PEJ	P. E. Jourdain
JMK	John Maynard Keynes
LL	Lydia Lopokova
GEM	G. E. Moore
NM	Norman Malcolm
OM	Lady Ottoline Morrell
CKO	C. K. Ogden
DP	David Pinsent
FP	Fanny Pinsent
GP	Gilbert Pattisson
BR	Bertrand Russell
FR	Frank Ramsey
RR	Rush Rhees
FS	Francis Skinner
LS	Lytton Strachey
MS	Moritz Schlick
FW	Friedrich Waismann
GHvW	G. H. von Wright

1 THE LABORATORY FOR SELF-DESTRUCTION

p. 3 'Why should one tell the truth': Wittgenstein's recollection of this
     episode is contained in a document found among Wittgenstein's

papers; quoted by Brian McGuinness in *Wittgenstein: A Life*, pp. 47–8.

p. 3 'Call me a truth-seeker': LW to Helene Salzer (née Wittgenstein); quoted in Michael Nedo and Michele Ranchetti, *Wittgenstein: Sein Leben in Bildern und Texten*, p. 292.

p. 4 'I can't understand that': Malcolm, *Memoir*, p. 116.

p. 6 'There is no oxygen in Cambridge': *Recollections*, p. 121.

p. 12 'our influence did not reach far enough': *Jahrbuch für sexuelle Zwischenstufen*, VI, p. 724; quoted by W. W. Bartley in *Wittgenstein*, p. 36.

p. 13 woken at three: this account was given by Wittgenstein to Rush Rhees, who mentioned it to the author in conversation.

p. 13 'I can begin to hear the sound of machinery': *Recollections*, p. 112.

p. 14 '*Du hast aber kein Rhythmus!*': quoted by Rush Rhees, in conversation with the author.

p. 14 'Whereas I in the same circumstances': from the document referred to on p. 3.

p. 16 '*Wittgenstein wandelt wehmütig*': recalled in a letter (12.4.76) from a fellow pupil of Wittgenstein's at Linz, J. H. Stiegler, to Adolf Hübner; quoted by Konrad Wünsche in *Der Volksschullehrer Ludwig Wittgenstein*, p. 35. I am indebted to Paul Wijdeveld for the translation.

p. 17 'A trial involving sexual morality': quoted by Frank Field in *Karl Kraus and his Vienna*, p. 56.

p. 17 'If I must choose': ibid., p. 51.

p. 17 Politics 'is what a man does': ibid., p. 75.

p. 20 'a time when art is content': Weininger, *Sex and Character*, pp. 329–30.

p. 21 'her sexual organs possess women': ibid., p. 92.

p. 22 'the male lives consciously': ibid., p. 102.

p. 22 'disposition for and inclination to prostitution': ibid., p. 217.

p. 22 'a characteristic which is really and exclusively feminine': ibid., p. 255.

p. 22 'the interest that sexual unions shall take place': ibid., p. 258.

p. 22 'but which has become actual': ibid., p. 303.

p. 23 'the most manly Jew': ibid., p. 306.

p. 23 'the extreme of cowardliness': ibid., p. 325.

p. 23 'conquered in himself Judaism': ibid., pp. 327–8.

p. 24 'it has the greatest, most limpid clearness and distinctness': ibid., p. 111.

p. 24 'they are no more than duty to oneself': ibid., p. 159.

p. 24 'Genius is the highest morality': ibid., p. 183.

p. 24 'many men first come to know of their own real nature': ibid.,
p. 244.

p. 24 'In love, man is only loving himself': ibid., p. 243.

p. 24 'what all the travels in the world': ibid., p. 239.

p. 24 'attached to the absolute': ibid., p. 247.

p. 25 'no one who is honest with himself': ibid., p. 346.

p. 26 'When these painful contradictions are removed': Hertz, *Principles of Mechanics*, p. 9.

2   MANCHESTER

p. 29 'I'm having a few problems': LW to Hermine Wittgenstein, 17.5.08.

p. 29 'Because I am so cut off': ibid.

p. 30 '. . . will try to solve': LW to Hermine Wittgenstein, Oct. 1908.

p. 32 'What the complete solution': Russell, *Principles of Mathematics*, p. 528.

p. 33 'Russell said': Jourdain, correspondence book, 20.4.09.

p. 34 'one of the very few people': LW to WE, 30.10.31.

p. 34 'his nervous temperament': J. Bamber to C. M. Mason, 8.3.54; printed as an appendix to Wolfe Mays, 'Wittgenstein in Manchester'.

p. 34 'He used to brag': ibid.

p. 34 'he used to sit through the concert': ibid.

p. 35 'in a constant, indescribable, almost pathological state': *Recollections*, p. 2.

3   RUSSELL'S PROTÉGÉ

p. 36 There exists some disagreement about whether Wittgenstein met Frege or Russell first. The account I give here agrees with that of Brian McGuinness in *Wittgenstein: A Life*, and follows that given by Hermine Wittgenstein in her memoir, 'My Brother Ludwig', *Recollections*, pp. 1–11. It is also supported by G. H. von Wright, who recounts in his 'Biographical Sketch' the story told to him by Wittgenstein that he went first to see Frege in Jena and then (on Frege's advice) to Cambridge to see Russell. Russell, however, was of the opinion that Wittgenstein had not met Frege before he came to Cambridge, and this opinion is shared by some of Wittgenstein's friends, including Elizabeth Anscombe and Rush Rhees (who expresses it in his editorial notes to Hermine's recollections). Professor Anscombe has suggested to me that, as Hermine Wittgenstein was an elderly woman by the time she wrote her reminiscences, her memory might have been at fault. However, in the absence of any conclusive reason for thinking this, I have trusted Hermine's account.

p. 36 'My intellect never recovered': Russell, *Autobiography*, p. 155.

p. 37 'I did think': BR to OM, 13.12.11.

p. 38 'What you call God': BR to OM, 29.12.11.

p. 38 '. . . now there is no prison': BR to OM, July 1911.

p. 38 '. . . an unknown German': BR to OM, 18.10.11.

p. 39 'I am much interested': ibid.

p. 39 'My German friend': BR to OM, 19.10.11.

p. 39 'My German engineer very argumentative': BR to OM, 1.11.11.

p. 39 'My German engineer, I think, is a fool': BR to OM, 2.11.11.

p. 40 '. . . was refusing to admit': BR to OM, 7.11.11.

p. 40 'My lecture went off all right': BR to OM, 13.11.11.

p. 40 'My ferocious German': BR to OM, 16.11.11.

p. 40 'My German is hesitating': BR to OM, 27.11.11.

p. 41 'literary, very musical, pleasant-mannered': BR to OM, 29.11.11.

p. 41 'very good, much better than my English pupils': BR to OM, 23.1.12.

p. 41 'Wittgenstein has been a great event in my life': BR to OM, 22.3.12.

p. 41 'a definition of logical *form*': BR to OM, 26.1.12.

p. 42 'brought a very good original suggestion': BR to OM, 27.2.12.

p. 42 'I found in the first hour': *Recollections*, p. 61.

p. 42 'At our first meeting': ibid.

p. 42 'While I was preparing my speech': BR to OM, 2.3.12.

p. 42 'Moore thinks enormously highly': BR to OM, 5.3.12.

p. 43 'ideal pupil': BR to OM, 17.3.12.

p. 43 'practically certain to do a good deal': BR to OM, 15.3.12.

p. 43 'full of boiling passion': ibid.

p. 43 'It is a rare passion': BR to OM, 8.3.12.

p. 43 'he has more passion': BR to OM, 16.3.12.

p. 43 'His disposition is that of an artist': BR to OM, 16.3.12.

p. 43 'I have the most perfect intellectual sympathy with him': BR to OM, 17.3.12.

p. 43 '. . . he even has the same similes': BR to OM, 22.3.12.

p. 43 'in argument he forgets': BR to OM, 10.3.12.

p. 44 'far more terrible with Christians': BR to OM, 17.3.12.

p. 45 'he says people who like philosophy': BR to OM, 17.3.12.

p. 45 'wears well': BR to OM, 23.4.12.

p. 46 'perhaps the most perfect example': Russell, *Autobiography*, p. 329.

p. 46 'I don't feel the subject neglected': BR to OM, 23.4.12.

p. 46 'He seemed surprised': ibid.

p. 47 'a model of cold passionate analysis': BR to OM, 24.4.12.

p. 47 'a trivial problem': BR to OM, 23.4.12

p. 47 'but only because of disagreement': BR to OM, 26.5.12.

p. 48 'Everybody has just begun to discover him': BR to OM, 2.5.12.

p. 48 'Somebody had been telling them': ibid.

p. 48 'Herr Sinckel-Winckel lunches with me': LS to JMK, 5.5.12.

p. 48 'Herr Sinckel-Winkel hard at it': LS to JMK, 17.5.12.

p. 49 'interesting and pleasant': Pinsent, Diary, 13.5.12.

p. 49 'I really don't know what to think': Pinsent, Diary, 31.5.12.

p. 50 '. . . he is reading philosophy up here': Pinsent, Diary, 30.5.12.

p. 50 'very communicative': Pinsent, Diary, 1.6.12.

p. 51 '. . . then went on to say': BR to OM, 30.5.12.

p. 51 'This book does me a lot of good': LW to BR, 22.6.12.

p. 52 'much pained, and refused to believe it': BR to OM, 1.6.12.

p. 52 '[Wittgenstein] said (and I believe him)': ibid.

p. 53 'since good taste is genuine taste': BR to OM, 17.5.12.

p. 53 'I am seriously afraid': BR to OM, 27.5.12.

p. 54 'I told him': ibid.

p. 54 'It is really amazing': BR to OM, 24.7.12.

p. 54 'I did seriously mean to go back to it': BR to OM, 21.5.12.

p. 54 'I do *wish* I were more creative': BR to OM, 7.9.12.

p. 55 '. . . the second part represented my opinions': BR to Anton Felton, 6.4.68.

p. 55 'Wittgenstein brought me the most lovely roses': BR to OM, 23.4.12.

p. 55 'I love him as if he were my son': BR to OM, 22.8.12.

p. 55 'We expect the next big step': *Recollections*, p. 2.

p. 55 'I went out': Pinsent, Diary, 12.7.12.

p. 56 'He is *very* fussy': BR to OM, 5.9.12.

p. 56 'rather quaint but not bad': Pinsent, Diary, 14.10.12.

p. 56 'arrogated base culture': Engelmann, *Memoir*, p. 130.

p. 56 'I am quite well again': LW to BR, summer 1912.

p. 57 'I am glad you read the lives of Mozart and Beethoven': LW to BR, 16.8.12.

p. 57 'a great contrast': BR to OM, 4.9.12.

p. 57 'This produced a wild outburst': BR to OM, 5.9.12.

p. 58 'Wittgenstein, or rather his father': Pinsent, Diary, 5.9.12.

p. 58 '. . . he is being very fussy': Pinsent, Diary, 7.9.12.

p. 58 'He has an enormous horror': Pinsent, Diary, 12.9.12.

p. 59 'Wittgenstein has been talking a lot': Pinsent, Diary, 19.9.12.

p. 59 'Wittgenstein however got terribly fussy': Pinsent, Diary, 13.9.12.

p. 59 'Wittgenstein was a bit sulky all the evening': Pinsent, Diary, 21.9.12.

p. 60 'His fussyness comes out': Pinsent, Diary, 15.9.12.

p. 60 'I am learning a lot': Pinsent, Diary, 18.9.12.

p. 60 'he simply won't speak to them': Pinsent, Diary, 24.9.12.

p. 61 'still fairly sulky': Pinsent, Diary, 25.9.12.

p. 61 'I really believe': Pinsent, Diary, 29.9.12.

p. 61 'I think father was interested': Pinsent, Diary, 4.10.12.

p. 61 'the most glorious holiday': Pinsent, Diary, 5.10.12.

4 RUSSELL'S MASTER

p. 62 'the infinite part of our life': Russell, 'The Essence of Religion', *Hibbert Journal*, XI (Oct. 1912), pp. 42–62.

p. 63 'Here is Wittgenstein': BR to OM, early Oct. 1912.

p. 63 'He felt I had been a traitor': BR to OM, 11.10.12.

p. 63 'Wittgenstein's criticisms': BR to OM, 13.10.12.

p. 63 'very much inclined': BR to OM, 14.10.12.

p. 63 'He was very displeased with them': Moore, undated letter to Hayek; quoted in Nedo, op. cit., p. 79.

p. 64 'pace up and down': Russell, *Autobiography*, p. 330.

p. 64 'not far removed from suicide': BR to OM, 31.10.12.

p. 64 'he strains his mind': BR to OM, 5.11.12.

p. 64 'I will remember the directions': BR to OM, 4.11.12.

p. 64 'passionate afternoon': BR to OM, 9.11.12.

p. 65 'I told Wittgenstein': BR to OM, 12.11.12.

p. 65 'I got into talking about his faults': BR to OM, 30.11.12.

p. 65 'a man Wittgenstein dislikes': Pinsent, Diary, 9.11.12.

p. 66 'but it was a failure': BR to OM, 31.10.12.

p. 66 'Wittgenstein is a most wonderful character': JMK to Duncan Grant, 12.11.12.

p. 66 'Have you heard': JMK to LS, 13.11.12.

p. 66 'Obviously from his point of view': BR to JMK, 11.11.12.

p. 67 'take him': James Strachey to Rupert Brooke, 29.1.12; see Paul Delany, *The Neo-pagans*, p. 142.

p. 67 'He can't stand him': BR to OM, 10.11.12.

p. 67 'Our brothers B and Wittgenstein': LS to JMK, 20.11.12.

p. 67 'The poor man is in a sad state': LS to Sydney Saxon Turner, 20.11.12.

p. 68 'The Witter-Gitter man': JS to LS, early Dec. 1912.

p. 68 'Wittgenstein has left the Society': BR to OM, undated, but either 6 or 13 Dec. 1912.

p. 69 'He is much the most apostolic': BR to 'Goldie' Lowes Dickenson, 13.2.13.

p. 69 'His latest': Pinsent, Diary, 25.10.12.

p. 70 'Mr Wittgenstein read a paper': minutes of the Moral Science Club, 29.11.12.

p. 70 'about our Theory of Symbolism': LW to BR, 26.12.12.

p. 70 'I think that there cannot be different Types of things!': LW to BR, Jan. 1913.

p. 71 'No good argument': see Ronald W. Clark, *The Life of Bertrand Russell*, p. 241.

p. 71 'Physics exhibits sensations': Russell, 'Matter', unpublished MS; quoted by Kenneth Blackwell in 'The Early Wittgenstein and the Middle Russell', in *Perspectives on the Philosophy of Wittgenstein*, ed. Irving Block.

p. 71 'I am sure I have hit upon a real thing': BR to OM, 9.11.12.

p. 72 'Then Russell appeared': Pinsent, Diary, 4.2.13.

p. 72 'fortunately it is his business': BR to OM, 23.2.13.

p. 72 'My dear father died': LW to BR, 21.1.13.

p. 72 'very much against it': Pinsent, Diary, 7.2.13.

p. 73 'terrific contest': BR to OM, 6.3.13.

p. 73 'I find I no longer talk to him about *my* work': BR to OM, 23.4.13.

p. 75 'I believe a certain sort of mathematicians': BR to OM, 29.12.12.

p. 76 'Whenever I try to think about Logic': LW to BR, 25.3.13.

p. 76 'Poor wretch!': BR to OM, 29.3.13.

p. 76 'Do you mean': PEJ to GF, 29.3.13.

p. 76 'shocking state': BR to OM, 2.5.13.

p. 76 'I played tennis with Wittgenstein': Pinsent, Diary, 29.4.13.

p. 76 'I had tea chez: Wittgenstein': Pinsent, Diary, 5.5.13.

p. 77 'The idea is this': Pinsent, Diary, 15.5.13.

p. 77 'talking to each other': BR to OM, 16.5.13.

p. 77 'went on the river': Pinsent, Diary, 4.6.13.

p. 78 '. . . we went to the C.U.M.C.': Pinsent, Diary, 30.11.12.

p. 78 'Wittgenstein and Lindley came to tea': Pinsent, Diary, 28.2.13.

p. 78 'I came with him': Pinsent, Diary, 24.5.13.

p. 79 'because ordinary crockery is too ugly': Pinsent, Diary, 16.6.13.

p. 79 'He affects me': BR to OM, 1.6.13.

p. 80 'His faults are exactly mine': BR to OM, 5.6.13.

p. 80 'an event of first-rate importance': BR to OM, 1916; the letter is reproduced in Russell, *Autobiography*, pp. 281–2.

p. 81 'It all flows out': BR to OM, 8.5.13.

p. 81 'He thinks it will be like the shilling shocker': BR to OM, 13.5.13.

p. 81 'He was right': BR to OM, 21.5.13.

p. 81 'We were both cross from the heat': BR to OM, 27.5.13.

p. 82 'But even if they are': BR to OM, undated.

p. 82 'I am very sorry': LW to BR, 22.7.13.

p. 82 'I must be much sunk': BR to OM, 20.6.13.

p. 82 'Ten years ago': BR to OM, 23.2.13.

p. 83 'Wittgenstein would like the work': BR to OM, 18.1.14.

p. 83 'You can hardly believe': BR to OM, 29.8.13.

p. 83 'latest discoveries': Pinsent, Diary, 25.8.13.

p. 84 'There are still some *very* difficult problems': LW to BR, 5.9.13.

p. 84 'He was very anxious': Pinsent, Diary, 25.8.13.

p. 84 'That is a splendid triumph': Pinsent, Diary, 29.8.13.

p. 84 'Soon after we had sailed': Pinsent, Diary, 30.8.13.

p. 85 'We have got on splendidly': Pinsent, Diary, 2.9.13.

p. 85 'absolutely sulky': ibid.

p. 86 'When he is working': Pinsent, Diary, 3.9.13.

p. 86 'which was the cause of another scene': Pinsent, Diary, 4.9.13.

p. 86 'just enough to do to keep one from being bored': Pinsent, Diary, 23.9.13.

p. 87 'I am sitting here': LW to BR, 5.9.13.

p. 87 'During all the morning': Pinsent, Diary, 17.9.13.

p. 88 '*as soon as possible*': LW to BR, 20.9.13.

p. 88 'but yet frightfully worried': Pinsent, Diary, 20.9.13.

p. 88 'I am enjoying myself pretty fairly': Pinsent, Diary, 23.9.13.

p. 89 'suddenly announced a scheme': Pinsent, Diary, 24.9.13.

p. 89 'He has settled many difficulties': Pinsent, Diary, 1.10.13.

p. 90 'sexual desire increases with physical proximity': Weininger, *Sex and Character*, p. 239.

5 NORWAY

p. 91 'I said it would be dark': BR to Lucy Donnelly, 19.10.13.

p. 92 'After much groaning': BR to OM, 9.10.13.

p. 92 'In philosophy there are no deductions': *Notes on Logic*; printed as Appendix I in *Notebooks 1914–16*, pp. 93–107.

p. 93 'It was sad': Pinsent, Diary, 8.10.13.

p. 93 'As I hardly meet a soul': LW to BR, 29.10.13.

p. 94 '*Then* my mind was on fire!': quoted by Basil Reeve in conversation with the author.

p. 94 'that the whole of Logic': LW to BR, 29.10.13.

p. 94 'In pure logic': Russell, *Our Knowledge of the External World*, preface, pp. 8–9.

p. 94 'An account of general indefinables?': LW to BR, Nov. 1913.

p. 95 'I beg you': LW to BR, Nov. or Dec. 1913.

p. 95 'All the propositions of logic': ibid.

p. 96 'My day passes': LW to BR, 15.12.13.

p. 97 'But deep inside me': LW to BR, Dec. 1913 or Jan. 1914. In *Letters to*

Russell, Keynes and Moore this letter is dated June/July 1914, but, as Brian McGuinness argues in *Wittgenstein: A Life*, p. 192, it seems more plausible to assume that it was written during the Christmas period of 1913.

- **p. 97** 'It's VERY sad': LW to BR, Jan. 1914.
- **p. 98** 'come to the conclusion': LW to BR, Jan. or Feb. 1914.
- **p. 99** 'I dare say': BR to OM, 19.2.14.
- **p. 99** '*so* full of kindness and friendship': LW to BR, 3.3.14.
- **p. 101** 'who is not yet stale': LW to GEM, 19.11.13.
- **p. 101** '*You must come*': LW to GEM, 18.2.14.
- **p. 101** 'I *think*, now': LW to GEM, March 1914.
- **p. 102** 'Logical so-called propositions': 'Notes Dictated to G. E. Moore in Norway'; printed as Appendix II in *Notebooks 1914–16*.
- **p. 102** 'I have now relapsed': LW to BR, early summer 1914.
- **p. 103** 'Your letter annoyed me': LW to GEM, 7.5.14.
- **p. 104** 'Upon clearing up some papers': LW to GEM, 3.7.14
- **p. 104** 'Think I won't answer it': Moore, Diary, 13.7.14; quoted on p. 273 of Paul Levy, *G. E. Moore and the Cambridge Apostles*.

6 BEHIND THE LINES

- **p. 105** 'I hope the little stranger': LW to WE, July 1914.
- **p. 106** 'The effect is greatly admired': WE to LW, 28.6.14.
- **p. 106** 'I am turning to you in this matter': LW to LF, 14.7.14.
- **p. 107** 'In order to convince you': LW to LF, 19.7.14.
- **p. 107** 'That Austria's only honest review': quoted in the notes to *Briefe an Ludwig von Ficker*, and translated by Allan Janik in 'Wittgenstein, Ficker and "*Der Brenner*"', C. G. Luckhardt, *Wittgenstein: Sources and Perspectives*, pp. 161–89.
- **p. 107** From the painter Max von Esterle: see Walter Methlagl, 'Erläuerungen zur Beziehung zwischen Ludwig Wittgenstein und Ludwig von Ficker', *Briefe an Ludwig von Ficker*, pp. 45–69.
- **p. 107** 'a picture of stirring loneliness': quoted by Janik, op cit., p. 166. The quotation comes from Ficker, 'Rilke und der Unbekannte Freund', first published in *Der Brenner*, 1954, and reprinted in *Denkzettel und Danksagungen*, 1967.
- **p. 108** 'It makes me *very* happy': LW to LF, 1.8.14.
- **p. 108** 'You are me!': reported by Engelmann, op. cit., p. 127.
- **p. 109** 'Once I helped him': LW to PE, 31.3.17.
- **p. 109** 'I do not know': LW to LF, 1.8.14.
- **p. 109** 'as thanks they were': LW to LF, 13.2.15.
- **p. 109** 'but a gift': see Methlagl, op. cit., p. 57.
- **p. 110** '[It] both moved and deeply gladdened me': LW to LF, 13.2.15.

p. 110 'I suppose Madeira wouldn't suit you': DP to LW, 29.7.14.

p. 111 'an intense desire': *Recollections*, p. 3.

p. 111 'average men and women': Russell, *Autobiography*, p. 239.

p. 112 'No matter what a man's frailties': James, *Varieties of Religious Experience*, p. 364.

p. 112 'Now I have the chance': this and the following extract from Wittgenstein's diaries are quoted by Rush Rhees in his 'Postscript' to *Recollections*, pp. 172–209.

p. 112 'People to whom thousands come': *'Leute, die von Tausenden täglich um Rat gefragt werden, gaben freundliche und ausführliche Antworten'*: MS 101, 9.8.14.

p. 113 'Will I be able to work now??!': *'Werde ich jetzt arbeite können??! Bin gespannt auf mein kommendes Leben!'*: ibid.

p. 113 'Such incredible news': *'Solche unmögliche Nachrichten sind immer ein sehr schlechtes Zeichen. Wenn wirklich etwas für uns Günstiges vorfällt, dann wird das berichtet und niemand verfällt auf solche Absurditäten. Fühle darum heute mehr als je die furchtbare Traurigkeit unserer – der deutschen Rasse – Lage. Denn dass wir gegen England nicht aufkommen können, scheint mir so gut wie gewiss. Die Engländer – die beste Rasse der Welt – können nicht verlieren. Wir aber können verlieren und werden verlieren, wenn nicht in diesem Jahr so im nächsten. Der Gedanke, dass undere Rasse geschlagen werden soll, deprimiert mich furchtbar, denn ich bin ganz und gar deutsch'*: MS 101, 25.10.14.

p. 114 'a bunch of delinquents': quoted by Rhees, op. cit., p. 196.

p. 114 'When we hear a Chinese talk': MS 101, 21.8.14; this translation is taken from *Culture and Value*, p. 1.

p. 114 'Today, when I woke up': MS 101, 10.8.14; quoted in Nedo, op. cit., p. 161.

p. 114 'It was terrible': MS 101, 25.8.14; quoted ibid., p. 70.

p. 114 'There is an enormously difficult time': ibid.; quoted in Rhees, op. cit., p. 196.

p. 115 'No news from David': *'Keine Nachricht von David. Bin ganz verlassen. Denke an Selbstmord'*: MS 102, 26.2.15.

p. 115 'I have never thought of you': SJ to LW, 25.10.14.

p. 115 'That you have enlisted': GF to LW, 11.10.14.

p. 116 'If you are not acquainted with it': LW to LF, 24.7.15.

p. 116 'If I should reach my end now': MS 101, 13.9.14; quoted (but translated slightly differently) in Rhees, op. cit., p. 194.

p. 116 'Don't be dependent on the external world': MS 102, Nov. 1914; quoted in Rhees, op. cit., p. 196.

p. 117 'All the concepts of my work': *'Ich bin mit allen den Begriffen meiner*

Arbeit ganz und gar "unfamiliar". Ich SEHE gar nichts!!!': MS 101,
21.8.14.

p. 117 'I am on the path': MS 101, 5.9.14; quoted in Nedo, op. cit., p. 168.

p. 117 'I feel more sensual': *'Bin sinnlicher als früher. Heute wieder o . . .'*: MS
101, 5.9.14.

p. 118 told by Wittgenstein to G. H. von Wright: see *Biographical Sketch*,
p. 8.

p. 118 'In the proposition': *Notebooks*, p. 7.

p. 118 'We can say': *Notebooks*, p. 8.

p. 118 'Worked the whole day': *'Den ganzen Tag gearbeitet. Habe das
Problem verzeifelt gestürmt! Aber ich will eher mein Blut von dieser
Festung lassen, ehe ich unverrichteter Dinge abziehe. Die grösste
Schwierigkeit ist, die einmal eroberten Forts zu halten bis man ruhig in
ihnen sitzen kann. Und bis nicht die Stadt gefallen ist, kann man nicht für
immer ruhig in einem der Forts sitzen'*: MS 102, 31.10.14.

p. 119 'I would be greatly obliged': Trakl to LW, Nov. 1914.

p. 119 'How happy I would be': *'Wie gerne möchte ich ihn kennen lernen!
Höffentlich treffe ich ihn, wenn ich nach Krakau komme! Vielleicht wäre es
mir eine grosse Stärkung'*: MS 102, 1.11.14.

p. 119 'I miss greatly': *'Ich vermisse sehr einen Menschen, mit dem ich mich ein
wenig ausreden kann . . . es würde mich sehr stärken . . . In Krakau. Es
ist schon zu spät, Trakl heute noch zu besuchen'*: MS 102, 5.11.14.

p. 120 'How often I think of him!': MS 102, 11.11.14.

p. 120 'When this war is over': DP to LW, 1.12.14.

p. 120 'For the first time in 4 months': MS 102, 10.12.14.

p. 121 'Perhaps they will have a good influence': MS 102, 15.11.14.

p. 121 'We recognize a condition of morbid susceptibility': Nietzsche, *The
Anti-Christ*, p. 141.

p. 122 'An extreme capacity for suffering': ibid., p. 142.

p. 122 'Christianity is indeed the only *sure* way to happiness': *'Gewiss, das
Christentum ist der einzige* sichere *Weg zum Glük; aber wie wenn einer
dies Glück verschmähte?! Könnte es nicht besser sien, unglücklich im
hoffnungslosen Kampf gegen die äussere Welt zu Grunde zu gehen? Aber
ein solches Leben ist sinnlos. Aber warum nicht ein sinnloses Leben führen?
Ist es unwürdig?'*: MS 102, 8.12.14.

p. 122 'It is false to the point of absurdity': Nietzsche, op. cit., p. 151.

p. 123 'Let us hope': GF to LW, 23.12.14.

p. 123 'I wish to note': *'Notieren will ich mir, dass mein moralischer Stand jetzt
viel tiefer ist als etwa zu Ostern'*: MS 102, 2.1.15.

p. 124 'spent many pleasant hours': MS 102, 10.1.15.

p. 124 'My thoughts are tired': *'Meine Gedanken sind müde. Ich sehe die
Sachen nicht frisch, sondern alltäglich, ohne Leben. Es ist als ob eine*

Flamme erloschen wäre und ich muss warten, bis sie von selbst wieder zu brennen anfängt': MS 102, 13.1.15.

p. 124 'Only through a miracle': *'Nur durch Wunder kann sie gelingen. Nur dadurch, indem von ausserhalb mir der Schleier von meinen Augen weggenommen wird. Ich muss mich ganz in mein Schicksal ergeben. Wie es über mich verhängt ist, so wird es werden. Ich lebe in der Hand des Schicksals'*: MS 102, 25.1.15.

p. 124 'When will I hear something from David?!': MS 102, 19.1.15.

p. 124 'I hope you have been safely taken prisoner': JMK to LW, 10.1.15.

p. 125 'Lovely letter from David!': MS 102, 6.2.15.

p. 125 'except that I hope to God': DP to LW, 14.1.15.

p. 125 'We all hope': Klingenberg to LW, 26.2.15.

p. 125 'If one wants to build as solidly': Halvard Draegni to LW, 4.2.15.

p. 126 'comical misunderstandings': *Recollections*, p. 3.

p. 126 'probably very good': MS 102, 8.2.15.

p. 126 'no desire to assimilate foreign thoughts': LW to LF, 9.2.15.

p. 127 'If I were to write what I think': AJ to LW, 12.2.15.

p. 127 'In any case': SJ to LW, 20.2.15.

p. 127 A draft of a reply: this draft (written in English) is now in the Brenner Archive, Innsbruck.

p. 127 'I hope he will write to you': DP to LW, 27.1.15.

p. 127 'I am so sorry': DP to LW, 6.4.15.

p. 127 'Dream of Wittgenstein': quoted in Levy, op. cit., p. 274.

p. 128 'I have been writing a paper on Philosophy': DP to LW, 2.3.15.

p. 129 'The great problem': 1.6.15; *Notebooks*, p. 53.

p. 129 'It does not go against our feeling': 17.6.15; ibid., p. 62.

p. 129 'The demand for simple things': ibid., p. 63.

p. 129 'I hope with all my heart': BR to LW, 10.5.15.

p. 130 'I'm extremely sorry': LW to BR, 22.5.15.

p. 131 'It looks as if the Russian offensive': SJ to LW, 16.4.15.

p. 131 'May poor Galicia': SJ to LW, 4.5.15.

p. 131 'I write rarely': AJ to LW, 8.4.15.

p. 131 'What kind of unpleasantness?': ibid.

p. 131 'Sometimes, dear friend': LF to LW, 11.7.15.

p. 132 'I understand your sad news': LW to LF, 24.7.15.

p. 132 'God protect you': LF to LW, 14.11.15.

p. 132 'Three weeks' holiday': AJ to LW, 12.8.15.

p. 132 'Already during the first meal': Dr Max Bieler, letter to G. Pitcher, quoted by Sister Mary Elwyn McHale in her MA dissertation: 'Ludwig Wittgenstein: A Survey of Source Material for a Philosophical Biography', p. 48. I have here preserved Dr Bieler's own English.

p. 133 'Whatever happens': LW to BR, 22.10.15.

p. 134 'I am enormously pleased': BR to LW, 25.11.15.

p. 134 'I am pleased that you still have time': GF to LW, 28.11.15.

p. 134 'The importance of "tautology"': Russell, *Introduction to Mathematical Philosophy*, p. 205.

p. 135 'sometimes absorbed us so completely': Dr Max Bieler, letter to G. Pitcher, 30.9.61; quoted in McGuinness, op. cit., pp. 234–5. The translation, one assumes, is either by McGuinness or Pitcher – it is certainly not Dr Bieler's English (compare previous extract).

p. 136 'Constantin was a good boy': Bieler, op. cit.

p. 136 'The decision came as a heavy blow': ibid.

7 AT THE FRONT

p. 137 'God enlighten me': MS 103, 29.3.16.

p. 137 'Do your best. You cannot do more': *'Tu du dein bestes. Mehr kannst du nicht tun: und sei heiter. Lass dir an dir selbst genügen. Denn andere werden dich nicht stützen oder doch nur für kurze Zeit. (Dann wirst du diesen lästig werden.) Hilf dir selbst und hilf andern mit deiner ganzen Kraft. Und dabei sei heiter! Aber wieviel Kraft soll man für sich und wieviel für die anderen brauchen? Schwer ist es gut zu leben!! Aber das gute Leben ist schön. Aber nicht mein, sondern dein Wille geschehe'*: MS 103, 30.3.16.

p. 138 'If that happens': MS 103, 2.4.16.

p. 138 'If only I may be allowed': MS 103, 15.4.16.

p. 138 'Was shot at': MS 103, 29.4.16.

p. 138 'Only then': *'Dann wird für mich erst der Krieg anfangen. Und – kann sein – auch das Leben. Vielleicht bringt mir die Nähe des Todes das Licht des Lebens. Möchte Gott mich erleuchten. Ich bin ein Wurm, aber durch Gott werde ich zum Menschen. Gott stehe mir bei. Amen'*: MS 103, 4.5.16.

p. 138 'like the prince': *'Bin wie der Prinz im verwünschten Schloss auf dem Aufklärerstand. Jetzt bei Tag ist alles ruhig aber in der Nacht da muss es fürchterlich zugehen! Ob ich es aushalten werde?? Die heutige Nacht wird es zeigen. Gott stehe mir bei!!'*: MS 103, 5.5.16.

p. 138 'From time to time': MS 103, 6.5.16.

p. 139 'Only death gives life its meaning': MS 103, 9.5.16.

p. 139 'The men, with few exceptions': MS 103, 27.4.16; quoted in Rhees, op. cit., p. 197.

p. 139 'The heart of a true believer': MS 103, 8.5.16.

p. 139 'Whenever you feel like hating them': MS 103, 6.5.16; quoted in Rhees, op. cit., p. 198.

p. 139 'The people around me': MS 103, 8.5.16; quoted in Rhees, op. cit., p. 198.

p. 139 'The whole modern conception of the world': see *Notebooks*, p. 72. I have here adopted the translation published in the Pear/McGuinness edition of the *Tractatus*.

p. 140 'Your desire not to allow': GF to LW, 21.4.16.

p. 140 'What do I know about God and the purpose of life?': *Notebooks*, p. 72.

p. 141 'Fear in the face of death': ibid., p. 75.

p. 141 'How terrible!': MS 101, 28.10. 14.

p. 141 'To believe in a God': *Notebooks*, p. 74.

p. 142 'How things stand, is God': ibid., p. 79.

p. 142 'Colossal exertions': MS 103, 6.7.16.

p. 142 'broadened out': MS 103, 2.8.16.

p. 142 'The solution to the problem of life': 6 and 7.7.16; *Notebooks*, p. 74; see *Tractatus*, 6.521.

p. 142 'Ethics does not treat of the world': 24.7.16; *Notebooks*, p. 77.

p. 143 'I am aware of the complete unclarity': ibid., p. 79.

p. 143 'There are, indeed': *Tractatus*, 6.522.

p. 143 'The work of art': 7.10.16; *Notebooks*, p. 83.

p. 143 'no longer consider the where': Schopenhauer, *The World as Will and Representation*, I, p. 179.

p. 144 'As my idea is the world': 17.10.16; *Notebooks*, p. 85.

p. 144 'a merely "inner" world': Nietzsche, *The Anti-Christ*, p. 141.

p. 144 'It is true': 12.10.16; *Notebooks*, p. 84.

p. 144 'What the solipsist *means*': *Tractatus*, 5.62.

p. 144 'This is the way I have travelled': 15.10.16; *Notebooks*, p. 85.

p. 145 'I can hardly say the same': GF to LW, 24.6.16.

p. 145 'I am always pleased': GF to LW, 29.7.16.

p. 145 'The war cannot change our personal relationships': DP to LW, 31.5.16.

p. 145 'This kind, lovely letter': MS 103, 26.7.16.

p. 145 'icy cold, rain and fog': *'eisige Käite, Regen und Nebel. Qualvolles Leben. Furchtbar schwierig sich nicht zu verlieren. Denn ich bin ja ein schwacher Mensch. Aber der Geist hilft mir. Am besten wärs ich wäre schon krank, dann hätte ich wenigstens ein bisschen Ruhe'*: MS 103, 16.7.16.

p. 146 'Was shot at': MS 103, 24.7.16.

p. 146 'Yesterday I was shot at': *'Wurde gestern beschossen. War verzagt! Ich hatte Angst vor dem Tode. Solch einen Wunsch habe ich jetzt zu leben. Und es ist schwer, auf das Leben zu verzichten, wenn man es einmal gern hat. Das ist eben "Sünde", unvernünftiges Leben, falsche*

Lebensauffassung. Ich werde von Zeit zu Zeit zum Tier. *Dann kann ich
an nichts denken als an essen, trinken, schlafen. Furchtbar! Und dann leide
ich auch wie ein Tier, ohne die Möglichkeit innerer Rettung. Ich bin dann
meinen Gelüsten und Abneigungen preisgegeben. Dann ist an ein wahres
Leben nicht zu denken'*: MS 103, 29.7.16.

p. 146 'You know what you have to do': MS 103, 12.8.16.

p. 146 'By this distinctive behaviour': quoted McGuinness, op. cit., p. 242.

p. 147 'In this way': GF to LW, 28.8.16.

p. 147 'one of the wittiest men': Engelmann, op. cit., p. 65.

p. 148 'My dear friend': ibid., p. 68.

p. 148 'I often think of you': LW to PE, 31.3.17.

p. 148 '. . . enabled me to understand': Engelmann, op. cit., p. 72.

p. 148 'If I can't manage': ibid., p. 94.

p. 149 'In me': ibid., p. 74.

p. 149 '[it] may be considered': ibid., p. 117.

p. 150 'the poem as a whole': PE to LW, 4.4.17.

p. 151 'really magnificent': LW to PE, 9.4.17.

p. 151 'Let's hope for the best': GF to LW, 26.4.17.

p. 151 'The journey to Vienna': GF to LW, 30.6.17.

p. 152 'If in saying it': PE to LW, 8.1.18.

p. 152 'It is true': LW to PE, 16.1.18.

p. 153 'Each of us': GF to LW, 9.4.18.

p. 153 'which you don't deserve': LW to PE, 1.6.18.

p. 154 'so that it doesn't get lost': GF to LW, 1.6.18.

p. 154 'His exceptionally courageous behaviour': quoted in McGuinness,
op. cit., p. 263.

p. 154 'I want to tell you': FP to LW, 6.7.18.

p. 154 'My first and my only friend': LW to FP; quoted in Nedo, op. cit.

p. 156 'as if it were a Czar's ukase': Russell, *My Philosophical Development*,
p. 88.

p. 156 'There is indeed the inexpressi' e': *TLP* 6.522.

p. 157 'May it be granted': GF to LW, 15.10.18.

p. 157 'and it gives me more and more joy': PE to LW, 7.11.18.

p. 157 'Still no reply': LW to PE, 22.10.18.

p. 157 'for technical reasons': LW to PE, 25.10.18.

p. 158 'the portrait of my sister': see *Recollections*, p. 9.

p. 159 'and to have read': Parak, *Am anderen Ufer*.

p. 159 'I am prisoner in Italy': LW to BR, 9.2.19.

p. 160 'Most thankful to hear': BR to LW, 2.3.19.

p. 160 'Very glad to hear from you': BR to LW, 3.3.19.

p. 160 'You can't imagine': LW to BR, 10.3.19.

p. 160 'I've written a book': LW to BR, 13.3.19.

p. 161 'I should never have believed': LW to BR, 12.6.19.

p. 161 'It is true': BR to LW, 21.6.19.

p. 162 'No writing between the lines!': PE to LW, 6.4.19.

p. 163 'Right at the beginning': *'Gleich zu Anfang treffe ich die Ausdrücke "der Fall sein" und "Tatsache" und ich vermute, dass der Fall sein und eine Tatsache sein dasselbe ist. Die Welt ist alles, was der Fall ist und die Welt ist die Gesamtheit der Tatsachen. Ist nicht jede Tatsache der Fall und ist nicht, was der Fall ist, eine Tatsache? Ist nicht dasselbe, wenn ich sage, A sei eine Tatsache wie wenn ich sage, A sei der Fall? Wozu dieser doppelte Ausdruck? . . . Nun kommt aber noch ein dritter Ausdruck: "Was der Fall ist, die Tatsache, ist das Bestehen von Sachverhalten". Ich verstehe das so, dass jede Tatsache das Bestehen eines Sachverhaltes ist, so dass eine andre Tatsache das Bestehen eines andern Sachverhaltes ist. Könnte man nun nicht die Worte "das Bestehen" streichen und sagen: "Jede Tatsache ist ein Sachverhalt, jede andre Tatsache ist ein anderer Sachverhalt. Könnte man vielleicht auch sagen "Jeder Sachverhalt ist das Bestehen einer Tatsache"? Sie sehen: ich verfange mich gleich anfangs in Zweifel über das, was Sie sagen wollen, und komme so nicht recht vorwärts'*; GF to LW, 28.6.19.

p. 164 'I gather he doesn't understand a word': LW to BR, 19.8.19.

p. 164 'I am convinced': BR to LW, 13.8.19.

p. 164 'The main point': LW to BR, 19.8.19.

p. 165 'a curious kind of logical mysticism': Russell, *My Philosophical Development*, pp. 84–5.

p. 165 'Sachverhalt is': LW to BR, 19.8.19.

p. 165 'The theory of types': BR to LW, 13.8.19.

p. 165 'That's exactly what one can't say': LW to BR, 19.8.19.

p. 165 '. . . Just think': ibid.

p. 166 'If you said': BR to LW, 13.8.19.

p. 166 'you know how difficult': LW to BR, 19.8.19.

p. 166 'I agree with what you say': BR to LW, 13.8.19.

p. 166 'I should like to come to England': LW to BR, 19.8.19.

8 THE UNPRINTABLE TRUTH

p. 170 'You remind me of somebody': *Recollections*, p. 4.

p. 171 'A hundred times': ibid.

p. 171 'So you want to commit financial suicide': quoted by Rush Rhees, *Recollections*, p. 215.

p. 172 'I'm not quite normal yet': LW to BR, 30.8.19.

p. 172 'I am not very well': LW to PE, 25.8.19.

p. 172 'for as you may know': BR to LW, 8.9.19.

p. 172 'horrified and nauseated': LW to PE, 2.9.19.

p. 172 'I can no longer behave like a grammar-school boy': LW to PE, 25.9.19.

p. 172 'The benches are full of boys': LW to BR, 6.10.19.

p. 173 'to find something of myself': LW to PE, 2.9.19.

p. 173 'Not very': LW to LH, Sept. 1919.

p. 173 'My book will be published': LW to FP, 24.3.19.

p. 173 'naturally neither knows my name': LW to BR, 30.8.19.

p. 174 'I consider it indecent': LW to LF, undated, but probably Nov. 1919.

p. 174 'You now write': *'Sie schreiben nun: "Was einem Elementarsatze entspricht, wenn er wahr ist, ist das Bestehen eines Sachverhaltes". Hiermit erklären Sie nicht den Ausdruck "Sachverhalt", sondern den ganzen Ausdruck, "das Bestehen eines Sachverhaltes" . . . Die Freude beim Lesen Ihres Buches kann also nicht mehr durch den schon bekannten Inhalt, sondern nur durch die Form erregt werden, in der sich etwa die Eigenart des Verfassers ausprägt. Dadurch wird das Buch eher eine künstlerische als eine wissenschaftliche Leistung; das, was darin gesagt wird, tritt zurück hinter das, wie es gesagt wird':* GF to LW, 16.9.19.

p. 175 'The sense of both propositions': quoted Frege, ibid.

p. 175 'The actual sense of a proposition': *'Der eigentliche Sinn des Satzes ist für alle derselbe; die Vorstellungen aber, die jemand mit dem Satze verbindet, gehören ihm allein an; er ist ihr Träger. Niemand kann die Vorstellungen eines Andern haben':* ibid.

p. 175 'He doesn't understand': LW to BR, 6.10.19.

p. 175 'that I have learnt to know you': GF to LW, 30.9.19.

p. 176 'mutilate it from beginning to end': LW to LF, op. cit.

p. 176 'About a year ago': ibid.

p. 177 'Why hadn't you thought of me': LF to LW, 19.10.19.

p. 178 'I am pinning my hopes on you': LW to LF, undated, but almost certainly Nov. 1919.

p. 179 'Do you remember': LW to BR, 27.11.19.

p. 179 'Your letter, naturally, wasn't pleasant': LW to LF, 22.11.19.

p. 179 'Don't worry': LF to LW, 28.11.19.

p. 179 'I think I can say': LW to LF, 4.12.19.

p. 179 Ficker wrote that he was still hoping: LF to LW, 29.11.19.

p. 180 'I couldn't accept': LW to LF, 5.12.19.

p. 180 Rilke's letter to Ficker: reproduced in full in Ficker, op. cit., pp. 212–14.

p. 180 'Is there a *Krampus*': LW to LF, 5.12.19.

p. 180 'Just how far': LW to PE, 16.11.19.

p. 181 'Normal human beings': ibid.

p. 181 'It is terrible': BR to LW, 14.10.19.

p. 182 'Come here as quick as you can': BR to LW, undated, but certainly Dec. 1919.

p. 182 'a vague, shadowy figure': Dora Russell, *The Tamarisk Tree*, I, p. 79.

p. 182 'so full of logic': BR to Colette, 12.12.19.

p. 182 'I besought him to admit': Russell, *My Philosophical Development*, p. 86.

p. 182 'He has penetrated deep into mystical ways': BR to OM, 20.12.19.

p. 183 'I enjoyed our time together': LW to BR, 8.1.20.

p. 183 'The book is now a much smaller risk': LW to LF, 28.12.19.

p. 183 'With or without Russell': LF to LW, 16.1.20.

p. 183 'There's so much of it': LW to BR, 9.4.20.

p. 183 'All the refinement': LW to BR, 6.5.20.

p. 184 'I don't care twopence': BR to LW, 1.7.20.

p. 184 *'you can do what you like'*: LW to BR, 7.7.20.

p. 184 'I have continually thought': LW to PE, 30.5.20.

p. 184 'This change of home': LW to PE, 24.4.20.

p. 185 'If I am unhappy': Engelmann, op. cit., pp. 76–7.

p. 185 'Before Christ': PE to LW, 31.12.19.

p. 186 'They are still not clear': LW to PE, 9.1.20.

p. 186 'But then I did something': PE to LW, 19.6.20.

p. 187 'Many thanks for your kind letter': LW to PE, 21.6.20.

p. 188 'The best for me': LW to BR, 7.7.20.

p. 188 'It pleases them': LW to PE, 19.2.20.

p. 188 'There is no wall': LH to LW, 17.1.20.

p. 188 'The professor of psychology': LH to LW, 5.3.20.

p. 190 'Of course I don't take exception': *'Natürlich nehme ich Ihnen Ihre Offenheit nicht übel. Aber ich möchte gerne wissen, welche tiefen Gründe des Idealismus Sie meinen, die ich nicht erfasst hätte. Ich glaube verstanden zu haben, dass Sie selbst den erkenntnistheoretischen Idealismus nicht für wahr halten. Damit erkennen Sie, meine ich, an, dass es tiefere Gründe für diesen Idealismus überhaupt nicht gibt. Die Gründe dafür können dann nur Scheingründe sein, nicht logische'*: GF to LW, 3.4.20.

p. 191 'In the evening': LW to PE, 20.8.20.

p. 191 'So I see that intelligence counts': see *Recollections*, p. 123.

p. 191 'He took half my life': LW to BR, 6.8.20.

p. 191 'For unless all the devils in hell': LW to LF, 20.8.20.

9 'AN ENTIRELY RURAL AFFAIR'

p. 193 'That is not for me': recalled by Leopold Baumrucker in an interview with Adolf Hübner, 18.4.75.

p. 193 'I am to be an elementary-school teacher': LW to BR, 20.9.20.

p. 193 'a beautiful and tiny place': LW to PE, 11.10.20.

p. 194 'the villagers take you': see Luise Hausmann, 'Wittgenstein als Volkschullehrer', *Club Voltaire*, IV, pp. 391–6.

p. 194 'He is interested in everything himself': *Recollections*, p. 5.

p. 195 'During the arithmetic lesson': Anna Brenner, interview with Adolf Hübner, 23.1.75.

p. 196 'Again and again': Berger in Hausmann, op. cit., p. 393.

p. 197 'I was in the office': Frau Bichlmayer, quoted in Nedo, op. cit., p. 164–5

p. 198 'I am indeed very grateful': Hermine to LH, 13.12.20.

p. 198 'I was sorry': LW to PE, 2.1.21.

p. 198 In the event, Engelmann did not understand: what follows is a summary of a letter from Engelmann to Wittgenstein, undated, but almost certainly Jan. 1921.

p. 198 'I cannot at present analyse my state in a letter': LW to PE, 7.2.21.

p. 199 'One night': Hänsel, 'Ludwig Wittgenstein (1889–1951)', *Wissenschaft und Weltbild*, Oct. 1951, pp. 272–8.

p. 199 'I was a priest': see Bartley, *Wittgenstein*, p. 29.

p. 199 'It puzzled Wittgenstein': ibid., p. 30.

p. 200 'I wonder how you like being an elementary school-teacher': BR to LW, 11.2.21.

p. 201 'I am sorry you find': BR to LW, 3.6.21.

p. 201 'here they are much more good-for-nothing': LW to BR, 23.10.21.

p. 201 'I am very sorry': BR to LW, 5.11.21.

p. 201 'You are right': LW to BR, 28.11.21.

p. 201 'a good mathematician': BR to LW, 3.6.21.

p. 202 'I could not grasp': Karl Gruber, interview with Adolf Hübner, 16.1.75; quoted in Wünsche, *Der Volkschullehrer Ludwig Wittgenstein*, p. 150.

p. 202 'It would in my opinion': LW to LH, 5.7.21.

p. 202 'I work from early in the morning': LW to LH, 23.8.21.

p. 202 'because I was living in open sin': Russell, note on a letter from Littlewood, 30.1.21; quoted in Clark, op. cit., p. 485.

p. 203 'As they can't drop less than £50': CKO to BR, 5.11.21; full text of the letter reproduced in Russell, *Autobiography*, pp. 353–4.

p. 203 'In any other case': Ostwald to Dorothy Wrinch, 21.2.21; quoted by G. H. von Wright in 'The Origin of the "*Tractatus*"', *Wittgenstein*, pp. 63–109.

p. 204 'I am sorry, as I am afraid you won't like that': BR to LW, 5.11.21.

p. 204 'I must admit': LW to BR, 28.11.21.

p. 205 'Enclosed from Wittgenstein': BR to CKO, 28.11.21.

p. 206 'As a selling title': CKO to BR, 5.11.21.

p. 206 'I think the Latin one is better': LW to CKO, 23.4.22.

p. 207 'What is this?': CKO to LW, 20.3.22.

p. 207 'There can be no thought': LW to CKO, 5.5.22.

p. 207 'in consideration of their issuing it': the declaration was enclosed by Ogden in a letter to Wittgenstein dated 18.6.22.

p. 208 'As to your note': LW to CKO, 4.8.22.

p. 208 'because I don't get on': LW to BR, 23.10.21.

p. 208 'I would have felt it as a humiliation': Gruber, op. cit.

p. 209 'Today I had a conversation': LW to LH, 16.2.22.

p. 209 'I wish': BR to LW. 7.2.22.

p. 209 'On the contrary!': LW to BR, undated, but no doubt Feb. 1922. The letter is not included in *Letters to Russell, Keynes and Moore*, but will, I believe, be published in a forthcoming edition of Wittgenstein's correspondence. It is among the collection held by the Brenner Archive.

p. 210 'The little boy is lovely': BR to LW, 9.5.22.

p. 210 'circumstances of the time': Dora Russell, op. cit., p. 160.

p. 210 'much pained by the fact': BR to GEM, 27.5.29.

p. 210 'at the height of his mystic ardour': Russell, *Autobiography*, p. 332.

p. 210 'assured me with great earnestness': ibid.

p. 211 wrote at least two letters: these are now in the Brenner Archive.

p. 211 'When, in the twenties': Engelmann, quoted in Nedo, op. cit.

p. 212 'a very disagreeable impression': LW to PE, 14.9.22.

p. 212 he told Russell: in a letter now in the possession of the Brenner Archive; undated, but probably Nov. or Dec. 1922.

p. 212 'They really look nice': LW to CKO, 15.11.22.

p. 213 'Just improve yourself': quoted by Postl in an interview with Adolf Hübner, 10.4.75.

p. 214 'I think I ought to confess': LW to CKO, March 1923.

p. 214 'A short time ago': LW to BR, 7.4.23; letter now in the possession of the Brenner Archive.

p. 214 'does not really think': FR to LW, 20.2.24; reproduced in *Letters to C. K. Ogden*, pp. 83–5.

p. 214 'To my great shame': LW to PE, 10.8.22.

p. 215 'I should have preferred': LW to JMK, 1923.

p. 215 'Did Keynes write to me?': LW to CKO, 27.3.23.

p. 215 'This is a most important book': Ramsey, 'Critical Notice of L. Wittgenstein's "Tractatus Logico-Philosophicus",' *Mind*, Oct. 1923, pp. 456–78.

p. 216 'It is most illuminating': FR to CKO, undated.

p. 216 'It's terrible': FR to his mother, 20.9.23.

p. 216 'I shall try': ibid.

p. 217 'He is very poor': ibid.

p. 218 'the £50 belong to Keynes': FR to LW, 20.12.23.

p. 218 'Keynes very much wants to see L. W.': FR to Thomas Stonborough, Nov. or Dec. 1923; letter now in the Brenner Archive.

p. 218 'but you mustn't give it any weight': FR to LW, 20.12.23.

p. 219 'You are quite right': FR to LW, 20.2.24.

p. 220 'looked just a prosperous American': FR to his mother, dated March 1924 ('In the train Innsbruck–Vienna Sunday').

p. 220 'As far as I could make out': FR to his mother, dated simply 'Sunday', but certainly written from Vienna, March 1924.

p. 220 'trying to get him': FR to JMK, 24.3.24; quoted in Nedo, op. cit., p. 191.

p. 221 'Wittgenstein seemed to me tired': FR to his mother, 30.3.24.

p. 221 '. . . if he were got away': FR to JMK, 24.3.24.

p. 222 'I'm afraid I think': ibid.

p. 222 'yet my mind': JMK to LW, 29.3.24.

p. 223 '. . . because I myself no longer': LW to JMK, 4.7.24.

p. 223 'he has spent weeks': FR to his mother; quoted in *Letters to C. K. Ogden*, p. 85.

p. 224 'We really live in a great time for thinking': FR to his mother, 22.7.24; quoted in Nedo, op. cit., p. 188.

p. 224 'I'm sorry so few have sold': FR to CKO, 2.7.24.

p. 224 'I don't much want to talk about mathematics': FR to LW, 15.9.24.

p. 224 'I would, naturally': Hermine to LH, autumn 1924.

p. 225 'People kiss each other': quoted in Josef Putre, 'Meine Erinnerungen an den Philosophen Ludwig Wittgenstein', 7 May 1953.

p. 225 'It's not going well': LW to LH, Oct. 1924.

p. 226 'He who works': Wittgenstein, preface to the *Wörterbuch für Volksschulen*, trans. into English in the edition prepared by Adolf Hübner, together with Werner and Elizabeth Leinfellner, Hölder-Pichler-Tempsky, 1977.

p. 227 'No word is too common': ibid., p. xxxiii.

p. 227 'the most pressing question': Buxbaum's report is quoted in full by Adolf Hübner in his editor's introduction to the *Wörterbuch*.

p. 228 'I suffer much': LW to PE, 24.2.25.

p. 229 'That you want to go to Palestine': ibid.

p. 229 'I was more than pleased': LW to WE, 10.3.25.

p. 230 'England may not have changed': LW to WE, 7.5.25.

p. 230 'I should rather like to': LW to JMK, 8.7.25.

p. 230 'I'm awfully curious': LW to JMK, July or Aug. 1925.

p. 231 'I know that brilliance': LW to PE, 19.8.25.

p. 231 'It was during this period': Eccles, op. cit., p. 63.

p. 231 'Tell Wittgenstein': W. E. Johnson to JMK, 24.8.25.

p. 231 'In case of need': LW to PE, 9.9.25.

p. 231 'as long as I feel': LW to JMK, 18.10.25.

p. 232 'It cannot be said': August Riegler, interview with Adolf Hübner, 3.6.76.

p. 233 'I called him all the names under the sun': Franz Piribauer, interview with Adolf Hübner, 20.4.75.

p. 233 'I can only advise you': quoted by August Wolf in an interview with Adolf Hübner, 10.4.75.

10   OUT OF THE WILDERNESS

p. 236 'he and not I was the architect': Engelmann in a letter to F. A. von Hayek; quoted in Nedo, op. cit., p. 206.

p. 236 'Tell me, Herr Ingenieur': *Recollections*, pp. 6–7.

p. 237 'Perhaps the most telling proof': ibid., p. 8.

p. 237 '. . . even though I admired the house': quoted in Leitner, *The Architecture of Ludwig Wittgenstein*, p. 23.

p. 238 'I felt again at home': Marguerite Sjögren (*née* Respinger, now de Chambrier), *Granny et son temps*, p. 101.

p. 239 'It doesn't matter': quoted by Marguerite de Chambrier in conversation with the author.

p. 239 'Why do you want': ibid.

p. 239 'the sort of Jew one didn't like': ibid.

p. 240 'Love of a woman': *Sex and Character*, p. 249.

p. 240 '. . . the house I built for Gretl': *Culture and Value*, p. 38.

p. 240 'Within all great art': ibid., p. 37.

p. 241 'As an admirer': MS to LW, 25.12.24; quoted in *Ludwig Wittgenstein and the Vienna Circle*, p. 13.

p. 242 'It was as if': Mrs Blanche Schlick to F. A. von Hayek, quoted in Nedo, op. cit.

p. 242 'Again': ibid.

p. 242 'He asks me': Gretl to MS, 19.2.27; quoted in *Ludwig Wittgenstein and the Vienna Circle*, p. 14.

p. 242 'returned in an ecstatic state': Mrs Schlick, ibid.

p. 242 'Wittgenstein found Schlick': Engelmann, op. cit., p. 118.

p. 243 'Before the first meeting': Carnap's recollections of Wittgenstein appeared first in his 'Autobiography' in Paul Schlipp, ed., *The Philosophy of Rudolf Carnap*, and are reprinted in K. T. Fann, *Ludwig Wittgenstein: The Man and His Philosophy*, pp. 33–9.

p. 244 'His point of view': ibid.

p. 245 'Only so can we preserve it': Ramsey, "The Foundations of

Mathematics', reprinted in *Essays in Philosophy, Logic, Mathematics and Economics*, pp. 152–212.

p. 246 'The way out of all these troubles': LW to FR, 2.7.27.

p. 246 '. . . he thought with the aim': *Culture and Value*, p. 17.

p. 247 'The philosopher is not a citizen': *Zettel*, p. 455.

p. 247 'I couldn't stand the hot-water bottle': LW to JMK, summer 1927.

p. 247 'a doctrine which sets up as its bible': Keynes, *A Short View of Russia*, p. 14.

p. 247 '. . . many, in this age without religion': ibid., p. 13.

p. 248 '. . . which may, in a changed form': ibid., p. 15.

p. 248 'One who believes as I do': Russell, *Practice and Theory of Bolshevism*, p. 18.

p. 249 '. . . it was fascinating': Feigl; quoted in Nedo, op. cit., p. 223.

p. 249 '. . . he has a lot of stuff about infinity': BR to GEM, 5.5.30.

p. 250 'Intuitionism is all bosh': *Lectures on the Foundations of Mathematics*, p. 237.

p. 251 'à la Corbusier': JMK to his wife, 18.11.28; quoted in Nedo, op. cit., p. 222.

II THE SECOND COMING

p. 255 'Well, God has arrived': JMK to LL, 18.1.29.

p. 255 'as though time had gone backwards': MS 105; quoted in Nedo, op. cit., p. 225.

p. 256 'brutally rude': Leonard Woolf, *An Autobiography*, II: *1911–1969*, p. 406.

p. 256 'in mixed company': Frances Partridge, *Memories*, p. 160.

p. 257 '. . . Julian, Maynard says': Virginia Woolf, *A Reflection of the Other Person: Letters 1929–31*, p. 51.

p. 257 'For he talks nonsense': Julian Bell, 'An Epistle On the Subject of the Ethical and Aesthetic Beliefs of Herr Ludwig Wittgenstein', first published in *The Venture*, No. 5, Feb. 1930, pp. 208–15; reprinted in Irving M. Copi and Robert W. Beard, ed., *Essays on Wittgenstein's Tractatus*.

p. 258 'the kindest people': *Recollections*, p. 17.

p. 258 'at last has succeeded': JMK to LL, 25.2.29.

p. 258 'We have seen a lot of Wittgenstein': Partridge, op. cit., p. 159.

p. 259 'delightful discussions': MS 105; quoted in Nedo, op. cit., p. 225.

p. 259 'A good objection': '*Ein guter Einwand hilft vorwärts, ein flacher Einwand, selbst wenn er recht hat, wirkt ermattend. Ramseys Einwände sind von dieser Art. Der Einwand fasst die Sache nicht an ihrer Wurzel, wo das Leben ist, sondern schon so weit aussen wo sich nichts mehr rectifizieren* *lässt, selbst wenn es falsch ist. Ein guter Einwand hilft unmittelbar zur Lösung, ein flacher muss erst überwunden werden und kann dann von weiter unten herauf (wie eine überwundene abgestorbene Stelle) zur Seite liegengelassen werden. Wie wenn sich der Baum an der vernarbten Stelle vorbei krümmt um weiter zu wachsen*': MS 107, p. 81.

p. 260 'I don't like your method': quoted in Moore, 'Wittgenstein's Lectures in 1930–33', *Philosophical Papers*, pp. 252–324.

p. 261 'What is the logical form of *that*?': see Malcolm, *Memoir*, p. 58.

p. 262 'Moore? he shows you': *Recollections*, p. 51.

p. 262 'a disaster for Cambridge': ibid., p. 103.

p. 262 'The mind gets stiff': ibid., p. 105.

p. 263 'My first encounter with Wittgenstein': this recollection is contained in a letter from S. K. Bose to John King, 5.4.78, a copy of which Mr King very kindly sent me.

p. 264 'Don't think I ridicule this': *Recollections*, p. 101.

p. 264 'well-meaning commentators': ibid., p. xi.

p. 266 'I would have known': LW to GP, summer 1931.

p. 266 'Somehow or other': LW to GP, summer 1930.

p. 267 'You may through my generosity': LW to GP, Oct. 1931.

p. 267 'If I remember rightly': LW to GP, 16.2.38.

p. 267 'that for so many years': MS 107, pp. 74–5.

p. 268 'What a statement seems to imply': LW to FR, undated; see *Briefe*, p. 261.

p. 268 'Please try to understand': LW to JMK, May 1929.

p. 269 'What a maniac you are!': JMK to LW, 26.5.29.

p. 270 'Now as it somehow appears': LW to GEM, 18.6.29.

p. 270 'I propose to do some work': LW to GEM, 15.6.29.

p. 270 'In my opinion': FR to GEM, 14.7.29; quoted in Nedo, op. cit., p. 227.

p. 271 'I think that unless Wittgenstein': BR to GEM, 27.5.29.

p. 271 'I have never known anything so absurd': quoted in Rhees; see Nedo, op. cit., p. 227.

p. 271 Then Russell: the account of the viva that follows is based on that given by Alan Wood in his biography of Russell, *The Passionate Sceptic*, p. 156.

p. 272 'Give up literary criticism!': *Recollections*, p. 59.

p. 272 'You don't understand': ibid., p. 61.

p. 273 'even supposing': Ramsey, review of *Tractatus*, Copi and Beard, op. cit., p. 18.

p. 274 'It is, of course': 'Some Remarks on Logical Form', reprinted in Copi and Beard, op. cit., pp. 31–7.

p. 275 'as your presence': LW to BR, July 1929.

p. 275 'I'm afraid there is a gathering': John Mabbott, *Oxford Memories*, p. 79.

p. 275 'for some time': Ryle, 'Autobiographical', in Oscar P. Wood and George Pitcher, ed., *Ryle*.

p. 276 'This morning I dreamt': MS 107, p. 153.

p. 277 'My whole tendency': the 'Lecture on Ethics' is published in *Philosophical Review*, Jan. 1965, pp. 3–26.

p. 278 'What is good is also divine': *Culture and Value*, p. 3.

p. 278 'What others think of me': *'Was die anderen von mir halten beschäftigt mich immer ausserordentlich viel. Es ist mir sehr oft darum zu tun, einen guten Eindruck zu machen. D.h. ich denke sehr häufig über den Eindruck den ich auf andere mache und es ist mir angenehm, wenn ich denke, dass er gut ist und unangenehm im anderen Fall'*: MS 107, p. 76.

p. 278 'In my father's house': *Recollections*, p. 54.

p. 279 'A strange dream': *'Ein seltsamer Traum:*
Ich sehe in einer Illustrierten Zeitschrift eine Photographie von Evighztg (Vertsagt), der ein viel besprochener Tagesheld ist. Das Bild stellt ihn in seinem Auto dar. Es ist von seinen Schandtaten die Rede; Hänsel steht bei mir und noch jemand anderer ähnlich meinem Bruder Kurt. Dieser sagt, dass Vertsag ein Jude sei aber die Erziehung eines reichen schottischen Lords genossen habe. Jetzt ist er Arbeiterführer. Seinen Namen habe er nicht geändert weil das dort nicht Sitte sei. Es ist mir neu dass Vertsagt den ich mit der Betonung auf der ersten Silbe ausspreche, ein Jude ist, und ich erkenne dass ja sein Name einfach verzagt heisst. Es fällt mir nicht auf, dass es mit "ts" geschrieben ist was ich ein wenig fetter als das übrige gedruckt sehe. Ich denke: muss denn hinter jeder Unanständigkeit ein Jude stecken. Nun bin ich und Hänsel auf der Terrasse eines Hauses etwa des grossen Blockhauses auf der Hochreit und auf der Strasse kommt in seinem Automobil Vertsag; er hat ein böses Gesicht ein wenig rötlich blondes Haar und einen solchen Schnauzbart (er sieht nicht jüdisch aus). Er feuert nach rückwärts mit einem Maschinengewehr auf einen Radfahrer, der hinter ihm fährt und sich vor Schmerzen krümmt und der unbarmherzig durch viele Schüsse zu Boden geschossen wird. Vertsag ist vorbei und nun kommt ein junges Mädchen ärmlich aussehend auf einem Rade daher und auch sie empfängt die Schüsse von dem weiterfahrenden Vertsag. Und diese Schüsse die ihre Brust treffen machen ein brodelndes Geräusch wie ein Kessel in dem sehr wenig Wasser ist über einer Flamme. Ich hatte Mitleid mit dem Mädchen und dachte nur in Österreich kann es geschehen dass dieses Mädchen kein hilfreiches Mitleid findet und die Leute zusehen wie sie leidet und umgebracht wird. Ich selbst fürchte mich auch davor ihr zu helfen weil ich die Schüsse Vertsags fürchte. Ich nähere mich ihr, suche aber Deckung hinter einer Planke. Dann erwache ich. Ich muss nachtragen, dass in dem

*Gespräch ob Hänsel erst in Anwesenheit des anderen dann nachdem er uns
verlassen hat ich mich geniere und nicht sagen will dass ich ja selbst von
Juden abstamme oder dass der Fall Vertsags ja auch mein Fall ist. Nach dem
Erwachen komme ich darauf dass ja verzagt nicht mit "ts" geschrieben
wird, glaube aber sonderbarerweise dass es mit "pf" geschrieben wird
"pferzagt". Ich habe den Traum gleich nach dem Erwachen notiert. Die
Gegend die in dem Traum etwa der Gegend hinter der Hochreiter Kapelle
entspricht (die Seite gegen den Windhut) stelle ich mir im Traum als einen
steilen bewaldeten Abhang und eine Strasse im Tal vor wie ich es in einem
anderen Traum gesehen habe. Ähnlich einem Stück der Strasse von
Gloggnitz nach Schlagl. Als ich das arme Mädchen bedauere sehe ich
undeutlich ein altes Weib, welches sie bedauert aber sie nicht zu sich nimmt
und ihr hilft. Das Blockhaus auf der Hochreit ist auch nicht deutlich, wohl
aber die Strasse und was auf ihr vorgeht. Ich glaube ich hatte eine Idee dass
der Name wie ich ihn im Traume ausspreche "Vért-sagt" ungarisch ist.
Der Name hatte für mich etwas böses, boshaftes, und sehr männliches':*
MS 107, p. 219, 1.12.29.

12 THE 'VERIFICATIONIST PHASE'

p. 281 'For if the spirit': MS 108, p. 24, 19.12.29.

p. 281 'I am a beast': MS 108, p. 38, 25.12.29.

p. 281 'The spirit in which one can write the truth': *'Die Wahrheit über sich
selbst kann man in den verschiedensten Geiste schreiben. Im anständigsten
und unanständigsten. Und danach ist es sehr wünschenswert oder sehr
unrichtig, dass sie geschrieben werde. Ja, es gibt unter den wahrhaften
Autobiographien die man schreiben könnte, alle Stufen vom Höchsten zum
Niedrigsten. Ich zum Beispiel kann meine Biographie nicht höher schreiben
als ich bin. Und durch die blosse Tatsache, dass ich sie schreibe, hebe ich
mich nicht notwendigerweise, ich kann mich dadurch sogar schmutziger
machen als ich schon war. Etwas in mir spricht dafür, meine Biographie zu
schreiben und zwar möchte (m)ich mein Leben einmal klar ausbreiten, um
es klar vor mir zu haben und auch für andere. Nicht so sehr, um darüber
Gericht zu halten, als um jedenfalls Klarheit und Wahrheit zu schaffen':*
MS 108, pp. 46–7, 28.12.29.

p. 282 'the most serious book': *Recollections*, p. 90.

p. 282 'And woe to those': ibid.

p. 282 'What, you swine': *Ludwig Wittgenstein and the Vienna Circle*, p. 69.

p. 282 'I think it is definitely important': ibid.

p. 283 'Just because Schlick': quoted ibid., p. 18.

p. 284 '. . . at that time': ibid., p. 64.

p. 285 'Indeed!': ibid., p. 78.

p. 285 'Once I wrote': ibid., pp. 63–4.

p. 286 'Physics does not yield': ibid., p. 63.

p. 286 'I would reply': ibid., p. 68.

p. 286 'explains – I believe': *Philosophical Remarks*, p. 129.

p. 287 'If I say, for example': *Ludwig Wittgenstein and the Vienna Circle*, p. 47.

p. 287 'I used at one time to say': quoted in Gasking and Jackson, 'Wittgenstein as a Teacher'; see Fann, op. cit., pp. 49–55.

p. 288 'Imagine that there is a town': quoted Malcolm, op. cit., p. 55.

p. 289 'Wittgenstein's kindness': Partridge, op. cit., p. 170.

p. 289 'The subject of the lectures': recalled by S. K. Bose in the letter to John King of 5.4.78.

p. 290 'Your voice and his': I. A. Richards, 'The Strayed Poet', in *Internal Colloquies*, Routledge, 1972, pp. 183–6.

p. 291 'I think I summed up': *Culture and Value*, p. 24.

p. 291 'the attempt to be rid': *Lectures 1930–1932*, p. 1.

p. 291 'when the average hearer': Russell, *The Analysis of Mind*, p. 198.

p. 291 'If I wanted to eat an apple': *Philosophical Remarks*, p. 64.

p. 291 'for there seems': GEM to BR, 9.3.30.

p. 292 'I do not see how I can refuse': BR to GEM, 11.3.30.

p. 292 'Of course, we couldn't get very far': LW to GEM, March or April 1930.

p. 293 'Unfortunately I have been ill': BR to GEM, 5.5.30.

p. 294 'I find I can only understand Wittgenstein': BR to GEM, 8.5.30.

p. 294 'If a person tells me': *Recollections*, p. 112.

p. 294 'Arrived back in Cambridge': '*Nach den Osterferien wieder in Cambridge angekommen. In Wien oft mit Marguerite. Ostersonntag mit ihr in Neuwaldegg. Wir haben uns viel geküsst drei Stunden lang und es war sehr schön*': MS 108, p. 133, 25.4.30.

p. 294 'My life is now very economical': LW to GEM, 26.7.30.

p. 294 'Dear Gil (old beast)': LW to GP, summer 1930.

p. 296 'A proposition cannot say more': see *Ludwig Wittgenstein and the Vienna Circle*, p. 244.

p. 296 'If one tried to advance': *Philosophical Investigations*, I, 128.

p. 297 'I know that my method is right': *Recollections*, p. 110.

13 THE FOG CLEARS

p. 298 'The nimbus of philosophy': *Lectures: 1930–1932*, p. 21.

p. 298 'What we find out': ibid., p. 26.

p. 299 '. . . once a method has been found': ibid., p. 21.

p. 299 'I was walking about': *Recollections*, p. 112.

p. 300 'Telling someone something': *Culture and Value*, p. 7.

p. 300 'It is all one to me': ibid.

p. 301 'I would like to say': *Philosophical Remarks*, preface.

p. 301 'Philosophical analysis': *Lectures: 1930–1932*, p. 35.

p. 301 'We never arrive': ibid., p. 34.

p. 302 'The means whereby': Oswald Spengler, *The Decline of the West*, p. 4.

p. 302 'taking of spiritual-political events': ibid., p. 6.

p. 303 'so here we shall develop': ibid., p. 26.

p. 303 'recognize living forms': quoted by Erich Heller in 'Goethe and the Scientific Truth', *The Disinherited Mind*, pp. 4–34.

p. 303 'What I give': see Malcolm, op. cit., p. 43.

p. 303 'Our thought here': Waismann, *Principles of Linguistic Philosophy*, pp. 80–81.

p. 304 'Yes, this fellowship business': LW to JMK, Dec. 1930.

p. 304 '*For me*': *Ludwig Wittgenstein and the Vienna Circle*, p. 117.

p. 305 'For it cuts off': ibid , p. 115.

p. 305 'I would reply': ibid., p. 116.

p. 305 'I can well imagine a religion': ibid., p. 117.

p. 305 'If you and I': *Recollections*, p. 114.

p. 306 'As long as I can play the game': *Ludwig Wittgenstein and the Vienna Circle*, p. 120.

p. 306 'The following is a question': ibid., pp. 129–30.

p. 307 'What do we do': ibid., p. 120.

p. 307 'It is another calculus': ibid., pp. 121–2.

p. 307 '*You cannot*': ibid., p. 129.

p. 308 'A rule of syntax': ibid., p. 126.

p. 308 'If, then': ibid., p. 133.

p. 308 'the demonstration': ibid.

p. 308 'Things must connect directly': ibid., p. 155.

p. 308 'Here *seeing* matters': ibid., p. 123.

14   A NEW BEGINNING

p. 309 'I think now': *Remarks on Frazer's Golden Bough*, p. vi.

p. 310 'even those': *Recollections*, p. 102.

p. 310 'What narrowness': *Remarks on Frazer*, p. 5.

p. 311 'I can set out this law': ibid., pp. 8–9.

p. 311 'If I may explain': '*Wenn ich es durch einen Vergleich klar machen darf: Wenn ein "Strassenköter" seine Biographie schriebe, so bestünde die Gefahr a) dass er entweder seine Natur verleugnen, oder b) einen Grund ausfindig machen würde, auf sie stolz zu sein, oder c) die Sache so darstellen, als sei diese seine Natur eine nebensächliche Angelegenheit. Im ersten Falle lügt er, im zweiten ahmt er eine nur dem Naturadel natürliche Eigenschaft, den Stolz, nach, der ein vitium splendidum ist, das er* *ebensowenig wirklich besitzen kann, wie ein krüppelhafter Körper natürliche Gracie. Im dritten Fall macht er gleichsam die sozialdemokratische Geste, die die Bildung über die rohen Eigenschaften des Körpers stellt, aber auch das ist ein Betrug. Er ist was er ist und das ist zugleich wichtig und bedeutsam, aber kein Grund zum Stolz, andererseits immer Gegenstand der Selbstachtung. Ja ich kann den Adelsstolz des Andern und siene Verachtung meiner Natur anerkennen, denn ich erkenne ja dadurch nur meine Natur an und den andern der zur Umgebung meiner Natur, die Welt, deren Mittelpunkt dieser vielleicht hässliche Gegenstand, meine Person, ist'*: MS 110. pp. 252–3, 1.7.31.

p. 312 'Putting together a complete autobiography': quoted in Rhees, *Recollections*, p. 182.

p. 312 'I can quite imagine': LW to GEM, 23.8.31.

p. 313 'How wrong he was': *Recollections*, p. 91.

p. 313 'has something Jewish': *Culture and Value*, p. 20.

p. 313 'Mendelssohn is not a peak': ibid., p. 2.

p. 313 'Tragedy is something un-Jewish': ibid., p. 1.

p. 313 'who like a noxious bacillus': Hitler, *Mein Kampf*, p. 277.

p. 314 'the Jew lacks those qualities': ibid., p. 275.

p. 314 'since the Jew': ibid., p. 273.

p. 314 'It has sometimes been said': *Culture and Value*, p. 22.

p. 314 'Look on this tumour': ibid., p. 20.

p. 316 *Untergangsters*: quoted in Field, op. cit., p. 207.

p. 316 'a confession': *Culture and Value*, p. 18.

p. 316 'It is typical': ibid., p. 19.

p. 316 'Amongst Jews': ibid., pp. 18–19.

p. 317 'Often, when I have': ibid., p. 19.

p. 317 'The Jew must see to it': ibid.

p. 319 'My presence': Sjögren, op. cit., p. 122.

p. 319 'but that doesn't matter': see *Philosophical Grammar*, p. 487.

p. 320 'For the thing itself': LW to MS, 20.11.31.

p. 320 'There are *very, very* many statements': ibid.

p. 320 'If there were theses': *Ludwig Wittgenstein and the Vienna Circle*, p. 183.

p. 321 'still proceeded dogmatically': ibid., p. 184.

p. 321 'make head or tail': LW to MS, 4.3.32.

p. 322 'This is the right sort of approach': *Lectures: 1930–1932*, p. 73.

p. 322 '. . . the dialectical method': ibid., p. 74.

p. 322 'Philosophy is not a choice': ibid., p. 75.

p. 322 'The right expression is': ibid., p. 97.

p. 323 'Grammatical rules': ibid., p. 98.

p. 323 'You owe a great debt': see *Recollections*, p. 123.

p. 324 '. . . from the bottom of my heart': LW to MS, 8.8.32.

p. 324 'That I had not dealt': ibid. (I am indebted to Dr P.M.S. Hacker for this translation.)

p. 325 'All that philosophy can do': MS 213, p. 413; quoted by Anthony Kenny in 'Wittgenstein on the Nature of Philosophy', *The Legacy of Wittgenstein*, pp. 38–60. See also, in the same collection of essays, 'From the Big Typescript to the "*Philosophical Grammar*"', pp. 24–37.

p. 326 'Confusions in these matters': *Philosophical Grammar*, p. 375.

p. 327 'Philosophical clarity': ibid., p. 381.

p. 327 'Nothing seems to me less likely': *Culture and Value*, p. 62.

15   FRANCIS

p. 328 'Is there a substratum': *Wittgenstein's Lectures Cambridge 1932–1935*, p. 205.

p. 329 'no philosophy can possibly': Hardy, 'Mathematical Proof', *Mind*, Jan. 1929, pp. 1–25.

p. 329 'The talk of mathematicians': *Lectures: 1932–5*, p. 225.

p. 330 'Russell and I': ibid., p. 11.

p. 331 'I have wanted to show': ibid., pp. 12–13.

p. 332 'In the event of my death': MS 114.

p. 332 'I am glad': FS to LW, 28.12.32.

p. 332 'Dear Ludwig': FS to LW, 25.3.33.

p. 333 'I'm busy': quoted Pascal, *Recollections*, p. 23.

p. 333 'I feel much further': FS to LW, 2.10.33.

p. 335 'Come to Cambridge at once': *Recollections*, p. 124.

p. 335 'Part of [Braithwaite's] statements', *Mind*, 42 (1933), pp. 415–16.

p. 335 'The extent to which': ibid.

16   LANGUAGE-GAMES: *THE BLUE AND BROWN BOOKS*

p. 337 'I shall in the future': *Blue Book*, p. 17.

p. 338 'We are inclined': ibid.

p. 338 'Philosophers constantly see': ibid., p. 18.

p. 338 'What we say will be easy': *Lectures: 1932–5*, p. 77.

p. 338 'After I stopped': FS to LW, 17.12.33.

p. 339 'My despair': Sjögren, op. cit., p. 137.

p. 340 'He has the great gift': FW to MS, 9.8.34.

p. 340 'If I am with you': FS to LW, 25.3.34.

p. 340 'I thought of you a lot': ibid.

p. 341 'I long to be with you': FS to LW, 4.4.34.

p. 341 'I started off again': FS to LW, 24.7.34.

p. 342 'When I read this': FS to LW, 11.8.34.

p. 343 'growing political awareness': George Thomson, 'Wittgenstein: Some Personal Recollections', *Revolutionary World*, XXXVII, no. 9, pp. 86–8.

p. 343 'I am a communist': quoted by Rowland Hutt in conversation with the author.

p. 343 'I think Francis means': *Recollections*, pp. 125–6.

p. 344 'Imagine a people': *Brown Book*, p. 100.

p. 344 'Imagine a tribe': ibid., p. 103.

p. 344 'Imagine that human beings': ibid., p. 120.

p. 345 'Here is one of the most fertile sources': ibid., p. 108.

p. 345 'We are inclined to say': ibid.

p. 346 'Our answer is': ibid.

p. 346 'the way in which': LW to MS, 31.7.35.

17 JOINING THE RANKS

p. 347 'At the beginning of September': LW to MS, 31.7.35.

p. 348 'I am sure that you partly understand': LW to JMK, 6.7.35.

p. 348 'exceedingly careful': ibid.

p. 349 'May I venture': Keynes's introduction is reproduced in full in *Letters to Russell, Keynes and Moore*, pp. 135–6.

p. 349 'definitely nice': LW to JMK, July 1935.

p. 350 'My interview with Miss B': LW to GP, dated simply 'Tuesday', which is consistent with its being 20.8.35.

p. 350 'If you were a qualified technician': JKM to LW, 10.7.35.

p. 351 'Wittgenstein!': this story is told by George Sacks in *A Thinking Man as Hero*, a television play by Hugh Whitemore, first broadcast on BBC 2, April 1973. I am very grateful to Mr Whitemore for drawing my attention to this source.

p. 351 'we heard that Wittgenstein': ibid.

p. 351 'I wish I could be with you': FS to LW, 17.9.35.

p. 352 'My dear Gilbert!': LW to GP, Sept. 1935.

p. 353 'He had taken no decisions': *Recollections*, p. 29.

p. 353 'The important thing': ibid., p. 205.

p. 353 'Tyranny': ibid.

p. 353 'If anything': ibid.

p. 354 'perhaps I shall go to Russia': LW to PE, 21.6.37.

p. 354 according to Piero Sraffa: see John Moran, 'Wittgenstein and Russia', *New Left Review*, LXXIII (May–June 1972), pp. 83–96.

p. 354 'People have accused Stalin': *Recollections*, p. 144.

p. 355 'in a silly detective story': 'The Language of Sense Data and Private Experience – I (Notes taken by Rush Rhees of Wittgenstein's

Lectures, 1936)', *Philosophical Investigations*, VII, no.1 (Jan. 1984), pp. 1–45.

p. 356 'We have the feeling': ibid., no.2 (April 1984), p. 139.

p. 356 'Here at last': *Recollections*, p. 136.

p. 357 'It's all excellent similes': Moore, 'Wittgenstein's Lectures', op. cit., p. 316.

p. 357 'What I invent': *Culture and Value*, p. 19.

p. 357 'I still have a little money': *Recollections*, p. 209.

p. 359 'Sometimes his silence infuriates me': *Recollections*, p. 127.

p. 360 'I don't see how you *can* win!': quoted by Gilbert Pattisson in conversation with the author.

18 CONFESSIONS

p. 361 'When I got your letter': FS to LW, 6.9.36.

p. 362 'I don't feel clear': FS to LW, 1.11.36.

p. 362 'My feelings for you': FS to LW, 26.10.36.

p. 363 'I do believe': LW to GEM, Oct. 1936.

p. 363 'The weather has changed': LW to GP, Oct. 1936.

p. 363 '"Both fit and style are perfect"': LW to GP, 2.2.37.

p. 363 'or nearly all': LW to GEM, 20.11.36.

p. 364 'These words': *Philosophical Investigations*, I, 1.

p. 364 'A simile that has been': ibid., 112.

p. 365 'A *picture* held us': ibid., 115.

p. 365 'Our clear and simple': ibid., 130.

p. 365 'It is not our aim': ibid., 133.

p. 365 'The results of philosophy': ibid., 119

p. 366 'The edifice of your pride': *Culture and Value*, p. 26.

p. 366 'If anyone is unwilling': quoted in Rhees, *Recollections*, p. 174.

p. 367 'all sorts of things': LW to GEM, 20.11.36.

p. 367 'Whatever you say': FS to LW, 6.12.36.

p. 368 'Whatever you have to tell me': FS to LW, 9.12.36.

p. 368 'listened patiently': *Recollections*, p. 38.

p. 368 'He would have sat transfixed': ibid.

p. 368 'If ever a thing could wait': ibid., p. 35.

p. 369 remembered by Rowland Hutt: and told to me in the course of several conversations.

p. 369 'he had to keep a firmer control': *Recollections*, p. 37.

p. 371 'I myself was not a pupil': Georg Stangel, interview with Adolf Hübner, 19.2.75.

p. 371 'Ja, ja': Leopold Piribauer, interview with Adolf Hübner, 3.12.74.

p. 372 'Last year': quoted in Rhees, *Recollections*, p. 173.

p. 372 'I thought of having it removed': LW to GB, 18.11.37.

p. 372 'I feel it is wrong': FS to LW, 1.3.37.

p. 373 'I don't think I have ever understood': FS to LW, 27.5.37.

p. 373 'partly because I've been troubled': LW to GEM, 4.3.37.

p. 373 'vain, thoughtless, frightened': *'Eitel, gedankenlos, ängstlich . . . Ich möchte jetzt bei jemandem wohnen. In der Früh ein menschliches Gesicht sehen. Anderseits bin ich jetzt wieder so verweichlicht, dass es vielleicht gut wäre allein sein zu müssen. Bin jetzt ausserordentlich verächtlich . . . Ich habe das Gefühl, dass ich jetzt nicht ganz ohne Ideen wäre, aber dass mich die Einsamkeit bedrücken wird, dass ich nicht arbeiten werde können. Ich fürchte mich, dass in meinem Haus alle meine Gedanken werden getötet werden. Dass dort ein Geist der Niedergeschlagenheit von mir ganz Besitz ergreifen wird'*: MS 118, 16.8.37.

p. 374 'unhappy, helpless and thoughtless': *'Unglücklich, ratlos und gedankenlos . . . Und da kam mir wieder zum Bewusstsein, wie einzig Francis ist und unersetzlich. Und wie wenig ich doch das weiss, wenn ich mit ihm bin.*

Bin ganz in Kleinlichkeit verstrickt. Bin irritiert, denke nur an mich und fühle, dass mein Leben elend ist, und dabei habe ich auch gar keine Ahnung, wie elend es ist': MS 118, 17.8.37.

p. 374 'I am ashamed': MS 118, 18.8.37.

p. 374 'I do not know whether I have either a right': MS 118, 19.8.37.

p. 374 'Am now really ill': MS 118, 22.8.37.

p. 375 'showered with gifts': MS 118, 26.8.37.

p. 375 'You said in one of your letters': FS to LW, 23.8.37.

p. 375 'I would love very much to come': FS to LW, 30.8.37.

p. 375 'The way to solve the problem': MS 118, 27.8.37.

p. 375 'I conduct myself badly': MS 118, 26.8.37.

p. 375 'I am a coward': MS 118, 2.9.37.

p. 375 'Am irreligious': MS 118, 7.9.37.

p. 376 'Christianity is not a doctrine': MS 118, 4.9.37; see *Culture and Value*, p. 28.

p. 376 'just wicked and superstitious': MS 118, 7.9.37.

p. 376 'It's as though my work had been drained': MS 118, 17.9.37.

p. 376 'sensual, susceptible, indecent': MS 118, 22.9.37.

p. 376 'Lay with him two or three times': *'Zwei oder dreimal mit ihm gelegen. Immer zuerst mit dem Gefühl, es sei nichts Schlechtes,* dann *mit Scham. Bin auch ungerecht, auffahrend und auch falsch gegen ihn gewesen und quälerisch'*: ibid.

p. 377 'Am very impatient!': MS 119, 25.9.37.

p. 377 'The last 5 days': *'Die letzten 5 Tage waren schön: er hatte sich in das Leben hier hineingefunden und tat alles mit Liebe und Güte, und ich war, Gott sei Dank, nicht ungeduldig, und hatte auch wahrhaftig keinen Grund,* *ausser meine eigene böse Natur. Begleitete ihn gestern bis Sogndal; heute in meine Hütte zurück. Etwas bedrückt, auch müde'*: MS 119, 1.10.37.

p. 377 'I often remember': FS to LW, undated.

p. 377 'I think *constantly* of you': FS to LW, undated.

p. 377 'I am often thinking': FS to LW, 14.10.37.

p. 378 'I'm thinking of you a lot': FS to LW, 26.10.37.

p. 378 'Prof. Moore wasn't present': FS to LW, 22.10.37.

p. 378 'lovely letter from Fr.': *'Lieben Brief von Fr., er schreibt über eine Sitzung des Mor.Sc.Cl. und wie elend schlecht die Diskussion unter Braithwaits Vorsitz war. Es ist scheusslich. Aber ich wüsste nicht, was dagegen zu machen wäre, denn die andern Leute sind auch zu wenig ernst. Ich wäre auch zu feig, etwas Entscheidendes zu tun'*: MS 119, 27.10.37.

p. 378 'harsh and hectoring' letter: see *Recollections*, p. 32.

p. 379 'Have not heard from Francis': MS 119, 16.10.37.

p. 379 'Am relieved': MS 119, 17.10.37.

p. 379 'He made a *good* impression': MS 119, 10.10.37.

p. 379 '[I] just took some apples': *Culture and Value*, p. 31.

p. 380 'How bad is it?': *'Heute Nacht onaniert. Wie schlecht ist es? Ich weiss es nicht. Ich denke mir, es ist schlecht, aber habe keinen Grund'*: MS 120, 21.11.37.

p. 380 'Think of my earlier love': *'Denke an meine frühere Liebe, oder Verliebtheit, in Marguerite und an meine Liebe für Francis. Es ist ein schlimmes Zeichen für mich, dass meine Gefühle für M. so gänzlich erkalten konnten! Freilich ist hier ein Unterschied; aber* meine Herzenskälte *besteht.*

Möge mir vergeben werden; d.h. aber: möge es mir möglich sein, aufrichtig und liebevoll zu sein': MS 120, 1.12.37.

p. 380 'Masturbated tonight': *'Heute nacht onaniert. Gewissensbisse, aber auch die Überzeugung, dass ich zu schwach bin, dem Drang und der Versuchung zu widerstehen, wenn die und die Vorstellungen sich mir darbieten, ohne dass ich mich in andere* flüchten *kann. Gestern abend* noch hatte ich *Gedanken über die Notwendigkeit der Reinheit meines Wandels. (Ich dachte an Marguerite und Francis.)'*: MS 120, 2.12.37.

p. 380 'the bewitchment of our intelligence': *Philosophical Investigations*, I, 109.

p. 381 'Isn't there a truth': *Remarks on the Foundations of Mathematics*, I, p. 5.

p. 381 'I am merely': ibid., I, p. 110.

p. 382 'I am nervous': *'Ich bin beim Schreiben nervös und alle meine Gedanken kurz von Atem. Und ich fühle immer, dass ich den Ausdruck nicht ganz verteidigen kann. Dass er schlecht schmeckt'*: MS 119, 11.11.37.

p. 382 'I would like to run away': *'Ich möchte fliehen, aber es wäre unrecht und ich kann es gar nicht. Vielleicht aber könnte ich es auch – ich könnte* morgen *packen und den nächsten Tag abfahren. Aber möchte ich es? Wäre es richtig? Ist es nicht richtig, hier noch auszuhalten? Gewiss. Ich würde mit einem* schlechten *Gefühl morgen abfahren. "Halt es aus", sagt mir eine Stimme. Es ist aber auch Eitelkeit dabei, dass ich aushalten will; und auch etwas Besseres. – Der einzige triftige Grund hier früher oder gleich abzureisen wäre, dass ich anderswo jetzt vielleicht besser arbeiten könnte. Denn es ist Tatsache, dass der Druck, der jetzt auf mir liegt, mir das Arbeiten beinahe unmöglich macht und vielleicht in einigen Tagen wirklich unmöglich*': MS 120, 22.11.37.

p. 382   'It is the opposite of piety': MS 120, 28.11.37.

p. 382   'You must *strive*': ibid.

p. 382   'The ever-changing, difficult weather': MS 120, 30.11.37.

p. 383   'I'm sorry you are having storms': FS to LW, 1.11.37.

p. 383   '*He is dead and decomposed*': MS 120, 12.12.37. This long diary entry is given in full in *Culture and Value*, p. 33.

19   *FINIS AUSTRIAE*

p. 385   'German-Austria must return': Hitler, *Mein Kampf*, p. 3.

p. 385   'in my earliest youth': ibid., p. 15.

p. 386   'but cleverer people than I': Hermine Wittgenstein, *Familienerinnerungen*, p. 148.

p. 386   'When, at midnight': ibid.

p. 387   'Freud's idea': MS 120, 2.1.38, *Culture and Value*, p. 33.

p. 387   'and that is bad': MS 120, 5.1.38.

p. 387   'Thought: it would be good': MS 120, 4.1.38.

p. 387   'I am cold': ibid.

p. 388   'irreligious': MS 120, 10.2.38.

p. 388   'on the other hand': MS 120, 14.2.38.

p. 388   'It is entirely as though': MS 120, 15.2.38.

p. 389   'You didn't make a mistake': the letter is reproduced in full in *Recollections*, pp. 95–6.

p. 389   'Can't work': '*Kann nicht arbeiten. Denke viel über einen eventuellen Wechsel meiner Nationalität nach. Lese in der heutigen Zeitung, dass eine weitere zwangsweise Annäherung Österreichs an Deutschland erfolgt ist. – Aber ich weiss nicht, was ich eigentlich machen soll*': MS 120, 16.2.38.

p. 390   'You will either fulfil my demands': quoted in Roger Manvell and Heinrich Fraenkel, *Hitler: The Man and the Myth*, p. 142.

p. 390   'If Herr Hitler's suggestion': quoted in George Clare, *Last Waltz in Vienna*, p. 166.

p. 390   'That the first act': quoted ibid.

p. 390   'That is a ridiculous rumour': *Recollections*, p. 139.

p. 391 'What I hear about Austria': *'Was ich von Österreich höre, beunruhigt mich. Bin im Unklaren darüber, was ich tun soll, nach Wien fahren oder nicht. Denke hauptsächlich an Francis und dass ich ihn nicht verlassen will'*: MS 120, 12.3.38.

p. 392 'Before trying to discuss': Piero Sraffa to LW, 14.3.38.

p. 394 'I am now in an extraordinarily difficult situation': MS 120, 14.3.38; quoted in Nedo, op. cit., p. 296.

p. 394 'In my *head*': MS 120, 16.3.38; quoted ibid.

p. 394 'Sraffa advised me': *'In Cambridge: Sraffa riet mir gestern vorläufig auf keinen Fall nach Wien zu gehen, da ich meinen Leuten jetzt nicht helfen könnte und aller Wahrscheinlichkeit nach nicht mehr aus Österreich herausgelassen würde. Ich bin nicht völlig klar darüber, was ich tun soll, aber ich glaube vorläufig, Sraffa hat recht'*: MS 120, 18.3.38.

p. 394 'The same, of course': LW to JMK, 18.3.38. The letter is given in full in *Briefe*, pp. 278–9.

p. 396 'is a body who helps people': LW to GP, 26.3.38.

p. 396 'My dear Ludwig': reproduced in Nedo, op. cit., p. 300.

p. 396 'reassuring *sounding* news': MS 120, 25.3.38.

p. 396 Hermine recalls: see Hermine Wittgenstein, op. cit., pp. 154–81.

p. 397 'That these children': Brigitte Zwiauer, 'An die Reichstelle für Sippenforschung', 29 Sept. 1938.

p. 399 'the great nervous strain': LW to GEM, 19.10.38.

p. 399 'In case you want an Emetic': LW to GP, Sept. 1938.

p. 400 'And if': Hermine Wittgenstein, op. cit., p. 120.

p. 400 received certificates: these were issued from Berlin, and still survive. Hermine's is dated 30.8.39, and states: 'Hermine Maria Franziska Wittgenstein of 16 Argentinierstrasse, Vienna IV, born in Eichwald, Teplich on 1.12.1874, is of mixed Jewish blood, having two racially Jewish grandparents as defined by the first Reich Citizenship Law of 14 Nov. 1935'.

p. 400 'their racial classification': this document, dated 10 Feb. 1940, is reproduced in Nedo, op. cit., p. 303.

20   THE RELUCTANT PROFESSOR

p. 403 'If you write': *Recollections*, p. 141.

p. 404 'persuading people': *Lectures and Conversations on Aesthetics, Psychology & Religious Belief*, p. 28.

p. 404 'Jeans has written a book': ibid., p. 27.

p. 405 'You might think': ibid., p. 11.

p. 405 'Do you think I have a theory?': ibid., p. 10.

p. 405 'It is not only difficult': ibid., p. 7.

p. 406 'She was descending from a height': Freud, *The Interpretation of Dreams*, pp. 463–5.

p. 406 'I would say': *Lectures and Conversations*, p. 24.

p. 406 'he treated me quite as his equal': see Freud, *Jokes and their Relation to the Unconscious*, pp. 47–52.

p. 407 'If it is not causal': *Lectures and Conversations*, p. 18.

p. 407 'When I read his poems': ibid, p. 4.

p. 408 'It seems to me': LW to PE, 23.10.21.

p. 408 'I now believe': LW to LH, Nov. 1921.

p. 408 'THE KING OF THE DARK CHAMBER': This fragment is now in the possession of Mrs Peg Rhees; it was shown to me by Rush Rhees, who very kindly supplied me with a copy of it.

p. 410 'Russell and the parsons': *Recollections*, p. 102.

p. 411 'Suppose someone said: "This is poor evidence"': *Lectures and Conversations*, p. 61.

p. 411 'Suppose someone said: "What do you believe"': ibid., p. 70.

p. 412 'You are not beautiful': Tagore, *King of the Dark Chamber*, p. 199.

p. 412 'Dear Mrs Stewart': LW to Mrs Stewart, 28.10.38, now in the possession of Mrs Katherine Thomson.

p. 414 'I needn't say': LW to GEM, 2.2.39.

p. 415 'To refuse the chair': quoted in *Recollections*, p. 141.

p. 415 'Having got the professorship': LW to WE, 27.3.39.

p. 415 'I would do my utmost': *Lectures and Conversations*, p. 28.

p. 416 'I would say': *Wittgenstein's Lectures on the Foundations of Mathematics: Cambridge, 1939*, p. 103.

p. 416 'There is no religious denomination': *Culture and Value*, p. 1.

p. 416 'Take Russell's contradiction': *Lectures on the Foundations of Mathematics*, p. 222.

p. 417 'All the puzzles': ibid., p. 14.

p. 417 'Another idea': ibid.

p. 417 'The *mathematical* problems': *Remarks on the Foundations of Mathematics*, VII, p. 16.

p. 418 'somewhat parenthetical': *Lectures on the Foundations of Mathematics*, p. 67.

p. 418 'I shall try': ibid., p. 22.

p. 418 'I understand, but I don't agree': *Lectures on the Foundations of Mathematics*, p. 67.

p. 419 'I see your point': ibid., p. 95.

p. 419 'Turing thinks': ibid., p. 102.

p. 420 'Obviously': ibid., p. 55.

p. 420 'introducing Bolshevism': ibid., p. 67.

p. 420 'It is very queer': ibid., pp. 206–7.

p. 421 'will not come in': ibid., p. 211.

p. 421 *Turing*: 'You cannot be confident': ibid., pp. 217–18.

p. 421 'You seem to be saying': ibid., p. 219.

p. 422 Andrew Hodges: see *The Enigma of Intelligence*, note (3.39), pp. 547–8.

p. 422 'Wittgenstein was doing something important': Malcolm, *Memoir*, p. 23

p. 423 'I am not the deducting, deducing book type': Street & Smith's *Detective Story Magazine*, Jan. 1945. Race Williams was the creation of Carroll John Daly, the writer credited with having invented the 'hard-boiled' detective story.

p. 424 'what is the use of studying philosophy': this is Wittgenstein's reaction as it was remembered by him in a later letter, LW to NM, 16.11.44. See *Memoir*, pp. 93–4.

p. 424 'how should I find the strength': MS 118, 12.9.37; quoted in Baker and Hacker, *An Analytical Commentary*, p. 11.

p. 425 'I feel I will die slowly': quoted in a letter from John Ryle to his wife, Miriam. Letter now in the possession of Dr Anthony Ryle.

p. 425 'Because, unless I'm very much mistaken': LW to NM, 22.6.40.

p. 425 '*Only by a miracle*': LW to NM, 3.10.40.

p. 425 'I feel very unhappy': FS to LW, 11.10.39.

p. 426 'See K once or twice a week': '*Sehe K ein – bis zweimal die Woche; bin aber zweifelhaft darüber, inwieweit das Verhältnis das richtige ist. Möge es wirklich gut sein*': MS 117, 13.6.40.

p. 426 'Occupied myself the *whole* day': '*Habe den ganzen Tag mich mit Gedanken über mein Verhältnis zu Kirk beschäftigt. Grösstenteils sehr falsch und fruchtlos. Wenn ich diese Gedanken aufschriebe, so sähe man wie tiefstehend und ungerade //schlüpferig// meine Gedanken sind*': MS 123, 7.10.40.

p. 427 'My dear Ro[w]land': LW to RH, 12.10.41.

p. 427 'frightened wild animal': quoted in Pascal, *Recollections*, p. 26.

p. 428 'Think a lot about Francis': '*Denke viel an Francis, aber immer nur mit Reue wegen meiner Lieblosigkeit; nicht mit Dankbarkeit. Sein Leben und Tod scheint mich nur anzuklagen, denn ich war in den letzten 2 Jahren seines Lebens sehr oft lieblos und im Herzen untreu gegen ihn. Wäre er nicht so unendlich sanftmütig und treu gewesen, so wäre ich gänzlich lieblos gegen ihn geworden . . . Keit(h?) sehe ich oft, und was das eigentlich heisst, weiss ich nicht. Verdiente Enttäuschung, Bangen, Sorge, Unfähigkeit mich in eine Lebensweise niederzulassen*': MS 125, 28.12.41.

p. 428 'Think a great deal about the last time I was with Francis': '*Denke viel an die letzte Zeit mit Francis: an meine Abscheulichkeit mit ihm . . . Ich kann nicht sehen, wie ich je im Leben von dieser Schuld befreit werden kann*': MS 137, 11.7.48.

21 WAR WORK

p. 431 'He is one of the world's famousest philosophers': John Ryle, letter to Miriam Ryle, 29.9.41.

p. 432 'Good God': story told to me by Dr R. L. Waterfield.

p. 433 'Yes, very well': quoted by Ronald MacKeith in a letter to *Guy's Hospital Gazette*, XC (1976), p. 215.

p. 433 '*One word* that comes from your heart': LW to RH, 20.8.41.

p. 433 'I can't write about Francis': LW to RH, 27.11.41.

p. 433 'If, however': LW to RH, dated 'Sunday'.

p. 433 'It is on the whole': LW to RH, 'Wednesday'.

p. 434 'As long as you find it difficult': LW to RH, 26.1.42.

p. 434 'I feel, on the whole, lonely': LW to RH, 31.12.41.

p. 434 'Daddy and another Austrian': This diary is still in the possession of its author, Dr Anthony Ryle.

p. 435 'The hospital had scores of firebombs': letter from Dr H. Osmond to the author, 4.2.86.

p. 436 'Two – and one of them is Gilbert Ryle': told to the author by Miss Wilkinson.

p. 436 'Tonight I dreamt': MS 125, 16.10.42; quoted in Nedo, op. cit., p. 305.

p. 437 'we may then refer': *Lectures and Conversations*, p. 44.

p. 437 'and to me': ibid., p. 42.

p. 438 'it is an idea': ibid., p. 43.

p. 438 '. . . something which people are inclined to accept': ibid., p. 44.

p. 438 'One of the chief triumphs': Russell, 'Mathematics and the Metaphysicians', *Mysticism and Logic*, pp. 59–74.

p. 439 'Why do I want to take': *Remarks on the Foundations of Mathematics*, VII, p. 19.

p. 439 'is almost as if': ibid., V, p. 25.

p. 439 'completely deformed the thinking': ibid., VII, p. 11.

p. 442 'I no longer feel any hope': '*Ich fühle keine Hoffnung mehr für die Zukunft in meinem Leben. Es ist als hätte ich nur mehr eine lange Strecke lebendigen Todes vor mir. Ich kann mir für mich keine Zukunft als eine grässliche vorstellen. Freundlos und freudlos*': MS 125, 1.4.42.

p. 442 'I suffer greatly': '*Ich leide sehr unter Furcht vor der gänzlichen Vereinsamung, die mir jetzt droht. Ich kann nicht sehen, wie ich dieses Leben ertragen kann. Ich sehe es als ein Leben, in dem ich mich jeden Tag werde vor dem Abend fürchten müssen, der mir nur dumpfe Traurigkeit bringt*': MS 125, 9.4.42.

p. 442 'If you can't find happiness': '*"Wenn du das Glück nicht in der Ruhe finden kannst, finde es im Laufen!" Wenn ich aber müde werde, zu laufen? "Sprich nicht vom Zusammenbrechen, ehe du zusammenbrichst."*'

Wie ein Radfahrer muss ich nun beständig treten, mich beständig bewegen, um nicht umzufallen': MS 125, 9.4.42.

p. 442 'My unhappiness is so complex': *'Mein Unglück ist so komplex, dass es schwer zu beschreiben ist. Aber wahrscheinlich ist doch* Vereinsamung *die Hauptsache'*: MS 125, 26.5.42.

p. 442 'For ten days': *'Höre seit 10 Tagen nichts mehr von K, obwohl ich ihn vor einer Woche um dringende Nachricht gebeten habe. Ich denke, dass er vielleicht mit mir gebrochen hat. Ein tragischer Gedanke!'*: MS 125, 27.5.42.

p. 443 'I have suffered much': *'Ich habe viel gelitten, aber ich bin scheinbar unfähig aus meinem Leben zu lernen. Ich leide noch immer so wie vor vielen Jahren. Ich bin nicht stärker und nicht weiser geworden'*: ibid.

p. 444 'He could be cheerful': *Recollections*, p. 24.

p. 444 'I'm sorry to hear': LW to RF, 8.6.49.

p. 444 'I wonder': LW to RF, 15.12.50.

p. 444 'I'm glad to hear': LW to RF, 1.2.51.

p. 445 'Recent experience': Dr R. T. Grant, 'Memorandum on the Observations Required in Cases of Wound Shock', MRC Archives.

p. 446 'In my way of doing philosophy': MS 213 (The 'Big Typescript'), p. 421.

p. 446 'Quite a lot of the preamble': Colonel Whitby to Dr Landsborough Thomson, 5.7.41, MRC Archives.

p. 447 'Professor Ludwig Wittgenstein': Dr Grant to Dr Herrald, 30.4.43, MRC Archives.

p. 448 'He is proving very useful': Dr Grant to Dr Herrald, 1.6.43.

p. 448 'I *imagine*': LW to RH, 17.3.43.

p. 448 'On each of these': *Lectures and Conversations*, p. 45.

p. 449 'points to the sort of explanation': ibid., p. 47.

p. 449 'Freud very commonly': ibid.

p. 449 'Obviously': ibid., p. 48.

p. 449 'There was a vacant room': Miss Helen Andrews to the author, 12.11.85.

p. 450 'You think philosophy is difficult': *Recollections*, p. 106.

p. 451 'You do *decent* work': quoted by Dr Basil Reeve in conversation with the author.

p. 452 'In practice': introduction to *Observations on the General Effects of Injury in Man* (HMSO, 1951).

p. 452 '[It] threw grave doubt': *Medical Research in War*, Report of the MRC for the years 1939–45, p. 53.

p. 453 'After the end': *Recollections*, p. 147.

p. 454 'Why in the world': quoted in Drury, *Recollections*, p. 148.

p. 454 'It is obvious to me': quoted ibid., p. 147.

p. 454 'I haven't heard from Smythies': LW to NM, 11.9.43.

p. 454 'I am feeling lonely': LW to NM, 7.12.43.

p. 455 'I too regret': LW to NM, 11.9.43.

p. 456 'Wittgenstein has agreed': Dr Grant to Dr Landsborough Thomson, 13.12.43.

p. 456 'He was reserved': Dr E. G. Bywaters to the author, 9.11.85.

p. 457 'Professor Wittgenstein has been doing': Bywaters to Cuthbertson, 8.2.44.

p. 457 'Professor Wittgenstein left us today': Bywaters to Herrald, 16.2.44.

22 SWANSEA

p. 458 'I don't know if you remember Rhees': NM to LW, 7.12.43.

p. 458 'If, e.g., I leave here': LW to RR, 9.2.44.

p. 459 'The weather's foul': LW to NM, 15.12.45.

p. 459 'his remedies would be all too drastic': *Recollections*, p. 32.

p. 460 'I hadn't a good impression': LW to RH, 17.3.44.

p. 460 'If it ever happens': *Recollections*, p. 149.

p. 461 'is that you can read it': LW to NM, 24.11.42.

p. 461 'I think you must stop creeping': LW to RH, 17.3.44.

p. 461 'I wish I knew more': LW to RH, 24.3.44.

p. 462 'It seems to me': LW to RH, 20.4.44.

p. 463 'I wish you *luck*': LW to RH, 8.6.44.

p. 463 'Yes I do': quoted by Rush Rhees in conversation with the author.

p. 464 'If someone tells me': quoted in Drury, *Recollections*, p. 88.

p. 464 'An honest religious thinker': *Culture and Value*, p. 73.

p. 464 'A miracle is, as it were': ibid., p. 45.

p. 464 'I am not a religious man': *Recollections*, p. 79.

p. 464 'Isn't she an angel': quoted by Mrs Clement in conversation with the author.

p. 466 'Wittgenstein's chief contribution': quoted by Rush Rhees in conversation with the author. (Rhees had no doubt that his memory was correct, but it must be pointed out that Professor John Wisdom had, when I asked him, no recollection of the episode.)

p. 466 'What about your work on mathematics?': quoted by Rush Rhees in conversation with the author.

p. 467 'I want to call': MS 169, p. 37.

p. 469 'The application of the concept': *Remarks on the Foundations of Mathematics*, VI, p. 21.

p. 469 'I may give a new rule': ibid., p. 32.

p. 470 'I'll probably take on a war-job': LW to RH, 3.8.44.

p. 470 'What I'll do': LW to RH, 3.9.44.

23   THE DARKNESS OF THIS TIME

p. 471 'Russell's books': quoted in *Recollections*, p. 112.

p. 472 'Russell isn't going to kill himself': see Malcolm, op. cit., p. 57.

p. 472 'The earlier Wittgenstein': Russell, *My Philosophical Development*, p. 161.

p. 472 'I've seen Russell': LW to RR, 17.10.44.

p. 472 'It is not an altogether pleasant experience': Russell, op. cit., p. 159.

p. 473 'Moore is as nice as always': LW to RR, 17.10.44.

p. 473 'I fear': LW to GEM, 7.3.41; see *Briefe*, p. 254.

p. 474 'He did not realise': quoted in Sister Mary Elwyn McHale, op. cit., p. 77.

p. 474 'with his great love for truth': Malcolm, op. cit., p. 56.

p. 474 'Thinking is sometimes easy': LW to RR, 17.10.44.

p. 474 'I then thought': LW to NM, 16.11.44.

p. 475 'We sat in silence': Malcolm, op. cit., p. 36.

p. 475 'Had I had it before': LW to NM, 22.5.45.

p. 476 'This war': LW to RH, dated only 'Thursday', but probably autumn 1944.

p. 476 'I'm sorry to hear': LW to RR, 28.11.44.

p. 476 'you were right': ibid.

p. 477 'How does the philosophical problem': *Philosophical Investigations*, I, 308.

p. 478 'The "Self of selves"': William James, *Principles of Psychology*, I, 301.

p. 478 'not the meaning of the word': *Philosophical Investigations*, I, 410.

p. 478 'I always enjoy reading anything of William James': *Recollections*, p. 106.

p. 479 'The Term's over': LW to RR, 13.6.45.

p. 479 'going damn slowly': LW to NM, 26.6.45.

p. 479 'I might publish by Christmas': LW to NM, 17.8.45.

p. 480 'The last 6 months': LW to RH, 14.5.45.

p. 480 'this peace is only a truce': LW to NM, undated.

p. 480 'lots of luck': LW to RH, 8.9.45.

p. 480 'self-righteousness in international affairs': quoted in Ruth Dudley Edwards, *Victor Gollancz: A Biography*, p. 406.

p. 481 'glad to see that someone': LW to Victor Gollancz, 4.9.45; reproduced in full, ibid., pp. 406–7.

p. 482 'Polemic, or the art of throwing eggs': *Recollections*, p. 203.

p. 482 'L. Wiltgenstein, Esq.': quoted in Edwards, op. cit., p. 408. Wittgenstein's reaction was told to me by Rush Rhees.

p. 482 'enjoying my absence from Cambridge': LW to NM, 8.9.45.

p. 482 'My book is gradually': LW to NM, 20.9.45.

p. 484 'It is not without reluctance': *Culture and Value*, p. 66.

p. 484 'They mean to do it': see Britton, op. cit., p. 62.

p. 485 'The hysterical fear': *Culture and Value*, p. 49.

p. 485 'The truly apocalyptic view': ibid., p. 56.

p. 485 'Science and industry': ibid., p. 63.

p. 486 'My type of thinking': quoted Drury, *Recollections*, p. 160.

p. 486 'In fact, nothing is more *conservative*': quoted Rhees, *Recollections*, p. 202.

p. 486 'I find more and more': see *Recollections*, pp. 207–8.

p. 487 'I'll talk about anything': told to the author by Rush Rhees.

p. 487 'One day in July': Britton, op. cit., p. 62.

p. 488 'the disintegrating and putrefying English civilization': MS 134; quoted in Nedo, op. cit., p. 321.

24   A CHANGE OF ASPECT

p. 489 'cheaply wrapped': *Culture and Value*, p. 50.

p. 490 'I am by no means sure': ibid., p. 61.

p. 490 'Wisdom is cold': ibid., p. 56.

p. 490 '"Wisdom is grey"': ibid., p. 62.

p. 490 'I believe': ibid., p. 53.

p. 491 'it's as though my knees were stiff': ibid., p. 56.

p. 491 'I am very sad': '*Ich bin sehr traurig, sehr oft traurig. Ich fühle mich so, als sei das jetzt das Ende meines Lebens . . . Das eine, was die Liebe zu B. für mich getan hat ist: sie hat die übrigen kleinlichen Sorgen meine Stellung und Arbeit betreffend in den Hintergrund gejagt*': MS 130, p. 144, 8.8.46.

p. 491 'just as a boy': MS 131, 12.8.46.

p. 491 'I feel as though': MS 131, 14.8.46.

p. 492 'It is the mark of a *true* love': MS 131, 14.8.46; quoted in Nedo, op. cit., p. 325.

p. 492 'I feel that my mental health': '*Ich fühle, meine geistige Gesundheit hängt an einem dünnen Faden. Es ist natürlich die Sorge und Angst wegen B., die mich so abgenützt hat. Und doch könnte auch das nicht geschehen, wenn ich nicht eben leicht entzündbar wäre, "highly inflammable"*': MS 131, 18.8.46.

p. 492 'Were they stupid': MS 131, 20.8.46; *Culture and Value*, p. 49.

p. 492 'if a light shines on it': *Culture and Value*, pp. 57–8.

p. 492 '"For our desires shield us"': '"*Denn die Wünsche verhüllen uns selbst das Gewünschte. Die Gaben kommen herunter in ihren eignen Gestalten etc." Das sage ich mir wenn ich die Liebe B's empfange. Denn dass sie das grosse, seltene Geschenk ist, weiss ich wohl; dass sie ein seltener Edelstein ist, weiss ich wohl, – und auch, dass sie nicht ganz von der Art ist, von der ich geträumt hatte*': MS 132, 29.9.46.

p. 493 'Everything about the place': *'Alles an dem Ort stösst mich ab. Das Steife, Künstliche, Selbstgefällige der Leute. Die Universitätsatmosphäre ist mir ekelhaft'*: MS 132, 30.9.46.

p. 493 'What I miss most': LW to RF, 9.11.46.

p. 493 'So when you'll come back': LW to RF, Aug. 1946.

p. 493 'Sorry you don't get post': LW to RF, 7.10.46.

p. 493 'Why in hell': LW to RF, 21.10.46.

p. 494 'I'm feeling far better': LW to RF, 9.11.46.

p. 494 'I'm thinking every day': LW to RF, 21.10.46.

p. 495 'Not to threaten visiting lecturers': Popper's account is given in *Unended Quest: An Intellectual Autobiography*, pp. 122–3.

p. 495 'veneration for Wittgenstein': Ryle in Wood & Pitcher, op. cit., p. 11.

p. 496 'As little philosophy as I have read': MS 135, 27.7.47.

p. 496 'Practically every philosopher': Mary Warnock, diary, 14.5.47. I am very grateful to Lady Warnock, and to Oscar Wood and Sir Isaiah Berlin for their recollections of this meeting. The part of the exchange between Wittgenstein and Pritchard that is quoted comes from *A Wittgenstein Workbook*, p. 6.

p. 497 'For years': Anscombe, *Metaphysics and the Philosophy of Mind*, pp. vii–ix.

p. 498 'This man': quoted by Professor Anscombe in conversation with the author.

p. 498 'very unnerving': Iris Murdoch, quoted by Ved Mehta in *The Fly and the Fly Bottle*, p. 55.

p. 498 'More able than Ramsey?': story told to me by Rush Rhees.

p. 499 'were far from the centre': Kreisel, 'Wittgenstein's *"Remarks on the Foundations of Mathematics"'*, *British Journal for the Philosophy of Science*, IX (1958), pp. 135–58.

p. 499 'tense and often incoherent': Kreisel, 'Critical Notice: *"Lectures on the Foundations of Mathematics"'*, in *Ludwig Wittgenstein: Critical Assessments*, pp. 98–110.

p. 499 'Wittgenstein's views on mathematical logic': Kreisel, *British Journal for the Philosophy of Science*, op. cit., pp. 143–4.

p. 499 'As an introduction': Kreisel, 'Wittgenstein's Theory and Practice of Philosophy', *British Journal for the Philosophy of Science*, XI (1960), pp. 238–52.

p. 500 'These lectures are on the philosophy of psychology': from the notes taken by A. C. Jackson. These notes (together with those of the same lectures taken by P. T. Geach and K. J. Shah) have now been published as *Wittgenstein's Lectures on Philosophical Psychology: 1946–7*, but at the time of writing this I was dependent on privately circulated copies. There may be some slight variations between the notes as I give them and as they have been published.

p. 501 'Now let us go back to last day': ibid.

p. 501 'What I give is the morphology': Malcolm, op. cit., p. 43.

p. 502 'arose from the fact': Gasking and Jackson, 'Wittgenstein as a Teacher', Fann, op. cit., pp. 49–55.

p. 502 'I am showing my pupils': *Culture and Value*, p. 56.

p. 502 'In teaching you philosophy': Gasking and Jackson, op. cit., p. 51.

p. 503 'I still keep getting entangled': *Culture and Value*, p. 65.

p. 503 'Starting at the beginning': Malcolm, op. cit., p. 44.

p. 503 'All is happiness': '*Alles ist Glück. Ich könnte jetzt so nicht schreiben, wenn ich nicht die letzten 2 Wochen mit B. verbracht hätte. Und ich hätte sie nicht so verbringen können, wenn Krankheit oder irgend ein Unfall dazwischen gekommen wäre*': MS 132, 8.10.46.

p. 504 'In love': '*Ich bin in der Liebe zu wenig* gläubig *und zu wenig* mutig . . . *ich bin leicht verletzt und fürchte mich davor, verletzt zu werden, und sich in* dieser *Weise selbst schonen ist der Tod aller Liebe. Zur wirklichen Liebe braucht es Mut. Das heisst aber doch, man muss auch den Mut haben, abzubrechen, und zu entsagen, also den Mut eine Todeswunde zu ertragen. Ich aber kann nur hoffen, dass mir das Fürchterlichste erspart bleibt*': MS 132, 22.10.46.

p. 504 'I do not have the courage': '*Ich habe nicht den Mut und nicht die Kraft und Klarheit den Tatsachen meines Lebens gerade in's Gesicht zu schauen. – B. hat zu mir eine Vor-Liebe. Etwas, was nicht halten kann. Wie diese verwelken wird, weiss ich natürlich nicht. Wie etwas von ihr zu erhalten wäre, lebendig, nicht gepresst in einem Buch als Andenken, weiss ich auch nicht . . . Ich weiss nicht, ob und wie ich es aushalten werde, dies Verhältnis mit dieser Aussicht weiterzunähren . . . Wenn ich mir vorstelle, dass ich es abgebrochen hätte, so fürchte ich mich vor der Einsamkeit*': MS 133, 25.10.46.

p. 504 'love is a joy': '*Die Liebe ist ein* Glück. *Vielleicht ein Glück mit Schmerzen, aber ein Glück . . . In der Liebe muss ich sicher ruhen können. – Aber kannst du ein warmes Herz zurückweisen; Ist es ein Herz, das warm für mich schlägt;* – I'll rather do anything than to hurt the soul of friendship. – I must know: he won't hurt *our friendship. Der Mensch kann aus seiner Haut nicht heraus. Ich kann nicht eine Forderung, die tief in mir, meinem ganzen Leben verankert, liegt, aufgeben. Denn die Liebe ist mit der Natur verbunden; und würde ich unnatürlich, so würde / /müsste/ / die Liebe aufhören. – Kann ich sagen: "Ich werde vernünftig sein, und das nicht mehr verlangen."? . . . Ich kann sagen: Lass ihn gewähren, – es wird einmal anders werden. – Die Liebe, die ist die Perle von grossem Wert, die man am Herzen hält, für die man*

nichts *eintauschen will, die man als das wertvollste schätzt. Sie* zeigt
einem überhaupt – wenn man sie hat – was grosser Wert ist. *Man lernt,
was es* heisst: *ein Edelmetall von allen andern aussondern . . . Das
Furchtbare ist die Ungewissheit . . . "Auf Gott vertrauen". . . . Von da,
wo ich bin, zum Gottvertrauen ist ein* weiter *Weg. Freudevolle Hoffnung
und Furcht sind einander verschwistert. Ich kann die eine nicht haben ohne
dass sie an die andre grenzt'*: MS 133, 26.10.46.

p. 505 'Trust in God': ibid.

p. 505 'Ask yourself these questions: *'Frag dich diese Frage: Wenn du stirbst,
wer wird dir nachtrauern; und* wie tief *wird die Trauer sein? Wer trauert
um F.; wie tief trauere ich um ihn, der mehr Grund zur Trauer hat als
irgend jemand? Hat er* nicht *verdient, dass jemand sein ganzes Leben lang
um ihn trauert? Wenn jemand so er. Da möchte man sagen: Gott wird ihn
aufheben und ihm* geben, *was ein schlechter Mensch ihm versagt'*: MS
133, 10.11.46.

p. 506 'The fundamental insecurity': MS 133, 12.11.46.

p. 506 'Don't be too cowardly': MS 133, 15.11.46.

p. 506 'Can you not cheer up': *'Kannst du nicht auch ohne seine Liebe fröhlich
sein? Musst du ohne diese Liebe in Gram versinken? Kannst du ohne diese
Stütze nicht leben? Denn das ist die Frage: kannst du* nicht *aufrecht gehn,
ohne dich auf diesen Stab zu lehnen? Oder kannst du dich nur nicht
entschliessen ihn aufzugeben? Oder ist es beides? – Du darfst nicht
immer Briefe erwarten, die nicht kommen . . . Es ist nicht Liebe, was mich
zu dieser Stütze zieht, sondern, dass ich auf meinen zwei Beinen allein
nicht sicher stehen kann'*: MS 133, 27.11.46.

p. 506 'Some men': *'Mancher Mensch ist im ganzen Leben krank und kennt nur
das Glück, das der fühlt, der nach langen heftigen Schmerzen ein paar
schmerzlose Stunden hat. (Es ist ein seeliges Aufatmen.)'*: MS 133,
23.11.46.

p. 506 'Is it so unheard of': *'Ist es so unerhört, dass ein Mensch leidet, dass z.B.
ein ältlicher Mensch müde und einsam ist, ja selbst, dass er halb verrückt
wird?'*: MS 133, 2.12.46.

p. 506 'Only nothing theatrical': MS 133, 12.2.46.

p. 506 'The belief in a benevolent father': MS 134, 4.4.47.

p. 506 'What good does all my talent do me': *'Wozu dient mir all meine
Geschicklichkeit, wenn ich im Herzen unglücklich bin? Was hilft es mir,
philosophische Probleme zu lösen, wenn ich mit der Hauptsache nicht ins
Reine kommen kann?'*: MS 134, 13.4.47.

p. 507 'My lectures are going well': *'Meine Vorlesungen gehen gut, sie werden
nie besser gehen. Aber welche Wirkung lassen sie zurück? Helfe ich
irgendjemand? Gewiss nicht* mehr, *als wenn ich ein grosser Schauspieler
wäre, der ihnen Tragödien vorspielt. Was sie lernen, ist nicht wert gelernt*

*zu werden; und der persönliche Eindruck nützt ihnen nichts. Das gilt für
Alle, mit vielleicht einer, oder zwei Ausnahmen'*: MS 133, 19.11.46.

p. 507 'Suppose I show it to a child': notes taken by P. T. Geach; see
Wittgenstein's Lectures on Philosophical Psychology, p. 104 (but see also
reference for p. 500).

p. 508 'It would have made': *Philosophical Investigations*, II, p. 195.

p. 509 'In the German language': Wolfgang Köhler, *Gestalt Psychology*,
p. 148.

p. 510 'Here where': Goethe, *Italian Journey*, pp. 258–9.

p. 510 'The *Urpflanze*': ibid., p. 310.

p. 511 'Two uses': *Philosophical Investigations*, II, p. 193.

p. 511 'I explained to him': quoted Heller, op. cit., p. 6.

p. 512 'Well, so much the better': ibid.

p. 513 'When I tell the reader': Köhler, op. cit., p. 153.

p. 513 'Now Köhler said': see *Wittgenstein's Lectures on Philosophical
Psychology*, pp. 329–30.

p. 514 'It makes no sense to ask': see ibid., p. 104.

p. 514 'Now you try': *Recollections*, p. 159.

p. 514 'The expression of a change': *Philosophical Investigations*, II,
pp. 196–7.

p. 515 'Köhler says': *Remarks on the Philosophy of Psychology*, I, p. 982.

p. 516 'A philosopher says': *Culture and Value*, p. 61.

p. 516 'In this country': *'Für Leute wie mich liegt in diesem Lande nichts näher
als Menschenhass. Gerade dass man sich in all dieser Solidität auch keine
Revolution denken kann macht die Lage noch viel hoffnungsloser. Es ist als
hätte diese ganze grenzenlose Öde "come to stay". Es ist als könnte man
von diesem Land sagen, es habe ein nasskaltes geistiges Klima'*: MS 134,
13.4.47.

p. 516 'Cambridge grows more and more hateful': *'Cambridge wird mir mehr
und mehr verhasst.* The disintegrating and putrefying English
civilization. *Ein Land, in dem die Politik zwischen einem bösen Zweck
und keinem Zweck schwankt'*: MS 134, 23.4.47.

p. 516 '[I] feel myself to be an alien': *'fühle mich fremd //als Fremdling// in der
Welt. Wenn dich kein Band an Menschen und kein Band an Gott bindet, so
bist du ein Fremdling'*: MS 135, 28.7.47.

p. 517 'I wouldn't be altogether surprised': *Recollections*, p. 152.

p. 517 'This is an excellent book': ibid.

p. 517 '. . . go somewhere': LW to GHvW, 27.8.47.

p. 518 'he was reacting': quoted by John Moran, op. cit., p. 92.

p. 518 'It's mostly bad': LW to GHvW, 6.11.47.

25 IRELAND

p. 520 'cold and uncomfortable': LW to RR, 9.12.47.

p. 520 'Sometimes my ideas': *Recollections*, pp. 153–4.

p. 521 'the prospect of becoming English': LW to GHvW, 22.12.47.

p. 521 'Cambridge is a dangerous place': LW to GHvW, 23.2.48.

p. 521 'There is nothing like the Welsh coast': LW to RR, 5.2.48.

p. 521 'The country here': LW to Helene, 10.1.48; quoted in Nedo, op. cit., p. 326.

p. 522 'In a letter': *Culture and Value*, pp. 65–6.

p. 522 'Heaven knows if I'll ever publish': LW to GHvW, 22.12.47.

p. 522 'I am in very good bodily health': LW to RR, 5.2.48.

p. 522 'My work's going moderately well': LW to NM, 4.1.48.

p. 522 'Feel unwell': MS 137, 3.2.48.

p. 523 'occasionally queer states': LW to NM, 5.2.48.

p. 523 'My nerves, I'm afraid': LW to RR, 5.2.48.

p. 523 'I often believe': LW to GHvW, 17.3.48.

p. 523 'They are very quiet': LW to GHvW, 22.12.47.

p. 523 'As soon as he had arrived': *Recollections*, pp. 154–5.

p. 524 'I often thought of you': LW to RR, 15.4.48.

p. 525 'quite nice': LW to NM, 5.6.48.

p. 525 'the man upon whom': MS 137, 17.7.48; quoted in Nedo, op. cit., p. 326.

p. 526 'Tinned food': story told to the author by Thomas Mulkerrins.

p. 526 'I thought you had company': ibid.

p. 526 'Nearly all my writings': *Culture and Value*, p. 77.

p. 527 'I've had a bad time': LW to NM, 30.4.48.

p. 528 'it's undoubtedly a great blessing': LW to Lee Malcolm, 5.6.48.

p. 528 'For though as you know': LW to NM, 4.6.48.

p. 528 'As I recall': see footnote to above letter.

p. 529 Davis wrote to Raymond Chandler: see Frank MacShane, ed., *Selected Letters of Raymond Chandler* (Cape, 1981), p. 167.

p. 529 'All this was very boring': Norbert Davis, *Rendezvous with Fear*, p. 9.

p. 529 'Is he hurt?': ibid., p. 86.

p. 529 'Humour is not a mood': *Culture and Value*, p. 78.

p. 530 'So how do we explain': ibid., p. 70.

p. 531 'What would a person be lacking?': *Remarks on the Philosophy of Psychology*, II, p. 508.

p. 532 'What is lacking': ibid., pp. 464–8.

p. 532 'What is it like': *Culture and Value*, p. 83.

p. 533 'What is incomprehensible': *Remarks on the Philosophy of Psychology*, II, p. 474.

p. 533 'leaves everything as it is': *Philosophical Investigations*, I, 124.

p. 533 'Tradition is not something a man can learn': *Culture and Value*, p. 76.

p. 534 'I get tired': LW to GHvW, 26.5.48.

p. 534 'too soft, too weak': *Culture and Value*, p. 72.

p. 534 'Don't let the grief vex you!': *'Lass dich die Trauer nicht verdriessen! Du solltest sie ins Herz einlassen und auch den Wahnsinn nicht fürchten! Er kommt vielleicht als Freund und nicht als Feind zu dir und nur dein Wehren ist das Übel. Lass die Trauer ins Herz ein, verschliess ihr nicht die Tür. Draussen vor der Tür im Verstand stehend ist sie furchtbar, aber im Herzen ist sie's nicht'*: MS 137, 29.6.48.

p. 534 'Think a great deal': MS 137, 11.7.48.

p. 534 'But I have decided to *try*': MS 137, 17.7.48.

p. 535 'When I look at the faces': *Recollections*, p. 166.

p. 536 'I'm anxious to make hay': LW to NM, 6.11.48.

p. 536 'Just wait a minute': *Recollections*, p. 156.

p. 536 'I hear the words': *Last Writings*, I, p. 47.

p. 536 'Hegel seems to me': *Recollections*, p. 157.

p. 537 'hasn't the necessary multiplicity': ibid., p. 160.

p. 537 'Now you try': ibid., p. 159.

p. 537 '"Denken ist schwer"': *Culture and Value*, p. 74.

p. 537 'It is impossible for me': *Recollections*, p. 160.

p. 538 'We say that someone has the "eyes of a painter"': *Last Writings*, I, p. 782.

p. 538 'We say that someone doesn't have a musical ear': ibid., p. 783; cf. *Philosophical Investigations*, II, xi, p. 214.

p. 538 'I would like it': *Recollections*, p. 160.

p. 538 'I think he felt': ibid., p. 97.

p. 539 'some sort of infection': LW to NM, 28.1.49.

p. 539 'Drury, I think': MS 138, 29.1.49.

p. 539 'great weakness and pain': MS 138, 11.2.49.

p. 539 '[They] contain many excellent things': *Culture and Value*, p. 27.

p. 540 'for otherwise': MS 138, 2.3.49.

p. 540 'Nice time': MS 138, 15.3.49.

p. 540 'Often it is as though my soul were dead': MS 138, 17.3.49.

p. 540 'Of course it was rejected': *Recollections*, p. 161.

p. 540 'If Christianity is the truth': *Culture and Value*, p. 83.

p. 540 'I can't understand the Fourth Gospel': *Recollections*, p. 164.

p. 541 'The spring which flows gently': *Culture and Value*, p. 30.

p. 541 'It is one and the same': *Recollections*, p. 165.

p. 541 'If it is a good and godly picture': *Culture and Value*, p. 32.

p. 541 'Suppose someone were taught': ibid., p. 81.

p. 542 'What happens': LW to NM, 18.2.49.

p. 542 'While I was in Vienna': LW to NM, 17.5.49.

p. 543 'It is so characteristic': *Recollections*, p. 163.

p. 543 'has something to say': ibid., p. 159.

p. 543 'Now that is all I want': ibid., p. 168.

p. 544 'There is one thing that I'm afraid of': LW to GHvW, 1.6.49.

p. 545 'You have said something': LW to GEM, Oct. 1944.

p. 546 'Don't regard': *Philosophical Investigations*, II, p. 192.

p. 546 'But surely': ibid., p. 190.

p. 547 'We can imagine': ibid., p. 188.

p. 548 'Drury, just look at the expression': *Recollections*, p. 126.

p. 548 'If I see someone': *Philosophical Investigations*, II, p. 223.

p. 548 'It is important': *Culture and Value*, p. 74.

p. 548 'If a lion could talk': *Philosophical Investigations*, II, p. 223.

p. 548 'Is there such a thing': *ibid.*, p. 227.

p. 549 'It was said by many people': Dostoevsky, *The Brothers Karamazov*, p. 30.

p. 549 'Yes, there really have been people like that': *Recollections*, p. 108.

p. 549 'The confusion and barrenness': *Philosophical Investigations*, II, p. 232.

26 A CITIZEN OF NO COMMUNITY

p. 552 'My mind is tired & stale': LW to NM, 1.4.49.

p. 552 'I *know* you'd extend your hospitality': LW to NM, 4.6.49.

p. 552 'My anaemia': LW to NM, 7.7.49.

p. 552 'Ordinarily': Stuart Brown; quoted in McHale, op. cit., p. 78.

p. 553 'particularly because': LW to RF, 28.7.49.

p. 553 'probably the most philosophically strenuous': quoted ibid., p. 80.

p. 554 'But then, he added': Bouwsma's notes of his conversations with Wittgenstein have now been published; see *Wittgenstein Conversations 1949–1951*, p. 9.

p. 554 'I am a very vain person': ibid.

p. 555 'If I had planned it': ibid., p. 12.

p. 556 'I can prove now': Moore, 'Proof of an External World', *Philosophical Papers*, p. 146.

p. 556 'To understand a sentence': Malcolm, op. cit., p. 73.

p. 557 'Instead of saying': ibid., p. 72.

p. 557 'When the sceptical philosophers': ibid., p. 73.

p. 557 'Scepticism is *not* irrefutable': *Tractatus*, 6.51.

p. 557 'Certain propositions': Malcolm, op. cit., p. 74.

p. 558 'If I walked over to that tree': ibid., p. 71.

p. 558 'Just before the meeting': quoted in McHale, op. cit., pp. 79–80.

p. 559 'I don't want to die in America': Malcolm, op. cit., p. 77.

p. 559 'I am sorry that my life should be prolonged': LW to RR, 4.12.49.

p. 559 'My health is very bad': LW to Helene, 28.11.49; quoted in Nedo, op. cit., p. 337.

p. 560 'This is of the greatest importance': LW to NM, 11.12.49.

p. 560 'ARRIVED': LW to GHvW, 26.12.49.

p. 560 'I haven't been to a concert': LW to GHvW, 19.1.50.

p. 560 'I'm very happy': LW to Dr Bevan, 7.2.50.

p. 561 'Colours spur us to philosophise': *Culture and Value*, p. 66.

p. 561 'It's partly boring': LW to GHvW, 19.1.50.

p. 561 'I may find': *Culture and Value*, p. 79.

p. 562 'As I mean it': *On Colour*, II, p. 3.

p. 562 'If someone didn't find': ibid., p. 10.

p. 562 'Phenomenological analysis': ibid., p. 16.

p. 562 'We had expected her end': LW to GHvW, 12.2.50.

p. 562 'Wittgenstein, who took a long time': Paul Feyerabend, *Science in a Free Society*, p. 109.

p. 563 'everything descriptive': *On Certainty*, p. 56.

p. 563 'If "I know etc."': ibid., p. 58.

p. 564 'If language': *Philosophical Investigations*, I, 242.

p. 564 'woeful': see MS 173, 24.3.50.

p. 564 'I don't think I can give formal lectures': LW to NM, 5.4.50.

p. 565 'The thought': LW to NM, 17.4.50.

p. 566 'in my present state': LW to NM, 12.1.51.

p. 566 'I'm doing some work': LW to NM, 17.4.50.

p. 566 'That which I am writing about': *On Colour*, III, p. 295.

p. 566 'One and the same': ibid', p. 213.

p. 566 'Imagine someone': ibid., p. 263.

p. 567 'In the late spring': K. E. Tranøj, 'Wittgenstein in Cambridge, 1949–51', *Acta Philosophica Fennica*, XXVII, 1976; quoted in Nedo, op. cit., p. 335.

p. 567 'I like to stay': LW to NM, 17.4.50.

p. 567 'The house isn't very noisy': LW to GHvW, 28.4.50.

p. 567 'Pink wants to sit on six stools': quoted by Barry Pink in conversation with the author (he was perfectly sure that 'arse' was the word Wittgenstein used).

p. 568 'Certainly not!': quoted by Barry Pink in conversation with the author.

p. 568 'It is remarkable': *Culture and Value*, p. 48.

p. 568 'Shakespeare's similes': ibid., p. 49.

p. 568 'I believe': ibid., p. 85.

p. 569 'I could only stare': ibid., pp. 84–5.

p. 570 'If Moore were to pronounce': *On Certainty*, p. 155.

p. 570 'For months I have lived': ibid., pp. 70–71.

p. 570 'I could imagine': ibid., p. 264.

p. 571 'Everything that I have seen': ibid., p. 94.

p. 571 'The river-bed': ibid., p 97.

p. 571 'I believe': ibid., p. 239.

p. 572 'I have a world picture': ibid., p. 162.

p. 572 'Perhaps one could': *Culture and Value*, p. 85.

p. 572 'Life can educate one': ibid. p. 86.

p. 572 'The attitude that's in question': ibid., p. 85.

p. 573 'He wanted': Father Conrad to the author, 30.8.86.

p. 574 'we enjoyed our stay': LW to GHvW, 29.1.51.

27 STOREYS END

p. 576 'I can't even *think* of work': LW to NM, undated.

p. 576 'How lucky': this, and all other remarks of Wittgenstein's to Mrs Bevan quoted in this chapter, are given as they were told to me by Mrs Bevan in a series of conversations I had with her during 1985–7.

p. 576 'He was very demanding': extract from a written statement of her memories of Wittgenstein by Mrs Bevan.

p. 577 'I have been ill': LW to RF, 1.2.51.

p. 578 'I do philosophy': *On Certainty*, p. 532.

p. 578 'I believe': ibid., p. 387.

p. 578 'A doubt without an end': ibid., p. 625.

p. 578 'I am sitting': ibid., p. 467.

p. 578 'Doubting and non-doubting': ibid., p. 354.

p. 579 'Am I not': ibid., p. 501.

p. 579 'I remember': *Recollections*, p. 171.

p. 580 'Isn't it curious': ibid., p. 169.

p. 580 'God may say to me': *Culture and Value*, p. 87.

SELECT BIBLIOGRAPHY

Below are listed the principal printed sources used in the writing of this biography. For an exhaustive bibliography of works by and about Wittgenstein, see V. A. and S. G. Shanker, ed., *Ludwig Wittgenstein: Critical Assessments, V: A Wittgenstein Bibliography* (Croom Helm, 1986).

Anscombe, G. E. M. *Metaphysics and the Philosophy of Mind*, Collected Philosophical Papers, II (Blackwell, 1981)

Augustine, Saint *Confessions* (Penguin, 1961)

Ayer, A. J. *Wittgenstein* (Weidenfeld & Nicolson, 1985)

—— *Part of My Life* (Collins, 1977)

—— *More of My Life* (Collins, 1984)

Baker, G. P. *Wittgenstein, Frege and the Vienna Circle* (Blackwell, 1988)

Baker, G. P. and Hacker, P. M. S. *Wittgenstein: Meaning and Understanding* (Blackwell, 1983)

—— *An Analytical Commentary on Wittgenstein's Philosophical Investigations*, I (Blackwell, 1983)

—— *Wittgenstein: Rules, Grammar and Necessity: An Analytical Commentary on the Philosophical Investigations*, II (Blackwell, 1985)

—— *Scepticism, Rules and Language* (Blackwell, 1984)

Bartley, W. W. *Wittgenstein* (Open Court, rev. 2/1985)

Bernhard, Thomas *Wittgenstein's Nephew* (Quartet, 1986)

Block, Irving, ed., *Perspectives on the Philosophy of Wittgenstein* (Blackwell, 1981)

Bouwsma, O. K. *Philosophical Essays* (University of Nebraska Press, 1965)

—— *Wittgenstein: Conversations 1949–1951*, ed. J. L. Craft and Ronald E. Hustwit (Hackett, 1986)

Clare, George *Last Waltz in Vienna* (Pan, 1982)

Clark, Ronald W. *The Life of Bertrand Russell* (Jonathan Cape and Weidenfeld & Nicolson, 1975)

Coope, Christopher, et al. *A Wittgenstein Workbook* (Blackwell, 1971)

Copi, Irving M. and Beard, Robert W., ed., *Essays on Wittgenstein's Tractatus* (Routledge, 1966)

Dawidowicz, Lucy S. *The War Against the Jews 1933–45* (Weidenfeld & Nicolson, 1975)

Deacon, Richard *The Cambridge Apostles: A History of Cambridge University's Elite Intellectual Secret Society* (Robert Royce, 1985)

Delany, Paul *The Neo-pagans: Rupert Brooke and the Ordeal of Youth* (The Free Press, 1987)

Dostoevsky, Fyodor *The Brothers Karamazov* (Penguin, 1982)

Drury, M. O'C. *The Danger of Words* (Routledge, 1973)

Duffy, Bruce *The World As I Found It* (Ticknor & Fields, 1987)

Eagleton, Terry 'Wittgenstein's Friends', *New Left Review*, CXXXV (September–October 1982); reprinted in *Against the Grain* (Verso, 1986)

Fann, K. T., ed., *Ludwig Wittgenstein: The Man and His Philosophy* (Harvester, 1967)

Feyerabend, Paul *Science in a Free Society* (Verso, 1978)

Ficker, Ludwig von *Denkzettel und Danksagungen* (Kösel, 1967)

Field, Frank *The Last Days of Mankind: Karl Kraus and His Vienna* (Macmillan, 1967)

Frege, Gottlob *The Foundations of Arithmetic* (Blackwell, 1950)

—— *Philosophical Writings* (Blackwell, 1952)

—— *Philosophical and Mathematical Correspondence* (Blackwell, 1980)

—— *The Basic Laws of Arithmetic* (University of California Press, 1967)

Freud, Sigmund *The Interpretation of Dreams* (Penguin, 1976)

—— *Jokes and Their Relation to the Unconscious* (Penguin, 1976)

Gay, Peter *Freud: A Life for Our Time* (Dent, 1988)

Goethe, J. W. *Italian Journey* (Penguin, 1970)

—— *Selected Verse* (Penguin, 1964)

Grant, R. T. and Reeve, E. B. *Observations on the General E⁻⁻cts of Injury in Man* (HMSO, 1951)

Hacker, P. M. S. *Insight and Illusion: Themes in the Philosophy of Wittgenstein* (Oxford, rev. 2/1986)

Hänsel, Ludwig 'Ludwig Wittgenstein (1889–1951)', *Wissenschaft und Weltbild* (October 1951), p. 272–8

Haller, Rudolf *Questions on Wittgenstein* (Routledge, 1988)

Hayek, F. A. von 'Ludwig Wittgenstein' (unpublished, 1953)

Heller, Erich *The Disinherited Mind: Essays in Modern German Literature and Thought* (Bowes & Bowes, 1975)

Henderson, J. R. 'Ludwig Wittgenstein and Guy's Hospital', *Guy's Hospital Reports*, CXXII (1973), pp. 185–93

Hertz, Heinrich *The Principles of Mechanics* (Macmillan, 1899)

Hilmy, S. Stephen *The Later Wittgenstein: The Emergence of a New Philosophical Method* (Blackwell, 1987)

Hitler, Adolf *Mein Kampf* (Hutchinson, 1969)

Hodges, Andrew *Alan Turing: The Enigma of Intelligence* (Burnett, 1983)

Iggers, Wilma Abeles *Karl Kraus: A Viennese Critic of the Twentieth Century* (Nijhoff, 1967)

James, William *The Varieties of Religious Experience* (Penguin, 1982)

—— *The Principles of Psychology*, 2 vols (Dover, 1950)

Janik, Allan and Toulmin, Stephen *Wittgenstein's Vienna* (Simon & Schuster, 1973)

Jones, Ernest *The Life and Work of Sigmund Freud* (Hogarth, 1962)

Kapfinger, Otto *Haus Wittgenstein: Eine Dokumentation* (The Cultural Department of the People's Republic of Bulgaria, 1984)

Kenny, Anthony *Wittgenstein* (Allen Lane, 1973)

—— *The Legacy of Wittgenstein* (Blackwell, 1984)

Keynes, J. M. *A Short View of Russia* (Hogarth, 1925)

Köhler, Wolfgang *Gestalt Psychology* (G. Bell & Sons, 1930)

Kraus, Karl *Die Letzten Tage der Menschenheit*, 2 vols (Deutscher Taschenbuch, 1964)

—— *No Compromise: Selected Writings*, ed. Frederick Ungar (Ungar Publishing, 1984)

—— *In These Great Times: A Karl Kraus Reader*, ed. Harry Zohn (Carcanet, 1984)

Kreisel, G. 'Wittgenstein's "*Remarks on the Foundations of Mathematics*"', *British Journal for the Philosophy of Science*, IX (1958), pp. 135–58

—— 'Wittgenstein's Theory and Practice of Philosophy', *British Journal for the Philosophy of Science*, XI (1960), pp. 238–52

—— 'Critical Notice: "*Lectures on the Foundations of Mathematics*"', in *Ludwig Wittgenstein: Critical Assessments*, ed. S. G. Shanker (Croom Helm, 1986), pp. 98–110

Leitner, Bernhard *The Architecture of Ludwig Wittgenstein: A Documentation* (Studio International, 1973)

Levy, Paul *G. E. Moore and the Cambridge Apostles* (Oxford, 1981)

Luckhardt, C. G. *Wittgenstein: Sources and Perspectives* (Harvester, 1979)

Mabbott, John *Oxford Memories* (Thornton's, 1986)

Mahon, J. 'The great philosopher who came to Ireland' *Irish Medical Times*,

—— (February 14, 1986)

McGuinness, Brian *Wittgenstein: A Life. Young Ludwig 1889–1921* (Duckworth, 1988)

—— , ed., *Wittgenstein and His Times* (Blackwell, 1982)

McHale, Sister Mary Elwyn *Ludwig Wittgenstein: A Survey of Source Material for a Philosophical Biography* (MA thesis for the Catholic University of America, 1966)

Malcolm, Norman *Ludwig Wittgenstein: A Memoir* (with a Biographical Sketch by G. H. von Wright) (Oxford, rev. 2/1984)

Manvell, Roger and Fraenkel, Heinrich *Hitler: The Man and the Myth* (Grafton, 1978)

Mays, W. 'Wittgenstein's Manchester Period', *Guardian* (24 March 1961)

—— 'Wittgenstein in Manchester', in *'Language, Logic, and Philosophy':
Proceedings of the 4th International Wittgenstein Symposium* (1979), pp. 171–8

Mehta, Ved *The Fly and the Fly-Bottle* (Weidenfeld & Nicolson, 1963)

Moore, G. E. *Philosophical Papers* (Unwin, 1959)

Moran, John 'Wittgenstein and Russia', *New Left Review*, LXXIII (May–June 1972)

Morton, Frederic *A Nervous Splendour* (Weidenfeld & Nicolson, 1979)

Nedo, Michael and Ranchetti, Michele *Wittgenstein: Sein Leben in Bildern und Texten* (Suhrkamp, 1983)

Nietzsche, Friedrich *Twilight of the Idols* and *The Anti-Christ* (Penguin, 1968)

Ogden, C. K. and Richards, I. A. *The Meaning of Meaning* (Kegan Paul, 1923)

Parak, Franz *Am anderen Ufer* (Europäischer Verlag, 1969)

Partridge, Frances *Memories* (Robin Clark, 1982)

Popper, Karl *Unended Quest: An Intellectual Autobiography* (Fontana, 1976)

Ramsey, F. P. 'Critical Notice of L. Wittgenstein's "Tractatus Logico-Philosophicus"', *Mind*, XXXII, no. 128 (October 1923), pp. 465–78

—— *Foundations: Essays in Philosophy, Logic, Mathematics and Economics* (Routledge, 1978)

Rhees, Rush 'Wittgenstein' [review of Bartley, op. cit.] *The Human Word*, XIV (February 1974)

—— *Discussions of Wittgenstein* (Routledge, 1970)

—— *Without Answers* (Routledge, 1969)

——, ed., *Recollections of Wittgenstein* (Oxford, 1984)

Russell, Bertrand *The Principles of Mathematics* (Unwin, 1903)

—— *The Problems of Philosophy* (Home University Library, 1912)

—— *Our Knowledge of the External World* (Unwin, 1914)

—— *Mysticism and Logic* (Unwin, 1918)

—— *Introduction to Mathematical Philosophy* (Unwin, 1919)

—— *The Analysis of Mind* (Unwin, 1921)

—— *The Practice and Theory of Bolshevism* (Unwin, 1920)

—— *Marriage and Morals* (Unwin, 1929)

—— *The Conquest of Happiness* (Unwin, 1930)

—— *In Praise of Idleness* (Unwin, 1935)

—— *An Inquiry into Meaning and Truth* (Unwin, 1940)

—— *History of Western Philosophy* (Unwin, 1945)

—— *Human Knowledge: Its Scope and Limits* (Unwin, 1948)

Russell, Bertrand *Logic and Knowledge*, ed. R. C. March (Unwin, 1956)
—— *My Philosophical Development* (Unwin, 1959)
—— *Autobiography* (Unwin, 1975)
Russell, Dora *The Tamarisk Tree*, I: *My Quest for Liberty and Love* (Virago, 1977)
Ryan, Alan *Bertrand Russell: A Political Life* (Allen Lane, 1988)
Schopenhauer, Arthur *Essays and Aphorisms* (Penguin, 1970)
—— *The World as Will and Representation*, 2 vols (Dover, 1969)
Shanker, S. G. *Wittgenstein and the Turning Point in the Philosophy of Mathematics* (Croom Helm, 1987)
Sjögren, Marguerite *Granny et son temps* (privately printed in Switzerland, 1982)
Skidelsky, Robert *John Maynard Keynes*, I: *Hopes Betrayed 1883–1920* (Macmillan, 1983)
Spengler, Oswald *The Decline of the West* (Unwin, 1928)
Sraffa, Piero *Production of Commodities By Means of Commodities* (Cambridge, 1960)
Steiner, G. *A Reading Against Shakespeare*, W. P. Ker Lecture for 1986 (University of Glasgow, 1986)
Tagore, Rabindranath *The King of the Dark Chamber* (Macmillan, 1918)
Thomson, George 'Wittgenstein: Some Personal Recollections', *The Revolutionary World*, XXXVII–IX (1979), pp. 87–8
Tolstoy, Leo *A Confession and Other Religious Writings* (Penguin, 1987)
—— *Master and Man and Other Stories* (Penguin, 1977)
—— *The Kreutzer Sonata and Other Stories* (Penguin, 1985)
—— *The Raid and Other Stories* (Oxford, 1982)
Waismann, F. *The Principles of Linguistic Philosophy*, ed. R. Harré (Macmillan, 1965)
Walter, Bruno *Theme and Variations: An Autobiography* (Hamish Hamilton, 1947)
Weininger, Otto *Sex and Character* (Heinemann, 1906)
Wittgenstein, Hermine, *Familienerinnerungen* (unpublished)
Wood, Oscar P. and Pitcher, George, ed., *Ryle* (Macmillan, 1971)
Wright, G. H. von *Wittgenstein* (Blackwell, 1982)
—— 'Ludwig Wittgenstein, A Biographical Sketch', in Malcolm, op. cit.
Wuchterl, Kurt and Hübner Adolf *Ludwig Wittgenstein in Selbstzeugnissen und Bilddokumenten* (Rowohlt, 1979)
Wünsche, Konrad, *Der Volksschullehrer Ludwig Wittgenstein* (Suhrkamp, 1985)

TEXTS

Review of P. Coffey *The Science of Logic*, *The Cambridge Review*, XXXIV (1913), p. 351

'Notes on Logic', in *Notebooks 1914–16*, pp. 93–107

'Notes Dictated to G. E. Moore in Norway', in *Notebooks 1914–16*, pp. 108–19

Notebooks 1914–16, ed. G. E. M. Anscombe and G. H. von Wright (Blackwell, 1961)

Prototractatus – An Early Version of Tractatus Logico-Philosophicus, ed. B. F. McGuinness, T. Nyberg and G. H. von Wright (Routledge, 1971)

Tractatus Logico-Philosophicus, trans. C. K. Ogden and F. P. Ramsey (Routledge, 1922)

Tractatus Logico-Philosophicus, trans. D. F. Pears and B. F. McGuinness (Routledge, 1961)

Wörterbuch für Volksschulen, ed. Werner and Elizabeth Leinfelner and Adolf Hübner (Hölder-Pichler-Tempsky, 1977)

'Some Remarks on Logical Form', *Proceedings of the Aristotelian Society*, IX (1929), pp. 162–71; reprinted in *Essays on Wittgenstein's Tractatus*, ed. I. M. Copi and R. W. Beard (Routledge, 1966)

'A Lecture on Ethics', *Philosophical Review*, LXXIV, no. 1 (1968), pp. 4–14

Philosophical Remarks, ed. Rush Rhees (Blackwell, 1975)

Philosophical Grammar, ed. Rush Rhees (Blackwell, 1974)

Remarks on Frazer's Golden Bough, ed. Rush Rhees (Brynmill, 1979)

The Blue and Brown Books (Blackwell, 1975)

'Notes for Lectures on "Private Experience" and "Sense Data"', ed. Rush Rhees, *Philosophical Review*, LXXVII, no. 3 (1968), pp. 275–320; reprinted in *The Private Language Argument*, ed. O. R. Jones (Macmillan, 1971), pp. 232–75

'Cause and Effect: Intuitive Awareness', ed. Rush Rhees, *Philosophia*, VI, nos. 3–4 (1976)

Remarks on the Foundations of Mathematics, ed. R. Rhees, G. H. von Wright and G. E. M. Anscombe (Blackwell, 1967)

Philosophical Investigations, ed. G. E. M. Anscombe and R. Rhees (Blackwell, 1953)

Zettel, ed. G. E. M. Anscombe and G. H. von Wright (Blackwell, 1981)

Remarks on the Philosophy of Psychology, I, ed. G. E. M Anscombe and G. H. von Wright (Blackwell, 1980)

Remarks on the Philosophy of Psychology, II, ed. G. H. von Wright and Heikki Nyman (Blackwell, 1980)

Last Writings on the Philosophy of Psychology, I: *Preliminary Studies for Part II of Philosophical Investigations*, ed. G. H. von Wright and Heikki Nyman (Blackwell, 1982)

Remarks on Colour, ed. G. E. M. Anscombe (Blackwell, 1977)

On Certainty, ed. G. E. M. Anscombe and G. H. von Wright (Blackwell, 1969)

Culture and Value, ed. G. H. von Wright in collaboration with Heikki
    Nyman (Blackwell, 1980)

NOTES OF LECTURES AND CONVERSATIONS

*Ludwig Wittgenstein and the Vienna Circle: Conversations Recorded by Friedrich
    Waismann* ed. B. F. McGuinness (Blackwell, 1979)
'Wittgenstein's Lectures in 1930–33', in G. E. Moore, *Philosophical Papers*
    (Unwin, 1959), pp. 252–324
Wittgenstein's Lectures: Cambridge, 1930–1932, ed. Desmond Lee (Blackwell,
    1980)
Wittgenstein's Lectures: Cambridge, 1932–1935, ed. Alice Ambrose (Blackwell,
    1979)
'The Language of Sense Data and Private Experience – Notes taken by
    Rush Rhees of Wittgenstein's Lectures, 1936', *Philosophical Investigations*,
    VII, no. 1 (1984), pp. 1–45; continued in *Philosophical Investigations*, VII,
    no. 2 (1984), pp. 101–40
Lectures and Conversations on Aesthetics, Psychology and Religious Belief, ed.
    Cyril Barrett (Blackwell, 1978)
Wittgenstein's Lectures on the Foundations of Mathematics: Cambridge, 1939, ed.
    Cora Diamond (Harvester, 1976)
Wittgenstein's Lectures on Philosophical Psychology 1946–47, ed. P. T. Geach
    (Harvester, 1988)

CORRESPONDENCE

*Briefe, Briefwechsel mit B. Russell, G. E. Moore. J. M. Keynes, F. P. Ramsey,
    W. Eccles, P. Engelmann und L. von Ficker*, ed. B. F. McGuinness and
    G. H. von Wright (Suhrkamp, 1980)
Letters to Russell, Keynes and Moore, ed. G. H. von Wright assisted by B. F.
    McGuinness (Blackwell, 1974)
*Letters to C. K. Ogden with Comments on the English Translation of the Tractatus
    Logico-Philosophicus*, ed. G. H. von Wright (Blackwell/Routledge, 1973)
Letters from Ludwig Wittgenstein with a Memoir by Paul Engelmann, ed. B. F.
    McGuinness (Blackwell, 1967)
Briefe an Ludwig von Ficker, ed. G. H. von Wright with Walter Methlagl
    (Otto Müller, 1969)
'Letters to Ludwig von Ficker', ed. Allan Janik, in *Wittgenstein: Sources and
    Perspectives*, ed. C. G. Luckhardt (Harvester, 1979), pp. 82–98
'Some Letters of Ludwig Wittgenstein', in W. Eccles, *Hermathena*, XCVII
    (1963), pp. 57–65
Letter to the Editor, *Mind*, XLII, no. 167 (1933), pp. 415–16
'Some Hitherto Unpublished Letters from Ludwig Wittgenstein to Georg
    Henrik von Wright', *The Cambridge Review* (28 February 1983)

INDEX